T0255359

Lecture Notes in Computer Science

Lecture Notes in Computer Science

Edited by G. Goos and J. Hartmanis

231

Roland Hausser

NEWCAT: Parsing Natural Language Using Left-Associative Grammar

Springer-Verlag
Berlin Heidelberg New York London Paris Tokyo

Author

Roland Hausser
Institut für Deutsche Philologie, Universität München
Schellingstraße 3, 8000 München 40, FRG

CR Subject Classifications (1985): D.3.1, F.4.2, I.2.7, H.2.3, H.3.1, J.1.5

ISBN 3-540-16781-1 Springer-Verlag Berlin Heidelberg New York
ISBN 0-387-16781-1 Springer-Verlag New York Berlin Heidelberg

Printing and binding: Beltz Offsetdruck, Hemsbach/Bergstr.
2145/3140-543210

Preface

The verb *to parse* means "to describe grammatically by stating the part of speech and explaining the syntactical relationship" (Webster's New Collegiate Dictionary). The noun *parser* refers to computer programs which grammatically analyze sentences or text of a language. Parser programs have been written for both formal languages (programming languages)[1] and natural languages (e. g. English or German).

Natural language parsers are a precondition of comfortable man-machine communication. Automatic speech recognition, data base interfaces, machine translation, and a host of other important applications require efficient natural language parsers. For this reason natural language parsing has always been a primary goal of non-numeric programming.

The construction of natural language parsers is an interdisciplinary enterprise, requiring the cooperation of linguists and computer scientists. This cooperation is characterized by a convenient division of labor. The linguists take pride in basing their grammars solely on linguistic grounds, such as natural language "universals". Whether or not their grammar is suitable for parsing programs is not considered an issue. The computer scientists, on the other hand, take pride in their ability to implement any grammar as a computer program as long as the grammar is a reasonably explicit formalism. How a grammar is implemented on a computer is considered irrelevant as long as the program runs reasonably fast, and the display of the output closely resembles the syntactic representations envisioned by the linguist.

However, despite great efforts for over thirty years, the parsing of natural language is still an unsolved mystery. There are many different parsing algorithms, each with its own merits and limitations. But somehow the structures found in natural language do not seem amenable to a general and efficient analysis with existing parsing programs. This is taken by many people as evidence that it is simply impossible to build computers which analyze (and understand) natural language with the ease and efficiency of a native speaker.

Why is the computational analysis of natural language such a difficult task? Is natural language or the theoretical approach at fault? So far the widely accepted separation of the "declarative" (grammatical) and the "procedural" (computational) aspects of parsing has prevented the investigating of whether contemporary formal grammars of natural language provide a suitable basis for parsing programs.

In this book it is shown that constituent structure analysis, predominant in today's grammars, induces an irregular order of linear composition which is the direct cause of extreme computational inefficiency. An alternative left-associative grammar is proposed, which operates with a regular order of linear compositions. Left-associative grammar is based on building up and cancelling valencies. Left-associative parsers differ from all other systems in that the history of the parse doubles as the linguistic analysis. The efficiency and descriptive power of left-associative grammar is illustrated with two left-associative natural language parsers: one for German and one for English.

Munich/Stanford, May 1986   R. Hausser

---

[1] For conversion of higher level statements into assembly or machine language in compilers.

Acknowledgements

The research for this book was supported by a Heisenberg grant from the Deutsche Forschungsgemeinschaft, West Germany. The parser programs were written during two 3 month stays at the Center for the Study of Language and Information, Stanford University, in 1984 and 1985. The German parser NEW-CAT (a name derived from 'NEW CATegorial approach') was first described in the CSLI publication IN-CSLI-85-5 of December 1985.

Conceptually NEWCAT is based on many years of linguistic research in syntax and semantics which would have remained dormant in the form of paper and pencil studies without the opportunity to work with the computing facilities and the people maintaining them at CSLI. I would like to thank Betsy Macken, John Perry, and Stanley Peters for sponsoring my stays there.

At various stages in the development of the programs, I received help from people who were or still are working at CSLI. Doug Cutting, Frederic Vander Elst, Mike Moore, Atty Mullins, Paul Oppenheimer, and Greep (alias Steven Tepper) spent long hours figuring out what I wanted and how to write it in LISP. Brad Horak and Joe Zingheim maintained the dandytiger in my office in top running condition. Emma Pease helped me with formatting this book in Latex. David Brown, Marjorie Maxwell, and Susi Parker helped me with the practical aspects of life at CSLI.

I benefitted especially from discussions with Tryg Ager, Pentti Kanerva, Ron Kaplan, Martin Kay, Joachim Laubsch, Eric Ostrom, Carl Pollard, Stuart Shieber, and Hans Uszkoreit. Steven Tepper and Theo Vennemann made detailed comments on the semifinal draft. I am indebted to Dikran Kargueuzian for help and advice on several occasions. Last, but not least, I would like to thank Deborah Kerman for proofreading the book. All remaining mistakes of style and substance are the responsibility of the author.

This book was reproduced from a camera-ready copy supplied by the author who gladly acknowledges the generous access to computers provided by CSLI.

Contents

Introduction

This book describes a **left-associative** approach to the syntax and semantics of natural language. A left-associative system analyzes a sentence from left to right, first combining word 1 and word 2, then adding word 3, then adding word 4, etc., until there are no more 'next words'. Conceptually, the left-associative approach is based on the notion of **possible continuations**: after word n has been added, the grammar specifies precisely what the categories of word n+1 may be.

The formal description of the possible continuations at the end of a 'sentence start' may be used to choose a grammatically compatible 'next word' (generation), or it may be used to decide whether a given 'next word' is grammatically compatible with the sentence start (parsing). Left-associative grammar is suited equally well for generation and for parsing.

Analyzing language in a linear, left-associative fashion in terms of possible continuations represents a substantial departure from contemporary linguistic analysis, which works in terms of constituent structures. Constituent structure analysis takes place in the theoretical space between the root of the constituent structure tree (usually called the S-node), representing an abstract category, and the leaves of the tree, representing the concrete words of the sentence (called the terminal symbols). Constituent structure analysis views the whole sentence by looking from the root of the tree to the terminal symbols (top-down analysis), or from the terminal symbols to the root of the tree (bottom-up analysis).[1]

Left-associative analysis, on the other hand, takes place in the theoretical space between the first and last words of a sentence or text. The only combinations permitted are between sentence starts and next words. The resulting trees are of a completely regular, left-associative nature (see example 1.3.4 below). The 'root' of a left-associative tree is not an abstract start symbol, but the result of the last combination of a sentence start and a next word. Left-associative trees are built only from the bottom up; every combination of a sentence start and a next word results in a new 'root'.

In other respects, however, left-associative grammar is very traditional. Linguistically, left-associative analyses are based solely on the concepts of **valency**

---

[1] Constituent structure trees are usually drawn upside down, with the root at the top and the terminal symbols at the bottom. See 1.2.1 as an example.

and **agreement**. These, in turn, are implemented on the basis of such traditional notions as case (nominative, genitive, dative, accusative), number (singular, plural), gender (masculine, femine, neuter), and person. Other notions
used are traditional word classes such as verb (of a certain valency), noun (of a
certain number, gender, and - in German - case), adjective, adverb, preposition,
etc.

Left-associative grammar resulted from attempts to build a parser for the
context-free categorial system presented in **Surface Compositional Grammar** (SCG, Hausser 1984). **SCG** argues that **categorial grammar**[2] has formal properties which differ intuitively, methodologically, and heuristically from
phrase structure grammar[3] The point of departure for this argument is the
weak equivalence between certain categorial grammars and certain phrase
structure grammars proven informally in Bar-Hillel (1953).

This weak equivalence in generative power has been interpreted by linguists
working in the paradigm of phrase structure grammar as if there were no important differences between categorial grammar and phrase structure grammar.
They saw no reason to explore possible differences in the descriptive potential of
the two kinds of formal grammar. Instead, systems which had originated within
categorial grammar, such as the various systems of Montague (1974), where
quickly redesigned: one kept their characteristic model-theoretic semantics but
replaced their categorial surface syntax with a corresponding phrase structure
system (with or without a transformational component).

SCG sets out to show that "the choice between phrase structure grammar
and categorial grammar is not merely a matter of terminological habit or profes-
sional expedience", but has far reaching consequences on the resulting linguistic
analyses. For instance, the categories of categorial grammar are combinatorially and denotationally transparent, while those of phrase structure grammar
are opaque.[4] **SCG** illustrates the descriptive potential of pure (i.e. context-free)
categorial grammar by presenting the syntax and the semantics of a relatively
large fragment of English.

The implementation of the **SCG** system as a parser was intended to further
explore the descriptive potential of pure categorial grammer. Rather than attempting to cast the English fragment defined in **SCG** into an existing parser
framework, such as an ATN, a chart parser, or an Early algorithm, it seemed
more suitable for our purposes to program the categorial principles of **SCG** directly. In the course of this project it became apparent that, well-motivated as
the grammatical system of **SCG** seemed from a linguistic point of view, it was
not a very suitable basis for an efficient parsing program. The reason for this

---

[2] In the tradition of Lesniewski (1929), Ajdukiewicz (1935), Bar-Hillel (1953), and Montague
(1974).

[3] In the tradition of Post (1936), Chomsky (1957), and Jackendoff (1977). Phrase structure
grammars are a linguistic application of Post's rewriting rule systems.

[4] These notions are briefly explained in section 3.1. For a more detailed discussion see
SCG.

is not an inherent property of categorial grammar but the irregular nature of conventional constituent structure trees[5], which are common to both categorial grammar and phrase structure grammar.

After this experience we switched to building a parser for German. We wanted to apply the methodological and heuristic principles of **SCG** in a new context. The use of a different natural language as the object of formal description and the goal of a computationally efficient implementation of this description soon made the syntactic formalism develop independently of the earlier pencil and paper system. We realized that **SCG** had not gone far enough. In hindsight, the formalism of **SCG** may be regarded as a last ditch attempt to save constituent structure analysis, albeit in the form of 'orthogonal trees'[6], while the new research has led us to the conclusion that constituent structure analysis should be abandoned completely.

The basic idea of left-associative parsing was implemented as a LISP-program in December 1984. After returning to CSLI in March, 1985, the linguistic scope of the parser expanded very quickly. NEWCAT (for 'NEW CATegorial approach') handles the word order of German in declarative and interrogative main clauses with and without auxiliaries, as well as in subordinate clauses. It handles all free word order variations, center embedded relative clauses of arbitrary depth, extraposed relative clauses, auxiliaries, modals, passive voice in main and subordinate clauses, multiple infinitives, conjunction, gapping, obligatory and optional adverbs, adverbial clauses, prepositional clauses, discontinuous elements, and the agreement between determiners, adjectives, nouns and verbs. In May 1985 the parser NEWCAT was demonstrated at Stanford University and the Stanford Research Institute.

During a third stay at CSLI from late September to December 1985, the principles of NEWCAT were extended in three directions: a revised left-associative German parser, called DCAT, a new left-associative English parser, called ECAT, and a new left-associative parser for propositional logic with truth-value assignment, called LOGCAT. The purpose of these extensions was to demonstrate that left-associative grammar is a general approach, applicable to different natural languages as well as to formal languages.

Since left-associative grammar was abstracted from comprehensive and efficiently running parsing programs, it will be convenient and illuminating to describe the linguistic theory at least in part by explaining how the programs proceed in the analysis of sentences. When we discuss general principles of left-associative parsing, we will use the name of the first left-associative parsing system, NEWCAT. When we turn to the specifics of the parsers for German and English, we will use the names DCAT and ECAT, respectively.

Chapter 1 provides the linguistic background of left-associative grammar. It describes the problems of constituent structure analysis, and explains the

---

[5] Cf. section 1.2.
[6] See **SCG**, chapter 3.

relationship between categorial grammar and left-associative grammar. The potential of left-associative grammar is illustrated with some examples of parsing continuous text.

Chapter 2 explains the relationship between the motor, the linguistic rules, the rule packages, and the lexicon of a left-associative parser. NEWCAT is shown to be a highly modular system, with regard to both the relation between the grammar and the parsing procedure, and the different parts of the grammar itself. In NEWCAT the parsing history doubles as the linguistic analysis. This aspect of left-associative parsing is illustrated by going through the derivation of a sentence word by word.

Chapter 3 presents the category system of left-associative grammar. The principles of categorization and the relationship between categories and rules, are explained in terms of a detailed analysis of German noun phrases. It is shown that in German the noun should not be defined as the 'head' of the noun phrase.

Chapter 4 illustrates the descriptive power of left-associative grammar in the analysis of complex syntactic constructions, such as word order phenomena in German main and subordinate clauses, passive and complex auxiliary constructions, center-embedded and extraposed relative clause with arbitrary stacking depth, syntactic ambiguity, etc.

Chapter 5 describes the category system and the basic combinatorial properties of a left-associative analysis of English. It explains the treatment of agreement and word order, and discusses a number of constructions such as passive voice, relative clauses, and interrogatives. The linguistic analysis is implemented in the left-associative parser ECAT/ELEX.

In appendix A the LISP code of the parser program DCAT/DLEX is documented. For many years, linguists have used formal languages to describe natural languages, for methodological and heuristic reasons. LISP, like other programming languages, is a formal language. But in contrast to formalisms defined only on paper, LISP has the advantage of actually running on computers. By printing the LISP code of DCAT/DLEX we provide an explicit formal description of the grammatical system. The descriptive scope of DCAT/DLEX is further documented in appendix B, where 164 additional sample derivations are presented. Appendix C presents 114 sample derivations of the parser ECAT. Appendix D contains a list of all 335 computer-generated derivations presented in this book.

The development of left-associative grammar would not have been possible without the sophisticated programming tools of today's LISP work-stations. They sharpen the perceptions of the researcher in two ways: by demanding the explicit formulation of linguistic hypotheses in the simple and precise code of the programming language, and by being a powerful tool for testing these hypotheses over a much wider range of data than could be managed with paper and pencil.

A closer study will doubtlessly reveal much room for improvement. By documenting left-associative grammar as completely as possible, we hope to provide a solid foundation for future team efforts to **expand** the system, as well as continuing in the best tradition of science.

1. Left-associative grammar

The linguistic theory underlying left-associative grammar differs from other contemporary approaches in that the traditional notions of a constituent structure or a dependency structure (cf. Matthews 1981, p. 71-88) are not employed. But like any theory of natural language, left-associative grammar is based on the concept of constituents. Constituents and constituent structures are not the same: the notion of a constituent refers to intuitions of the native speaker, while constituent structure is one of the formalisms invented by linguists to account for these intuitions.

The intuitions underlying the notion of a constituent may be formalized either in terms of possible continuations or in terms of substitutions. For example, the sentence start *The man who saw a movie yesterday* is similar to the sentence starts *The man* and *John* in that each may be continued in the same way, e.g. *sleeps on the couch* . The expressions in question are also similar in that they may be substituted for each other in a sentence without changing its grammaticality. So on this level the definitions of constituents, in terms of continuations and substitutions, are roughly equivalent.

Substitution tests are an essential tool of linguistic research and constitute the methodological basis for establishing different classes or categories of words, and of word groups or sentence parts. But in the context of left-associative grammar we prefer the definition of constituents in terms of possible continuations rather than in terms of substitutions because it is psychologically more natural: hearers often continue incomplete sentences, but nobody outside of linguistics has any cause to substitute constituents from one sentence into another. The substitution process runs counter to the linear nature of coding and decoding natural language.

1.1 The constituent structure paradox

Constituent structures are defined as trees which fulfill the following two conditions. First, words or constituents which belong together semantically are to be dominated directly and exhaustively by a node; thus *gave Mary* in the sentence

> *John gave Mary a book.*

is directly dominated by the node VP, while there is no node that directly and exhaustively dominates *John gave.*[1] Second, the branches of the constituent structure tree may not cross. This condition is also known as the 'non-tangling' condition. The term "constituent structure analysis" refers to grammars based on tree structures (or equivalent representations) which attempt to fulfill these two conditions whenever possible.

Constituent structure analysis is subject to a deeply rooted paradox, caused by the attempt to express linguistic intuitions in a way that is formally inadequate. The paradox of constituent structure analysis appears whenever two parts of a sentence which belong together semantically are not adjacent to each other in the sentence. Constructions which cannot be represented in standard constituent structure terms are not a problem of natural language but rather of the descriptive apparatus.

A classic example of the constituent structure paradox is 'discontinuous elements', as in 1.1.1.

1.1.1 *John looked the word up.*

Given the intuition that *looked* and *up* belong more closely together semantically than *look* and *the word*, the constituent structure tree for this example should be 1.1.2.

1.1.2 An illustration of the constituent structure paradox:

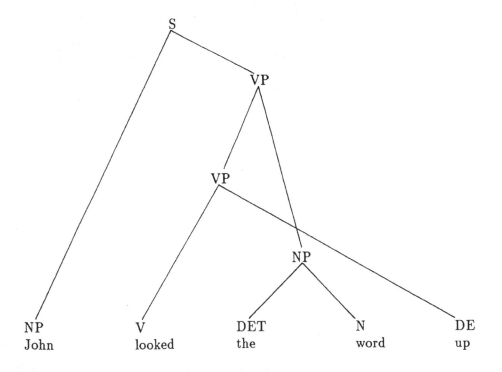

---

[1]See 1.2.1 below for the constituent structure tree of this example.

A tree like 1.1.2 is prohibited, because it violates the requirement that the lines of the tree may not cross. Yet an alternative tree without the crossing would violate the assumption that parts which belong together semantically must be dominated directly and exhaustively by a node characterizing them as a constituent. The paradox of constituent structure analysis is caused by the empirical fact of natural language that expressions which belong together from the viewpoint of semantic intuition need not be adjacent in the surface.

One way of salvaging constituent structure analysis from this dilemma is by postulating two separate structures, one for each of the two incompatible assumptions. For example, in transformational grammar the semantic intuitions of constituent structure are captured in the 'deep structure', and the facts of the surface serialization in the 'surface structure'.

Another way to resolve the dilemma is to give up one of the two incompatible assumptions. LFG[2] and GPSG[3] abandon the requirement that discontinuous elements must be directly and exhaustively dominated by a node in the constituent structure. Instead, LFG encodes the semantic intuition in the F-structure, defined as a directed acyclic graph, or DAG, while GPSG encodes it in the form of a feature system. Abandoning the semantic aspect of constituent structure analysis in those cases where it leads to problems is an *ad hoc* procedure.[4] It seriously weakens the status of constituent structure, and one might well ask why constituent structure should not be relinquished altogether.

There remains the possibility of abandoning or circumventing the condition that the lines of a tree may not cross in a constituent structure. The latter approach is taken by 'tree-linking grammar', which proposes three-dimensional trees. Given the linear, one-dimensional nature of natural language, three-dimensional constituent structures have a charming touch of extravagance. But the problem with any weakening of the 'non-tangling condition' is that the well-studied mathematical properties of two-dimensional trees, as well as the linguistic concepts and constraints based on the notions of **dominance** and **precedence**, are lost.

Left-associative grammar does not propose a new way to circumvent the paradox of constituent structure analysis.[5] Instead left-associative grammar avoids the use of constituent structures altogether. A natural language analysis without constituent structures may seem inconceivable to most contemporary

---

[2] Cf. Bresnan (1982).

[3] Cf. Gazdar et al. (1985).

[4] Despite appeal in GPSG to an 'autonomy of syntax' hypothesis offered as theoretical justification. Curiously, the 'autonomy of syntax' hypothesis was first championed in what GPSG considers its main opponent, i.e. Chomsky's later theories. LFG uses the C-structure only for treating language dependent facts of surface serialization and morphology. Thus constituent structure has a comparatively low status in LFG. What LFG takes to be the universal semantic properties of natural language are encoded in the F-structure.

[5] This was done in **SCG**. In hindsight orthogonal trees may be regarded as a rather abstract attempt to save the basic intuitions of constituent structure analysis by giving up the traditional tree structure.

formal linguists. But this reaction would be based on mistakenly equating syntactic structure and constituent structure — a terminological confusion similar to equating generative grammar and transformational grammar.

Constituent structure analysis is by no means the only kind of syntactic analysis proposed in the literature. There is also, for example, the tradition of dependency structure analysis. "A dependency grammar is a set of grammatical rules, stating the controlling and dependent relations that each class of units can, and by implication cannot, enter into." (Matthews, 1981, p. 81). However, dependency grammar, like constituent structure grammar, views the complete sentence as a two-dimensional hierarchical structure. This leads to problems similar to the dilemma of constituent structure analysis described above. Left-associative grammar differs from dependency grammar in that dependency relations are not defined between individual words or constituents, but solely between the 'sentence start' and the 'next word'.

1.2   The irregular left-to-right order of constituent structure

The descriptive problems of constituent structure analysis are only one reason for adopting a substantially different approach. The second and perhaps more important reason is the fact that constituent structure trees induce an irregular order of left-to-right combinations. Consider the standard constituent structure analysis of a simple example which does not involve the constituent structure paradox, e.g. *John gave Mary a book.*

1.2.1 Example of a constituent structure tree:

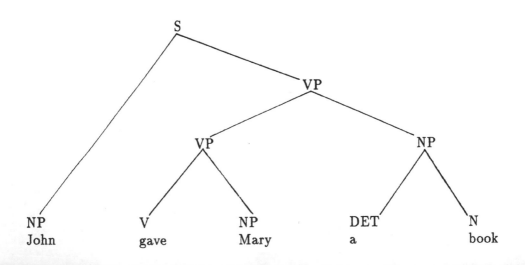

Natural language is encoded and decoded in a linear order, from beginning to end.[6] But within constituent structure analysis, intermediate structures like *John gave* or *John gave Mary a* are not acceptable; they do not satisfy the kinds of substitution tests on which this analysis is conceptually based. Thus there are no **categories** within constituent structure analysis that could be assigned to such expressions.

Left-associative grammar, on the other hand, is based on the notion of 'possible continuations'. *John gave* and *John gave Mary a* are acceptable intermediate structures because these expressions may be continued into complete well-formed sentences. In left-associative grammar *John gave* has the category (V D A), indicating a sentential expression (V) that still needs a dative (D) and an accusative (A) to be a complete sentence. Similarly, *John gave Mary a* has the category (V SN), indicating a sentential expression which needs a singular noun to be a complete sentence (see 1.3.4 below for the left-associative tree). The categories and the rules of left-associative grammar are designed to cancel off as well as build up valencies, and to encode the relevant agreement features.

From a linear point of view, constituent structures induce an irregular order of combinations that is very difficult to predict, and therefore extremely costly computationally. Consider the work of a conventional parser which uses the above constituent structure tree as the basis of its linguistic analysis. Such a parser would first combine *gave* and *Mary* into *gave Mary*. Then it would combine *a* and *book* into *a book*. Then it would combine *gave Mary* and *a book* into *gave Mary a book*. And finally it would combine the first word of the sentence, *John*, with *gave Mary a book*. Every time a conventional parser scans a new word, it is an open question (to be decided by the grammar) whether this word should be combined with expressions already analyzed, or set aside to be combined later with the words not yet scanned.

But each theoretical framework fosters its own kinds of intuitions and rationalizations. Linguists committed to constituent structure analysis refuse to consider the resulting irregular order of left-to-right composition as an issue, by claiming that the combination order of the **words** in a sentence is generally irrelevant for the essence of constituent structure analysis: the trees are supposed to represent grammatical relations *in abstracto*.[7]

That parsing necessarily involves a certain combination order of the words in the input string is treated as a 'procedural' problem and as such regarded as irrelevant for, or extraneous to, theoretical linguistic analysis. Natural language parsers which make no use of constituent structure are often dismissed as 'hacks', i.e. pieces of *ad hoc* programming which lack generality and have no theoretical foundation. While it is true that a natural language parser should be based on a general and clear linguistic theory, it is by no means certain that the theory must be a version of constituent structure analysis.

---

[6]Or left to right, assuming the writing conventions of most Western cultures.

[7]Instead the discussion within linguistics has centered on the ordering of **rules**, e.g. intrinsic versus extrinsic ordering of transformations and of phonological rules.

Today's natural language parsers vary widely as to whether they analyze constituent structures top-down, bottom-up, left-to-right, right-to-left, left-corner, right-corner, etc. Each ordering has its own merits and faults depending on the constructions handled by the grammar[8]. So it may seem that the order of combination is something of dubious theoretical status, best handled by purely computational considerations.

But one may interpret this situation quite differently: that no dominant order of combination has emerged in contemporary natural language parsing is a direct result of the fact that the underlying linguistic analysis imposes an irregular order of left-to-right composition. The widely acknowledged lack of substantial progress in natural language parsing during the last 25 years[9] must be largely attributed to the overwhelming dominance of constituent structure analysis in theoretical and computational linguistics.

1.3   Left-associative versus categorial grammar

Left-associative grammar developed in the course of attempting to program the orthogonal syntax of **Surface Compositional Grammar** (SCG, Hausser 1984), which uses the insights of categorial grammar from Lesniewski 1929 to Montague 1974 in describing the syntax and semantics of a fairly large fragment of natural language. But **SCG** is still a conventional categorial system in that it makes great efforts to satisfy traditional concepts of constituent structure, although in the form of orthogonal trees. The purpose of the orthogonal trees is to solve the constituent structure paradox by separating the surface order (specified vertically) and the semantic order (specified horizontally).

In our initial project to implement the **SCG** grammar as a parser, the constituent structure nature of **SCG** was reflected in the bracketing structure of the input string:

1.3.1 Bracketing structure of a categorial **SCG** analysis:
   (John,((gave,Mary),(the,book)))

This attempt at writing a categorial parser, a system called CATG (for CATegorial Grammar), worked very nicely on the basis of categorial cancelling rules. But it would analyze inputs only if the proper bracketing was provided, as in 1.3.1. Since a bracketing that reflects constituent structure is of an irregular nature which cannot be predicted, we had to either provide the bracketing of the input string by hand, or test the string automatically for all possible bracketings. Both possibilities where unacceptable, the first because of its dependence on human preprocessing, and the second because of its staggering computational inefficiency.

---

[8]See Winograd (1984) for a description of the different systems proposed in the literature.
[9]See Rich (1983), p. 295.

As an alternative we explored the idea of using a completely regular bracketing structure, conceptually based on the notion of possible continuations.

1.3.2 Bracketing structure of a left-associative analysis:
((((John,gave),Mary),the),book)

Rewriting the rules of CATG to accommodate this regular bracketing structure turned out to be surprisingly easy. Further study of this new approach led to the development of left-associative grammar and the parser NEWCAT.

To clarify the conceptual difference between a left-associative grammar and a categorial grammar, consider the following linguistic analyses of the sentence *"John gave Mary the book."* (1.3.3 and 1.3.4 below).

1.3.3 Analysis in traditional categorial grammar

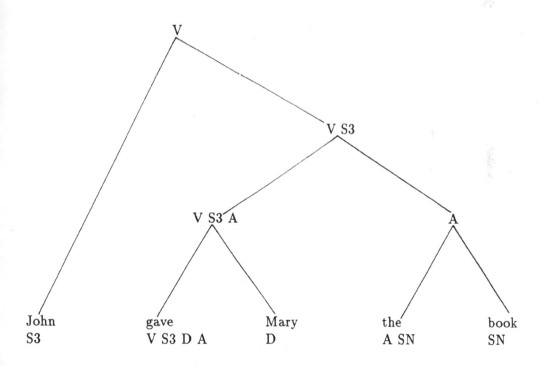

| John | gave | Mary | the | book |
| S3 | V S3 D A | D | A SN | SN |

1.3.4 Analysis in left-associative grammar

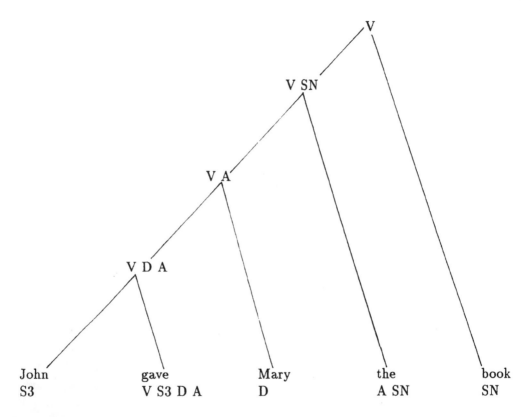

Which grammar is preferable? 1.3.3 and 1.3.4 assign exactly the same categories to the words. These categories are well-motivated. S3 indicates a nominative of third person singular, V S3 D A indicates a verb that takes an S3, a D (for dative noun phrase) and an A (for accusative noun phrase) as its obligatory arguments, and A SN indicates a determiner which takes a singular noun to render an accusative. On the basis of these categories, quite similar categorial combination rules may be defined in 1.3.3 and 1.3.4. So what is the difference?

The difference is in the order of the combinations of words in the sentence. Consider a bottom-up analysis of the two trees. In 1.3.4 the grammar combines *John* with *gave*, takes that and combines it with *Mary*, takes that and combines it with *the*, and so on. In 1.3.3, on the other hand, the grammar cannot combine *John* with anything until it has reached the end of the sentence and built up the (V S3)[10] constituent *gave Mary the book*. As far as parsing is concerned, the structure in 1.3.4 is computationally more efficient than the structure in 1.3.3, for reasons that are intuitively obvious. Whenever a new word is scanned in 1.3.3, it is difficult to decide whether this word should be combined with

---

[10]or VP, to use a more familiar notation

something already analyzed, or stored away to be combined later with something else.

The difference in the order of linear combinations implies other profound distinctions between constituent structure trees and left-associative trees. While it is meaningful to talk about a top-down versus bottom-up analysis in a constituent structure tree like 1.3.3[11], this alternative makes no conceptual sense in a left-associative tree like 1.3.4. The only way a left-associative tree can be meaningfully interpreted is bottom-up from left to right, such that the last combination of a sentence start and a next word results in the 'root'. This left-associative order holds for both parsing and generation.

In the final analysis, the choice between examples 1.3.3 and 1.3.4 comes down to the question of whether or not left-associative combinations like *John + gave* or *John gave Mary + the* should be permitted in a categorial style grammar. Given the present state of the field, one is initially inclined to reject a system that uses exclusively left-associative combinations, because the resulting structures seem to violate what we feel to be strong and solid intuitions about constituent structure. But our interpretation of these intuitions is at least in part determined by the contemporary state of linguistics. Therefore, the answer to the question at hand should be based not on our initial reaction, but on a careful evaluation of how well a system using only left-associative combinations will actually work, what kind of constructions it will account for, and what kind of generalizations it will render.

Furthermore, it should be noted that our naive intuitions about constituent structure are made quite explicit in a left-associative analysis, although in an unfamiliar, 'linear' way. The beginning of a constituent in a left-associative analysis is the place in the sentence where a word is added whose first category segment is a 'result category', such as S3 (third person singular nominative) or ADV-T (temporal adverb), etc.[12] Thus the first category segment of the 'next word' will indicate what kind of a constituent has been initiated.

If there are no further category segments, the 'next word' is considered a complete basic constituent, such as a proper name like ((Maria)(S3)). If there are additional category segments, however, as in the German article ((der) (S3 MS -EN))), the constituent initialized by this word may or must be followed by words which complete the constituent. In this case the end of a constituent is the place in the sentence where the argument segments imported by the category of the word initiating the constituent have all been cancelled off by subsequent words (which make up the inside of the constituent). In nested constructions a new constituent of lower rank may begin in the middle of an incomplete constituent.[13]

In short, the question is not whether or not constituents exist, but rather

---

[11] Irrespective of whether such a tree uses categorial or phrase structure categories.

[12] The notation of categories may vary depending on the agreement properties of the language in question.

[13] See 4.3.1 for an extreme example of this process.

how to represent them. In constituent structure analysis, the relevant intuitions
are encoded in terms of non-linear, hierarchical tree structures; these irregular
trees correspond to an irregular order of combining the words in the sentence.
In left-associative grammar, on the other hand, the order of combinatorial operations and the characterization of constituents are separated. The order of
combinatorial operations is left to right, word by word, and may be represented
by a left-associative tree; it reflects the linear nature of coding and decoding in
natural language. The intuitions regarding constituents, on the other hand, are
expressed by the categories of left-associative grammar.[14]

1.4 Left-associative trees as structured lists

Consider now the actual ECAT analysis of the sentence *John gave Mary a book*
in 1.4.1 below. The input typed on the terminal consists of a left parenthesis, the
function name R (for 'read'), the sentence to be parsed, and a right parenthesis.

1.4.1 *John gave Mary a book.*

```
(R John gave Mary a book .)
((*CMPLT ((John gave Mary a book %.)
        (DECL)
        1
        (*START (John)
               (SH)
               (gave)
               (V N D A))
        2
        (*NOM+FVERB (John gave)
               (V D A SH)
               (Mary)
               (SH))
        3
        (*FVERB+MAIN (John gave Mary)
               (V A SH SH)
               (a)
               (C))
        4
        (*FVERB+MAIN (John gave Mary a)
               (V C SH SH)
               (book)
               (C-H))
        5
        (*DET+NOUN (John gave Mary a book)
               (V SH SH S-H)
               (%.)
               (DECL V))
        6)))
```

---

[14] For further discussion of the relation of constituent structure analysis and left-associative
grammar see section 4.4.

The linguistic analysis of a left-associative parse is a structured list which represents the history of the computation. The history consists of numbered history segments. Each history segment characterizes the combination of a sentence start with a next word. A sentence start is made up of the name of a rule package, a surface, and a category, while the next word consists only of a surface and a category. For example, the sentence start of history section 2 is 1.4.2:

1.4.2 Example of a sentence start in a history section:

```
2
(*NOM+FVERB (John gave)
            (V D A SH)
```

while the next word in this history section is 1.4.3:

1.4.3 Example of a next word in a history section:

```
            (Mary)
            (SH))
```

The category (SH) in 1.4.3 indicates a singular noun phrase, while the category (V D A) in 1.4.2 indicates a sentential expression that still needs a dative and an accusative.

The last combination of a successful left-associative parse results in a sentence start without a next word. It is called the resulting sentence start and is printed at the beginning of the analysis. The resulting sentence start of analysis 1.4.1 is repeated below:

1.4.4 Example of a resulting sentence start:

```
(*CMPLT ((John gave Mary a book %.)
         (DECL))
```

Like all sentence starts, it consists of a rule package (in this case *CMPLT, indicating a complete sentence), a surface (here (*John gave Mary a book %.*)[15]), and a category (here (DECL), indicating declarative sentence mood).[16]

Given a left-associative analysis like 1.4.1, we generally distinguish between the **sentence start**, meaning the 'resulting sentence start', and the **history**, meaning the sequence of numbered history segments. If the input sentence is **n** words long, there will be **n-1** history segments in the left-associative parser analysis. The number of words in a sentence is indicated by the last number of

---

[15] The '%'-sign is added automatically by INTERLISPD and serves to distinguish the punctuation sign from the LISP '.' .

[16] The sentence starts in the numbered history sections have a simpler bracketing structure than the resulting sentence start for the sake of perspicuity.

the history. Counting the punctuation mark as a word, the input sentence in 1.4.1 consists of 6 words.

The linguistic content of a left-associative analysis is encoded in **rule packages, rules,** and **categories**. The analysis of a sentence (parsing) by a left-associative grammar proceeds as follows. The rule package *START, which contains all the rules that may apply at the beginning of a sentence, is applied to the Cartesian product of all readings of the first two words of the sentence. If a rule in *START accepts one of these ordered pairs, for example NOM+FVERB, it produces a new sentence start. The rule package of this new sentence start, e.g. *NOM+FVERB, contains all the rules which may apply after NOM+FVERB has succeeded.

The name of a rule package is closely related to the name of the rule which calls the rule package. For example, since the rule package in history section 5 of 1.4.1 is named *DET+NOUN, we know that the rule responsible for the combination of the parts indicated in history section 4 is DET+NOUN. Thus a left-associative parse like 1.4.1 specifies not only the categories and the names of the rule packages at each stage of the derivation, but also the names of the rules. The name of the rule package in history section **n** specifies the name of the rule which applied in history section **n-1**.

At each left-associative combination, the grammar forms the Cartesian product of the last resulting sentence start(s) and the next word, and applies the rule package(s) of the sentence start(s) to the expressions of these pairs. Each successful application of a rule will result in a new sentence start. This process continues until either the end of the input expression is reached (no more 'next words'), or the analysis fails because at some point none of the available rules accepted any of the pairs.

Next consider the process of generation in a left-associative grammar. It begins by choosing two words readings of which are accepted by one of the rules in the rule package *START. The output of this rule produces a sentence start, containing another rule package. The third word chosen must be accepted as the 'next word' by one of the rules in this second rule package, resulting again in a sentence start. This process can be continued indefinitely.

If a combination attempt produces several sentence starts, the grammar will pursue their continuation in parallel. If the input expression is unambiguous, only one of these intermediate structures will be continued to the end. If the input has more than one reading, several output analyses will result. As an example consider 1.4.5:

1.4.5 Left-associative analysis of an ambiguous sentence:
   John was given a book by Mary.

```
(R John was given a book by Mary .)
((*CMPLT ((John was given a book by Mary %.)
        (DECL)
        1
        (*START (John)
```

```
                  (SH)
                  (was)
                  (V S3 B))
          2
          (*NOM+FVERB (John was)
                     (V B SH)
                     (given)
                     (HV D A))
          3
          (*ADD-VERB (John was given)
                     (V A AG SH)
                     (a)
                     (C))
          4
          (*FVERB+MAIN (John was given a)
                       (V C AG SH)
                       (book)
                       (C-H))
          5
          (*DET+NOUN (John was given a book)
                     (V AG SH S-H)
                     (by)
                     (PNM NP))
          6
          (*NOUN+PNM (John was given a book by)
                     (V NP AG SH)
                     (Mary)
                     (SH))
          7
          (*PREP+NP (John was given a book by Mary)
                    (V AG SH)
                    (%.)
                    (DECL V))
          8))
(*CMPLT ((John was given a book by Mary %.)
        (DECL)
        1
        (*START (John)
                (SH)
                (was)
                (V S3 B))
        2
        (*NOM+FVERB (John was)
                   (V B SH)
                   (given)
                   (HV D A))
        3
        (*ADD-VERB (John was given)
                   (V A AG SH)
                   (a)
                   (C))
        4
        (*FVERB+MAIN (John was given a)
                     (V C AG SH)
                     (book)
```

```
                    (C-H))
        5
        (*DET+NOUN  (John was given a book)
                    (V AG SH S-H)
                    (by)
                    (AG NP))
        6
        (*FVERB+MAIN (John was given a book by)
                    (V NP SH S-H)
                    (Mary)
                    (SH))
        7
        (*PREP+NP (John was given a book by Mary)
                    (V SH SH)
                    (%.)
                    (DECL V))
        8)))
```

The rule package *NOUN+PNM in history section 6 of the first analysis indicates that the combination in section 5 is of a noun and (the beginning of) a PNM, or postnominal modifier. This is the adnominal reading of *by Mary*. In contrast, the rule package in section 6 of the second analysis is *FVERB+MAIN, indicating that section 5 initiates a constituent serving as an argument to the verb. This is the reading where *by Mary* characterizes the agent of the giving.

The categories, the rules, and the rule packages of the German parser DCAT and the English parser ECAT will be discussed in detail below. For the moment consider the relationship between the two kinds of representation we have used for left-associative analysis, namely a **left-associative tree** like 1.3.4 and a **structured list** like 1.4.1. 1.3.4 and 1.4.1 look different: the tree 1.3.4 is to be read diagonally from left to right, while the list 1.4.1 is to be read from top to bottom. But they encode exactly the same structural information.

As proof consider the abstract left-associative tree 1.4.6(i) and the corresponding structured lists 1.4.6(ii) and 1.4.6(iii):

1.4.6 Left-associative trees and structured lists:

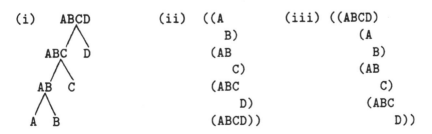

The structured list 1.4.6(ii) is isomorphic to the binary tree 1.4.6(i): the last line of (ii) corresponds to the root of the tree in (i); the elements of the next higher pair in (ii) correspond to the daughters of the root in (ii); and so on.

Each left-associative combination takes a sentence start, e.g. A, and a new word, e.g. B, and derives a new sentence start, AB. The sentence start completing the derivation, e.g. ABCD, is represented in (i) as the root of the tree, and in (ii) as the last line of the structured list. Since we would like the result of a derivation to appear at the beginning rather than the end of the structured list, we define the output of NEWCAT analyses in accordance with (iii) rather than (ii). The difference between (ii) and (iii) is that the last line in (ii) appears as the first line in (iii). Since (iii) is a simple transformation of (ii), the isomorphism between the left-associative tree (i) and the structured list (ii) also holds between (i) and the structured list (iii). The first element of the structured list in (iii) is the 'resulting sentence start', while the remaining elements constitute the 'history' of the derivation.

Since left-associative trees like 1.3.4 are always of the same completely regular form, they have no intrinsic heuristic or descriptive value within left-associative grammar. Furthermore, since trees are comparatively difficult to display and to print, left-associative analyses are presented in the form of structurally equivalent lists, as shown in 1.4.1.

1.5 Parsing continuous text

We have seen that left-associative trees are always built bottom-up and left-to-right, so that the 'root' of the tree is the result of the last combination of a sentence start and a next word. In other words, the start of the derivation coincides with the start of the sentence, and the end of the derivation describes the addition of the last word of the input. Whether this last word happens to be the beginning of a constituent, as in 1.5.1, the end of a constituent, as in 1.5.2, or a complete sentence followed by the beginning of another sentence, as in 1.5.3, is of no consequence whatsoever.

1.5.1 Analyzing a sentence start ending in an incomplete constituent:
John gave Mary a

```
(R John gave Mary a)
((*FVERB+MAIN ((John gave Mary a)
             (V C SH SH)
      1
      (*START (John)
              (SH)
              (gave)
              (V N D A))
      2
      (*NOM+FVERB (John gave)
              (V D A SH)
              (Mary)
              (SH))
      3
      (*FVERB+MAIN (John gave Mary)
```

```
                      (V A SH SH)
                      (a)
                      (C))
              4)))
```

1.5.2 Analyzing a sentence start ending in a complete constituent:
An old beautiful book

```
(R an old beautiful book)
((*DET+NOUN ((an old beautiful book)
            (S-H)
            1
            (*START (an)
                    (-C)
                    (old)
                    (-CA))
            2
            (*DET+ADJ (an old)
                      (S)
                      (beautiful)
                      (CA))
            3
            (*DET+ADJ (an old beautiful)
                      (S)
                      (book)
                      (C-H))
            4)))
```

1.5.3 Analyzing a sentence followed by the beginning of another sentence:
John gave Mary a book. The book[17]

```
(R John gave Mary a book . the book)
((*DET+NOUN ((John gave Mary a book %. the book)
            (S-H)
            1
            (*START (John)
                    (SH)
                    (gave)
                    (V N D A))
            2
            (*NOM+FVERB (John gave)
                        (V D A SH)
                        (Mary)
                        (SH))
            3
            (*FVERB+MAIN (John gave Mary)
                         (V A SH SH)
                         (a)
                         (C))
            4
            (*FVERB+MAIN (John gave Mary a)
                         (V C SH SH)
```

---

[17]Capital letters at the beginning of sentences are not handled by ECAT.

```
                        (book)
                        (C-H))
            5
            (*DET+NOUN  (John gave Mary a book)
                        (V SH SH S-H)
                        (%.)
                        (DECL V))
            6
            (*CMPLT  (John gave Mary a book %,)
                     (DECL.)
                     (the)
                     (U))
            7
            (*START  (John gave Mary a book %. the)
                     (U)
                     (book)
                     (C-H))
            8)))
```

Due to the strictly linear nature of left-associative grammar, the linguistic analysis is not restricted by the boundaries of the sentence. A continuous text, consisting of a sequence of sentences (as in a book or a newspaper article), is analyzed in left-associative grammar like any other well-formed string of natural language. Given a sequence of grammatical input sentences, NEWCAT will analyze one sentence after the other without interruption. The completion of a sentence in the text is indicated by the application the rule package CMPLT (or *CMPLT in ECAT) , while the beginning of a new sentence is indicated by the rule package START (or *START in ECAT). As an example consider 1.5.4:

1.5.4 Analysis of a brief text in DCAT:

```
(CMPLT ((DER MANN KAUFTE EIN BUCH %. DAS BUCH LIEGT AUF DEM TISCH %. ER WILL
 DAS BUCH DEM MAEDCHEN GEBEN %.)
(DECL)))
1
(START (DER)
       (S3 MS -E)
       (MANN)
       (MS))
2
(DET+NOUN (DER MANN)
          (S3 MS)
          (KAUFTE)
          (V S3 A))
3
(MAIN+FVERB (DER MANN KAUFTE)
            (V A MS)
            (EIN)
            (A NS -ES))
4
(FVERB+MAIN (DER MANN KAUFTE EIN)
            (V MS NS -ES)
            (BUCH)
```

```
                    (NS))
5
(DET+NOUN (DER MANN KAUFTE EIN BUCH)
          (V MS NS)
          (%.)
          (V DECL))
6
(CMPLT (DER MANN KAUFTE EIN BUCH %.)
       (DECL)
       (DAS)
       (S3 NS -E))
7
(START (DER MANN KAUFTE EIN BUCH %. DAS)
       (S3 NS -E)
       (BUCH)
       (NS))
8
(DET+NOUN (DER MANN KAUFTE EIN BUCH %. DAS BUCH)
          (S3 NS)
          (LIEGT)
          (V S3 ADV-L))
9
(MAIN+FVERB (DER MANN KAUFTE EIN BUCH %. DAS BUCH LIEGT)
            (V ADV-L NS)
            (AUF)
            (ADV-L (D)))
10
(FVERB+MAIN (DER MANN KAUFTE EIN BUCH %. DAS BUCH LIEGT AUF)
            (V NS (D))
            (DEM)
            (D MS -EN))
11
(PREP+MAIN (DER MANN KAUFTE EIN BUCH %. DAS BUCH LIEGT AUF DEM)
           (V NS MS -EN)
           (TISCH)
           (MS))
12
(DET+NOUN (DER MANN KAUFTE EIN BUCH %. DAS BUCH LIEGT AUF DEM TISCH)
          (V NS MS)
          (%.)
          (V DECL))
13
(CMPLT (DER MANN KAUFTE EIN BUCH %. DAS BUCH LIEGT AUF DEM TISCH %.)
       (DECL)
       (ER)
       (S3))
14
(START (DER MANN KAUFTE EIN BUCH %. DAS BUCH LIEGT AUF DEM TISCH %. ER)
       (S3)
       (WILL)
       (V S3 W))
15
(MAIN+FVERB (DER MANN KAUFTE EIN BUCH %. DAS BUCH LIEGT AUF DEM TISCH %. ER
             WILL)
            (V W)
```

```
                (DAS)
                (A NS -E))
16
(FVERB+MAIN (DER MANN KAUFTE EIN BUCH %. DAS BUCH LIEGT AUF DEM TISCH %. ER
                WILL DAS)
                (V W A NS -E)
                (BUCH)
                (NS))
17
(DET+NOUN (DER MANN KAUFTE EIN BUCH %. DAS BUCH LIEGT AUF DEM TISCH %. ER
                WILL DAS BUCH)
                (V W A NS)
                (DEM)
                (D NS -EN))
18
(FVERB+MAIN (DER MANN KAUFTE EIN BUCH %. DAS BUCH LIEGT AUF DEM TISCH %. ER
                WILL DAS BUCH DEM)
                (V W A NS D NS -EN)
                (MAEDCHEN)
                (NS))
19
(DET+NOUN (DER MANN KAUFTE EIN BUCH %. DAS BUCH LIEGT AUF DEM TISCH %. ER
                WILL DAS BUCH DEM MAEDCHEN)
                (V W A NS D NS)
                (GEBEN)
                (W D A INF))
20
(MAINCL+NFVERB (DER MANN KAUFTE EIN BUCH %. DAS BUCH LIEGT AUF DEM TISCH %. ER
                WILL DAS BUCH DEM MAEDCHEN GEBEN)
                (V NS NS INF)
                (%.)
                (V DECL))
21))
```

The above example shows that NEWCAT parses a text just as it would parse a single sentence or part of a single sentence.[18]

Analyzing continuous text is of great practical potential. One application is automatic conversion of a text into a database. Assume, for example, that a left-associative analysis like 1.4.1 includes an automatic restatement of the grammatical relations in a PROLOG-like form[19], such as

give(john,mary,book).

---

[18]Those versions of NEWCAT which parse continuous text are actually more systematic than those which do not. In earlier versions of NEWCAT which were restricted to parsing single sentences, the first rule package START is not called by any rule and the last rule (then called INTERPUNCT, now called CMPLT) does not call a rule package. The present version of NEWCAT with text parsing is more consistent in that every rule calls a rule package and every rule package is called by a rule. Instead of carrying along the surface of the whole previous text at each combination step, one might prefer a version in which only the surface of the last incomplete sentence was given in the history. This version of NEWCAT is easily implemented by specifying that the output surface of RSTART should consist only of the surface of the second input expression.

[19]See Clocksin and Mellish (1984).

This would result in a system which not only can analyze newspaper articles or other texts grammatically, but which automatically creates a database-like presentation of the content. Such a system of Automatic Data Base Conversion (ADBC) would read continuous text and transform the content into a database. The database may be accessed either in the standard way, such as a PROLOG-question like

    ?- give(X,mary,book),

or with the corresponding natural language expressions.

Another application is literary analysis. Rather than merely counting the frequency of words in a text, one may use continuous left-associative analysis to automatically investigate the text for certain kinds of syntactic constructions. Furthermore, the continuous left-associative analysis may be implemented as a 'grammar and style checker', in analogy to the existing orthography checkers.

Besides these practical applications, analysis of continuous text is also very interesting linguistically. For example, anaphoric pronouns may have their antecedent not only in the same sentence, as in

    After John came home, he took a bath.

but also in a previous sentence, such as

    John came home at six. He was looking forward to a bath.

The latter cases are usually ignored in constituent structure grammar. This is because constituent structure grammar is limited to single sentences. Each constituent structure is a tree with the start symbol S as the abstract root and the words of the sentence as the terminal symbols. The relation between sentences and continuous text is problematic in constituent structure based approaches, because there is no obvious way to adapt the left-to-right order of sentences in a text to the peculiar viewpoint of constituent structure analysis.

The parsing of continuous text presents a vast field with enormous theoretical and practical potential. The list of descriptive tasks and their possible technical solutions is long and would serve little purpose in the present context. It may suffice that we have opened the door and considered a field to which the standard methods of theoretical linguistics have not seemed applicable.

2. Left-associative parsing

A good way of demonstrating the formal rigor as well as the descriptive scope of a grammatical theory is by implementing it as a parser. This has several scientific advantages. Formulating a grammatical system as a computer program requires a level of explicitness that enhances linguistic insight. Furthermore, testing a grammar electronically for a wide range of data is heuristically valuable for the analysis of language. Implementation also has practical applications: natural language parsers are needed for data base front ends, machine translation, and dialogue systems.[1].

Writing parsers for natural language is one of the oldest projects in non-numeric programming. Yet building good natural language parsers has turned out to be very difficult. There are some powerful formal parsing systems which can analyze structures of high complexity. But there are no parsers which analyze natural language with the ease and efficiency of a native speaker. The basis of a good parser is a good theory of natural language syntax. The transparency, transportability and expandability of parser programs should be well-grounded in linguistic theory.

2.1 A production system with a simple control structure

NEWCAT is the result of a linguist's attempt to implement his own theory as a computer program. The programming environment imposes constraints: some things are easy to program and others very hard. Given the formal grammar of **SCG**, the choice was between implementing it in its original form (which turned out to be difficult), or reformulating its linguistic content to adapt to the simple and straightforward constructs of standard LISP. From a linguistic point of view the second choice seemed easier and much more interesting.

As an alternative to a general purpose programming language like LISP, linguists have the choice of using 'specialized programming environments' such as the LFG system or the PATR-II system. These specialized environments are

---

[1] There are of course many more applications, such as computer assisted instruction (CAI) in foreign language teaching, style checkers, literary analysis, etc.

written in LISP and provide particular features, such as constituent structure tree generators (which are intended to facilitate the use of computers for syntactic analysis). Along with a simplified programming task, the user of these environments must accept a specific linguistic theory, which includes not only all the notational details, but also the conceptual approach underlying them. Since the goal was to implement a new type of categorial grammar, the use of a specialized programming environment was not an option. A general purpose programming language is preferable to a specialized programming environment because general purpose languages are not laden with particular linguistic assumptions, and provide for implementations which are ultimately faster, more versatile, and more transparent.

NEWCAT was written in INTERLISP-D and runs on a XEROX 1108 or 1109 Lisp machine. The refined NEWCAT version called DCAT, which is described in chapters 3 and 4 has been translated in Common Lisp and runs on the SUN 3 work station, VAX computers, and other machines supporting Common Lisp. The principles of the parser are quite general, and not restricted to a particular programming language or machine. NEWCAT is a data-driven, bottom-up, breadth-first, strictly left-associative parser. Furthermore, NEWCAT is a production system, consisting of an interpretive part and a control part. The interpretive part comprises the linguistic rules of the grammar, defined as productions: that is, pairs consisting of a condition part (called the **input condition**) and an action part (called the **output specification**). The conditional structure of these rules and their formal linguistic content can easily be expressed in any standard programming environment, or formulated on paper as 'declarative' rules (cf. 3.3.5, 3.3.7, 3.4.3, and 3.4.5). In NEWCAT the linguistic rules are implemented as LISP functions.

The control structure of NEWCAT is defined as follows. Given an input sentence, the parser looks at the first two words, forms the Cartesian product of all category readings of the first word and the second word, and applies to the resulting set of ordered pairs a **rule package** called START. The readings of each word are defined in the lexicon.

The lexicon of the parser NEWCAT is called NEWLX. NEWLX is a 'full form lexicon' in the sense that different surface forms like *gibt* ('gives') and *gab* ('gave') are regarded as different words. Different readings of a word are treated in terms of different categories. For example, the unanalyzed surface *las*[2] is defined in NEWLX as in 2.1.1:

2.1.1 Lexical analysis of a word in NEWLX:

```
(LAS ((V S1 A)
      (V S3 A)))
```

The two different categories in 2.1.1 indicate that *las* is a transitive verb of first or third person singular.

---

[2] *las* is the first or third person singular past tense of *lesen* or 'read'.

At the beginning of a parse, the lexical analysis of the first word is expanded into complete sentence starts. For example, 2.1.1 would be expanded into 2.1.2.

2.1.2 Expanding a lexical analysis into sentence starts:

```
[(START ((LAS)
         (V S1 A)))
 (START ((LAS)
         (V S3 A)))]
```

The verb form *las* may occur at the beginning of a yes/no-interrogative, such *Las Maria das Buch?*. By expanding the first word of a parse into complete sentence starts, consisting of the rule package (START) and a list of the surface and category of the word, the combination of the first two words of a sentence or text is treated exactly the same as any subsequent combination: the parser forms the Cartesian product of the sentence start and the next word and applies the rule package listed as the first element of the first member of the pair to the second elements of the first and second members of the pair.

START[3] comprises all productions that may apply at the beginning of a sentence. If the input condition of a production Rp-i in START is satisfied by an ordered pair, the output specification of Rp-i produces a new 'sentence start' consisting of (i) the name of a new rule package p-i which lists all productions that may apply after Rp-i has been successful, and (ii) an output expression which consists of (iia) an output surface consisting of the concatenation of the surfaces of the input expressions, and (iib) the category of the output surface. The state of the machine after the application of production Rp-i is partially characterized in terms of the rule package p-i.

With the rule package and the output expression, the parser is ready for the next left-associative combination. Given a new next word, the parser will form pairs of the previously generated output expression and all readings of the next word. Then it applies the rule package p-i, which, if successful, results in a new sentence start consisting of another rule package and a new output expression with a surface one word longer than its predecessor.

In other words, the output of the first left-associative combination readies the parser for the second combination: all it needs is a suitable next word. Then the output of the second combination readies the parser for the third combination, and so on. The process continues in this way until it either (i) fails because none of the rules of the rule package called at a given point in the sentence is successful (because none of the categories of the 'next word' is grammatically compatible), or (ii) succeeds by reaching the end of the sentence or text. The end is reached when there is no further 'next word'.

If more than one input pair is accepted by the different rules in a rule package, there will be several sentence starts, all with the same surface but with different rule packages and different categories. These sentence starts are continued in

---

[3]Or *START in ECAT.

parallel. For each sentence start the parser forms the Cartesian product of its output expression and all category readings of the next word. Then the rule package of each sentence start is applied to its set of ordered pairs. The state of the machine after the application of a set of rule packages to sets of input pairs is characterized by the set of resulting sentence starts.

In summary, the control structure of NEWCAT is characterized by a coupling of each production Rp-i with the set of those productions that are applied just when Rp-i is successful. At the beginning of a text the initial rule package (i.e. START) is provided lexically by the first word. If a sentence S occurs within a continuous text, the rule package START is provided by the rule RSTART, which combines the text ending with the last complete sentence and the first word of the new sentence S. The parsing of continuous text is illustrated in section 1.5 above.

2.2   Modularity and expansion of the grammar

Given the scope of NEWCAT analyses (see appendix C), the program is relatively small. DCAT includes 18 linguistic rules and has a length of 78,000 bytes (uncompiled) or 28,000 bytes (compiled). But as with any complex program, the question arises whether the system is really **modular**. A system is modular if changing one part does not necessitate rewriting all the other parts. In complex computer programs, modularity is highly desirable.

One kind of modularity in natural language parsing is the distinction between the 'procedural' and 'declarative' aspects of the system. This distinction may be intuitively described as follows. The procedural aspect is represented by an external framework which performs a sequence of computational operations controlling the application of linguistic rules. The declarative aspect, on the other hand, is represented by the content of the linguistic rules called by the external framework.

There are two reasons for the separation of the procedural and declarative aspects of parsing. One is to keep a given grammatical system, for example a transformational grammar, independent of different possible parsing implementations. The other is to keep a given parser, for example an augmented transition network, independent of the description of particular natural languages or particular versions of a grammatical theory.

But this kind of modularity does not mean that the grammar could or should be completely independent of the parsing system, or the parsing system completely independent of the grammar. This would be highly impractical. The grammatical rules and the computational operations which apply them in the course of a parse must be **compatible** if the result is to be of any theoretical or practical interest. For example, implementing a fairly large fragment of categorial grammar, such as the orthogonal syntax of **SCG**, as an ATN parser (which was designed for transformational grammars) would involve so much rewriting of the respective systems, to adapt the grammar to the parser or the parser to the grammar, that one would arrive at a new system - a result clearly contrary to the idea of modularity. In short, grammars are modular only relative to compatible types of parsers and parsers are modular only relative to compatible types of grammars.

In left-associative systems the compatibility between the grammar and the parser is based on the general principle of left-associative combinations. This principle is well-founded computationally, as well as linguistically and psychologically. Furthermore, it provides the basis for a close cooperation between the grammar and the parser: the computational history can double as the linguistic analysis because the computational operations of left-associative combination are regular and simple, and because the linguistic rules are adapted to this mode of combination.

At the same time the principle of left-associative combinations provides for a clear separation of the procedural and the declarative aspects of the system. The procedural aspect is represented by a computational routine which goes through the sentence from left to right, generates the Cartesian product of the sentence start and the next word, sets up the system to attempt left-associative combinations on each of the pairs, takes the result and the next word, and repeats the process. This procedure is completely independent of the properties of the particular natural language described. The German parser DCAT, the English parser ECAT, and the parser for propositional calculus LOGCAT use exactly the same procedure, described in A.1 as the 'motor of a left-associative parser'.

The declarative aspect of a left-associative parser, on the other hand, is represented by the linguistic rules and rule packages used by the general procedure. While these rules and rule packages always have the same form, their grammatical content will differ for different languages. The linguistic control structure of NEWCAT, based on the interaction of linguistic rules and rule packages, may be displayed in the form of an undirected graph by the MASTERSCOPE program and BROWSER package. These two INTERLISP-D packages are designed to analyze complex programming structures. MASTERSCOPE has calls such as 'analyze functions on record' and 'show paths from function to function'.

The most natural way to display the control structure of NEWCAT using MASTERSCOPE is to 'show paths from START to CMPLT'. In the resulting graph each rule package is shown once. The beginning of the graph characterizing the German parser DCAT is shown in 2.2.1 below.

2.2.1 The initial part of the MASTERSCOPE graph of DCAT:

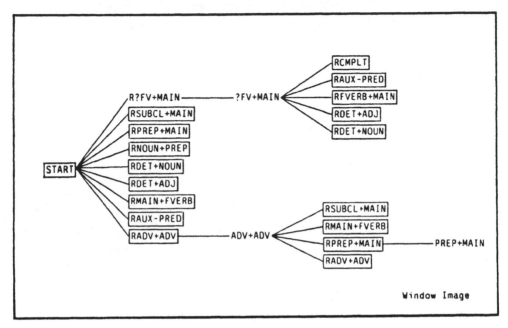

We see that ADV+ADV (called by RADV+ADV) contains four rules. In practice, all four rules will be active[4] if the derivation happens to run through RADV+ADV and ADV+ADV. For the purpose of representation, however, the chart continues only one or two rules of each rule package. The rules mentioned in the graph, along with the lines connecting them, give a complete picture of the structure of the program. Inasmuch as the program is an accurate representation of the language analyzed, the MASTERSCOPE graph may be regarded as a 'floor plan' of (the syntax of) the language.

The graph partly given in 2.2.1 has a certain practical interest as a potential floor plan of a "German chip", i.e. as the basic layout for a hardwired or microcoded version of DCAT. Furthermore, it is linguistically interesting to write NEWCAT parsers for other languages and compare the various graphs typologically. It is already apparent that the floor plan of an English NEWCAT parser would differ substantially from the graph of the corresponding German grammar. For example, while the rule package NOUN+RELPRO in the parser of German contains the rule RSUBCL+VERB (to handle a linear combination such as *Der Vogel, der + gesungen (hatte)*), this rule would not appear in the corresponding rule package of an English parser, because *The bird that + sung (had)* is ungrammatical. Instead, the English NOUN+RELPRO package would use RSUBCL+FVERB in order to derive *The bird that + had (sung)*.

As 2.2.1 shows, the basic layout of NEWCAT is essentially a finite state network (non-deterministic finite automaton). What goes beyond finite state

---

[4]In that they are potential continuation points for a transition.

and makes NEWCAT a context-free system is the fact that there is no upper bound on the number of categories. The empirical necessity of this feature of NEWCAT is discussed in section 4.3, which deals with center-embedding relative clauses to arbitrary depth. In this construction the grammatical categories are used as a stack; the more center-embedded relative clauses started, the longer the category (argument adding). When the finite verbs of the respective relative clauses are appended in a last-in, first-out fashion, the category becomes shorter again (wholesale cancelling up to the last V). Since there is no upper bound on the number of center-embedded relative clauses, there is no upper bound on the length of categories. Since there is no upper bound on the length of categories, there is no upper bound on the number of categories.

A striking feature of the program is the high degree of parallel computing inherent in the NEWCAT approach. Each time a new word is added in the course of a derivation, a rule package is called. In theory, all the rules of the rule package apply **in parallel** to the pairs derived from the sentence start and the new word. With present technology, the rules of each rule package must be applied in sequence. But the new parallel architecture would make it possible to utilize the inherent parallelism of NEWCAT, resulting in a system which would be considerably faster than the present sequential implementation.

We have seen that left-associative parsers and left-associative grammars are highly modular in the sense that the procedural and the declarative aspect the system are clearly separated. Let us turn now to another kind of modularity which concerns not the relation between the grammar and the parsing algorithm, but rather the relation between different parts of the grammar. Linguists working within constituent structure analysis use modularity to mean separating the syntactic analysis into several **levels**. But left-associative grammar, as a strictly linear, one-dimensional approach, does not postulate different levels of syntactic generation.

In the general sense of the word, however, modularity of grammar means that change of one part of the system does not affect the functioning of other parts. This is particularly important for redesigning the linguistic description of a specific construction and for expanding an existing system by adding new constructions. Is the left-associative approach modular as a grammatical system? Let us consider what would be required to add a new construction to a left-associative system. Prepositional phrases in adverbial use are already handled in DCAT.[5] But what would be required to add them to an earlier version of the system?

First, we have to know which expressions may be followed by a preposition. As it happens, prepositional phrases occur in the same positions as noun phrases and adverbs (constituents called MAIN in NEWCAT). By categorizing adverbial prepositions as (ADV-L (D)) (indicating a local adverb, initiated by a preposition, that still needs a dative) or (ADV-D (A)) (indicating a directional

---

[5]Chapter 4 presents DCAT analyses of several sentences containing prepositional phrases.

adverb that still needs an accusative), the addition of prepositions in the right places is already accounted for: wherever we can add a determiner, a name, or an elementary adverb, the existing rules will also accept a preposition. This is because the linguistic rules in question only look at the first category segment of the second expression. Thus RFVERB+MAIN does not care whether the second expression is a full noun phrase (proper name) or only the beginning of one (determiner), or whether the second expression is a full adverb, as in *Peter gab Maria + hier*, or only the beginning of one (i.e. a preposition), as in *Peter gab Maria + in*.

Next we have to write a linguistic rule that handles what may happen after a preposition has been added. This rule is called RPREP+MAIN. According to the input specification of RPREP+MAIN, the first expression must end in a preposition and the second expression must begin a noun phrase of the proper case. Take for example *Peter gab Maria in*, which is of category (V A (D)), indicating a declarative sentence still missing an accusative argument and a dative argument for a prepositional clause, and *der*, which may be of category (D MS -EN), indicating a dative, masculine, singular determiner that would agree with an adjective ending in -EN. RPREP+MAIN will form *Peter gab Maria in der* of category (V A MS -EN).

Finally we have to write the rule package PREP+MAIN to make sure that the prepositional phrase is properly completed. This rule package contains only rules that already exist, such as RDET+NOUN (to produce something like *Peter gab Maria in der Schule*), RDET+ADJ, RFVERB+MAIN, etc.

We have seen that adding the construction of adverbial prepositional phrases involved three simple and clearly defined steps: (i) the right categorization of prepositions ensured that the beginnings of prepositional phrases branched off at the right spots in the existing system; (ii) the definition of the linguistic rule RPREP+MAIN ensured that prepositions were followed by the right expressions; and (iii) the definition of the rule package PREP+MAIN not only made sure that the constituent was completed correctly, but also guided the continuation of the sentence back into the existing transition network.

The reason for the strong grammatical modularity of left-associative grammar is the linear nature of the derivations. No matter how long a sentence start is, the number of possible continuations will always depend on the number of readings of the sentence start and the number of rules in the rule packages of the respective readings. New constructions are basically new kinds of possible continuations. The rule packages, the input conditions of the rules, and the design of the categories completely control the flow of continuations in left-associative grammar.

2.3   The parsing history as linguistic analysis

Once the basic framework of NEWCAT had been completed it turned out that new constructions could be added very easily. It took only a few days (or weeks, for gapping) to incorporate any new construction into the system. The author is not aware of any construction types of German that would pose a basic computational or linguistic difficulty to the left-associative approach of NEWCAT. There are a few syntactic constructions, however, which are omitted for the sake of simplicity[6]; for example imperatives and the syntax of mass nouns.

One reason for the speed of NEWCAT is that the linguistic analysis printed by the parser consists simply of the derivational/computational history of the parse. This is possible because the linguistic analysis is based on left-associative combinations. In other words, the linguistic analysis and the computation are treated as different aspects of the same basic procedure. This is advantageous from a computational point of view, because it eliminates the need for the design of additional display facilities.

Using the parse history as the linguistic analysis is also desirable from a scientific point of view. It is well known that syntactic phenomena may be analyzed in many different ways. Within constituent structure analysis the choice between alternative possible analyses is motivated by appealing to 'universals' and other theory-internal principles. In NEWCAT, on the other hand, there is a direct correlation between the linguistic analysis chosen and the speed of the parser.

In the course of building the parser an analysis initially chosen for its intuitive linguistic appeal often turned out to be computationally costly.[7] Subsequent improvements aiming at a reduction of the number of combinatorial steps (by reducing the number of rules and the number of lexical readings) always turned out to be superior from a linguistic point of view as well, since the concrete morphological facts of the surface played a more dominant role.

Because the linguistic analysis and the computation are seen merely as different aspects of the same procedure, improvements of the syntactic analysis translate directly into a faster computation. Conversely, analyzing the computation of linguistic examples with the standard tracing facilities of LISP provides excellent heuristics for improving the linguistic description, leading to a better, i.e. more minimal, syntactic theory.

Left-associative combinations and the use of the parse history as the linguistic analysis, however, cannot alone guarantee an efficient system. It might very well have turned out that the number of readings in a breadth-first, left-associative NEWCAT parse increased so enormously with the length of the sentence that the approach was not computationally feasible. The speed of

---

[6]It is also useful to leave small, well-defined problems for students.

[7]As an example see the discussion of exhaustive versus distinctive categorization in section 3.1.

NEWCAT ultimately depends on the empirical linguistic fact that the number of possible readings at each step of the analysis is to be relatively small.

The intermediate steps of a left-associative derivation may be shown either in form of a trace, or by inputting longer and longer sentence starts. The latter method permits linguistic analysis even in LISP implementations which are not equipped with comfortable tracing facilities. The generation and elimination of readings in the course of deriving longer and longer sentence starts is illustrated in the following step by step derivation of the sentence 2.3.1:

2.3.1 *Das Mädchen gab dem Kind den Teller.*

This sentence, which means '*The girl gave the child the plate.*', is unambiguous. But the first two words of 2.3.1 in isolation have the following two DCAT analyses:

2.3.2 All readings of *Das Mädchen*

```
(R DAS MAEDCHEN)
((DET+NOUN ((DAS MAEDCHEN)
           (S3 NS))
          1
          (START (DAS)
                 (S3 NS -E)
                 (MAEDCHEN)
                 (NS))
          2)
 (DET+NOUN ((DAS MAEDCHEN)
           (A NS))
          1
          (START (DAS)
                 (A NS -E)
                 (MAEDCHEN)
                 (NS))
          2))
```

The two sentence starts represent the nominative and accusative readings of the noun phrase.

2.3.3 All readings of *Das Mädchen gab*

```
(R DAS MAEDCHEN GAB)
((MAIN+FVERB ((DAS MAEDCHEN GAB)
             (V D A NS))
            1
            (START (DAS)
                   (S3 NS -E)
                   (MAEDCHEN)
                   (NS))
            2
            (DET+NOUN (DAS MAEDCHEN)
                      (S3 NS)
                      (GAB)
```

```
                              (V S3 D A))
                     3)
(MAIN+FVERB ((DAS MAEDCHEN GAB)
            (V S1 D NS))
            1
            (START (DAS)
                   (A NS -E)
                   (MAEDCHEN)
                   (NS))
            2
            (DET+NOUN (DAS MAEDCHEN)
                      (A NS)
                      (GAB)
                      (V S1 D A))
                     3)
(MAIN+FVERB ((DAS MAEDCHEN GAB)
            (V S3 D NS))
            1
            (START (DAS)
                   (A NS -E)
                   (MAEDCHEN)
                   (NS))
            2
            (DET+NOUN (DAS MAEDCHEN)
                      (A NS)
                      (GAB)
                      (V S3 D A))
                     3))
```

The first sentence start represents the reading in which the noun phrase is a
nominative and the verb is third person singular. The second sentence start
represents the reading in which the noun phrase is an accusative and the verb is
first person singular. The third sentence start represents the reading in which
the noun phrase is an accusative and the verb is third person singular.

2.3.4 All readings of *Das Mädchen gab dem*

```
(R DAS MAEDCHEN GAB DEM)
((FVERB+MAIN ((DAS MAEDCHEN GAB DEM)
             (V A NS MS -EN))
             1
             (START (DAS)
                    (S3 NS -E)
                    (MAEDCHEN)
                    (NS))
             2
             (DET+NOUN (DAS MAEDCHEN)
                       (S3 NS)
                       (GAB)
                       (V S3 D A))
             3
             (MAIN+FVERB (DAS MAEDCHEN GAB)
                         (V D A NS)
                         (DEM)
```

```
                                (D MS -EN))
                    4)
(FVERB+MAIN ((DAS MAEDCHEN GAB DEM)
            (V A NS NS -EN))
            1
            (START (DAS)
                   (S3 NS -E)
                   (MAEDCHEN)
                   (NS))
            2
            (DET+NOUN (DAS MAEDCHEN)
                      (S3 NS)
                      (GAB)
                      (V S3 D A))
            3
            (MAIN+FVERB (DAS MAEDCHEN GAB)
                        (V D A NS)
                        (DEM)
                        (D NS -EN))
                    4)
(FVERB+MAIN ((DAS MAEDCHEN GAB DEM)
            (V S1 NS MS -EN))
            1
            (START (DAS)
                   (A NS -E)
                   (MAEDCHEN)
                   (NS))
            2
            (DET+NOUN (DAS MAEDCHEN)
                      (A NS)
                      (GAB)
                      (V S1 D A))
            3
            (MAIN+FVERB (DAS MAEDCHEN GAB)
                        (V S1 D NS)
                        (DEM)
                        (D MS -EN))
                    4)
(FVERB+MAIN ((DAS MAEDCHEN GAB DEM)
            (V S1 NS NS -EN))
            1
            (START (DAS)
                   (A NS -E)
                   (MAEDCHEN)
                   (NS))
            2
            (DET+NOUN (DAS MAEDCHEN)
                      (A NS)
                      (GAB)
                      (V S1 D A))
            3
            (MAIN+FVERB (DAS MAEDCHEN GAB)
                        (V S1 D NS)
                        (DEM)
                        (D NS -EN))
```

```
                4)
(FVERB+MAIN ((DAS MAEDCHEN GAB DEM)
            (V S3 NS MS -EN))
            1
            (START (DAS)
                   (A NS -E)
                   (MAEDCHEN)
                   (NS))
            2
            (DET+NOUN (DAS MAEDCHEN)
                      (A NS)
                      (GAB)
                      (V S3 D A))
            3
            (MAIN+FVERB (DAS MAEDCHEN GAB)
                        (V S3 D NS)
                        (DEM)
                        (D MS -EN))
                4)
(FVERB+MAIN ((DAS MAEDCHEN GAB DEM)
            (V S3 NS NS -EN))
            1
            (START (DAS)
                   (A NS -E)
                   (MAEDCHEN)
                   (NS))
            2
            (DET+NOUN (DAS MAEDCHEN)
                      (A NS)
                      (GAB)
                      (V S3 D A))
            3
            (MAIN+FVERB (DAS MAEDCHEN GAB)
                        (V S3 D NS)
                        (DEM)
                        (D NS -EN))
            4))
```

The six sentence starts derive from the three readings of 2.3.3 and the fact that *dem* may be a determiner of masculine singular dative or neuter singular dative. In the first, third, and fifth sentence starts *dem* is of masculine gender; in the second, fourth, and sixth sentence starts, of neuter.[8]

2.3.5 All readings of *Das Mädchen gab dem Kind*

```
(R DAS MAEDCHEN GAB DEM KIND)
((DET+NOUN ((DAS MAEDCHEN GAB DEM KIND)
            (V A NS NS))
```

---

[8]An earlier version of NEWCAT implemented the constraint that if the nominative of a declarative main clause was not in initial position, it had to come as the first obligatory argument after the finite verb (which is in second position). This constraint eliminated all but the first two readings in 2.3.4. Theo Vennemann argued, however, that sentences like *Den Teller gab dem Kind das Mädchen.* are grammatical. Removal of the constraint resulted in the additional readings and a simplified parser.

```
            1
            (START (DAS)
                   (S3 NS -E)
                   (MAEDCHEN)
                   (NS))
            2
            (DET+NOUN (DAS MAEDCHEN)
                      (S3 NS)
                      (GAB)
                      (V S3 D A))
            3
            (MAIN+FVERB (DAS MAEDCHEN GAB)
                        (V D A NS)
                        (DEM)
                        (D NS -EN))
            4
            (FVERB+MAIN (DAS MAEDCHEN GAB DEM)
                        (V A NS NS -EN)
                        (KIND)
                        (NS))
            5)
  (DET+NOUN ((DAS MAEDCHEN GAB DEM KIND)
            (V S1 NS NS))
            1
            (START (DAS)
                   (A NS -E)
                   (MAEDCHEN)
                   (NS))
            2
            (DET+NOUN (DAS MAEDCHEN)
                      (A NS)
                      (GAB)
                      (V S1 D A))
            3
            (MAIN+FVERB (DAS MAEDCHEN GAB)
                        (V S1 D NS)
                        (DEM)
                        (D NS -EN))
            4
            (FVERB+MAIN (DAS MAEDCHEN GAB DEM)
                        (V S1 NS NS -EN)
                        (KIND)
                        (NS))
            5)
  (DET+NOUN ((DAS MAEDCHEN GAB DEM KIND)
            (V S3 NS NS))
            1
            (START (DAS)
                   (A NS -E)
                   (MAEDCHEN)
                   (NS))
            2
            (DET+NOUN (DAS MAEDCHEN)
                      (A NS)
                      (GAB)
```

```
                    (V S3 D A))
         3
      (MAIN+FVERB (DAS MAEDCHEN GAB)
                   (V S3 D NS)
                   (DEM)
                   (D NS -EN))
         4
      (FVERB+MAIN (DAS MAEDCHEN GAB DEM)
                   (V S3 NS NS -EN)
                   (KIND)
                   (NS))
         5))
```

Three of the previous six readings were eliminated, namely those where *dem* was categorized as of masculine gender.

2.3.6 All readings of *Das Mädchen gab dem Kind den*

```
(R DAS MAEDCHEN GAB DEM KIND DEN)
((FVERB+MAIN ((DAS MAEDCHEN GAB DEM KIND DEN)
              (V NS NS MS -EN))
         1
      (START (DAS)
             (S3 NS -E)
             (MAEDCHEN)
             (NS))
         2
      (DET+NOUN (DAS MAEDCHEN)
                (S3 NS)
                (GAB)
                (V S3 D A))
         3
      (MAIN+FVERB (DAS MAEDCHEN GAB)
                   (V D A NS)
                   (DEM)
                   (D NS -EN))
         4
      (FVERB+MAIN (DAS MAEDCHEN GAB DEM)
                   (V A NS NS -EN)
                   (KIND)
                   (NS))
         5
      (DET+NOUN (DAS MAEDCHEN GAB DEM KIND)
                (V A NS NS)
                (DEN)
                (A MS -EN))
         6))
```

Two of the three previous readings were eliminated, namely those where *das Mädchen* is interpreted as an accusative.

2.3.7 All readings of *Das Mädchen gab dem Kind den Teller*

```
(R DAS MAEDCHEN GAB DEM KIND DEN TELLER)
((DET+NOUN ((DAS MAEDCHEN GAB DEM KIND DEN TELLER)
```

```
(V NS NS MS))
1
(START (DAS)
       (S3 NS -E)
       (MAEDCHEN)
       (NS))
2
(DET+NOUN (DAS MAEDCHEN)
          (S3 NS)
          (GAB)
          (V S3 D A))
3
(MAIN+FVERB (DAS MAEDCHEN GAB)
            (V D A NS)
            (DEM)
            (D NS -EN))
4
(FVERB+MAIN (DAS MAEDCHEN GAB DEM)
            (V A NS NS -EN)
            (KIND)
            (NS))
5
(DET+NOUN (DAS MAEDCHEN GAB DEM KIND)
          (V A NS NS)
          (DEN)
          (A MS -EN))
6
(FVERB+MAIN (DAS MAEDCHEN GAB DEM KIND DEN)
            (V NS NS MS -EN)
            (TELLER)
            (MS))
7))
```

No previous reading was eliminated and no new reading arose.

2.3.8 All readings of *Das Mädchen gab dem Kind den Teller.*

```
(R DAS MAEDCHEN GAB DEM KIND DEN TELLER .)
((CMPLT ((DAS MAEDCHEN GAB DEM KIND DEN TELLER %.)
        (DECL))
    1
    (START (DAS)
           (S3 NS -E)
           (MAEDCHEN)
           (NS))
    2
    (DET+NOUN (DAS MAEDCHEN)
              (S3 NS)
              (GAB)
              (V S3 D A))
    3
    (MAIN+FVERB (DAS MAEDCHEN GAB)
                (V D A NS)
                (DEM)
                (D NS -EN))
```

```
4
(FVERB+MAIN (DAS MAEDCHEN GAB DEM)
            (V A NS NS -EN)
            (KIND)
            (NS))
5
(DET+NOUN (DAS MAEDCHEN GAB DEM KIND)
          (V A NS NS)
          (DEN)
          (A MS -EN))
6
(FVERB+MAIN (DAS MAEDCHEN GAB DEM KIND DEN)
            (V NS NS MS -EN)
            (TELLER)
            (MS))
7
(DET+NOUN (DAS MAEDCHEN GAB DEM KIND DEN TELLER)
          (V NS NS MS)
          (%.)
          (V DECL))
8))
```

In this last analysis the rule RCMPLT applied and the sentence is completed. The sequence 2.3.2 - 2.3.8 illustrates the breadth first approach of NEWCAT, which is based on eliminating incompatible readings at each step. Theoretically, the number of readings could have increased with each new word. We see, however, that after the third combination (i.e. after the fourth word of this eight word sentence), the number of readings drops and in the end only one reading survives.

Presumably, a native speaker would use intonational and contextual clues to pursue only a limited number of possible readings in the course of interpreting a sentence. Sentences which surprise the hearer with an unexpected grammatical interpretation are called 'garden path sentences'. Since NEWCAT derives all possible readings of all sentence starts of a sentence (as the examples 2.3.2 - 2.3.8 illustrate), 'garden path sentences' are derived by NEWCAT just like any other readings.

Each reading produced at the different steps of the above derivation is linguistically well-motivated in the sense that it could be continued to result in a complete grammatical sentence. This stands in marked contrast to other parsers, in which intermediate structures which admittedly have no linguistic motivation are generated 'on the fly'. The only intermediate structures used in a left-associative derivation are sentence starts which have grammatical continuations.

The order in which NEWCAT returns several readings of an input expression depends on the ordering of the word readings in the lexicon and the rules in the rule packages. This fact may be used to ensure that the grammatically most common reading is returned first. For example, in 2.3.3 the first reading analyzes *das Mädchen* as a nominative and *gab* as categorized for third person singular;

on the second reading *das Mädchen* is an accusative and *gab* is categorized for first person singular; on the third reading *das Mädchen* is an accusative and *gab* is categorized for third person singular.

If we wanted to invert the order of the first and the other two readings, we would have to list the accusative of *das* before the nominative. If we wanted to invert the second and the third reading, we would have to list the third person singular reading of *gab* before the first person singular reading in the DLEX.

Instead of having the system return all readings at once, one might prefer a version which returns only the first and grammatically most likely reading, with the other readings returned upon further prompting. Such a version, which is easily implemented, would simulate a depth first analysis. An altogether different matter is the construction of a genuine depth first left-associative parser. While this is theoretically possible, it would involve a major redesigning of the system. Conceptually the left-associative approach is neither primarily breadth first nor primarily depth first but rather of a genuinely parallel nature (cf. 2.2.1 above).

One might expect the number of possible continuations in a left-associative analysis to be prohibitively high, but given the linear structure of natural language, it is quite plausible that there would be a limited number of readings. The attempt at something like left-associative grammar in the 1950s by Yngve and others, which many regard as a conclusive failure, may be another reason, why left-associative grammar has not been successfully implemented before.

That the present attempt succeeded can be explained only in terms of its new **linguistic** approach. The linguistic approach underlying NEWCAT differs from that of other parsers by being conceptually based on the principles of categorial grammar. But this approach differs from categorial grammar (as well as from all other current syntactic theories) because it is strictly left-associative and conceptually based on the notion of possible continuations.[9] NEWCAT is computationally efficient because left-associative structures are computationally simple, and happen to provide a heuristically fruitful basis for linguistic analyses which are concretely motivated.

2.4   Parsing ungrammatical input

Whether or not the combination of a sentence start and a next word is grammatical depends on three factors: (i) the rule package of the sentence start; (ii) the category of the sentence start; and (iii) the category of the next word. A combination is grammatical if the rule package in question contains at least one rule which accepts the categories of the two input expressions and produces a

---

[9]The notion of continuations has been employed in the construction of compilers (continuation descriptors, cf. Abelson and Sussman, p. 446), but has not been used in the syntactic analysis of natural language.

new sentence start. If all rules of the rule package produce NIL for the two
categories, the reading represented by the sentence start is eliminated.

The elimination of a sentence start does not necessarily mean that the expression under analysis is determined at that point to be ungrammatical. This
depends on whether or not there are other, parallel sentence starts which continue to be viable readings. The continuation of an expression at a certain word
is ungrammatical if, and only if, none of the sentence starts derived in parallel
up to that word produces a grammatical combination with a reading of the
word.

In such a case NEWCAT gives the following output: (i) an error message
reading 'ERROR "Ungrammatical continuation at:"'; (ii) the last of the sentence
starts active at the point where the derivation failed; and (iii) the last reading
of the next word.[10] As an example consider 2.4.1.

2.4.1 Parsing an ungrammatical sentence in ECAT:

```
(R John read a old beautiful book .)
[ERROR "Ungrammatical continuation at:"
        ((*FVERB+MAIN ((John read a)
                      (V C SH)
                      1
                      (*START (John)
                      (SH)
                      (read)
                      (V N A))
                      2
                      (*NOM+FVERB (John read)
                                  (V A SH)
                                  (a)
                                  (C))
                      3))
        (*START ((old)
                (-CA]
```

Word 4 in 2.4.1 constitutes an ungrammatical continuation because the word
after the article *a* must begin with a consonant.

As an example from German consider 2.4.2:

2.4.2 Parsing an ungrammatical sentence in DCAT:

```
(R EIN KLUGES SCHOENES JUNGE MAEDCHEN)
[ERROR "Ungrammatical continuation at:"
        ((DET+ADJ ((EIN KLUGES SCHOENES)
                  (A NS -ES))
                  ((history:)
                  1
                  (START (EIN)
                        (A NS -ES)
                        (KLUGES)
```

---

[10]One may imagine further development of the error message feature which would be an
important factor in computer aided foreign language instruction.

```
                (-ES))
        2
        (DET+ADJ (EIN KLUGES)
                 (A NS -ES)
                 (SCHOENES)
                 (-ES))
            3))
   (START ((JUNGE)
           (A P -E]
```

Word 4 in 2.4.2 constitutes an ungrammatical continuation because *junge* violates the agreement conditions of German adjectives. Up to *ein kluges schönes* the expression actually has two readings, one representing the nominative, the other the accusative. The error message in 2.4.2 returns only the sentence start representing the last reading. The category of JUNGE in 2.4.2 represents the reading that happens to be the last in the lexicon; (A P -E) is the category of an adjective used as a determiner, as in *Peter mag junge Katzen*.

Earlier versions, which were not equipped with the error message feature illustrated above, simply return NIL if an expression is not accepted by the parser. The fact that the present version of NEWCAT returns the successful part of an unsuccessful derivation is not only of theoretical interest, when the input expression is actually ungrammatical (as in 2.4.2), but is also of practical use, in cases were the parser fails to accept a grammatical sentence (debugging). The latter case is a normal occurrence during the development of a parsing system of natural language. In the earlier systems the breakpoint was determined by going through the sentence word by word (as illustrated in section 2.2), up to the point where NIL was returned. The present version indicates the breakpoint automatically.

2.5   Some computational contrasts with other parsers

The formal structure of NEWCAT as a 'virtual machine' is very simple. We described it in section 2.1 as a production system with a control structure based on coupling productions with partial production sets. Let us compare it now with other virtual machines described in the literature. What is the relationship between NEWCAT and more standard parsers, for example recursive transition networks (RTNs)?

An obvious difference between NEWCAT and RTNs is that NEWCAT is left-associative, while RTNs are not. Consider for example *John gave Mary + the*. After finding the article *the*, an RTN pushes down into a lower NP network, continues there until the NP analysis is completed, and pops up to insert the whole NP analysis into the higher network. But if the next word is a basic NP, as in *John gave Mary + cookies*, the RTN processes *cookies* at the top level without pushing into a lower network. Thus RTNs characterize complex constituents in terms of a structure with levels where several networks are embedded in each other.

In contrast, a left-associative parser like NEWCAT always adds a next word to a sentence start in the same way, whether the next word is a complete basic constituent, the beginning of a complex constituent, or the continuation of a complex constituent. What RTNs treat in terms of different networks is handled in NEWCAT in terms of the **grammar**. For example, the category assigned to *John gave Mary the* is such that only rules like RDET+ADJ and RDET+NOUN in the next rule package are applicable (because only their input conditions will accept this category). In contrast, the category of *John gave Mary cookies* is such that only rules like RCMPLT and RADD+CONJ are applicable.

Its left-associative nature differentiates NEWCAT not only from ATNs and chart parsers, which are extensions of RTNs, but also from PDAs, bounded context automata, deterministic PDAs and other systems using stacks. This difference leads to many other contrasts with conventional parsers. For example, NEWCAT is strictly bottom-up and data-driven, whereas other systems such as RTNs and ATNs are largely top-down and hypothesis-driven. In contrast to bounded context automata and deterministic PDAs, NEWCAT employs no limited 'look ahead', but derives all possible readings of a sentence start word by word in a parallel, breadth-first manner.

Conceptually, the most basic divergence from conventional parsers is the fact that NEWCAT handles complex structures of natural language, such as center embedding[11], solely in terms of the grammar. Other systems treat such structures in terms of special parsing procedures involving queues or stacks. The completely regular and simple left-associative parsing algorithm of NEWCAT is possible because the **categories** of the grammar are designed that they encode information which other systems, using combinatorially opaque categories like S, NP, VP, have to treat by building stacks or other complications into the parser.

Since NEWCAT handles certain aspects of the analysis in the grammar, which other parsers treat as part of the parsing algorithm, there is no simple way to generalize complexity results from other systems to left-associative parsing. The overall structure of NEWCAT is that of a non-deterministic finite state automaton. However, since the linguistic categories are used to encode information which other parsers handle with stacks or queues, NEWCAT accepts context-free structures. NEWCAT goes beyond the generative power of finite state automata because there is no upper bound on the length of categories, and therefore no upper bound on the number of categories (see section 4.3).

Some conventional parsers, such as the Early algorithm (cf. Aho and Ullman (1972)), may be interpreted as procedures which transform left-associative structures into linguistically motivated constituent structures like 1.2.1. But in these cases the left-associative structure is justified only in terms of computa-

---

[11]See section 4.3 for a detailed discussion.

tional considerations; it has no linguistic motivation whatsoever. Within linguistics based on constituent structure an intermediate structure like *John gave Mary a* is simply unacceptable. In other words, if a parser implementing a constituent structure grammar happens to go through a stage where left-associative structures are generated (for computational reasons), this is considered at best irrelevant for the linguistic analysis.

NEWCAT differs both linguistically and computationally from existing systems in that it does not employ constituent structure analysis. Instead the linguistic analysis and the computation are based on the same strictly left-associative structures. This is desirable for the following reasons.

1. Computational simplicity and efficiency:

   The transformation of left-associative structures into hierarchical constituent structures in some conventional parsers makes them much more costly computationally than a system like NEWCAT, which uses only left-associative structures. Furthermore, since NEWCAT bases both the computation and the linguistic analysis on a common (left-associative) structure, the history of a left-associative parse also constitutes a left-associative **linguistic analysis** of the sentence. More conventional parsers require additional displays that show the syntactic analysis within the given linguistic theory, but that do not reflect the actual parse.

2. Syntactic and semantic basis for speech recognition:

   A major obstacle in building computers that would recognize natural language speech is the fact that the electronic analysis of the acoustical signal allows too many possible interpretations. Speech recognition systems, such as the HEARSAY and HEARSAY-II systems (Erman 1980), provide ample evidence that speech recognition depends to a large degree on the hearer's hypotheses about what is being said. By restricting the **context** to extremely simple environments, such as a chess game, speech recognition systems may be made rather accurate. But there is no way to expand these systems to meet the diversities of even simple real life situations. Left-associative parsing complements context-based hypotheses with additional syntactic hypotheses: each time a new word is added in the sentence under analysis, NEWCAT has to consider only a very limited number of possible continuations. Furthermore, since left-associative combinations are semantically interpretable, the grammar may provide additional semantic hypotheses at each step.

3. The psychology of natural language:

   There is widespread agreement in older, classical treatments of natural language (e.g. those of Hermann Paul, Ferdinand de Saussure, and Karl Bühler) that natural language is organized along the one dimensional time axis. Furthermore, natural language expressions are coded and decoded linearly from beginning to end. This fact is accommodated in a left-associative analysis. NEWCAT parses incomplete expressions like *Yesterday John*, *Yesterday John saw*, *Yesterday John saw a*, etc. As long as there are possible continuations, NEWCAT will provide syntactic analyses of all readings of a sentence start.

4. The syntax of natural language:

   A strictly left-associative analysis permits a syntactic analysis of natural language which has a high degree of descriptive and explanatory power. For example, NEWCAT handles all major syntactic constructions of German; NEWCAT is fast and highly modular, so that new constructions can be added easily; and the printed analyses have concrete linguistic motivations. The syntactic side of NEWCAT will be illustrated in chapters 3, 4, and 5.

5. The semantic interpretation of natural language:

   The semantic components defined in the literature vary considerably in content and form. In most contemporary grammars the semantic component accounts only for 'grammatical roles', such as the specification of the cases, or of subject, direct object, indirect object, etc. This aspect of semantics is already handled by left-associative grammar (see chapters 3, 4, and 5). Furthermore, definition of a left-associative model-theoretic semantics for a left-associative syntax is straightforward, given the powers of higher order lambda calculus. From the present viewpoint, however, automatic conversion of texts into data bases ('ADBC', see section 1.5) seems a more useful and theoretically more interesting alternative than translation into formulas of intensional logic.

   The psychological fact that natural language is encoded and decoded lineary is not accommodated in contemporary linguistic analyses based on constituent structures. Constituent structures correspond to irregular trees (see example 1.2.1) without a dominant left-to-right orientation. Constituent structure analysis takes place in the theoretical space between the root of the tree, representing an abstract category (e.g. S in example 1.2.1), and the leaves of the tree, representing the concrete words of the sentence. The viewpoint of a left-associative analysis is orthogonal to that of constituent structure analysis. There is no abstract root of the tree; rather, a left-associative analysis takes place in the space between the first and last words of the input expression.

   In summary, NEWCAT is a parser in which the linguistic analysis and the computation are treated as different aspects of the same basic (left-associative) procedure. This results in a powerful linguistic analysis and a fast computation. It also eliminates the need for additional display facilities. But there is still much room for improvement by optimizing the LISP code and by utilizing the parallel structure of the program.

3. The category system of left-associative grammar

At each step of a grammatical analysis, we refer to the categories of words and expressions. Therefore, the choice of categories for a grammatical system is extremely important both from a conceptual and a heuristic point of view. In a sense, the categories of a grammatical system are the most basic conceptual tools of analysis, and the quality of the analysis will depend directly on the quality of the underlying category system. In this chapter we would like to present and motivate the category system of a left-associative grammar by discussing the treatment of different kinds of noun phrases in DCAT.

3.1 Syntactic categories and syntactic rules

What are the properties of a good category system? First, it should be descriptively adequate, in the sense that it allows the data to be classified simply and systematically. A body of data may be classified in many different ways, and the choice of a particular kind of classification has far-reaching consequences for the overall system.

Furthermore, the basic symbols should have good mnemonic qualities. From a purely formal point of view, the choice of the basic symbols could be considered a mere matter of notation. But conceptually, not all notations are alike. Even if 010110101 and ADD are provably equivalent labels for the same operation in some hypothetical system, the first one is meaningless for all practical purposes of human communication, while the latter is recognized by nearly everyone as indicating addition. 010110101 is bad mnemonically: it provides no clue to the intended meaning and is therefore hard to remember.

The mnemonic appeal of a notation depends not only on the conceptual clarity and coherence of the underlying system, but also on extraneous factors such as language, convention, and habit. For example, the reason for the good mnemonics of the symbol ADD is its similarity to the English word 'addition'. Other symbols are remembered simply because their use is widely established. Sometimes the original motivation for choosing certain symbols is forgotten. Examples of such 'demotivation' are the LISP expressions CAR and CDR, which used to stand for Content of Address Register and Content of Decrement Register, respectively. Today CAR simply means 'first element of a list', while CDR means 'tail of a list'.

If a system of classification and the associated notation is widely established in a field of research, it provides good mnemonics for a large group of people. An accepted category system can be a valuable asset for a research community by providing the basis for communicating ideas. But it can also be a serious obstacle to scientific progress. In research areas where fundamental issues are still unresolved, an unsuitable system of classification may cause decades or centuries of stagnation. This point is clearly illustrated in the histories of biology, chemistry, and physics.

In the last thirty years an abundance of different syntactic theories has been developed within theoretical linguistics. Syntactic analyses of numerous constructions have been critically evaluated, arguments for new solutions have been advanced, and various new schools have been founded. But the original categories of phrase structure grammar changed very little in this process. Instead, phrase structure categories, like the basic structures of constituent analysis, are widely accepted as the common core of the different theories of contemporary syntax. Today any arguments for adopting new categorial conventions will be weighed against the comfort of the accepted phrase structure system.

However, the reasons for considering category systems other than those of phrase structure grammar are very good. The category system of a syntactic theory not only serves to classify words and expressions, but is also the basis of the **syntactic rules**, which refer to the categories. Therefore the choice of the category system has far-reaching consequences for the syntax. Depending on the formal syntax system chosen, the **combinatorial role** of the categories in the syntactic rules varies greatly.

In systems based on phrase structure grammar, e.g. transformational grammar, REST[1], GPSG[2], or LFG[3], the syntactic rules are formulated as **rewriting rules** such as 3.1.1.

3.1.1 Example of rewriting rules in phrase structure grammar:

NP → DET+NOUN
DET → the
NOUN → book

The categories in rewriting rule systems do not directly contribute to the combinatorics of the system, because their structure does not indicate how they can combine with each other. Instead, this information is specified solely in the system of interlocking rewriting rules. In other words, the categories of grammars

---

[1]Chomsky (1981)
[2]Gazdar et al.(1985)
[3]Bresnan (1982)

based on phrase structure are 'combinatorially opaque'.[4]

In systems based on categorial grammar, on the other hand, the categories have an internal structure which indicates combinatorial properties of the corresponding expressions. For example, categorizing an article like *the* as (T/CN) indicates that *the* is a functor that takes a common noun like *book* of category (CN) as its argument and results in a noun phrase or term of category (T). Given the internal structure of the categories, only a few general syntactic rule schemas or combinatorial conventions are needed to build up complex expressions, e.g. *the book* of category T. For example, 3.1.2:

3.1.2 Rule schemata of categorial grammar:

$$(A/B) \cdot (B) \rightarrow (A)$$
$$(B) \cdot (A \backslash B) \rightarrow (A)$$

In this way one may build grammars in which the categories of expressions completely specify how they may combine with categories of other expressions, on the basis of which combinatorial conventions. In other words, the categories of a pure (i.e. context-free) categorial grammar are 'combinatorially transparent'.

SCG approached the choice of a category system by considering whether the combinatorics of a natural language should be encoded in the rule system alone, as in phrase structure based systems, or in the categories alone, as in a pure categorial grammar. **SCG** argued for the second option and explored its consequences by presenting a formal grammar for a relatively large fragment of English. But the attempt to program the syntactic system of **SCG** brought to light the problem[5] of irregular left-to-right orderings induced by the constituent structure analysis implicit in **SCG**.

The attempt to resolve this problem developed into left-associative grammar, which differs from both phrase structure grammar and categorial grammar because of its completely regular order of linear combinations. Implementing this regular order of combinations, however, required a new approach to the combinatorics of natural language. Rather than encoding all combinatorial information in a system of rewriting rules, as in phrase structure grammar, or in combinatorially transparent categories, as in **SCG**, left-associative grammar distinguishes two kinds of combinatorial information: one concerning agreement and valency, the other concerning word order.

Combinatorial information relating to agreement and valency is encoded in the **categories** of left-associative grammar. Combinatorial information concerning the word order, on the other hand, is encoded in terms of (i) **syntactic rules** (productions), which resemble the categorial rules of PTQ[6] in that they are defined for specific input categories rather than being a general schemata,

---

[4]See **SCG** for a detailed discussion of the notions of 'combinatorial' and 'denotational opaqueness', as well as 'combinatorial' and 'denotational transparency'.

[5]Described in chapter 1.

[6]Montague 1974, chapter 8.

and (ii) associated **rule packages** that specify which of the syntactic rules are
to apply next.

The lexicon of left-associative grammar analyzes each word as a pair consisting of a surface and a list of categories:

3.1.3 Lexical analysis of an ambiguous word:

```
(Surface ((CAT1)
          (CAT2)
           ...

          (CATn)))
```

Each category represents a possible reading. If a word is lexically unambiguous,
the list of categories has only one element.

3.1.4 Lexical analysis of an unambiguous word:

```
(Surface ((CAT1)))
```

A category is formally defined in left-associative grammar as a **list**. Take for
example the third person singular present tense form *reads* in ELEX, which is
defined as follows:

3.1.5 Analysis of *reads* in ELEX:

```
(reads ((V S3 A)))
```

We see that *reads* is specified with only one category, characterizing it as an
unambiguous word. The category (V S3 A) is a list consisting of three elements.
We call the elements of a left-associative category the **segments** of the category.
The segment V indicates a verb. The segments S3 and A indicate valencies for
a third person singular nominative and an accusative noun phrase, respectively.
The category (V S3 A) may be interpreted intuitively as indexing a class of
expressions which take a third person singular nominative and an accusative as
arguments and result in a sentence.

There are no internal parentheses, slashes or bars in the categories of left-
associative grammar, in contrast to categorial grammar. The function of these
diacritic markers in the categories of categorial grammar, e.g. (A/B), ((A/B)/C),
(A\B), is to indicate which categorial operation is to apply (if the categorial
grammar permits more than one type of combination). The categories of left-
associative grammar are defined as simple lists of category segments, because
the exact nature of the categorial operation is decided locally by the rules.

The categories of left-associative grammar are combinatorially transparent in
that they explicitly encode which arguments are still missing, what agreement
features arguments and optional modifiers must have, etc. Furthermore, the
syntactic rules of left-associative grammar are categorial, since they derive the
output category from the input categories. However, left-associative grammar

differs from a pure context-free categorial system like **SCG**, as well as from a less stringent categorial system like PTQ, in that the word order aspect of the combinatorics (the 'serialization') is treated neither in terms of the categories alone (**SCG**), nor in terms of the rules alone (PTQ), but in terms of a novel left-associative control structure.

In contrast to phrase structure analysis, left-associative grammar does not assume that there is a set of basic categories, such as V, N, VP, NP, AUX[7], which are shared by all natural languages. Notions such as "noun", "verb", "determiner", etc. are derivative concepts in left-associative grammar, defined in terms of language-dependent sets of formal categories. For example, there is no category 'noun' formally used to index a word like *Tisch*. Instead, *Tisch* is indexed by the category (MS). In DLEX, a noun is any word with the category (MS), (MG), (FS), (NS), (NG), (P), or (PD).

This particular indirect characterization of the notion 'noun', which is described and motivated in the following sections, holds only for German. In other natural languages the agreement properties of nouns will be defined in terms of other parameters. In English, for example, determiner/noun agreement depends on number and on whether the noun begins with a vowel or a consonant, whereas in German it depends on gender, number, and case. Relative clause agreement depends in English on whether the noun refers to a human or non-human object, whereas in German it depends on gender and number of the noun. Unlike German, English does not allow using determiners as full noun phrases (cf. section 3.5). Also, adjective agreement in is different in English and German.

The definition of left-associative categories of a natural language is solely concerned with encoding the specific agreement features of that language in a manner that is complete and minimal at the same time. We illustrate the language dependent left-associative approach to categorization by giving a detailed description of the category systems of two different natural languages, German (sections 3.2 - 3.5) and English (chapter 5). The principles of a distinctive versus an exhaustive approach to left-associative categorization are presented in the following section, and will be presupposed in chapter 5.

3.2 Determiner-noun agreement in DCAT

Let us explain the basic linguistic questions of left-associative categorization by discussing the grammatical nature of German noun phrases. Traditional grammars of German distinguish nouns with regard to gender, number and case. There are three genders: masculine, feminine and neuter, henceforth M, F, and N, respectively. There are two numeri: singular and plural, henceforth S and P, respectively. Finally, there are four cases: nominative, genitive, dative, and accusative, henceforth N, G, D, and A, respectively.

---

[7]See "The Category AUX in Universal Grammar" by Akmajian, Steele, and Wasow (1979).

Postulating the parameters of gender, number, and case for German noun phrases is concretely motivated insofar as they contribute to agreement and disagreement between determiners and nouns. For example, *das Kind* is well-formed, but **das Tisch*[8] is not. The reason is that *Kind* is of neuter, while *Tisch* is of masculine gender. Furthermore, *des Mannes* is well-formed, but **des Mann* is not. The reason is that *Mannes* is of genitive case, while *Mann* can only combine with determiners of nominative, dative, or accusative singular case. Finally, *dem Mann* is well-formed, while **dem Männer* is not. The reason is that *Mann* is singular, while *Männer* is plural.

Having established the role of gender, number, and case for the definition of agreement between determiners and nouns of German, we must decide whether to postulate complete paradigms of German nouns, or to categorize nouns only for the maximum number of distinct surface forms. This is a profound alternative in the design of a category system, which has not yet been discussed in the literature. We call it the alternative between an **exhaustive** and a **distinctive** approach to categorization.

Categorizing German nouns exhaustively with respect to gender, number, and case results in altogether 24 noun forms: three genders times two numbers times four cases. As an example of a complete paradigm analysis in a system of exhaustive categorization consider 3.2.1:

3.2.1 Exhaustive categorization of the masculine noun *Tisch:*

	singular:	plural:
nominative:	TISCH (MSN)	TISCHE (MPN)
genitive:	TISCHES (MSG)	TISCHE (MPG)
dative:	TISCH (MSD)	TISCHEN (MPD)
accusative:	TISCH (MSA)	TISCHE (MPA)

The exhaustive categorization in 3.2.1 represents the traditional category analysis influenced by the paradigms of Latin grammar. It is found in traditional German grammars, and schoolbooks for teaching German as a foreign language.

The categorization in 3.2.1 postulates eight different forms. But there are only four different surfaces, namely *Tisch, Tisches, Tische,* and *Tischen.* Categorizing a noun like *Tisch* exhaustively with respect to the parameters gender, number, and case amounts to saying: the form *Tisch* is three-ways ambiguous;

---

[8] Following linguistic tradition, ungrammatical expressions are marked by an asterisk.

it could be (MSN), (MSD), or (MSA). The form *Tische* is also three-ways ambiguous; it could be (MPN), (MPG), (MPA). The exhaustive approach is based on the assumption that if a certain parameter is crucial for the categorization of some forms of a word class[9], then all forms of the word class have to be specified for this parameter.

Yet it is not an isolated fact that the noun analyzed in 3.2.1 happens to have only four surface forms. Rather, it holds in general that German nouns of masculine or neuter gender may have at most four forms, while German nouns of feminine gender may have at most three forms. This means that an exhaustive approach to the categorization of German nouns systematically generates an enormous number of lexical ambiguities.

The distinctive method, on the other hand, uses a parameter like gender or case only where it is necessary for the proper characterization of agreement. Compare 3.2.1 and 3.2.2:

3.2.2 Distinctive categorization of the masculine noun *Tisch* in DLEX:

(TISCH ((MS)))	(TISCHE ((P)))
(TISCHES ((MG)))	(TISCHEN ((PD)))

According to the distinctive approach, none of the four surface forms of the noun *Tisch* is analyzed as ambiguous.[10] In 3.2.2 gender is specified in the categories of two forms, number is specified in the categories of three forms, and case is specified in the categories of two forms. (MS) stands for masculine singular, (MG) stands for masculine genitive, (P) stands for plural and (PD) stands for plural dative.

Let us compare the exhaustive and the distinctive system of categorization with respect to the treatment of agreement. Assume that a determiner and a noun are compatible if the second category segment of the determiner is identical to the first (and only) category segment of the noun.

3.2.3 Schema of determiner/noun composition in left-associative grammar:

(determiner) · (noun) → (determiner noun)
(A B)   (B)   (A)

This preliminary[11] rule combining a determiner and a compatible noun simply cancels the identical category segments. What remains becomes the result category.

Comparison of the alternative categorizations of *Tisch* and the definite article in 3.2.4 and 3.2.5, respectively, shows that, as far as the treatment of determiner/noun agreement is concerned, there is no difference between the exhaustive and the distinctive approach.

---

[9] For example, case is crucial for properly distinguishing the noun forms *Tisches* and *Tisch*.

[10] The present discussion is limited to nouns in the narrow sense. The treatment of bare plurals and mass nouns discussed in section 3.5 will result in additional readings.

[11] See 3.3.7 for the final formulation of this rule.

3.2.4 Determiner/noun-agreement in an *exhaustive* category system:

```
der       Tisch    des     Tisches    dem     Tisch    den     Tisch
(S3 MSN)(MSN)       (G MSG)(MSG)       (D MSD)(MSD)      (A MSA)(MSA)

die       Tische   der     Tische     den     Tischen  die     Tische
(P3 MPN)(MPN)       (G MPG)(MPG)       (D MPD)(MPD)      (A MPA)(MPA)
```

3.2.5 Determiner/noun-agreement in a *distinctive* category system:

```
der       Tisch    des     Tisches    dem     Tisch    den     Tisch
(S3 MS) (MS)        (G MG) (MG)        (D MS) (MS)       (A MS)(MS)

die       Tische   der     Tische     den     Tischen  die     Tische
(P3 P)  (P)         (G P)  (P)         (D PD) (PD)       (A P) (P)
```

Both 3.2.4 and 3.2.5 obey the simple rule of category cancelling indicated in 3.2.3 above. Furthermore, the two approaches render exactly the same result categories, namely S3 (third person singular nominative), P3 (third person plural nominative), G (genitive), D (dative), and A (accusative). This means that an exhaustive specification of gender, number, and case is not **necessary** for handling determiner-noun agreement in German. Left-associative grammar adopts distinctive categorization, for both German and English, because it avoids the redundancies of the exhaustive approach and is thus computationally far more efficient.

As further illustrations of distinctive categorization, consider the analyses of feminine and neuter nouns below:

3.2.6 Distinctive categorization of a feminine noun in DLEX:

```
(MUTTER ((FS)))          (MUETTER ((P)))

                         (MUETTERN ((PD)))
```

3.2.7 Distinctive categorization of a neuter noun in DLEX:

```
(BUCH ((NS)))            (BUECHER ((P)))

(BUCHES ((NG)))          (BUECHERN ((PD)))
```

But what about nouns that do not have the maximum number of forms? For example, the maximum number of forms for neuter nouns is 4, but *Mädchen* has only 2, namely MAEDCHEN and MAEDCHENS. In such a case the surface forms of the noun are categorized for the standard number of 4 readings:

3.2.8 Analysis of a noun with fewer than the maximum number of forms:

```
(MAEDCHEN ((NS)          (MAEDCHENS ((NG)))
          (P)
          (PD)))
```

By categorizing nouns in principle for the maximum number of forms for their class[12], the agreement between determiners and nouns can be maintained syntactically on a completely general level.

The advantage of the distinctive approach is that the words have considerably fewer readings than in the exhaustive approach. In the case of nouns, the exhaustive approach postulates a total of 24 categories, while the distinctive approach assumes only 11 categories, reflecting the maximal number of surface forms (four for masculine plus three for feminine plus four for neuter nouns). For the definite article, which has six different surface forms in German, namely *der, die, das, des, dem,* and *den,* the exhaustive approach postulates 24 readings, while the distinctive approach assumes only 16 readings.[13]

The difference in the number of lexical ambiguities assumed by the two approaches to categorization makes a considerable computational difference. For example, the words *der* and *Tisch* produce 18 ordered pairs in the exhaustive approach, but only 4 ordered pairs in the distinctive approach. This is because in the distinctive approach *Tisch* has only 1 (instead of 3) readings, and *der* has only 4 (instead of 6) readings.

3.3   Adjective agreement in DCAT

An analysis of German noun phrases must account not only for the agreement between determiners and nouns, but also for the agreement restrictions of noun modifiers such as adjectives and relative clauses. In German adjectives come in four morphological flavors, e.g. *alte, alten, alter,* and *altes*[14]. Which of these forms is appropriate depends not only on the case, number, and gender specified in the determiner category, but also on whether the determiner is definite or indefinite. Consider for example 3.3.1:

3.3.1 Adjectives and the definite/indefinite distinction:

1. das alte Haus

2. ein altes Haus

---

[12] The class of a noun in German, for the purposes of agreement, is determined by the gender. Our analysis of nouns ignores marginal paradigms, such as *der Rabe, des Raben, das Herz, des Herzen,* etc, where the dative and accusative have forms different from the nominative. There are also nouns which inflect differently depending on whether the determiner is definite or indefinite, e.g *der Beamte, ein Beamter.* These paradigms may all be implemented on the basis of a separate categorization and special clauses in the rule RDET+NOUN specifying correspondence between these new categories and the relevant segments of the determiner categories. The notion of categories which correspond without being identical is explained in section 4.5.

[13] See 3.3.2 and 3.3.3 for the DLEX analysis of the definite and the indefinite article in German.

[14] There is a fifth form *altem,* which we disregard in the present context because it does not occur with determiners.

The noun *Haus* is of category (NS), i.e. neuter singular, in both cases. Furthermore, both noun phrases are in nominative (or accusative) case. The different endings of the adjective are due solely to the fact that the determiner in (1) is definite, while the determiner in (2) is indefinite.

Traditional German grammars claim that adjectives are inflected to agree in gender, number, and case with the noun. The formal implementation of this claim requires an exhaustive categorization of adjectives, nouns, and determiners. Taking into account the agreement-relevant distinction between definite and indefinite articles illustrated in 3.3.1, an exhaustive categorization would postulate a total of 48 readings for the 4 surface forms of each German adjective: four cases, times three genders, times two numbers, times two kinds of determiners (+definite, -definite).

DCAT, on the other hand, proceeds on the assumption that German adjectives agree with the determiner, and not with the noun. This stems from the fact that the definiteness property of the determiner affects the agreement of adjectives. Since the left-associative treatment of determiner-noun agreement (presented in section 3.2) insures that the second category segment of the determiner is identical to the category of compatible nouns, the category of a noun contributes nothing to the agreement of the adjectives in a noun phrase.

Which categorial feature should control the agreement between determiners and adjectives? While the definiteness property is relevant for the agreement of determiners and adjectives, it does not suffice by itself because an adjective like *alte* may occur in an indefinite noun phrase such as *eine alte Frau* as well as in a definite noun phrase such as *der alte Mann*. But if we use the grammatical parameters of gender, number, and case in addition to the definiteness property, the resulting number of possibilities is too large for an effective treatment of adjective agreement.

What could we use instead of grammatical parameters like gender, number, or case for a distinctive treatment of adjective agreement? Note that the endings of German adjectives are morphologically completely regular. The four surface forms of an adjective always end in -E, -EN, -ES, or -ER. Let us define the agreement of adjectives **morphologically** by referring to the characteristic endings of the respective adjective forms:

1. ((der) (S3 MS -E)) ((alte) (-E)) ((Mann)(MS))

2. ((den) (S3 MS -EN)) ((alten)(-EN)) ((Mann)(MS))

3. ((ein) (S3 NS -ES)) ((altes)(-ES)) ((Haus)(FN))

4. ((ein) (S3 MS -ER)) ((alter)(-ER)) ((Mann)(MS))

The formal implementation of adjective agreement requires a change in the definition of the determiner categories. Instead of the tentative two-segment categories used in section 3.2, DCAT defines determiners as three segment categories. The first segment indicates the result category, the second segment takes care of the agreement with the noun, and the third segment handles the agreement with the optional adjective.

The final analysis of the definite and the indefinite article in DLEX is given in 3.3.2 and 3.3.3 below:

3.3.2 Analysis of the *definite* article in DLEX:

```
(DER ((S3 MS -E)          (DIE ((P3 P -EN)          (DAS ((S3 NS -E)
     (G P -EN)                 (S3 FS -E)                 (A NS -E)))
     (G FS -EN)                (A FS -E)
     (D FS -EN)))              (A P -EN)))

(DES ((G MG -EN)          (DEM ((D MS -EN)          (DEN ((A MS -EN)
     (G NG -EN)))              (D NS -EN)))              (D PD -EN)))
```

3.3.3 Analysis of the *indefinite* article in DLEX:

```
(EIN ((S3 MS -ER)         (EINE ((S3 FS -E)         (EINER ((G FS -EN)
     (S3 NS -ES)                (A FS -E)))                (D FS -EN)))
     (A NS -ES)))

(EINES (G MG -EN)         (EINEM ((D MS -EN)        (EINEN ((A MS -EN)))
       (G NG -EN)))              (D NS -EN)))
```

The definite article has six surface forms and 16 readings, while the indefinite article has six surface forms and 12 readings. The indefinite article combines only with singular nouns, which explains the smaller number of readings.[15]

Consider now the DCAT analysis of *der schöne alte Tisch*:

3.3.4 *Der schöne alte Tisch* / the beautiful old table

```
(R DER SCHOENE ALTE TISCH)
(DET+NOUN ((DER SCHOENE ALTE TISCH)
          (S3 MS))
          1
          (START (DER)
                 (S3 MS -E)
                 (SCHOENE)
                 (-E))
          2
          (DET+ADJ (DER SCHOENE)
                   (S3 MS -E)
                   (ALTE)
                   (-E))
          3
          (DET+ADJ (DER SCHOENE ALTE)
                   (S3 MS -E)
                   (TISCH)
                   (MS))
          4)))
```

---

[15]Other indefinite determiners like *kein, mein, dein*, etc. do combine with plural nouns and have the full number of 16 readings.

The history in this example consists of three sections, because the expression analyzed consists of four words. The first history section indicates the application of the rule package START. The result is the sentence start in section 2, which indicates the application of the linguistic rule RDET+ADJ in section 1. RDET+ADJ is defined as follows:[16]

3.3.5 Formal declarative statement of the rule RDET+ADJ:

> If (S1,C1) is an expression ending in a determiner and (S2,C2) is an adjective, where S1 and S2 are the respective surfaces, and C1 and C2 the respective categories, then RDET+NOUN((S1,C1)(S2,C2)) equals (DET+NOUN(S3,C3)) if and only if the last segment of C1 equals the first segment of C2, where S3 is the concatenation of S1 and S2, and C3 equals C1.

An expression ending in a determiner is formally characterized by a category where the last segment is -E, -EN, -ES, or -ER and the next to last segment is MS, FS, NS, MG, NG, P, or PD.[17] An adjective is formally characterized by a one-segment category consisting of -E, -EN, -ES, or -ER.

Left-associative rules all have in common that the input consists of an ordered pair the elements of which consist of a surface and a category. Furthermore, the output surface of a left-associative rule is always the concatenation of the two input surfaces. Finally, the name of the rule package in the output is always systematically derived from the name of the rule itself. The only information that is linguistically relevant in left-associative rules is the specification of the input and the output categories. We may therefore reformulate the content of 3.3.5 as in 3.3.6 without loss of information.

3.3.6 Simplified declarative statement of the rule RDET+ADJ:

> The **input condition** of the rule RDET+ADJ specifies that (i) the first expression must end in a determiner, (ii) the second expression must be an adjective, and (iii) the last category segment of the first expression must agree with the first category segment of the second expression. The **output specification** of RDET+ADJ says that the output category is the same as the category of the first input expression.

The derivation in 3.3.4 illustrates the fact that a determiner may be followed by an indefinite number of adjectives. Note that the output of the second section, i.e. *Der schöne alte*, has exactly the same category as *der* in history section 1. Thus we may either add more adjectives (iteratively), or continue with the noun (as in the third section of 3.3.4).

---

[16]See A.2.2 for the corresponding LISP code.
[17]See A.3.14 for the corresponding LISP code.

Let us return now to the rule RDET+NOUN, which describes the left-associative combination of a determiner and a noun. The change of determiners from two-segment to three-segment categories (due to the implementation of adjective agreement) necessitates a reformulation of this rule, which was tentatively specified in 3.2.3. We state it in the informal style of 3.3.6.[18]

3.3.7 Declarative statement of the rule RDET+NOUN:

> The **input condition** of the rule RDET+NOUN specifies that (i) the first expression must end in a determiner, (ii) the second expression must be a noun, and (iii) the next to last category segment of the first expression must agree with the first category segment of the second expression. The **output specification** of RDET+NOUN says that the output category is the category of the first expression minus the last segment.

The input conditions of the rules RDET+NOUN and RDET+ADJ require that the last category segment of the first input expression is an adjective segment, i.e. -E, -EN, -ER, or -ES.[19] The output condition of RDET+ADJ preserves the adjective segment in the result category, allowing the addition of further adjectives or a noun. The output condition of RDET+NOUN, on the other hand, removes the adjective segment from the result category, ensuring that no additional nouns or adjectives can be added.[20] The noun segment remains in the output of RDET+NOUN because it contains information needed for agreement with an optional relative clause.

As another example of a noun phrase consider the left-associative analysis of *der Tisch* in 3.3.8.

3.3.8 *der Tisch* / the table

```
(R DER TISCH)
(DET+NOUN ((DER TISCH)
          (S3 MS))
        1
        (START (DER)
               (S3 MS -E)
               (TISCH)
               (MS))
        2))
```

The result category (S3 MS) in 3.3.8 is exactly the same as in 3.3.4. Thus the presence or absence of adjectives between the determiner and the noun does not affect the category of the resulting noun phrase. Each noun phrase is an S3, i.e.

---

[18]The LISP code is given in appendix A.2.4.

[19]This is implicit in the condition that the first expression must end in a determiner.

[20]In contrast to the preliminary formulation 3.2.3, the combination of a determiner and a noun does not result in cancelling the noun segment in the determiner category, but rather the adjective segment.

a nominative of third person singular. And each noun phrase may be continued with a relative clause of MS, or masculine singular, agreement, e.g. *den Peter kaufte*. For a detailed discussion of relative clauses see section 4.3.

3.4   Combining noun phrases and verbs in DCAT

The combination of noun phrases with verbs in DCAT is based on the same agreement principles as the combination of determiners and nouns. Consider the following examples:

3.4.1 *Ich schlafe.* / I sleep. - I am asleep.

```
(R ICH SCHLAFE .)
((CMPLT ((ICH SCHLAFE %.)
        (DECL))
        1
        (START (ICH)
               (S1)
               (SCHLAFE)
               (V S1))
        2
        (MAIN+FVERB (ICH SCHLAFE)
                    (V)
                    (%.)
                    (V DECL))
        3))
```

3.4.2 *Du schläfst.* / You sleep. - You are asleep.

```
(R DU SCHLAEFST .)
((CMPLT ((DU SCHLAEFST %.)
        (DECL))
        1
        (START (DU)
               (S2)
               (SCHLAEFST)
               (V S2))
        2
        (MAIN+FVERB (DU SCHLAEFST)
                    (V)
                    (%.)
                    (V DECL))
        3))
```

The finite verb in German is inflected to agree with the nominative in **person** and **number**. The treatment of nominative-verb aggreement is analogous to that of determiner-adjective-noun agreement described in sections 3.2 and 3.3 above. Since the person parameter has three values and the number parameter two, there is a total of six possible nominatives in German. They are categorially defined in DCAT as S1, S2, S3, P1, P2, and P3. Thus the class of nominative noun phrases is specified in terms of a set of categories, just as the class of nouns is specified in terms of the set of categories (MS), (MG), (FS), (NS), (NG), (P), and (PD).

A nominative noun phrase and a finite verb are compatible only if the initial category segment of the noun phrase agrees with a non-initial category segment of the verb. In 3.4.1 the pronoun *ich* has the category (S1), indicating a first person singular nominative noun phrase. The combination of *ich* and the verb form *schlafe* simply cancels the S1 segment in the category of the verb, indicating that the argument for this particular type of nominative has been filled. The derivation in 3.4.2 is similar. The crucial rule in both derivations is RMAIN+FVERB, which handles the combination of any 'Vorfeld'-constituent[21] with the finite verb.

3.4.3 Declarative statement of RMAIN+FVERB:

> The **input condition** of the rule RMAIN+FVERB specifies that (i) the first expression must be a main constituent such as a noun phrase or adverb, (ii) the second expression must be a finite verb, and (iii) the first category segment of the first expression must agree with a non-initial category segment of the second expression, unless the first expression is an adverb, or the first expression is not a nominative and the second expression is an auxiliary. The **output specification** of RMAIN+FVERB says: the output category is the result of cancelling the first with the second category.

All notions used in the above declarative statement have precise counterparts in LISP. In fact, the actual LISP code of the rule, stated in A.2.12 of appendix A, was written before the declarative paraphrase 3.4.3. The notions 'main constituent' and 'finite verb' in the input condition of 3.4.3 have precise definitions in terms of their possible categories. The notion 'cancelling' in the output condition of 3.4.3 is defined in terms of the LISP function ADIFF (atom difference)[22]. The ADIFF of two lists consists of all elements of the first list which are not in the second list. For example, (ADIFF '(A B B C) '(C D)) renders (A B B). The cancelling of two categories is defined as the ADIFF of the first and second category plus the ADIFF of the second and first category. For example, (CANCEL '(A B B C) '(C D)) renders (A B B D).[23]

The simple and concise method of matching category segments not only accounts for the number and person agreement between the nominative and the finite verb, but also characterizes the **grammatical role** of the nominative in the sentence. The grammatical role of a nominative is characterized in left-associative grammar as cancelling the corresponding valency position in the valency carrier. The valency carrier may be a sentence start (if the verb has

---

[21] In German declarative sentences the finite verb is in second position. The position before the finite verb is called the 'Vorfeld'.

[22] Cf. A.3.2 for the definition of ADIFF.

[23] Cf. A.3.1 for the definition of CANCEL.

already been added, as in *Mary gave +* ...), or a next word (if the next word is
the verb, as in *The beautiful young girl + gave.*

The oblique cases of German, i.e. genitive, dative, and accusative, have
no morphological agreement requirements with the verb. This simplifies the
categorization. While the nominative is specified in terms of two-parameter
category segments indicating different numbers and persons, genitive, dative,
and accusative are characterized by the single-parameter category segments G,
D, and A, respectively. The grammatical role of non-nominative noun phrases
is characterized in the same way as that of nominatives, namely in terms of
cancelling the corresponding valency position in the valency carrier. Consider
example 3.4.4:

3.4.4 *Der Mann gab dem Mädchen ein Buch.* / The man gave the girl a book.

```
(R DER MANN GAB DEM MAEDCHEN EIN BUCH .)
((CMPLT ((DER MANN GAB DEM MAEDCHEN EIN BUCH %.)
        (DECL))
    1
    (START (DER)
           (S3 MS -E)
           (MANN)
           (MS))
    2
    (DET+NOUN (DER MANN)
              (S3 MS)
              (GAB)
              (V S3 D A))
    3
    (MAIN+FVERB (DER MANN GAB)
                (V D A MS)
                (DEM)
                (D NS -EN))
    4
    (FVERB+MAIN (DER MANN GAB DEM)
                (V A MS NS -EN)
                (MAEDCHEN)
                (NS))
    5
    (DET+NOUN (DER MANN GAB DEM MAEDCHEN)
              (V A MS NS)
              (EIN)
              (A NS -ES))
    6
    (FVERB+MAIN (DER MANN GAB DEM MAEDCHEN EIN)
                (V MS NS NS -ES)
                (BUCH)
                (NS))
    7
    (DET+NOUN (DER MANN GAB DEM MAEDCHEN EIN BUCH)
              (V MS NS NS)
              (%.)
              (V DECL))
    8))
```

In section 3 the first category segment D (dative) of the second expression, i.e. *dem*, cancels the corresponding segment in the category of the sentence start *Der Mann gab*. The rule responsible for this combination is RFVERB+MAIN.[24]

3.4.5 Declarative statement of RFVERB+MAIN:

> The **input condition** of the rule RFVERB+MAIN specifies that (i) the category of the first expression must begin with a V, indicating presence of a finite verb, (ii) the second expression must be the beginning of a main constituent, and (iii) the first category segment of the second expression must agree with a non-initial category segment of the first expression, unless the second expression is an adverb, or the second expression is not a nominative and the verb in the first expression is an auxiliary. The **output specification** of RFVERB+MAIN says: the output category is the result of cancelling the first with the second category.

The category resulting in history section 4 of 3.4.4, namely (V A MS NS -EN), indicates a sentence which may be continued with an adjective ending in -EN, requires a noun of category (NS), may have an extraposed relative clause with (MS) agreement, and needs an accusative noun phrase (A) in order to be complete. For the purposes of the next rule, RDET+NOUN in history section 4 of 3.4.4, the category (V A MS NS -EN) simply indicates an expression ending in a determiner. Categorially speaking, we may call the operation of RFVERB+MAIN in history section 3 'argument cancelling with appending of the remainder'. The argument cancelled is the dative valency and the non-initial category segments of the determiner *dem* are the remainder.

As another example of argument cancelling with appending of the remainder consider history section 5. The first category segment A (accusative) of the second expression, i.e. *ein*, cancels the corresponding segment in the category of the sentence start *Der Mann gab dem Mädchen*. The non-initial category segments of the determiner *ein* are appended. The resulting category (V MS NS NS -ES) indicates a sentence, which may be continued with an adjective ending in -ES, must be continued with a noun of category NS, and may have an extraposed relative clause of NS or MS agreement.

The operations of RFVERB+MAIN in example 3.4.4 are strictly left-associative. The rule does not add a whole noun phrase, but only the beginning of one. The rule package FVERB+MAIN ensures that the rules RDET+NOUN and RDET+ADJ will be tried on the next set of ordered pairs. The categorially formulated input conditions of the rules in the rule package FVERB+MAIN ensure that the next word will be a grammatical continuation.

---

[24]See A.2.14 for the LISP code.

3.5   Treating different kinds of noun phrases in DCAT

Left-associative rules specify input categories and output categories by referring either to particular positions or segments of a particular form in the lists representing the categories. This method of categorial specification is simple and descriptively powerful. For example, if we wanted to ensure that an article were necessarily followed either by an adjective or a noun, we could easily tighten the input conditions of RMAIN+FVERB and RFVERB+MAIN by prohibiting the presence of any adjective segments -E, -EN, -ES, or -ER, in the category of the MAIN-expression.

It turns out, however, that most determiners may function as full noun phrases in German. Consider for example 3.5.1:

3.5.1 *Der gab einem das.*

This 'pronominal' use of determiners in German touches upon a profound question about the correct grammatical analysis of noun phrases. There is an ancient controversy in traditional grammar about whether one should treat the noun as the 'head' and the determiner as the 'complement', or the other way around. The notion of a 'head' has been defined in many different ways, but pre-theoretically it means 'central part of a constituent'.[25]

Assuming that the noun is the head of a noun phrase, one will be inclined to argue that *Der* used as a pronoun in 3.5.1 is a completely different word from *Der* used as a determiner in 3.4.4. In 3.4.4 the head of the first noun phrase is the noun *Mann*, while in 3.5.1 the head of the first noun phrase is the determiner/pronoun *der*. The disadvantage of this approach is that it would result in a large number of additional readings for all the determiners of German which can function as full noun phrases.

On the other hand, if the determiner is treated as the head of a noun phrase, the grammatical difference between the prenominal and the pronominal use of a determiner is much smaller. In both uses the determiner is the head of the constituent; the pronominal use is simply characterized by the absence of a complement. For German this approach would have the advantage that no additional determiner readings would have to be postulated in order to account for the pronominal use.

Theories of constituent structure analysis try to motivate specific analyses by appealing to 'universals', such as certain 'deep structure' configurations which

---

[25]In GPSG the head is formally defined as that daughter which subcategorizes the other daughters. This definition builds on a formal theory of constituent structure. In the analysis of noun phrases, GPSG defines the noun as the head and the determiner as the complement. LFG does not use the notion of a head, but one may regard a node marked with '↑ = ↓' as equivalent to a head. Given this assumption, one may say that LFG is like GPSG in that it treats the noun as the head of a noun phrase.

are claimed to be characteristic of all natural languages. Therefore the question whether the noun or the determiner should be treated as the head of noun phrases would seem to be an important and profound issue within constituent structure analysis. However, some languages encode the grammatical information specifying the noun phrase in the determiner (which suggests treating the determiner as the head), while other languages have only rudimentary determiners and encode the relevant grammatical information in the noun instead (which suggests treating the noun as the head). Thus it is difficult to justify a universal claim, which in turn explains why the discussion of this ancient controversy has been rather subdued within constituent structure analysis.

Left-associative grammar, with its linear outlook, takes no position on the issue. Instead, it proceeds on the assumption that the grammatical role of a noun phrase is specified in its initial or left-most word. For example, if a noun phrase begins with a determiner, the determiner specifies its grammatical role. The grammatical role of a noun phrase in German is represented by its case, and for nominative case, the number and the person as well. Once the first word of a new noun phrase has been added to a sentence start in German, one is free to complete the noun phrase, for example by adding a noun after a determiner. But one may also choose to leave the noun phrase incomplete, for example by using only the determiner, or the determiner with one or more adjectives, in lieu of a full noun phrase. The different possible degrees of completeness of a German noun phrase beginning with a determiner are illustrated in 3.5.2.

3.5.2 Possible degrees of completeness of German noun phrases beginning with a determiner:

1. *Peter kaufte die.*

2. *Peter kaufte die kleinen.*

3. *Peter kaufte die kleinen grünen.*

4. *Peter kaufte die kleinen grünen Tomaten.*

5. *Peter kaufte die, die so bitter schmecken.*

6. *Peter kaufte die kleinen, die so bitter schmecken.*

7. *Peter kaufte die kleinen grünen, die so bitter schmecken.*

8. *Peter kaufte die kleinen grünen Tomaten, die so bitter schmecken.*

The assumption that the grammatical role of a noun phrase is specified in its initial or left-most word leads to a very simple syntactic treatment of the different kinds of noun phrases illustrated in 3.5.2. Let us begin with the pronominal use of determiners in German. It is handled by letting the input conditions of RMAIN+FVERB and RFVERB+MAIN accept MAIN-expressions which have -E or -EN segments in their categories. The DCAT analysis of example 3.5.1 is given in 3.5.3:

3.5.3 *Der gab einem das.* / He gave someone that.

```
(R DER GAB EINEM DAS .)
((CMPLT ((DER GAB EINEM DAS %.)
        (DECL)
        1
        (START (DER)
               (S3 MS -E)
               (GAB)
               (V S3 D A))
        2
        (MAIN+FVERB (DER GAB)
                    (V D A MS)
                    (EINEM)
                    (D NS -EN))
        3
        (FVERB+MAIN (DER GAB EINEM)
                    (V A MS NS -EN)
                    (DAS)
                    (A NS -E))
        4
        (FVERB+MAIN (DER GAB EINEM DAS)
                    (V MS NS NS -E)
                    (%.)
                    (V DECL))
        5))
```

The pronominal use of a determiner is characterized categorially by the presence of an adjective segment that has not been cancelled by RDET+NOUN. Consider history segment 1 of 3.5.3: The rule RMAIN+FVERB 'knows' that it is dealing with a determiner used pronominally because the sentence start contains a -E segment in its category. If we were to write a semantic interpretation for RMAIN+FVERB, the adjective segment would trigger the required pronominal interpretation of *der*. Similarly in history section 3: the rule RFVERB+MAIN 'knows' that it is dealing with a determiner used pronominally because the category of the sentence start contains -EN. This characterization of a determiner as being used pronominally is strictly local: the output conditions of RMAIN+FVERB and RFVERB+MAIN remove the adjective segments from the result category.

But what about the few determiner forms of German which do not allow pronominal use? For example, instead of *Ein schläft* one has to say *Einer schläft*. Determiners which do not allow pronominal use happen to have the adjective segments -ER or -ES in their category. By specifying in the input condition of RMAIN+FVERB and RFVERB+MAIN that -ER or -ES may not occur in the category of the MAIN-expression, we insure that ungrammatical pronominal uses of determiners are not accepted by DCAT.[26]

---

[26] In the lexicon DLEX presented in appendix A.5, *einer* has one more reading than in 3.3.3. It is characterized by the category (S3 MS) and accounts for the possible use of this word as a full noun phrase. The form *eines* in DLEX has two additional readings of category (S3 NS) and (A NS) for the same reason.

Since a determiner-adjective sequence like *die kleinen* or *die kleinen grünen* has the same category as the determiner by itself, the syntactic treatment of pronominal determiner uses described above also accounts for examples like 3.5.4 and 3.5.5:

3.5.4 *Peter kaufte die kleinen.* / Peter bought the small (ones).

```
(R PETER KAUFTE DIE KLEINEN .)
((CMPLT ((PETER KAUFTE DIE KLEINEN %.)
        (DECL)
        1
        (START (PETER)
               (S3 MS)
               (KAUFTE)
               (V S3 A))
        2
        (MAIN+FVERB (PETER KAUFTE)
                    (V A MS)
                    (DIE)
                    (A P -EN))
        3
        (FVERB+MAIN (PETER KAUFTE DIE)
                    (V MS P -EN)
                    (KLEINEN)
                    (-EN))
        4
        (DET+ADJ (PETER KAUFTE DIE KLEINEN)
                 (V MS P -EN)
                 (%.)
                 (V DECL))
        5)))
```

3.5.5 *Peter kaufte die kleinen grünen.* / Peter bought the small green (ones).

```
(R PETER KAUFTE DIE KLEINEN GRUENEN .)
((CMPLT ((PETER KAUFTE DIE KLEINEN GRUENEN %.)
        (DECL)
        1
        (START (PETER)
               (S3 MS)
               (KAUFTE)
               (V S3 A))
        2
        (MAIN+FVERB (PETER KAUFTE)
                    (V A MS)
                    (DIE)
                    (A P -EN))
        3
        (FVERB+MAIN (PETER KAUFTE DIE)
                    (V MS P -EN)
                    (KLEINEN)
                    (-EN))
        4
        (DET+ADJ (PETER KAUFTE DIE KLEINEN)
                 (V MS P -EN)
```

```
                (GRUENEN)
                (-EN))
        5
        (DET+ADJ (PETER KAUFTE DIE KLEINEN GRUENEN)
                (V MS P -EN)
                (%.)
                (V DECL))
        6)))
```

After an indefinite number of adjectives, a noun phrase may be continued
by adding a noun of proper agreement. Note that the adjective segment -EN in
section 5 of 3.5.6 below is absent in section 6. Thus no adjectives may be added
once a noun is in place.

3.5.6 *Peter kaufte die kleinen grünen Tomaten.* / Peter bought the small
green tomatoes.

```
(R PETER KAUFTE DIE KLEINEN GRUENEN TOMATEN .)
((CMPLT ((PETER KAUFTE DIE KLEINEN GRUENEN TOMATEN %.)
        (DECL)
        1
        (START (PETER)
                (S3 MS)
                (KAUFTE)
                (V S3 A))
        2
        (MAIN+FVERB (PETER KAUFTE)
                (V A MS)
                (DIE)
                (A P -EN))
        3
        (FVERB+MAIN (PETER KAUFTE DIE)
                (V MS P -EN)
                (KLEINEN)
                (-EN))
        4
        (DET+ADJ (PETER KAUFTE DIE KLEINEN)
                (V MS P -EN)
                (GRUENEN)
                (-EN))
        5
        (DET+ADJ (PETER KAUFTE DIE KLEINEN GRUENEN)
                (V MS P -EN)
                (TOMATEN)
                (P))
        6
        (DET+NOUN (PETER KAUFTE DIE KLEINEN GRUENEN TOMATEN)
                (V MS P)
                (%.)
                (V DECL))
        7)))
```

If we assumed that the head of a noun phrase is the noun and that every noun
phrase must have a head, we would have to make a categorial distinction between

'adjectival' and 'nominal' uses of adjectives: adjectives in noun phrases with a noun, like *die kleinen grünen Tomaten*, would be categorized as adjectives, but the last adjective in a noun phrase without a noun, like *die kleinen grünen*, would be categorized as a noun. This would result in numerous additional readings. Instead of 4 readings, each adjective would have 11 readings: 4 for the adjectival use, represented by the segments -E, -EN, -ES, -ER, and 7 for the nominal uses, represented by the segments MS, MG, FS, NS, NG, P, and PD - assuming the distinctive approach to categorization. In an exhaustive system each adjective would have 72 readings, 48 for the adjectival use plus 24 for the nominal use! Instead of treating the pronomonial use of determiners and the nominal use of adjectives lexically by postulating additional readings, these different kinds of noun phrases are handled in DCAT by the syntactic rules.

Let us turn now to postnominal modifiers in German. German noun phrases consisting only of a determiner (e.g. 3.5.3) or a determiner-adjective combination (e.g. 3.5.4, 3.5.5) may be continued with a relative clause of proper agreement, just as any 'complete' noun phrase consisting of a determiner, a number of adjectives, and a noun (e.g. 3.5.6).[27] The second category segment of determiners specifies the agreement properties not only of a possible noun, but also of a possible relative clause. For example, the category of the accusative plural determiner *die* is (A P -EN). The second category segment P indicates that a possible noun must be a non-dative plural form and that a possible relative clause must begin with a relative pronoun of plural agreement.

The presence of the relative clause agreement feature in the determiner permits a very simple treatment of 'incomplete' noun phrases with relative clauses. Modification of a determiner by a relative clause is handled in DCAT by relaxing the input conditions of the rule RNOUN+RELPRO to accept sentence starts with -E or -EN segments in their categories. This is similar to the treatment of determiners as full noun phrases, which is handled by relaxing the input condition of RMAIN+FVERB and RFVERB+MAIN to accept MAIN-expressions with -E and -EN segments in their categories (see 3.5.3 above).

3.5.7 *Peter kaufte die, die so bitter schmecken.* / Peter bought the (ones) that taste so bitter.

```
(R PETER KAUFTE DIE DIE SO BITTER SCHMECKEN .)
((CMPLT ((PETER KAUFTE DIE , DIE SO BITTER SCHMECKEN %.)
        (DECL)
        1
        (START (PETER)
               (S3 MS)
               (KAUFTE)
               (V S3 A))
        2
        (MAIN+FVERB (PETER KAUFTE)
                    (V A MS)
                    (DIE)
```

---

[27]The internal structure of German relative clauses is discussed in detail in section 4.3.

```
                      (A P -EN))
           3
     (FVERB+MAIN (PETER KAUFTE DIE)
                 (V MS P -EN)
                 (DIE)
                 (P3 P -EN))
           4
     (NOUN+RELPRO (PETER KAUFTE DIE , DIE)
                  (V MS -EN V P3)
                  (SO)
                  (ADV-M))
           5
     (SUBCL+MAIN (PETER KAUFTE DIE , DIE SO)
                 (V MS V P3 ADV-M)
                 (BITTER)
                 (ADV-M))
           6
     (SUBCL+MAIN (PETER KAUFTE DIE , DIE SO BITTER)
                 (V MS V P3 ADV-M ADV-M)
                 (SCHMECKEN)
                 (V P3))
           7
     (SUBCL+LASTVERB (PETER KAUFTE DIE , DIE SO BITTER SCHMECKEN ,)
                     (V MS)
                     (%.)
                     (V DECL))
        8)))
```

The modification of an 'incomplete' noun phrase by a relative clause illustrated in 3.5.7 extends naturally to noun phrases consisting of a determiner and any number of adjectives. The reason is that determiners and corresponding determiner/adjective combinations have the same category. As examples consider 3.5.8 and 3.5.9:

3.5.8 *Peter kaufte die kleinen, die so bitter schmecken.* / Peter bought the small (ones) that taste so bitter.

```
(R PETER KAUFTE DIE KLEINEN DIE SO BITTER SCHMECKEN .)
((CMPLT ((PETER KAUFTE DIE KLEINEN , DIE SO BITTER SCHMECKEN %.)
         (DECL)
         1
         (START (PETER)
                (S3 MS)
                (KAUFTE)
                (V S3 A))
         2
         (MAIN+FVERB (PETER KAUFTE)
                     (V A MS)
                     (DIE)
                     (A P -EN))
         3
         (FVERB+MAIN (PETER KAUFTE DIE)
                     (V MS P -EN)
                     (KLEINEN)
```

```
                    (-EN))
            4
        (DET+ADJ (PETER KAUFTE DIE KLEINEN)
                (V MS P -EN)
                (DIE)
                (P3 P -EN))
            5
        (NOUN+RELPRO (PETER KAUFTE DIE KLEINEN , DIE)
                    (V MS -EN V P3)
                    (SO)
                    (ADV-M))
            6
        (SUBCL+MAIN (PETER KAUFTE DIE KLEINEN , DIE SO)
                    (V MS V P3 ADV-M)
                    (BITTER)
                    (ADV-M))
            7
        (SUBCL+MAIN (PETER KAUFTE DIE KLEINEN , DIE SO BITTER)
                    (V MS V P3 ADV-M ADV-M)
                    (SCHMECKEN)
                    (V P3))
            8
        (SUBCL+LASTVERB (PETER KAUFTE DIE KLEINEN , DIE SO BITTER
                            SCHMECKEN ,)
                    (V MS)
                    (%.)
                    (V DECL))
        9)))
```

3.5.9 *Peter kaufte die kleinen grünen, die so bitter schmecken.* / Peter bought
the small green (ones) that taste so bitter.

```
(R PETER KAUFTE DIE KLEINEN GRUENEN DIE SO BITTER SCHMECKEN .)
((CMPLT ((PETER KAUFTE DIE KLEINEN GRUENEN , DIE SO BITTER SCHMECKEN %.)
        (DECL)
        1
        (START (PETER)
            (S3 MS)
            (KAUFTE)
            (V S3 A))
        2
        (MAIN+FVERB (PETER KAUFTE)
                (V A MS)
                (DIE)
                (A P -EN))
        3
        (FVERB+MAIN (PETER KAUFTE DIE)
                (V MS P -EN)
                (KLEINEN)
                (-EN))
        4
        (DET+ADJ (PETER KAUFTE DIE KLEINEN)
                (V MS P -EN)
                (GRUENEN)
                (-EN))
        5
```

```
      (DET+ADJ (PETER KAUFTE DIE KLEINEN GRUENEN)
              (V MS P -EN)
              (DIE)
              (P3 P -EN))
      6
      (NOUN+RELPRO (PETER KAUFTE DIE KLEINEN GRUENEN , DIE)
                   (V MS -EN V P3)
                   (SO)
                   (ADV-M))
      7
      (SUBCL+MAIN (PETER KAUFTE DIE KLEINEN GRUENEN , DIE SO)
                  (V MS V P3 ADV-M)
                  (BITTER)
                  (ADV-M))
      8
      (SUBCL+MAIN (PETER KAUFTE DIE KLEINEN GRUENEN , DIE SO BITTER)
                  (V MS V P3 ADV-M ADV-M)
                  (SCHMECKEN)
                  (V P3))
      9
      (SUBCL+LASTVERB (PETER KAUFTE DIE KLEINEN GRUENEN , DIE SO BITTER
                              SCHMECKEN ,)
                      (V MS)
                      (%.)
                      (V DECL))
   10)))
```

Note that the rule RNOUN+RELPRO automatically adds the comma required before a relative pronoun in German. For the sake of completeness, we also present an example of a full noun phrase modified by a relative clause.[28] As mentioned above (see 3.3.7), the rule RDET+NOUN cancels the adjective segment in the determiner category, rather than the segment used for the agreement with the noun. The latter is retained for controlling agreement with a possible relative clause.

3.5.10 *Peter kaufte die kleinen grünen Tomaten, die so bitter schmecken. /* Peter bought the small green tomatoes that taste so bitter.

```
(R PETER KAUFTE DIE KLEINEN GRUENEN TOMATEN DIE SO BITTER SCHMECKEN .)
((CMPLT ((PETER KAUFTE DIE KLEINEN GRUENEN TOMATEN , DIE SO BITTER SCHMECKEN %.)
        (DECL)
        1
        (START (PETER)
               (S3 MS)
               (KAUFTE)
               (V S3 A))
        2
        (MAIN+FVERB (PETER KAUFTE)
                    (V A MS)
                    (DIE)
                    (A P -EN))
        3
```

---
[28]For additional examples of relative clauses with 'complete' head nouns see 4.3.

```
(FVERB+MAIN (PETER KAUFTE DIE)
            (V MS P -EN)
            (KLEINEN)
            (-EN))
4
(DET+ADJ (PETER KAUFTE DIE KLEINEN)
         (V MS P -EN)
         (GRUENEN)
         (-EN))
5
(DET+ADJ (PETER KAUFTE DIE KLEINEN GRUENEN)
         (V MS P -EN)
         (TOMATEN)
         (P))
6
(DET+NOUN (PETER KAUFTE DIE KLEINEN GRUENEN TOMATEN)
          (V MS P)
          (DIE)
          (P3 P -EN))
7
(NOUN+RELPRO (PETER KAUFTE DIE KLEINEN GRUENEN TOMATEN , DIE)
             (V MS V P3)
             (SO)
             (ADV-M))
8
(SUBCL+MAIN (PETER KAUFTE DIE KLEINEN GRUENEN TOMATEN , DIE SO)
            (V MS V P3 ADV-M)
            (BITTER)
            (ADV-M))
9
(SUBCL+MAIN (PETER KAUFTE DIE KLEINEN GRUENEN TOMATEN , DIE SO
                          BITTER)
            (V MS V P3 ADV-M ADV-M)
            (SCHMECKEN)
            (V P3))
10
(SUBCL+LASTVERB (PETER KAUFTE DIE KLEINEN GRUENEN TOMATEN , DIE
                       SO BITTER SCHMECKEN ,)
                (V MS)
                (%.)
                (V DECL))
11)))
```

Our discussion of German noun phrases beginning with determiners has shown that the treatment of 'incomplete' noun phrases does not require postulating additional lexical readings. Instead it is based simply on relaxing the input conditions of certain rules (e.g RMAIN+FVERB, RFVERB+MAIN, RNOUN+RELPRO) to accept MAIN-expressions with uncancelled adjective segments.

Let us turn now to noun phrases which do not begin with determiners. Consider the following examples:

3.5.11 Possible degrees of completeness of determiner-less noun phrases in German:

1. *Peter schwieg.*
2. *Peter, der Maria das Buch gegeben hatte, schwieg.*
3. *Maria liest gerne Bücher.*
4. *Maria liest gerne Bücher, die traurig enden.*
5. *Maria liest gerne gute Bücher.*
6. *Maria liest gerne gute.*
7. *Maria liest gerne gute lange.*
8. *Maria liest gerne gute lange, die traurig enden.*
9. *Maria liest gerne gute lange Bücher, die traurig enden.*
10. *Peter trank Wein.*
11. *Peter trank Wein, den ihm Maria geschenkt hatte.*
12. *Peter trank roten.*
13. *Peter trank roten Wein.*
14. *Peter trank roten Wein, den ihm Maria geschenkt hatte.*
15. *Peter trank guten roten.*
16. *Peter trank guten roten, den ihm Maria geschenkt hatte.*
17. *Peter trank guten roten Wein, den ihm Maria geschenkt hatte.*

There are five kinds of noun phrases without initial determiners in German. First, noun phrases beginning with a proper name, e.g. 1 and 2 in 3.5.11. These almost always occur in the singular. Second, plural noun phrases beginning with a noun, e.g. 3 and 4. Third, noun phrases beginning with a plural adjective, e.g. 5 - 9. These nouns and adjectives are restricted to nominative, dative, and accusative plural, and are called 'bare plurals'. Four, the noun phrases beginning with a singular noun, e.g. 10 and 11. And fifth, noun phrases beginning with a singular adjective, e.g. 12 - 17. The last two kinds of noun phrases are called 'mass nouns'.

The first word of a noun phrase beginning with a proper name, a noun, or an adjective may function alone as a full noun phrase, as illustrated in the examples 1, 3, 6, 10, and 12 of 3.5.11, respectively. This fact lends further support to the hypothesis that the grammatical role of German noun phrases should be encoded in the first word of the clause, regardless of whether this first word is a determiner, a proper name, an adjective or a noun. The kinds of continuations possible depend on the category of the initial word. Thus, clause-initial proper names or nouns may be continued only with a relative clause (cf. 2 and 4, respectively). Clause-initial adjectives, on the other hand, may be continued with another adjective (e.g. 7, 15, and 16), a noun (e.g. 5, 13, and 14), a relative clause (e.g. 8 and 16), or a combination of adjectives, a noun, and a relative clause (e.g. 9 and 17).

While conventional approaches that treat the noun as the **head** of a noun phrase must supply noun phrase readings for proper names, determiners and adjectives in order to handle noun phrases without nouns, left-associative grammar must supply noun phrase readings for proper names, adjectives, and nouns in order to handle noun phrases without determiners. This is necessary in order to maintain the principle that the grammatical role of German noun phrases is always specified in the initial or left-most word. As a first example of our lexical treatment of determiner-less noun phrases in German, consider the following categorization of a proper name in DLEX:

3.5.12 Categorization of a proper name in DLEX:

```
(PETER ((S3 MS)
        (D MS)
        (A MS)
        (MS)))
```

The first three readings characterize *Peter* as a full noun phrase of nominative (S3), dative (D), or accusative (A) case which may be continued by a relative clause of MS agreement. The fact that noun phrases beginning with a proper name may not be continued with an adjective is formally handled by the absence of any adjective segments in the category. The last reading in 3.5.12 handles the use of proper names as nouns, as in *Ich habe den Peter gesehen* or *der alte Peter*, which is quite common in German.

Sentences with noun phrases beginning with a proper name are illustrated in 3.5.13 and 3.5.14. 3.5.14 shows that a proper names is not necessarily an elementary noun phrase, but rather may be continued with a relative clause.

3.5.13 *Peter schwieg.* / Peter was silent.

```
(R PETER SCHWIEG .)
((CMPLT ((PETER SCHWIEG %.)
          (DECL)
          1
          (START (PETER)
                 (S3 MS)
                 (SCHWIEG)
                 (V S3))
          2
          (MAIN+FVERB (PETER SCHWIEG)
                      (V MS)
                      (%.)
                      (V DECL))
          3)))
```

3.5.14 *Peter, der Maria das Buch gegeben hatte, schwieg.* / Peter, who had
given the book to Mary, was silent.

```
(R PETER DER MARIA DAS BUCH GEGEBEN HATTE SCHWIEG .)
((CMPLT ((PETER , DER MARIA DAS BUCH GEGEBEN HATTE , SCHWIEG %.)
        (DECL)
        1
        (START (PETER)
               (S3 MS)
               (DER)
               (S3 MS -E))
        2
        (NOUN+RELPRO (PETER , DER)
                    (S3 V S3)
                    (MARIA)
                    (D FS))
        3
        (SUBCL+MAIN (PETER , DER MARIA)
                    (S3 V S3 D FS)
                    (DAS)
                    (A NS -E))
        4
        (SUBCL+MAIN (PETER , DER MARIA DAS)
                    (S3 V S3 D FS A NS -E)
                    (BUCH)
                    (NS))
        5
        (DET+NOUN (PETER , DER MARIA DAS BUCH)
                  (S3 V S3 D FS A NS)
                  (GEGEBEN)
                  (H D A))
        6
        (SUBCL+VERB (PETER , DER MARIA DAS BUCH GEGEBEN)
                    (S3 V S3 FS NS INF H)
                    (HATTE)
                    (V S3 H))
        7
        (SUBCL+LASTVERB (PETER , DER MARIA DAS BUCH GEGEBEN HATTE ,)
                        (S3 FS NS)
                        (SCHWIEG)
                        (V S3))
        8
        (MAIN+FVERB (PETER , DER MARIA DAS BUCH GEGEBEN HATTE , SCHWIEG)
                    (V FS NS)
                    (%.)
                    (V DECL))
        9)))
```

The second kind of determiner-less noun phrases in German is 'bare plurals'
beginning with a noun. The use of nouns as full 'bare plural' noun phrases is
also treated lexically. For example, instead of the four unambiguous forms of
the noun *Buch* in 3.2.7, DLEX actually provides the following 7 readings for the
four forms:

3.5.15 All readings of the noun *Buch* in DLEX:

```
(BUCH ((NS)))              (BUECHER ((P)
&                (P3 P)
&                (A P)))

(BUCHES (SG)))            (BUECHERN ((PD)
&                (D P)))
```

The additional lexical readings are indicated by the '&' in 3.5.15. The fact that plural forms generally have the readings indicated by '&' may be captured in the form of a lexical derivation rule. The categories of these readings specify the case of the noun phrase and the agreement property (P) of a possible relative clause. The absence of adjective segments in the categories of the new readings ensures that a noun phrase beginning with a bare plural noun cannot be continued with an adjective.

This lexical treatment of bare plurals raises the total number of readings of masculine and neuter nouns from 4 to 7 (for the usual four surface forms), and of feminine nouns from 3 to 6 (for the usual three surface forms). Because of the categorization of bare plurals as standard noun phrases, the rules of DCAT are unaffected. As an example of a sentence containing a noun phrase with an initial noun, consider 3.5.16.

3.5.16 *Maria liest gerne Bücher.* / Mary likes to read books.

```
(R MARIA LIEST GERNE BUECHER .)
((CMPLT ((MARIA LIEST GERNE BUECHER %.)
         (DECL)
         1
         (START (MARIA)
                (S3 FS)
                (LIEST)
                (V S3 A))
         2
         (MAIN+FVERB (MARIA LIEST)
                     (V A FS)
                     (GERNE)
                     (ADV-M))
         3
         (FVERB+MAIN (MARIA LIEST GERNE)
                     (V A FS)
                     (BUECHER)
                     (A P))
         4
         (FVERB+MAIN (MARIA LIEST GERNE BUECHER)
                     (V FS P)
                     (%.)
                     (V DECL))
         5)))
```

Bare plural noun phrases beginning with a noun are like noun phrases beginning with a proper name, in that they do not allow any adjectives to follow, but may be continued with a relative clause. This similarity is reflected in the respective categories. As an example of a bare plural beginning with a noun and continued with a relative clause, consider 3.5.17:

3.5.17 *Maria liest gerne Bücher, die traurig enden.* / Mary likes to read books that have sad endings.

```
(R MARIA LIEST GERNE BUECHER DIE TRAURIG ENDEN .)
((CMPLT ((MARIA LIEST GERNE BUECHER , DIE TRAURIG ENDEN %.)
        (DECL)
        1
        (START (MARIA)
               (S3 FS)
               (LIEST)
               (V S3 A))
        2
        (MAIN+FVERB (MARIA LIEST)
                    (V A FS)
                    (GERNE)
                    (ADV-M))
        3
        (FVERB+MAIN (MARIA LIEST GERNE)
                    (V A FS)
                    (BUECHER)
                    (A P))
        4
        (FVERB+MAIN (MARIA LIEST GERNE BUECHER)
                    (V FS P)
                    (DIE)
                    (P3 P -EN))
        5
        (NOUN+RELPRO (MARIA LIEST GERNE BUECHER , DIE)
                     (V FS V P3)
                     (TRAURIG)
                     (ADV-M))
        6
        (SUBCL+MAIN (MARIA LIEST GERNE BUECHER , DIE TRAURIG)
                    (V FS V P3 ADV-M)
                    (ENDEN)
                    (V P3))
        7
        (SUBCL+LASTVERB (MARIA LIEST GERNE BUECHER , DIE TRAURIG ENDEN ,)
                        (V FS)
                        (%.)
                        (V DECL))
        8)))
```

Finally consider noun phrases beginning with an adjective, as in *Maria liest gerne gute* or *Maria liest gerne gute Bücher*. In accordance with the hypothesis that the grammatical role of a noun phrase is specified in its first word, the bare plural uses of adjectives are treated by means of additional readings in DLEX. For example, instead of four unambiguous forms, the adjective *gut-* actually has the following analysis in DLEX:

3.5.18 All readings of the adjective *gut-* in DLEX:

```
(GUTE ((-E)                (GUTEN ((-EN)
&      (P3 P -E)      &            (D P -EN)))
&      (A P -E)))

(GUTES ((-ES)))            (GUTER ((-ER)))
```

As in 3.5.15, the additional readings in 3.5.18 are marked with '&'. The treatment of bare plurals beginning with adjectives requires three additional readings in the analysis of the four adjective forms of German ending in -E, -EN, -ES, and -ER. Note that their respective categories are those of determiners. As an example of a bare plural noun phrase beginning with an adjective, consider 3.5.19:

3.5.19 *Maria liest gerne gute.* / Mary likes to read good (ones).

```
(R MARIA LIEST GERNE GUTE .)
((CMPLT ((MARIA LIEST GERNE GUTE %.)
        (DECL)
        1
        (START (MARIA)
               (S3 FS)
               (LIEST)
               (V S3 A))
        2
        (MAIN+FVERB (MARIA LIEST)
                    (V A FS)
                    (GERNE)
                    (ADV-M))
        3
        (FVERB+MAIN (MARIA LIEST GERNE)
                    (V A FS)
                    (GUTE)
                    (A P -E))
        4
        (FVERB+MAIN (MARIA LIEST GERNE GUTE)
                    (V FS P -E)
                    (%.)
                    (V DECL))
        5)))
```

Since the bare plural readings of adjectives have categories like those of determiners, they may be continued with an indefinite number of additional adjectives - unlike bare plurals beginning with a noun. Instances of noun phrases consisting of adjectives without a noun are already treated by the provisions for the pronominal use of determiners (cf. 3.5.3, 3.5.4 and 3.5.5 above). As an example of a bare plural noun phrase consisting of two adjectives, consider 3.5.20:

3.5.20 *Maria liest gerne gute lange.* / Mary likes to read good long (ones).

```
(R MARIA LIEST GERNE GUTE LANGE .)
((CMPLT ((MARIA LIEST GERNE GUTE LANGE %.)
        (DECL)
        1
        (START (MARIA)
               (S3 FS)
               (LIEST)
               (V S3 A))
        2
        (MAIN+FVERB (MARIA LIEST)
                    (V A FS)
                    (GERNE)
                    (ADV-M))
        3
        (FVERB+MAIN (MARIA LIEST GERNE)
                    (V A FS)
                    (GUTE)
                    (A P -E))
        4
        (FVERB+MAIN (MARIA LIEST GERNE GUTE)
                    (V FS P -E)
                    (LANGE)
                    (-E))
        5
        (DET+ADJ (MARIA LIEST GERNE GUTE LANGE)
                 (V FS P -E)
                 (%.)
                 (V DECL))
        6)))
```

Noun phrases beginning with an adjective are like all the other kinds of noun phrases in that they may be continued with a relative clause of proper agreement. Consider 3.5.21 and 3.5.22 as examples:

3.5.21 *Maria liest gern gute lange, die traurig enden.* / Mary likes to read good long (ones) that have sad endings.

```
(R MARIA LIEST GERN GUTE LANGE DIE TRAURIG ENDEN .)
((CMPLT ((MARIA LIEST GERN GUTE LANGE , DIE TRAURIG ENDEN %.)
        (DECL)
        1
        (START (MARIA)
               (S3 FS)
               (LIEST)
               (V S3 A))
        2
        (MAIN+FVERB (MARIA LIEST)
                    (V A FS)
                    (GERN)
                    (ADV-M))
        3
        (FVERB+MAIN (MARIA LIEST GERN)
                    (V A FS)
                    (GUTE)
                    (A P -E))
```

```
        4
        (FVERB+MAIN (MARIA LIEST GERN GUTE)
                    (V FS P -E)
                    (LANGE)
                    (-E))
        5
        (DET+ADJ (MARIA LIEST GERN GUTE LANGE)
                 (V FS P -E)
                 (DIE)
                 (P3 P -EN))
        6
        (NOUN+RELPRO (MARIA LIEST GERN GUTE LANGE , DIE)
                     (V FS -E V P3)
                     (TRAURIG)
                     (ADV-M))
        7
        (SUBCL+MAIN (MARIA LIEST GERN GUTE LANGE , DIE TRAURIG)
                    (V FS V P3 ADV-M)
                    (ENDEN)
                    (V P3))
        8
        (SUBCL+LASTVERB (MARIA LIEST GERN GUTE LANGE , DIE TRAURIG ENDEN ,)
                        (V FS)
                        (%.)
                        (V DECL))
        9)))
```

3.5.22 *Maria liest gern gute lange Bücher, die traurig enden.* / Mary likes to read good long books that have sad endings.

```
(R MARIA LIEST GERN GUTE LANGE BUECHER DIE TRAURIG ENDEN .)
((CMPLT ((MARIA LIEST GERN GUTE LANGE BUECHER , DIE TRAURIG ENDEN %.)
        (DECL)
        1
        (START (MARIA)
               (S3 FS)
               (LIEST)
               (V S3 A))
        2
        (MAIN+FVERB (MARIA LIEST)
                    (V A FS)
                    (GERN)
                    (ADV-M))
        3
        (FVERB+MAIN (MARIA LIEST GERN)
                    (V A FS)
                    (GUTE)
                    (A P -E))
        4
        (FVERB+MAIN (MARIA LIEST GERN GUTE)
                    (V FS P -E)
                    (LANGE)
                    (-E))
        5
        (DET+ADJ (MARIA LIEST GERN GUTE LANGE)
                 (V FS P -E)
```

```
                  (BUECHER)
                  (P))
      6
      (DET+NOUN (MARIA LIEST GERN GUTE LANGE BUECHER)
                (V FS P)
                (DIE)
                (P3 P -EN))
      7
      (NOUN+RELPRO (MARIA LIEST GERN GUTE LANGE BUECHER , DIE)
                   (V FS V P3)
                   (TRAURIG)
                   (ADV-M))
      8
      (SUBCL+MAIN (MARIA LIEST GERN GUTE LANGE BUECHER , DIE TRAURIG)
                  (V FS V P3 ADV-M)
                  (ENDEN)
                  (V P3))
      9
      (SUBCL+LASTVERB (MARIA LIEST GERN GUTE LANGE BUECHER , DIE TRAURIG
                                                          ENDEN ,)
                      (V FS)
                      (%.)
                      (V DECL))
      10)))
```

Besides noun phrases beginning with a plural noun or a plural adjective (bare plurals), there are also noun phrases beginning with a singular noun or a singular adjective, such as in *Peter fand Gold* or *Schönes klares Wasser war in dem Bach.* These kinds of noun phrases are called **mass nouns**. Mass nouns are not treated in DCAT, but their implementation would be very similar to the implementation of bare plurals. It would be a lexical treatment, consisting in the specification of additional readings for the singular forms of certain nouns and adjectives.

The approach of DCAT describes the variety of German noun phrases by treating certain words as lexically ambiguous, but it uses lexical ambiguity very sparingly. This is due to the use of a distinctive rather than an exhaustive method of categorization (cf. sections 3.2 and 3.3). Handling the different kinds of noun phrases with a lexical rather than syntactic approach is motivated in part by the fact that not all nouns and adjectives may be used as bare plurals or mass nouns; whether or not a noun or adjective may be so used, is encoded directly into its lexical analysis. A much more important reason for choosing a lexical treatment, however, is the principle of surface compositionality: the syntax should not operate below the word level, but rather be limited to combining completely analyzed word forms.[29]

In a lexical approach the underlying theory determines which words are treated as ambiguous. Since the present approach assumes that the grammatical function of a noun phrase is encoded in its first word, additional readings must

---

[29]The principle of surface compositionality was proposed in **SCG**. See chapter 2 of **SCG** for a detailed discussion.

be postulated for adjectives and nouns, while no additional readings are needed for determiners and proper names. An alternative lexical account of different noun phrases in German which assumes that the noun is the 'head' of the noun phrase would have to postulate at least as many readings as the left-associative approach, in order to account for the pronominal use of determiners, the nominal use of adjectives in bare plurals and mass nouns, and the use of nouns as bare plurals and mass nouns.

Specifying additional readings for the initial word of each type of noun phrase, instead of treating the noun as the head, has the advantage that varying degrees of 'completeness' of any kind of noun phrase (beginning with a determiner, a proper name, a singular adjective, a singular noun, a plural adjective, or a plural noun) may be handled without any special syntactic or lexical provisions. Once the initial word of a German noun phrase has been added in left-associative grammar, one may choose whether or not to continue the noun phrase. The grammatical function of the noun phrase is accomplished by adding the first word. We will return to this subject matter in chapter 5 in connection with our left-associative treatment of noun phrases in English.

4. The local nature of possible continuations

Each left-associative combination is inherently asymmetric. Left-associative combinations take a sentence start and a next word as input, and render a new sentence start as output. The sentence start represents the state of the left-associative transition network that has been reached by analyzing the sentence up to the point where the most recent sentence start ended. The rule package responsible for a left-assssociative combination is provided by the sentence start, and not by the next word.

Given a sentence start with its rule package and its category, the function of the next word is to trigger another transition step, resulting in a new sentence start. The syntactic function of a next word is represented by its category alone, while the syntactic function of a sentence start is represented by both the rule package and the category. The next word is always an elementary lexical item, while the sentence start will usually be a derived expression.

4.1 The treatment of word order in DCAT

In left-associative grammar, there are no sentence frames representing the 'basic' or 'underlying' word order of a natural language, and there are no 'derived' word orders. Instead, word order is treated locally in terms of the input conditions of the rules, the categorial operations of the output conditions, and the content of the rule packages. This section illustrates the handling of word order in left-associative grammar by discussing several examples from German.

In declarative main clauses of German the finite verb must be in second position. If the finite verb is an auxiliary, the non-finite main verb must be in final or initial position. Otherwise the word order is free. In subordinate clauses the word order is also free except that the subordinating conjunction is clause initial and the verb complex is clause final. As an example of a declarative sentence with a three-place finite main verb consider 4.1.1.[1]

---

[1] For a step-by-step derivation of this sentence see 2.3.1 - 2.3.8 above.

4.1.1 *Das Mädchen gab dem Kind den Teller.* / The girl gave the child the plate.

```
(R DAS MAEDCHEN GAB DEM KIND DEN TELLER .)
((CMPLT ((DAS MAEDCHEN GAB DEM KIND DEN TELLER %.)
        (DECL)
        1
        (START (DAS)
               (S3 NS -E)
               (MAEDCHEN)
               (NS))
        2
        (DET+NOUN (DAS MAEDCHEN)
               (S3 NS)
               (GAB)
               (V S3 D A))
        3
        (MAIN+FVERB (DAS MAEDCHEN GAB)
               (V D A NS)
               (DEM)
               (D NS -EN))
        4
        (FVERB+MAIN (DAS MAEDCHEN GAB DEM)
               (V A NS NS -EN)
               (KIND)
               (NS))
        5
        (DET+NOUN (DAS MAEDCHEN GAB DEM KIND)
               (V A NS NS)
               (DEN)
               (A NS -EN))
        6
        (FVERB+MAIN (DAS MAEDCHEN GAB DEM KIND DEN)
               (V NS NS NS -EN)
               (TELLER)
               (NS))
        7
        (DET+NOUN (DAS MAEDCHEN GAB DEM KIND DEN TELLER)
               (V NS NS NS)
               (%.)
               (V DECL))
        8)))
```

The combination of noun phrases and the verb in this example is based on the categorial operation of 'cancelling'. As explained in section 3.4, in left-associative grammar the result of cancelling two lists is defined as a new list, consisting of all elements of the first list not contained in the second plus all elements of the second list not contained in the first. Example 4.1.1 is a syntactic construction where arguments immediately cancel corresponding segments in the valency carrier, either because the argument is sentence initial and the valency carrier is the next word, or because the valency carrier is part of the sentence start and the argument is the next word.

In history section 2, the argument precedes the valency carrier. As indicated in the sentence start of history section 3, the nominative noun phrase *das Mädchen* of category (S3 NS) and the verb form *gab* of category (V S3 D A) cancel, resulting in (V D A NS). The operation differs from cancelling in categorial grammar insofar as the non-initial segment of the first category (also called the 'remainder), appears in the output category. The segment NS is carried along because it may be needed to specify the agreement properties of a possible extraposed relative clause modifying the nominative.

Next consider history section 3 of 4.1.1, which shows the input of a left-associative combination where the valency carrier of category (V D A NS) precedes the argument of category (D NS -ES). The rule responsible for this combination is RFVERB+MAIN. It differs from RMAIN+FVERB in several respects (see 3.4.3 and 3.4.5 for the declarative formulation of these two rules). In RMAIN+FVERB the sentence start is the noun phrase and the next word is the finite verb, while in RFVERB+MAIN the sentence start includes the finite verb and the next word is the beginning of a noun phrase. Furthermore, the two rules call different rule packages and generally represent quite different states of syntactic transition. But in both rules the categorial operation is cancelling. The category resulting in history section 4 is (V A NS NS -ES).

In history section 5 of example 4.1.1 the rule RFVERB+MAIN applies again. The categories of the input expressions are (V A NS NS) and (A MS -EN), the output category specified in history section 6 is (V NS NS MS -EN). Note that the rule RMAIN+FVERB, unlike to RFVERB+MAIN, may apply only once. For example, 4.1.2 is ungrammatical and treated as such by DCAT.

4.1.2 *Das Mädchen dem Kind gab den Teller.

```
(R DAS MAEDCHEN DEM KIND GAB DEN TELLER .)
[ERROR "Ungrammatical continuation at:"
              ((NOUN+RELPRO ((DAS MAEDCHEN , DEM)
                       (A V D)
                       1
                       (START (DAS)
                       (A NS -E)
                       (MAEDCHEN)
                       (NS))
                       2
                       (DET+NOUN (DAS MAEDCHEN)
                       (A NS)
                       (DEM)
                       (D NS -EN))
                       3))
         (START ((KIND)
                 (NS]
```

4.1.2 is ungrammatical[2] because declarative sentences in German have the finite verb in second position. The position before the finite verb, (the Vorfeld), may

---

[2]In 4.1.2 DCAT tries to interpret *dem* as a relative pronoun, but the subsequent singular noun *Kind* is not a possible continuation and the derivation fails at this point. If a treatment

be filled by a noun phrase of any case, by an adverb, by an adverbial sentence, etc. But it is not acceptable to have more than one constituent in the Vorfeld (as in 4.1.2).

How does DCAT know that RMAIN+FVERB can apply only once in a sentence, while RFVERB+MAIN may apply several times? RMAIN+FVERB and RFVERB+MAIN are both listed in the rule package DET+NOUN of RDET+NOUN, which in 4.1.1 precedes the applications RMAIN+FVERB and RFVERB+MAIN. Thus the different number of applications of the two rules in 4.1.1 does not originate in the external control structure, but rather in the respective input conditions. As specified in 3.4.3 and 3.4.5, respectively, RMAIN+FVERB may apply only if the initial category segment of the sentence is not V, while RFVERB+MAIN requires that the initial segment of the sentence start is V (indicating presence of a finite verb). RMAIN+FVERB can apply only once because it cannot apply to its own output.

For convenience the declarative formulations of the rules RMAIN+FVERB and RFVERB+MAIN are repeated in 4.1.3 and 4.1.4 below.

4.1.3 Declarative statement of RMAIN+FVERB:

> The **input condition** of the rule RMAIN+FVERB specifies that (i) the first expression must be a main constituent such as a noun phrase or adverb, (ii) the second expression must be a finite verb, and (iii) the first category segment of the first expression must agree with a non-initial category segment of the second expression, unless the first expression is an adverb, or the first expression is not a nominative and the second expression is an auxiliary. The **output specification** of RMAIN+FVERB says: the output category is the result of cancelling the first with the second category.

4.1.4 Declarative statement of RFVERB+MAIN:

> The **input condition** of the rule RFVERB+MAIN specifies that (i) the category of the first expression must begin with a V, indicating the presence of a finite verb, (ii) the second expression must be (the beginning of) a main constituent, and (iii) the first category segment of the second expression must agree with a non-initial category segment of the first expression, unless the second expression is an adverb, or the second expression is not a nominative and the first expression is an auxiliary. The **output specification** of RFVERB+MAIN says: the output category is the result of cancelling the first with the second category.

---

of mass nouns were incorporated in DCAT, the parser would accept some apparent sequences of two noun phrases and a verb, such as *Das Mädchen dem Wein schmeckt.* But as in 4.1.2, the analysis would make clear that the construction involves a relative clause.

While RFVERB+MAIN may apply more than once, it may not apply arbitrarily many times. For example, if we added another noun phrase to 4.1.1, the result would be ungrammatical:

4.1.5 **Das Mädchen gab dem Kind den Teller ein Buch.*

```
(R DAS MAEDCHEN GAB DEM KIND DEN TELLER EIN BUCH .)
[ERROR "Ungrammatical continuation at:"
             ((DET+NOUN ((DAS MAEDCHEN GAD DEM KIND DEN TELLER)
                        (V NS NS MS)
                        1
                        (START (DAS)
                               (S3 NS -E)
                               (MAEDCHEN)
                               (NS))
                        2
                        (DET+NOUN (DAS MAEDCHEN)
                               (S3 NS)
                               (GAB)
                               (V S3 D A))
                        3
                        (MAIN+FVERB (DAS MAEDCHEN GAB)
                               (V D A NS)
                               (DEM)
                               (D NS -EN))
                        4
                        (FVERB+MAIN (DAS MAEDCHEN GAB DEM)
                               (V A NS NS -EN)
                               (KIND)
                               (NS))
                        5
                        (DET+NOUN (DAS MAEDCHEN GAB DEM KIND)
                               (V A NS NS)
                               (DEN)
                               (A MS -EN))
                        6
                        (FVERB+MAIN (DAS MAEDCHEN GAB DEM KIND DEN)
                               (V NS NS MS -EN)
                               (TELLER)
                               (MS))
                        7))
        (START ((EIN)
               (A NS -ES]
```

How does DCAT know that another application of RFVERB+MAIN would be inappropriate? The input condition of RFVERB+MAIN requires that the first category segment of the next word must have a counterpart among the non-initial segments of the category of the sentence start. Since the two earlier applications of RFVERB+MAIN in history sections 3 and 5 removed the dative (D) and accusative (A) valency positions originally introduced by the finite verb, any further addition of noun phrases is prevented. Both the introduction and the cancelling of valency positions is handled by the categorial operation of cancelling.

The input conditions of the rules RMAIN+FVERB and RFVERB+MAIN and the categorial operation of cancelling in the output condition of these two rules not only prevent the acceptance of ungrammatical sentences; they also constitute an extremely simple and powerful method of handling free word order in German. Consider for example 4.1.6.

4.1.6 *Dem Kind gab das Mädchen den Teller.*

```
(R DEM KIND GAB DAS MAEDCHEN DEN TELLER .)
((CMPLT ((DEM KIND GAB DAS MAEDCHEN DEN TELLER %.)
        (DECL)
        1
        (START (DEM)
               (D NS -EN)
               (KIND)
               (NS))
        2
        (DET+NOUN (DEM KIND)
                  (D NS)
                  (GAB)
                  (V S3 D A))
        3
        (MAIN+FVERB (DEM KIND GAB)
                    (V S3 A NS)
                    (DAS)
                    (S3 NS -E))
        4
        (FVERB+MAIN (DEM KIND GAB DAS)
                    (V A NS NS -E)
                    (MAEDCHEN)
                    (NS))
        5
        (DET+NOUN (DEM KIND GAB DAS MAEDCHEN)
                  (V A NS NS)
                  (DEN)
                  (A MS -EN))
        6
        (FVERB+MAIN (DEM KIND GAB DAS MAEDCHEN DEN)
                    (V NS NS MS -EN)
                    (TELLER)
                    (MS))
        7
        (DET+NOUN (DEM KIND GAB DAS MAEDCHEN DEN TELLER)
                  (V NS NS MS)
                  (%.)
                  (V DECL))
        8)))
```

The sentences in 4.1.1 and 4.1.6 are closely related. They contain exactly the same words, and the combination of the words involves exactly the same grammatical functions. The only difference is the word order: in 4.1.1 the first constituent is the nominative, while in 4.1.6 the first constituent is the topicalized dative.

The close syntactic relation between 4.1.1 and 4.1.6 is expressed by the fact that the two left-associative derivations use exactly the same categories, the same rules, and even the same order of rule packages (and rules), namely

START
DET+NOUN
MAIN+FVERB
FVERB+MAIN
DET+NOUN
FVERB+MAIN
DET+NOUN
CMPLT

The difference in the serialization is shown only in a different order of cancelling the valencies. For example, in history section 2 of 4.1.6 the dative is cancelled, while in history section 2 of 4.1.1 it is the nominative. The rules RMAIN+FVERB and RFVERB+MAIN handle all alternative serializations of 4.1.1 without any special provisions.

In each left-associative combination of the examples 4.1.1 and 4.1.6, arguments immediately cancel corresponding segments in the valency carrier, either because the argument is sentence initial and the valency carrier is the next word, or because the valency carrier is part of the sentence start and the argument is the next word. Let us turn now to another construction of German, where the valency carrier is not yet available when certain arguments are combined with the sentence start. Consider for example 4.1.7.

4.1.7 *Das Mädchen hat dem Kind den Teller gegeben.* / The girl has given the child the plate.

```
(R DAS MAEDCHEN HAT DEM KIND DEN TELLER GEGEBEN .)
((CMPLT ((DAS MAEDCHEN HAT DEM KIND DEN TELLER GEGEBEN %.)
        (DECL)
        1
        (START (DAS)
               (S3 NS -E)
               (MAEDCHEN)
               (NS))
        2
        (DET+NOUN (DAS MAEDCHEN)
                  (S3 NS)
                  (HAT)
                  (V S3 H))
        3
        (MAIN+FVERB (DAS MAEDCHEN HAT)
                    (V H NS)
                    (DEM)
                    (D NS -EN))
        4
        (FVERB+MAIN (DAS MAEDCHEN HAT DEM)
                    (V H NS D NS -EN)
                    (KIND)
                    (NS))
```

```
     5
 (DET+NOUN  (DAS MAEDCHEN HAT DEM KIND)
            (V H NS D NS)
            (DEN)
            (A MS -EN))
     6
 (FVERB+MAIN (DAS MAEDCHEN HAT DEM KIND DEN)
            (V H NS D NS A MS -EN)
            (TELLER)
            (MS))
     7
 (DET+NOUN  (DAS MAEDCHEN HAT DEM KIND DEN TELLER)
            (V H NS D NS A MS)
            (GEGEBEN)
            (H D A))
     8
 (MAINCL+NFVERB (DAS MAEDCHEN HAT DEM KIND DEN TELLER GEGEBEN)
            (V NS NS MS)
            (%.)
            (V DECL))
 9)))
```

4.1.7 is an example of what is called a 'Satzklammer' in German. The finite verb
in second position is an auxiliary which carries the valency for the nominative.
The valencies for the other arguments of the verb phrase are carried by the
non-finite main verb (past participle), which is positioned at the end.

The relation between the finite auxiliary *hat* and the non-finite main verb
gegeben is expressed in the respective categories, (V S3 H) and (H D A). Cancelling of these two categories renders (V S3 D A), which is the same as the
category of the finite main verb *gab* used in 4.1.1 and 4.1.6. Other auxiliaries,
for example *war* of category (V S3 S) of the paradigm *sein*, are not compatible
with *gegeben*, because they have no counterpart for cancelling the H segment.

Let us consider now the building up and cancelling of valencies in 4.1.7. In
history section 2 the sentence start is a nominative which agrees with the S3 in
the finite verb. RMAIN+FVERB applies, and cancelling renders *Das Mädchen
hat* of category (V H NS). Next comes the dative, *dem* of category (D NS -EN).
Notice that the sentence start *Das Mädchen hat* contains no valency position
to cancel with the dative. Rather, the valencies for the non-nominative noun
phrases in 4.1.7 are carried by the non-finite main verb *gegeben* of category (H
D A), which occurs at the very end of the sentence.

DCAT handles this situation by accumulating argument positions in the
sentence start, which are cancelled off at the end when the derivation reaches
the non-finite main verb. For example, the application of RFVERB+MAIN in
history section 3 results in the category (V H NS D NS -EN). This category results from standard cancelling; the only special provision for handling auxiliary
constructions in RFVERB+MAIN is in the input condition: "(iii) the first category segment of the second expression must agree with a non-initial category
segment of the first expression, unless ... the second expression is not a nom-

inative and the verb in the first expression is an auxiliary." (cf. 4.1.4 above). Cancelling of two categories which have no segments in common is called argument adding, whereas cancelling of two categories which have one segment in common is called argument cancelling[3].

Since left-associative continuations are purely local, application of the rule RDET+NOUN in history section 4 is not affected by the fact that the dative has been argument-added in the previous combination. For RDET+NOUN, the only relevant property of the sentence start *Das Mädchen hat dem* is the fact that it ends in a determiner, which is clearly encoded in the last two segments of its category, (V H NS D NS -EN). The category (NS) of the next word *Kind* is compatible and the output condition of RDET+NOUN renders the category (V H NS D NS).[4]

Once the auxiliary is in place in second position, indefinitely many arguments may be added, as long as a non-finite verb may still be found that would provide valencies for all the added arguments. For example, in history section 5 of 4.1.7, RFVERB+MAIN applies again. After another application of RDET+NOUN in history section 6, the category of the sentence start *Das Mädchen hat dem Kind den Teller* is (V H NS D NS A MS). This category indicates an incomplete declarative sentence with a finite auxiliary verb (H), an argument-added dative (D), and an argument-added accusative (A). The segments NS, NS, and MS are carried along for specifying agreement with a possible extraposed relative clause.

Cancelling of two categories which have several segments in common is called 'wholesale cancelling', which is the intuitive counterpart of 'argument adding'. Consider history section 7 of 4.1.7, where the new rule RMAINCL+NFVERB (mainclause plus nonfinite verb) applies. The input expressions are *Das Mädchen hat dem Kind den Teller* of category (V H NS D NS A MS) and *gegeben* of category (H D A). The output category, specified in the sentence start of history section 8, is (V NS NS MS) and results from cancelling the input categories. In its basic form, RMAINCL+NFVERB may be stated as follows:

4.1.8 Simplified declarative statement of RMAINCL+NFVERB

> The **input condition** of the rule RMAINCL+NFVERB specifies
> that (i) the finite verb in the first expression must be an auxiliary,
> (ii) the second expression must be a non-finite verb, and (iii) all
> segments of the category of the second expression must have coun-
> terparts in the category of the first expression, and all case segments
> in the category of the first expression must have counterparts in the
> category of the second expression. The **output specification** of

---

[3]If the two lists have an empty intersection, cancelling results in adding the second list to the first (argument adding). If the two sets have a non-empty intersection, the corresponding elements of each list are removed (argument cancelling)

[4]See 3.3.7 for a statement of the rule RDET+NOUN.

RMAINCL+NFVERB says: the output category is the result of cancelling the first with the second category.

The actual LISP-code of this rule in appendix A.2 is more complicated than 4.1.8 in order to handle iteration of non-finite verb forms at the end of declarative and interrogative sentences, as in *Das Mädchen hat dem Kind den Teller geben können wollen.*

The input condition of RMAINCL+NFVERB ensures that the rule will be successful only if the arguments accumulated in the sentence start correspond precisely to the valency positions in the non-finite verb. This in turn takes into account the fact that the non-finite verb must occur at the end of the sentence. If the non-finite verb occurred before the end, there would be too few argument-added segments in the sentence start to match the category of the non-finite verb. Also, combination with the non-finite verb cancels the auxiliary segment in the category of the sentence start, preventing any further argument adding.

Because of the general nature of category cancelling, the rules RMAIN-+FVERB and RFVERB+MAIN handle the possible variations of word order in constructions involving 'Satzklammer's without any special provisions. As an example consider 4.1.9:

4.1.9 *Dem Kind hat das Mädchen den Teller gegeben.*

```
(R DEM KIND HAT DAS MAEDCHEN DEN TELLER GEGEBEN .)
((CMPLT ((DEM KIND HAT DAS MAEDCHEN DEN TELLER GEGEBEN %.)
         (DECL)
         1
         (START (DEM)
                (D NS -EN)
                (KIND)
                (NS))
         2
         (DET+NOUN (DEM KIND)
                   (D NS)
                   (HAT)
                   (V S3 H))
         3
         (MAIN+FVERB (DEM KIND HAT)
                     (V S3 H D NS)
                     (DAS)
                     (S3 NS -E))
         4
         (FVERB+MAIN (DEM KIND HAT DAS)
                     (V H D NS NS -E)
                     (MAEDCHEN)
                     (NS))
         5
         (DET+NOUN (DEM KIND HAT DAS MAEDCHEN)
                   (V H D NS NS)
                   (DEN)
                   (A NS -EN))
         6
```

```
(FVERB+MAIN (DEM KIND HAT DAS MAEDCHEN DEN)
            (V H D NS NS A MS -EN)
            (TELLER)
            (MS))
7
(DET+NOUN (DEM KIND HAT DAS MAEDCHEN DEN TELLER)
          (V H D NS NS A MS)
          (GEGEBEN)
          (H D A))
8
(MAINCL+NFVERB (DEM KIND HAT DAS MAEDCHEN DEN TELLER GEGEBEN)
               (V NS NS MS)
               (%.)
               (V DECL))
9)))
```

Example 4.1.9 is closely related to 4.1.7. Both sentences contain exactly the same words, and the combination of the words involves the same grammatical functions. The only syntactic difference is the word order: in 4.1.9 the Vorfeld-position is taken by the dative, while the arguments after the finite auxiliary are the nominative and the accusative; in 4.1.7 the Vorfeld is taken by the nominative, while the arguments after the finite auxiliary are the dative and the accusative. As in the earlier examples 4.1.1 and 4.1.6, DCAT handles these variations in word order in terms of different orders of building up and cancelling valencies.

Sentences like 4.1.7 and 4.1.9 are impossible to analyze within constituent structure theory. There is not only the discontinuous Satzklammer *hat ... gegeben* to account for, but also the word order variation. The only way to capture the obvious relation between 4.1.7 and 4.1.9, or between 4.1.1 and 4.1.6, is by using transformations or other techniques to circumvent the inherent limitations of constituent structure analysis. In contrast, left-associative grammar uses the same simple rules RMAIN+FVERB and RFVERB+MAIN (with the additional rule RMAINCL+NFVERB) to handle both construction types and all possible word order variations. Since all words are used in their standard categorization in the above constructions, the left-associative treatment captures significant syntactic generalizations simply and straightforwardly.

Argument adding and wholesale cancelling comprise the intuitively obvious method for treating constructions in which the valency carrier is added at the end. Other constructions involving argument adding in German are subordinate clauses. These instances are even more striking than in Satzklammer-constructions with auxiliaries. In the latter the valency carrier for the nominative (i.e. the auxiliary) will be available no matter where the nominative appears, but in subordinate clauses even the nominative is argument-added.

As a simple example of a subordinate clause in German consider 4.1.10:

4.1.10 *Der schöne alte Tisch, den Peter kaufte,/* The beautiful old table, which Peter bought

```
(R DER SCHOENE ALTE TISCH DEN PETER KAUFTE)
((SUBCL+LASTVERB ((DER SCHOENE ALTE TISCH , DEN PETER KAUFTE ,)
                (S3))
            1
            (START (DER)
                  (S3 MS -E)
                  (SCHOENE)
                  (-E))
            2
            (DET+ADJ (DER SCHOENE)
                  (S3 MS -E)
                  (ALTE)
                  (-E))
            3
            (DET+ADJ (DER SCHOENE ALTE)
                  (S3 MS -E)
                  (TISCH)
                  (MS))
            4
            (DET+NOUN (DER SCHOENE ALTE TISCH)
                  (S3 MS)
                  (DEN)
                  (A MS -EN))
            5
            (NOUN+RELPRO (DER SCHOENE ALTE TISCH , DEN)
                     (S3 V A)
                     (PETER)
                     (S3 MS))
            6
            (SUBCL+MAIN (DER SCHOENE ALTE TISCH , DEN PETER)
                     (S3 V A S3 MS)
                     (KAUFTE)
                     (V S3 A))
            7)))
```

The first three history sections of analysis 4.1.10 are identical to those of
3.3.4. The rule combining the sentence start *Der schöne alte Tisch* of category
(S3 MS) with the article *den* of category (A MS -EN) in history section 4 is
RNOUN+RELPRO, which is defined as follows:

4.1.11 Simplified declarative statement of RNOUN+RELPRO:

> The **input condition** of the rule RNOUN+RELPRO specifies that
> (i) the first expression must end in a determiner[5] or a noun[6], (ii)
> the second expression must be a determiner with the surface *der,*
> *die, das, dessen, dem, den,* or *deren,* and (iii) the second segment of
> the category of the second expression must agree with the last noun
> segment of the category of the first expression. The **output spec-**
> **ification** of RNOUN+RELPRO says: the output category consists

---

[5]Cf. 3.5.7, 3.5.8, 3.5.9, 3.5.21.
[6]Cf. 3.5.10, 3.5.14, 3.5.17, 3.5.22.

of the first input category up to the last noun segment, plus the segment V, plus the initial segment of the category of the second expression.

In the simplified form of 4.1.11, the rule RNOUN+RELPRO handles only relative clauses which are positioned directly after the noun phrase they modify. The additional clauses in the actual LISP-code of this rule in appendix A.2 account for other forms of extraposed relative clauses in German.

RNOUN+RELPRO requires agreement between the last noun segment of the sentence start and the second category segment of the next word (see history section 4; the segment in question is MS). The determiners *der, die, das, dessen, dem,* and *den* are used both as determiners and as relative pronouns.[7] The output condition of RNOUN+RELPRO derives the result category by combining the category of the first input expression minus the last segment, the segment V, and the first category segment of the second expression, e.g. (S3 V A).

This category has the following interpretation. The result segment S3 tells us that we will obtain a third person singular nominative once the remaining segments have been cancelled. The segment V indicates that a relative clause has been initiated. The A indicates that the verb of this relative clause, which in German is in clause final position, must have a valency position for an accusative. The accusative in question is grammatically represented by the determiner *den,* which functions in 4.1.10 as a relative pronoun.

RNOUN+RELPRO, like RDET+NOUN and RDET+ADJ, does not derive the output category on the basis of cancelling the input categories, but on the basis of more specific instructions. The formulation in 4.1.11 has the advantage that determiners are used as relative pronouns. We could define RNOUN+RELPRO in a way that uses cancelling but it would require postulating numerous additional readings for the forms *der, die, das, dessen, deren, dem,* and *den.* This would fail to exploit the linguistic fact that the agreement properties of determiners suffice for their use as relative pronouns in German[8]. Also, it would be computationally costly. Every time a word like *der* appeared in a parse, ordered pairs would be generated for determiner as well as relative pronoun readings. The rules of the rule package would have to apply to a considerably larger number of ordered pairs, which would slow down the computation.[9].

In history section 5 of our example, the rule RSUBCL+MAIN combines *Der schöne alte Tisch, den* of category (S3 V A) with the (S3 MS) noun phrase *Peter.* Here we see another instance of argument adding. The output category is (S3 V A S3 MS) and results from adding the category of the second expression

---

[7]A third use of determiners in DCAT, which likewise avoids multiple categorization, is as full noun phrases, i.e. the pronominal use of determiners described in section 3.5.

[8]Presuming the analysis of noun phrases presented in section 3.5.

[9]See the related calculations in the discussion of exhaustive versus distinctive categorization in the sections 3.2 and 3.3.

to the category of the first. Intuitively, argument adding is necessary in a left-associative analysis of German subordinate clauses because the verb comes at the end. Once a subordinate clause is initiated, e.g. after the relative pronoun, indefinitely many arguments may be added using RSUBCL+MAIN, as long as a verb can still be found to cancel all the accumulated valencies at the end.

4.1.12 Simplified declarative statement of RSUBCL+MAIN:

> The **input condition** of the rule RSUBCL+MAIN specifies that (i) the category of the first expression must contain a non-initial V segment, indicating that a subordinate clause has been initiated, and (ii) the second expression must be (the beginning of) a main constituent. The **output specification** of RSUBCL+MAIN says: the output category consists of the first input category plus the second input category.[10]

In history section 6 of 4.1.10, the rule RSUBCL+LASTVERB closes the relative clause by adding a finite verb of category (V S3 A), which has the proper valency. This is another instance of wholesale-cancelling.

4.1.13 Simplified declarative statement of RSUBCL+LASTVERB

> The **input condition** of the rule RSUBCL+LASTVERB specifies that (i) the first expression must have a non-initial V segment, (ii) the second expression must be a finite verb, (iii) all segments of the second category must have counterparts in the tail of the first category beginning with the last V, and (iv) there may be no case segments in the tail of the first category beginning with the last V, which do not have counterparts in the category of the second expression. The **output specification** of RSUBCL+LASTVERB says: the output category consists of the first input category up to, but not including, the last V.

The above statements of the rules RSUBCL+MAIN and RSUBCL+LASTVERB are simplified insofar as they do not account for complex verb constructions, in particular cases like *Der Tisch, den Peter hat kaufen können wollen*, where the finite verb is not in clause final position. For complete formulations of these rules see the actual LISP code in appendix A.2. The rules do account for possible word order variations in subordinate clauses, such as *Das Buch, das den Kindern ein alter Mann gab* versus *Das Buch, das ein alter Mann den Kindern gab*. The order in which arguments are added is free as long as all arguments have counterparts in the clause final verb construction.

---

[10]We do not use cancelling here, because in subordinate clauses the category of the next word could accidentally match a category segment in the sentence start. The situation is different in the case of RMAIN+FVERB and RFERB+MAIN, which operate on the top level of sentences.

So far, the discussion of basic constructions of German has been restricted to the relation between noun phrases and verbs. The grammatical role of a noun phrase was explained in terms of cancelling a corresponding case segment in the category of the valency carrier. Let us turn now to a type of main constituent which does not involve case, namely **adverbs**. How does left-associative grammar characterize the grammatical role of adverbs?

There are both obligatory and optional uses of adverbs. An adverb is obligatory if it cancels a corresponding valency position in the verb. Verbs which take obligatory adverbs distinguish between different kinds of adverbs. In DCAT there are adverbs of location (ADV-L), time (ADV-T), direction (ADV-D), manner (ADV-M), and cause (ADV-C). Some verbs require an adverb of a certain kind as their argument. The verb *wohnen*, for example, requires a nominative and an adverb of location. Consequently, *wohnt* has the category (V S3 ADV-L).

An adverb is optional if there is no corresponding valency position in the valency carrier. Optional adverbs may be added freely wherever a noun phrase could occur. There are no agreement restrictions on the optional use of adverbs.

Consider the following derivation:

4.1.14 *Früher wohnte Peter in Hamburg.* / Peter lived in Hamburg earlier. Peter used to live in Hamburg.

```
(R FRUEHER WOHNTE PETER IN HAMBURG .)
((CMPLT ((FRUEHER WOHNTE PETER IN HAMBURG %.)
        (DECL))
    1
    (START (FRUEHER)
           (ADV-T)
           (WOHNTE)
           (V S3 ADV-L))
    2
    (MAIN+FVERB (FRUEHER WOHNTE)
                (V S3 ADV-L)
                (PETER)
                (S3 MS))
    3
    (FVERB+MAIN (FRUEHER WOHNTE PETER)
                (V ADV-L MS)
                (IN)
                (ADV-L (D)))
    4
    (FVERB+MAIN (FRUEHER WOHNTE PETER IN)
                (V MS (D))
                (HAMBURG)
                (D NS))
    5
    (PREP+MAIN (FRUEHER WOHNTE PETER IN HAMBURG)
               (V MS NS)
               (%.)
               (V DECL))
    6)))
```

In section 1 of example 4.1.14, the time adverb *Früher* combines with the finite main verb *wohnte*. Since this verb does not have a valency position for an ADV-T, *früher* is an optional adverb. In main clauses with a finite main verb the addition of an optional adverb simply does not register in the output category. The grammatical function of an optional adverb is to modify the whole clause.

In section 3 of example 4.1.14, the beginning of the local adverb *in Hamburg* is added. Here we have an obligatory adverb, because the valency carrier (in this case the sentence start) has a corresponding ADV-L segment in its category. In main clauses with a finite main verb the addition of an obligatory adverb cancels the corresponding segment in the valency carrier. The grammatical function of an obligatory adverb is similar to that of a dative or accusative noun phrase.

In constructions involving argument adding, such as main clauses with auxiliaries and subordinate clauses, whether an adverb is optional or obligatory can be decided only when the verb is added at the end. In these constructions the category of any adverb is 'argument added'. Consider for example 4.1.15:

4.1.15 *Weil Peter früher gern in Hamburg wohnte,* / Because Peter had earlier liked living in Hamburg - Since Peter used to like living in Hamburg

```
(R WEIL PETER FRUEHER GERN IN HAMBURG WOHNTE)
((SUBCL+LASTVERB ((WEIL PETER FRUEHER GERN IN HAMBURG WOHNTE ,)
                  (ADCL MS NS)
                1
                (START (WEIL)
                       (ADCL V)
                       (PETER)
                       (S3 MS))
                2
                (SUBCL+MAIN (WEIL PETER)
                            (ADCL V S3 MS)
                            (FRUEHER)
                            (ADV-T))
                3
                (SUBCL+MAIN (WEIL PETER FRUEHER)
                            (ADCL V S3 MS ADV-T)
                            (GERN)
                            (ADV-M))
                4
                (SUBCL+MAIN (WEIL PETER FRUEHER GERN)
                            (ADCL V S3 MS ADV-T ADV-M)
                            (IN)
                            (ADV-L (D)))
                5
                (SUBCL+MAIN (WEIL PETER FRUEHER GERN IN)
                            (ADCL V S3 MS ADV-T ADV-M ADV-L (D))
                            (HAMBURG)
                            (D NS))
                6
                (PREP+MAIN (WEIL PETER FRUEHER GERN IN HAMBURG)
                           (ADCL V S3 MS ADV-T ADV-M ADV-L NS)
                           (WOHNTE)
                           (V S3 ADV-L))
```

7)))

When wholesale-cancelling applies at the end, 'argument added' adverb categories without a counterpart in the valency carrier are forgotten, because they represent optional adverbs. But if there are adverb segments in the valency carrier which do not have counterparts in the sentence start, they remain in the output category to indicate the lack of an obligatory adverb. In 4.1.15 the ADV-L segment in the valency carrier *wohnte* has a counterpart in the category of the sentence start and the result is a well-formed sentence.

Many of the rules discussed above are based on the categorial operation of cancelling. This operation is useful for a concise description of German, which permits noun phrases to occur in any order, as long as the finite verb is in second position (in a declarative main clause) or in final position (in a subordinate clause). But sometimes the operation of cancelling is modified by special conditions, in order to handle specific syntactic phenomena of the language. For example, the rule RMAIN+FVERB does not always add all remaining segments of the first category to the output; if the category of the noun phrase contains an adjective segment (because of the pronominal use of a determiner), it will be filtered from the output category, for reasons explained in section 3.5. Other rules, like RDET+ADJ, RDET+NOUN, and RDET+RELPRO do not use cancelling at all; instead they check for corresponding segments in the two input categories and then derive the output category on the basis of rather specific instructions.

It would be more pleasing aesthetically or mathematically if the output category were always derived from the input categories by the same operation, e.g. cancelling. But the cost of maintaining this kind of regularity is considerable. What are the options? One may omit from the grammar constructions which are presently treated in terms of operations other than pure cancelling, such as determiners used pronominally, or relative clauses. Or one may treat these constructions using only pure cancelling on the basis of additional lexical readings. Neither of these methods is attractive: the first one achieves the goal by disregarding much of the data, while the second slows down the computation because of additional lexical readings.

Furthermore, it is important to realize that cancelling is not suitable for all languages, useful as it is for German. In English, for example, the combination of noun phrases and the verb is subject to a rigid word order. The cancelling operation is not suitable for describing this aspect of English, because it is not sensitive to the order of the segments in the category of the valency carrier. [11] In other words, left-associative grammar does not attempt to describe certain kinds of combination (e.g. noun phrase and verb, determiner and noun, etc.) with a small number of categorial operations which are 'universal' for all natural languages. Rather, the categorial operations used by left-associative grammar are characteristic of the particular natural language described.

---

[11] This point is explained in detail in chapter 5.

Each left-associative rule represents a particular transition in the transition network of a natural language. The transition network reflects general properties of the natural language in question, such as word order and agreement. Special conditions for the categorial operations of rules are simply a way to account for the natural properties of transitions which evolved and changed in the history of a language. In natural languages many historical strata combine into complex, multi-layered systems. A desire for linguistic universals should not mislead one to expect that the categorial operations of left-associative grammar should be the same in all rules, or even all languages. Instead, uniformity may be found in the systematic, linear nature of left-associative combinations.

4.2 Passive and other constructions with auxiliaries in DCAT

New grammatical constructions may be added to a left-associative grammar in two ways: by defining new rules, and by addition of new words, with appropriate categories, to the lexicon. In the previous section we explained how the rules RMAIN+FVERB, RFVERB+MAIN, and RMAINCL+NFVERB handle word order and word order variation in declarative main clauses of German, and how the rules RNOUN+RELPRO, RSUBCL+MAIN, and RSUBCL+LASTVERB handle the word order and word order variation in relative clauses of German. In this section we show that these rules will also account for the passive construction, provided that the relevant verb forms are categorized appropriately. As a first example of a passive sentence in German consider 4.2.1:

4.2.1 *Dem Mann wurde von dem Mädchen ein Buch gegeben.* / The man was given a book by the girl.

```
(R DEM MANN WURDE VON DEM MAEDCHEN EIN BUCH GEGEBEN .)
((CMPLT ((DEM MANN WURDE VON DEM MAEDCHEN EIN BUCH GEGEBEN %.)
        (DECL))
      1
      (START (DEM)
             (D MS -EN)
             (MANN)
             (MS))
      2
      (DET+NOUN (DEM MANN)
               (D MS)
               (WURDE)
               (V S3 WP))
      3
      (MAIN+FVERB (DEM MANN WURDE)
                 (V S3 WP D MS)
                 (VON)
                 (-AG (D)))
      4
      (FVERB+MAIN (DEM MANN WURDE VON)
```

```
                    (V S3 WP D MS -AG (D))
                    (DEM)
                    (D NS -EN))
        5
        (PREP+MAIN (DEM MANN WURDE VON DEM)
                    (V S3 WP D MS -AG NS -EN)
                    (MAEDCHEN)
                    (NS))
        6
        (DET+NOUN (DEM MANN WURDE VON DEM MAEDCHEN)
                    (V S3 WP D MS -AG NS)
                    (EIN)
                    (S3 NS -ES))
        7
        (FVERB+MAIN (DEM MANN WURDE VON DEM MAEDCHEN EIN)
                    (V WP D MS -AG NS NS -ES)
                    (BUCH)
                    (NS))
        8
        (DET+NOUN (DEM MANN WURDE VON DEM MAEDCHEN EIN BUCH)
                    (V WP D MS -AG NS NS)
                    (GEGEBEN)
                    (WP D -AG))
        9
        (MAINCL+NFVERB (DEM MANN WURDE VON DEM MAEDCHEN EIN BUCH GEGEBEN)
                    (V MS NS NS)
                    (%.)
                    (V DECL))
        10)))
```

The treatment of passives in DCAT is lexical in the sense that there are no special passive rules; instead it is based on the categories of the auxiliary, e.g. (V S3 WP), and the non-finite main verb, e.g. (WP D A)[12]. The passives of main clauses are derived with the same linguistic rules as are active main clauses with auxiliaries. Compare the passive example 4.2.1 with the active sentence 4.2.2:

4.2.2 *Das Mädchen hat dem Mann ein Buch gegeben.* / The girl has given the man a book.

```
(R DAS MAEDCHEN HAT DEM MANN EIN BUCH GEGEBEN .)
((CMPLT ((DAS MAEDCHEN HAT DEM MANN EIN BUCH GEGEBEN %.)
        (DECL))
        1
        (START (DAS)
                (S3 NS -E)
                (MAEDCHEN)
                (NS))
```

---

[12] Note that treatment of case in left-associative grammar is purely surface compositional. There are no 'deep cases', and a nominative in an active sentence is not different from a nominative in a passive sentence. Many conventional grammars use concepts like 'subject', 'direct object', and 'indirect object' in addition to or instead of the cases. Left-associative grammar uses only cases for characterizing the grammatical relations. Cf. Vennemann 1980.

```
2
(DET+NOUN (DAS MAEDCHEN)
          (S3 NS)
          (HAT)
          (V S3 H))
3
(MAIN+FVERB (DAS MAEDCHEN HAT)
          (V H NS)
          (DEM)
          (D MS -EN))
4
(FVERB+MAIN (DAS MAEDCHEN HAT DEM)
          (V H NS D MS -EN)
          (MANN)
          (MS))
5
(DET+NOUN (DAS MAEDCHEN HAT DEM MANN)
          (V H NS D MS)
          (EIN)
          (A NS -ES))
6
(FVERB+MAIN (DAS MAEDCHEN HAT DEM MANN EIN)
          (V H NS D MS A NS -ES)
          (BUCH)
          (NS))
7
(DET+NOUN (DAS MAEDCHEN HAT DEM MANN EIN BUCH)
          (V H NS D MS A NS)
          (GEGEBEN)
          (H D A))
8
(MAINCL+NFVERB (DAS MAEDCHEN HAT DEM MANN EIN BUCH GEGEBEN)
              (V NS MS NS)
              (%.)
              (V DECL))
9)))
```

From the viewpoint of left-associative grammar the syntactic structures of the active and the passive sentences are very similar. Both have the finite auxiliary in second position and the non-finite main verb in final position. This similarity is reflected in the sequence of rules in the passive example 4.2.1 and the syntactically corresponding active 4.2.2:

passive	active
RDET+NOUN	RDET+NOUN
RMAIN+FVERB	RMAIN+FVERB
RFVERB+MAIN	RFVERB+MAIN
RPREP+MAIN	
RDET+NOUN	RDET+NOUN
RFVERB+MAIN	RFVERB+MAIN
RDET+NOUN	RDET+NOUN
RMAINCL+NFVERB	RMAINCL+NFVERB

RCMPLT   RCMPLT

Apart from the additional rule RPREP+MAIN in section 4 of the passive example, the sequence of rules is exactly the same for the passive and active sentences.

The difference between active and passive is a difference in the respective valency structures. In the active example 4.2.2 the nominative noun phrase represents the giver, while in the passive example 4.2.1 the nominative represents what is given. The verb determines what arguments are required and how they relate to one another. Therefore the different valency structure of active and passive constructions must be reflected in different categories of the respective finite auxiliaries and non-finite main verbs.

Consider the verb constructions of 4.2.1 and 4.2.2, which are schematically indicated below:

passive: ((wurde)(V S3 WP)) ((gegeben)(WP -AG D))
active: ((hat)   (V S3 H))   ((gegeben)(H D A))

The passive-forming auxiliary *wurde* is characterized by the segment WP, which agrees with the first segment of the passive category of the participle. The passive participle also has the segment -AG indicating an optional agent, formed with the preposition *von*, and the segment D indicating the obligatory dative. WP indicates a passive-forming auxiliary in the paradigm of *werden*. The fact that the S3 has a different role in the active and the passive, in terms of what is given (*gegeben*) and who gives, is indicated by the presence or absence of the category segment WP.

Active-forming auxiliaries are characterized categorially by the segments H (haben), S (sein), or W (werden), which ensure agreement with the correct non-finite main verbs at the end of the sentence. There are four different kinds of auxiliaries in German:

((hat)   (V S3 H)) ((gesehen) (H A))
((ist)   (V S3 S)) ((gegangen)(S))
((wird) (V S3 W)) ((gehen)   (W))
((wurde) (V S3 WP   ((gesehen) (WP -AG))

In its present tense forms *wird* is the only auxiliary which is multiply categorized: e.g. (V S3 W) versus (V S3 WP). *wurde*, on the other hand, occurs only as a passive forming auxiliary and is categorized only as (V S3 WP). Compare:
Peter wird Maria sehen.
Peter wird von Maria gesehen.
*Peter wurde Maria sehen.
Peter wurde von Maria gesehen.

Auxiliaries with the category segments S or WP are also used as predicates, as in *Peter ist klein*, *Peter ist ein guter Arzt*, *Peter wurde gross*, *Peter wurde ein guter Arzt*, etc. In order to avoid an excess of multiple categorization, agreement is handled in these cases on the basis of corresponding rather than identical category segments (see section 4.5).

As an example of an active sentence with the auxiliary *sein* and the predicative use of *geworden* consider 4.2.3:

4.2.3 *Peter ist ein guter Arzt geworden.* / Peter has become a good doctor.

```
(R PETER IST EIN GUTER ARZT GEWORDEN .)
((CMPLT ((PETER IST EIN GUTER ARZT GEWORDEN %.)
         (DECL))
       1
       (START (PETER)
              (S3 MS)
              (IST)
              (V S3 S))
       2
       (MAIN+FVERB (PETER IST)
                   (V S MS)
                   (EIN)
                   (S3 MS -ER))
       3
       (FVERB+MAIN (PETER IST EIN)
                   (V S MS S3 MS -ER)
                   (GUTER)
                   (-ER))
       4
       (DET+ADJ (PETER IST EIN GUTER)
                (V S MS S3 MS -ER)
                (ARZT)
                (MS))
       5
       (DET+NOUN (PETER IST EIN GUTER ARZT)
                 (V S MS S3 MS)
                 (GEWORDEN)
                 (S WP))
       6
       (MAINCL+NFVERB (PETER IST EIN GUTER ARZT GEWORDEN)
                      (V MS MS)
                      (%.)
                      (V DECL))
       7)))
```

The intermediate expression *Peter ist ein guter Arzt* actually has two readings. The first reading is characterized by the category (V MS MS). Here *ist* is interpreted as a predicate combining with *ein guter Arzt*. Since there are no obligatory segments in the category, the sentence may be completed by adding a punctuation sign or continued with an optional relative clause. The second reading is characterized by the category (V S MS S3 MS) (see history section 5 above). Here *ist* is interpreted as an auxiliary. Since the category contains the obligatory segments S and S3, the sentence is still incomplete at this point. By adding the word *geworden* of category (S WP), the first reading is eliminated and the second reading continued into a potentially complete sentence. Note that S3 is cancelled by WP, because RMAINCL+FVERB specifies that these segments correspond.

The first category segment S of *geworden* (which is the perfect participle of the main verb *werden*) ensures that this word will combine only with a sentence start that has a corresponding segment in its category, indicating that the sentence start contains a finite auxiliary which is a form of *sein*, such as *ist* or *war*. Ungrammatical sentences like **Peter hat ein guter Arzt geworden* or **Peter wird ein guter Arzt geworden* are not accepted by DCAT.

In German, the passive uses the same verb forms in subordinate clauses as in main clauses. Also, the word order for passive subordinate clauses is analogous to that of subordinate clauses in active voice. For these reasons, passive in subordinate clauses is handled in DCAT without either additional rules or additional lexical readings. As an example consider 4.2.4, which is a 'transformation' of 4.2.1.

4.2.4 *Der Mann, dem von dem Mädchen ein Buch gegeben wurde,* / The man who was given a book by the girl

```
(R DER MANN DEM VON DEM MAEDCHEN EIN BUCH GEGEBEN WURDE)
((SUBCL+LASTVERB ((DER MANN , DEM VON DEM MAEDCHEN EIN BUCH GEGEBEN WURDE ,)
                (S3 NS)
                1
                (START (DER)
                       (S3 MS -E)
                       (MANN)
                       (MS))
                2
                (DET+NOUN (DER MANN)
                          (S3 MS)
                          (DEM)
                          (D MS -EN))
                3
                (NOUN+RELPRO (DER MANN , DEM)
                             (S3 V D)
                             (VON)
                             (-AG (D)))
                4
                (SUBCL+MAIN (DER MANN , DEM VON)
                            (S3 V D -AG (D))
                            (DEM)
                            (D NS -EN))
                5
                (PREP+MAIN (DER MANN , DEM VON DEM)
                           (S3 V D -AG NS -EN)
                           (MAEDCHEN)
                           (NS))
                6
                (DET+NOUN (DER MANN , DEM VON DEM MAEDCHEN)
```

```
                         (S3 V D -AG NS)
                         (EIN)
                         (S3 NS -ES))
              7
              (SUBCL+MAIN (DER MANN , DEM VON DEM MAEDCHEN EIN)
                         (S3 V D -AG NS S3 NS -ES)
                         (BUCH)
                         (NS))
              8
              (DET+NOUN (DER MANN , DEM VON DEM MAEDCHEN EIN BUCH)
                         (S3 V D -AG NS S3 NS)
                         (GEGEBEN)
                         (WP D -AG))
              9
              (SUBCL+VERB (DER MANN , DEM VON DEM MAEDCHEN EIN BUCH
                              GEGEBEN)
                         (S3 V NS S3 NS INF WP)
                         (WURDE)
                         (V S3 WP))
              10)))
```

Besides simple passives such as *wurde ... gesehen* there are also complex passives such as *ist ... gesehen worden*. In the first case there is only one auxiliary, the passive-forming *wurde* of category (V S3 WP). But in the case of a complex passive there are two auxiliaries, the finite auxiliary *ist* and the non-finite auxiliary *worden*. Consider the derivation in example 4.2.5:

4.2.5 *Peter ist von Maria gesehen worden.* / Peter has been seen by Mary.

```
(R PETER IST VON MARIA GESEHEN WORDEN .)
((CMPLT ((PETER IST VON MARIA GESEHEN WORDEN %.)
         (DECL))
        1
        (START (PETER)
               (S3 MS)
               (IST)
               (V S3 S))
        2
        (MAIN+FVERB (PETER IST)
               (V S MS)
               (VON)
               (-AG (D)))
        3
        (FVERB+MAIN (PETER IST VON)
               (V S MS -AG (D))
               (MARIA)
               (D FS))
        4
        (PREP+MAIN (PETER IST VON MARIA)
               (V S MS -AG FS)
               (GESEHEN)
               (WP -AG))
        5
        (MAINCL+NFVERB (PETER IST VON MARIA GESEHEN)
```

```
                    (V S MS FS WP)
                    (WORDEN)
                    (S WP))
      6
(MAINCL+NFVERB (PETER IST VON MARIA GESEHEN
                    WORDEN)
                    (V MS FS)
                    (%.)
                    (V DECL))
      7)))
```

The category of the second expression in history section 1 indicates that *ist* is categorized as the usual active-forming auxiliary (V S3 S). In section 4 the rule RMAINCL+NFVERB, based on wholesale-cancelling, applies (see the result in history section 5). The second expression is the usual passive participle *gesehen* of category (WP -AG). The two categories in question have only the segment -AG in common, which is cancelled; the remainder of the second category is attached to the output category. The result is the category (V S WP), where the S comes from the auxiliary and the WP from the passive reading of *gesehen*. In section 5, RMAINCL+NFVERB applies again. The second expression, *worden*, has the category (S WP). Wholesale-cancelling renders the output category V (plus the optional relative clause agreement segments MS and FS), indicating a complete declarative sentence.

In other words, in complex passives the second valency carrier *gesehen* of category (WP -AG) has the WP cancelled by the passive-forming non-finite auxiliary *worden* of category (S WP). The categories of the finite auxiliary (V S3 S) and the non-finite auxiliary (S WP) jointly amount to the category of a regular passive-forming auxiliary: if we assume that the S's in the two categories cancel each other, the result category is (V S3 WP).

The other complex passive construction with the auxiliary *werden* is based on the categorization illustrated in the following example:

4.2.6 *Peter wird von Maria gesehen werden.* / Peter will be seen by Mary.

```
(R PETER WIRD VON MARIA GESEHEN WERDEN .)
((CMPLT ((PETER WIRD VON MARIA GESEHEN WERDEN %.)
        (DECL)
        1
        (START (PETER)
               (S3 MS)
               (WIRD)
               (V S3 W))
        2
        (MAIN+FVERB (PETER WIRD)
               (V W MS)
               (VON)
               (-AG (D)))
        3
        (FVERB+MAIN (PETER WIRD VON)
               (V W MS -AG (D))
```

```
                        (MARIA)
                        (D FS))
            4
      (PREP+MAIN (PETER WIRD VON MARIA)
                        (V W MS -AG FS)
                        (GESEHEN)
                        (WP -AG))
            5
      (MAINCL+NFVERB (PETER WIRD VON MARIA GESEHEN)
                        (V W MS FS WP)
                        (WERDEN)
                        (W WP INF))
            6
      (MAINCL+NFVERB (PETER WIRD VON MARIA GESEHEN WERDEN)
                        (V MS FS INF)
                        (%.)
                        (V DECL))
            7)))
```

In contrast to *ist*, *wird* is both active- and passive-forming:

((Peter)(S3)) ((wird)(V S3 W))((schlafen)(W))

versus

((Peter)(S3)) ((wird)(V S3 WP)) ((von Maria)(-AG)) ((gesehen)(WP -AG)).

The treatment of complex passives extends to subordinate clauses, just as does the treatment of simple passives (see 4.2.4 above). As an example of a complex passive in a relative clause consider 4.2.7, which is a 'transformation' of 4.2.5.

4.2.7 *Der Mann, der von Maria gesehen worden ist, /* The man who has been seen by Mary

```
(R DER MANN DER VON MARIA GESEHEN WORDEN IST)
((SUBCL+LASTVERB ((DER MANN , DER VON MARIA GESEHEN WORDEN IST ,)
                        (S3 FS)
                        1
                        (START (DER)
                                (S3 MS -E)
                                (MANN)
                                (MS))
                        2
                        (DET+NOUN (DER MANN)
                                (S3 MS)
                                (DER)
                                (S3 MS -E))
                        3
                        (NOUN+RELPRO (DER MANN , DER)
                                (S3 V S3)
                                (VON)
                                (-AG (D)))
                        4
                        (SUBCL+MAIN (DER MANN , DER VON)
                                (S3 V S3 -AG (D))
```

```
                        (MARIA)
                        (D FS))
            5
            (PREP+MAIN (DER MANN , DER VON MARIA)
                        (S3 V S3 -AG FS)
                        (GESEHEN)
                        (WP -AG))
            6
            (SUBCL+VERB (DER MANN , DER VON MARIA GESEHEN)
                        (S3 V S3 FS INF WP)
                        (WORDEN)
                        (S WP))
            7
            (SUBCL+VERB (DER MANN , DER VON MARIA GESEHEN WORDEN)
                        (S3 V S3 FS S)
                        (IST)
                        (V S3 S))
            8)))
```

The multiple application of RMAINCL+NFVERB in complex main clause passives may also be observed in active sentences. Consider example 4.2.8:

4.2.8 *Peter hätte ein guter Arzt werden können.* / Peter could have become a good doctor.

```
(R PETER HAETTE EIN GUTER ARZT WERDEN KOENNEN .)
((CMPLT ((PETER HAETTE EIN GUTER ARZT WERDEN KOENNEN %.)
        (DECL))
        1
        (START (PETER)
                (S3 MS)
                (HAETTE)
                (V S3 H))
        2
        (MAIN+FVERB (PETER HAETTE)
                    (V H MS)
                    (EIN)
                    (S3 MS -ER))
        3
        (FVERB+MAIN (PETER HAETTE EIN)
                    (V H MS S3 MS -ER)
                    (GUTER)
                    (-ER))
        4
        (DET+ADJ (PETER HAETTE EIN GUTER)
                 (V H MS S3 MS -ER)
                 (ARZT)
                 (MS))
        5
        (DET+NOUN (PETER HAETTE EIN GUTER ARZT)
                  (V H MS S3 MS)
                  (WERDEN)
                  (W WP INF))
        6
        (MAINCL+NFVERB (PETER HAETTE EIN GUTER ARZT WERDEN)
```

```
                         (V H MS MS W INF)
                         (KOENNEN)
                         (H W INF))
         7
         (MAINCL+NFVERB (PETER HAETTE EIN GUTER ARZT WERDEN
                            KOENNEN)
                         (V MS MS INF)
                         (%.)
                         (V DECL))
         8)))
```

As in example 4.2.5, the first application of RMAINCL+NFVERB in 4.2.8 involves a remainder from the category of the second expression, which is attached to the output category. Another application of RMAINCL+NFVERB is needed to obtain an output category acceptable to RCMPLT. The iteration of modals, as in *Peter hätte ein guter Arzt werden können sollen*, is based on the presence of the segment INF (see section 7), which is ignored by RCMPLT as an optional segment like MS, but which permits addition of possible further modal infinitives. Note that the first expression of section 6 is not a complete sentence because there are still non-optional segments present, namely H and W.

Multiple infinitives occur also in subordinate clauses. Consider 4.2.9, which is a 'transformation' of 4.2.5.

4.2.9 *Weil Peter ein guter Arzt hätte werden können,* / Because Peter could have become a good doctor

```
(R WEIL PETER EIN GUTER ARZT HAETTE WERDEN KOENNEN)
((SUBCL+LASTVERB ((WEIL PETER EIN GUTER ARZT HAETTE WERDEN KOENNEN ,)
                 (ADCL)
                 1
                 (START (WEIL)
                        (ADCL V)
                        (PETER)
                        (S3 MS))
                 2
                 (SUBCL+MAIN (WEIL PETER)
                             (ADCL V S3 MS)
                             (EIN)
                             (S3 MS -ER))
                 3
                 (SUBCL+MAIN (WEIL PETER EIN)
                             (ADCL V S3 MS S3 MS -ER)
                             (GUTER)
                             (-ER))
                 4
                 (DET+ADJ (WEIL PETER EIN GUTER)
                          (ADCL V S3 MS S3 MS -ER)
                          (ARZT)
                          (MS))
                 5
                 (DET+NOUN (WEIL PETER EIN GUTER ARZT)
```

```
                           (ADCL V S3 MS S3 MS)
                           (HAETTE)
                           (V S3 H))
              6
              (SUBCL+VERB (WEIL PETER EIN GUTER ARZT HAETTE)
                           (ADCL INF H MS S3 MS)
                           (WERDEN)
                           (W WP INF))
              7
              (SUBCL+VERB (WEIL PETER EIN GUTER ARZT HAETTE WERDEN)
                           (ADCL INF H MS S3 MS W WP INF)
                           (KOENNEN)
                           (H W INF))
        8))
```

The existence of examples like 4.2.9 is one reason for the complications in the LISP code of RSUBCL+VERB and RSUBCL+LASTVERB. Normally, the finite auxiliary is last in a subordinate clause, e.g. *weil Peter den Brief geschrieben hat.* But if there are infinitives and the auxiliary is a form of *haben* (or possibly *werden*), then the auxiliary is verb phrase initial, as in 4.2.9. As an example with several infinitives and a clause final modal consider 4.2.10:

4.2.10 *Weil Peter ein guter Arzt werden können wollte,* / Because Peter wanted to be able to become a good doctor

```
(R WEIL PETER EIN GUTER ARZT WERDEN KOENNEN WOLLTE)
((SUBCL+LASTVERB ((WEIL PETER EIN GUTER ARZT WERDEN KOENNEN WOLLTE ,)
                   (ADCL MS)
              1
              (START (WEIL)
                      (ADCL V)
                      (PETER)
                      (S3 MS))
              2
              (SUBCL+MAIN (WEIL PETER)
                           (ADCL V S3 MS)
                           (EIN)
                           (S3 MS -ER))
              3
              (SUBCL+MAIN (WEIL PETER EIN)
                           (ADCL V S3 MS S3 MS -ER)
                           (GUTER)
                           (-ER))
              4
              (DET+ADJ (WEIL PETER EIN GUTER)
                        (ADCL V S3 MS S3 MS -ER)
                        (ARZT)
                        (MS))
              5
              (DET+NOUN (WEIL PETER EIN GUTER ARZT)
                         (ADCL V S3 MS S3 MS)
                         (WERDEN)
                         (W WP INF))
              6
```

```
(SUBCL+VERB (WEIL PETER EIN GUTER ARZT WERDEN)
            (ADCL V MS S3 MS W INF)
            (KOENNEN)
            (H W INF))
7
(SUBCL+VERB (WEIL PETER EIN GUTER ARZT WERDEN KOENNEN)
            (ADCL V MS S3 MS W INF)
            (WOLLTE)
            (V S3 W))
8)))
```

German has a wide variety of complex verb constructions with intricate agreement properties, but their treatment in a left-associative grammar is simple. Once the rules for the basic construction with a finite auxiliary and a non-finite main verb were implemented for main and subordinate clauses, the other constructions were added solely on the basis of pertinent categorizations of the expressions involved.

The main work in implementing these constructions was figuring out the categorization. Once the categories were established, we only had to add the words or the relevant readings to the lexicon DLEX. The implementation of passives, for example, including the word order variation of main and subordinate clauses, and the distinction between declaratives and interrogatives, took no more than a couple of hours. No new rules had to be added and the existing rules were edited only minimally to accept the new category segment WP.

4.3   Center-embedded versus extraposed relative clauses in DCAT

We have seen in the previous sections that the DCAT analysis of a grammatical expression explicitly specifies which rule applies for each addition of a new word. It also specifies the categories of each sentence start expression and each new word. This in turn provides an implicit characterization of the categorial operations of each linguistic rule. If the input expression is ambiguous, a complete description is provided for each reading. This kind of analysis works for simple examples as well as for the most complicated constructions imaginable.

Since complex expressions usually use more words than simple ones, the main difference between DCAT analyses of simple and complicated expressions is a difference in the number of history sections. Consider the analysis of a noun phrase with several center embedded relative clauses:

4.3.1 *Der Mann, den die Frau, die das Kind, das schläft, liebt, sieht, /* The man who the woman who the child who sleeps loves sees

```
((SUBCL+LASTVERB ((DER MANN , DEN DIE FRAU , DIE DAS KIND , DAS SCHLAEFT ,
                   LIEBT , SIEHT ,)
(S3))
1
```

```
(START (DER)
       (S3 MS -E)
       (MANN)
       (MS))
2
(DET+NOUN (DER MANN)
          (S3 MS)
          (DEN)
          (A MS -EN))
3
(NOUN+RELPRO (DER MANN , DEN)
             (S3 V A)
             (DIE)
             (S3 FS -E))
4
(SUBCL+MAIN (DER MANN , DEN DIE)
            (S3 V A S3 FS -E)
            (FRAU)
            (FS))
5
(DET+NOUN (DER MANN , DEN DIE FRAU)
          (S3 V A S3 FS)
          (DIE)
          (S3 FS -E))
6
(NOUN+RELPRO (DER MANN , DEN DIE FRAU , DIE)
             (S3 V A S3 V S3)
             (DAS)
             (A NS -E))
7
(SUBCL+MAIN (DER MANN , DEN DIE FRAU , DIE DAS)
            (S3 V A S3 V S3 A NS -E)
            (KIND)
            (NS))
8
(DET+NOUN (DER MANN , DEN DIE FRAU , DIE DAS KIND)
          (S3 V A S3 V S3 A NS)
          (DAS)
          (S3 NS -E))
9
(NOUN+RELPRO (DER MANN , DEN DIE FRAU , DIE DAS KIND , DAS)
             (S3 V A S3 V S3 A V S3)
             (SCHLAEFT)
             (V S3))
10
(SUBCL+LASTVERB (DER MANN , DEN DIE FRAU , DIE DAS KIND ,  DAS SCHLAEFT ,)
                (S3 V A S3 V S3 A)
                (LIEBT)
                (V S3 A))
11
(SUBCL+LASTVERB (DER MANN , DEN DIE FRAU , DIE DAS KIND , DAS SCHLAEFT , LIEBT ,)
                (S3 V A S3)
                (SIEHT)
                (V S3 A))
12))
```

The sentence above is 12 words long. Accordingly, the DCAT history consists of 11 sections. In the sentence start of history section 4 of 4.3.1 the rule RSUBCL+MAIN combines the sentence start *Der Mann, den* with the determiner *die* (not with a proper name representing a full noun phrase, as in section 6 of example 4.1.10). Since RSUBCL+MAIN is based on argument adding, the whole determiner category is simply added to the category of the first expression, resulting in (S3 V A S3 FS -E).

Sections 5 and 6 of example 4.3.1 illustrate the rule RDET+NOUN once again. RDET+NOUN may be applied because the first expression of section 5 ends in a determiner and the second category segment of the second expression of section 5 matches the last obligatory category segment of the first expression. The result category is (S3 V A S3 V S3), which has the following interpretation. The first segment S3 indicates that the expression will result in a third person singular nominative when all the other segments have been cancelled off. The segments V A S3 indicate that a relative clause has been opened which will require a clause final verb with valency positions for A and S3. The last two segments V S3 indicate that another relative clause has been opened, which has a valency requirement of S3 for the verb that will eventually close it.

The process of opening new relative clauses by encoding the valency requirements, resulting in a longer and longer category, can be continued indefinitely in DCAT. Example 4.3.1 shows another instance of this process. In sections 6 and 7 the accusative noun phrase *das Kind* is added, resulting in the category (S3 V A S3 V S3 A NS). The last segment indicates that a relative clause of neuter singular agreement (modifying *das Kind*) may follow. In section 8 the rule RNOUN+RELPRO applies again (see sentence start of section 9). This time the result category is lengthened to (S3 V A S3 V S3 A V S3), which indicates three incomplete center-embedded relative clauses.

We saw in example 4.3.1 that the counterpart to argument adding by the rules RNOUN+RELPRO and RSUBCL+MAIN is wholesale cancelling by the rule RSUBCL+LASTVERB. Note also that open center-embedded relative clauses of German are closed in a 'last in - first out' fashion. In history section 9 the finite verb *schläft* of category (V S3) is added with the rule RSUBCL+LAST-VERB, which closes the last opened relative clause and shortens the output category to (S3 V A S3 V S3 A) (see section 10).

RSUBCL+LASTVERB applies again in section 10, closing the relative clause opened next to last and shortening the output category to (S3 V A S3) using wholesale-cancelling. This process is repeated once more in section 11, resulting in the output category (S3), which indicates a complete nominative noun phrase of third person singular which may be continued in exactly the same way as simpler noun phrases of the same kind.[13]

The rules of DCAT which analyze center-embedded relative clauses also

---

[13] The analysis of several center-embedded relative clauses given above shows the context-free nature of DCAT. The build-up of the category resembles the context-free formal language $a^n b^n$: the number of relative pronouns added requires an equal number of verbs.

analyze extraposed relative clauses of German. The extraposed analogue of
example 4.3.1 is presented below:

4.3.2 *Der Mann, den die Frau sieht, die das Kind liebt, das schläft, /* The
man whom the woman sees who the child who sleeps loves

```
((SUBCL+LASTVERB ((DER MANN , DEN DIE FRAU SIEHT , DIE DAS KIND LIEBT ,
                    DAS SCHLAEFT ,)
(SS))
1
(START (DER)
       (S3 MS -E)
       (MANN)
       (MS))
2
(DET+NOUN (DER MANN)
          (S3 MS)
          (DEN)
          (A MS -EN))
3
(NOUN+RELPRO (DER MANN , DEN)
             (S3 V A)
             (DIE)
             (S3 FS -E))
4
(SUBCL+MAIN (DER MANN , DEN DIE)
            (S3 V A S3 FS -E)
            (FRAU)
            (FS))
5
(DET+NOUN (DER MANN , DEN DIE FRAU)
          (S3 V A S3 FS)
          (SIEHT)
          (V S3 A))
6
(SUBCL+LASTVERB (DER MANN , DEN DIE FRAU SIEHT ,)
                (S3 FS)
                (DIE)
                (S3 FS -E))
7
(NOUN+RELPRO (DER MANN , DEN DIE FRAU SIEHT , DIE)
             (S3 V S3)
             (DAS)
             (A NS -E))
8
(SUBCL+MAIN (DER MANN , DEN DIE FRAU SIEHT , DIE DAS)
            (S3 V S3 A NS -E)
            (KIND)
            (NS))
9
(DET+NOUN (DER MANN , DEN DIE FRAU SIEHT , DIE DAS KIND)
          (S3 V S3 A NS)
          (LIEBT)
          (V S3 A))
10
```

```
(SUBCL+LASTVERB (DER MANN , DEN DIE FRAU SIEHT , DIE DAS KIND LIEBT ,)
                (S3 NS)
                (DAS)
                (S3 NS -E))
11
(NOUN+RELPRO (DER MANN , DEN DIE FRAU SIEHT , DIE DAS KIND LIEBT , DAS)
             (S3 V S3)
             (SCHLAEFT)
             (V S3))
12))
```

According to the grammar of DCAT, the only difference between the center-embedded and the extraposed versions of multiple relative clauses is in the flow of the continuations. In 4.3.1 the nouns are immediately continued with the beginnings of relative clauses, which build up valencies cancelled at the end by adding a series of finite verbs. In 4.3.2 the second relative clause is opened after the first relative clause is finished, the third relative clause after the second relative clause is finished, and so on.

The fact that DCAT analyzes embedded and extraposed relative clauses without postulating a syntactic difference other than the order of building up and eliminating valencies may seem mysterious to those who have wrestled with these constructions in more conventional frameworks. Consider the point where the examples 4.3.1 and 4.3.2 diverge, namely the respective sections 6 and 7, which are repeated in 4.3.3 and 4.3.4 for convenience:

4.3.3 Sections 5 and 6 of example 4.3.1

```
5
(DET+NOUN (DER MANN , DEN DIE FRAU)
          (S3 V A S3 FS)
          (DIE)
          (S3 FS -E))
6
(NOUN+RELPRO (DER MANN , DEN DIE FRAU , DIE)
             (S3 V A S3 V S3)
             (DAS)
             (A NS -E))
```

4.3.4 Sections 5 and 6 of example 4.3.2

```
5
(DET+NOUN (DER MANN , DEN DIE FRAU)
          (S3 V A S3 FS)
          (SIEHT)
          (V S3 A))
6
(SUBCL+LASTVERB (DER MANN , DEN DIE FRAU SIEHT ,)
                (S3 FS)
                (DIE)
                (S3 FS -E))
```

Both 4.3.3 and 4.3.4 follow the application of the rule RDET+NOUN. Also, the first input expressions in 4.3.3 and 4.3.4 are the same, namely *Der Mann, den die Frau*, and have the same category (S3 V A S3 FS).

The difference is in the respective next words. In 4.3.3 the second expression in section 6 is the relative pronoun *die* of category (S3 FS -E), whereas in 4.3.4 it is the verb *sieht* of category (V S3 A). Correspondingly, the combination rule is RNOUN+RELPRO in 4.3.3, but RSUBCL+LASTVERB in 4.3.4. Both of these rules are contained in the rule package DET+NOUN, which is called after the successful application of RDET+NOUN.

Both examples inherit from their parallel beginnings the valency specifications (S3 V A S3 FS) of the first category of the respective sections 6. But since RNOUN+RELPRO (in 4.3.3) and RSUBCL+LASTVERB (in 4.3.4) call different rule packages, the derivations of the remainders of the two examples will be completely independent. After section 5 the two sentence starts may be continued in any way at all, as long as care is taken to cancel the outstanding valencies properly and to steer the sentence to a grammatical conclusion. Thus the grammatical relation between the center-embedded example 4.3.1 and the extraposed example 4.3.2 is not one of similar constituent structure, but rather follows from the fact that the two sentences happen to contain the same words with the same categories, and moreover build up and cancel the same valency positions (although in a different order).

The difference of continuation in 4.3.3 and 4.3.4 may be interpreted either in terms of **generation** or in terms of **parsing**. Consider the interpretation of the DCAT grammar in terms of generation. We arrive at the expression *Der Mann, den die Frau* by most recently applying RDET+NOUN and are now faced with the question of continuations. A first answer is given by the rule package DET+NOUN, which contains 11 rules (see appendix A.2).

A further narrowing of the possible continuations results from the fact that many of the 11 rules in DET+NOUN are not applicable; the category (S3 V A S3 FS) produced by RDET+NOUN in our particular example(s) is not accepted by the input conditions of these rules. For instance, the rules RMAIN+FVERB and RFVERB+MAIN are not candidates for continuation, because their input conditions prohibit any non-initial V segment (indicating an unfinished subordinate clause) in the category of their first input expression; RCMPLT is not a candidate, because its input condition requires that the category of the first expression does not contain any A, S3, etc. segments (indicating unfilled argument positions), and so on.

The remaining rules in DET+NOUN which accept the category (S3 V A S3 FS) for their first input expression, such as RSUBCL+MAIN, RSUBCL+VERB, and RSUBCL+LASTVERB, are all viable candidates for continuations of *Der Mann, den die Frau*. We need only choose a word with a category which is accepted as the second input expression of one of these rules. If we choose to continue with RSUBCL+VERB, for example, we have to find a word that has a suitable category for this rule, such as *gesehen*.

In summary, from a generation point of view the different continuations in 4.3.3 and 4.3.4 result from choosing different viable rules from the last rule package, which in turn delimit the categories of the respective next words. The particular category of the next word chosen will uniquely determine the output category, which in combination with the next rule package opens up a new set of continuation possibilities.

Let us turn now to the interpretation of the DCAT grammar in terms of parsing. We refer again to sections 5 and 6 of the examples 4.3.1 and 4.3.2, reprinted in 4.3.3 and 4.3.4, respectively. The parser has arrived at the expression *Der Mann, den die Frau*. Next the rule package DET+NOUN is applied non-deterministically. That is, all 11 rules of DET+NOUN apply to all ordered pairs consisting of *Der Mann, den die Frau* of category (S3 V A S3 FS) and a reading of the next word.

In 4.3.3 the next word is *die* of category (S3 FS -E)[14]. The relevant rule in DET+NOUN that can apply is RNOUN+RELPRO. In 4.3.4 the 'next word' is *sieht* of category (V S3 A)[15], so the only applicable rule in DET+NOUN is RSUBCL+FVERB. In each case the parser specifies a new sentence start, consisting of (i) a rule package (i.e. NOUN+RELPRO and SUBCL+LASTVERB, respectively), and (ii) a new expression. In each case the parser is ready for the next cycle. All that is needed for another left-associative combination is a new next word.

The difference between the generation aspect and the parsing aspect in DCAT may be summarized as follows. In the case of generation the next word is not a given. Rather, the problem is to choose a next word that is grammatically compatible with the sentence start. The control structure of DCAT solves this problem by telling us exactly which categories the next word may have, and, once a choice has been made, how to continue from there.

In the case of parsing the next word is given in the input string. Here the problem is to find out whether the combination of the sentence start with (some reading of) the given next word is grammatical, and if so, what the grammatical nature of the combination is. The control structure of DCAT solves this problem by telling us, for each sentence start, which syntactic rule in the presently active rule package is compatible with which possible reading of the next word.

---

[14]This word has other readings, categorized as (A FS -E), (P3 P -EN) and (A P -EN), of which only the first would result in a grammatical continuation. This reading, representing the case where the woman is loved by the child, is generated by the parser, but omitted from this discussion for the sake of simplicity.

[15]This word has only one category.

4.4 Syntactic equivalence in left-associative grammar

Left-associative grammar is not merely a new formalism for describing natural language. It takes a linear point of view and thus promotes intuitions quite different from those evoked by grammars that view natural language as hierarchical structures. Now that the survey of various constructions in German and their treatment in left-associative grammar is complete[16], let us consider whether the intuitions of hierarchical constituent structure analysis could be reconstructed within a left-associative framework.

Syntactic equivalence is a crucial intuitive notion of constituent structure analysis, and defined in terms of substitutional equivalence: if part A of a sentence may be substituted for another expression B without a change of grammaticality, then A and B are syntactically equivalent. Syntactically equivalent expressions are assigned the same category in constituent structure analysis[17].

Left-associative grammar differs from constituent structure analysis in that categorial equivalence does not imply syntactic equivalence. Two sentence starts may have the same category, yet be completely different syntactically. The syntactic properties of a sentence start in left-associative grammar are not defined in terms of the category alone, but rather in terms of the category and the rule package. The category and the rule package jointly define the set of possible continuations of a sentence start. As an illustration consider examples 4.4.1 and 4.4.2:

4.4.1 *Dem Kind, das geschlafen hatte, gab Maria einen Teller.* / Mary gave a plate to the child who had slept.

```
(R DEM KIND DAS GESCHLAFEN HATTE GAB MARIA EINEN TELLER .)
((CMPLT ((DEM KIND , DAS GESCHLAFEN HATTE , GAB MARIA EINEN TELLER %.)
         (DECL)
         1
         (START (DEM)
                (D NS -EN)
                (KIND)
                (NS))
         2
         (DET+NOUN (DEM KIND)
                   (D NS)
                   (DAS)
                   (S3 NS -E))
         3
         (NOUN+RELPRO (DEM KIND , DAS)
                      (D V S3)
                      (GESCHLAFEN)
                      (H))
         4
```

---

[16] Additional constructions are illustrated in appendix B.

[17] Whether that analysis is based on phrase structure or an categorial grammar.

```
        (SUBCL+VERB (DEM KIND , DAS GESCHLAFEN)
                    (D V S3 INF H)
                    (HATTE)
                    (V S3 H))
        5
        (SUBCL+LASTVERB (DEM KIND , DAS GESCHLAFEN HATTE ,)
                        (D)
                        (GAB)
                        (V S3 D A))
        6
        (MAIN+FVERB (DEM KIND , DAS GESCHLAFEN HATTE , GAB)
                    (V S3 A)
                    (MARIA)
                    (S3 FS))
        7
        (FVERB+MAIN (DEM KIND , DAS GESCHLAFEN HATTE , GAB MARIA)
                    (V A FS)
                    (EINEN)
                    (A MS -EN))
        8
        (FVERB+MAIN (DEM KIND , DAS GESCHLAFEN HATTE , GAB MARIA EINEN)
                    (V FS MS -EN)
                    (TELLER)
                    (MS))
        9
        (DET+NOUN (DEM KIND , DAS GESCHLAFEN HATTE , GAB MARIA EINEN TELLER)
                  (V FS MS)
                  (%.)
                  (V DECL))
        10)))
```

4.4.2 *Hatte Maria einen Teller?* / Did Mary have a plate?

```
(R HATTE MARIA EINEN TELLER ?)
((CMPLT ((HATTE MARIA EINEN TELLER ?)
        (INTERROG)
        1
        (START (HATTE)
               (V S3 A)
               (MARIA)
               (S3 FS))
        2
        (?FV+MAIN (HATTE MARIA)
                  (V I A FS)
                  (EINEN)
                  (A MS -EN))
        3
        (FVERB+MAIN (HATTE MARIA EINEN)
                    (V I FS MS -EN)
                    (TELLER)
                    (MS))
        4
        (DET+NOUN (HATTE MARIA EINEN TELLER)
                  (V I FS MS)
                  (?)
                  (I INTERROG))
```

        5)))

The sentence starts in history section 6 of example 4.4.1, and in history section
1 of example 4.4.2 have the same category:

4.4.3 Two sentence starts with the category (V S3 A):

1.   6
         (MAIN+FVERB (DEM KIND , DAS GESCHLAFEN HATTE , GAB)
                 (V S3 A)

2.   1
         (START (HATTE)
                 (V S3 A)

The category of the first sentence start is the result of combining a dative
noun phrase with the three-place verb *geben*. The category of the second sentence start is the lexical characterization of a reading of the two-place verb
haben. Both sentence starts need a third person singular nominative and an
accusative in order to become complete sentences. This is the reason why they
have the same category, (V S3 A), in DCAT. But the two sentence starts are
completely different syntactically. The first example has a three-place verb in
second position and may result in a declarative sentence, while the second example has a two-place verb in initial position and can only result in a yes/no
interrogative.

The two sentence starts have similar valency requirements, but different
possible continuations. This syntactic difference is expressed by the fact that
the sentence starts have different rule packages, namely MAIN+FVERB and
START, respectively. Only the rule package START contains the rule R?FV-
+MAIN, which combines the sentence initial finite verb with the beginning
of a main constituent in yes/no interrogatives like 4.4.2. The rule package
MAIN+FVERB, on the other hand, contains the rule RFVERB+MAIN, which
is not contained in START. The different contents of the two rule packages
explain the different continuations in history sections 7 and 2 of 4.4.1 and 4.4.2,
respectively.

Two sentence starts are syntactically equivalent in left-associative grammar
if, and only if, they have the same rule package and the same category. Consider
for example 4.4.4 and 4.4.5.

4.4.4 *Dem Kind, das geschlafen hatte, gab das junge Mädchen einen*

(R DEM KIND DAS GESCHLAFEN HATTE GAB DAS JUNGE MAEDCHEN EINEN)
((FVERB+MAIN ((DEM KIND , DAS GESCHLAFEN HATTE , GAB DAS JUNGE MAEDCHEN EINEN)
             (V NS MS -EN)
         1
         (START (DEM)
                 (D NS -EN)
                 (KIND)
                 (NS))

```
          2
(DET+NOUN (DEM KIND)
              (D NS)
              (DAS)
              (S3 NS -E))
          3
(NOUN+RELPRO (DEM KIND , DAS)
                 (D V S3)
                 (GESCHLAFEN)
                 (H))
          4
(SUBCL+VERB (DEM KIND , DAS GESCHLAFEN)
                (D V S3 INF H)
                (HATTE)
                (V S3 H))
          5
(SUBCL+LASTVERB (DEM KIND , DAS GESCHLAFEN HATTE ,)
                    (D)
                    (GAB)
                    (V S3 D A))
          6
(MAIN+FVERB (DEM KIND , DAS GESCHLAFEN HATTE , GAB)
                (V S3 A)
                (DAS)
                (S3 NS -E))
          7
(FVERB+MAIN (DEM KIND , DAS GESCHLAFEN HATTE , GAB DAS)
                (V A NS -E)
                (JUNGE)
                (-E))
          8
(DET+ADJ (DEM KIND , DAS GESCHLAFEN HATTE , GAB DAS JUNGE)
             (V A NS -E)
             (MAEDCHEN)
             (NS))
          9
(DET+NOUN (DEM KIND , DAS GESCHLAFEN HATTE , GAB DAS JUNGE
                  MAEDCHEN)
              (V A NS)
              (EINEN)
              (A NS -EN))
      10)))
```

4.4.5 *Das kleine Kind sah den*

```
(R DAS KLEINE KIND SAH DEN)
((FVERB+MAIN ((DAS KLEINE KIND SAH DEN)
             (V NS MS -EN)
          1
          (START (DAS)
                 (S3 NS -E)
                 (KLEINE)
                 (-E))
          2
          (DET+ADJ (DAS KLEINE)
                   (S3 NS -E)
```

```
                   (KIND)
                   (NS))
         3
         (DET+NOUN (DAS KLEINE KIND)
                   (S3 NS)
                   (SAH)
                   (V S3 A))
         4
         (MAIN+FVERD (DA3 KLEINE KIND SAH)
                     (V A NS)
                     (DEN)
                     (A MS -EN))
         5))
```

4.4.4 and 4.4.5 result in syntactically equivalent sentence starts because they have the same rule package, FVERB+MAIN, and the same category, (V NS MS -EN). Syntactic equivalence in left-associative grammar has little to do with a similarity in sentence structure; 4.4.4 contains a three-place verb, while 4.4.5 contains a two-place verb; there is a relative clause in 4.4.4, but not in 4.4.5, and so on. Instead, syntactic equivalence is defined locally in terms of the range of possible continuations at a given point in the linear sequence of left-associative combinations. The range of possible continuations of a sentence start is specified precisely in terms of its category and its rule package.

The intuitions underlying constituent structure analysis are reflected in left-associative analysis in two very different ways, depending on whether or not the constituent occurs, or could occur, at the beginning of a sentence. For example, the sentence initial expressions in 4.4.6 are considered to be constituents of the same kind.

4.4.6 Examples of initial constituents which are possible sentence starts:

1. *Peter*

2. *The funny old man*

3. *The funny old man who made this movie*

All three expressions in 4.4.6 have the category NP (noun phrase) in phrase structure grammar. They are also characterized as syntactically similar in left-associative grammar; all three expressions result in equivalent sentence starts.

Certain expressions which are not sentence initial, like those in 4.4.7, are also considered constituents of the same kind.

4.4.7 Examples of non-initial constituents which are not possible sentence starts:

1. *walked to the store*

2. *is reading a book*

3. *gave Mary a cookie*

The expressions in 4.4.7 satisfy substitution tests and are called VPs (verb phrases) in phrase structure grammar. But they do not constitute well-formed sentence starts. Therefore the concept of equivalent sentence starts cannot be utilized to reconstruct the concept of non-initial constituents in left-associative grammar.

One possible proposal for reconstructing non-initial constituents may be based on the fact that there are expressions similar to those in 4.4.7 which are equivalent sentence starts. Consider 4.4.8:

4.4.8 Examples of sentence starts limited to imperative mood:

1. *walk to the store*

2. *read a book*

3. *give Mary a cookie*

However, the expression in 4.4.8 may be completed only as imperative sentences. This means that explaining the postulation of non-initial constituents (e.g. 4.4.7) 'transderivationally' within left-associative grammar is rather tenuous. Also, it is doubtful that this kind of indirect explanation can account for all instances of non-initial constituents, because one may not be able to find corresponding well-formed sentence starts for every non-initial constituent postulated.

A more general way to reconstruct the alleged syntactic similarity of the expressions in 4.4.7 within left-associative grammar is in terms of equivalent possible continuations. The expressions in question are equivalent possible continuations in the sense that, given a sentence start of the right kind, they may be used to continue it to result in equivalent new sentence starts. For example, the expressions in 4.4.7 are syntactically similar since they may be used to continue the sentence starts in 4.4.6 into the following complete declarative sentences.

4.4.9 Examples of 'equivalent continuations':

1. (a) *John + walked to the store*

    (b) *John + is reading a book*

    (c) *John + gave Mary a cookie*

2. (a) *The funny old man + walked to the store*

    (b) *The funny old man + is reading a book*

    (c) *The funny old man + gave Mary a cookie*

3. (a) *The funny old man who made the movie + walked to the store*

    (b) *The funny old man who made the movie + is reading a book*

    (c) *The funny old man who made the movie + gave Mary a cookie*

The notion of equivalent sentence starts is formally defined in left-associative grammar. But only certain sentence starts correspond to potentially sentence initial constituents. Thus additional work has to be done if the notion of initial constituents is to be reconstructed in left-associative grammar on the basis of the concept of equivalent sentence starts. The notion of equivalent possible continuations illustrated in 4.4.9, on the other hand, has no formal definition in left-associative grammar, because possible continuations are only considered one next word at a time.

The notions of equivalent sentence starts and equivalent possible continuations may appear suitable for introducing the concepts of initial and non-initial constituents, respectively. But there is no reason to reconstruct constituent structure analysis in left-associative grammar, which is founded on the concept of possible continuations. The intuitions of hierarchical constituent structure analysis, based on substitution tests, constitute a mere epiphenomenon within the framework of left-associative grammar. Given the problems of constituent structure analysis described in sections 1.1 and 1.2, we may leave it behind and concentrate on a linear analysis of natural language.

Let us turn to expressions in which one surface has several readings, or put differently, in which several readings have an identical surface. Such expressions are called syntactically ambiguous.[18] Normally if two expressions have exactly the same surface, they are equivalent, and in particular syntactically equivalent. But in ambiguous sentences, sentence starts with the same surface are not syntactically equivalent.

Left-associative grammar handles syntactic ambiguities in terms of multiple categorization, alternative rule applications, or both. If the different uses of a word come from the fact that certain morphological distinctions present in other members of the same word class happen to be absent, the proper method of treating these different uses is with multiple categorization. But if each member of a given word class can be used for two different grammatical functions, then the proper method of treating these different uses is with alternative rule applications, without multiple categorizations of the expressions involved.

In section 4.2 we suggested characterizing the different grammatical roles of the non-finite main verb *gegeben* in active versus passive sentences by assigning it different categories: (H D A) for active sentences with the auxiliary *haben* and (WP D -AG) for passive sentences with the auxiliary *werden*. In other words, the difference in possible grammatical function of the surface *gegeben* is treated on the basis of a lexical ambiguity. In the present section we turn to syntactic ambiguities. For example,

4.4.10 *Flying airplanes can be dangerous.*

is syntactically ambiguous because *flying* may be used as an adjective (airplanes that fly) or as a gerund (for someone to fly airplanes). Another example is

---

[18]See **SCG**, chapter 2.2, for an extensive discussion of the theoretical nature of ambiguity and paraphrase.

4.4.11 *John saw the girl with a telescope.*

This sentence is ambiguous because *with a telescope* can be used as adverbially modifying *saw* or as adnominally modifying *girl*.

In German, ambiguities abound. It is not always obvious at first glance whether a certain ambiguity should be based on alternative rule applications alone, or whether there should also be multiple categorization of the words involved. For example, depending on the intonation and the context of use,

4.4.12 *Peter gab Maria Susi.*

can mean that Peter gave Maria to Susi, or that Maria gave Peter to Susi, or that Maria gave Susi to Peter, etc. The DCAT analyses of all readings of 4.4.12 are presented in 4.4.13:

4.4.13 *Peter gab Maria Susi.* / Peter gave Mary to Susi. Peter gave Susi to Mary. Mary gave Peter to Susi. Mary gave Susi to Peter. Susi gave Peter to Mary. Susi gave Mary to Peter.

```
(R PETER GAB MARIA SUSI .)
((CMPLT ((PETER GAB MARIA SUSI %.)
        (DECL)
        1
        (START (PETER)
               (S3 MS)
               (GAB)
               (V S3 D A))
        2
        (MAIN+FVERB (PETER GAB)
                    (V D A MS)
                    (MARIA)
                    (D FS))
        3
        (FVERB+MAIN (PETER GAB MARIA)
                    (V A MS FS)
                    (SUSI)
                    (A FS))
        4
        (FVERB+MAIN (PETER GAB MARIA SUSI)
                    (V MS FS FS)
                    (%.)
                    (V DECL))
        5))
 (CMPLT ((PETER GAB MARIA SUSI %.)
        (DECL)
        1
        (START (PETER)
               (S3 MS)
               (GAB)
               (V S3 D A))
        2
        (MAIN+FVERB (PETER GAB)
                    (V D A MS)
```

```
                         (MARIA)
                         (A FS))
             3
             (FVERB+MAIN (PETER GAB MARIA)
                         (V D MS FS)
                         (SUSI)
                         (D FS))
             4
             (FVERB+MAIN (PETER GAB MARIA SUSI)
                         (V MS FS FS)
                         (%.)
                         (V DECL))
             5))
 (CMPLT ((PETER GAB MARIA SUSI %.)
         (DECL)
         1
         (START (PETER)
                (D MS)
                (GAB)
                (V S3 D A))
         2
         (MAIN+FVERB (PETER GAB)
                     (V S3 A MS)
                     (MARIA)
                     (S3 FS))
         3
         (FVERB+MAIN (PETER GAB MARIA)
                     (V A MS FS)
                     (SUSI)
                     (A FS))
         4
         (FVERB+MAIN (PETER GAB MARIA SUSI)
                     (V MS FS FS)
                     (%.)
                     (V DECL))
         5))
 (CMPLT ((PETER GAB MARIA SUSI %.)
         (DECL)
         1
         (START (PETER)
                (D MS)
                (GAB)
                (V S3 D A))
         2
         (MAIN+FVERB (PETER GAB)
                     (V S3 A MS)
                     (MARIA)
                     (A FS))
         3
         (FVERB+MAIN (PETER GAB MARIA)
                     (V S3 MS FS)
                     (SUSI)
                     (S3 FS))
         4
         (FVERB+MAIN (PETER GAB MARIA SUSI)
```

```
                         (V MS FS FS)
                         (%.)
                         (V DECL))
            5))
(CMPLT ((PETER GAB MARIA SUSI %.)
        (DECL)
        1
        (START (PETER)
                (A MS)
                (GAB)
                (V S3 D A))
        2
        (MAIN+FVERB (PETER GAB)
                    (V S3 D MS)
                    (MARIA)
                    (S3 FS))
        3
        (FVERB+MAIN (PETER GAB MARIA)
                    (V D MS FS)
                    (SUSI)
                    (D FS))
        4
        (FVERB+MAIN (PETER GAB MARIA SUSI)
                    (V MS FS FS)
                    (%.)
                    (V DECL))
        5))
(CMPLT ((PETER GAB MARIA SUSI %.)
        (DECL)
        1
        (START (PETER)
                (A MS)
                (GAB)
                (V S3 D A))
        2
        (MAIN+FVERB (PETER GAB)
                    (V S3 D MS)
                    (MARIA)
                    (D FS))
        3
        (FVERB+MAIN (PETER GAB MARIA)
                    (V S3 MS FS)
                    (SUSI)
                    (S3 FS))
        4
        (FVERB+MAIN (PETER GAB MARIA SUSI)
                    (V MS FS FS)
                    (%.)
                    (V DECL))
        5)))
```

The ambiguity in 4.4.12 comes from a morphological deficiency of proper names in German, since analogous sentences using noun phrases with determiners are morphologically disambiguated. Therefore DCAT handles this particular ambiguity on the basis of alternative categorizations of proper names in the lexicon, which in turn control the standard application of different existing rules. In other words, the ambiguity in 4.4.12 is simply the syntactic result of lexical ambiguities.

Theoretically, the syntactic ambiguities in 4.4.10 and 4.4.11 could also be based on a lexical ambiguity of some of the words involved. However, this would require a computationally costly multiple categorization. Instead, such ambiguities may be derived in left-associative grammar by defining special rules which apply to the same input expressions and render different output expressions. In this way the different grammatical functions of the expressions involved are captured in terms of the rules alone, avoiding a multiple categorization.

As an illustration of the treatment of syntactic ambiguity based on alternative rule applications without concomitant multiple categorizations, consider example 4.4.14, which is ambiguous in a way similar to 4.4.11 above.

4.4.14 *Der Mann brachte dem Mädchen ein Buch aus München.* / The man brought the girl a book from Munich.
(a) The adverbial reading:

```
(R DER MANN BRACHTE DEM MAEDCHEN EIN BUCH AUS MUENCHEN .)
((CMPLT ((DER MANN BRACHTE DEM MAEDCHEN EIN BUCH AUS MUENCHEN %.)
 (DECL))
 1
 (START (DER)
        (S3 MS -E)
        (MANN)
        (MS))
 2
 (DET+NOUN (DER MANN)
           (S3 MS)
           (BRACHTE)
           (V S3 D A))
 3
 (MAIN+FVERB (DER MANN BRACHTE)
             (V D A MS)
             (DEM)
             (D NS -EN))
 4
 (FVERB+MAIN (DER MANN BRACHTE DEM)
             (V A MS NS -EN)
             (MAEDCHEN)
             (NS))
 5
 (DET+NOUN (DER MANN BRACHTE DEM MAEDCHEN)
           (V A MS NS)
           (EIN)
           (A NS -ES))
 6
 (FVERB+MAIN (DER MANN BRACHTE DEM MAEDCHEN EIN)
             (V MS NS NS -ES)
             (BUCH)
```

```
            (NS))
7
(DET+NOUN (DER MANN BRACHTE DEM MAEDCHEN EIN BUCH)
          (V MS NS NS)
          (AUS)
          (ADV-L (D)))
8
(FVERB+MAIN (DER MANN BRACHTE DEM MAEDCHEN EIN BUCH AUS)
            (V MS NS NS (D))
            (MUENCHEN)
            (D NS))
9
(PREP+MAIN (DER MANN BRACHTE DEM MAEDCHEN EIN BUCH AUS MUENCHEN)
           (V MS NS NS NS)
           (%.)
           (V DECL))
10))
```

(b) The adnominal reading:

```
(CMPLT ((DER MANN BRACHTE DEM MAEDCHEN EIN BUCH AUS MUENCHEN %.)
(DECL))
1
(START (DER)
       (S3 MS -E)
       (MANN)
       (MS))
2
(DET+NOUN (DER MANN)
          (S3 MS)
          (BRACHTE)
          (V S3 D A))
3
(MAIN+FVERB (DER MANN BRACHTE)
            (V D A MS)
            (DEM)
            (D NS -EN))
4
(FVERB+MAIN (DER MANN BRACHTE DEM)
            (V A MS NS -EN)
            (MAEDCHEN)
            (NS))
5
(DET+NOUN (DER MANN BRACHTE DEM MAEDCHEN)
          (V A MS NS)
          (EIN)
          (A NS -ES))
6
(FVERB+MAIN (DER MANN BRACHTE DEM MAEDCHEN EIN)
            (V MS NS NS -ES)
            (BUCH)
            (NS))
7
(DET+NOUN (DER MANN BRACHTE DEM MAEDCHEN EIN BUCH)
          (V MS NS NS)
```

```
            (AUS)
            (ADV-L (D)))
  8
(NOUN+PREP (DER MANN BRACHTE DEM MAEDCHEN EIN BUCH AUS)
            (V MS NS NS (D))
            (MUENCHEN)
            (D NS))
  9
(PREP+MAIN (DER MANN BRACHTE DEM MAEDCHEN EIN BUCH AUS MUENCHEN)
            (V MS NS NS NS)
            (%.)
            (V DECL))
10)))
```

Intuitively, this sentence is ambiguous between a reading in which *aus Mün-chen* modifies the verb (adverbial interpretation of the prepositional phrase) and a reading in which *aus München* modifies the noun (adnominal interpretation of the prepositional phrase). On the first reading we would have a constituent like 'bring from Munich', corresponding to the reading 'see with a telescope' in 4.4.11; on the second reading we would have a constituent like 'book from Munich', corresponding to the reading 'girl with a telescope' in 4.4.11.

Note that the categorizations and the sequences of rules in analyses 4.4.14a and 4.4.14b are exactly alike, except for the rules applying in section 7. For convenience, the respective sections 7 and 8 are repeated below as 4.4.15 and 4.4.16[19]:

4.4.15 Adverbial reading:

```
  7
(DET+NOUN (DER MANN BRACHTE DEM MAEDCHEN EIN BUCH)
            (V MS NS NS)
            (AUS)
            (ADV-L (D)))
  8
(FVERB+MAIN (DER MANN BRACHTE DEM MAEDCHEN EIN BUCH AUS)
            (V MS NS NS (D))
            (MUENCHEN)
            (D))
```

4.4.16 Adnominal reading:

```
  7
(DET+NOUN (DER MANN BRACHTE DEM MAEDCHEN EIN BUCH)
            (V MS NS NS)
            (AUS)
            (ADV-L (D)))
  8
(NOUN+PREP (DER MANN BRACHTE DEM MAEDCHEN EIN BUCH AUS)
            (V MS ND NS (D))
```

---

[19]The parentheses around the D in (ADV-L (D)) indicate that the dative is part of a prepositional clause. This categorization ensures that the dative will be added by no rule other than RPREP+MAIN.

```
          (MUENCHEN)
          (D))
```

In section 7 of 4.4.15 the rule is RFVERB+MAIN, while in section 7 of
4.4.16 the rule is RNOUN+PREP. This analysis involves minimal of grammatical difference between the two readings. Yet the difference in grammatical
function is captured in terms of the application of two different rules. The basis
of this treatment is the definition of agreement in terms of corresponding (rather
than identical) categories.

As a third use of prepositions (in additions to the adverbial and the postnominal) consider example 4.4.17:

4.4.17 *Das Haus, aus dem Maria kam, gehört Peter.* The house out of which
Mary came is owned by Peter.

```
(R DAS HAUS AUS DEM MARIA KAM GEHOERT PETER .)
((CMPLT ((DAS HAUS , AUS DEM MARIA KAM , GEHOERT PETER %.)
        (DECL))
        1
        (START (DAS)
               (S3 NS -E)
               (HAUS)
               (NS))
        2
        (DET+NOUN (DAS HAUS)
                  (S3 NS)
                  (AUS)
                  (ADV-L (D)))
        3
        (NOUN+SUBPREP (DAS HAUS , AUS)
                      (S3 NS V ADV-L (D))
                      (DEM)
                      (D NS -EN))
        4
        (SUBPREP+PRO (DAS HAUS , AUS DEM)
                     (S3 V ADV-L)
                     (MARIA)
                     (S3 FS))
        5
        (SUBCL+MAIN (DAS HAUS , AUS DEM MARIA)
                    (S3 V ADV-L S3 FS)
                    (KAM)
                    (V S3))
        6
        (SUBCL+LASTVERB (DAS HAUS , AUS DEM MARIA KAM ,)
                        (S3 FS)
                        (GEHOERT)
                        (V S3 D))
        7
        (MAIN+FVERB (DAS HAUS , AUS DEM MARIA KAM , GEHOERT)
                    (V D FS)
                    (PETER)
                    (D NS))
```

```
      8
      (FVERB+MAIN (DAS HAUS , AUS DEM MARIA KAM , GEHOERT
         PETER)
                   (V FS MS)
                   (%.)
                   (V DECL))
      9)))
```

Note that the category of the preposition *aus* in 4.4.17 is the same as in
the two readings analyzed in 4.4.14. The different grammatical function of
the preposition in the construction in 4.4.17 is captured by the rule RNOUN-
+SUBPREP. RNOUN+SUBPREP is like RNOUN+RELPRO in that it adds a
comma between the noun and the next word in the surface, and a V indicating
an open subordinate clause in the output category (see history sections 2 and
3).

The rule package called by RNOUN+SUBPREP, i.e. NOUN+SUBPREP,
contains only the rule RSUBPREP+PRO (see 3.4.2), ensuring that prepositions
functioning as subordinating conjunctions are properly followed by the required
pronoun. After the application of RSUBPREP+PRO the derivation continues
like that of any other subordinate clause.

DCAT handles many other constructions, for example sentential complements, separable verbal prefixes, yes/no interrogatives, wh-interrogatives, infinitives with *zu*, and adsentential clauses. For reasons of space, these will not
be discussed in detail here. Instead the reader is referred to appendix B, where
additional DCAT derivations of various constructions are presented. Given the
discussion of examples on the previous pages, the linguistic content of the sample derivations in appendix B may be deduced directly from the printouts. Furthermore, since the LISP-code of DCAT and DLEX is reprinted in appendix A,
the formal background of all 221 DCAT derivations in this book is completely
documented.

4.5 Remarks on the lexicon of left-associative grammar

The lexicon of left-associative grammar is implemented as a 'full-form lexicon':
for each word all the different forms are listed, not only the infinitive of verbs,
the nominative   singular of nouns, etc. The analysis of word forms in the
lexicon of left-associative grammar is minimal, in that only the surface and a
list of categories are specified. Consider for example the lexical analysis of the
past participle of the verb *essen* in DLEX:

4.5.1 The DLEX analysis of *gegessen*:

```
(GEGESSEN ((H A)
           (WP -AG)))
```

If this word occurs at the very beginning of a parse, as in 4.5.2 below, the system provides the rule package START, which is applied as usual to all ordered pairs consisting of readings of the first two words, e.g., *gegessen*[20] and *hat*.

4.5.2 *Gegessen hat Maria den Apfel.* Mary has eaten the apple.

```
(R GEGESSEN HAT MARIA DEN APFEL .)
((CMPLT ((GEGESSEN HAT MARIA DEN APFEL %.)
        (DECL)
        1
        (START (GEGESSEN)
               (H A)
               (HAT)
               (V S3 H))
        2
        (MAIN+FVERB (GEGESSEN HAT)
                    (V S3 A)
                    (MARIA)
                    (S3 FS))
        3
        (FVERB+MAIN (GEGESSEN HAT MARIA)
                    (V A FS)
                    (DEN)
                    (A MS -EN))
        4
        (FVERB+MAIN (GEGESSEN HAT MARIA DEN)
                    (V FS MS -EN)
                    (APFEL)
                    (MS))
        5
        (DET+NOUN (GEGESSEN HAT MARIA DEN APFEL)
                  (V FS MS)
                  (%.)
                  (V DECL))
        6)))
```

But if the word analyzed in 4.5.1 occurs as a next word, as in 4.5.3 below, it is not preceded by a rule package in the history section:

4.5.3 *Den Apfel hat Maria gegessen.* Mary has eaten the apple.

```
(R DEN APFEL HAT MARIA GEGESSEN .)
((CMPLT ((DEN APFEL HAT MARIA GEGESSEN %.)
        (DECL)
        1
        (START (DEN)
               (A MS -EN)
               (APFEL)
               (MS))
        2
        (DET+NOUN (DEN APFEL)
                  (A MS)
```

---

[20]The word form *gegessen* is listed in the lexicon with two readings, one for active, the other for passive.

```
             (HAT)
             (V S3 H))
3
(MAIN+FVERB (DEN APFEL HAT)
            (V S3 H A MS)
            (MARIA)
            (S3 FS))
4
(FVERB+MAIN (DEN APFEL HAT MARIA)
            (V H A MS FS)
            (GEGESSEN)
            (H A))
5
(MAINCL+NFVERB (DEN APFEL HAT MARIA GEGESSEN)
               (V MS FS)
               (%.)
               (V DECL))
6)))
```

In left-associative grammar, the different serializations in 4.5.2 and 4.2.3 are reflected in alternative orders of building up and cancelling valencies, a procedure discussed in detail in the previous sections of this chapter.

If a word is lexically ambiguous, it is listed with several different categories, representing the different readings. The readings of a word form are tied together by a common surface. For example, if we type *Bücher* on the terminal, DLEX returns:

4.5.4 The DLEX analysis of *Bücher:*

```
(BUECHER ((P)
          (P3 P)
          (A P)))
```

The first reading represents the use of *Bücher* as a plural noun; the second reading represents the use as a nominative plural noun phrase, as in *Bücher sind teuer;* and the third reading represents the use as an accusative plural noun phrase, as in *Peter kaufte Bücher* (cf. section 3.5 above).

But what about morphology? What about the relation between *Buch, Buches, Bücher,* and *Büchern,* for example? This relation is irrelevant for syntactic composition. When confronted with the task of replacing *Büchern* in the sentence *Peter las in den Büchern* by either *Bücher* or *Zeitungen,* the grammatically correct choice is *Zeitungen,* because it is morphologically compatible with the required dative plural reading, while *Bücher,* despite its morphological relation to *Büchern,* is not.

This conclusion does not preclude a morphological analysis in the lexicon of a surface compositional grammar. On the contrary, the linguistic issues of morphology, such as derivation, inflection, and composition, the formation of new words, the handling of regular versus irregular forms in lexical derivation rules, the treatment of word semantics on the basis of roots, and so on, are discussed in detail in chapter 4 of **SCG**.[21] But for the purposes of syntactic composition, a surface compositional grammar does not need a morphological component.

A related issue is computational economy. Would implementation of a morphological component result in a faster system requiring less memory or space? Or is the present system, without a morphological component more economical? The answer to this question depends in part on whether the language under analysis is isolating, inflectional, or polysynthetic. Let us consider an example from German, which is an inflectional language.

4.5.5 *Die Gesandten wären gestern gegangen.*

A parser using a morphological component has to analyze each word. For instance, the past participle form *gegangen* consists of the prefix *ge-*, the stem *gang*, which is an irregular form of *geh*, and the suffix *-en*. The boundaries of the regular, productive morphemes in 4.5.5 are indicated in 4.5.6:

4.5.6 *Die Gesandte-n wär-en gestern ge-gangen.*

Possible, but nonproductive or incorrect morpheme boundaries are illustrated in 4.5.7:

4.5.7 *Die Ge-sandt-en wären ge-stern gegang-en.*

Determining the boundaries of productive morphemes in an inflectional or isolating language is a very complicated task for a parser. A word initial sequence of letters like 'ge' may be a morpheme without a regular or productive function, as in *Gesandten*, a *bona fide* productive morpheme, as in *gegangen*, or may not be a morpheme at all, as in *gestern*,

In the current approach, without a morphological analysis, each word form is listed in the lexicon. Its syntactic function is specified completely by a list of categories. Computationally, surface forms are treated as global LISP variables, which is a most efficient and convenient method offered by LISP, at least for present purposes.[22] If we type a word form such as *gegangen* on the terminal, the lexical analysis appears instantly on the screen.[23]

---

[21] According to the SCG approach the connection between different forms like *Buch, Buches, Bücher* and *Büchern* is not the surface, which may differ completely between forms, e.g. *go* versus *went*, but is rather a semantic one. In the lexicon it is expressed on the semantic level by a common root representing the basic semantic concept underlying these different surface forms.

[22] In a full implementation, an access function would retrieve the value of a word. This has the advantages that: (i) potential conflicts between lexical entries and LISP atoms are avoided; (ii) the lexicon is independent of the details of the particular LISP version used, and (iii) control over the search procedure is ensured.

[23] This particular LISP implementation of the lexicon in left-associative grammar is theory-neutral, however, since the principles of a 'full-form lexicon' can also be satisfied in terms of other data structures.

4.5.8 The DLEX analysis of *gegangen*

```
(GEGANGEN ((S)))
```

This analysis characterizes *gegangen* as an unambiguous word. The category (S) indicates a past participle which combines with an auxiliary form of *sein* (rather than *haben*). The absence of additional category segments characterizes the word as the past participle of an intransitive verb.

Gegangen is a form of the verb *gehen*. This verb has a total of 9 forms: *gehe, gehst, geht, gehen, ging, gingst, gingen, gingt,* and *gegangen*[24]. The analysis of these forms in DLEX is given below:

4.5.9 Lexical analysis of all forms of the verb *gehen:*

```
(RPAQQ GEGANGEN (GEGANGEN ((S))))
(RPAQQ GEHE (GEHE ((V S1))))
(RPAQQ GEHEN (GEHEN ((W INF)
                     (V P1)
                     (V P3))))
(RPAQQ GEHST (GEHST ((V S2))))
(RPAQQ GEHT (GEHT ((V S3)
                   (V P2))))
(RPAQQ GING (GING ((V S1)
                   (V S3))))
(RPAQQ GINGEN (GINGEN ((V P1))
                      (V P3))))
(RPAQQ GINGST (GINGST ((V S2))))
(RPAQQ GINGT (GINGT ((V P2))))
```

In INTERLISP-D 'RPAQQ A B' indicates that the variable A has been set to the value B. For the sake of simplicity we usually list only the values of word forms, as in 4.5.8. If we wanted to define a new word, e.g. the masculine singular noun GEHER, we would type (SETQ GEHER '(GEHER ((MS)))) on the terminal.

Other words have fewer forms than the verb *gehen*. For example, prepositions and conjunctions have only one form each, and nouns in German have at most four forms (cf. sections 3.2 and 3.3). But let us assume for the sake of argument that the average number of forms of a word or lexeme is 10. This number will vary from language to language; 10 forms per word is higher than the average of German and much higher than that of English.

Let us assume furthermore that the common vocabulary of a natural language is about 50,000 words.[25] Therefore the complete lexical analysis of a

---

[24]Ignoring the outmoded subjunctive forms *ginge, gingest,* and *ginget.*

[25]Jespersen (1938) provides the following estimates of the number of words in English: "Shakespeare's vocabulary is often stated to be the richest ever employed by a single man. It has been calculated to comprise 21,000 words ('rough calculation, found in Mrs. Clark's Concordance... without counting inflected forms as distinct words', Craik), or, according to others, 24,000 or 15,000. In order to appreciate what that means we must look a little at various statements that have been given of the number of words used by other authors and by

natural language involves roughly 500,000 word forms. How much space would these forms require in a 'full-form' lexicon? At present DLEX contains well over 1000 word forms (see appendix A.5, where DLEX is reprinted in its entirety). This would correspond to 100 lexemes, by our assumption. DLEX has a size of 58 kilobytes compiled, and 47 kilobytes uncompiled. Thus the complete lexical treatment of 100 words (lexemes) requires roughly 50 kilobytes in a left-associative system.

It follows that the lexical treatment of 500,000 word forms or 50,000 words will require no more than 25 megabytes. In other words, the full-form lexicon of a natural language, in its present unoptimized code, may easily be stored on one hard disk of today's LISP work-stations. The size of such a full-form lexicon may be reduced to about 3 megabytes by using a technique called "byte encoding". Thus the full-form lexicon of an entire language may be loaded into the working memory of today's LISP machines. Analysis of each word form in a sentence is extremely fast, since it merely requires finding a matching surface in the lexicon. The implementation of DLEX as a full-form lexicon, where each entry is defined as a global LISP variable, provides for an instantaneous recognition of word forms.

Next let us turn to the relation of syntax and morphology in the context of language change. During the historical change of a natural language, fixed sequences of words contract into single words. In such cases the syntax of the phrase from which the new word resulted may still be visible. How does left-associative grammar handle such transitions from syntactic structure to morphological structure? Let us consider a simple example. If the German preposition *an* is followed by the definite article form *dem*, the two words may be contracted into *am*. Since left-associative grammar is a surface compositional system, the forms *an* and *am* are treated in the lexicon as two full words with different categories.[26] But what about the obvious linguistic relation between the two words? Compare the following two DCAT analyses.

4.5.10 *Das Haus an dem See gehört Maria.* / The house on the lake belongs to Mary.

```
(R DAS HAUS AN DEM SEE GEHOERT MARIA .)
((CMPLT ((DAS HAUS AN DEM SEE GEHOERT MARIA %.)
        (DECL)
        1
        (START (DAS)
```

---

ordinary beings, educated and uneducated. Unfortunately, these statements are in many cases given and repeated without any indication of the manner in which they have been arrived at. ... People who had never been to college, but, with an ordinary common school education, were regular readers of books and periodicals, according to the same writer [E.H. Babbit] reported generally from 25,000 to 35,000 words, though some went higher, even to 50,000." (op.cit. p. 199, 201)

[26]Theo Vennemann has pointed out that the contracted and the non-contracted forms may differ in their uses. For example, *Peter geht zur Schule* can mean that Peter walks to school or that Peter is a student. But *Peter geht zu der Schule*, has only the first interpretation.

```
                (S3 NS -E)
                (HAUS)
                (NS))
        2
        (DET+NOUN (DAS HAUS)
                (S3 NS)
                (AN)
                (ADV-L (D)))
        3
        (NOUN+PREP (DAS HAUS AN)
                (S3 NS (D))
                (DEM)
                (D MS -EN))
        4
        (PREP+MAIN (DAS HAUS AN DEM)
                (S3 NS MS -EN)
                (SEE)
                (MS))
        5
        (DET+NOUN (DAS HAUS AN DEM SEE)
                (S3 NS MS)
                (GEHOERT)
                (V S3 D))
        6
        (MAIN+FVERB (DAS HAUS AN DEM SEE GEHOERT)
                (V D NS MS)
                (MARIA)
                (D FS))
        7
        (FVERB+MAIN (DAS HAUS AN DEM SEE GEHOERT MARIA)
                (V NS MS FS)
                (%.)
                (V DECL))
        8)))
```

4.5.11 *Das Haus am See gehört Maria.*

```
(R DAS HAUS AM SEE GEHOERT MARIA .)
((CMPLT ((DAS HAUS AM SEE GEHOERT MARIA %.)
        (DECL)
        1
        (START (DAS)
                (S3 NS -E)
                (HAUS)
                (NS))
        2
        (DET+NOUN (DAS HAUS)
                (S3 NS)
                (AM)
                (ADV-L MS -EN))
        3
        (NOUN+PREP (DAS HAUS AM)
                (S3 NS MS -EN)
                (SEE)
                (MS))
        4
```

```
(DET+NOUN (DAS HAUS AM SEE)
          (S3 NS MS)
          (GEHOERT)
          (V S3 D))
5
(MAIN+FVERB (DAS HAUS AM SEE GEHOERT)
            (V D NS MS)
            (MARIA)
            (D FS))
6
(FVERB+MAIN (DAS HAUS AM SEE GEHOERT MARIA)
            (V NS MS FS)
            (%.)
            (V DECL))
7)))
```

Analysis 4.5.10 has 8 history sections, while analysis 4.5.11 has only 7. The reason is that 4.5.11 is one word shorter than 4.5.10, due to the contraction of *an dem* into *am*. The two derivations diverge in history section 2; the respective next words have different surfaces and different categories. But in history section 4 of 4.5.10 and history section 3 of 4.5.11 the sentence starts are equivalent again. The relevant portions of 4.5.10 and 4.5.11 are repeated in 4.5.12 and 4.5.13, respectively, for convenience:

4.5.12

```
    2
    (DET+NOUN (DAS HAUS)
              (S3 NS)
              (AN)
              (ADV-L (D)))
    3
    (NOUN+PREP (DAS HAUS AN)
               (S3 NS (D))
               (DEM)
               (D MS -EN))
    4
    (PREP+MAIN (DAS HAUS AN DEM)
               (S3 NS MS -EN)
               (SEE)
               (MS))
    5
    (DET+NOUN (DAS HAUS AN DEM SEE)
              (S3 NS MS)
```

4.5.13

```
    2
    (DET+NOUN (DAS HAUS)
              (S3 NS)
              (AM)
              (ADV-L MS -EN))
    3
```

```
(NOUN+PREP (DAS HAUS AM)
           (S3 NS MS -EN)
           (SEE)
           (MS))
4
(DET+NOUN (DAS HAUS AM SEE)
           (S3 NS MS)
```

In 4.5.12 the derivation proceeds from the sentence start in history section
2 to the sentence start in history section 5 via the rules RNOUN+PREP and
RPREP+MAIN. In 4.5.13 the derivation proceeds from the corresponding sentence start in history section 2 to the sentence start in history section 4, which
is equivalent to that in history section 5 of 4.5.12, via the rule RNOUN+PREP
alone. Thus the contraction of *an dem* into *am* not only involves a new surface
with a different category, but also represents a shortcut in the syntactic transition network. The category of *dem* has incorporated the rule RPREP+MAIN
and the corresponding rule package.

Finally, we return to the discussion of category segments in DCAT. In sections 3.2 and 3.3 we explained the motivation for the choice of category segments
such as MS (masculine singular) and D (dative). In subsequent sections most
of the category segments used by DCAT and DLEX were explained. But there
are still a few which have not yet been mentioned. Consider the derivation in
4.5.14:

4.5.14 *Das Buch ist von Maria zu lesen.* / The book is to be read by Mary.

```
(R DAS BUCH IST VON MARIA ZU LESEN .)
((CMPLT ((DAS BUCH IST VON MARIA ZU LESEN %.)
         (DECL)
         1
         (START (DAS)
                (S3 NS -E)
                (BUCH)
                (NS))
         2
         (DET+NOUN (DAS BUCH)
                   (S3 NS)
                   (IST)
                   (V S3 S))
         3
         (MAIN+FVERB (DAS BUCH IST)
                     (V S NS)
                     (VON)
                     (-AG (D)))
         4
         (FVERB+MAIN (DAS BUCH IST VON)
                     (V S NS -AG (D))
                     (MARIA)
                     (D FS))
         5
         (PREP+MAIN (DAS BUCH IST VON MARIA)
                    (V S NS -AG FS)
```

```
                    (ZU)
                    (Z))
        6
   (MAINCL+NFVERB (DAS BUCH IST VON MARIA ZU)
                  (V NS -AG FS Q)
                  (LESEN)
                  (Q -AG))
        7
   (MAINCL+NFVERB (DAS BUCH IST VON MARIA ZU LESEN)
                  (V NS FS)
                  (%.)
                  (V DECL))
        8)))
```

4.5.14 is a kind of passive in German. Like the constructions in section 4.2, it is implemented lexically. The form *lesen* is categorized not only as an infinitive and as the first and third person plural present tense, but also as a 'Q-passive'. The category of *lesen* in history section 6 is (Q -AG). '-AG' is the usual segment indicating the agent in passives, while 'Q' is a category segment not previously mentioned. The choice of 'Q' was rather arbitrary; 'Q' had not been used for anything and it happens to be the letter after P (passive). Another new segment is 'Z', which categorizes the subordinating conjunction *zu*.

Example 4.5.14 is notable also for the fact that agreement is not based only on identical categories, but exhibits an instance of agreement based on corresponding categories. In history section 5 the 'Z' of *zu* cancels the 'S' introduced by the auxiliary. The rule RMAINCL+NFVERB derives the resulting category (see history section 6) by saying roughly: if category **a** contains a segment S and category **b** contains a segment Z, then the result category is the sum of **a** and **b** minus S and Z.

Agreement in terms of corresponding categories is not quite as perspicuous as that based on identical categories. For example, in history section 5 we have to remember that Z may correspond to S. In history section 2, on the other hand, it is obvious that the S3 in the sentence start cancels the identical segment in the next word. Almost all constructions of DCAT handle agreement on the basis of identical category segments, and use of corresponding categories could be completely avoided. But the price is a considerable increase of certain lexical readings, for example of *ist*. In a language with a highly reduced morphology, like English, the use of corresponding categories is practically unavoidable.

Another construction using *zu* and a Q-passive is illustrated in 4.5.15, which also employs the new category segment 'ADJ', for adjective:

4.5.15 *Das Buch ist schwierig zu lesen.* / The book is difficult to read.

```
(R DAS BUCH IST SCHWIERIG ZU LESEN .)
((CMPLT ((DAS BUCH IST SCHWIERIG ZU LESEN %.)
        (DECL)
        1
        (START (DAS)
               (S3 NS -E)
```

```
                (BUCH)
                (NS))
    2
    (DET+NOUN (DAS BUCH)
                (S3 NS)
                (IST)
                (V S3 S))
    3
    (MAIN+FVERB (DAS BUCH IST)
                (V S NS)
                (SCHWIERIG)
                (ADJ S))
    4
    (AUX-PRED (DAS BUCH IST SCHWIERIG)
                (V NS S)
                (ZU)
                (Z))
    5
    (MAINCL+NFVERB (DAS BUCH IST SCHWIERIG ZU)
                (V NS Q)
                (LESEN)
                (Q -AG))
    6
    (MAINCL+NFVERB (DAS BUCH IST SCHWIERIG ZU LESEN)
                (V NS -AG)
                (%.)
                (V DECL))
    7)))
```

In history section 3 of 4.5.15 'ADJ' cancels 'S' and introduces a new 'S', which is cancelled in history section 4 by 'Z'. Constructions similar to 4.5.14 and 4.5.15 can become quite complex in German. See appendix B, where the derivations of several additional examples are given.

The soundness of using corresponding categories for handling agreement in German is particulary obvious in 'copula'-constructions like 4.5.16, 4.5.17, and 4.5.18, where an auxiliary of paradigm S ('*sein*') combines with an adjective, a nominative noun phrase, and a local adverb, respectively.

4.5.16 *Maria ist jung.* / Mary is young.

```
(R MARIA IST JUNG .)
((CMPLT ((MARIA IST JUNG %.)
        (DECL)
        1
        (START (MARIA)
                (S3 FS)
                (IST)
                (V S3 S))
        2
        (MAIN+FVERB (MARIA IST)
                (V S FS)
                (JUNG)
                (ADJ))
```

```
        3
(AUX-PRED (MARIA IST JUNG)
             (V FS)
             (%.)
             (V DECL))
        4)))
```

4.5.17 *Maria ist ein junges Mädchen.* / Mary is a young girl.

```
(R MARIA IST EIN JUNGES MAEDCHEN .)
((CMPLT ((MARIA IST EIN JUNGES MAEDCHEN %.)
        (DECL)
        1
        (START (MARIA)
             (S3 FS)
             (IST)
             (V S3 S))
        2
        (MAIN+FVERB (MARIA IST)
             (V S FS)
             (EIN)
             (S3 NS -ES))
        3
        (AUX-PRED (MARIA IST EIN)
             (V FS NS -ES)
             (JUNGES)
             (-ES))
        4
        (DET+ADJ (MARIA IST EIN JUNGES)
             (V FS NS -ES)
             (MAEDCHEN)
             (NS))
        5
        (DET+NOUN (MARIA IST EIN JUNGES MAEDCHEN)
             (V FS NS)
             (%.)
             (V DECL))
        6)))
```

4.5.18 *Maria ist in der Schule.* / Mary is in the school.

```
(R MARIA IST IN DER SCHULE .)
((CMPLT ((MARIA IST IN DER SCHULE %.)
        (DECL)
        1
        (START (MARIA)
             (S3 FS)
             (IST)
             (V S3 S))
        2
        (MAIN+FVERB (MARIA IST)
             (V S FS)
             (IN)
             (ADV-L (D)))
        3
        (AUX-PRED (MARIA IST IN)
```

```
                (V FS (D))
                (DER)
                (D FS -EN))
    4
    (PREP+MAIN (MARIA IST IN DER)
               (V FS FS -EN)
               (SCHULE)
               (FS))
    5
    (DET+NOUN (MARIA IST IN DER SCHULE)
              (V FS FS)
              (%.)
              (V DECL))
    6)))
```

In 4.5.16, the segment S in the sentence start of history section 2 corresponds to the segment 'ADJ', in 4.5.17 it corresponds to the segment 'S3', and in 4.5.18 it corresponds to the segment 'ADV-L'. An alternative implementation of these constructions on the basis of identical categories would result in a considerably slower analysis. An annotated list of all category segments used in DCAT and DLEX is given in appendix B.1.

Concluding the presentation of the German parser DCAT/DLEX let us briefly consider the following qestion: is the approach of left-associative grammar illustrated above suitable also for other natural languages? Natural languages are known to show marked structural differences. Some have a free word order, others a fixed one. Some have a varied morphology, others a simplified one. Some languages have the verb usually in second position, some in last position, some in first position.

However, there are several specific reasons for the conjecture that a left-associative approach would be suitable for the description of a wide range of natural languages. German has a fairly varied morphology with associated agreement conditions. DCAT's treatment of this aspect of German, based on a suitable categorization, can be used to treat morphological agreement in other languages as well.

German has some strict word order rules: for example, in declarative main clauses the finite verb must be in second position, while in subordinate clauses the finite verb is usually in final position. DCAT's treatment of word order regularities in terms of a control structure based on rule packages can be used in the description of similar phenomena in other languages.

In other respects the word order of German is fairly free. Noun phrases, for example, may occur in any order. DCAT's handling of free word order in terms of cancelling corresponding category segments in the valency carrier (cf. examples in section 4.1, 4.2, and 4.3) can be used for the treatment of similar phenomena in other languages.

There are languages in which the valency carrier, e.g. the verb, comes at the very end of the sentence. At first glance, one might consider this a problem for the left-associative approach. But German exhibits this phenomenon too:

in main clauses with finite auxiliaries the non-finite main verb is usually clause final (cf. example 4.1.7); and in subordinate clauses the whole verb construction is clause final (cf. example 4.1.10). The treatment in DCAT, based on argument adding and wholesale cancelling, can also be used for the description of similar phenomena in other languages.

Some languages have intricate structures of nested relative clauses which seem to defy context-free analysis. Such constructions may also be found in German (cf. example 4.3.1). DCAT's context-free treatment of these structures, as well as their extraposed counterparts (cf. example 4.3.2), would also work in other languages.

A more general reason for thinking that the left-associative approach would work for all natural languages is the fact that natural languages code and decode information in a linear manner, from the beginning to the end of the sentence. But the best way to show that left-associative grammar works for a given natural language is to write a parser for it. The following chapter presents a small left-associative parser for English.

5. A left-associative fragment of English

In the previous chapters we presented an application of left-associative grammar to an inflectional language, contemporary German. The present chapter describes the left-associative analysis of an isolating language, contemporary English. English, like Chinese, is considered an isolating language because of its simplified morphology. In English, grammatical relations are encoded by word order to a much greater degree than in German.

The left-associative analysis of English is implemented as the parser ECAT/-ELEX. In order to permit ECAT and DCAT to be loaded at the same time, the two parsers use different notational conventions. Words are written in upper case in DCAT, e.g (AN ((ADV-L D))), and in lower case in ECAT, e.g. (an ((-C))).[1] Rule packages in ECAT are marked with an asterisk: *DET+NOUN is a rule package in ECAT, while DET+NOUN is a rule package of DCAT. Combination rules are marked with an initial '/', e.g. /DET+NOUN, in ECAT, and an initial 'R', e.g. RDET+NOUN, in DCAT.

At present ECAT has 15 combination rules. The complete program, including the motor and auxiliary functions, has a size of 80 KB (uncompiled) or 34 KB compiled. A commented list of the category segments used by ECAT/ELEX is provided in appendix C.1. In C.2 - C.21 the linguistic analysis of ECAT is illustrated with additional examples. These deal with a variety of constructions, such as yes/no-interrogatives, WH-interrogatives, *that*-clauses, relative clauses, active versus passive, and "Wh-movement".

5.1 A distinctive categorization for English noun phrases

What is required for writing a left-associative English parser? The general system of the parser, consisting of the motor and the format of interacting rules and rule packages, is already available, so we may begin the linguistic

---

[1] Not all LISP dialects distinguish between upper and lower case (as does INTERLISP). In such LISP dialects other means for distinguishing the lexica of two different languages must be found. Loading more than one lexicon is necessary for the purposes of machine translation, for example.

analysis immediately. The first task of this analysis is the design of a suitable category system.[2] The category system is built up using the simple grammatical properties which control agreement and valency in the natural language under investigation.

English noun phrases are not marked for case. Consider for example 5.1.1.

5.1.1 The same noun phrases performing different grammatical functions:

1. *John gave the girl the mother.*

2. *The girl gave the mother John.*

3. *The mother gave John the girl.*

The noun phrase *John* is used as a nominative in (1), an accusative in (2), and a dative in (3). Similarly, the noun phrase *the girl* is used as a nominative in (2), an accusative in (3), and a dative in (1). Finally, the noun phrase *the mother* is used as a nominative in (3), an accusative in (1), and a dative in (2). The different grammatical functions of the noun phrases in 5.1.1 are expressed by the word order.

An apparent exception to the thesis that nouns and noun phrases of English are not morphologically marked for case is the genitive, e.g. *Bill's* or *girl's.* Closer inspection, however, suggests categorization of genitives as determiners (in the case of proper names) or adjectives (in the case of nouns). Consider for example 5.1.2.

5.1.2 The function of genitives as determiners or adjectives:

1. *the book* versus *Bill's book*

2. *the beautiful book* versus *the girl's book*

Determiners combine with nouns into noun phrases. Many determiners agree with the noun in number, but there are also determiners that combine with both singular and plural nouns. Consider the examples in 5.1.3.

5.1.3 Number agreement of determiner-noun combinations:

1. *a girl* versus **a girls*

2. **all girl* versus *all girls*

3. *every girl* versus **every girls*

4. **several girl* versus *several girls*

5. *the girl* versus *the girls*

6. *some girl* versus *some girls*

---

[2] See the general discussion of left-associative categories in chapter 3.

Let us use the category segments S (singular), P (plural), and U (universal) to characterize the agreement properties of articles with respect to number. *Every* has the category (S), because it combines only with singular nouns; *all* has the category (P), because it combines only with plural nouns; and *the* has the category (U), because it combines with both singular and plural nouns. The interrogative determiner *which* has the category (WU): the U indicates that it has the combinatorial properties of U determiners, while the W indicates membership in the special class of words like *who, what, why*, etc.[3]

One determiner, the indefinite article *a(n)*, is sensitive to whether the next word starts with a consonant or a vowel. Consider for example 5.1.4.

5.1.4 Agreement properties of the singular indefinite article:

1. *a book* versus **an book*

2. **a auto* versus *an auto*

3. *a beautiful auto* versus **an beautiful auto*

4. **a old book* versus *an old book*

Let us use the category segments C (consonant) and -C (no consonant) to characterize the agreement properties of the indefinite article with respect to the first phoneme of the next word. Thus *a* has the category (C) and *an* has the category (-C). C and -C are regarded as specializations of S.

5.1.5 ELEX definition of various determiners:

```
(the ((U)))        (some ((U)))
(all ((P)))        (several ((P)))
(every ((S)))      (each ((S)))
(a ((C)))          (an ((-C)))
(which ((WU)))
```

The relationships between articles of the different categories (U)/(WU), (S), (C), (-C), and (P) and compatible nouns may be represented in the form of the following tree:

---

[3]The use of *which* as a relative pronoun is characterized by another category, (W-H), because it can modify only -H (non-human) nouns. The pronouns *who* and *whom*, on the other hand, are lexically unambiguous and serve as both interrogative and relative pronouns.

5.1.6 The agreement properties of determiners and nouns in English:

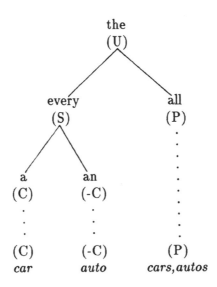

If a noun is singular, it is categorized as (C) or (-C), depending on whether or not its first phoneme is a consonant. If a noun is plural, it is categorized as (P). A noun of category C may combine with determiners of category (C), (S), or (U)/(WU); a noun of category (-C) may combine with determiners of category (-C), (S), or (U)/(WU); and a noun of category (P) may combine with determiners of category (P) or (U)/(WU). The fact that certain letters may function either as consonants or as vowels, e.g. *a hotel* versus *an hour*, is not a problem, because the agreement property of a noun is written into its category.

The categorization of nouns in 5.1.6 is not yet complete. The agreement between nouns and relative clauses in English depends on whether the noun denotes a person or a thing. Consider the following examples.

5.1.7 Agreement with relative clauses:

  1. *the man who walks* versus **the man which walks*

  2. **the car who runs* versus *the car which runs*

Let us use the category segments H and -H to indicate whether or not a noun denotes something human. Adding this segment to the distinction between C and -C nouns, we arrive at the following noun categories in English:

5.1.8 ELEX definition of various nouns:

```
(man  ((CH)))        (men   ((PH)))
(aunt ((-CH)))       (aunts ((PH)))
(car  ((C-H)))       (cars  ((P-H)))
(auto ((-C-H)))      (autos ((P-H)))
```

The above analysis of English noun phrases represents a minimal distinctive categorization. All the nouns and determiners mentioned are categorized unambiguously. The determiner categories U, P, S, C, -C, and WU make up a rather diverse set, but they capture the concrete facts of English. The same holds for the noun categories CH, -CH, C-H, -C-H, PH, and P-H. Furthermore, compared with the three-segment determiner categories and the three or four forms of nouns in German, the English system is parsimonious, despite the unschematic nature of the categorial combinations.

Once a determiner and a noun are combined, a certain uniformity of categories results: third person noun phrases of English may be SH (singular human), S-H (singular non-human), PH (plural human), P-H (plural non-human), WS (interrogative singular), or WP (interrogative plural). Consider the following ECAT analyses illustrating determiner-noun agreement in English.

5.1.9 Some examples of determiner-noun agreement in ECAT:

1. the man versus *the men*

```
(R the man)                      (R the men)
((*DET+NOUN ((the man)           ((*DET+NOUN ((the men)
            (SH)                             (PH)
            1                                1
            (*START (the)                    (*START (the)
                    (U)                              (U)
                    (man)                            (men)
                    (CH))                            (PH))
            2)))                             2)))
```

2. *all man versus *all men*

```
(R all man)                                      (R all men)
[ERROR "Ungrammatical continuation at:"          ((*DET+NOUN ((all men)
            ((*START ((all)                                   (PH)
                     (P)))                                    1
            (*START ((man)                                    (*START (all)
                    (CH]                                              (P)
                                                                      (men)
                                                                      (PH))
                                                              2)))
```

3. every man versus **every men*

```
(R every man)                          (R every men)
((*DET+NOUN ((every man)               [ERROR "Ungrammatical continuation at:"
            (SH)                                   ((*START ((every)
            1                                                (S)))
            (*START (every)                        (*START ((men)
                    (S)                                     (PH]
                    (man)
                    (CH))
            2)))
```

4. a man versus **an men*

```
(R a man)                        (R an man)
((*DET+NOUN ((a man)             [ERROR "Ungrammatical continuation at:"
      (SH)                              ((*START ((an)
      1                                        (-C)))
      (*START (a)                      (*START ((man)
            (C)                               (CH]
            (man)
            (CH))
      2)))
```

5. *a auto versus *an auto*

```
(R a auto)                               (R an auto)
[ERROR "Ungrammatical continuation at:"  ((*DET+NOUN ((an auto)
      ((*START ((a)                            (S-H)
            (C)))                              1
      (*START ((auto)                          (*START (an)
            (-C-H]                                   (-C)
                                                     (auto)
                                                     (-C-H))
                                             2)))
```

6. which man versus *which cars*

```
(R which man)                    (R which cars)
((*DET+NOUN ((which man)         ((*DET+NOUN ((which cars)
      (WS)                             (WP)
      1                                1
      (*START (which)                  (*START (which)
            (WU)                             (WU)
            (man)                            (cars)
            (CH))                            (P-H))
      2)))                             2)))
```

/DET+NOUN handles all agreement distinctions of determiner-noun combinations in English. It specifies exactly what the categories of the sentence start and the next word must be in order to combine into well-formed noun phrases, and what the category of the resulting new sentence start will be. An English paraphrase of /DET+NOUN is given in 5.1.10:

5.1.10 Declarative statement of /DET+NOUN:

If the category of the first expression consists of a single segment x, the value of the local variable ARG is set to x. Otherwise the value of ARG is set to the second segment of the category of the first input expression. The **input condition** of the rule /DET+NOUN specifies that (i) the value of ARG must be U, S, C, or WU, and the category of the second expression must be (CH) or (C-H), or (ii) the value of ARG must be U, S, -C, or WU, and the category of the second expression must (-CH) or (-C-H), or (iii) the value of ARG must be U, P, CA, -CA[4], or WU, and the category of the second expression must be (PH) or (P-H). The **output specification** of /DET+NOUN says: (i) if the value of ARG is WU, and if the first category segment of the second expression is CH, -CH, C-H, or -C-H, then the output category is WS; otherwise it is WP. (ii) if the category of the second expression is (CH) or (-CH), then the output category is the category of the first expression minus the ARG segment, plus SH; (iii) if the category of the second expression is (C-H) or (-C-H), then the output category is the category of the first expression minus the ARG segment, plus S-H; (iv) if the category of the second expression is (PH) or (P-H), then the output category is the category of the first expression minus the ARG segment plus the category of the second expression.

An earlier, simpler version of /DET+NOUN is based on the convention that the determiner segment in a sentence start is always the last segment (as in DCAT). It turned out, however, that the category segment in the sentence start which is being changed in the process of a left-associative ECAT combination is usually the second segment. For reasons of generality, /DET+NOUN and /DET+ADJ (see below) were changed to conform to this principle wherever possible, i.e. in those cases where the determiner is not in sentence-initial position.

Note that the category of plural noun phrases is the same as that of plural nouns. For example, *books* and *all books* are both of category P-H. Thus the treatment of bare plurals in sentence initial position has a straightforward categorial solution in ECAT. In non-initial position, bare plurals and plural noun phrases behave differently because the first are elementary noun phrases while the second are complex. Compare for example 5.1.11 and 5.1.12:

5.1.11 *John likes all movies.*

```
(R John likes all movies .)
((*CMPLT ((John likes all movies %.)
         (DECL)
         1
         (*START (John)
                 (SH)
                 (likes)
                 (V S3 A))
         2
         (*NOM+FVERB (John likes)
                     (V A SH)
                     (all)
                     (P))
         3
         (*FVERB+MAIN (John likes all)
```

---

[4]CA and -CA are category segments representing adjectives (see below). These segments are listed in order to handle bare plurals beginning with an adjective, as in *beautiful books*.

```
        (V P SH)
        (movies)
        (P-H))
4
(*DET+NOUN (John likes all movies)
        (V SH P-H)
        (%.)
        (DECL V))
5)))
```

5.1.12 *John likes movies.*

```
(R John likes movies .)
((*CMPLT ((John likes movies %.)
        (DECL)
        1
        (*START (John)
                (SH)
                (likes)
                (V S3 A))
        2
        (*NOM+FVERB (John likes)
                (V A SH)
                (movies)
                (P-H))
        3
        (*FVERB+MAIN (John likes movies)
                (V SH P-H)
                (%.)
                (DECL V))
        4)))
```

In 5.1.11 the accusative valency position is changed by the rule /FVERB-+MAIN into the determiner category P. The only way to eliminate the P is by adding a noun of category PH or P-H. In history section 3 /DET+NOUN cancels the P and adds P-H at the end of the category, where it provides the agreement features for a possible relative clause. In 5.1.12, on the other hand, the /FVERB+MAIN cancels the accusative valency in one step and adds the category of the bare plural at the end.

The difference between 5.1.11 and 5.1.12 stems from the fact that left-associative combinations proceed word by word. Complex noun phrases occuring to the right of the valency carrier cancel the valency position before they are completed, while complex noun phrases occurring to the left of the valency carrier are first completed and then cancel the valency position. This is why elementary noun phrases behave like complex noun phrases in sentence initial position, whereas elementary and complex noun phrases seem to differ in post-verbal positions.

The interrogative determiner *which* switches the category segment V (indicating the presence of a finite verb) to VI. Sentence starts with a VI segment must end in a question mark. Consider 5.1.13:

5.1.13 *Which movies does John like?*

```
(R which movies does John like ?)
((*CMPLT ((which movies does John like ?)
         (INTERROG)
         1
         (*START (which)
                 (WU)
                 (movies)
                 (P-H))
         2
         (*DET+NOUN (which movies)
                 (WP)
                 (does)
                 (V S3 DO))
         3
         (*TOP-MAIN (which movies does)
                 (VI S3 DO WP)
                 (John)
                 (SH))
         4
         (*FVERB+NOM (which movies does John)
                 (VI DO WP SH)
                 (like)
                 (V NOM A))
         5
         (*ADD-VERB (which movies does John like)
                 (VI SH)
                 (?)
                 (INTERROG V))
         6)))
```

We turn next to the categorization of the genitives of proper nouns, for example *Bill's*. By categorizing them as U determiners, ECAT also handles constructions like *Bill's car, Bill's uncle, Bill's cars* and *Bill's uncles*. As an example consider 5.1.14:

5.1.14 *Bill's car is fast.*

```
(R Bill's car is fast %.)
((*CMPLT ((Bill's car is fast %.)
         (DECL)
         1
         (*START (Bill's)
                 (U)
                 (car)
                 (C-H))
         2
         (*DET+NOUN (Bill's car)
                 (S-H)
                 (is)
                 (V S3 B))
         3
         (*NOM+FVERB (Bill's car is)
                 (V B S-H)
```

```
                    (fast)
                    (CA))
         4
         (*ADD-VERB (Bill's car is fast)
                    (V S-H)
                    (%.)
                    (DECL V))
            5)))
```

Next let us turn to adjective agreement in English. In left-associative grammar, adjectives combine with the determiner and not with the noun. Apart from the nature of left-associative combinations, this is motivated by the fact that in English, as in German, there are specific agreement restrictions between the determiner and the adjective, but not between the adjective and the noun. Consider for example:

5.1.15 Agreement properties of adjectives:

1. a beautiful old car versus **a old beautiful car*

*2. *an beautiful old car* versus *an old beautiful car*

3. a beautiful old auto versus **a old beautiful auto*

*4. *an beautiful old auto* versus *an old beautiful auto*

Determiners of category U, P, S, or WU may combine with any adjectives; if the determiner is of category C, the adjective must begin with a consonant; if the determiner is of category -C, the adjective may not begin with a consonant. Adjectives beginning with a consonant have the category CA; other adjectives have the category -CA.

5.1.16 ELEX definition of various adjectives:

```
(beautiful ((CA)))                    (old ((-CA)))
```

The result of a determiner-adjective combination is regarded as a complex determiner which may combine with another adjective into another complex determiner, and so on. If the determiner is of category U, P, or S, the result of the determiner-adjective combination has the same category as the determiner; if the determiner is of category C or -C, the result has the determiner category S. Determiner-adjective combinations are handled by the rule /DET+ADJ, which is stated below:

5.1.17 Declarative statement of /DET+ADJ:

> If the category of the first expression consists of a single segment x, the value of the local variable ARG is set to x. Otherwise the value of ARG is set to the second segment of the category of the first input expression. The **input condition** of the rule /DET+ADJ specifies

that (i) if ARG is U, S, P, CA, or -CA, then the second expression
must have the category (CA) or (-CA), (ii) if ARG is (-C), then the
second expression must have the category (-CA), and (iii) if ARG is
(C), then the second expression must have the category (CA). The
output specification of /DET+ADJ says: (i) if ARG is U, S, or P,
then the output category is the category of the first input expression;
(ii) if ARG is CA or -CA, then the output category is the category
of the first input expression except that ARG is replaced by P[5]; (iii)
if ARG is C or -C, then the output category is the category of the
first input expression except that ARG is replaced by S.

Consider the following examples:

5.1.18 *An old beautiful car*

```
(R an old beautiful car)
((*DET+NOUN ((an old beautiful car)
            (S-H)
            1
            (*START (an)
                    (-C)
                    (old)
                    (-CA))
            2
            (*DET+ADJ (an old)
                    (S)
                    (beautiful)
                    (CA))
            3
            (*DET+ADJ (an old beautiful)
                    (S)
                    (car)
                    (C-H))
            4)))
```

5.1.19 **a old beautiful car*

```
(R a old beautiful car)
[ERROR "Ungrammatical continuation at:" ((*START ((a)
                                                  (C)))
        (*START ((old)
                 (B]
```

5.1.20 *a beautiful old car*

```
(R a beautiful old car)
((*DET+NOUN ((a beautiful old car)
            (S-H)
            1
            (*START (a)
```

---

[5]This clause handles bare plurals beginning with several adjectives, such as *old beautiful
books.*

```
                    (C)
                    (beautiful)
                    (CA))
            2
        (*DET+ADJ (a beautiful)
                    (S)
                    (old)
                    (-CA))
            3
        (*DET+ADJ (a beautiful old)
                    (S)
                    (car)
                    (C-H))
            4)))
```

5.1.21 **an beautiful old car*

```
(R an beautiful old car)
[ERROR "Ungrammatical continuation at:" ((*START ((an)
                                                    (-C)))
        (*START ((beautiful)
                (CA]
```

By categorizing the genitive of common nouns like *man's* as adjectives, ECAT handles constructions like *the man's book, the old man's nice books, an uncle's car*, etc. As an example consider 5.1.22:

5.1.22 *The nice old man's car*

```
(R the nice old man's car)
((*DET+NOUN ((the nice old man's car)
            (S-H)
            1
            (*START (the)
                    (U)
                    (nice)
                    (CA))
            2
            (*DET+ADJ (the nice)
                    (U)
                    (old)
                    (-CA))
            3
            (*DET+ADJ (the nice old)
                    (U)
                    (man's)
                    (CA))
            4
            (*DET+ADJ (the nice old man's)
                    (U)
                    (car)
                    (C-H))
            5)))
```

But genitive common nouns differ semantically from regular adjectives. Compare for example *a nice old man's beautiful car* and *a nice man's old beautiful car*. Adjectives preceding a genitive noun modify the genitive; the genitive together with the preceding adjectives modifies what follows as a whole.

The rules /DET+NOUN and /DET+ADJ also handle bare plurals beginning with one or several adjectives. Consider 5.1.23 and 5.1.24:

5.1.23 *Old movies*

```
(R old movies)
((*DET+NOUN ((old movies)
           (P-H)
           1
           (*START (old)
                   (-CA)
                   (movies)
                   (P-H))
           2)))
```

5.1.24 *Old beautiful movies*

```
(R old beautiful movies)
((*DET+NOUN ((old beautiful movies)
           (P-H)
           1
           (*START (old)
                   (-CA)
                   (beautiful)
                   (CA))
           2
           (*DET+ADJ (old beautiful)
                     (P)
                     (movies)
                     (P-H))
           3)))
```

In both examples the first adjective is treated as a determiner. Note that /DET+ADJ assigns the plural category P to *old beautiful*. The combination of an adjective without a preceding determiner and a singular noun, as in *John likes old wine*, is acceptable only in the mass noun interpretation, just as in German.

The ECAT treatment of bare plurals beginning with adjectives is generally quite similar to that in DCAT (see chapter 3). But in other respects the analysis of determiners, adjectives, and nouns in ECAT is very different. The most striking difference is the fact that in ECAT determiner categories have only one segment. At first glance, one might prefer two- or three-segment categories for determiners (as in DCAT), because this characterizes the determiner intuitively as a functor: the non-initial segments represent the arguments and the first segment the result. However, the morphology of English determiner-adjective-noun combinations does not provide a basis for singling out one of these word classes as the functor.

Treating the determiner as a two-segment category in English would make sense only if the categorial correspondence between the determiner and the noun were defined in terms of the identity of the second determiner segments and the category of compatible nouns. But this would result in the postulation of unwarranted lexical ambiguities in English. Consider the following possible analysis: the indefinite article is categorized as (a ((S C))) and (an ((S -C))). Assuming that nouns are categorized as, e.g. (uncle ((-C H))) and (man ((C H))), determiner-adjective combination could be based on cancelling the last segment of the determiner category with the first segment of the adjective category with appending of the remainder, resulting in (S H). Making this work for an S determiner like *every* would require postulating a neutral segment, e.g. X, that could cancel both C and -C in the noun. The real problem arises with U/WU determiners like *the*, *some*, and *which*, where both a singular and a plural reading would have to be postulated: (the ((S X)))(car ((C -H))) versus (the ((P P))) (cars ((P -H))).

Such a multiple categorization of *the* and similar determiners for the purpose of having two-segment determiner categories in English may not seem such a costly move. But if its only purpose is to maintain a certain linguistic schema, it might as well be discarded. In the long run a minimal categorization which avoids any unwarranted lexical ambiguities will not only result in a faster computation, but also prove more descriptively adequate. The categories assigned in ECAT to determiners, adjectives, and nouns are combinatorially transparent, in that they supply the crucial information for handling agreement.

5.2   Combining noun phrases and verbs in ECAT

The word order of English sentences is interpreted in left-associative grammar in terms of a strict order of cancelling valencies. The valencies are encoded in a certain order in the category of the verb. For example, one category of *gave* is (V N D A). The non-initial segments N (nominative), D (dative) and A (accusative) are cancelled in the order of their occurrence. The valency to be filled next is always the second segment of the valency carrier. Consider the following example:

5.2.1 *John gave...*

```
(R John gave)
((*NOM+FVERB ((John gave)
            (V D A SH)
            1
            (*START (John)
                    (SH)
                    (gave)
                    (V N D A))
            2))
```

In history section 1 the valency carrier is the next word *gave* of category (V N D A). The rule /NOM+FVERB applies and cancels the nominative with the noun of category (SH). The result is the sentence start *John gave* of category (V D A SH). The next valency to be filled is the dative (D), which is now in second position.[6]

The addition of the dative is shown in example 5.2.2:

5.2.2 *John gave Mary...*

```
(R John gave Mary)
((*FVERB+MAIN ((John gave Mary)
              (V A SH SH)
              1
              (*START (John)
                      (SH)
                      (gave)
                      (V N D A))
              2
              (*NOM+FVERB (John gave)
                          (V D A SH)
                          (Mary)
                          (SH))
              3))
```

In history section 2 the rule /FVERB+MAIN applies and cancels the dative with the noun *Mary* of category (SH). The result is the sentence start *John gave Mary* of category (V A SH SH). The next and last valency to be filled is the accusative (A), which is now in second position. The completion of the derivation is shown in 5.2.3:

5.2.3 *John gave Mary a book.*

```
(R John gave Mary a book .)
((*CMPLT ((John gave Mary a book %.)
          (DECL)
          1
          (*START (John)
                  (SH)
                  (gave)
                  (V N D A))
          2
          (*NOM+FVERB (John gave)
                      (V D A SH)
                      (Mary)
                      (SH))
          3
          (*FVERB+MAIN (John gave Mary)
                       (V A SH SH)
                       (a)
                       (C))
```

---

[6]The category SH of the noun phrase is added at the end in order to provide agreement features for a possible extraposed relative clause.

```
      4
      (*FVERB+MAIN  (John gave Mary a)
                    (V C SH SH)
                    (book)
                    (C-H))
      5
      (*DET+NOUN  (John gave Mary a book)
                  (V SH SH S-H)
                  (%.)
                  (DECL V))
      6)))
```

In history section 3 the valency carrier is the sentence start *John gave Mary* of category (V A SH SH). The rule /FVERB+MAIN applies again and cancels the accusative with the determiner *a* of category C. The result is the sentence start *John gave Mary a* of category (V C SH SH). The segment C in this category indicates a sentence start ending in a determiner which requires an adjective or a singular noun beginning with a consonant. In history section 4 the rule /DET+NOUN applies (see 5.1.10 for its definition). The result is the sentence start *John gave Mary a book* of category (V SH SH S-H). Next the rule /CMPLT may apply because there are only the optional agreement segments SH SH S-H left. /CMPLT adds the punctuation mark %. of category (DECL V). The result is a complete declarative sentence of category (DECL).

Analysis in ECAT differs considerably from that in DCAT. In DCAT, noun phrases are categorized for case; a noun phrase fulfills its grammatical role by cancelling an identical segment in the valency carrier. There is no prescribed order in which valencies must be cancelled in DCAT, and therefore noun phrases may be added in any order. In ECAT, on the other hand, noun phrases are not categorized for case. Rather, the grammatical role of the noun phrase is specified indirectly by the valency position filled by the noun phrase. For example, a noun phrase filling a dative position has the grammatical role of a dative. Which valency positions are filled by which noun phrases is controlled by the order in which valencies are cancelled in ECAT. Consider for example 5.2.4, which is exactly like 5.2.3 except that *John* and *Mary* are swapped.

5.2.4 *Mary gave John a book.*

```
(R Mary gave John a book .)
((*CMPLT  ((Mary gave John a book %.)
          (DECL)
          1
          (*START  (Mary)
                   (SH)
                   (gave)
                   (V N D A))
          2
          (*NOM+FVERB  (Mary gave)
                       (V D A SH)
                       (John)
                       (SH))
```

```
    3
    (*FVERB+MAIN  (Mary gave John)
                  (V A SH SH)
                  (a)
                  (C))
    4
    (*FVERB+MAIN  (Mary gave John a)
                  (V C SH SH)
                  (book)
                  (C-H))
    5
    (*DET+NOUN  (Mary gave John a book)
                (V SH SH S-H)
                (%.)
                (DECL V))
    6)))
```

The derivation in 5.2.4 shows clearly how *Mary* happens to fulfill the role of the nominative, while *John* is the dative.

Instead of *John gave Mary the book* one may also say *John gave the book to Mary*. This construction is handled in ECAT on the basis of a second categorization of *gave* as (V N A TO). Consider 5.2.5:

5.2.5 *John gave the book to Mary.*

```
(R John gave the book to Mary .)
((*CMPLT ((John gave the book to Mary %.)
         (DECL)
         1
         (*START (John)
                 (SH)
                 (gave)
                 (V N A TO))
         2
         (*NOM+FVERB (John gave)
                     (V A TO SH)
                     (the)
                     (U))
         3
         (*FVERB+MAIN (John gave the)
                      (V U TO SH)
                      (book)
                      (C-H))
         4
         (*DET+NOUN (John gave the book)
                    (V TO SH S-H)
                    (to)
                    (TO NP))
         5
         (*FVERB+MAIN (John gave the book to)
                      (V NP SH S-H)
                      (Mary)
                      (SH))
         6
```

```
      (*PREP+NP (John gave the book to Mary)
               (V SH S-H SH)
               (%.)
               (DECL V))
  7)))
```

The noun phrase *the book* is characterized in history section 2 as an accusative:
the determiner category U cancels the A segment in the valency carrier. The
sentence start *John gave the book* is ambiguous in ECAT:

5.2.6 The two readings of *John gave the book*

```
(R John gave the book)
((*DET+NOUN ((John gave the book)
            (V A SH S-H)
            1
            (*START (John)
                    (SH)
                    (gave)
                    (V N D A))
            2
            (*NOM+FVERB (John gave)
                        (V D A SH)
                        (the)
                        (U))
            3
            (*FVERB+MAIN (John gave the)
                         (V U A SH)
                         (book)
                         (C-H))
            4))
  (*DET+NOUN ((John gave the book)
             (V TO SH S-H)
             1
             (*START (John)
                     (SH)
                     (gave)
                     (V N A TO))
             2
             (*NOM+FVERB (John gave)
                         (V A TO SH)
                         (the)
                         (U))
             3
             (*FVERB+MAIN (John gave the)
                          (V U TO SH)
                          (book)
                          (C-H))
             4)))
```

The first sentence start in 5.2.6 may only be continued with a noun phrase which
can serve as an accusative, e.g. *John gave the book a thorough reading.* When
the beginning of such a noun phrase is added to 5.2.6, the second sentence start
is eliminated because its category (V TO SH S-H) signals that a *to*-phrase is
needed at this point.

5.2.7 Elimination of the second reading in 5.2.6:

```
(R John gave the book a)
((*FVERB+MAIN ((John gave the book a)
              (V C SH S-H)
              1
              (*START (John)
                      (SH)
                      (gave)
                      (V N D A))
              2
              (*NOM+FVERB (John gave)
                          (V D A SH)
                          (the)
                          (U))
              3
              (*FVERB+MAIN (John gave the)
                           (V U A SH)
                           (book)
                           (C-H))
              4
              (*DET+NOUN (John gave the book)
                         (V A SH S-H)
                         (a)
                         (C))
              5)))
```

If the sentence start in 5.2.6 is continued with the word *to*, however, the first reading is eliminated.

Both constructions are handled by the same rules. The forms of the verb *give* have the following lexical analysis:

5.2.8 The ELEX analysis of the verb *give:*

```
(gave ((V N D A)
       (V N A TO)))
(give ((V NOM D A)
       (V NOM A TO)
(given ((HV D A)
        (HV A TO)
(gives ((V S3 D A)
        (V S3 A TO)))
(giving ((B D A)
         (B A TO)))
```

The category segment HV indicates a form which combines with an auxiliary of the *have* paradigm, while the segment B indicates a form which combines with an auxiliary of the *be* paradigm. As illustrations consider 5.2.9 and 5.2.11:

5.2.9 *John has given a book to Mary.*

```
(R John has given Mary a book .)
((*CMPLT ((John has given Mary a book %.)
         (DECL)
```

```
        1
        (*START (John)
                (SH)
                (has)
                (V S3 HV))
        2
        (*NOM+FVERB (John has)
                    (V HV SH)
                    (given)
                    (HV D A))
        3
        (*ADD-VERB (John has given)
                   (V D A SH)
                   (Mary)
                   (SH))
        4
        (*FVERB+MAIN (John has given Mary)
                     (V A SH SH)
                     (a)
                     (C))
        5
        (*FVERB+MAIN (John has given Mary a)
                     (V C SH SH)
                     (book)
                     (C-H))
        6
        (*DET+NOUN (John has given Mary a book)
                   (V SH SH S-H)
                   (%.)
                   (DECL V))
        7)))
```

5.2.10 *John was giving Mary a book.*

```
(R John was giving Mary a book .)
((*CMPLT ((John was giving Mary a book %.)
         (DECL)
         1
         (*START (John)
                 (SH)
                 (was)
                 (V S3 B))
         2
         (*NOM+FVERB (John was)
                     (V B SH)
                     (giving)
                     (B D A))
         3
         (*ADD-VERB (John was giving)
                    (V D A SH)
                    (Mary)
                    (SH))
         4
         (*FVERB+MAIN (John was giving Mary)
                      (V A SH SH)
                      (a)
```

```
                        (C))
        5
        (*FVERB+MAIN  (John was giving Mary a)
                      (V C SH SH)
                      (book)
                      (C-H))
        6
        (*DET+NOUN  (John was giving Mary a book)
                    (V SH SH S-H)
                    (%.)
                    (DECL V))
        7)))
```

In 5.2.9 and 5.2.10 the categorial operations of /ADD-VERB are based on correspondence defined in terms of identity. For example, in history section 2 of 5.2.10, the sentence start *John was* of category (V B SH) combines with the next word *giving* of category (B D A) into a new sentence start of category (V D A SH). /ADD-VERB may apply because the second segment of the sentence start is identical to the first segment of the next word. But in the case of modal verbs, the agreement condition of /ADD-VERB is not based on identity, as illustrated in 5.2.11.

5.2.11 *John might give Mary a book.*

```
(R John might give Mary a book .)
((*CMPLT ((John might give Mary a book %.)
         (DECL)
         1
         (*START (John)
                 (SH)
                 (might)
                 (V N M))
         2
         (*NOM+FVERB (John might)
                     (V M SH)
                     (give)
                     (V NOM D A))
         3
         (*ADD-VERB (John might give)
                    (V D A SH)
                    (Mary)
                    (SH))
         4
         (*FVERB+MAIN (John might give Mary)
                      (V A SH SH)
                      (a)
                      (C))
         5
         (*FVERB+MAIN (John might give Mary a)
                      (V C SH SH)
                      (book)
                      (C-H))
         6
```

```
(*DET+NOUN (John might give Mary a book)
           (V SH SH S-H)
           (%.)
           (DECL V))
7)))
```

The categorial operations of rules like /ADD-VERB will be discussed in more detail in the following section. Our present concern is showing that the valency to be cancelled next is almost always the second segment of the valency carrier. This general principle of ECAT is illustrated in the derivations 5.2.3, 5.2.4, 5.2.5, 5.2.9, 5.2.11 and 5.2.10 above. Leaving aside the details of specifying agreement, let us call this type of cancelling '2-cancel', in contrast to the type of cancelling used in DCAT, which we call A-cancelling (for anywhere-cancelling). Just as A-cancelling emerged as the main type of categorial operation in DCAT, providing for a natural treatment of free word order in German, 2-cancelling emerges as the main type of categorial operation in ECAT, providing for a natural treatment of the rigid word order of English.

Before we continue our discussion of different syntactic constructions in ECAT in section 5.3, let us explain some basic issues regarding the agreement of noun phrases and verbs in English. The analysis of noun phrases in the previous section distinguishes noun phrases as to number (S versus P) and as to whether the object denoted is a person or a thing (H versus -H).[7] The H/-H distinction anticipates the treatment of relative clauses, while the S/P distinction arises from the combination of determiners and nouns.

The number distinction in noun phrases is relevant for the definition of agreement between nominative noun phrases and verbs. Consider for example 5.2.12.

5.2.12 Number agreement in the combination of nominative noun phrases and verbs:

1. *The man walks* versus ***The men walks*
2. ***The man walk** versus *The men walk*

Another parameter affecting the agreement between a nominative noun phrase and a verb is person. Consider for example 5.2.13.

5.2.13 Person agreement in the combination of noun phrases and verbs:

1. *I am* versus **I are*
2. **You am* versus *You are*
3. *I walk* versus **The man walk*
4. **I walks* versus *The man walks*

---

[7]The present discussion applies *mutatis mutandis* to the special class of interrogative noun phrases of category WS, WP, WH, and W-H.

In older forms of English, the person parameter had a more varied morphology, in both the personal pronouns and the verbs.

5.2.14 Old and new morphology of the person parameter in the indicative present tense:

Old forms:	Today's forms:
I walk	*I walk*
thou walkest	*you walk*
he, she, it walketh	*he, she, it walks*
we walk	*we walk*
ye walk	*you walk*
they walk	*they walk*

We see that the four different forms of the verb have decreased to two, *walk* and *walks*. In the past tense, furthermore, there is only one verb form for all six person/number combinations, namely *walked*. Also, the second person pronouns *thou* and *ye* are now represented by only one form, *you*.

Similar simplifications occurred in the paradigms of the auxiliaries and modals *have, do, can, may,* etc.[8]: there are at most two forms in the present tense (one for the third person singular and one for the other person/number instances), and one form in the past tense. The auxiliary *be* is the only complex paradigm that remains.

In verbs other than the auxiliary *be*, the nominative is represented by the category segments N, S3, and NOM. The nominative is represented in the past tense of verbs by N, in third person singular present tense forms by S3, and by NOM in the other present tense forms. As an illustration consider the following ELEX analyses of the different finite forms of *walk, see, have, do,* and *can*:

5.2.15 ELEX analysis of the finite forms of *walk, see, have, do,* and *can*:

```
(walk ((V NOM)))      (walks ((V S3)))      (walked ((V N)))
(see  ((V NOM A)))    (sees  ((V S3 A)))    (saw    ((V N A)))
(have ((V NOM HV)))   (has   ((V S3 HV)))   (had    ((V N HV)))
(do   ((V NOM DO)))   (does  ((V S3 DO)))   (did    ((V N DO)))
                                            (can    ((V N M)))
                                            (could  ((V N M)))
```

HV indicates a form of the auxiliary *have*, DO a form of the auxiliary *do*, and M a form of a modal verb like *can*.

Noun phrases of category (SH) or (S-H) may fill N and S3 positions in the verb. This is illustrated by the following ECAT derivations:

5.2.16 *The man walks.*

---

[8]See Curme (1947)

```
(R the man walks .)
((*CMPLT ((the man walks %.)
          (DECL)
          1
          (*START (the)
                  (U)
                  (man)
                  (CH))
          2
          (*DET+NOUN (the man)
                  (SH)
                  (walks)
                  (V S3))
          3
          (*NOM+FVERB (the man walks)
                  (V SH)
                  (%.)
                  (DECL V))
          4)))
```

5.2.17 *The man walked.*

```
(R the man walked .)
((*CMPLT ((the man walked %.)
          (DECL)
          1
          (*START (the)
                  (U)
                  (man)
                  (CH))
          2
          (*DET+NOUN (the man)
                  (SH)
                  (walked)
                  (V N))
          3
          (*NOM+FVERB (the man walked)
                  (V SH)
                  (%.)
                  (DECL V))
          4)))
```

5.2.18 *The car runs.*

```
(R the car runs .)
((*CMPLT ((the car runs %.)
          (DECL)
          1
          (*START (the)
                  (U)
                  (car)
                  (C-H))
          2
          (*DET+NOUN (the car)
                  (S-H)
                  (runs)
```

```
                    (V S3))
        3
        (*NOM+FVERB (the car runs)
                    (V S-H)
                    (%.)
                    (DECL V))
        4)))
```

5.2.19 *The car ran.*

```
(R the car ran .)
((*CMPLT ((the car ran %.)
        (DECL)
        1
        (*START (the)
                (U)
                (car)
                (C-H))
        2
        (*DET+NOUN (the car)
                   (S-H)
                   (ran)
                   (V N))
        3
        (*NOM+FVERB (the car ran)
                    (V S-H)
                    (%.)
                    (DECL V))
        4)))
```

Noun phrases of category (PH) and (P-H) may fill NOM and N positions.
This is illustrated by the following ECAT analyses:

5.2.20 *The men walk.*

```
(R the men walk .)
((*CMPLT ((the men walk %.)
        (DECL)
        1
        (*START (the)
                (U)
                (men)
                (PH))
        2
        (*DET+NOUN (the men)
                   (PH)
                   (walk)
                   (V NOM))
        3
        (*NOM+FVERB (the men walk)
                    (V PH)
                    (%.)
                    (DECL V))
        4)))
```

5.2.21 *The men walked.*

```
(R the men walked .)
((*CMPLT ((the men walked %.)
          (DECL)
          1
          (*START (the)
                  (U)
                  (men)
                  (PH))
          2
          (*DET+NOUN (the men)
                     (PH)
                     (walked)
                     (V N))
          3
          (*NOM+FVERB (the men walked)
                      (V PH)
                      (%.)
                      (DECL V))
          4)))
```

5.2.22 *The cars run.*

```
(R the cars run .)
((*CMPLT ((the cars run %.)
          (DECL)
          1
          (*START (the)
                  (U)
                  (cars)
                  (P-H))
          2
          (*DET+NOUN (the cars)
                     (P-H)
                     (run)
                     (V NOM))
          3
          (*NOM+FVERB (the cars run)
                      (V P-H)
                      (%.)
                      (DECL V))
          4)))
```

5.2.23 *The cars ran.*

```
(R the cars ran .)
((*CMPLT ((the cars ran %.)
          (DECL)
          1
          (*START (the)
                  (U)
                  (cars)
                  (P-H))
          2
          (*DET+NOUN (the cars)
                     (P-H)
                     (ran)
```

```
                (V N))
     3
     (*NOM+FVERB (the cars ran)
                (V P-H)
                (%.)
                (DECL V))
     4)))
```

It is not grammatical, however, to fill a NOM position with an SH or S-II noun phrase, or to fill an S3 position with a PH or P-H noun phrase, as illustrated in 5.2.24 and 5.2.25:

5.2.24 *The man walk.*

```
(R the man walk .)
[ERROR "Ungrammatical continuation at:"
((*DET+NOUN ((the man)
            (SH)
            1
            (*START (the)
                    (U)
                    (man)
                    (CH))
            2))
        (*START ((walk)
                (V NOM]
```

5.2.25 *The cars runs.*

```
(R the cars runs .)
[ERROR "Ungrammatical continuation at:"
((*DET+NOUN ((the cars)
            (P-H)
            1
            (*START (the)
                    (U)
                    (cars)
                    (P-H))
            2))
        (*START ((runs)
                (V S3]
```

This completes discussion of the correlation between the third person noun phrase categories (SH), (S-H), (PH), and (P-H), and N, NOM, and S3 nominative valencies.

The nominative segments N, NOM, and S3 suffice for all main verbs, auxiliaries, and modals of English except the auxiliary *be*.

5.2.26 The present and past tense indicative of *be:*

I am   *I was*
you are   *you were*
he, she, it is   *he, she, it was*

we are   we were
you are   you were
they are   they were

Because of the special forms *am* and *was* for first person singular, nominative valencies in the *be* paradigm are represented by the segments S1, S3, and NM.

5.2.27 ELEX analysis of the finite forms of *be:*

```
(am  ((V S1 B)))  (is  ((V S3 B)))  (are  ((V NM B)))
(was ((V S1 B)))  (was ((V S3 B)))  (were ((V NM B)))
```

The nominative is represented by S1 in the first person singular present and past tense of *be*, by S3 in the third person singular present and past tense, and by NM in the remaining forms, which may combine with noun phrases of second person singular and first, second, and third person plural. The segment B indicates a form of the auxiliary *be*. [9]

The distinction between different persons is also reflected in the categorization of the personal pronouns.

5.2.28 Categorization of the nominative and non-nominative forms of the personal pronouns in ELEX:

```
(I  ((S1)))          (he  ((S3)))  (she ((S3)))

        (you ((PH)))                          (it ((S-H)))

   (me ((:S1)))      (him ((:S3))) (her ((:S3)))

 (we ((P1)))         (they ((P3)))
 (us ((:P1)))        (them ((:P3)))
```

The personal pronouns differ from regular (SH), (S-H), (PH), and (P-H) noun phrases in that most of them distinguish morphologically between nominative and non-nominative uses. The non-nominative form of a personal pronoun has the same category as the nominative form, except for the added ':'. The person and number information in non-nominative forms is needed for relative clause agreement.

Some personal pronouns denote persons, such as *I, you, he, she, we,* and *they.* One says *I, who...*, not **I, which.* This fact is treated in the rule /NOM+REL-PRO, which has a clause saying that the next word must be *who* rather than *which* if the category of the sentence start ends with the segment SH, PH, S1, :S1,

---

[9]If we wanted to represent nominative valencies with the same segments for all verbs of English, including the auxiliary *be*, we would have to extend the distinction between first and third person singular from *be* to all present tense and past tense forms. This would lead to two additional lexical readings for all verbs.

S3, :S3, P1, :P1, P3 or :P3. The pronoun *you* may be used to address one or more persons. For the sake of simplicity, *you* has the category (PH), which accounts for nominative and non-nominative use and includes the singular as a default. The pronoun *it* has the category (S-H), because it has both nominative and non-nominative functions and may denote only things: one says *it, which...,* not **it, who....* The pronouns *he* and *she* have the special S3 category, because they can be used only as nominatives. The pronouns *they* and *them,* finally, may denote either persons or things. This fact is treated in the rule /NOM+RELPRO, which has a clause saying that the next word must be *which* if the category of the sentence start ends with the segment S-H, P-H, P3 or :P3. In other words, the fact that *they* and *them* can be followed by either *who* or *which* is handled by listing them in both relevant clauses of /NOUN+RELPRO.

The combination of a nominative with the finite verb in simple declarative sentences is handled by the ECAT rule /NOM+FVERB, which is stated below:

5.2.29 Simplified declarative statement of /NOM+FVERB:

> If the category of the first expression contains a WH, W-H, WS, or WP segment, the value of the local variable ARG is set to the last category segment of the first expression. Otherwise the value of ARG is set to the first category segment of the first input expression. The **input condition** of /NOM+FVERB specifies that the category of the sentence start may not contain a DO, HV, or B segment, and the next word must be a finite verb. Furthermore, (i) if ARG is S1, then the second category segment of the next word must be S1, NOM, or N; (ii) if ARG is PH, P-H, WP, P1, or P3, then the second category segment of the next word must be NM, NOM, or N; (iii) if ARG is SH, S-H, S3, WH, W-H, or WS, then the second category segment of the second expression must be S3 or N. The **output condition** of /NOM+FVERB says: if ARG is (SH), (S-H), (PH), or (P-H), then the output category is the category of the second expression minus the second segment, plus the value of ARG added at the end.

This definition describes all /NOM+FVERB applications in the examples given above. The actual formulation of /NOM+FVERB is more complicated because of certain possible inversions in relative clauses, e.g. *the man whom Mary + loves.* Since word order in English main clauses is essentially the same as in subordinate clauses, main clauses and subordinate clauses are derived with the same rules.

5.3   Passive and other constructions with auxiliaries in ECAT

The ELEX definition of all forms of the verb *give* in 5.2.8 above provides no special category segments to indicate passive forms. Instead a passive category results when a sentence start with a B segment (indicating presence of the auxiliary *be*) in second position combines with a next word which has HV as its first category segment:

```
John was + given     >   John was given
(V B SH)   (HV D A)      (V A AG SH)
```

This categorial operation is performed by the rule /ADD-VERB. Consider the following derivation.

5.3.1 *John was given a book by Mary.*

```
(R John was given a book by Mary .)
((*CMPLT ((John was given a book by Mary %.)
         (DECL)
         1
         (*START (John)
                 (SH)
                 (was)
                 (V S3 B))
         2
         (*NOM+FVERB (John was)
                 (V B SH)
                 (given)
                 (HV D A))
         3
         (*ADD-VERB (John was given)
                 (V A AG SH)
                 (a)
                 (C))
         4
         (*FVERB+MAIN (John was given a)
                 (V C AG SH)
                 (book)
                 (C-H))
         5
         (*DET+NOUN (John was given a book)
                 (V AG SH S-H)
                 (by)
                 (AG NP))
         6
         (*FVERB+MAIN (John was given a book by)
                 (V NP SH S-H)
                 (Mary)
                 (SH))
         7
         (*PREP+NP (John was given a book by Mary)
```

```
                    (V SH SH)
                    (%.)
                    (DECL V))
              8))
 (*CMPLT ((John was given a book by Mary %.)
          (DECL)
          1
          (*START (John)
                  (SH)
                  (was)
                  (V S3 B))
          2
          (*NOM+FVERB (John was)
                      (V B SH)
                      (given)
                      (HV D A))
          3
          (*ADD-VERB (John was given)
                     (V A AG SH)
                     (a)
                     (C))
          4
          (*FVERB+MAIN (John was given a)
                       (V C AG SH)
                       (book)
                       (C-H))
          5
          (*DET+NOUN (John was given a book)
                     (V AG SH S-H)
                     (by)
                     (PNM NP))
          6
          (*NOUN+PNM (John was given a book by)
                     (V NP AG SH)
                     (Mary)
                     (SH))
          7
          (*PREP+NP (John was given a book by Mary)
                    (V AG SH)
                    (%.)
                    (DECL V))
          8)))
```

The above derivation characterizes the input sentence as ambiguous. In the first reading, *by Mary* is analyzed as the agent; in the second, as a postnominal modifier of *book*. In other words, in the first reading *Mary* gives the book to John, while in the second reading *Mary* is the author of the book. The AG segment in passive sentence starts represents an optional valency position. As an example of a passive without an agent phrase consider 5.3.2.

5.3.2 *John was given a book.*

```
(R John was given a book .)
((*CMPLT ((John was given a book %.)
```

```
(DECL)
1
(*START  (John)
         (SH)
         (was)
         (V S3 B))
2
(*NOM+FVERB  (John was)
             (V B SH)
             (given)
             (HV D A))
3
(*ADD-VERB  (John was given)
            (V A AG SH)
            (a)
            (C))
4
(*FVERB+MAIN  (John was given a)
              (V C AG SH)
              (book)
              (C-H))
5
(*DET+NOUN  (John was given a book)
            (V AG SH S-H)
            (%.)
            (DECL V))
6)))
```

The rule /CMPLT, which adds the punctuation mark, treats AG as an optional segment, like S-H or PH. Sentences may be completed without filling the AG valency, as shown by the above derivation.

English does not indicate whether the nominative of a passive sentence represents the 'direct object' or the 'indirect object'. Consider the 5.3.3:

5.3.3 The inherent ambiguity of certain English passives:

A child was given a father.

reading 1: Someone gives a child to a father

reading 2: Someone gives a father to a child

This ambiguity occurs only with three-place verbs like *give*. Furthermore, it is restricted to the forms of *give* characterized by the category (V N D A); the forms characterized by the category (V N A TO) indicate the 'indirect object' with the preposition *to*.

Since the alternative interpretations are always theoretically possible, there is no reason to define alternative syntactic derivations. The only way of determining the 'underlying' function of the nominative in 5.3.3 is by using the context and knowledge of the world. The fact that *John* in 5.3.2 should be interpreted as the 'direct object' rather than the 'indirect object' is not treated as part of the grammatical analysis in ECAT. As an example in which the most likely interpretation of the nominative is as the 'direct object', consider 5.3.4:

5.3.4 *A book was given John by Mary.*

```
(R a book was given John by Mary .)
((*CMPLT ((a book was given John by Mary %.)
        (DECL)
        1
        (*START (a)
                (C)
                (book)
                (C-H))
        2
        (*DET+NOUN (a book)
                (S-H)
                (was)
                (V S3 B))
        3
        (*NOM+FVERB (a book was)
                (V B S-H)
                (given)
                (HV D A))
        4
        (*ADD-VERB (a book was given)
                (V A AG S-H)
                (John)
                (SH))
        5
        (*FVERB+MAIN (a book was given John)
                (V AG S-H SH)
                (by)
                (AG NP))
        6
        (*FVERB+MAIN (a book was given John by)
                (V NP S-H SH)
                (Mary)
                (SH))
        7
        (*PREP+NP (a book was given John by Mary)
                (V S-H SH)
                (%.)
                (DECL V))
        8)))
```

Passives formed with the second reading of the past participle *given*, characterized by the category (HV A TO), are derived in the same way as the passives described above. Consider 5.3.5:

5.3.5 *A book was given to John by Mary.*

```
(R a book was given to John by Mary .)
((*CMPLT ((a book was given to John by Mary %.)
```

```
(DECL)
1
(*START (a)
        (C)
        (book)
        (C-H))
2
(*DET+NOUN (a book)
           (S-H)
           (was)
           (V S3 B))
3
(*NOM+FVERB (a book was)
            (V B S-H)
            (given)
            (HV A TO))
4
(*ADD-VERB (a book was given)
           (V TO AG S-H)
           (to)
           (TO NP))
5
(*FVERB+MAIN (a book was given to)
             (V NP AG S-H)
             (John)
             (SH))
6
(*PREP+NP (a book was given to John)
          (V AG S-H SH)
          (by)
          (AG NP))
7
(*FVERB+MAIN (a book was given to John by)
             (V NP S-H SH)
             (Mary)
             (SH))
8
(*PREP+NP (a book was given to John by Mary)
          (V S-H SH SH)
          (%.)
          (DECL V))
9)))
```

Once ADD-VERB has combined the sentence start *a book was* of category
(V B S-H) with *given* of category (HV A TO) into the new sentence start *a
book was given* of category (V TO AG S-H), the second segment is TO and the
only possible continuation at this point is with a *to*-phrase. After adding the
to-phrase, the optional segment AG moves into second position.

The rule /ADD-VERB handles not only passive, but all other complex auxiliary constructions as well. The most simple case is illustrated in 5.2.9 and
5.2.10 above (compare their history sections 2 and 3). In 5.2.9, the input expressions of /ADD-VERB have the categories (V HV SH) and (HV D A); the
output category (V D A SH) results from 2-cancelling the HV segment in the

sentence start, adding both the remainder of the category of the next word and the remainder of the sentence start category. Similarly in 5.2.10: there the input categories are (V B SH) and (B D A), and the output category is (V D A SH).

A more interesting case is illustrated in 5.2.11, where the sentence start *John might* of category (V M SH) combines with the next word *give*. If we wanted to provide the categorial operation of this combination an analysis exactly parallel to those described above, we would have to assign *give* the reading (M D A) in addition to the reading of the finite present tense form of category (V NOM D A)[10]. But little would be gained by postulating such a lexical ambiguity. Instead, /ADD-VERB has a clause saying: if the second segment of the sentence start is M and the first two segments of the next word are V and NOM, then the output category consists of the first segment of the first category, and the tails of the second and first input categories beginning with the third segment. In other words, the category of *John might give* is (V D A SH) or (V A TO SH), depending on which paradigm of *give* is chosen. Thus *John gave, John has given, John was giving,* and *John might give* all have the same categories. They constitute equivalent sentence starts (see 4.4 above).

The forms of the auxiliary *do* are characterized by the segment DO. For example, *did* and *didn't* have the category (V N DO). *Do* behaves like the modals in that it combines with unmarked present tense forms, as illustrated in 5.3.6:

5.3.6 *The man didn't give Mary a book.*

```
(R the man didn't give Mary a book .)
((*CMPLT ((the man didn't give Mary a book %.)
         (DECL)
         1
         (*START (the)
                 (U)
                 (man)
                 (CH))
         2
         (*DET+NOUN (the man)
                    (SH)
                    (didn't)
                    (V N DO))
         3
         (*NOM+FVERB (the man didn't)
                     (V DO SH)
                     (give)
                     (V NOM D A))
         4
         (*ADD-VERB (the man didn't give)
                    (V D A SH)
                    (Mary)
```

---

[10]For the sake of simplicity, the present discussion is limited to (V N D A) forms of *give*. It applies *mutatis mutandis* to the (V N A TO) forms as well as to two-place and one-place verbs, e.g. *John is sleeping, John has slept,* and *John is sleeping*.

```
                  (SH))
        5
        (*FVERB+MAIN  (the man didn't give Mary)
                      (V A SH SH)
                      (a)
                      (C))
        6
        (*FVERB+MAIN  (the man didn't give Mary a)
                      (V C SH SH)
                      (book)
                      (C-H))
        7
        (*DET+NOUN  (the man didn't give Mary a book)
                    (V SH SH S-H)
                    (%.)
                    (DECL V))
        8)))
```

The categorial operation of /ADD-VERB in history section 3 is analogous to example 5.2.11: the input categories (V DO SH) and (V NOM D A) combine into (V D A SH). Modals and *do* behave similarly in other respects (e.g. interrogatives), but they differ with regard to complex verb constructions involving *have* or *be*. Compare 5.3.7 and 5.3.8:

5.3.7 **The man didn't have given Mary a book.*

```
(R the man didn't have given Mary a book %.)
[ERROR "Ungrammatical continuation at:"
        ((*NOM+FVERB ((the man didn't)
                      (V DO SH)
                      1
                      (*START (the)
                              (U)
                              (man)
                              (CH))
                      2
                      (*DET+NOUN (the man)
                                 (SH)
                                 (didn't)
                                 (V N DO))
                      3))
        (*START ((have)
                 (V NOM HV]
```

5.3.8 *The man couldn't have given Mary a book.*

```
(R the man couldn't have given Mary a book %.)
((*CMPLT ((the man couldn't have given Mary a book %.)
         (DECL)
         1
         (*START (the)
                 (U)
                 (man)
                 (CH))
```

```
      2
      (*DET+NOUN (the man)
                 (SH)
                 (couldn't)
                 (V N M))
      3
      (*NOM+FVERB (the man couldn't)
                 (V M SH)
                 (have)
                 (V NOM HV))
      4
      (*ADD-VERB (the man couldn't have)
                 (V HV SH)
                 (given)
                 (HV D A))
      5
      (*ADD-VERB (the man couldn't have given)
                 (V D A SH)
                 (Mary)
                 (SH))
      6
      (*FVERB+MAIN (the man couldn't have given Mary)
                 (V A SH SH)
                 (a)
                 (C))
      7
      (*FVERB+MAIN (the man couldn't have given Mary a)
                 (V C SH SH)
                 (book)
                 (C-H))
      8
      (*DET+NOUN (the man couldn't have given Mary a book)
                 (V SH SH S-H)
                 (%.)
                 (DECL V))
      9)))
```

Also, *The man did be giving Mary a book* and *The man did have been giving Mary a book* are ungrammatical and rejected by ECAT, while the corresponding sentences with a modal are grammatical:

5.3.9 *The man could be giving Mary a book.*

```
(R the man could be giving Mary a book %.)
((*CMPLT ((the man could be giving Mary a book %.)
         (DECL)
      1
      (*START (the)
                 (U)
                 (man)
                 (CH))
      2
      (*DET+NOUN (the man)
                 (SH)
                 (could)
```

```
                        (V N M))
        3
        (*NOM+FVERB (the man could)
                    (V M SH)
                    (be)
                    (M B))
        4
        (*ADD-VERB (the man could be)
                   (V B SH)
                   (giving)
                   (B D A))
        5
        (*ADD-VERB (the man could be giving)
                   (V D A SH)
                   (Mary)
                   (SH))
        6
        (*FVERB+MAIN (the man could be giving Mary)
                     (V A SH SH)
                     (a)
                     (C))
        7
        (*FVERB+MAIN (the man could be giving Mary a)
                     (V C SH SH)
                     (book)
                     (C-H))
        8
        (*DET+NOUN (the man could be giving Mary a book)
                   (V SH SH S-H)
                   (%.)
                   (DECL V))
        9)))
```

Since *do* cannot combine with *have*, it is not possible to form passives with *do*. But the corresponding constructions with a modal are grammatical:

5.3.10 *A book could have been given to Mary by the man.*

```
(R a book could have been given to Mary by the man .)
((*CMPLT ((a book could have been given to Mary by the man %.)
         (DECL)
         1
         (*START (a)
                 (C)
                 (book)
                 (C-H))
         2
         (*DET+NOUN (a book)
                    (S-H)
                    (could)
                    (V N M))
         3
         (*NOM+FVERB (a book could)
                     (V M S-H)
                     (have)
```

```
                   (V NOM HV))
        4
        (*ADD-VERB (a book could have)
                   (V HV S-H)
                   (been)
                   (HV B))
        5
        (*ADD-VERB (a book could have been)
                   (V B C H)
                   (given)
                   (HV A TO))
        6
        (*ADD-VERB (a book could have been given)
                   (V TO AG S-H)
                   (to)
                   (TO NP))
        7
        (*FVERB+MAIN (a book could have been given to)
                   (V NP AG S-H)
                   (Mary)
                   (SH))
        8
        (*PREP+NP (a book could have been given to Mary)
                   (V AG S-H SH)
                   (by)
                   (AG NP))
        9
        (*FVERB+MAIN (a book could have been given to Mary by)
                   (V NP S-H SH)
                   (the)
                   (U))
        10
        (*PREP+NP (a book could have been given to Mary by the)
                   (V U S-H SH)
                   (man)
                   (CH))
        11
        (*DET+NOUN (a book could have been given to Mary by the man)
                   (V S-H SH SH)
                   (%.)
                   (DECL V))
        12)))
```

Note that in the examples 5.3.8 and 5.3.9 the rule /ADD-VERB applies twice, and in 5.3.10 three times in a row. Each application of /ADD-VERB uses the standard categorial operations described above. In other words, the different combinations for different inputs are not only used in constructions where /ADD-VERB applies only once, and thus provide a complete and simple explanation of complex verb constructions in English.

For example, in history section 3 of 5.2.22 the sentence start *a book could* of category (V M S-H) combines with *have* of category (V NOM HV). The result category is (V HV S-H). As far as /ADD-VERB is concerned, this combination is exactly like the combination of *the man could* of category (V M SH) with *see* of category (V NOM A). In the latter case the output category is (V A SH). The difference in the respective output categories (V HV S-H) and (V A SH) is a matter of the different tails of the respective second categories.

In history section 4 of 5.3.8 the sentence start *a book could have* of category (V HV S-H) combines with *been* of category (HV B). The result category is (V B S-H). As far as /ADD-VERB is concerned, this combination is exactly like the combination of *the man has* of category (V HV SH) with the next word *seen* of category (HV A). In the latter case the output category is (V A SH). The difference in the respective output categories is again a matter of the different tails of the respective second categories.

In history section 5 of 5.3.8 the sentence start *a book could have been* of category (V B S-H) combines with the next word *given* of category (HV A TO). The result category is (V TO AG S-H). As far as /ADD-VERB is concerned, this combination is exactly like the combination of *the man was* of category (V B SH) with the next word *seen* of category (HV A). In the latter case the output category is (V AG SH). Thus the local nature of possible continuations may also be observed in English.

5.4   Relative clauses in ECAT

Relative clauses of English are characterized by the following alternation in word order:

5.4.1 Word order alternations in English relative clauses:

1. *The man who loves Mary is reading a book.*

2. *The man who Mary loves is reading a book.*

In both examples the relative pronoun *who* serves as a subordinating conjunction and a valency filler in the relative clause.[11] The two examples differ, however, in that *who* functions as a nominative in the first case, and as an accusative in the second. This difference in grammatical function is encoded by means of the different word order. Compare the ECAT derivations 5.4.2 and 5.4.3:

5.4.2 *The man who loves Mary is reading a book.*

```
(R the man who loves Mary is reading a book .)
((*CMPLT ((the man who loves Mary is reading a book %.)
        (DECL)
        1
        (*START (the)
                (U)
                (man)
```

---

[11]Strictly speaking, the relative pronoun should be *whom* in the second example. But for most speakers of English this distinction is becoming obsolete. ECAT allows both *who* and *whom* in oblique case positions, but rejects *whom* in nominative positions.

```
                    (CH))
            2
            (*DET+NOUN (the man)
                        (SH)
                        (who)
                        (WH))
            3
            (*START-RELCL (the man who)
                            (SH WS #)
                            (loves)
                            (V S3 A))
            4
            (*NOM+FVERB (the man who loves)
                        (SH A)
                        (Mary)
                        (SH))
            5
            (*FVERB+MAIN (the man who loves Mary)
                            (SH SH)
                            (is)
                            (V S3 B))
            6
            (*NOM+FVERB (the man who loves Mary is)
                        (V B)
                        (reading)
                        (B A))
            7
            (*ADD-VERB (the man who loves Mary is reading)
                        (V A)
                        (a)
                        (C))
            8
            (*FVERB+MAIN (the man who loves Mary is reading a)
                            (V C)
                            (book)
                            (C-H))
            9
            (*DET+NOUN (the man who loves Mary is reading a book)
                        (V S-H)
                        (%.)
                        (DECL V))
            10)))
```

5.4.3 *The man who Mary loves is reading a book.*

```
(R the man who Mary loves is reading a book .)
((*CMPLT ((the man who Mary loves is reading a book %.)
            (DECL)
            1
            (*START (the)
                    (U)
                    (man)
                    (CH))
            2
            (*DET+NOUN (the man)
                        (SH)
```

```
                    (who)
                    (WH))
        3
        (*START-RELCL (the man who)
                    (SH WS #)
                    (Mary)
                    (SH))
        4
        (*ADD-NOM (the man who Mary)
                    (SH WS SH #)
                    (loves)
                    (V S3 A))
        5
        (*NOM+FVERB (the man who Mary loves)
                    (SH)
                    (is)
                    (V S3 B))
        6
        (*NOM+FVERB (the man who Mary loves is)
                    (V B)
                    (reading)
                    (B A))
        7
        (*ADD-VERB (the man who Mary loves is reading)
                    (V A)
                    (a)
                    (C))
        8
        (*FVERB+MAIN (the man who Mary loves is reading a)
                    (V C)
                    (book)
                    (C-H))
        9
        (*DET+NOUN (the man who Mary loves is reading a book)
                    (V S-H)
                    (%.)
                    (DECL V))
        10)))
```

The difference in word order is reflected in the two sequences of rules. Consider
5.4.4

5.4.4 The rule sequences in sentences 5.4.2 and 5.4.3:

5.4.2:	5.4.3:
*START	*START
*DET+NOUN	*DET+NOUN
*START-RELCL	*START-RELCL
*NOM+FVERB	*ADD-NOM
*FVERB+MAIN	*NOM+FVERB
*NOM+FVERB	*NOM+FVERB
*ADD+VERB	*ADD+VERB

```
        *FVERB+MAIN              *FVERB+VERB
        *DET+NOUN                *DET+NOUN
        *COMPLT                  *CMPLT
```

The rule package *START-RELCL contains both /NOM+FVERB and /ADD-NOM. In sentences 5.4.2 and 5.4.3, these two rules apply to the same sentence starts but to different next words. /NOM+FVERB and /ADD-NOM differ not only in their input conditions, but also in their output specifications: /NOM+FVERB is based on 'argument cancelling' while /ADD-NOM is 'argument adding' (see 4.1 above). The relevant history sections are repeated below:

5.4.5 The categorial operations of /NOM+FVERB in sentence 5.4.2 and /ADD-NOM in sentence 5.4.3:

```
3                                   3
(*START-RELCL (the man who)         (*START-RELCL (the man who)
              (SH WS #)                           (SH WS #)
              (loves)                             (Mary)
              (V S3 A))                           (SH))
4                                   4
(*NOM+FVERB (the man who loves)     (*ADD-NOM (the man who Mary)
            (SH A)                            (SH WS SH #)
```

/NOM+FVERB combines the categories (SH WS #) and (V S3 A) into (SH A). In other words, the first two segments of (V S3 A) cancel the last two segments of (SH WS #). The output category consists of the initial segment of the first category and the remainder of the second. The result category (SH A) is just what is needed in order for /FVERB+MAIN to apply. After the accusative valency has been cancelled, the result is the noun phrase *the man who loves Mary* of category (SH SH). The difference between the category (SH SH) and the category (SH), as in (John ((SH))), only concerns possible relative clauses.[12] As far as the main clause is concerned, the expression *the man who loves Mary* behaves just like a simple proper name.

/ADD-NOM, on the other hand, combines the categories (SH WS #) and (SH) into (SH WS SH #). The category of the second expression is added between the WH and the subclause delimiter # of the first category. *the man who Mary* is an expression which needs a verb that will cancel the accumulated valencies. This operation is performed by the next rule, /NOM+FVERB. The relevant history section of derivation 5.4.3 is repeated below:

5.4.6 Wholesale cancelling in 5.4.3:

```
4
(*ADD-NOM (the man who Mary)
```

---

[12]If *the man who loves Mary* is continued with a relative clause, it will modify the second SH, representing *Mary* (assuming it is not extraposed); but if *John* is continued with a relative clause, it will modify the first (and only) SH, representing *John*.

```
               (SH WS SH #)
               (loves)
               (V S3 A))
      5
      (*NOM+FVERB (the man who Mary loves)
                  (SH)
```

/NOM+FVERB cancels the WS in (SH WS SH #) with the first two segments
of (V S3 A), and the A with the SH #. The result category is (SH). After
completion of the relative clauses in history sections 5 of sentences 5.4.2 and
5.4.3, the derivations represent syntactically equivalent sentence starts. In both
derivations the rule package is *NOM+FVERB and the category (V B).

Next let us consider the alternation discussed above in relative clauses with
complex verb phrases. Compare the derivations 5.4.7 and 5.4.8.

5.4.7 *The man who doesn't love Mary is reading a book.*

```
(R the man who doesn't love Mary is reading a book .)
((*CMPLT ((the man who doesn't love Mary is reading a book %.)
         (DECL)
      1
      (*START (the)
              (U)
              (man)
              (CH))
      2
      (*DET+NOUN (the man)
                 (SH)
                 (who)
                 (WH))
      3
      (*START-RELCL (the man who)
                    (SH WS #)
                    (doesn't)
                    (V S3 DO))
      4
      (*NOM+FVERB (the man who doesn't)
                  (SH DO)
                  (love)
                  (V NOM A))
      5
      (*ADD-VERB (the man who doesn't love)
                 (SH A)
                 (Mary)
                 (SH))
      6
      (*FVERB+MAIN (the man who doesn't love Mary)
                   (SH SH)
                   (is)
                   (V S3 B))
      7
      (*NOM+FVERB (the man who doesn't love Mary is)
                  (V B)
                  (reading)
```

```
                       (B A))
            8
            (*ADD-VERB (the man who doesn't love Mary is reading)
                       (V A)
                       (a)
                       (C))
            9
            (*FVERB+MAIN (the man who doesn't love Mary is reading a)
                         (V C)
                         (book)
                         (C-H))
            10
            (*DET+NOUN (the man who doesn't love Mary is reading a book)
                       (V S-H)
                       (%.)
                       (DECL V))
            11)))
```

5.4.8 *The man who Mary doesn't love is reading a book.*

```
(R the man who Mary doesn't love is reading a book .)
((*CMPLT ((the man who Mary doesn't love is reading a book %.)
         (DECL)
         1
         (*START (the)
                 (U)
                 (man)
                 (CH))
         2
         (*DET+NOUN (the man)
                    (SH)
                    (who)
                    (WH))
         3
         (*START-RELCL (the man who)
                       (SH WS #)
                       (Mary)
                       (SH))
         4
         (*ADD-NOM (the man who Mary)
                   (SH WS SH #)
                   (doesn't)
                   (V S3 DO))
         5
         (*NOM+FVERB (the man who Mary doesn't)
                     (SH DO WS)
                     (love)
                     (V NOM A))
         6
         (*ADD-VERB (the man who Mary doesn't love)
                    (SH)
                    (is)
                    (V S3 B))
         7
         (*NOM+FVERB (the man who Mary doesn't love is)
                     (V B)
```

```
                    (reading)
                    (B A))
        8
        (*ADD-VERB (the man who Mary doesn't love is reading)
                   (V A)
                   (a)
                   (C))
        9
        (*FVERB+MAIN (the man who Mary doesn't love is reading a)
                     (V C)
                     (book)
                     (C-H))
        10
        (*DET+NOUN (the man who Mary doesn't love is reading a book)
                   (V S-H)
                   (%.)
                   (DECL V))
        11)))
```

The rule sequence in the derivations 5.4.7 and 5.4.8 differs from that in sentences 5.4.2 and 5.4.3: after the first application of /NOM+FVERB there is the additional rule /ADD-VERB, which is already familiar from section 5.3.

5.4.9 The rule sequences in 5.4.7 and 5.4.8:

5.4.7:	5.4.8:
*START	*START
*DET+NOUN	*DET+NOUN
*START-RELCL	*START-RELCL
*NOM+FVERB	*ADD-NOM
*ADD-VERB	*NOM+FVERB
*FVERB+MAIN	*ADD-VERB
*NOM+FVERB	*NOM+FVERB
*ADD+VERB	*ADD+VERB
*FVERB+MAIN	*FVERB+VERB
*DET+NOUN	*DET+NOUN
*COMPLT	*CMPLT

Let us compare the sentences 5.4.2 and 5.4.7, which have in common that the relative pronouns function as the nominatives of the subordinate clauses. The two derivations diverge after the third combination. The relevant history sections are repeated below for convenience:

5.4.10 The operations of /NOM+FVERB in the derivations 5.4.2 and 5.4.7:

```
3                                          3
(*START-RELCL (the man who)               (*START-RELCL (the man who)
              (SH WS #)                                  (SH WS #)
              (loves)                                    (doesn't)
              (V S3 A))                                  (V S3 DO))
4                                          4
(*NOM+FVERB (the man who loves)           (*NOM+FVERB (the man who doesn't)
            (SH A)                                    (SH DO)
```

We see that the categorial operations of /NOM+FVERB are the same in the
two derivations. The output categories differ because the respective next words
have different segments in the third positions of their categories.

The rule package *NOM+FVERB contains the rules /FVERB+MAIN and
/ADD-VERB. These rules apply in history sections 4 of sentences 5.4.2 and
5.4.7, respectively, which are repeated below for convenience:

5.4.11 The operation of /FVERB+MAIN in derivation 5.4.2 and /ADD-VERB
in 5.4.7:

```
4                                          4
(*NOM+FVERB (the man who loves)           (*NOM+FVERB (the man who doesn't)
            (SH A)                                    (SH DO)
            (Mary)                                    (love)
            (SH))                                     (V NOM A))
5                                          5
(*FVERB+MAIN (the man who loves Mary)     (*ADD-VERB (the man who doesn't love)
             (SH SH)                                 (SH A)
```

Different rules apply in history sections 5 of sentences 5.4.2 and 5.4.7 because
of the different categories of the input expressions. However, after the standard
application of /ADD-VERB (see section 5.3), the two derivations are similar
again, as shown by the comparison of history section 5 of sentence 5.4.2 and 6
of sentence 5.4.7:

5.4.12 Sentence start of sentence 5.4.7 which is equivalent to that of sentence
5.4.2 reprinted in 5.4.11:

```
5
(*ADD-VERB (the man who doesn't love)
           (SH A)
           (Mary)
           (SH))
6
(*FVERB+MAIN (the man who doesn't love Mary)
             (SH SH)
```

The sentence starts in history section 5 of sentence 5.4.2 and history section
6 of sentence 5.4.7 are equivalent because they have the same rule package,
*FVERB+MAIN, and the same category, (SH SH).

We turn now to the examples 5.4.3 and 5.4.8, which have in common that the relative pronouns function as the accusatives of the subordinate clauses. These two derivations diverge after the fourth rather than the third combination. The relevant history sections are repeated below for convenience:

5.4.13 The operations of /NOM+FVERB in derivations 5.4.3 and 5.4.8:

```
4                                          4
(*ADD-NOM (the man who Mary)               (*ADD-NOM (the man who Mary)
          (SH WS SH #)                               (SH WS SH #)
          (loves)                                    (doesn't)
          (V S3 A))                                  (V S3 DO))
5                                          5
(*NOM+FVERB (the man who Mary loves)       (*NOM+FVERB (the man who Mary doesn't)
            (SH)                                       (SH DO WS)
```

The categorial operation of /NOM+FVERB in the right-hand history section above has not yet been discussed. The output category (V DO WS) represents a sentence start which needs a verb form compatible with DO. Furthermore, this verb form must have a oblique valency position for the Wh-noun phrase represented by WS. /NOM+FVERB handles this particular case with a clause which exactly specifies the nature of the input categories and the resulting output category.

The rule package *NOM+FVERB contains the rules /NOM+FVERB and /ADD-VERB. These rules apply in history sections 5 of derivations 5.4.3 and 5.4.8. The former combination is already well-known; it simply involves combination of a complex noun phrase with a finite verb. But derivation 5.4.8 shows a categorial operation of /ADD-VERB which has not yet been discussed. Consider the relevant history section, which is repeated below for convenience:

5.4.14 The operation of /ADD-VERB in history section 6 of derivation 5.4.8:

```
5
(*NOM+FVERB (the man who Mary doesn't)
            (SH DO WS)
            (love)
            (V NOM A))
6
(*ADD-VERB (the man who Mary doesn't love)
           (SH)
```

/ADD-VERB cancels the DO in the first input category with the first two segments of (V NOM A) and the A in the second input category with the WS. The result is a complete noun phrase of category (SH). The subsequent combinations in the derivation of this sentence are already familiar. For more examples of different kinds of relative clauses see appendix C.

5.5   Wh-interrogatives in ECAT

The W-words, such as *who* and *which*, function not only as relative pronouns but also as interrogative pronouns in "Wh-interrogatives". Wh-interrogatives exhibit an alternation in word order similar to that of relative clauses. Consider the following examples.

5.5.1 Word order alternations in English Wh-interrogatives:

1. *Who loves Mary?*
2. *Who does love Mary?*
3. ** Who Mary loves?*
4. *Who does Mary love?*

The sentence initial W-word may function as a nominative (e.g. 1 and 2) or as an oblique case (e.g. 4). In the latter case 'do-support' is obligatory in interrogatives. In relative clauses, on the other hand, a W-word with an oblique case function may occur either with or without do-support: *the man who Mary loves / the man who Mary does(n't) love.*

The ECAT derivation of the first example in 5.5.1 is straightforward:

5.5.2 *Who loves Mary?*

```
(R who loves Mary ?)
((*CMPLT ((who loves Mary ?)
         (INTERROG)
         1
         (*START (who)
                 (WH)
                 (loves)
                 (V S3 A))
         2
         (*NOM+FVERB (who loves)
                     (VI A)
                     (Mary)
                     (SH))
         3
         (*FVERB+MAIN (who loves Mary)
                      (VI SH)
                      (?)
                      (INTERROG V))
         4)))
```

In history section 1, /NOM+FVERB cancels the S3 in (V S3 A) with the category (WH)[13] of *who* and changes the V to VI, requiring the sentence to end with a question mark.

Next let us compare the derivations of *Who does love Mary?* and *Who does Mary love?*. Consider 5.5.3 and 5.5.4

---

[13]Remember that the H in WH stands for 'human'. The W-word *which* has the category (W-H).

5.5.3 *Who does love Mary?*

```
(R who does love Mary ?)
((*CMPLT ((who does love Mary ?)
         (INTERROG)
         1
         (*START (who)
                 (WH)
                 (does)
                 (V S3 DO))
         2
         (*NOM+FVERB (who does)
                 (VI DO)
                 (love)
                 (V NOM A))
         3
         (*ADD-VERB (who does love)
                 (VI A)
                 (Mary)
                 (SH))
         4
         (*FVERB+MAIN (who does love Mary)
                 (VI SH)
                 (?)
                 (INTERROG V))
         5)))
```

5.5.4 *Who does Mary love?*

```
(R who does Mary love ?)
((*CMPLT ((who does Mary love ?)
         (INTERROG)
         1
         (*START (who)
                 (WH)
                 (does)
                 (V S3 DO))
         2
         (*TOP-MAIN (who does)
                 (VI S3 DO WH)
                 (Mary)
                 (SH))
         3
         (*FVERB+NOM (who does Mary)
                 (VI DO WH SH)
                 (love)
                 (V NOM A))
         4
         (*ADD-VERB (who does Mary love)
                 (VI SH)
                 (?)
                 (INTERROG V))
         5)))
```

Compare history sections 1 of 5.5.3 and 5.5.4, which are repeated below for convenience:

5.5.5 History sections 1 of 5.5.3 and 5.5.4:

```
1                               1
(*START (who)                   (*START (who)
        (WH)                            (WH)
        (does)                          (does)
        (V S3 DO))                      (V S3 DO))
2                               2
(*NOM+FVERB (who does)          (*TOP-MAIN (who does)
            (VI DO)                        (VI S3 DO WH)
```

The rule package *START contains the rules /NOM+FVERB and /TOP-MAIN (for 'topicalized main constituent'). Both accept the same input expressions: *who* of category (WH) and *does* of category (V S3 DO). But their specifications of the output category are different: /NOM+FVERB is argument cancelling while /TOP+MAIN is argument adding.

More specifically, the category (VI DO) produced by /NOM+FVERB indicates an interrogative sentence (VI rather than V) with an unsaturated form of *do* (DO). The category (VI S3 DO WH) produced by /TOP+MAIN, on the other hand, represents a sentence start which is marked as an interrogative (VI rather than V), has a nominative third person singular valency (S3) carried by a finite verb form of *do* (DO), and has an argument-added filler for an oblique noun phrase valency (WH).

So even though the first combinations of 5.5.3 and 5.5.4 use exactly the same input expressions, the resulting sentence starts are not equivalent: they have different rule packages (*NOM+FVERB versus *TOP-MAIN) and different categories ((VI DO) versus (VI S3 DO WH)).

Next compare history sections 2 of 5.5.3 and 5.5.4, which are repeated in 5.5.6 for convenience:

5.5.6 The history sections 2 of 5.5.3 and 5.5.4:

```
2                               2
(*NOM+FVERB (who does)          (*TOP-MAIN (who does)
            (VI DO)                        (VI S3 DO WH)
            (love)                         (Mary)
            (V NOM A))                     (SH))
3                               3
(*ADD-VERB (who does love)      (*FVERB+NOM (who does Mary)
           (VI A)                           (VI DO WH SH))
```

In 5.5.3 the familiar rule /ADD-VERB applies. It cancels the DO segment in the first category with the segments V NOM in the second category and attaches the remainder(s), resulting in (VI A). (VI A) indicates an interrogative sentence start with an accusative valency. In 5.5.4, on the other hand, the rule /FVERB+NOM applies in a completely standard way: the category (SH) of the second expression 2-cancels the S3 valency in the category of the first. The result category (VI DO WH SH) indicates an interrogative sentence start with an unsaturated form of *do* (DO) and an argument-added filler for an oblique noun phrase valency (WH); the segment SH, finally, specifies agreement for a possible relative clause modifying the nominative (e.g. *Who does Mary, who loves John, give a cookie?*).

The valencies represented by DO and WH in the output of history section 2 of 5.5.4 are cancelled in the next combination step by /ADD-VERB.

5.5.7 History section 3 of 5.5.4:

```
3
(*FVERB+NOM (who does Mary)
            (VI DO WH SH)
            (love)
            (V NOM A))
4
(*ADD-VERB (who does Mary love)
           (VI SH))
```

The /ADD-VERB cancels the DO segment of the first input category with the segments V NOM of the second. In contrast, the accusative valency of the second category is cancelled by the argument-added WH segment of the first. We have previously observed this categorial operation in a relative clause (derivation 5.4.8, history section 5; see also 5.4.14). The output category (VI SH) indicates a saturated interrogative sentence start. The SH segment specifies agreement for a possible extraposed relative clause, e.g *Who does the man love who gave Mary the book?*.

Another case where two similar sentence starts are continued in very different ways is illustrated by pairs like *Who does John believe?* versus *Who does John believe that Mary saw?*. Up to and including the word *believe*, the surfaces of the sentence starts are alike. But the grammatical role of the W-word *who* is very different in the two examples. In the first case, *who* fills the accusative valency of *believe*, while in the second case it fills the accusative valency of *saw*. Consider the ECAT derivations of the two examples in 5.5.8 and 5.5.9:

5.5.8 *Who does John believe?*

```
(R who does John believe ?)
((*CMPLT ((who does John believe ?)
          (INTERROG)
          1
          (*START (who)
                  (WH)
                  (does)
                  (V S3 DO))
          2
          (*TOP-MAIN (who does)
                     (VI S3 DO WH)
                     (John)
                     (SH))
          3
          (*FVERB+NOM (who does John)
                      (VI DO WH SH)
```

```
                    (believe)
                    (V NOM A))
         4
      (*ADD-VERB (who does John believe)
                 (VI SH)
                 (?)
                 (INTERROG V))
         5)))
```

5.5.9 *Who does John believe that Mary saw?*

```
(R who does John believe that Mary saw ?)
((*CMPLT ((who does John believe that Mary saw ?)
          (INTERROG)
          1
          (*START (who)
                  (WH)
                  (does)
                  (V S3 DO))
          2
          (*TOP-MAIN (who does)
                     (VI S3 DO WH)
                     (John)
                     (SH))
          3
          (*FVERB+NOM (who does John)
                      (VI DO WH SH)
                      (believe)
                      (V NOM A))
          4
          (*WH+VERB (who does John believe)
                    (VI A WH SH)
                    (that)
                    (SC))
          5
          (*START-SUBCL (who does John believe that)
                        (VI SC WH SH)
                        (Mary)
                        (SH))
          6
          (*ADD-NOM (who does John believe that Mary)
                    (VI SC SH # WH SH)
                    (saw)
                    (V S3 A))
          7
          (*NOM+FVERB (who does John believe that Mary saw)
                      (VI SH)
                      (?)
                      (INTERROG V))
          8)))
```

In history sections 1 and 2 of 5.5.8 and 5.5.9 the derivations are identical. The rule package *FVERB+NOM contains the rules /ADD-VERB and /WH+VERB, which take the same input expressions but produce different outputs. While /ADD-VERB is argument cancelling, /WH+VERB is argument

adding. If we type (R who does John believe) on the terminal, ECAT returns
the following ambiguous sentence start:

5.5.10 *Who does John believe*

```
(R who does John believe)
((*ADD-VERB ((who does John believe)
            (VI SH)
            1
            (*START (who)
                    (WH)
                    (does)
                    (V S3 DO))
            2
            (*TOP-MAIN (who does)
                       (VI S3 DO WH)
                       (John)
                       (SH))
            3
            (*FVERB+NOM (who does John)
                        (VI DO WH SH)
                        (believe)
                        (V NOM A))
            4))
 (*WH+VERB ((who does John believe)
            (VI A WH SH)
            1
            (*START (who)
                    (WH)
                    (does)
                    (V S3 DO))
            2
            (*TOP-MAIN (who does)
                       (VI S3 DO WH)
                       (John)
                       (SH))
            3
            (*FVERB+NOM (who does John)
                        (VI DO WH SH)
                        (believe)
                        (V NOM A))
            4)))
```

The first result category (VI SH) indicates an interrogative sentence without
unsaturated valencies; after adding the question mark in the next combination,
the derivation results in 5.5.8. The second result category (VI A WH SH), on
the other hand, indicates a sentence with an accusative valency (A) and an
argument-added noun phrase (WH).

Let us follow the subsequent combination steps in the derivation of 5.5.9. In
history section 4, the rule /START-SUBCL replaces the accusative valency in
the sentence start with the segment SC. (SC) is the category of the subordinating
conjunction *that*.

5.5.11 History section 4 of derivation 5.5.9:

```
4
(*WH+VERB (who does John believe)
         (VI A WH SH)
         (that)
         (SC))
5
(*START-SUBCL (who does John believe that)
              (VI SC WH SH)
```

The result category (VI SC WH SH) indicates an interrogative sentence start
with the beginning of a subordinate clause (SC) and an argument-added noun
phrase valency (WH). The next word in the sentence is *Mary*, which functions
as the nominative of the subordinate clause. *Mary* is added by the rule /ADD-
NOM, familiar from derivations 5.4.3 (history section 3; see also 5.4.5) and 5.4.8
(history section 3).

5.5.12 History section 5 of derivation 5.5.9:

```
5
(*START-SUBCL (who does John believe that)
              (VI SC WH SH)
              (Mary)
              (SH))
6
(*ADD-NOM (who does John believe that Mary)
          (VI SC SH # WH SH))
```

The categorial operation of /ADD-NOM places the category segment SH of
the next word *Mary* between the segments SC and WH of the sentence start
category, adding the subclause delimiter #. The result category (VI SC SH
WH SH) indicates an interrogative sentence start with the beginning of a
subordinate clause (SC) which already has the nominative in place (SH #);
furthermore, there is an argument-added noun phrase valency (WH).

The rule package *ADD-NOM contains the rules /WH+VERB and /NOM-
+FVERB, each of which may apply to the sentence start which resulted in
5.5.12 and the next word *saw*. In other words, ECAT analyzes the sentence
start *Who does John believe that Mary saw* as ambiguous. The analysis is given
in 5.5.13:

5.5.13 The two readings of *Who does John believe that Mary saw*

```
(R who does John believe that Mary saw)
((*WH+VERB ((who does John believe that Mary saw)
           (VI A WH SH)
           1
           (*START (who)
                   (WH)
                   (does)
                   (V S3 DO))
           2
           (*TOP-MAIN (who does)
```

```
                           (VI S3 DO WH)
                           (John)
                           (SH))
                3
                (*FVERB+NOM (who does John)
                           (VI DO WH SH)
                           (believe)
                           (V NOM A))
                4
                (*WH+VERB (who does John believe)
                           (VI A WH SH)
                           (that)
                           (SC))
                5
                (*START-SUBCL (who does John believe that)
                           (VI SC WH SH)
                           (Mary)
                           (SH))
                6
                (*ADD-NOM (who does John believe that Mary)
                           (VI SC SH # WH SH)
                           (saw)
                           (V N A))
                7))
(*NOM+FVERB ((who does John believe that Mary saw)
            (VI SH)
            1
            (*START (who)
                    (WH)
                    (does)
                    (V S3 DO))
            2
            (*TOP-MAIN (who does)
                       (VI S3 DO WH)
                       (John)
                       (SH))
            3
            (*FVERB+NOM (who does John)
                       (VI DO WH SH)
                       (believe)
                       (V NOM A))
            4
            (*WH+VERB (who does John believe)
                       (VI A WH SH)
                       (that)
                       (SC))
            5
            (*START-SUBCL (who does John believe that)
                       (VI SC WH SH)
                       (Mary)
                       (SH))
            6
            (*ADD-NOM (who does John believe that Mary)
                       (VI SC SH # WH SH)
                       (saw)
```

```
                  (V N A))
         7)))
```

Note that the resultant sentence start of the first reading is equivalent to
the sentence start of history section 4 of that reading:

5.5.14 The output of history section 4 and the resultant sentence start of the
first reading in 5.5.13

```
        4
        (*WH+VERB (who does John believe)
                  (VI A WH SH))

        (*WH+VERB ((who does John believe that Mary saw)
                  (VI A WH SH))
```

In other words, in the first reading of 5.5.13 the grammar (and the parser)
is getting ready for another subordinate clause. In the next combination the
accusative valency will be replaced by SC (just like in history section 4); then
another nominative will be added (just like in history section 5), etc. The first
reading of 5.5.13 may be continued in this way indefinitely, e.g. *Who does John
believe that Mary saw that Bill wrote that Susi kissed?* or *... that Susi said that
Peter kissed?*, etc. Each time a nominative is added in a new subordinate clause,
an ambiguity arises just as in 5.5.13. Note that the WH segment introduced by
the initial *who* is not affected by the rules making up the recursion loop, namely
/WH+VERB, /START-SUBCL, and /ADD-NOM.

The rule that stops the recursion is /NOM+FVERB, which applies in the
second reading of 5.5.13 as well as at the end of derivation 5.5.9.

5.5.15 History section 6 of derivation 5.5.9:

```
        6
        (*ADD-NOM (who does John believe that Mary)
                  (VI SC SH # WH SH)
                  (saw)
                  (V S3 A))
        7
        (*NOM+FVERB (who does John believe that Mary saw)
                    (VI SH)
```

/NOM+FVERB cancels the valency position A in the second input carrier with
the argument-added noun phrase filler WH.

Examples like 5.5.9 have been called "unbounded dependencies". In left-
associative analysis unbounded dependencies arise in terms of a sentence initial
argument added noun phrase filler, e.g. WH, and a recursion consisting of a two-
place verb like *believe*, a subordinating conjunction filling the second valency,
and an added nominative. After the nominative another two place verb may
be added, and the recursion starts over again. This process may be continued
until the second position of the last two-place verb is filled with the WH rather
than another subordinating conjunction.

Note that the subordinating conjunction need not be explicit in the surface. For example, instead of *Who does John believe that Mary saw?* one may also say *Who does John believe Mary saw?*. These cases are also handled by ECAT. Consider 5.5.16:

5.5.16 *Who does John believe Mary saw?*

```
(R who does John believe Mary saw ?)
((*CMPLT ((who does John believe Mary saw ?)
         (INTERROG)
         1
         (*START (who)
                 (WH)
                 (does)
                 (V S3 DO))
         2
         (*TOP-MAIN (who does)
                    (VI S3 DO WH)
                    (John)
                    (SH))
         3
         (*FVERB+NOM (who does John)
                     (VI DO WH SH)
                     (believe)
                     (V NOM A))
         4
         (*WH+VERB (who does John believe)
                   (VI A WH SH)
                   (Mary)
                   (SH))
         5
         (*START-SUBCL (who does John believe Mary)
                       (VI SC SH # WH SH)
                       (saw)
                       (V N A))
         6
         (*NOM+FVERB (who does John believe Mary saw)
                     (VI SH)
                     (?)
                     (INTERROG V))
         7)))
```

If the two place verb, e.g. *believe* is followed directly by a noun phrase, e.g. *Mary*, then /START-SUBCL changes the accusative valency to SC and adds the nominative. In other words, in such cases the rule /START-SUBCL assumes the function of /ADD-NOM.

Traditional approaches attempt to explain unbounded dependencies in terms of the relation between, e.g. 5.5.9 and 5.5.17.

5.5.17   *John believes that Mary saw Bill.*

```
(R John believes that Mary saw Bill .)
((*CMPLT ((John believes that Mary saw Bill %.)
```

```
(DECL)
1
(*START (John)
        (SH)
        (believes)
        (V S3 A))
2
(*NOM+FVERB (John believes)
            (V A)
            (that)
            (SC))
3
(*START-SUBCL (John believes that)
              (V SC)
              (Mary)
              (SH))
4
(*ADD-NOM (John believes that Mary)
          (V SC SH *)
          (saw)
          (V N A))
5
(*NOM+FVERB (John believes that Mary saw)
            (V A)
            (Bill)
            (SH))
6
(*FVERB+MAIN (John believes that Mary saw Bill)
             (V SH)
             (%.)
             (DECL V))
7)))
```

As far as left-associative grammar is concerned, the only relation between 5.5.9 and 5.5.17 consists in the fact that both sentences use largely the same words and assign similar grammatical roles. But as far as the building up and cancelling of valencies are concerned, the two derivations are quite different. Our explanation of 5.5.9 is independent of 5.5.17. The analysis is similar in spirit to the treatment of German center-embedded and extraposed relative clauses in 4.4 above, where the extraposed version is also derived completely independently from the center-embedded one.

Appendices

A. The LISP functions of DCAT

In this appendix we present the definitions of the parser DCAT/DLEX. The definitions are written in the programming language LISP and implement the left-associative grammar of German explained in chapters 3 and 4 as a computer program. The actual LISP code of DCAT and DLEX is printed here because it is the most concise statement available of the linguistic analysis.

In chapters 3 and 4 we paraphrased some of the left-associative rules of DCAT in English, but doing this for all rules of the grammar would be extremely tedious. Also, the source code of the linguistic rules, which is only 16 pages long (see section A.2), contains a wealth of information which would only be implicit in the English paraphrases. Explaining the linguistic theory in terms of the program has the advantages of explicitness and precision, and will also lead to the discovery of further syntactic generalizations, which in turn result in improvement of the program.

Programming languages are formal languages. But in contrast to many formal languages that are defined only on paper, programming languages have the advantage of actually running on computers.[1] Formulating a definition in a particular programming language does not imply a loss of generality[2]. Some languages are more suitable for certain purposes than others, but if a program lacks clarity or generality it is usually not the fault of the language.

LISP (for LISt Programming) is the *lingua franca* of artificial intelligence.[3] It is a general purpose programming language, and next to FORTRAN, the oldest programming language still in use. During its long history[4] it has evolved into several different dialects, such as MACLISP, INTERLISP, ZETALISP, and Common Lisp.

Theoretically, all general purpose programming languages are intertranslatable. This follows from the fact that general purpose programming languages are Turing equivalent. Therefore, the parser program presented below could be

---

[1] Attempts by Weyhrauch (1980) and others to program the proof theory of first order logic have met with great difficulties. This is surprising, given the supposedly mechanical nature of deriving proofs in first order logic.

[2] Just as saying something in French rather than English doesn't imply a loss of generality.

[3] See Winston (1977), Charniak, Riesbeck, and McDermott (1980), Rich (1983).

[4] The inception of LISP is dated with McCarthy (1960).

implemented in any other programming language.[5] The left-associative parsers DCAT, ECAT, and LOGCAT were written in INTERLISP-D and run on XE-ROX 1108 (dandelion) or 1109 (dandytiger) work-stations. They also run in INTERLISP-10 on DEC2060 mainframe computers, VAX computers, and other machines supporting INTERLISP.

On May 4, 1986, Steven Tepper translated the INTERLISP versions of DCAT and ECAT into Common Lisp. DCAT and ECAT run in Kyoto Common Lisp both on the Vax and on SUN-3 work-stations. In theory, the Common Lisp versions of the two parsers should also run on all other machines supporting Common Lisp. Only minor editing would be required to change the code of DCAT and ECAT to run the programs in other LISP dialects on, e.g. SYMBOL-ICS 3640/70 (MACLISP) or Hewlett-Packard Bobcats (Standard Basic Lisp).

A left-associative parser consists of a motor (appendix A.1), the linguistic combination rules and rule packages (appendix A.2), and auxiliary functions for the combination rules (appendix A.3). A commented alphabetical list of all DCAT LISP functions is given in appendix A.4. The lexicon DLEX is presented in appendix A.5.

A.1 The motor of a left-associative parser

Due to the regular nature of left-associative combinations, the same motor can be used for all left-associative systems. The motor defined below has been used in the systems DCAT, ECAT, and LOGCAT. The present design evolved through a number of stages. Different versions of a left-associative motor are like the different designs of a combustion engine. They differ in details, but the main thing — as far as the overall system is concerned — is that they run.[6]

The expressions used in the following definitions are either standard INTER-LISP-D functions, like MAPCAR, EVAL, LIST, COND, AND, CAR, CADR, CDDR, etc., which are explained in the INTERLISP-D reference manual (Teitelman et al. 1983), or functions written in INTERLISP-D, which are defined in this appendix. The latter are listed in alphabetical order in appendix A.4 with

---

[5]In practice, translating a program from one language into another is simplest if the new environment is another LISP dialect. In very different programming languages like PASCAL or FORTRAN, on the other hand, there are basically three options: (i) rewriting the program to take advantage of the basic constructs of PASCAL (FORTRAN); (ii) defining equivalents of the data structures characteristic of LISP in PASCAL (FORTRAN) and retain the general form of the program; or (iii) writing a LISP interpreter running on top of PASCAL (FORTRAN), leaving the original program completely unchanged. Many versions of FORTRAN do not allow recursion or run-time storage allocation (and certainly not automatic garbage collection). For such systems only the third option is practically feasible.

[6]Consider the following alternative design: at present, the top level function R evaluates and expands all the words in the input before TR2 is applied to the first two input expressions. For a number of reasons one may prefer an alternative version where words are evaluated one by one as they come up in the left-associative parse. For tasks like this a left-associative grammar team should have an experienced programmer.

the place of their definition indicated in parentheses. For easier reference, all D-CAT functions are marked with an '@'. This graphical distinction is limited to this appendix and not contained in the actual source code.

In the process of loading the parser, the variable SYSPRETTYFLG is set to the value T. This activates the "pretty-printer" of INTERLISP-D. [7]

A.1.1 Turning on the pretty printer:

```
(RPAQQ SYSPRETTYFLG T)
```

In other LISP environments, a pretty printing function must be defined by the programmer in order to have the derivations printed as structured lists. For the Common Lisp versions of DCAT and ECAT such a function was defined by Steven Tepper. Consider the following example:

A.1.2 An illustration of the pretty-printer in the Common Lisp versions of DCAT and ECAT:

```
(z John gave Mary a book %.)

  *CMPLT
  JOHN GAVE MARY A BOOK %. (DECL)

     *START
     1
        JOHN (SH)
        GAVE (V N D A)
     *NOM+FVERB
     2
        JOHN GAVE (V D A)
        MARY (SH)
     *FVERB+MAIN
     3
        JOHN GAVE MARY (V A SH)
        A (C)
     *FVERB+MAIN
     4
        JOHN GAVE MARY A (V C SH)
        BOOK (C-H)
     *DET+NOUN
     5
        JOHN GAVE MARY A BOOK (V SH S-H)
        %. (DECL V)
```

The above analysis presents the left-associative derivation of a sentence in a format somewhat different from that of the general purpose pretty-printer of INTERLISP-D used elsewhere in this book. The new pretty-printer groups the input expressions of a combination with the following rule package, while the other analyses group the input expressions with the previous rule package. Both

---

[7] The LISP functions presented below are also pretty-printed. RPAQQ is the INTERLISP-D code for SETQ.

formats are well-motivated, and faithfully reflect the underlying computational operations. Without a pretty-printer, the parsing analyses are not printed as structured lists, but rather dumped into continuous lines. The top-level function of the motor of a left-associative parser is called @R (for 'read'). @R appears in the input line of each sentence to be analyzed and triggers the parse.

A.1.3 The motor function @R:

```
(@R
    [NLAMBDA SENT
        (@TR2 (MAPCAR (MAPCAR SENT (FUNCTION EVAL))
                (FUNCTION @EXPAND])
```

@R applies the function @TR2 to the lexical evaluation and expansion of the input sentence.[8] For example, if the input sentence is 'PETER SCHLAEFT', then (MAPCAR PETER SCHLAEFT (FUNCTION EVAL)) replaces PETER and SCHLAEFT by their lexically analyzed counterparts, i.e.

A.1.4

```
(PETER ((S3 MS)
        (D MS)
        (A MS)))
```

and

A.1.5

```
(SCHLAEFT ((V S3)))
```

respectively. Application of (MAPCAR...(FUNCTION @EXPAND)) to the expressions A.1.4 and A.1.5 expands the lexical analyses of these words into the corresponding sentence starts[9]:

A.1.6

```
[(@START ((PETER)
          (S3)))
 (@START ((PETER)
          (D)))
 (@START ((PETER)
          (A]
```

---

[8] The square brackets '[,]' in A.1.3 and other places are inserted by the INTERLISP-D pretty-printer. In MACLISP and Common Lisp mapping functions like MAPCAR take the arguments in opposite order. The MACLISP function corresponding to no-spread NLAMBDA is called FEXPR.

[9] That next words are expanded into the form of elementary sentence starts is a remnant of an earlier stage, where the lexicon listed all words in the form of A.1.6, i.e. as elementary sentence starts. Since the expanded form of a word is used only once at the beginning of the parse, and since listing of the words as elementary sentence starts requires about 40 percent more disk space, we changed the lexical analysis to the simplified form illustrated in A.1.4 and A.1.5. In order to retain the rather intricate definitions of @COMB, @BUILDHIST, and @MAKEHIST, the function @EXPAND, which adjusts the new lexical input to the earlier format, was built into @R.

A.1.7

```
[(@START ((SCHLAEFT)
          (V S3],
```

Next consider the function @TR2, which is called by @R.

A.1.8 The motor function **@TR2**:

```
(@TR2
  [LAMBDA (SENT)
    (COND
      ((EQ (CAR SENT)
           (QUOTE ERROR))

         SENT)
      ((EQ (CAAR SENT)
           (QUOTE ERROR))
       (CAR SENT))
      ((NULL (CDDR SENT))
        (@COMB (CAR SENT)
               (CADR SENT)))
      (T (@TR2 (CONS (@COMB (CAR SENT)
                            (CADR SENT))
                     (CDDR SENT])
```

The task of the function @TR2 is to apply the function @COMB to (the evaluated versions of) a sentence start and the next word, call the result a sentence start and apply @COMB to it and the next word, call the result a sentence start and apply @COMB to it and the next word, etc., until either (i) there is no next word, in which case @TR2 returns the result of the final combination, or (ii) @COMB fails in the course of the recursive operation of @TR2 (e.g. (EQ (CAR SENT)(QUOTE ERROR))). In the latter case @TR2 returns the expression provided by @COMB, consisting of an error message and the successful part of the derivation.

Finally consider the function @COMB, which is called by @TR2.

A.1.9 The motor function **@COMB**:

```
(@COMB
  [LAMBDA (EXPR1 EXPR2)
    (PROG ((PAIRS (@MAKEPAIR EXPR1 EXPR2))
           (PAIR NIL)
           (TEMP NIL)
           (OLDPAIR NIL)
           (RESULT NIL)
           (HIST NIL))
          (SETQ PAIR (pop PAIRS))
      LP  [COND
            ((CAAR PAIR)
              (SETQ TEMP (REMOVE NIL (APPLY* (CAAR PAIR)
                                             (CADAR PAIR)
                                             (CADADR PAIR]
```

```
(COND
    ((CAR TEMP)
     (SETQ RESULT (APPEND RESULT (@BUILDHIST TEMP PAIR]
(SETQ OLDPAIR PAIR)
(SETQ PAIR (pop PAIRS))
(COND
  (PAIR (GO LP))
  (T (RETURN (COND
                ((NULL RESULT)
                 (LIST (QUOTE ERROR)

                    "Ungrammatical continuation at:"
                        OLDPAIR))
                (T RESULT]))
```

The function @COMB takes a sentence start and the next word, and forms the Cartesian product of all readings of the sentence start and all readings of the next word (see (@MAKEPAIR EXPR1 EXPR2)). For each pair, @COMB applies the first element of the first member (i.e. the rule package), to the second element of the first and second members (i.e. the expressions, each consisting of a surface and a category). The code of this operation is (APPLY* (CAAR PAIR)(CADAR PAIR)(CADADR PAIR)). For each successful @COMBination, @COMB builds a history section (@BUILDHIST TEMP PAIR), complete with section numbers. If the APPLY* operation[10] does not succeed on any member of a given set of pairs, @COMB returns the error message "Ungrammatical continuation at:" and the last pair.

The three rules @R, @TR2, and @COMB described above execute the same operations regardless of the grammatical constructions contained in the analyzed sentence. The linguistic analysis is completely controlled by the input expressions. The crucial clause is (APPLY* (CAAR PAIR) (CADAR PAIR) (CADADR PAIR)) in @COMB. Consider the first pair derived from the words PETER and SCHLAEFT:

A.1.10   ((@START ((PETER)   (@START ((SCHLAEFT)
               (S3)))   (V S3))))

(CAAR PAIR) refers to the rule package of the sentence start, i.e. @START in the analysis of PETER. (CADAR PAIR) refers to the expression of the sentence start, ((PETER)(S3)). (CADADR PAIR) refers to the expression of the next word, ((SCHLAEFT)(V S3)). (APPLY* (CAAR PAIR) (CADAR PAIR) (CADADR PAIR)) applies all rules of the rule package mentioned by its first element, @START, to the second and third element.

Depending on the rules in the rule package applied, the   combination   will result in either NIL or a new sentence start. In the example A.1.10 the result is the following:

A.1.11   (@MAIN+FVERB ((PETER SCHLAEFT)
                 (V)))

---

[10] APPLY* is called FUNCALL in MACLISP and Common Lisp

The rule in the package @START responsible for this combination was @RMAIN-+FVERB, so the rule package of the new sentence start is @MAIN+FVERB which contains all rules applicable after @RMAIN+FVERB has been successful.

Next @TR2 fetches a new next word and the process starts over again: @MAKEPAIR renders a new set of pairs and (APPLY* (CAAR PAIR) (CA-DAR PAIR) (CADADR PAIR)) applies to each pair in the set. Whether or not (APPLY*...) is successful for a given pair depends completely on the nature of the pair; specifically, on the rule package of the first member of the pair and the respective categories of the two expressions.

The rules @R, @TR2, and @COMB call a number of auxiliary functions, which are defined below:

A.1.12 The auxiliary motor function **@EXPAND**:

```
(@EXPAND
  [LAMBDA (WORD)
    (@UNFOLD (CAR WORD)
             (CADR WORD])
```

A.1.13 The auxiliary motor function **@UNFOLD**:

```
(@UNFOLD
  [LAMBDA (S C)
    (COND
      [(EQ (CDR C)
           NIL)
        (LIST (LIST (QUOTE @START)
                    (LIST (LIST S)
                          (CAR C]
      (T (APPEND [LIST (LIST (QUOTE @START)
                             (LIST (LIST S)
                                   (CAR C]
                 (@UNFOLD S (CDR C])
```

A.1.14 The auxiliary motor function **@BUILDHIST**:

```
(@BUILDHIST
  [LAMBDA (TEMP PAIR)
    (PROG ((PV TEMP)
           (PV1 NIL)
           (R1 NIL)
           (HIST NIL))
      (SETQ PV1 (pop PV))
  LP  (COND
        ((CAR PV1)
          (@MAKEHIST PAIR)))
      (SETQ COUNT (PLUS 1 (QUOTIENT (LENGTH HIST)
                                    2)))
      (SETQ HIST (APPEND HIST (LIST COUNT)))
      [COND
        ((CAR PV1)
          (SETQ R1 (CONS (LIST (CAR PV1)
                               (APPEND (CADR PV1)
```

```
                    HIST))
              R1]
     (SETQ PV1 (pop PV))
     (COND
      (PV1 (GO LP))
      (T (RETURN R1])
```

A.1.15 The auxiliary motor function @MAKEPAIR:

```
(@MAKEPAIR
 [LAMBDA (EXPR1 EXPR2)
  (BIND PAIRS FOR SEXPR1 IN EXPR1 DO [FOR SEXPR2 IN EXPR2
               DO (SETQ PAIRS (APPEND PAIRS
                              (CONS (CONS SEXPR1
                                     (CONS SEXPR2 NIL)) NIL]
     FINALLY (RETURN PAIRS])
```

A.1.16 The auxiliary motor function @MAKEHIST:

```
(@MAKEHIST
 [LAMBDA (PAIR)
  (SETQ HIST (COND
    [(EQ (CDR (CDADAR PAIR))
      (QUOTE NIL))
     (LIST (QUOTE 1)
       (LIST (CAAR PAIR)
         (CAR (CADAR PAIR))
         (CADR (CADAR PAIR))
         (CAR (CADADR PAIR))
         (CADR (CADADR PAIR]
    (T (APPEND (CDR (CDADAR PAIR))
       (LIST (LIST (CAAR PAIR)
         (CAR (CADAR PAIR))
         (CADR (CADAR PAIR))
         (CAR (CADADR PAIR))
         (CADR (CADADR PAIR]])
```

The rules @R, @TR2, and @COMB, as well as the auxiliary rules are computationally straightforward and simple. Since general purpose programming languages are intertranslatable, the motor of a left-associative parser can be duplicated in other general purpose programming languages.

A.2   The linguistic rules and rule packages

The linguistic combination rules of DCAT are all based on the same pattern. A DCAT combination rule consists of two parts: an input condition and an output specification. The input condition specifies which categories the input expressions may have. If the input condition of a rule is not satisfied by (the categories of) a given pair of input expressions, the output is NIL. If it is satisfied, the output specification of the rule gives a new sentence start.

DCAT has the following linguistic rules:

1. @RDET+NOUN: combines a sentence start ending with a determiner and a noun (e.g. *Peter las das + Buch*).

2. @RDET+ADJ: combines a sentence start ending with a determiner and an adjective (e.g. *Peter las das + dicke (Buch)*).

3. @RNOUN+PREP: combines a sentence start ending with a noun and a preposition (e.g. *Das Haus + auf (dem Berg)*).

4. @RPREP+MAIN: combines a sentence start ending with a preposition and the beginning of a noun phrase (e.g. *Das Haus auf + dem (Berg)*).

5. @RNOUN+RELPRO: combines a sentence start ending with a noun and a relative pronoun (e.g. *Der Mann + der (das Buch las schläft auf dem Sofa)*[11]).

6. @RMAIN+FVERB: combines a sentence start consisting of a main constituent (i.e. noun phrase, adverb, adverbial clause, etc.) and a finite verb (main verb or auxiliary) in declarative sentences (e.g. *Der Mann + hat (geschlafen)*).

7. @RFVERB+MAIN: combines a sentence start ending with a finite verb and the beginning of a main constituent (e.g. *Der Mann hat + dem (Mädchen ein Buch gegeben)*).

8. @RMAINCL+NFVERB: combines a sentence start consisting of a main clause and the clause final non-finite verb (e.g. *Der Mann hat dem Mädchen ein Buch + gegeben*).

9. @R?FV+MAIN: combines a finite verb and the beginning of a main constituent, forming the beginning of a yes/no-interrogative (e.g. *Gab + Peter (Maria ein Buch ?)* or *Hat + Peter (Maria ein Buch gegeben?)*).

10. @RADV+ADV: combines an initial adverb and another adverb (e.g. *Gestern + nach (der Schule las Peter ein Buch)*).

11. @RAUX+PRED: combines a sentence start with an auxiliary used as a copula with the predicate (e.g. *Das Mädchen ist + klug, Maria ist + ein (kluges Mädchen), Maria ist + in (der Schule)*).

12. @RSUBCL+MAIN: combines a sentence start with an initiated subordinate clause and the beginning of a main constituent of the subordinate clause (e.g. *Der Mann, der + das (dicke Buch las, schläft auf dem Sofa)*).

---

[11] This rule also handles extraposed relative clauses, as in *Der Mann schläft auf dem Sofa + der (das Buch las)*

13. @RSUBCL+VERB: combines a sentence start with an initiated subordinate clause and a non-clause final part of the verb phrase of the subordinate clause (e.g. *Der Mann, der das Buch + lesen (wollte, schläft auf dem Sofa)* or *Der Mann, der das Buch + gelesen (hatte, schläft auf dem Sofa))*.

14. @RSUBCL+LASTVERB: combines a sentence start with an initiated subordinate clause and the clause final part of the verb phrase of the subordinate clause (e.g. *Der Mann, der das Buch gelesen + hatte, (schläft auf dem Sofa))*.

15. @RNOUN+SUBPREP: combines a sentence start ending in a noun with subordinating preposition (e.g. *Der Ofen, + hinter (dem die Katze schläft, ...))*.

16. @RSUBPREP+PRO: combines a sentence start ending with a subordinating preposition with a pronoun (e.g. *Der Ofen hinter + dem (die Katze schläft)...)*.

17. @RCMPLT: combines a sentence start without missing obligatory arguments and a punctuation sign (e.g. *Die Katze schläft + .* or *Die Katze schläft + ?)*.

18. @RSTART: combines a complete sentence (or a sequence of complete sentences) and the beginning of the next sentence (e.g. *Die Katze schlief. + Maria (ass einen Apfel))*.

Intermediate versions of DCAT contained as many as 50 rules. The number of rules was reduced by the discovery of more and more syntactic generalizations of left-associative analysis.

The linguistic rules of DCAT all have exactly the same form. A linguistic rule consists of an input condition (as described above) and an output specification which specifies a new sentence start consisting of (i) a new rule package, (ii) a surface (resulting from simple concatenation of the input surfaces), and (iii) a category. The linguistic content of a DCAT rule is found in the input categories and the output category, since the derivation of the surface and the name of the new rule package are completely regular.

If a linguistic rule has the name @RX, the associated rule package has the name @X. For example, the rule package associated with (and called by) @RDET+NOUN has the name @DET+NOUN. The rule package @DET+NOUN lists all the rules which may be applied after the rule @RDET+NOUN has been successful. The following list of rules and rule packages begins with the rule package @START and ends with the rule @RSTART.

Some of the linguistic rules defined below, the auxiliary rules in appendix A.3, and the lexical definitions in appendix A.5, mention category segments like D (dative), ADV-L (local adverb), etc. For a commented list of all category segments used by DCAT and DLEX see appendix B.1.

A.2.1 The rule package **@START**:

```
(@START
 [LAMBDA (E1 E2)
  (LIST (@RADV+ADV E1 E2)
        (@RAUX+PRED E1 E2)
        (@RMAIN+FVERB E1 E2)
        (@RDET+ADJ E1 E2)
        (@RDET+NOUN E1 E2)
        (@RNOUN+PREP E1 E2)
        (@RPREP+MAIN E1 E2)
        (@RSUBCL+MAIN E1 E2)
        (@R?FV+MAIN E1 E2)])
```

A.2.2 The combination rule **@RDET+ADJ**:

```
(@RDET+ADJ
 [LAMBDA (EXPR1 EXPR2)
  (COND
    ([AND (@END-DET EXPR1)
       (@EQ-ADJ EXPR2)
       (EQ (CAR (LAST (CADR EXPR1)))
          (CAR (CADR EXPR2)]
     (LIST (FUNCTION @DET+ADJ)
        (LIST (APPEND (CAR EXPR1)
                (CAR EXPR2))
           (CADR EXPR1])
```

A.2.3 The rule package **@DET+ADJ**:

```
(@DET+ADJ
 [LAMBDA (E1 E2)
  (LIST (@RDET+ADJ E1 E2)
        (@RDET+NOUN E1 E2)
        (@RNOUN+PREP E1 E2)
        (@RMAIN+FVERB E1 E2)
        (@RFVERB+MAIN E1 E2)
        (@RNOUN+SUBPREP E1 E2)
        (@RSUBCL+VERB E1 E2)
        (@RSUBCL+LASTVERB E1 E2)
        (@RSUBCL+MAIN E1 E2)
        (@RNOUN+RELPRO E1 E2)
        (@RMAINCL+NFVERB E1 E2)
        (@RADV+ADV E1 E2)
        (@RCMPLT E1 E2)])
```

A.2.4 The combination rule **@RDET+NOUN**:

```
(@RDET+NOUN
 [LAMBDA (EXPR1 EXPR2)
  (COND
    ([AND (@END-DET EXPR1)
       (@EQ-NOUN EXPR2)
       (EQ (CAR (NLEFT (CADR EXPR1)
              2))
          (CAR (CADR EXPR2)]
```

```
(LIST (FUNCTION @DET+NOUN)
   (LIST (APPEND (CAR EXPR1)
          (CAR EXPR2))
      (REVERSE (CDR (REVERSE (CADR EXPR1])
```

A.2.5 The rule package @DET+NOUN:

```
(@DET+NOUN
 [LAMBDA (E1 E2)
  (LIST (@RMAINCL+NFVERB E1 E2)
     (@RNOUN+PREP E1 E2)
     (@RFVERB+MAIN E1 E2)
     (@RNOUN+SUBPREP E1 E2)
     (@RMAIN+FVERB E1 E2)
     (@RSUBCL+VERB E1 E2)
     (@RSUBCL+LASTVERB E1 E2)
     (@RSUBCL+MAIN E1 E2)
     (@RNOUN+RELPRO E1 E2)
     (@RADV+ADV E1 E2)
     (@RCMPLT E1 E2])
```

A.2.6 The combination rule @RNOUN+PREP:

```
(@RNOUN+PREP
 [LAMBDA (EXPR1 EXPR2)
  (COND
   ((AND (OR (@END-NOUN EXPR1)
        (@END-DET EXPR1))
     (MEMB (CAR (CADR EXPR2))
        (QUOTE (-AG ADV-L ADV-D ADV-M ADV-C ADV-T)))
     (NOT (EQ (CADR (CADR EXPR2))
          NIL)))
    (LIST (FUNCTION @NOUN+PREP)
       (LIST (APPEND (CAR EXPR1)
            (CAR EXPR2))
          (APPEND (@ADIFF (CADR EXPR1)
               (QUOTE (-E -EN -ES -ER)))
             (CDR (CADR EXPR2])
```

A.2.7 The rule package @NOUN+PREP:

```
(@NOUN+PREP
 [LAMBDA (E1 E2)
  (LIST (@RPREP+MAIN E1 E2)
     (@RDET+NOUN E1 E2])
```

A.2.8 The combination rule @RPREP+MAIN:

```
(@RPREP+MAIN
 [LAMBDA (EXPR1 EXPR2)
  (COND
   ([AND (NOT (EQ (CAR (CADR EXPR1))
          (QUOTE -PP)))
     (MEMB (CAR (CADR EXPR2))
        (QUOTE (G D A)))
     (EQ [CAR (CAR (REVERSE (CADR EXPR1]
```

```
         (CAR (CADR EXPR2]
    (LIST (FUNCTION @PREP+MAIN)
       (LIST (APPEND (CAR EXPR1)
             (CAR EXPR2))
          (APPEND [LDIFFERENCE (CADR EXPR1)
                      (LIST (LIST (CAR (CADR EXPR2]
             (CDR (CADR EXPR2])
```

A.2.9 The rule package @PREP+MAIN:

```
(@PREP+MAIN
 [LAMBDA (E1 E2)
  (LIST (@RDET+NOUN E1 E2)
     (@RDET+ADJ E1 E2)
     (@RNOUN+PREP E1 E2)
     (@RMAIN+FVERB E1 E2)
     (@RFVERB+MAIN E1 E2)
     (@RSUBCL+MAIN E1 E2)
     (@RSUBCL+VERB E1 E2)
     (@RSUBCL+LASTVERB E1 E2)
     (@RMAINCL+NFVERB E1 E2)
     (@RADV+ADV E1 E2)
     (@RCMPLT E1 E2])
```

A.2.10 The combination rule @RNOUN+RELPRO:

```
(@RNOUN+RELPRO
 [LAMBDA (EXPR1 EXPR2)
  (COND
   ([AND (@END-NOUN EXPR1)
      (OR (@EQ-DET EXPR2)
        (EQ (CAAR EXPR2)
          (QUOTE DESSEN)))
      (MEMB (CAAR EXPR2)
         (QUOTE (DER DES DEM DEN DIE DAS DESSEN)))
      (COND
       [(@LASTV (CADR EXPR1))
        (INTERSECTION (CDR (@LASTV (CADR EXPR1)))
             (QUOTE (S1 S2 S3 P1 P2 P3]
       (T T))
      (AND [COND
          [(AND (@LASTV (CADR EXPR1))
            (EQ (INTERSECTION (@LASTV (CADR EXPR1))
                  (QUOTE (S1 S2 S3 P1 P2 P3 G D A ADV-L
                           ADV-T ADV-D ADV-M ADV-C)))
              NIL))
           (SETQ ARG (@LASTV (CADR EXPR1]
          ((EQ (INTERSECTION (CADR EXPR1)
                 (QUOTE (S1 S2 S3 P1 P2 P3 G D A ADV-L
                          ADV-T ADV-D ADV-M ADV-C)))
             NIL)
           (SETQ ARG (CADR EXPR1)))
          (T (SETQ ARG (LAST (CADR EXPR1]
         [OR [AND (INTERSECTION ARG (QUOTE (MS MSG)))
            (MEMB (CADR (CADR EXPR2))
               (QUOTE (MS MSG]
```

```
          (AND (MEMB (QUOTE FS)
                 ARG)
            (EQ (CADR (CADR EXPR2))
               (QUOTE FS)))
          [AND (INTERSECTION ARG (QUOTE (NS NSG)))
            (MEMB (CADR (CADR EXPR2))
               (QUOTE (NS NSG]
          (AND (INTERSECTION ARG (QUOTE (P PD)))
            (MEMB (CADR (CADR EXPR2))
               (QUOTE (P PD]
        (SETQ CAT (APPEND [@ADIFF (CADR EXPR1)
                   (LIST (CADR (CADR EXPR2]
               (LIST (QUOTE V))
               (LIST (CAR (CADR EXPR2)))
               (COND
                 ((MEMB (CADDR (CADR EXPR2))
                    (QUOTE (MS FS NS P)))
                  (CDDR (CADR EXPR2)))
                 (T NIL]
    (LIST (FUNCTION @NOUN+RELPRO)
       (LIST [COND
          ((EQ (CAR (LAST (CAR EXPR1)))
             (QUOTE ,))
           (APPEND (CAR EXPR1)
              (CAR EXPR2)))
          (T (APPEND (CAR EXPR1)
                (QUOTE (,))
                (CAR EXPR2]
        CAT])
```

A.2.11 The rule package @NOUN+RELPRO:

```
(@NOUN+RELPRO
 [LAMBDA (E1 E2)
  (LIST (@RSUBCL+MAIN E1 E2)
     (@RSUBCL+VERB E1 E2)
     (@RSUBCL+LASTVERB E1 E2)
     (@RDET+NOUN E1 E2)
     (@RDET+ADJ E1 E2)
     (@RPREP+MAIN E1 E2)
     (@RMAIN+FVERB E1 E2])
```

A.2.12 The combination rule @RMAIN+FVERB:

```
(@RMAIN+FVERB
  [LAMBDA (EXPR1 EXPR2)
    (COND
      ((AND (OR (@EQ-MAINC EXPR1)
               (@EQ-NFVERB EXPR1))
            (NOT (MEMB (QUOTE V)
                    (CADR EXPR1)))
            (NOT (@END-PREP EXPR1))
            [NOT (INTERSECTION (CADR EXPR1)
                            (QUOTE (-ES -ER]
          (@EQ-FVERB EXPR2)
          (COND
```

```
            [[NOT (INTERSECTION (CADR EXPR2)
                                 (QUOTE (H S W WP]
              (OR (INTERSECTION (LIST (CAR (CADR EXPR1)))
                                 (CADR EXPR2))
                  (MEMB (CAR (CADR EXPR1))
                        (QUOTE (-AG -FA ADCL ADV-T ADV-L ADV-M
                                   ADV-D ADV-C]
            ((MEMB (CAR (CADR EXPR1))
                   (QUOTE (S H W WP S1 S2 S3 P1 P2 P3)))
              (MEMB (CAR (CADR EXPR1))
                    (CADR EXPR2)))
            (T T)))
       (LIST
         (FUNCTION @MAIN+FVERB)
         (LIST
           (APPEND (CAR EXPR1)
                   (CAR EXPR2))
           (COND
             [(MEMB (CADDR (CADR EXPR2))
                    (QUOTE (S H W WP)))
              (@CANCEL (CADR EXPR2)
                       (LDIFFERENCE (CADR EXPR1)
                                    (QUOTE (ADCL -E -EN]
             (T (@ADIFF [@CANCEL (CADR EXPR2)
                                 (LDIFFERENCE (CADR EXPR1)
                                              (QUOTE (-E -EN]
                        (INTERSECTION (CADR EXPR1)
                                      (QUOTE (ADCL ADV-M ADV-C
                                                 ADV-T ADV-D
                                                 ADV-L]) )
```

A.2.13 The rule package @MAIN+FVERB:

```
(@MAIN+FVERB
 [LAMBDA (E1 E2)
  (LIST (@RFVERB+MAIN E1 E2)
     (@RMAINCL+NFVERB E1 E2)
     (@RSUBCL+MAIN E1 E2)
     (@RCMPLT E1 E2)
     (@RAUX+PRED E1 E2])
```

A.2.14 The combination rule @RFVERB+MAIN:

```
(@RFVERB+MAIN
 [LAMBDA (EXPR1 EXPR2)
  (COND
   ([AND (EQ (CAR (CADR EXPR1))
         (QUOTE V))
     (EQ (@LASTV (CDR (CADR EXPR1)))
       NIL)
     (NOT (@END-PREP EXPR1))
     [NOT (INTERSECTION (CADR EXPR1)
               (QUOTE (-ER -ES]
     (@EQ-MAINC EXPR2)
     (COND
      [[AND (@UNTERMENGE (QUOTE (SC I))
```

```
                        (CADR EXPR1))
            (MEMB (QUOTE I)
                (CDR (CADR EXPR2]
         (SETQ CAT (APPEND [REVERSE (CDR (MEMB (QUOTE SC)
                               (REVERSE (CADR EXPR1]
                     (QUOTE (V))
                     (@ADIFF (CADR EXPR2)
                         (QUOTE (I]
     [(AND (INTERSECTION (CADR EXPR1)
               (QUOTE (H S W WP)))
        (COND
          [(MEMB (CAR (CADR EXPR2))
              (QUOTE (G D A)))
            (NOT (MEMB (CAR (CADR EXPR2))
                 (@ADIFF (CADR EXPR1)
                     (QUOTE (A]
          [(MEMB (CAR (CADR EXPR2))
              (QUOTE (S1 S2 S3 P1 P2 P3)))
            (NOT (INTERSECTION (CADR EXPR1)
                      (QUOTE (S1 S2 S3 P1 P2 P3 G D A]
          (T T)))
        (SETQ CAT (APPEND (LDIFFERENCE (CADR EXPR1)
                     (QUOTE (-E -EN)))
                 (CADR EXPR2]
      ([AND [OR (MEMB (CAR (CADR EXPR2))
             (CADR EXPR1))
           (MEMB (CAR (CADR EXPR2))
               (QUOTE (ADV-L ADV-T ADV-M ADV-C ADV-D ADCL]
         (OR [AND (INTERSECTION (QUOTE (H S W WP))
                    (CADR EXPR1))
               (MEMB (CAR (CADR EXPR2))
                  (QUOTE (S1 S2 S3 P1 P2 P3)))
               (MEMB (CADR (MEMB (CAR (CADR EXPR2))
                      (CADR EXPR1)))
                  (QUOTE (H S W WP]
             (NOT (INTERSECTION (QUOTE (H S W WP))
                      (CADR EXPR1]
         (SETQ CAT (APPEND [@ADIFF (LDIFFERENCE (CADR EXPR1)
                      (QUOTE (I -E -EN)))
                   (LIST (CAR (CADR EXPR2]
                 (CDR (CADR EXPR2]
     (LIST (FUNCTION @FVERB+MAIN)
        (LIST [COND
            ((MEMB (CAR (CADR EXPR2))
                (QUOTE (SC ADCL)))
             (APPEND (CAR EXPR1)
                 (QUOTE (,))
                 (CAR EXPR2)))
            (T (APPEND (CAR EXPR1)
                 (CAR EXPR2]
          CAT])
```

A.2.15 The rule package @FVERB+MAIN:

```
(@FVERB+MAIN
 [LAMBDA (E1 E2)
```

```
(LIST (@RFVERB+MAIN E1 E2)
    (@RAUX+PRED E1 E2)
    (@RDET+NOUN E1 E2)
    (@RDET+ADJ E1 E2)
    (@RNOUN+PREP E1 E2)
    (@RNOUN+RELPRO E1 E2)
    (@RPREP+MAIN E1 E2)
    (@RMAINCL+NFVERB E1 E2)
    (@RSUBCL+MAIN E1 D2)
    (@RCMPLT E1 E2)])
```

A.2.16 The combination rule @RMAINCL+NFVERB:

```
(@RMAINCL+NFVERB
 [LAMBDA (EXPR1 EXPR2)
  (COND
   ([AND (@EQ-NFVERB EXPR2)
       (NOT (@END-PREP EXPR1))
       [NOT (INTERSECTION (CADR EXPR1)
                  (QUOTE (-ER -ES]
       [COND
        [(INTERSECTION (CADR EXPR1)
               (QUOTE (H S W WP Q Z INF)))
         (MEMB (CAR (CADR EXPR2))
             (QUOTE (H S W WP Q Z]
         (T (MEMB (CAR (CADR EXPR2))
             (QUOTE (Z DE1 DE2 DE3 DE4 DE5 DE6]
       (COND
        [[AND (MEMB (CADR (CADR EXPR2))
              (QUOTE (WP)))
           (INTERSECTION (CADR EXPR1)
                 (QUOTE (ADJ S3 P3]
         (SETQ CAT (@CANCEL (@ADIFF (CADR EXPR1)
                   (QUOTE (ADJ S3 P3)))
                (@ADIFF (CADR EXPR2)
                   (QUOTE (WP]
        [[AND (EQ (CADR (CADR EXPR2))
              (QUOTE S))
           (INTERSECTION (CADR EXPR1)
                 (QUOTE (ADJ ADV-L S3 P3]
         (SETQ CAT (@CANCEL (@ADIFF (CADR EXPR1)
                   (QUOTE (ADJ S3 P3)))
                (@ADIFF (CADR EXPR2)
                   (QUOTE (S]
        [[AND (EQUAL (CADR EXPR2)
              (QUOTE (H W INF)))
           (OR (EQUAL (@STRIP (CADR EXPR1))
                 (QUOTE (V INF)))
             (EQUAL (@STRIP (CADR EXPR1))
                 (QUOTE (V H W INF)))
             (EQUAL (@STRIP (CADR EXPR1))
                 (QUOTE (V W WP INF]
         (SETQ CAT (APPEND (@ADIFF (CADR EXPR1)
                   (CADR EXPR2))
                (QUOTE (INF]
        [[AND (EQUAL (CADR EXPR2)
```

```
                (QUOTE (Z)))
         (INTERSECTION (CADR EXPR1)
                (QUOTE (S H W Z]
   (COND
    [(EQUAL (INTERSECTION (CADR EXPR1)
                (QUOTE (S H W)))
          (QUOTE (H)))
     (SETQ CAT (APPEND (@ADIFF (CADR EXPR1)
                (QUOTE (H)))
            (QUOTE (W]
    [(EQUAL (INTERSECTION (CADR EXPR1)
                (QUOTE (S H W)))
          (QUOTE (S)))
     (COND
      [(INTERSECTION (CADR EXPR1)
                (QUOTE (D A)))
       (SETQ CAT (APPEND (@ADIFF (CADR EXPR1)
                   (QUOTE (S)))
              (QUOTE (W]
      (T (SETQ CAT (APPEND (@ADIFF (CADR EXPR1)
                   (QUOTE (S)))
              (QUOTE (Q]
    [(EQUAL (INTERSECTION (CADR EXPR1)
                (QUOTE (S H W)))
          (QUOTE (W)))
     (SETQ CAT (APPEND (@ADIFF (CADR EXPR1)
                (QUOTE (W)))
            (QUOTE (Q W S]
    ((EQUAL (INTERSECTION (CADR EXPR1)
                (QUOTE (S H W Z)))
          (QUOTE (Z)))
     (SETQ CAT (APPEND (@ADIFF (CADR EXPR1)
                (QUOTE (Z)))
            (QUOTE (W]
    (T (SETQ CAT (APPEND (@ADIFF (@ADIFF (CADR EXPR1)
                   (CADR EXPR2))
              (QUOTE (ADV-L ADV-T ADV-C ADV-M ADV-D ADCL)))
           (@ADIFF (CADR EXPR2)
              (CADR EXPR1]
(LIST (FUNCTION @MAINCL+NFVERB)
   (LIST (APPEND (CAR EXPR1)
          (CAR EXPR2))
      (LDIFFERENCE CAT (QUOTE (-E - EN])
```

A.2.17 The rule package @MAINCL+NFVERB:

```
(@MAINCL+NFVERB
 [LAMBDA (E1 E2)
  (LIST (@RCMPLT E1 E2)
     (@RMAINCL+NFVERB E1 E2)
     (@RNOUN+RELPRO E1 E2)
     (@RFVERB+MAIN E1 E2)
     (@RMAIN+FVERB E1 E2)])
```

A.2.18 The combination rule @R?FV+MAIN:

```
(@R?FV+MAIN
 [LAMBDA (EXPR1 EXPR2)
  (COND
   ((AND (EQ (CAR (CADR EXPR1))
         (QUOTE V))
      (@EQ-MAINC EXPR2)
      (NOT (MEMB (QUOTE I)
            (CADR EXPR2)))
      (COND
       [[NOT (INTERSECTION (CADR EXPR1)
               (QUOTE (H S W WP]
        (OR (MEMB (CAR (CADR EXPR2))
             (CADR EXPR1))
          (MEMB (CAR (CADR EXPR2))
             (QUOTE (ADV-T ADV-L ADV-M ADV-D ADV-C ADCL]
       (T T)))
     (LIST (FUNCTION @?FV+MAIN)
        (LIST (APPEND (CAR EXPR1)
              (CAR EXPR2))
           (APPEND (QUOTE (V))
              (QUOTE (I))
              (COND
               ((INTERSECTION (CADR EXPR1)
                    (QUOTE (H S W WP)))
                (@CANCEL (CDR (CADR EXPR1))
                    (CADR EXPR2)))
               (T (@ADIFF (@CANCEL (CDR (CADR EXPR1))
                       (CADR EXPR2))
                    (INTERSECTION (CADR EXPR2)
                        (QUOTE (ADCL ADV-M ADV-C ADV-T
                              ADV-D ADV-L])
```

A.2.19 The rule package @?FV+MAIN:

```
(@?FV+MAIN
 [LAMBDA (E1 E2)
  (LIST (@RDET+NOUN E1 E2)
     (@RDET+ADJ E1 E2)
     (@RFVERB+MAIN E1 E2)
     (@RAUX+PRED E1 E2)
     (@RCMPLT E1 E2)])
```

A.2.20 The combination rule @RADV+ADV:

```
(@RADV+ADV
 [LAMBDA (EXPR1 EXPR2)
  (COND
   ([AND (MEMB (CAR (CADR EXPR1))
          (QUOTE (ADCL ADV-T ADV-L ADV-M ADV-D ADV-C)))
      (NOT (@END-DET EXPR1))
      (NOT (MEMB (QUOTE V)
           (CADR EXPR1)))
      (MEMB (CAR (CADR EXPR2))
          (QUOTE (ADCL ADV-T ADV-L ADV-M ADV-D ADV-C)))
      (NOT (MEMB (QUOTE I)
           (CADR EXPR2]
    (LIST (FUNCTION @ADV+ADV)
       (LIST (APPEND (CAR EXPR1)
            (CAR EXPR2))
         (@ADIFF (APPEND (CADR EXPR1)
             (CADR EXPR2))
            (QUOTE (MS FS NS MSG NSG P PD])
```

A.2.21 The rule package @ADV+ADV:

```
(@ADV+ADV
 [LAMBDA (E1 E2)
  (LIST (@RADV+ADV E1 E2)
    (@RPREP+MAIN E1 E2)
    (@RMAIN+FVERB E1 E2)
    (@RSUBCL+MAIN E1 E2])
```

A.2.22 The combination rule @RAUX+PRED:

```
(@RAUX+PRED
 [LAMBDA (EXPR1 EXPR2)
  (COND
   ([AND (NOT (@END-PREP EXPR1))
      (COND
       [[OR [AND (@UNTERMENGE (QUOTE (V S))
              (CADR EXPR2))
          (MEMB (CAR (CADR EXPR1))
            (QUOTE (ADJ ADV-L]
         (AND (@UNTERMENGE (QUOTE (V WP))
              (CADR EXPR2))
          (MEMB (CAR (CADR EXPR1))
            (QUOTE (ADJ]
        (SETQ CAT (APPEND (LDIFFERENCE (CADR EXPR2)
                (QUOTE (S WP)))
              (CDR (CADR EXPR1]
       ([OR [AND (@UNTERMENGE (QUOTE (V S))
              (CADR EXPR1))
          (MEMB (CAR (CADR EXPR2))
            (QUOTE (ADJ ADV-L S1 S2 S3 P1 P2 P3]
         (AND (@UNTERMENGE (QUOTE (V WP))
              (CADR EXPR1))
          (MEMB (CAR (CADR EXPR2))
            (QUOTE (ADJ S1 S2 S3 P1 P2 P3]
        (SETQ CAT (APPEND (LDIFFERENCE (CADR EXPR1)
                (QUOTE (S WP ADV-L ADV-T ADV-M
```

```
                              ADV-C ADV-D)))
                   (CDR (CADR EXPR2]
      (LIST (FUNCTION AUX-PRED)
         (LIST (APPEND (CAR EXPR1)
                (CAR EXPR2))
            CAT])
```

A.2.23 The rule package AUX-PRED:

```
(AUX-PRED
 [LAMBDA (E1 E2)
  (LIST (@RCMPLT E1 E2)
     (@RNOUN+RELPRO E1 E2)
     (@RFVERB+MAIN E1 E2)
     (@RMAIN+FVERB E1 E2)
     (@RMAINCL+NFVERB E1 E2)
     (@RDET+ADJ E1 E2)
     (@RDET+NOUN E1 E2)
     (@RPREP+MAIN E1 E2])
```

A.2.24 The combination rule @RSUBCL+MAIN:

```
(@RSUBCL+MAIN
 [LAMBDA (EXPR1 EXPR2)
  (COND
   ((AND (NOT (@END-PREP EXPR1))
      [OR (END-SUBCL EXPR1)
        (EQ (CAR (CADR EXPR1))
           (QUOTE (V ADCL)))
        (MEMB (QUOTE H)
           (MEMB (QUOTE INF)
              (CADR EXPR1]
      (@EQ-MAINC EXPR2)
      (NOT (MEMB (QUOTE I)
           (CADR EXPR2)))
      (COND
       [(MEMB (CAR (CADR EXPR2))
           (QUOTE (G D A)))
        (AND [NOT (MEMB (CAR (CADR EXPR2))
              (@ADIFF (@LASTV (CADR EXPR1))
                 (QUOTE (A]
           (NOT (@UNTERMENGE (QUOTE (D A))
                 (@LASTV (CADR EXPR1]
       ((MEMB (CAR (CADR EXPR2))
           (QUOTE (ADJ)))
        (EQ (@ADIFF [CDR (@STRIP (@LASTV (CADR EXPR1]
              (QUOTE (S1 S2 S3 P1 P2 P2 ADV-L ADV-M ADV-T
                    ADV-C ADV-D -E -EN)))
           NIL))
       [(MEMB (CAR (CADR EXPR2))
           (QUOTE (S1 S2 S3 P1 P2 P3)))
        (COND
         [(INTERSECTION (QUOTE (G D A))
               (@LASTV (CADR EXPR1)))
          (NOT (INTERSECTION (QUOTE (INF S1 S2 S3 P1 P2 P3))
                 (@LASTV (CADR EXPR1]
```

```
          (T (NOT (INTERSECTION (QUOTE (S1 S2 S3 P1 P2 P3))
                      (@ADIFF (CADR EXPR1)
                          (QUOTE (S1 S2 S3 P1 P2 P3]
        (T T)))
      (LIST (FUNCTION @SUBCL+MAIN)
        (LIST (APPEND (CAR EXPR1)
              (CAR EXPR2))
          (APPEND (@ADIFF (CADR EXPR1)
                (QUOTE (-E -EN)))
              (CADR EXPR2]))
```

A.2.25 The rule package @SUBCL+MAIN:

```
(@SUBCL+MAIN
 [LAMBDA (E1 E2)
  (LIST (@RSUBCL+MAIN E1 E2)
     (@RDET+NOUN E1 E2)
     (@RDET+ADJ E1 E2)
     (@RPREP+MAIN E1 E2)
     (@RSUBCL+VERB E1 E2)
     (@RSUBCL+LASTVERB E1 E2]))
```

A.2.26 The combination rule @RSUBCL+VERB:

```
(@RSUBCL+VERB
 [LAMBDA (EXPR1 EXPR2)
  (COND
   ([AND (NOT (@END-PREP EXPR1))
      [COND
       [[AND (INTERSECTION (CADR EXPR2)
               (QUOTE (S1 S2 S3 P1 P2 P3)))
          (NOT (MEMB (QUOTE D)
              (CADR EXPR2]
        (AND (MEMB (QUOTE H)
            (CADR EXPR2))
          (MEMB (CADR (CADR EXPR2))
            (@LASTV (CADR EXPR1)))
          (NOT (MEMB (QUOTE INF)
              (@LASTV (CADR EXPR1]
       [(EQUAL (CADR EXPR2)
          (QUOTE (Z)))
        (NOT (@DOUBLE-NOM (@LASTV (CADR EXPR1]
       (T (AND (INTERSECTION (CADR EXPR2)
               (QUOTE (H S W Q WP ADJ)))
          (@UNTERMENGE (INTERSECTION (CADR EXPR2)
                  (QUOTE (ADV-L ADV-D ADV-T ADV-C ADV-M)))
              (@LASTV (CADR EXPR1)))
          (OR (@UNTERMENGE (@STRIP (@CANCEL (CDR (@LASTV
                            (CADR EXPR1)))
                      (CADR EXPR2)))
              (QUOTE (S1 S2 S3 P1 P2 P3 ADV-L ADV-D
                  ADV-T ADV-C ADV-M H S W WP Z Q INF ADJ)))
            (@UNTERMENGE (@STRIP (@CANCEL (MEMB (QUOTE INF)
                      (CADR EXPR1))
                  (CADR EXPR2)))
              (QUOTE (S1 S2 S3 P1 P2 P3 ADV-L ADV-D
```

```
                         ADV-T ADV-C ADV-M H S W WP INF)))
        (@UNTERMENGE (@STRIP (@CANCEL (CDR (@LASTV (CADR EXPR1)))
                             (CADR EXPR2)))
                  (QUOTE (D ADJ S]
[COND
 [[AND (@LASTV (CADR EXPR1))
    (NOT (MEMB (QUOTE H)
          (@LASTV (CADR EXPR1]
  (AND [SETQ ARG1 (REVERSE (CDR (MEMB (QUOTE V)
                       (REVERSE (CADR EXPR1]
     (SETQ ARG2 (@LASTV (CADR EXPR1]
 ([MEMB (QUOTE H)
     (CDR (MEMB (QUOTE INF)
          (CADR EXPR1]
  (AND (SETQ ARG1 [REVERSE (MEMB (QUOTE INF)
                   (REVERSE (CADR EXPR1]
     (SETQ ARG2 (CDR (MEMB (QUOTE INF)
                (CADR EXPR1]
(COND
 ((AND (EQUAL (CADR EXPR2)
        (QUOTE (H W INF)))
    (@UNTERMENGE (QUOTE (W INF))
          ARG2))
  (SETQ CAT (CADR EXPR1)))
 [(AND (MEMB (CAR (CADR EXPR2))
        (QUOTE (W Q)))
    (MEMB (QUOTE Z)
      ARG2))
  (SETQ CAT (APPEND ARG1 (@CANCEL (@ADIFF ARG2 (QUOTE (Z)))
                  (CDR (CADR EXPR2)))
          (COND
            ((EQ (CAR (CADR EXPR2))
               (QUOTE W))
             (QUOTE (H)))
            ((EQ (CAR (CADR EXPR2))
               (QUOTE Q))
             (QUOTE (S]
 [(AND [OR (@DOUBLE-NOM (@LASTV (CADR EXPR1)))
      (MEMB (QUOTE ADJ)
          (@LASTV (CADR EXPR1]
    (MEMB (CAR (CADR EXPR2))
      (QUOTE (S W)))
    (EQ (CADR (CADR EXPR2))
      (QUOTE WP)))

  (AND [COND
      [(INTERSECTION (CDR (MEMB (QUOTE S3)
                 (REVERSE ARG2)))
             (QUOTE (S3 P3)))
       (SETQ ARG2 (@ADIFF ARG2 (QUOTE (S3]
      [(INTERSECTION (CDR (MEMB (QUOTE P3)
                 (REVERSE ARG2)))
             (QUOTE (S3 P3)))
       (SETQ ARG2 (@ADIFF ARG2 (QUOTE (P3]
      ((MEMB (QUOTE ADJ)
         ARG2)
```

```
                  (SETQ ARG2 (@ADIFF ARG2 (QUOTE (ADJ]
                  (SETQ CAT (APPEND ARG1 ARG2 (@ADIFF (CADR EXPR2)
                                   (QUOTE (WP]
            [[COND
              [(EQ (CAR ARG2)
                  (QUOTE V))
               (AND (@UNTERMENGE (@ADIFF (CADR EXPR2)
                           (QUOTE (H S W WP INF -AG)))
                       ARG2)
                  [NOT (EQUAL (CADR EXPR2)
                       (QUOTE (H W]
                  (NOT (EQUAL (CADR EXPR2)
                       (QUOTE (S Q]
             ((EQ (CAR (LAST ARG1))
                  (QUOTE INF))
               (NOT (INTERSECTION (@ADIFF ARG2 (CADR EXPR2))
                       (QUOTE (G D A]
             (SETQ CAT (APPEND ARG1 (COND
                       [(AND (EQ (CADDR (CADR EXPR2))
                           (QUOTE S))
                          (MEMB (QUOTE ADJ)
                             ARG2))
                         (APPEND (@CANCEL (@ADIFF ARG2 (QUOTE (ADJ)))
                               (CADR EXPR2))
                             (QUOTE (S]
                       ((OR (EQ (CAR (CADR EXPR2))
                           (QUOTE V))
                          (EQ (CAR ARG2)
                             (QUOTE INF)))
                        (@CANCEL (UNION (QUOTE (INF))
                               (CADR EXPR2))
                             ARG2))
                       (T (@CANCEL ARG2 (UNION (QUOTE (INF))
                                 (CADR EXPR2]
             (T (SETQ CAT (APPEND ARG1 (@CANCEL (@LASTV (CADR EXPR1))
                       (CADR EXPR2]
          (LIST (FUNCTION @SUBCL+VERB)
             (LIST (APPEND (CAR EXPR1)
                   (CAR EXPR2))
                CAT])
```

A.2.27 The rule package @SUBCL+VERB:

```
(@SUBCL+VERB
 [LAMBDA (E1 E2)
   (LIST (@RSUBCL+VERB E1 E2)
      (@RSUBCL+LASTVERB E1 E2])
```

A.2.28 The combination rule @RSUBCL+LASTVERB:

```
(@RSUBCL+LASTVERB
 [LAMBDA (EXPR1 EXPR2)
   (COND
    ([COND
       [[AND (@LASTV (CADR EXPR1))
          (EQ (CAR (CADR EXPR2))
```

```
                 (QUOTE V))
          (OR [AND (@UNTERMENGE (@ADIFF [@STRIP (@ADIFF (@LASTV
                                                  (CADR EXPR1))
                              (QUOTE (INF]
                        (CADR EXPR2))
                     (QUOTE (ADV-D ADV-L ADV-M ADV-C ADV-T)))
              (@UNTERMENGE (CADR EXPR2)
                       (@LASTV (CADR EXPR1]
             (AND (@UNTERMENGE [@ADIFF (CADR EXPR2)
                        (@STRIP (@ADIFF (@LASTV (CADR EXPR1))
                              (QUOTE (INF]
                       (QUOTE (S WP)))
                 (@UNTERMENGE (@ADIFF (@STRIP (@ADIFF (@LASTV (CADR EXPR1))
                              (QUOTE (INF)))
                        (CADR EXPR2))
                     (QUOTE (ADJ S1 S2 S3 P1 P2 P3]
           (SETQ CAT (APPEND [REVERSE (CDR (MEMB (QUOTE V)
                         (REVERSE (CADR EXPR1]
                 (INTERSECTION (@LASTV (CADR EXPR1))
                       (QUOTE (MS FS NS MSG NSG P PD]
          ([AND [@UNTERMENGE (QUOTE (H W INF))
                (CDR (MEMB (QUOTE INF)
                     (CADR EXPR1]
             (@UNTERMENGE (CADR EXPR2)
                    (QUOTE (H W INF]
             (SETQ CAT (APPEND [REVERSE (CDR (MEMB (QUOTE INF)
                          (CDR (REVERSE (CADR EXPR1]
                   (INTERSECTION (@LASTV (CADR EXPR1))
                         (QUOTE (MS FS NS MSG NSG P PD]
          (LIST (FUNCTION @SUBCL+LASTVERB)
            (LIST (APPEND (CAR EXPR1)
                  (CAR EXPR2)
                  (QUOTE (,)))
               CAT])
```

A.2.29 The rule package @SUBCL+LASTVERB:

```
(@SUBCL+LASTVERB
 [LAMBDA (E1 E2)
  (LIST (@RFVERB+MAIN E1 E2)
     (@RSUBCL+VERB E1 E2)
     (@RSUBCL+LASTVERB E1 E2)
     (@RMAIN+FVERB E1 E2)
     (@RNOUN+RELPRO E1 E2)
     (@RCMPLT E1 E2])
```

A.2.30 The combination rule @RNOUN+SUBPREP:

```
(@RNOUN+SUBPREP
 [LAMBDA (EXPR1 EXPR2)
  (COND
   ([AND (@END-NOUN EXPR1)
      (MEMB (CAR (CADR EXPR2))
         (QUOTE (ADV-L ADV-T ADV-D ADV-M ADV-C)))
      (MEMBER (CADR (CADR EXPR2))
         (QUOTE ((D)
```

```
                        (A]
        (LIST (FUNCTION @NOUN+SUBPREP)
            (LIST (APPEND (CAR EXPR1)
                    (QUOTE (,))
                    (CAR EXPR2))
                (APPEND (CADR EXPR1)
                    (QUOTE (V))
                    (CADR EXPR2])
```

A.2.31 The rule package @NOUN+SUBPREP:

```
(@NOUN+SUBPREP
 [LAMBDA (E1 E2)
  (LIST (@RSUBPREP+PRO E1 E2)])
```

A.2.32 The combination rule @RSUBPREP+PRO:

```
(@RSUBPREP+PRO
 [LAMBDA (EXPR1 EXPR2)
  (COND
    ([AND [MEMBER [CAR (LAST (@LASTV (CADR EXPR1]
            (QUOTE ((D)
                  (A]
        [EQ (CAR (CADR EXPR2))
          (CAAR (LAST (CADR EXPR1]
        [EQ (CADR (CADR EXPR2))
          (CADR (MEMB (QUOTE V)
                (REVERSE (CADR EXPR1]
        (MEMB (CAAR EXPR2)
            (QUOTE (DER DES DEM DEN DIE DAS]
      (LIST (FUNCTION @SUBPREP+PRO)
          (LIST (APPEND (CAR EXPR1)
                (CAR EXPR2))
            (REVERSE (CDR (REVERSE (CADR EXPR1])])
```

A.2.33 The rule package @SUBPREP+PRO:

```
(@SUBPREP+PRO
 [LAMBDA (E1 E2)
  (LIST (@RSUBCL+MAIN E1 E2)])
```

A.2.34 The combination rule @RCMPLT:

```
(@RCMPLT
 [LAMBDA (EXPR1 EXPR2)
  (COND
    ((AND (@UNTERMENGE (CADR EXPR1)
            (QUOTE (V I -AG -FA -E -EN MS FS NS MSG NSG P
                    PD INF)))
        [MEMBER (CADR EXPR2)
            (QUOTE ((V DECL)
                  (I INTERROG]
        (COND
          ((MEMB (QUOTE I)
              (CADR EXPR1))
            (MEMB (QUOTE I)
```

```
           (CADR EXPR2)))
      (T T)))
  (LIST (FUNCTION @CMPLT)
     (LIST [COND
         ((EQ (CAR (LAST (CAR EXPR1)))
             (QUOTE ,))
          (APPEND [REVERSE (CDR (REVERSE (CAR EXPR1]
              (CAR EXPR2)))
         (T (APPEND (CAR EXPR1)
               (CAR EXPR2]
        (CDR (CADR EXPR2])
```

A.2.35 The rule package **@CMPLT**:

```
(@CMPLT
 [LAMBDA (E1 E2)
  (LIST (@RSTART E1 E2])
```

A.2.36 The combination rule **@RSTART**:

```
(@RSTART
 [LAMBDA (EXPR1 EXPR2)
  (COND
   ((AND (MEMB (CAR (CADR EXPR1))
          (QUOTE (DECL INTERROG)))
      (OR (@EQ-MAINC EXPR2)
        (@EQ-NFVERB EXPR2)))
    (LIST (FUNCTION @START)
       (LIST (APPEND (CAR EXPR1)
             (CAR EXPR2))
          (CADR EXPR2])
```

A.3   Auxiliary functions of the linguistic rules

The 18 linguistic combination rules of DCAT use a number of auxiliary functions, which are defined below.

A.3.1 The auxiliary function **@CANCEL**:

```
(@CANCEL
 [LAMBDA (EXPR1 EXPR2)
  (APPEND (@ADIFF EXPR1 EXPR2)
     (@ADIFF EXPR2 EXPR1])
```

A.3.2 The auxiliary function **@ADIFF**:

```
(@ADIFF
 [LAMBDA (EXPR1 EXPR2)
  (COND
   (EXPR2 (@ADIFF (@AREMOVE EXPR1 (CAR EXPR2))
        (CDR EXPR2)))
   (T EXPR1])
```

A.3.3 The auxiliary function **@STRIP**:

```
(@STRIP
 [LAMBDA (EXPRN)
  (LDIFFERENCE EXPRN (QUOTE (MS FS NS MG NG P PD ADCL
                            -AG -FA])
```

A.3.4 The auxiliary function @AREMOVE:

```
(@AREMOVE
 [LAMBDA (EXPR1 EXPR2)
  (COND
   ((NULL EXPR1)
    NIL)
   ((EQ (CAR EXPR1)
       EXPR2)
    (CDR EXPR1))
   (T (CONS (CAR EXPR1)
          (@AREMOVE (CDR EXPR1)
              EXPR2])
```

A.3.5 The auxiliary function @EQ-DET:

```
(@EQ-DET
 [LAMBDA (EXPRN)
  (COND
   ([AND (MEMBER (CAR (CADR EXPRN))
          (QUOTE (S3 P3 G D A)))
     (MEMB (CADR (CADR EXPRN))
          (QUOTE (MS FS NS MG NG P PD)))
     (MEMB (CADDR (CADR EXPRN))
          (QUOTE (-E -EN -ES -ER]
    T])
```

A.3.6 The auxiliary function @DOUBLE-NOM:

```
(@DOUBLE-NOM
 [LAMBDA (EXPRN)
  (COND
   ([OR (INTERSECTION (CDR (MEMB (QUOTE S1)
                  EXPRN))
          (QUOTE (S1 S2 S3 P1 P2 P3)))
     (INTERSECTION (CDR (MEMB (QUOTE S2)
                  EXPRN))
          (QUOTE (S1 S2 S3 P1 P2 P3)))
     (INTERSECTION (CDR (MEMB (QUOTE S3)
                  EXPRN))
          (QUOTE (S1 S2 S3 P1 P2 P3)))
     (INTERSECTION (CDR (MEMB (QUOTE P1)
                  EXPRN))
          (QUOTE (S1 S2 S3 P1 P2 P3)))
     (INTERSECTION (CDR (MEMB (QUOTE P2)
                  EXPRN))
          (QUOTE (S1 S2 S3 P1 P2 P3)))
     (INTERSECTION (CDR (MEMB (QUOTE P3)
                  EXPRN))
          (QUOTE (S1 S2 S3 P1 P2 P3]
    T])
```

A.3.7 The auxiliary function @EQ-ADJ:

```
(@EQ-ADJ
 [LAMBDA (EXPRN)
  (COND
   ([MEMBER (CADR EXPRN)
        (QUOTE ((-E)
            (-EN)
            (-ER)
            (-ES]
     T])
```

A.3.8 The auxiliary function @EQ-MAINC:

```
(@EQ-MAINC
 [LAMBDA (EXPRN)
  (COND
   ([AND [OR (EQ (@LASTV (CADR EXPRN))
          NIL)
        (MEMB (CAR (CADR EXPRN))
           (QUOTE (ADCL SC]
     (MEMB (CAR (CADR EXPRN))
        (QUOTE (S1 S2 S3 P1 P2 P3 G D A -AG -FA ADCL ADV-T ADV-L
ADV-M ADV-C ADV-D SC SCI]
     T])
```

A.3.9 The auxiliary function @EQ-NOUN:

```
(@EQ-NOUN
 [LAMBDA (EXPRN)
  (COND
   ((MEMB (CAADR EXPRN)
       (QUOTE (MS FS NS MG NG P PD)))
     T])
```

A.3.10 The auxiliary function @EQ-FVERB:

```
(@EQ-FVERB
 [LAMBDA (EXPRN)
  (COND
   ((AND (EQ (CAR (CADR EXPRN))
       (QUOTE V)))
     T])
```

A.3.11 The auxiliary function @EQ-NFVERB:

```
(@EQ-NFVERB
 [LAMBDA (EXPRN)
  (COND
   ([AND (MEMB (CAR (CADR EXPRN))
        (QUOTE (H S W WP INF Q Z DE1 DE2 DE3 DE4 DE5 DE6)))
     (@UNTERMENGE (CDR (CADR EXPRN))
          (QUOTE (S1 S2 S3 P1 P2 P3 G D A -AG -FA MS FS NS MG NS
          G P PD ADV-T ADV-L ADV-M ADV-D ADV-C H S W WP SC INF Q Z]
     T])
```

A.3.12 The auxiliary function @UNTERMENGE:

```
(@UNTERMENGE
 [LAMBDA (EXPR1 EXPR2)
  (COND
   ((NULL EXPR1)
    T)
   ((MEMBER (CAR EXPR1)
         EXPR2)
    (@UNTERMENGE (CDR EXPR1)
         EXPR2))
   (T NIL])
```

A.3.13 The auxiliary function @LASTV:

```
(@LASTV
 [LAMBDA (X)
  (PROG [(RESULT (MEMBER (QUOTE V)
              (CDR X]
     (COND
      ((NULL RESULT)
       (RETURN NIL))
      ((NOT (MEMBER (QUOTE V)
             (CDR RESULT)))
       (RETURN RESULT))
      (T (RETURN (@LASTV (CDR RESULT])
```

A.3.14 The auxiliary function @END-DET:

```
(@END-DET
 [LAMBDA (EXPRN)
  (COND
   ([AND (MEMB (CAR (LAST (CADR EXPRN)))
         (QUOTE (-E -EN -ES -ER)))
      (MEMB (CAR (NLEFT (CADR EXPRN)
               2))
         (QUOTE (MS FS NS MG NG P PD]
    T])
```

A.3.15 The auxiliary function @END-NOUN:

```
(@END-NOUN
 [LAMBDA (EXPRN)
  (COND
   ([AND (MEMBER (CAR (LAST (CADR EXPRN)))
         (QUOTE (MS FS NS MG NG P PD]
    T])
```

A.3.16 The auxiliary function @END-PREP:

```
(@END-PREP
 [LAMBDA (EXPRN)
  (INTERSECTION (CADR EXPRN)
        (QUOTE ((D)
             (A])
```

A.4 Alphabetical list of DCAT-functions

For easier reference, an annotated list of all LISP functions of DCAT is given below. The functions are ordered alphabetically. The place of the actual definition is stated in parentheses before the name of the function.

1. (A.3.2) **@ADIFF**: Auxiliary DCAT function called by @CANCEL. ADDIFF of two lists results in a new list containing all elements of the first list which are not elements of the second list.

2. (A.2.2) **@ADV+ADV**: DCAT rule package.

3. (A.3.4) **@AREMOVE**: Auxiliary DCAT function called by @ADIFF.

4. (A.2.23) **@AUX+PRED**: DCAT rule package.

5. (A.1.13) **@BUILDHIST**: Auxiliary motor function. Builds numbered history sections of DCAT printouts.

6. (A.3.1) **@CANCEL**: Auxiliary DCAT function. Called by @RMAIN+FVERB,@RMAINCL+NFVERB,@R?FV+MAIN, @RSUBCL+VERB. @CANCEL of two lists A and B results in the union of A and B minus the intersection of A and B.

7. (A.1.8) **@COMB**: Motor function. Called by @TR2. Applies rule package of sentence start to ordered pairs derived from sentence start and next word.

8. (A.2.35) **@CMPLT**: DCAT rule package.

9. (A.2.3) **@DET+ADJ**: DCAT rule package

10. (A.2.5) **@DET+NOUN**: DCAT rule package.

11. (A.3.6) **@DOUBLE-NOM**: Auxiliary DCAT function. Called by @RSUBCL+VERB. Checks for sentence starts with double nominatives in subordinate clauses, as in *Weil Peter ein guter Arzt geworden ist.*

12. (A.3.14) **@END-DET**: Auxiliary DCAT function. Called by@RDET+ADJ, @RDET+NOUN, @RNOUN+PREP, @RADV+ADV. Returns T if a sentence start ends in a determiner.

13. (A.3.15) **@END-NOUN**:Auxiliary DCAT function. Calledby@RNOUN+PREP, @RNOUN+RELPRO, @RNOUN+SUBPREP. Returns T if a sentence start ends in a noun.

14. (A.3.16) **@END-PREP**: Auxiliary DCAT function. Called by RMAIN+FVERB, @RFVERB+MAIN, @RMAINCL+NFVERB, @RAUX+PRED,@RSUBCL+MAIN,@RSUBCL+VERB. Returns T if a sentence start ends in a noun.

15. (A.3.7) **@EQ-ADJ**: Auxiliary DCAT function. Called by @RDET+ADJ. Returns T if argument is an adjective.

16. (A.3.5) **@EQ-DET**: Auxiliary DCAT function. Called by @RNOUN-+RELPRO. Returns T if argument is a determiner.

17. (A.3.10) **@EQ-FVERB**: Auxiliary DCAT function. Called by @RMAIN-+FVERB. Returns T if argument is a finite verb.

18. (A.3.8) **@EQ-MAINC**: Auxiliary DCAT function. Called by @RMAIN-+FVERB, @RFVERB+MAIN, @R?FV+MAIN, @RSUBCL+MAIN, @RSTART. Returns T if argument is a main constituent.

19. (A.3.11) **@EQ-NFVERB**: Auxiliary DCAT function. Called by @RMAIN+FVERB, @RMAINCL+NFVERB, @RSTART. Returns T if argument is a non-finite verb.

20. (A.3.9) **@EQ-NOUN**: Auxiliary DCAT function. Called by @RDET-+NOUN. Returns T if argument is a noun.

21. (A.1.11) **@EXPAND**: Auxiliary motor function. Called by R. Expands DLEX analysis of words into sentence starts.

22. (A.2.15) **@FVERB+MAIN**: DCAT rule package.

23. (A.2.19) **@?FV+MAIN**: DCAT rule package.

24. (A.3.13) **@LASTV**: Auxiliary DCAT function. Called by @RNOUN-+RELPRO, @RFVERB+MAIN, @RSUBCL+MAIN, @RSUBCL-+VERB, @RSUBCL+LASTVERB, @RSUBPREP+PRO, @EQ-MAINC. If argument is category with non-initial V-segment, @LASTV returns tail beginning with the last V. Otherwise NIL.

25. (A.1.14) **@MAKEPAIR**: Auxiliary motor function. Called by @COMB. Forms Cartesian product of two lists.

26. (A.1.15) **@MAKEHIST**: Auxiliary motor function. Called by @BUILD-HIST. Makes history segments out of sentence starts and next words.

27. (A.2.13) **@MAIN+FVERB**: DCAT rule package.

28. (A.2.17) **@MAINCL+NFVERB**: DCAT rule package.

29. (A.2.7) **@NOUN+PREP**: DCAT rule package.

30. (A.2.11) **@NOUN+RELPRO**: DCAT rule package.

31. (A.2.31) **@NOUN+SUBPREP**: DCAT rule package.

32. (A.2.9) **@PREP+MAIN**: DCAT rule package.

33. (A.1.2) **@R**: Top motor function.

34. (A.2.20) **@RADV+ADV**: DCAT combination rule.

35. (A.2.22) **@RAUX+PRED**: DCAT combination rule.

36. (A.2.34) **@RCMPLT**: DCAT combination rule.

37. (A.2.2) **@RDET+ADJ**: DCAT combination rule.

38. (A.2.4) **@RDET+NOUN**: DCAT combination rule.

39. (A.2.14) **@RFVERB+MAIN**: DCAT combination rule.

40. (A.2.18) **@R?FV+MAIN**: DCAT combination rule.

41. (A.2.12) **@RMAIN+FVERB**: DCAT combination rule.

42. (A.2.16) **@RMAINCL+NFVERB**: DCAT combination rule.

43. (A.2.6) **@RNOUN+PREP**: DCAT combination rule.

44. (A.2.10) **@RNOUN+RELPRO**: DCAT combination rule.

45. (A.2.30) **@RNOUN+SUBPREP**: DCAT combination rule.

46. (A.2.8) **@RPREP+MAIN**: DCAT combination rule.

47. (A.2.36) **@RSTART**: DCAT combination rule.

48. (A.2.24) **@RSUBCL+MAIN**: DCAT combination rule.

49. (A.2.28) **@RSUBCL+LASTVERB**: DCAT combination rule.

50. (A.2.26) **@RSUBCL+VERB**: DCAT combination rule.

51. (A.2.32) **@RSUBPREP+PRO**: DCAT combination rule.

52. (A.2.1) **@START**: Initial DCAT rule package.

53. (A.3.3) **@STRIP**: Auxiliary DCAT function. Called by @RMAIN-CL+NFVERB, @RSUBCL+MAIN, @RSUBCL+VERB, @RSUBCL-+LASTVERB. Strips noun, agent, and adsentential clause segments from argument. Used to compare categories where stripped segments would interfer.

54. (A.2.25) **@SUBCL+MAIN**: DCAT rule package.

55. (A.2.29) **@SUBCL+LASTVERB**: DCAT rule package.

56. (A.2.27) **@SUBCL+VERB**: DCAT rule package.

57. (A.2.23) **@SUBPREP+PRO**: DCAT rule package.

58. (A.1.7) **@TR2**: Motor function. Called by @R. Applies @COMB recursively.

59. (A.1.12) **@UNFOLD**: Auxiliary motor function. Called by @EXPAND.

60. (A.3.12) **@UNTERMENGE**: Auxiliary DCAT function. Checks whether members of a list form subset of another list. There is a function called SUBSET in INTERLISP-D, but it has the quite different purpose of selecting certain kinds of values from a list, e.g. select all the numbers from a list containing both letters and numbers.

A.5   The definitions of DLEX

```
(%. ((V DECL)))                    (ALTES ((-ES)))
(? ((I INTERROG)))                 (AM ((ADV-L MS -EN)
(AELTER ((ADJ)))                       (ADV-L NS -EN)))
(AELTERE ((-E)                     (AN ((ADV-L (D))
        (P3 P -E)                      (ADV-D (A))
        (A P -E)))                     (DE1)))
(AELTEREN ((-EN)                   (ANTIK ((ADJ)))
         (D P -EN)                 (ANTIKE ((-E)
         (P -EN)))                        (P3 P -E)
(AELTERER ((-ER)                          (A P -E)))
         (G P -ER)))               (ANTIKEN ((-EN)
(AELTERES ((-ES)))                          (D P -EN)
(AEPFEL ((P)                                (P)
        (P3 P)                              (P3 P)
        (A P)))                             (D P)
(AEPFELN ((PD)                              (A P)))
         (D P)))                   (ANTIKER ((-ER)
(AERZTE ((P)                                (G P -ER)))
        (P3 P)                     (ANTIKES ((-ES)))
        (A P)))                    (APFEL ((MS)))
(AERZTEN ((PD)                     (APFELS ((MG)))
         (D P)))                   (ARZT ((MS)
(AESSE ((V S1 A)                          (ADJ)))
       (V S3 A)))                  (ARZTES ((MG)))
(AESSEN ((V P1 A)                  (ASS ((V S1 A)
        (V P3 A)))                       (V S3 A)))
(AESST ((V S2 A)                   (ASSEN ((V P1 A)
       (V P2 A)))                         (V P3 A)))
(ALLE ((P3 P -EN)                  (ASST ((V S2 A)
      (A P -EN)))                         (V P2 A)))
(ALLEM ((D NS -EN)))               (AUF ((ADV-L (D))
(ALLEN ((D P -EN)))                      (ADV-D (A))
(ALLER ((G P -ER)))                      (DE1)))
(ALLES ((S3 NS -E)                 (AUS ((ADV-L (D))))
       (A NS -E)))                 (AUTO ((NS)))
(ALS ((ADCL V)))                   (AUTOS ((P)
(ALT ((ADJ)))                             (NG)
(ALTE ((-E)                               (P3 P)
      (P3 P -E)                           (D P)
      (A P -E)))                          (A P)))
(ALTEN ((-EN)                      (BALD ((ADV-T)))
       (D P -EN)))                 (BEI ((ADV-L (D))
(ALTER ((-ER)                            (DE1)))
       (G P -ER)))                 (BEREIT ((ADJ)
```

```
               (ADJ S)))          (BRACHTEST ((V S2 D A)))
(BERG ((MS)))                      (BRACHTET ((V P2 D A)))
(BERGE ((P)                        (BRAECHTE ((V S1 D A)
        (P3 P)                               (V S3 D A)))
        (A P)))                    (BRAECHTEN ((V P1 D A)
(BERGEN ((PD)                                 (V P3 D A)))
         (D P)))                   (BRAECHTEST ((V S2 D A)))
(BERGES ((MG)))                    (BRAECHTET ((V P2 D A)))
(BETT ((NS)))                      (BRIEF ((MS)))
(BETTEN ((P)                       (BRIEFE ((P)
         (P3 P)                             (P3 P)
         (D P)                              (A P)))
         (A P)))                   (BRIEFEN ((PD)
(BETTES ((NG)))                             (D P)))
(BESSER ((ADJ)                     (BRIEFES ((MG)))
         (ADV-M)))                 (BRINGE ((V S1 D A)))
(BESSERE ((-E)                     (BRINGEN ((W D A INF)
          (P3 P -E)                          (Q D -AG)
          (A P -E)))                         (V P1 D A)
(BESSEREN ((-EN)                              (V P3 D A)))
           (D P -EN)))             (BRINGST ((V S2 D A)))
(BESSERER ((-ER)                   (BRINGT ((V S3 D A)))
           (G P -ER)))             (BRUECKE ((FS)))
(BESSERES ((-ES)))                 (BRUECKEN ((P)
(BEVOR ((ADV-T V)))                          (PD)
(BIN ((V S1 S)))                             (P3 P)
(BISHER ((ADV-T)))                           (D P)
(BIST ((V S2 S)))                            (A P)))
(BITTER ((ADV-M)))                 (BUCH ((NS)))
(BLAU ((ADJ)))                     (BUCHES ((NG)))
(BLAUE ((-E)                       (BUECHER ((P)
         (P3 P -E)                           (P3 P)
         (A P -E)))                          (A P)))
(BLAUEN ((-EN)                     (BUECHERN ((PD)
          (D P -EN)))                         (D P)))
(BLAUER ((-ER)                     (DARF ((V S3 A)
          (G P -ER)))                       (V S3 W)))
(BLAUES ((-ES)))                   (DARFST ((V S2 W)))
(BLUME ((FS)))                     (DAS ((S3 NS -E)
(BLUMEN ((P)                                (A NS -E)))
         (PD)                      (DASS ((SC V)))
         (P3 P)                    (DEIN ((S3 MS -ER)
         (D P)                               (S3 NS -ER)
         (A P)))                             (A NS -ER)))
(BRACHTE ((V S1 D A)              (DEINE ((P3 P -EN)
          (V S3 D A)))                      (A P -EN)))
(BRACHTEN ((V P1 D A)             (DEINEM ((D NS -EN)
            (V P3 D A)))                     (D MS -EN)))
```

```
(DEINES ((G MG -ES)
        (G NG -ES)))
(DEINEN ((D P -EN)
        (A MS -EN)))
(DEINER ((G P NPG -EN)
        (G FS -EN)
        (D FS -EN)))
(DEM ((D MS -EN)
      (D NS -EN)))
(DEN ((A MS -EN)
      (D PD -EN)))
(DENEN ((D P)))
(DER ((S3 MS -E)
      (G P -EN)
      (G FS -EN)
      (D FS -EN)))
(DEREN ((FS V A MS -EN)
        (P V A P -EN)))
(DES ((G SG -EN)))
(DESSEN ((A MS MS -EN)
         (A MS FS -E)
         (A MS NS -ES)
         (A MS P -E)
         (A NS MS -EN)
         (A NS FS -E)
         (A NS NS -ES)
         (A NS P -E)))
(DICH ((A)))
(DIE ((P3 P -EN)
      (S3 FS -E)
      (A FS -E)
      (A P -EN)))
(DIES ((S3)
       (A)))
(DIR ((D)))
(DORT ((ADV-L)))
(DU ((S2 MS)))
(DUERFEN ((H W INF)
          (V P1 W)
          (V P3 W)))
(DUERFE ((V S1 W)
         (V S3 W)))
(DUERFEST ((V S2 W)))
(DUERFT ((V P2 A)
         (V P2 W)))
(DUERFTE ((V S1 W)
          (V S3 W)))
(DUERFTEN ((V P1 W)
           (V P3 W)))
(DUERFTEST ((V S2 W)))
(DUERFTET ((V P2 W)))
(DURFTE ((V S1 W)
         (V S3 W)))
(DURFTEN ((V P1 W)
          (V P3 W)))
(DURFTEST ((V S2 W)))
(DURFTET ((V P2 W)))
(EIN ((S3 MS -ER)
      (S3 NS -ES)
      (A NS -ES)
      (DE2)))
(EINE ((S3 FS -E)
       (A FS -E)))
(EINEM ((D MS -EN)
        (D NS -EN)))
(EINEN ((A MS -EN)))
(EINER ((G FS -EN)
        (D FS -EN)
        (S3 MS)))
(EINES ((G MG -EN)
        (G NG -EN)
        (S3 NS)
        (A NS)))
(EINGELADEN ((H A)
             (WP -AG)))
(EINLADEN ((W A INF)
           (Q -AG)))
(EINLUD ((V S1 A)
         (V S3 A)))
(EINLUDEN ((V P1 A)
           (V P3 A)))
(EINLUDET ((V P2 A)))
(EINLUDST ((V S2 A)))
(EINLUED ((V S1 A)
          (V S3 A)))
(EINLUEDEN ((V P1 A)
            (V P3 A)))
(EINLUEDST ((V S2 A)))
(EINLUEDET ((V P2 A)))
(EINIGE ((P3 P -E)
         (A P -E)))
(EINIGEN ((D P -EN)))
(EINIGER ((G P -ER)))
(EINIGES ((S3 NS -ES)
          (A NS -ES)))
```

```
(ENDE ((V S1)                          (Q -AG)
      (NS)))                           (V P1 A)
(ENDEN ((W INF)                        (V P3 A)
       (V P1)                          (W ADV-L INF)
       (V P3)))                        (V P1 ADV-L)
(ENDEST ((V S2)))                      (V P3 ADV-L)))
(ENDET ((V S3)                  (FAHRT ((V P2 A)
       (V P2)))                        (V P2 ADV-L)
(ENDETE ((V S1)                        (FS)))
        (V S3)))                (FAEHRT ((V S2 A)
(ENDETEN ((V P1)                       (V S3 A)
         (V P3)))                      (V S2 ADV-L)
(ENDETEST ((V S2)))                    (V S3 ADV-L)))
(ER ((S3 MS)))                  (FAEHRST ((V S2 A)
(ES ((S3 NS)                           (V S3 A)
     (A NS)))                          (V S2 ADV-L)
(ESSE ((V S1 A)))                      (V S3 ADV-L)))
(ESSEN ((W A INF)               (FENSTER ((NS)
        (V P1 A)                       (P)
        (V P3 A)                       (P3 P)
        (NS)                           (A P)))
        (P)                     (FENSTERN ((PD)
        (PD)))                         (D P)))
(ESSENS ((NG)))                 (FENSTERS ((NG)))
(ESST ((V P2 A)))               (FILM ((MS)))
(EUCH ((D P)                    (FILME ((P)
       (A P)))                        (P3 P)
(EUER ((S3 MS -ER)                     (A P)))
       (S3 NS -ER)              (FILMEN ((PD)
       (A NS -ER)))                    (D P)))
(EURE ((P3 P -EN)               (FILMES ((MG)))
       (A P -EN)                (FISCH ((MS)))
       (S3 FS -E)               (FISCHE ((P)
       (A FS -E)))                     (P3 P)
(EUREM ((D NS -EN)                     (A P)))
        (D MS -EN)))            (FISCHEN ((PD)
(EURES (((EURES)                        (D P)))
        (G NS -ES))             (FISCHES ((MG)))
       ((EURES)                 (FRISCH ((ADJ)))
        (G MS -ES))))           (FRISCHER ((ADJ)))
(EUREN ((D P -EN)               (FRISCHERE ((-E)
        (A MS -EN)))                   (P3 P -E)
(EURER ((G P -EN)                      (A P -E)))
        (G FS -EN)              (FRISCHEREN ((-EN)
        (D FS -EN)))                    (D P -EN)))
(FAHRE ((V S1 A)                (FRISCHERER ((-ER)
        (V S1 ADV-L)))                  (G P -ER)))
(FAHREN ((W A INF)              (FRISCHERES ((-ES)))
```

```
(FRAGE ((FS)))                              (V P1 A)
(FRAGEN ((P)                                (V P3 A)))
        (PD)                        (FUEHRST ((V S2 A)
        (P3 P)                               (V S3 A)
        (D P)                                (V S2 ADV-L)
        (A P)))                              (V S3 ADV-L)))
(FRAU ((FS)))                       (FUEHRT ((V S2 A)
(FRAUEN ((P)                                (V S3 A)
        (PD)                                 (V S2 ADV-L)
        (P3 P)                               (V S3 ADV-L)))
        (D P)                       (FUHR ((V S1 A)
        (A P)))                             (V S3 A)
(FREUND ((MS)))                             (V S1 ADV-L)
(FREUNDE ((P)                               (V S3 ADV-L)))
         (P3 P)                     (FUHRST ((V S2 A)
         (A P)))                            (V P2 A)))
(FREUNDEN ((PD)                     (FUHREN ((V P1 A)
          (D P)))                           (V P3 A)
(FREUNDES ((MG)))                           (V P1 ADV-L)
(FRIERE ((V S1)))                           (V P3 ADV-L)))
(FRIEREN ((W INF)                   (FUHRT ((V S2 ADV-L)
         (W S3 D INF)                       (V P2 ADV-L)))
         (V P1)                     (GAB ((V S1 D A)
         (V P3)))                          (V S3 D A))
(FRIERST ((V S2)))                  (GABEL ((FS)))
(FRIERT ((V A)                      (GABELN ((P)
         (V P2)))                           (PD)
(FRITZ ((S3)                                (P3 P)
        (D)                                 (D P)
        (A)))                               (A P)))
(FRITZENS ((G)))                    (GABEN ((V P1 D A)
(FROR ((V S1)                               (V P3 D A)))
       (V S3)))                     (GABST ((V S2 D A))
(FROERE ((V S1)                     (GABT ((V P2 D A))
         (V A)))                    (GAEBE ((V S1 D A)
(FROERST ((V S2)))                          (V S3 D A)))
(FROEREN ((V P1)                    (GAEBEN ((V P1 D A)
          (V P3)))                           (V P3 D A)))
(FROERT ((V P2)))                   (GAEBST ((V S2 D A)))
(FROREN ((V P1)                     (GAEBT .((V P2 D A)))
         (V P3)))                   (GAERTEN ((P)
(FRORST ((V S2)))                            (PD)
(FRORT ((V P2)))                             (P3 P)
(FRUEHER ((ADV-T)))                          (D P)
(FUEHRE ((V S1 A)                            (A P)))
         (V S1 ADV-L)))             (GARTEN ((MS)))
(FUEHREN ((W A INF)                 (GARTENS ((MG)))
          (Q -AG)                   (GEBE ((V S1 D A)
```

```
            (V S1 D DE1)                    (GEHT ((V S3)
            (V S1 DE1)))                          (V P2)))
(GEBEN ((W D A INF)                     (GEKAUFT ((H A)
       (W D)                                      (WP -AG)))
       (Q D -AG)                         (GEKOCHT ((H A)
       (V P1 D A)                                 (WP -AG)))
       (V P3 D A)                        (GEKOMMEN ((S)))
(GEBRACHT ((H D A)                      (GEKONNT ((H A)
          (WP D -AG)))                           (W H)))
(GEBT ((V P2 D A)                       (GELACHT ((H)))
(GEDURFT ((H A)                         (GELEGEN ((H ADV-L)))
         (W H)))                        (GELESEN ((H A)
(GEENDET ((H)))                                  (H ADV-L)
(GEFAHREN ((H A)                                 (WP -AG)
          (WP -AG)))                             (S -AG)))
(GEFROREN ((H)                          (GELIEBT ((H A)
          (S)))                                  (WP -AG)))
(GEGANGEN ((S)))                        (GEMACHT ((H D A)
(GEGEBEN ((H D A)                                (H A)
         (WP D -AG)))                            (WP -AG)
(GEGESSEN ((H A)                                 (WP D -AG)))
          (WP -AG)))                    (GEMOCHT ((H A)
(GEGLAUBT ((H SC)                                (W H)))
          (WP D -AG)))                  (GENANNTE ((-E -E)))
(GEHABT ((H A)))                        (GENANNTEN ((-EN -EN)))
(GEHE ((V S1)))                         (GENANNTER ((-ER -ER)))
(GEHEN ((W INF)                         (GENANNTES ((-ES -ES)))
       (V P1)                           (GERN ((ADV-M)))
       (V P3)))                         (GERNE ((ADV-M)))
(GEHOERE ((V S1 D)))                    (GESOLLT ((H A)
(GEHOEREN ((W D INF)                             (W H)))
          (V P1 D)                      (GESUNGEN ((H A)
          (V P3 D)))                             (WP -AG)
(GEHOERST ((V S2 D)))                            (H)))
(GEHOERT ((V S3 D)                      (GEWESEN ((S S)))
         (V P2 D)                       (GEWOLLT ((H A)
         (H D)                                   (W H)))
         (WP -AG)))                     (GEWORDEN ((S WP)))
(GEHOERTE ((V S1 D)                     (GESCHLAFEN ((H)))
          (V S3 D)))                    (GESCHMECKT ((H)))
(GEHOERTEN ((V P1 D)                    (GESCHRIEBEN ((H D A)
           (V P3 D)))                                (H A)
(GEHOERTEST ((V S2 D)))                              (WP D -AG)
(GEHOERTET ((V P2 D)))                               (WP -AG)
(GEHOLFEN ((H D)                                     (S -AG)))
          (WP S3 D -AG)               (GESCHWIEGEN ((H)))
          (S S3 D -AG)))              (GESEHEN ((H A)
(GEHST ((V S2)))                              (WP -AG)))
```

```
(GESPROCHEN ((H)                              (V P2 A)))
          (H A)                       (GROSS ((ADJ)))
          (WP -AG)))                  (GROESSER ((ADJ)
(GESTAUNT ((H)))                                (ADV-M)))
(GESTERN ((ADV-T)))                   (GROESSERE ((-E)
(GEWOHNT ((H ADV-L)))                           (P3 P -E)
(GEWUSST ((H SC)                                (A P -E)))
        (H SCI)                       (GROESSEREN ((-EN)
        (H A)                                   (D P -EN)))
        (WP -AG)))                    (GROESSERER ((-ER)
(GEZEIGT ((H D A)                               (G P -ER)))
        (H A)                         (GROESSERES ((-ES)))
        (WP D -AG)))                  (GROSSE ((-E)
(GIBST ((V S2 D A)                              (P3 P -E)
(GIBT ((V S3 D A)                               (A P -E)))
(GING ((V S1)                         (GROSSEN ((-EN)
      (V S3)))                                  (D P -EN)))
(GINGE ((V S1)                        (GROSSER ((-ER)
       (V S3)))                                 (G P -ER)))
(GINGEN ((V P1)                       (GROSSES ((-ES)))
        (V P3)))                      (GRUEN ((ADJ)))
(GINGST ((V S2)))                     (GRUENE ((-E)
(GINGT ((V P2)))                                (P3 P -E)
(GLAUBE ((V S1 SC)                              (A P -E)))
        (V S1 A)))                    (GRUENEN ((-EN)
(GLAUBEN ((W SC INF)                            (D P -EN)))
         (V P1 SC)                    (GRUENER ((-ER)
         (V P3 SC)                              (G P -ER)
         (W A INF)                              (ADJ)))
         (V P1 A)                     (GRUENES ((-ES)))
         (V P3 A)))                   (GUT ((ADJ)))
(GLAUBST ((V S2 SC)                   (GUTE ((-E)
         (V S2 A)))                           (P3 P -E)
(GLAUBT ((V S3 SC)                            (A P -E)))
        (V P2 SC)                     (GUTEN ((-EN)
        (V S3 A)                              (D P -EN)))
        (V P2 A)))                    (GUTER ((-ER)
(GLAUBTE ((V S1 SC)                           (G P -ER)))
         (V S3 SC)                    (GUTES ((-ES)))
         (V S1 A)                     (HABE ((V S1 H)
         (V S3 A)))                         (V S1 A)))
(GLAUBTEN ((V P1 SC)                  (HABEST ((V S2 H)
          (V P3 SC)                           (V S2 A)))
          (V P1 A)                    (HABEN ((V P1 H)
          (V P3 A)))                          (V P3 H)
(GLAUBTEST ((V S2 SC)                          (V P1 A)
           (V S2 A)))                          (V P3 A)
(GLAUBTET ((V P2 SC)                           (Q S)
```

```
              (W A INF)))            (HELFEN ((W D INF)
(HABT ((V P2 H)                                (W S3 D -FA)
       (V P2 A)))                              (Q S3 D -FA)
(HAETTE ((V S1 H)                              (Q D -FA)
         (V S3 H)                              (V P1 D)
         (V S1 A)                              (V P3 D)))
         (V S3 A)))            (HELFT ((V P2 D)))
(HAETTEN ((V P1 H)             (HALF ((V S1 D)
          (V P3 H)                     (V S3 D)))
          (V P1 A)             (HALFST ((V S2 D)))
          (V P3 A)))           (HALFEN ((V P1 D)
(HAETTEST ((V S2 H)                     (V P3 D)))
           (V S2 A)))          (HALFT ((V P2 D)))
(HAETTET ((V P2 H)             (HEUTE ((ADV-T)))
          (V P2 A)))           (HIER ((ADV-L)))
(HAEUSER ((P)                  (HINTER ((ADV-L (D))
          (P3 P)                         (ADV-D (A))))
          (A P)))              (HUELFE ((V S1 D)
(HAEUSERN ((PD)                         (V S3 D)))
           (D P)))             (HUELFEST ((V S2 D)))
(HAMBURG ((S3 NS)              (HUELFEN ((V P1 D)
          (D NS)                         (V P3 D)))
          (A NS)))             (HUELFET ((V P2 D)))
(HAMBURGS ((G)))               (ICH ((S1 MS)))
(HANS ((S3 MS)                 (IHM ((D MS)))
       (D MS)                  (IHN ((A MS)))
       (A MS)))                (IHNEN ((D P)))
(HAST ((V S2 H)                (IHR ((D FS)
       (V S2 A)))                     (D FS -ES)
(HAT ((V S3 H)                        (P2 P)
      (V S3 A)))                      (S3 MS -ER)
(HATTE ((V S1 H)                      (S3 NS -ES)
        (V S3 H)                      (A NS -ES)))
        (V S1 A)               (IHRE ((P3 P -EN)
        (V S3 A)))                    (A P -EN)
(HATTEN ((V P1 H)                     (S3 FS -E)
         (V P3 H)                     (A FS -E)))
         (V P1 A)              (IHREN ((D P -EN)
         (V P3 A)))                    (A MS -EN)))
(HATTEST ((V S2 H)             (IHREM ((D NS -EN)
          (V S2 A)))                   (D MS -EN)))
(HATTET ((V P2 H)              (IHRER ((G P -EN)
         (V P2 A)))                    (G FS -EN)
(HAUS ((NS)))                          (D FS -EN)))
(HAUSES ((NG)))                (IHRES ((G NS -ES)
(HELFE ((V S1 D)))                     (G MS -ES)))
(HILFST ((V S2 D)))            (IM ((ADV-L MS -EN)
(HILFT ((V S3 D)))                   (ADV-L NS -EN)))
```

```
(IN ((ADV-L (D))                      (KAMST ((V S2)))
     (ADV-D (A))                      (KAMT ((V P2)))
     (DE6)))                          (KANN ((V S3 W)))
(INDEM ((ADCL V)))                    (KANNST ((V S2 W)))
(INTERESSANT ((ADV-M)                 (KATZE ((FS)))
          (ADJ)))                     (KATZEN ((P)
(ISST ((V S2 A)                                (PD)
       (V S3 A)))                              (P3 P)
(IST ((V S3 S)))                               (D P)
(JETZT ((ADV-T)))                              (A P)))
(JUENGER ((ADJ)))                     (KAUFE ((V S1 A)))
(JUENGERE ((-E)                       (KAUFEN ((W A INF)
         (P3 P -E)                              (V P1 A)
         (A P -E)))                             (V P3 A)))
(JUENGEREN ((-EN)                     (KAUFST ((V S2 A)))
          (D P -EN)))                 (KAUFT ((V S3 A)
(JUENGERER ((-ER)                             (V P2 A)))
          (G P -ER)))                 (KAUFTE ((V S1 A)
(JUENGERES ((-ES)))                            (V S3 A)))
(JUNG ((ADJ)))                        (KAUFTEN ((V P1 A)
(JUNGE ((-E)                                    (V P3 A)))
       (P3 P -E)                      (KAUFTEST ((V S2 A)))
       (A P -E)))                     (KAUFTET ((V P2 A)))
(JUNGEN ((-EN)                        (KIND ((NS)))
        (D P -EN)))                   (KINDER ((P)
(JUNGER ((-ER)                                 (P3 P)
        (G P -ER)))                            (A P)))
(JUNGES ((-ES)))                      (KINDERN ((PD)
(KAELTER ((ADJ)))                              (D P)))
(KAEME ((V S1)                        (KINDES ((NG)))
       (V S3)))                       (KLEIN ((ADV-M)
(KAEMEN ((V P1)                                (ADJ)))
        (V P3)))                      (KLEINE ((-E)
(KAEMST ((V S2)))                              (P3 P -E)
(KAEMT ((V P2)))                               (A P -E)))
(KALT ((ADJ)))                        (KLEINEN ((-EN)
(KALTE ((-E)                                   (D P -EN)))
       (P3 P -E)                      (KLEINER ((-ER)
       (A P -E)))                             (G P -ER)
(KALTEN ((-EN)                                (ADJ)))
        (D P -EN)))                   (KLEINERE ((-E)
(KALTER ((-ER)                                 (P3 P -E)
        (G P -ER)))                            (A P -E)))
(KALTES ((-ES)))                      (KLEINEREN ((-EN)
(KAM ((V S1)                                    (D P -EN)))
     (V S3)))                         (KLEINERER ((-ER)
(KAMEN ((V P1)                                  (G P -ER)))
       (V P3)))                       (KLEINERES ((-ES)))
```

```
(KLEINES ((-ES)))                    (KOMMT ((V S3)
(KLUEGER ((ADV-M)))                         (V P2)))
(KLUEGERE ((-E)                      (KONNTE ((V S1 A)
        (P3 P -E)                            (V S1 W)
        (A P -E)))                           (V S3 A)
(KLUEGEREN ((-EN)                            (V S3 W)))
          (D P -EN)))                (KONNTEST ((V S2 A)
(KLUEGERER ((-ER)                             (V S2 W)))
          (G P -ER)))                (KONNTEN ((V P1 A)
(KLUEGERES ((-ES)))                          (V P1 W)
(KLUG ((ADJ)                                 (V P3 A)
      (ADV-M)))                              (V P3 W)))
(KLUGE ((-E)                         (KONNTET ((V P2 A)
       (P3 P -E)                             (V P2 W)))
       (A P -E)))                    (KUCHEN ((MS)))
(KLUGEN ((-EN)                       (KUCHENS ((MG)))
        (D P -EN)))                  (LACHE ((V S1)))
(KLUGER ((-ER)                       (LACHEN ((NS)
        (G P -ER)))                          (W INF)
(KLUGES ((-ES)))                             (V P1)
(KOCHE ((V S1 A)))                           (V P3)))
(KOCHST ((V S2 A)))                  (LACHENS ((NG)))
(KOCHT ((V S3 A)))                   (LACHST ((V S2)))
(KOCHEN ((W D INF)                   (LACHT ((V S3)
        (V P1 A)                             (V P2)))
        (V P3 A)                     (LACHTE ((V S1)
        (NS)))                               (V S3)))
(KOCHENS ((NG)))                     (LACHTEST ((V S2)))
(KOCHTE ((V S1 A)                    (LACHTEN ((V P1)
        (V S3 A)))                           (V P3)))
(KOCHTEST ((V S2 A)))                (LACHTET ((V P2)))
(KOCHTEN ((V P1 A)                   (LADE ((V S1 A DE2)))
         (V P3 A)))                  (LADEN ((MS)
(KOCHTET ((V P2 A)))                         (V P1 A DE2)
(KOENNEN ((H W INF)                          (V P3 A DE2)))
         (V P1 W)                    (LADET ((V P2 A DE2)))
         (V P3 W)))                  (LAED ((V S3 A DE2)))
(KOENNT ((V P2 W)))                  (LAEDST ((V S2 A DE2)))
(KOENNTE ((V S3 W)))                 (LAESE ((V S1 A)
(KOENNTEN ((V P1 W)                          (V S1 ADV-L)
          (V P3 W)))                         (V S3 A)
(KOENNTEST ((V S2 W)))                       (V S3 ADV-L)))
(KOENNTET ((V P2 W)))                (LAESEN ((V P1 A)
(KOMME ((V S1)))                             (V P3 A)
(KOMMEN ((W INF)                             (V P1 ADV-L)
        (V P1)                               (V P3 ADV-L)))
        (V P3)))                     (LAEST ((V S2 A)
(KOMMST ((V S2)))                            (V P2 A)
```

```
        (V S2 ADV-L)                    (LEST ((V P2 A)
        (V P2 ADV-L)))                        (V P2 ADV-L)))
(LAEGE ((V S1 ADV-L)                   (LEXIKA ((P)
       (V S3 ADV-L)))                           (PD)
(LAEGST ((V S2 ADV-L)))                         (P3 P)
(LAEGEN ((V P1 ADV-L)                           (D P)
        (V P3 ADV-L)))                          (A P)))
(LAEGT ((V P2 ADV-L)))                 (LEXIKON ((NS)))
(LAG ((V S1 ADV-L)                     (LEXIKONS ((NG)))
     (V S3 ADV-L)))                    (LIEBE ((V S1 A)
(LAGEN ((V P1 ADV-L)                           (FS)))
       (V P3 ADV-L)))                  (LIEBEN ((W A INF)
(LAGST ((V S2 ADV-L)))                          (V P1 A)
(LAGT ((V P2 ADV-L)))                           (V P3 A)
(LANG ((ADJ)                                    (P)
      (ADV-M)))                                 (PD)))
(LANGE ((-E)                           (LIEBST ((V S2 A)))
       (P3 P -E)                       (LIEBT ((V S3 A)
       (A P -E)))                             (V P2 A)))
(LANGEN ((-EN)                         (LIEBTE ((V S1 A)
        (D P -EN)))                            (V S3 A)))
(LANGER ((-ER)                         (LIEBTEN ((V P1 A)
        (G P -ER)))                             (V P3 A)))
(LANGES ((-ES)))                       (LIEBTEST ((V S2 A)))
(LAS ((V S1 A)                         (LIEBTET ((V P2 A)))
     (V S3 A)                          (LIEGE ((V S1 ADV-L)))
     (V S1 ADV-L)                      (LIEGEN ((W ADV-L INF)
     (V S3 ADV-L)))                            (V P1 ADV-L)
(LASEN ((V P1 A)                               (V P3 ADV-L)))
       (V P3 A)                        (LIEGST ((V S2 ADV-L)))
       (V P1 ADV-L)                    (LIEGT ((V S3 ADV-L)
       (V P3 ADV-L)))                         (V P2 ADV-L)))
(LAST ((V S2 A)                        (LIEST ((V S2 A)
      (V P2 A)                                (V S3 A)
      (V S2 ADV-L)                            (V S2 ADV-L)
      (V P2 ADV-L)))                          (V S3 ADV-L)))
(LEICHT ((ADJ)                         (LOEFFEL ((MS)
        (ADJ S)))                               (P)
(LESE ((V S1 A)                                 (P3 P)
      (V S1 ADV-L)))                            (A P)))
(LESEN ((W A INF)                      (LOEFFELN ((PD)
       (Q -AG)                                  (D P)))
       (V P1 A)                        (LOEFFELS ((MG)))
       (V P3 A)                        (LUD ((V S1 A DE2)
       (W ADV-L INF)                         (V S3 A DE2)))
       (V P1 ADV-L)                    (LUEDE ((V S1 A DE2)))
       (V P3 ADV-L)))                  (LUEDEST ((V S2 A DE2)))
(LESENS ((NG)))                        (LUEDEN ((V P1 A DE2)
```

```
               (V P3 A DE2)))          (MEHRERE ((P3 P -E)
(LUEDET ((V P2 A DE2)))                    (A P -E)))
(LUDEN ((V P1 A DE2)               (MEHREREM ((D NS)))
        (V P3 A DE2)))             (MEHREREN ((-EN)
(LUDET ((V P2 A DE2)))                      (D P -EN)))
(LUDST ((V S2 A DE2)))             (MEHRERER ((G P -ER)))
(MACHE ((V S1 D A)))               (MEHRERES ((S3 NS)
(MACHEN ((W D A INF)                         (A NS)))
         (V P1 D A)                (MEIN ((S3 MS -ER)
         (V P3 D A)                       (S3 NS -ER)
         (W A INF)                        (A NS -ER)))
         (V P1 A)                  (MEINE ((P3 P -EN)
         (V P3 A)))                        (A P -EN)
(MACHST ((V S2 D A)))                      (S3 FS -E)
(MACHT ((V S3 D A)                         (A FS -E)))
        (V P2 D A)))               (MEINEM ((D NS -EN)
(MACHTE ((V S1 D A)                         (D MS -EN)))
         (V S3 D A)))              (MEINES ((A NS)
(MACHTEN ((V P1 D A)                        (G NS -ES)
          (V P3 D A)))                      (G MS -ES)))
(MACHTEST ((V S2 D A)))            (MEINEN ((D P -EN)
(MACHTET ((V P2 D A)))                      (A MS -EN)))
(MAEDCHEN ((NS)                    (MEINER ((G P -EN)
          (P)                               (G FS -EN)
          (PD)                              (D FS -EN)))
          (P3 P)                   (MICH ((A MS)))
          (D P)                    (MIR ((D MS)))
          (A P)))                  (MIT ((ADV-M (D))))
(MAEDCHENS ((NG)))                 (MOCHTE ((V S1 A)
(MAENNER ((P)                               (V S1 W)
          (P3 P)                            (V S3 A)
          (A P)))                           (V S3 W)))
(MAENNERN ((PD)                    (MOCHTEN ((V P1 A)
           (D P)))                           (V P1 W)
(MANCHMAL ((ADV-T)))                         (V P3 A)
(MANN ((MS)))                                (V P3 W)))
(MANNES ((MG)))                    (MOCHTEST ((V S2 A)
(MARIA ((S3 FS)                               (V S2 W)))
        (D FS)                     (MOCHTET ((V P2 A)
        (A FS)))                             (V P2 W)))
(MARIAS ((G)))                     (MOEBEL ((NS)
(MEER ((NS)))                               (P)
(MEERE ((P)                                 (P3 P)
        (P3 P)                              (A P)))
        (A P)))                    (MOEBELN ((PD)
(MEEREN ((PD)                               (D P)))
         (D P)))                   (MOEBELS ((NG)))
(MEERES ((NG)))                    (MOECHTE ((V S1 A)
```

```
              (V S3 A)                    (NACHSEHE ((V S1 A)
              (V S1 W)                               (V S3 A)))
              (V S3 W)))                  (NACHSEHEN ((W A)
(MOECHTEN ((V P1 A)                                  (V P1 A)
           (V P3 A)                                  (V P3 A)))
           (V P1 W)                       (NEBEN ((ADV-L (D))
           (V P3 W)))                             (ADV-D (A))
(MOECHTEST ((V S2 A)                              (DE1)))
            (V S2 W)))                    (NEU ((ADJ)))
(MOECHTET ((V P2 A)                       (NEUE ((-E)
           (V P2 W)))                            (P3 P -E)
(MOEGEN ((H W INF)                               (A P -E)))
         (V P1 W)                         (NEUEN ((-EN)
         (V P3 W)))                              (D P -EN)))
(MORGEN ((ADV-T)                          (NEUER ((-ER)
         (MS)                                    (G P -ER)
         (SD)))                                  (ADJ)))
(MUENCHEN ((S3 NS)                        (NEUERE ((-E)
           (D NS)                                 (P3 P -E)
           (A NS)))                               (A P -E)))
(MUENCHENS ((G)))                         (NEUEREN ((-EN)
(MUETTER ((P)                                      (D P -EN)))
          (P3 P)                          (NEUERER ((-ER)
          (A P)))                                  (G P -ER)))
(MUETTERN ((PD)                           (NEUERES ((-ES)))
           (D P)))                        (NEUES ((-ES)))
(MUSS ((V S3 W)))                         (OBWOHL ((ADCL V)))
(MUTTER ((FS)))                           (OFT ((ADV-M)))
(NACH ((ADV-T (D))                        (PETER ((S3 MS)
        (ADV-D (D))                               (D MS)
        (DE1)))                                   (A MS)))
(NACHDEM ((ADCL V)))                      (PETERS ((G)))
(NACHGEBE ((V S1 A)                       (PORCELLAN ((NS)))
           (V S3 A)))                     (PORCELLANS ((NG)))
(NACHGEBEN ((V P1 A)                      (PUPPE ((FS)))
            (V P3 A)))                    (PUPPEN ((P)
(NACHGEBT ((V P2)))                               (PD)
(NACHGESEHEN ((H A)                               (P3 P)
              (WP -AG)))                          (D P)
(NACHGIBST ((V S2 A)))                            (A P)))
(NACHGIBT ((V S3 A)))                     (RENOVIERE ((V S1 A)))
(NACHHAUSE ((ADV-D)))                     (RENOVIEREN ((W A INF)
(NACHSAEHE ((V S1 A)                                  (V P1 A)
            (V S3 A)))                                (V P3 A)))
(NACHSAEHT ((V P2 A)))                    (RENOVIERST ((V S2 A)))
(NACHSAEHST ((V S2 A)))                   (RENOVIERT ((V S3 A)
(NACHSAEHEN ((V P1 A)                                 (V P2 A)
             (V P3 A)))                               (H A)))
```

```
(RENOVIERTE ((V S1 A)                      (V P1)
            (V S3 A)))                     (V P3)))
(RENOVIERTEN ((V P1 A)              (SCHLAFT ((V P2)))
             (V P3 A)))             (SCHLIEF ((V S1)
(RENOVIERTEST ((V S2 A)))                     (V S3)))
(ROT ((ADJ)))                       (SCHLIEFE ((V S1)
(ROTE ((-E)                                    (V S3)))
      (P3 P -E)                     (SCHLIEFEN ((V P1)
      (A P -E)))                                (V P3)))
(ROTEN ((-EN)                       (SCHLIEFST ((V S2)))
       (D P -EN)))                  (SCHLIEFT ((V P2)))
(ROTER ((-ER)                       (SCHMECKE ((V S1)))
       (G P -ER)))                  (SCHMECKEN ((NS)
(ROTES ((-ES)))                                (W INF)
(SAH ((V S1 A)                                 (V P1)
      (V S3 A)                                 (V P3)))
      (V S1 A DE1)                  (SCHMECKST ((V S2)))
      (V S3 A DE1)))                (SCHMECKT ((V S3)
(SANG ((V S1 A)                               (V P2)))
       (V S3 A)                     (SCHMECKTE ((V S1)
       (V S1)                                  (V S3)))
       (V S3)))                     (SCHMECKTEN ((V P1)
(SANGEN ((V P1 A)                                (V P3)))
        (V P3 A)                    (SCHMECKTEST ((V S2)))
        (V P1)                      (SCHMECKTET ((V P2)))
        (V P3)))                    (SCHOEN ((ADJ)
(SANGST ((V S2 A)                            (ADV-M)))
        (V S2)))                    (SCHOENE ((-E)
(SANGT ((V P2 A)                              (P3 P -E)
       (V P2)))                               (A P -E)))
(SAEHE ((V S1 A)))                  (SCHOENEN ((-EN)
(SAEHEN ((V P1 A)                              (D P -EN)))
        (V P3 A)))                  (SCHOENER ((-ER)
(SAEHST ((V S2 A)))                            (G P -ER)
(SAEHT ((V S3 A)                               (ADJ)))
       (V P2 A)))                   (SCHOENES ((-ES)))
(SAHEN ((V P1 A)                    (SCHWEIGE ((V S1)))
       (V P3 A)                     (SCHWEIGEN ((NS)
       (V P1 A DE1)                            (W INF)
       (V P3 A DE1)))                          (V P1)
(SAHST ((V S2 A)                               (V P3)))
       (V S2 A DE1)))               (SCHWEIGST ((V S2)))
(SAHT ((V P2 A)                     (SCHWEIGT ((V S3)
      (V P2 A DE1)))                           (V P2)))
(SCHLAEFST ((V S2)))                (SCHWIEG ((V S1)
(SCHLAEFT ((V S3)))                           (V S3)))
(SCHLAFE ((V S1)))                  (SCHWIEGEN ((V P1)
(SCHLAFEN ((W INF)                            (V P3)))
```

```
(SCHWIEGST ((V S2)))
(SCHWIEGT ((V P2)))
(SCHWIERIG ((ADJ)
          (ADJ S)))
(SCHNELL ((ADV-M)
          (ADJ)))
(SCHNELLE ((-E)
          (P3 P -E)
          (A P -E)))
(SCHNELLEN ((-EN)
          (D P -EN)))
(SCHNELLER ((ADJ)
          (ADV-M)))
(SCHNELLERE ((-E)
          (P3 P -E)
          (A P -E)))
(SCHNELLEREN ((-EN)
          (D P -EN)))
(SCHNELLERER ((-ER)
          (G P -ER)))
(SCHNELLERES ((-ES)))
(SCHNELLES ((-ES)))
(SCHREIBE ((V S1 D A)
          (V S1 A)))
(SCHREIBEN ((W D A INF)
          (V P1 D A)
          (V P3 D A)
          (W A INF)
          (V P1 A)
          (V P3 A)))
(SCHREIBST ((V S2 D A)
          (V S2 A)))
(SCHREIBT ((V S3 D A)
          (V P2 D A)
          (V S3 A)
          (V P2 A)))
(SCHRIEB ((V S1 D A)
          (V S3 D A)
          (V S1 A)
          (V S3 A)))
(SCHRIEBE ((V S1 D A)
          (V S3 D A)
          (V S1 A)
          (V S3 A)))
(SCHRIEBEN ((V P1 D A)
          (V P3 D A)
          (V P1 A)
          (V P3 A)))
```

```
(SCHRIEBST ((V S2 D A)
          (V S2 A)))
(SCHRIEBT ((V P2 D A)
          (V P2 A)))
(SCHULE ((FS)))
(SCHULEN ((P)
          (PD)
          (P3)
          (D)
          (A)))
(SEE ((MS)))
(SEEN ((P)
          (P3 P)
          (A P)
          (PD)
          (D P)))
(SEES ((MG)))
(SEHE ((V S1 A)
          (V S1 A DE1)))
(SEHEN ((W A INF)
          (V P1 A)
          (V P3 A)
          (W A DE1)
          (V P3 A DE1)))
(SEHT ((V P2 A)
          (V P2 A DE1)))
(SEID ((V P2 S)))
(SEIN ((S3 MS -ER)
          (S3 NS -ER)
          (A NS -ER)
          (W S INF)))
(SEINE ((P3 P -EN)
          (A P -EN)
          (S3 FS -E)
          (A FS -E)))
(SEINEM ((D NS -EN)
          (D MS -EN)))
(SEINEN ((D P -EN)
          (A MS -EN)))
(SEINER ((G P -EN)
          (G FS -EN)
          (D FS -EN)))
(SEINES ((A NS)
          (G NS -ES)
          (G MS -ES)))
(SIE ((S3 FS)
          (A FS)
          (P3 P)
```

```
         (A P)))                        (SOLLTET ((V P2 A)
(SIEHST ((V S2 A)                                (V P2 W)))
        (V S2 A DE1)))              (SOFA ((NS)))
(SIEHT ((V S3 A)                     (SOFAS ((NG)
        (V S3 A DE1)))                      (P)
(SIND ((V P1 S)                             (PD)
       (V P3 S)))                           (P3 P)
(SINGE ((V S1 A)                            (D P)
        (V S1)))                            (A P)))
(SINGEN ((W A INF)                   (SPRACH ((V S1)
         (V P1 A)                            (V S3)))
         (V P3 A)                    (SPRACHE ((FS)))
         (W INF)                     (SPRACHEN ((V P1)
         (V P1)                               (V P3)
         (V P3)                               (P)
         (Q -FA)))                            (PD)
(SINGST ((V S2 A)                            (P3 P)
         (V S2)))                            (D P)
(SINGT ((V S3 A)                             (A P)))
        (V S3)                      (SPRACHST ((V S2)))
        (V P2 A)                    (SPRACHT ((V P2)))
        (V P2)))                    (SPRAECHE ((V S1)
(SO ((ADV-M)))                               (V S3)))
(SOLL ((V S1 A)                     (SPRAECHEN ((V P1)
       (V S3 A)                               (V P3)))
       (V S1 W)                     (SPRAECHST ((V S2)))
       (V S3 W)))                   (SPRAECHT ((V P2)))
(SOLLE ((V S1 A)                    (SPRECHE ((V S1)
        (V S3 A)                             (V S1 A)))
        (V S1 W)                    (SPRECHEN ((W INF)
        (V S3 W)))                           (V P1)
(SOLLST ((V S2 A)                            (V P3)
         (V S2 W)))                          (W A INF)
(SOLLEN ((H W INF)                           (V P1 A)
         (V P1 W)                            (V P3 A)))
         (V P3 W)))                 (SPRECHT ((V P2)
(SOLLT ((V P2 A)                             (V P2 A)))
        (V P2 W)))                  (SPRICHST ((V S2)
(SOLLTE ((V S1 A)                            (V S2 A)))
         (V S1 W)                   (SPRICHT ((V S3)
         (V S3 A)                            (V S3 A)))
         (V S3 W)))                 (STADT ((FS)))
(SOLLTEST ((V S2 A)                 (STAEDTE ((P)
           (V S2 W)))                        (P3 P)
(SOLLTEN ((V P1 A)                           (A P)))
          (V P1 W)                  (STAEDTEN ((PD)
          (V P3 A)                            ((D P))))
          (V P3 W)))                (STAUNE ((V S1)))
```

```
(STAUNEN ((NS)                          (P3 P)
         (W INF)                        (D P)
         (V P1)                         (A P)))
         (V P3)))                (TRAURIG ((ADV-M)))
(STAUNENS ((NG)))               (TROTZ ((ADV-C G)))
(STAUNST ((V S2)))              (UEBER ((ADV-L (D))
(STAUNT ((V S3)))                       (ADV-D (A))
(STAUNTE ((V S1)                        (DE1)))
         (V S3)))               (UEBERZEUGE ((V S1 A)))
(STAUNTEN ((V P1)               (UEBERZEUGEN ((Q -AG)
          (V P3)))                          (W A INF)
(STAUNTEST ((V S2)))                        (V P1 A)
(STAUNTET ((V P2)))                         (V P3 A)))
(SUPPE ((FS)))                  (UEBERZEUGST ((V S2 A)))
(SUPPEN ((P)                    (UEBERZEUGT ((V S3 A)
        (PD)                                (H A)
        (P3 P)                              (WP -AG)))
        (D P)                   (UEBERZEUGTE ((V S1 A)
        (A P)))                              (V S3 A)))
(SUSI ((S3 FS)                  (UEBERZEUGTEN ((V P1 A)
       (D FS)                                 (V P3 A)))
       (A FS)))                 (UEBERZEUGTEST ((V S2 A)))
(SUSIS ((G FS)))                (UEBERZEUGTET ((V P2 A)))
(TAG ((MS)))                    (UHR ((FS)))
(TAGE ((P)                      (UHREN ((P)
       (P3 P)                           (PD)
       (A P)))                          (P3 P)
(TAGEN ((PD)                             (D P)
        (D)))                            (A P)))
(TAGES ((MG)))                  (UND ((CNJ)))
(TELLER ((MS)                   (UNS ((D P)
         (SD)                          (A P)))
         (P)                    (UNSERE ((P3 P -EN)
         (P3 P)                          (A P -EN)
         (A P)))                         (S3 FS -E)
(TELLERN ((PD)                           (A FS -E)))
          (D)))                 (UNSER ((S3 MS -ER)
(TELLERS ((SG)))                         (S3 NS -ER)
(TISCH ((MS)))                           (A NS -ER)))
(TISCHE ((P)                    (UNSEREN ((D P -EN)
         (P3 P)                           (A MS -EN)))
         (A P)))                (UNSEREM ((D NS -EN)
(TISCHEN ((PD)                            (D MS -EN)))
          (D P)))               (UNSERES ((G NS -ES)
(TISCHES ((MG)))                          (G MS -ES)))
(TOMATE ((FS)))                 (UNSERER ((G P -EN)
(TOMATEN ((P)                             (G FS -EN)
          (PD)                            (D FS -EN)))
```

```
(UNTER ((ADV-L (D))                        (V S3 S)))
       (ADV-D (A))            (WAEREN ((V P1 S)
       (DE1)))                         (V P3 S)))
(VERKAUFE ((V S1 A)))          (WAERST ((V S2 S)))
(VERKAUFEN ((W A INF)          (WAERT ((V P2 S)))
          (V P1 A)             (WANN ((ADV-T)))
          (V P3 A)))           (WAR ((V S1 S)
(VERKAUFST ((V S2 A)))                (V S3 S)))
(VERKAUFT ((V S3 A)            (WAREN ((V P1 S)
          (V P2 A)                    (V P3 S)))
          (H A)                (WARM ((ADJ)))
          (WP A)))             (WARST ((V S2 S)))
(VERKAUFTE ((V S1 A)           (WART ((V P2 S)))
           (V S3 A)))          (WARUM ((ADV-C I)
(VERKAUFTEN ((V P1 A)                 (SCI V)))
            (V P3 A)))         (WAS ((A I)))
(VERKAUFTEST ((V S2 A)))       (WEGEN ((ADV-C G)))
(VERSUCHE ((V S1 Z)))          (WEIL ((ADCL V)))
(VERSUCHEN ((W INF Z)          (WEISS ((V S1 SC I)
           (V P1 Z)                   (V S1 A)
           (V P3 Z)))                 (V S3 SC I)
(VERSUCHST ((V S2 Z)))                (V S3 A)))
(VERSUCHT ((V S3 Z)            (WEISST ((V S2 SC)
          (V P2 Z)                     (V S2 SCI)
          (WP -AG)                     (V S2 A)))
          (H Z)))              (WEM ((D I)
(VERSUCHTE ((V S1 Z)                  (SCI V D)))
           (V S3 Z)))          (WEN ((A I)
(VERSUCHTEN ((V P1 Z)                 (SCI V A)))
            (V P3 Z)))         (WER ((S3 I)
(VERSUCHTEST ((V S2 Z)))              (SCI V S3)))
(VERSUCHTET ((V P2 Z)))        (WERDE ((V S1 W)
(VIEL ((S3 NS)                        (V S1 WP)))
      (A NS)                   (WERDEN ((V P1 W)
      (ADV-M)))                        (V P1 WP)
(VIELE ((P3 P -E)                      (V P3 W)
       (A P -E)))                      (V P3 WP)
(VIELEM ((D NS)))                      (W WP INF)))
(VIELEN ((-EN)                 (WERDET ((V P2 W)
        (D P -EN)))                    (V P2 WP)))
(VIELER ((G P -ER)))           (WESHALB ((ADV-C I)))
(VIELES ((S3 NS)               (WESSEN ((G I)
        (A NS)))                       (G I MS -ER)
(VON ((-AG (D))))                      (G I FS -E)
(VOR ((ADV-L (D))                      (G I NS -ES)))
     (ADV-D (A))               (WIE ((ADV-M I)
     (DE1)))                          (SCI V ADV-M)))
(WAERE ((V S1 S)               (WILL ((V S1 A)
```

```
        (V S3 A)                              (V P3 W)))
        (V S1 W)                   (WOLLT ((V P2 A)
        (V S3 W)))                        (V P2 W)))
(WILLST ((V S2 A)                  (WOLLTE ((V S1 A)
         (V S2 W)))                        (V S1 W)
(WIR ((P1 P)))                             (V S3 A)
(WIRD ((V S3 W)                            (V S3 W)))
       (V S3 WP)))                 (WOLLTEST ((V S2 A)
(WIRST ((V S2 W)                             (V S2 W)))
        (V S2 WP)))                (WOLLTEN ((V P1 A)
(WISSEN ((W SC INF)                         (V P1 W)
         (W SCI INF)                        (V P3 A)
         (V P1 SC)                          (V P3 W)))
         (V P1 SCI)                (WOLLTET ((V P2 A)
         (V P3 SC)                          (V P2 W)))
         (V P3 SCI)                (WORDEN ((S WP)))
         (W A INF)                 (WORT ((NS)))
         (V P1 A)                  (WORTES ((NG)))
         (V P3 A)))                (WUERDE ((V S1 W)
(WISST ((V P2 SC)                          (V S3 W)
        (V P2 SCI)                         (V S1 WP)
        (V P2 A)))                         (V S3 WP)))
(WO ((ADV-L I)                     (WUERDEN ((V P1 W)
     (SCI V ADV-L)))                        (V P3 W)
(WOERTER ((P)                                (V P1 WP)
          (P3)                               (V P3 WP)))
          (A)))                    (WUERDEST ((V S2 W)
(WOERTERN ((PD)                               (V S2 WP)))
           (D P)))                 (WUERDET ((V P2 W)
(WOHIN ((ADV-D I)                            (V P2 WP)))
        (SCI V ADV-D)))            (WURDE ((V S1 WP)
(WOHNE ((V S1 ADV-L)))                      (V S3 WP)))
(WOHNEN ((W ADV-L INF)             (WURDEST ((V S2 WP)))
         (V P1 ADV-L)              (WURDEN ((V P1 WP)
         (V P3 ADV-L)))                     (V P3 WP)))
(WOHNST ((V S2 ADV-L)))            (WURDET ((V P2 WP)))
(WOHNT ((V S3 ADV-L)               (WUSSTE ((V S1 SC)
        (V P2 ADV-L)))                     (V S1 SCI)
(WOHNTE ((V S1 ADV-L)                       (V S3 SC)
         (V S3 ADV-L)))                     (V S3 SCI)))
(WOHNTEN ((V P1 ADV-L)             (WUSSTEN ((V P1 SC)
          (V P3 ADV-L)))                    (V P1 SCI)
(WOHNTEST ((V S2 ADV-L)))                   (V P3 SC)
(WOHNTET ((V P2 ADV-L)))                    (V P3 SCI)))
(WOLLEN ((V P1 A)                  (WUSSTEST ((V S2 SC)
         (V P3 A)                            (V S2 SCI)))
         (H W INF)                 (WUSSTET ((V P2 SC)
         (V P1 W)                            (V P2 SCI)))
```

```
(ZEIGE ((V S1 D A)))
(ZEIGEN ((W D A INF)
        (V P1 D A)
        (V P3 D A)))
(ZEIGST ((V S2 D A)))
(ZEIGT ((V S3 D A)))
(ZEIGTE ((V S1 D A)
        (V S3 D A)))
(ZEIGTEN ((V P1 D A)
        (V P3 D A)))
(ZEIGTEST ((V S2 D A)))
(ZEIT ((FS)))
(ZEITEN ((P)
        (PD)
        (P3 P)
        (D P)
        (A P)))
(ZU ((Z)
     (ADV-D (D))))
(ZWEI ((P3 P -E)
       (D P -EN)
       (A P -E)
       (-EN)))
(ZWEIER ((G P -ER)))
```

B. A selection of DCAT test examples

As with all large parsers, one cannot rule out the possibility that this system might accept an expression or generate a reading which is not grammatical, or conversely reject an expression as ungrammatical that is in fact grammatical. Because of the complexity of the grammar, such instances can only be discovered through extensive testing of sample expressions. Each left-associative parser is tested on a set of examples which is continuously expanded as new constructions are added to the system.[1]

To give a realistic impression of the fragments analyzed by DCAT and ECAT, selections of the actual test examples are presented below. Each example consists of an abstract statement of the expression in italics, the input line, e.g. (R Sentence), and a list of the resulting DCAT derivations. If the input expression is analyzed as unambiguous, the list of derivations contains only one element. Expressions which are ungrammatical are marked with an asterisk in the abstract statement. The analysis of expressions rejected by the parser begins with the line

```
ERROR "Ungrammatical continuation at:"
```

The DCAT test examples are presented in B.2 - B.22. B.1 contains an annotated list of all category segments used in DCAT and DLEX. The ECAT test examples are presented in appendix C.2 -C.21. C.1 contains an annotated list of all ECAT/ELEX category segments. A consecutive list of all 335 computer-generated sample derivations reprinted in this book may be found in appendix D.

---

[1] In order to test the parser for selected examples without retyping, the following method was devised. A list of sample sentences ((R Sent1)(R Sent2) (R Sent3) ...) is defined as the value of a variable SAMPLE-N. After calling SAMPLE-N into the editor, the DCAT derivation of (e.g.) Sent3 is be obtained by underlining (R Sent3) in the edit window and choosing the EVAL option in the menu; subsequently the DCAT derivation of Sent3 appears in another window. The interactive programming environment required for this method of selective testing is standard on today's LISP work-stations. For testing of all test examples a function was defined which evaluates the sample sentences consecutively. During the development of DCAT and ECAT, systematic testing of old and new sets of sample sentences proved to be of great heuristic value.

B.1 List of category segments used in DCAT and DLEX

In DCAT/DLEX, category segments will usually represent either a valency position or a grammatical role, depending on their position. For example, the accusative segment 'A' indicates an accusative valency in the category (V S3 D A); (V S3 D A) is interpreted as a sentence which still needs an accusative, among other things, to become complete. In the category (A FS -E), on the other hand, the accusative segment indicates an accusative noun phrase. In other words, the category segments of DCAT/DLEX are normally used to characterize both the 'slot' and the 'filler'.

There are, however, some instances where the 'filler'-segment has a different name than the 'slot'-segment. For example, the segment S in category (V S MS) of *Peter ist* may be filled not only with a suitable verb form, e.g. *gekommen* of category (S), but also with a noun phrase, e.g. *ein guter Arzt* of category (S3 ...), an adjective, e.g. *jung* of category (ADJ), an adverb, etc. But these cases of categorial correspondence without identity of the 'slot' and the 'filler' are the exception in DCAT/DLEX.

1. **A** (accusative)

2. **ADCL** (adverbial clause)

3. **ADJ** (predicative adjective)

4. **ADV-C** (adverb of cause)

5. **ADV-D** (adverb of direction)

6. **ADV-L** (adverb of location)

7. **ADV-M** (adverb of manner)

8. **ADV-T** (adverb of time)

9. **-AG** (agent)

10. **D** (dative)

11. **DECL** (declarative)

12. **DE1** (discontinuous element type 1)

13. **DE2** (discontinuous element type 2)

14. **DEn** (discontinuous element type n)

15. **-E** (adjective ending in -e)

16. **-EN** (adjective ending in -en)

17. **-ES** (adjective ending in -es)

18. **-ER** (adjective ending in -er)

19. **FS** (feminine singular)

20. **G** (genitive)

21. **H** (auxiliary *haben*)

22. **I** (interrogative)

23. **INF** (infinitive)

24. **MS** (masculine singular)

25. **MG** (masculine genitive)

26. **NS** (neuter singular)

27. **NG** (neuter genitive)

28. **P** (plural)

29. **PD** (plural dative)

30. **P1** (first person plural nominative)

31. **P2** (second person plural nominative)

32. **P3** (third person plural nominative)

33. **Q** (Q-passive)

34. **S** (auxiliary *sein*)

35. **SC** (subordinate clause)

36. **SCI** (open, "interrogative", subordinate clause)

37. **S1** (first person singular nominative)

38. **S2** (second person singular nominative)

39. **S3** (third person singular nominative)

40. **V** (verb)

41. **W** (auxiliary *werden*)

42. **WP** (passive forming auxiliary *werden*)

43. **Z** (subordinating conjunction *zu*)

The category segments listed above suffice to handle all agreement and valency properties of the German fragment presented above and illustrated further in appendix B. The formal grammar DCAT/DLEX uses no additional features.

B.2   Declaratives with finite main verbs

B.2.1 *Das Mädchen gab dem Kind den Teller.*

```
(R DAS MAEDCHEN GAB DEM KIND DEN TELLER .)
((CMPLT ((DAS MAEDCHEN GAB DEM KIND DEN TELLER %.)
        (DECL)
        1
        (START (DAS)
               (S3 NS -E)
               (MAEDCHEN)
               (NS))
        2
        (DET+NOUN (DAS MAEDCHEN)
                  (S3 NS)
                  (GAB)
                  (V S3 D A))
        3
        (MAIN+FVERB (DAS MAEDCHEN GAB)
                    (V D A NS)
                    (DEM)
                    (D NS -EN))
        4
        (FVERB+MAIN (DAS MAEDCHEN GAB DEM)
                    (V A NS NS -EN)
                    (KIND)
                    (NS))
        5
        (DET+NOUN (DAS MAEDCHEN GAB DEM KIND)
                  (V A NS NS)
                  (DEN)
                  (A MS -EN))
        6
        (FVERB+MAIN (DAS MAEDCHEN GAB DEM KIND DEN)
                    (V NS NS MS -EN)
                    (TELLER)
                    (MS))
        7
        (DET+NOUN (DAS MAEDCHEN GAB DEM KIND DEN TELLER)
                  (V NS NS MS)
                  (%.)
                  (V DECL))
        8)))
```

B.2.2 *Das Mädchen gab den Teller dem Kind.*

```
(R DAS MAEDCHEN GAB DEN TELLER DEM KIND .)
```

```
((CMPLT ((DAS MAEDCHEN GAB DEN TELLER DEM KIND %.)
        (DECL)
        1
        (START (DAS)
              (S3 NS -E)
              (MAEDCHEN)
              (NS))
        2
        (DET¹NOUN (DAS MAEDCHEN)
              (S3 NS)
              (GAB)
              (V S3 D A))
        3
        (MAIN+FVERB (DAS MAEDCHEN GAB)
              (V D A NS)
              (DEN)
              (A MS -EN))
        4
        (FVERB+MAIN (DAS MAEDCHEN GAB DEN)
              (V D NS MS -EN)
              (TELLER)
              (MS))
        5
        (DET+NOUN (DAS MAEDCHEN GAB DEN TELLER)
              (V D NS MS)
              (DEM)
              (D NS -EN))
        6
        (FVERB+MAIN (DAS MAEDCHEN GAB DEN TELLER DEM)
              (V NS MS NS -EN)
              (KIND)
              (NS))
        7
        (DET+NOUN (DAS MAEDCHEN GAB DEN TELLER DEM KIND)
              (V NS MS NS)
              (%.)
              (V DECL))
        8)))
```

B.2.3 *Dem Kind gab das Mädchen den Teller.*

```
(R DEM KIND GAB DAS MAEDCHEN DEN TELLER .)
((CMPLT ((DEM KIND GAB DAS MAEDCHEN DEN TELLER %.)
        (DECL)
        1
        (START (DEM)
              (D NS -EN)
              (KIND)
              (NS))
        2
        (DET+NOUN (DEM KIND)
              (D NS)
              (GAB)
              (V S3 D A))
        3
        (MAIN+FVERB (DEM KIND GAB)
```

```
                        (V S3 A NS)
                        (DAS)
                        (S3 NS -E))
            4
        (FVERB+MAIN (DEM KIND GAB DAS)
                        (V A NS NS -E)
                        (MAEDCHEN)
                        (NS))
            5
        (DET+NOUN (DEM KIND GAB DAS MAEDCHEN)
                        (V A NS NS)
                        (DEN)
                        (A MS -EN))
            6
        (FVERB+MAIN (DEM KIND GAB DAS MAEDCHEN DEN)
                        (V NS NS MS -EN)
                        (TELLER)
                        (MS))
            7
        (DET+NOUN (DEM KIND GAB DAS MAEDCHEN DEN TELLER)
                        (V NS NS MS)
                        (%.)
                        (V DECL))
            8)))
```

B.2.4 *Dem Kind gab den Teller das Mädchen.*

```
(R DEM KIND GAB DEN TELLER DAS MAEDCHEN .)
((CMPLT ((DEM KIND GAB DEN TELLER DAS MAEDCHEN %.)
        (DECL)
            1
        (START (DEM)
                (D NS -EN)
                (KIND)
                (NS))
            2
        (DET+NOUN (DEM KIND)
                (D NS)
                (GAB)
                (V S3 D A))
            3
        (MAIN+FVERB (DEM KIND GAB)
                (V S3 A NS)
                (DEN)
                (A MS -EN))
            4
        (FVERB+MAIN (DEM KIND GAB DEN)
                (V S3 NS MS -EN)
                (TELLER)
                (MS))
            5
        (DET+NOUN (DEM KIND GAB DEN TELLER)
                (V S3 NS MS)
                (DAS)
                (S3 NS -E))
            6
```

```
        (FVERB+MAIN (DEM KIND GAB DEN TELLER DAS)
                    (V NS MS NS -E)
                    (MAEDCHEN)
                    (NS))
        7
        (DET+NOUN (DEM KIND GAB DEN TELLER DAS MAEDCHEN)
                  (V NS MS NS)
                  (%.)
                  (V DECL))
        8)))
```

B.2.5 *Den Teller gab das Mädchen dem Kind.*

```
(R DEN TELLER GAB DAS MAEDCHEN DEM KIND .)
((CMPLT ((DEN TELLER GAB DAS MAEDCHEN DEM KIND %.)
        (DECL)
        1
        (START (DEN)
               (A MS -EN)
               (TELLER)
               (MS))
        2
        (DET+NOUN (DEN TELLER)
                  (A MS)
                  (GAB)
                  (V S3 D A))
        3
        (MAIN+FVERB (DEN TELLER GAB)
                    (V S3 D MS)
                    (DAS)
                    (S3 NS -E))
        4
        (FVERB+MAIN (DEN TELLER GAB DAS)
                    (V D MS NS -E)
                    (MAEDCHEN)
                    (NS))
        5
        (DET+NOUN (DEN TELLER GAB DAS MAEDCHEN)
                  (V D MS NS)
                  (DEM)
                  (D NS -EN))
        6
        (FVERB+MAIN (DEN TELLER GAB DAS MAEDCHEN DEM)
                    (V MS NS NS -EN)
                    (KIND)
                    (NS))
        7
        (DET+NOUN (DEN TELLER GAB DAS MAEDCHEN DEM KIND)
                  (V MS NS NS)
                  (%.)
                  (V DECL))
        8)))
```

B.2.6 *Den Teller gab dem Kind das Mädchen.*

```
(R DEN TELLER GAB DEM KIND DAS MAEDCHEN .)
```

```
((CMPLT ((DEN TELLER GAB DEM KIND DAS MAEDCHEN %.)
        (DECL)
        1
        (START (DEN)
               (A MS -EN)
               (TELLER)
               (MS))
        2
        (DET+NOUN (DEN TELLER)
                  (A MS)
                  (GAB)
                  (V S3 D A))
        3
        (MAIN+FVERB (DEN TELLER GAB)
                    (V S3 D MS)
                    (DEM)
                    (D NS -EN))
        4
        (FVERB+MAIN (DEN TELLER GAB DEM)
                    (V S3 MS NS -EN)
                    (KIND)
                    (NS))
        5
        (DET+NOUN (DEN TELLER GAB DEM KIND)
                  (V S3 MS NS)
                  (DAS)
                  (S3 NS -E))
        6
        (FVERB+MAIN (DEN TELLER GAB DEM KIND DAS)
                    (V MS NS NS -E)
                    (MAEDCHEN)
                    (NS))
        7
        (DET+NOUN (DEN TELLER GAB DEM KIND DAS MAEDCHEN)
                  (V MS NS NS)
                  (%.)
                  (V DECL))
        8)))
```

B.3   Declaratives with auxiliaries and non-finite main verbs

B.3.1 *Das Mädchen hat dem Kind den Teller gegeben.*

```
(R DAS MAEDCHEN HAT DEM KIND DEN TELLER GEGEBEN .)
((CMPLT ((DAS MAEDCHEN HAT DEM KIND DEN TELLER GEGEBEN %.)
        (DECL)
        1
        (START (DAS)
               (S3 NS -E)
               (MAEDCHEN)
               (NS))
        2
```

```
(DET+NOUN (DAS MAEDCHEN)
          (S3 NS)
          (HAT)
          (V S3 H))
3
(MAIN+FVERB (DAS MAEDCHEN HAT)
            (V H NS)
            (DEM)
            (D NO EN))
4
(FVERB+MAIN (DAS MAEDCHEN HAT DEM)
            (V H NS D NS -EN)
            (KIND)
            (NS))
5
(DET+NOUN (DAS MAEDCHEN HAT DEM KIND)
          (V H NS D NS)
          (DEN)
          (A MS -EN))
6
(FVERB+MAIN (DAS MAEDCHEN HAT DEM KIND DEN)
            (V H NS D NS A MS -EN)
            (TELLER)
            (MS))
7
(DET+NOUN (DAS MAEDCHEN HAT DEM KIND DEN TELLER)
          (V H NS D NS A MS)
          (GEGEBEN)
          (H D A))
8
(MAINCL+NFVERB (DAS MAEDCHEN HAT DEM KIND DEN TELLER GEGEBEN)
               (V NS NS MS)
               (%.)
               (V DECL))
9)))
```

B.3.2 *Das Mädchen hat den Teller dem Kind gegeben.*

```
(R DAS MAEDCHEN HAT DEN TELLER DEM KIND GEGEBEN .)
((CMPLT ((DAS MAEDCHEN HAT DEN TELLER DEM KIND GEGEBEN %.)
         (DECL)
         1
         (START (DAS)
                (S3 NS -E)
                (MAEDCHEN)
                (NS))
         2
         (DET+NOUN (DAS MAEDCHEN)
                   (S3 NS)
                   (HAT)
                   (V S3 H))
         3
         (MAIN+FVERB (DAS MAEDCHEN HAT)
                     (V H NS)
                     (DEN)
                     (A MS -EN))
```

```
        4
        (FVERB+MAIN (DAS MAEDCHEN HAT DEN)
                    (V H NS A MS -EN)
                    (TELLER)
                    (MS))
        5
        (DET+NOUN (DAS MAEDCHEN HAT DEN TELLER)
                  (V H NS A MS)
                  (DEM)
                  (D NS -EN))
        6
        (FVERB+MAIN (DAS MAEDCHEN HAT DEN TELLER DEM)
                    (V H NS A MS D NS -EN)
                    (KIND)
                    (NS))
        7
        (DET+NOUN (DAS MAEDCHEN HAT DEN TELLER DEM KIND)
                  (V H NS A MS D NS)
                  (GEGEBEN)
                  (H D A))
        8
        (MAINCL+NFVERB (DAS MAEDCHEN HAT DEN TELLER DEM KIND GEGEBEN)
                       (V NS MS NS)
                       (%.)
                       (V DECL))
        9)))
```

B.3.3 *Dem Kind hat das Mädchen den Teller gegeben.*

```
(R DEM KIND HAT DAS MAEDCHEN DEN TELLER GEGEBEN .)
((CMPLT ((DEM KIND HAT DAS MAEDCHEN DEN TELLER GEGEBEN %.)
        (DECL)
        1
        (START (DEM)
               (D NS -EN)
               (KIND)
               (NS))
        2
        (DET+NOUN (DEM KIND)
                  (D NS)
                  (HAT)
                  (V S3 H))
        3
        (MAIN+FVERB (DEM KIND HAT)
                    (V S3 H D NS)
                    (DAS)
                    (S3 NS -E))
        4
        (FVERB+MAIN (DEM KIND HAT DAS)
                    (V H D NS NS -E)
                    (MAEDCHEN)
                    (NS))
        5
        (DET+NOUN (DEM KIND HAT DAS MAEDCHEN)
                  (V H D NS NS)
                  (DEN)
```

```
                (A MS -EN))
        6
        (FVERB+MAIN (DEM KIND HAT DAS MAEDCHEN DEN)
                    (V H D NS NS A MS -EN)
                    (TELLER)
                    (MS))
        7
        (DET+NOUN (DEM KIND HAT DAS MAEDCHEN DEN TELLER)
                  (V H D NS NS A MS)
                  (GEGEBEN)
                  (H D A))
        8
        (MAINCL+NFVERB (DEM KIND HAT DAS MAEDCHEN DEN TELLER GEGEBEN)
                       (V NS NS MS)
                       (%.)
                       (V DECL))
        9)))
```

B.3.4 *Dem Kind hat den Teller das Mädchen gegeben.*

```
(R DEM KIND HAT DEN TELLER DAS MAEDCHEN GEGEBEN .)
((CMPLT ((DEM KIND HAT DEN TELLER DAS MAEDCHEN GEGEBEN %.)
         (DECL)
         1
         (START (DEM)
                (D NS -EN)
                (KIND)
                (NS))
         2
         (DET+NOUN (DEM KIND)
                   (D NS)
                   (HAT)
                   (V S3 H))
         3
         (MAIN+FVERB (DEM KIND HAT)
                     (V S3 H D NS)
                     (DEN)
                     (A MS -EN))
         4
         (FVERB+MAIN (DEM KIND HAT DEN)
                     (V S3 H D NS A MS -EN)
                     (TELLER)
                     (MS))
         5
         (DET+NOUN (DEM KIND HAT DEN TELLER)
                   (V S3 H D NS A MS)
                   (DAS)
                   (S3 NS -E))
         6
         (FVERB+MAIN (DEM KIND HAT DEN TELLER DAS)
                     (V H D NS A MS NS -E)
                     (MAEDCHEN)
                     (NS))
         7
         (DET+NOUN (DEM KIND HAT DEN TELLER DAS MAEDCHEN)
                   (V H D NS A MS NS)
```

```
                    (GEGEBEN)
                    (H D A))
        8
    (MAINCL+NFVERB (DEM KIND HAT DEN TELLER DAS MAEDCHEN GEGEBEN)
                    (V NS MS NS)
                    (%.)
                    (V DECL))
        9)))
```

B.3.5 *Den Teller hat das Mädchen dem Kind gegeben.*

```
(R DEN TELLER HAT DAS MAEDCHEN DEM KIND GEGEBEN .)
((CMPLT ((DEN TELLER HAT DAS MAEDCHEN DEM KIND GEGEBEN %.)
        (DECL)
        1
        (START (DEN)
                (A MS -EN)
                (TELLER)
                (MS))
        2
        (DET+NOUN (DEN TELLER)
                (A MS)
                (HAT)
                (V S3 H))
        3
        (MAIN+FVERB (DEN TELLER HAT)
                (V S3 H A MS)
                (DAS)
                (S3 NS -E))
        4
        (FVERB+MAIN (DEN TELLER HAT DAS)
                (V H A MS NS -E)
                (MAEDCHEN)
                (NS))
        5
        (DET+NOUN (DEN TELLER HAT DAS MAEDCHEN)
                (V H A MS NS)
                (DEM)
                (D NS -EN))
        6
        (FVERB+MAIN (DEN TELLER HAT DAS MAEDCHEN DEM)
                (V H A MS NS D NS -EN)
                (KIND)
                (NS))
        7
        (DET+NOUN (DEN TELLER HAT DAS MAEDCHEN DEM KIND)
                (V H A MS NS D NS)
                (GEGEBEN)
                (H D A))
        8
        (MAINCL+NFVERB (DEN TELLER HAT DAS MAEDCHEN DEM KIND GEGEBEN)
                        (V MS NS NS)
                        (%.)
                        (V DECL))
        9)))
```

B.3.6 *Den Teller hat dem Kind das Mädchen gegeben.*

```
(R DEN TELLER HAT DEM KIND DAS MAEDCHEN GEGEBEN .)
((CMPLT ((DEN TELLER HAT DEM KIND DAS MAEDCHEN GEGEBEN %.)
        (DECL)
        1
        (START (DEN)
               (A MS -EN)
               (TELLER)
               (MS))
        2
        (DET+NOUN (DEN TELLER)
                  (A MS)
                  (HAT)
                  (V S3 H))
        3
        (MAIN+FVERB (DEN TELLER HAT)
                    (V S3 H A MS)
                    (DEM)
                    (D NS -EN))
        4
        (FVERB+MAIN (DEN TELLER HAT DEM)
                    (V S3 H A MS D NS -EN)
                    (KIND)
                    (NS))
        5
        (DET+NOUN (DEN TELLER HAT DEM KIND)
                  (V S3 H A MS D NS)
                  (DAS)
                  (S3 NS -E))
        6
        (FVERB+MAIN (DEN TELLER HAT DEM KIND DAS)
                    (V H A MS D NS NS -E)
                    (MAEDCHEN)
                    (NS))
        7
        (DET+NOUN (DEN TELLER HAT DEM KIND DAS MAEDCHEN)
                  (V H A MS D NS NS)
                  (GEGEBEN)
                  (H D A))
        8
        (MAINCL+NFVERB (DEN TELLER HAT DEM KIND DAS MAEDCHEN GEGEBEN)
                       (V MS NS NS)
                       (%.)
                       (V DECL))
        9)))
```

B.4 Declaratives with topicalized non-finite verbs

B.4.1 *Gegeben hat das Mädchen dem Kind den Teller.*

```
(R GEGEBEN HAT DAS MAEDCHEN DEM KIND DEN TELLER .)
((CMPLT ((GEGEBEN HAT DAS MAEDCHEN DEM KIND DEN TELLER %.)
        (DECL)
```

```
        1
        (START (GEGEBEN)
               (H D A)
               (HAT)
               (V S3 H))
        2
        (MAIN+FVERB (GEGEBEN HAT)
                    (V S3 D A)
                    (DAS)
                    (S3 NS -E))
        3
        (FVERB+MAIN (GEGEBEN HAT DAS)
                    (V D A NS -E)
                    (MAEDCHEN)
                    (NS))
        4
        (DET+NOUN (GEGEBEN HAT DAS MAEDCHEN)
                  (V D A NS)
                  (DEM)
                  (D NS -EN))
        5
        (FVERB+MAIN (GEGEBEN HAT DAS MAEDCHEN DEM)
                    (V A NS NS -EN)
                    (KIND)
                    (NS))
        6
        (DET+NOUN (GEGEBEN HAT DAS MAEDCHEN DEM KIND)
                  (V A NS NS)
                  (DEN)
                  (A MS -EN))
        7
        (FVERB+MAIN (GEGEBEN HAT DAS MAEDCHEN DEM KIND DEN)
                    (V NS NS MS -EN)
                    (TELLER)
                    (MS))
        8
        (DET+NOUN (GEGEBEN HAT DAS MAEDCHEN DEM KIND DEN TELLER)
                  (V NS NS MS)
                  (%.)
                  (V DECL))
        9)))
```

B.4.2 *Gegeben hat das Mädchen den Teller dem Kind.*

```
(R GEGEBEN HAT DAS MAEDCHEN DEN TELLER DEM KIND .)
((CMPLT ((GEGEBEN HAT DAS MAEDCHEN DEN TELLER DEM KIND %.)
         (DECL)
         1
         (START (GEGEBEN)
                (H D A)
                (HAT)
                (V S3 H))
         2
         (MAIN+FVERB (GEGEBEN HAT)
                     (V S3 D A)
                     (DAS)
```

```
                    (S3 NS -E))
        3
        (FVERB+MAIN (GEGEBEN HAT DAS)
                    (V D A NS -E)
                    (MAEDCHEN)
                    (NS))
        4
        (DET+NOUN (GEGEBEN HAT DAS MAEDCHEN)
                    (V D A NS)
                    (DEN)
                    (A MS -EN))
        5
        (FVERB+MAIN (GEGEBEN HAT DAS MAEDCHEN DEN)
                    (V D NS MS -EN)
                    (TELLER)
                    (MS))
        6
        (DET+NOUN (GEGEBEN HAT DAS MAEDCHEN DEN TELLER)
                    (V D NS MS)
                    (DEM)
                    (D NS -EN))
        7
        (FVERB+MAIN (GEGEBEN HAT DAS MAEDCHEN DEN TELLER DEM)
                    (V NS MS NS -EN)
                    (KIND)
                    (NS))
        8
        (DET+NOUN (GEGEBEN HAT DAS MAEDCHEN DEN TELLER DEM KIND)
                    (V NS MS NS)
                    (%.)
                    (V DECL))
        9)))
```

B.4.3 *Gegeben hat den Teller das Mädchen dem Kind.*

```
(R GEGEBEN HAT DEN TELLER DAS MAEDCHEN DEM KIND .)
((CMPLT ((GEGEBEN HAT DEN TELLER DAS MAEDCHEN DEM KIND %.)
        (DECL)
        1
        (START (GEGEBEN)
                    (H D A)
                    (HAT)
                    (V S3 H))
        2
        (MAIN+FVERB (GEGEBEN HAT)
                    (V S3 D A)
                    (DEN)
                    (A MS -EN))
        3
        (FVERB+MAIN (GEGEBEN HAT DEN)
                    (V S3 D MS -EN)
                    (TELLER)
                    (MS))
        4
        (DET+NOUN (GEGEBEN HAT DEN TELLER)
                    (V S3 D MS)
```

```
                    (DAS)
                    (S3 NS -E))
          5
          (FVERB+MAIN (GEGEBEN HAT DEN TELLER DAS)
                      (V D MS NS -E)
                      (MAEDCHEN)
                      (NS))
          6
          (DET+NOUN (GEGEBEN HAT DEN TELLER DAS MAEDCHEN)
                    (V D MS NS)
                    (DEM)
                    (D NS -EN))
          7
          (FVERB+MAIN (GEGEBEN HAT DEN TELLER DAS MAEDCHEN DEM)
                      (V MS NS NS -EN)
                      (KIND)
                      (NS))
          8
          (DET+NOUN (GEGEBEN HAT DEN TELLER DAS MAEDCHEN DEM KIND)
                    (V MS NS NS)
                    (%.)
                    (V DECL))
          9)))
```

B.4.4 *Gegeben hat den Teller dem Kind das Mädchen.*

```
(R GEGEBEN HAT DEN TELLER DEM KIND DAS MAEDCHEN .)
((CMPLT ((GEGEBEN HAT DEN TELLER DEM KIND DAS MAEDCHEN %.)
         (DECL)
         1
         (START (GEGEBEN)
                (H D A)
                (HAT)
                (V S3 H))
         2
         (MAIN+FVERB (GEGEBEN HAT)
                     (V S3 D A)
                     (DEN)
                     (A MS -EN))
         3
         (FVERB+MAIN (GEGEBEN HAT DEN)
                     (V S3 D MS -EN)
                     (TELLER)
                     (MS))
         4
         (DET+NOUN (GEGEBEN HAT DEN TELLER)
                   (V S3 D MS)
                   (DEM)
                   (D NS -EN))
         5
         (FVERB+MAIN (GEGEBEN HAT DEN TELLER DEM)
                     (V S3 MS NS -EN)
                     (KIND)
                     (NS))
         6
         (DET+NOUN (GEGEBEN HAT DEN TELLER DEM KIND)
```

```
                    (V S3 MS NS)
                    (DAS)
                    (S3 NS -E))
          7
          (FVERB+MAIN (GEGEBEN HAT DEN TELLER DEM KIND DAS)
                    (V MS NS NS -E)
                    (MAEDCHEN)
                    (NS))
          8
          (DET+NOUN (GEGEBEN HAT DEN TELLER DEM KIND DAS MAEDCHEN)
                    (V MS NS NS)
                    (%.)
                    (V DECL))
          9)))
```

B.4.5 *Gegeben hat dem Kind das Mädchen den Teller.*

```
(R GEGEBEN HAT DEM KIND DAS MAEDCHEN DEN TELLER .)
((CMPLT ((GEGEBEN HAT DEM KIND DAS MAEDCHEN DEN TELLER %.)
          (DECL)
          1
          (START (GEGEBEN)
                    (H D A)
                    (HAT)
                    (V S3 H))
          2
          (MAIN+FVERB (GEGEBEN HAT)
                    (V S3 D A)
                    (DEM)
                    (D NS -EN))
          3
          (FVERB+MAIN (GEGEBEN HAT DEM)
                    (V S3 A NS -EN)
                    (KIND)
                    (NS))
          4
          (DET+NOUN (GEGEBEN HAT DEM KIND)
                    (V S3 A NS)
                    (DAS)
                    (S3 NS -E))
          5
          (FVERB+MAIN (GEGEBEN HAT DEM KIND DAS)
                    (V A NS NS -E)
                    (MAEDCHEN)
                    (NS))
          6
          (DET+NOUN (GEGEBEN HAT DEM KIND DAS MAEDCHEN)
                    (V A NS NS)
                    (DEN)
                    (A MS -EN))
          7
          (FVERB+MAIN (GEGEBEN HAT DEM KIND DAS MAEDCHEN DEN)
                    (V NS NS MS -EN)
                    (TELLER)
                    (MS))
          8
```

```
(DET+NOUN (GEGEBEN HAT DEM KIND DAS MAEDCHEN DEN TELLER)
          (V NS NS MS)
          (%.)
          (V DECL))
9)))
```

B.4.6 *Gegeben hat dem Kind den Teller das Mädchen.*

```
(R GEGEBEN HAT DEM KIND DEN TELLER DAS MAEDCHEN .)
((CMPLT ((GEGEBEN HAT DEM KIND DEN TELLER DAS MAEDCHEN %.)
        (DECL)
        1
        (START (GEGEBEN)
               (H D A)
               (HAT)
               (V S3 H))
        2
        (MAIN+FVERB (GEGEBEN HAT)
                    (V S3 D A)
                    (DEM)
                    (D NS -EN))
        3
        (FVERB+MAIN (GEGEBEN HAT DEM)
                    (V S3 A NS -EN)
                    (KIND)
                    (NS))
        4
        (DET+NOUN (GEGEBEN HAT DEM KIND)
                  (V S3 A NS)
                  (DEN)
                  (A MS -EN))
        5
        (FVERB+MAIN (GEGEBEN HAT DEM KIND DEN)
                    (V S3 NS MS -EN)
                    (TELLER)
                    (MS))
        6
        (DET+NOUN (GEGEBEN HAT DEM KIND DEN TELLER)
                  (V S3 NS MS)
                  (DAS)
                  (S3 NS -E))
        7
        (FVERB+MAIN (GEGEBEN HAT DEM KIND DEN TELLER DAS)
                    (V NS MS NS -E)
                    (MAEDCHEN)
                    (NS))
        8
        (DET+NOUN (GEGEBEN HAT DEM KIND DEN TELLER DAS MAEDCHEN)
                  (V NS MS NS)
                  (%.)
                  (V DECL))
        9)))
```

B.4.7 **Gegeben dem Kind hat das Mädchen den Teller.*

```
(R GEGEBEN DEM KIND HAT DAS MAEDCHEN DEN TELLER .)
```

```
[ERROR "Ungrammatical continuation at"
       ((START ((GEGEBEN)
                (WP D -AG)))
        (START ((DEM)
                (D NS -EN]
```

B.5 Various predicate constructions in declarative main clauses

B.5.1 *Der Film wird gut sein.*

```
(R DER FILM WIRD GUT SEIN .)
((CMPLT ((DER FILM WIRD GUT SEIN %.)
         (DECL)
         1
         (START (DER)
                (S3 MS -E)
                (FILM)
                (MS))
         2
         (DET+NOUN (DER FILM)
                   (S3 MS)
                   (WIRD)
                   (V S3 W))
         3
         (MAIN+FVERB (DER FILM WIRD)
                     (V W MS)
                     (GUT)
                     (ADJ))
         4
         (FVERB+MAIN (DER FILM WIRD GUT)
                     (V W MS ADJ)
                     (SEIN)
                     (W S INF))
         5
         (MAINCL+NFVERB (DER FILM WIRD GUT SEIN)
                        (V MS INF)
                        (%.)
                        (V DECL))
         6)))
```

B.5.2 *Die Suppe wird gut werden.*

```
(R DIE SUPPE WIRD GUT WERDEN .)
((CMPLT ((DIE SUPPE WIRD GUT WERDEN %.)
         (DECL)
         1
         (START (DIE)
                (S3 FS -E)
                (SUPPE)
                (FS))
         2
         (DET+NOUN (DIE SUPPE)
```

```
                    (S3 FS)
                    (WIRD)
                    (V S3 W))
          3
          (MAIN+FVERB (DIE SUPPE WIRD)
                    (V W FS)
                    (GUT)
                    (ADJ))
          4
          (FVERB+MAIN (DIE SUPPE WIRD GUT)
                    (V W FS ADJ)
                    (WERDEN)
                    (W WP INF))
          5
          (MAINCL+NFVERB (DIE SUPPE WIRD GUT WERDEN)
                         (V FS INF)
                         (%.)
                         (V DECL))
          6)))
```

B.5.3 *Das kleine Mädchen ist nachhause gekommen.*

```
(R DAS KLEINE MAEDCHEN IST NACHHAUSE GEKOMMEN .)
((CMPLT ((DAS KLEINE MAEDCHEN IST NACHHAUSE GEKOMMEN %.)
        (DECL)
        1
        (START (DAS)
               (S3 NS -E)
               (KLEINE)
               (-E))
        2
        (DET+ADJ (DAS KLEINE)
                 (S3 NS -E)
                 (MAEDCHEN)
                 (NS))
        3
        (DET+NOUN (DAS KLEINE MAEDCHEN)
                  (S3 NS)
                  (IST)
                  (V S3 S))
        4
        (MAIN+FVERB (DAS KLEINE MAEDCHEN IST)
                    (V S NS)
                    (NACHHAUSE)
                    (ADV-D))
        5
        (FVERB+MAIN (DAS KLEINE MAEDCHEN IST NACHHAUSE)
                    (V S NS ADV-D)
                    (GEKOMMEN)
                    (S))
        6
        (MAINCL+NFVERB (DAS KLEINE MAEDCHEN IST NACHHAUSE GEKOMMEN)
                       (V NS)
                       (%.)
                       (V DECL))
        7)))
```

B.5.4 *Es ist jetzt an der Zeit.*

```
(R ES IST JETZT AN DER ZEIT .)
((CMPLT ((ES IST JETZT AN DER ZEIT %.)
        (DECL)
        1
        (START (ES)
               (S3)
               (IST)
               (V S3 S))
        2
        (MAIN+FVERB (ES IST)
                    (V S)
                    (JETZT)
                    (ADV-T))
        3
        (FVERB+MAIN (ES IST JETZT)
                    (V S ADV-T)
                    (AN)
                    (ADV-L (D)))
        4
        (AUX-PRED (ES IST JETZT AN)
                  (V (D))
                  (DER)
                  (D FS -EN))
        5
        (PREP+MAIN (ES IST JETZT AN DER)
                   (V FS -EN)
                   (ZEIT)
                   (FS))
        6
        (DET+NOUN (ES IST JETZT AN DER ZEIT)
                  (V FS)
                  (%.)
                  (V DECL))
        7)))
```

B.5.5 *Der Brief ist leicht geschrieben.*

```
(R DER BRIEF IST LEICHT GESCHRIEBEN .)
((CMPLT ((DER BRIEF IST LEICHT GESCHRIEBEN %.)
        (DECL)
        1
        (START (DER)
               (S3 MS -E)
               (BRIEF)
               (MS))
        2
        (DET+NOUN (DER BRIEF)
                  (S3 MS)
                  (IST)
                  (V S3 S))
        3
        (MAIN+FVERB (DER BRIEF IST)
                    (V S MS)
                    (LEICHT)
```

```
                    (ADJ S))
        4
        (AUX-PRED (DER BRIEF IST LEICHT)
                 (V MS S)
                 (GESCHRIEBEN)
                 (S -AG))
        5
        (MAINCL+NFVERB (DER BRIEF IST LEICHT GESCHRIEBEN)
                      (V MS -AG)
                      (%.)
                      (V DECL))
        6)))
```

B.5.6 *Peter ist ein guter Freund.*

```
(R PETER IST EIN GUTER FREUND .)
((CMPLT ((PETER IST EIN GUTER FREUND %.)
        (DECL)
        1
        (START (PETER)
               (S3 MS)
               (IST)
               (V S3 S))
        2
        (MAIN+FVERB (PETER IST)
                   (V S MS)
                   (EIN)
                   (S3 MS -ER))
        3
        (AUX-PRED (PETER IST EIN)
                 (V MS MS -ER)
                 (GUTER)
                 (-ER))
        4
        (DET+ADJ (PETER IST EIN GUTER)
                (V MS MS -ER)
                (FREUND)
                (MS))
        5
        (DET+NOUN (PETER IST EIN GUTER FREUND)
                 (V MS MS)
                 (%.)
                 (V DECL))
        6)))
```

B.5.7 *Peter hat einen guten Freund.*

```
(R PETER HAT EINEN GUTEN FREUND .)
((CMPLT ((PETER HAT EINEN GUTEN FREUND %.)
        (DECL)
        1
        (START (PETER)
               (S3 MS)
               (HAT)
               (V S3 A))
        2
```

```
              (MAIN+FVERB (PETER HAT)
                          (V A MS)
                          (EINEN)
                          (A MS -EN))
          3
          (FVERB+MAIN (PETER HAT EINEN)
                          (V MS MS -EN)
                          (GUTEN)
                          (-EN))
          4
          (DET+ADJ (PETER HAT EINEN GUTEN)
                      (V MS MS -EN)
                      (FREUND)
                      (MS))
          5
          (DET+NOUN (PETER HAT EINEN GUTEN FREUND)
                        (V MS MS)
                        (%.)
                        (V DECL))
          6)))
```

B.5.8 *Peter hat Freunde.*

```
(R PETER HAT FREUNDE .)
((CMPLT ((PETER HAT FREUNDE %.)
          (DECL)
          1
          (START (PETER)
                  (S3 MS)
                  (HAT)
                  (V S3 A))
          2
          (MAIN+FVERB (PETER HAT)
                          (V A MS)
                          (FREUNDE)
                          (A P))
          3
          (FVERB+MAIN (PETER HAT FREUNDE)
                          (V MS P)
                          (%.)
                          (V DECL))
          4)))
```

B.5.9 *Peter hat viele Freunde.*

```
(R PETER HAT VIELE FREUNDE .)
((CMPLT ((PETER HAT VIELE FREUNDE %.)
          (DECL)
          1
          (START (PETER)
                  (S3 MS)
                  (HAT)
                  (V S3 A))
          2
          (MAIN+FVERB (PETER HAT)
                          (V A MS)
```

```
                        (VIELE)
                        (A P -E))
            3
            (FVERB+MAIN (PETER HAT VIELE)
                        (V MS P -E)
                        (FREUNDE)
                        (P))
            4
            (DET+NOUN (PETER HAT VIELE FREUNDE)
                        (V MS P)
                        (%.)
                        (V DECL))
            5)))
```

B.5.10 *Peter hat viele gute Freunde, die ihm oft helfen.*

```
(R PETER HAT VIELE GUTE FREUNDE DIE IHM OFT HELFEN .)
((CMPLT ((PETER HAT VIELE GUTE FREUNDE , DIE IHM OFT HELFEN %.)
            (DECL)
            1
            (START (PETER)
                        (S3 MS)
                        (HAT)
                        (V S3 A))
            2
            (MAIN+FVERB (PETER HAT)
                        (V A MS)
                        (VIELE)
                        (A P -E))
            3
            (FVERB+MAIN (PETER HAT VIELE)
                        (V MS P -E)
                        (GUTE)
                        (-E))
            4
            (DET+ADJ (PETER HAT VIELE GUTE)
                        (V MS P -E)
                        (FREUNDE)
                        (P))
            5
            (DET+NOUN (PETER HAT VIELE GUTE FREUNDE)
                        (V MS P)
                        (DIE)
                        (P3 P -EN))
            6
            (NOUN+RELPRO (PETER HAT VIELE GUTE FREUNDE , DIE)
                        (V MS V P3)
                        (IHM)
                        (D MS))
            7
            (SUBCL+MAIN (PETER HAT VIELE GUTE FREUNDE , DIE IHM)
                        (V MS V P3 D MS)
                        (OFT)
                        (ADV-M))
            8
            (SUBCL+MAIN (PETER HAT VIELE GUTE FREUNDE , DIE IHM OFT)
```

```
                   (V MS V P3 D MS ADV-M)
                   (HELFEN)
                   (V P3 D))
        9
        (SUBCL+LASTVERB (PETER HAT VIELE GUTE FREUNDE , DIE IHM OFT HELFEN ,)
                        (V MS MS)
                        (%.)
                        (V DECL))
        10))))
```

B.5.11 *Ihr wurdet Ärzte.*

```
(R IHR WURDET AERZTE .)
((CMPLT ((IHR WURDET AERZTE %.)
        (DECL)
        1
        (START (IHR)
               (P2 P)
               (WURDET)
               (V P2 WP))
        2
        (MAIN+FVERB (IHR WURDET)
                    (V WP P)
                    (AERZTE)
                    (P3 P))
        3
        (AUX-PRED (IHR WURDET AERZTE)
                  (V P P)
                  (%.)
                  (V DECL))
        4)))
```

B.5.12 *Ihr wolltet Ärzte werden.*

```
(R IHR WOLLTET AERZTE WERDEN .)
((CMPLT ((IHR WOLLTET AERZTE WERDEN %.)
        (DECL)
        1
        (START (IHR)
               (P2 P)
               (WOLLTET)
               (V P2 W))
        2
        (MAIN+FVERB (IHR WOLLTET)
                    (V W P)
                    (AERZTE)
                    (P3 P))
        3
        (FVERB+MAIN (IHR WOLLTET AERZTE)
                    (V W P P3 P)
                    (WERDEN)
                    (W WP INF))
        4
        (MAINCL+NFVERB (IHR WOLLTET AERZTE WERDEN)
                       (V P P INF)
                       (%.)
```

```
                                (V DECL))
            5)))
```

B.5.13 *Ihr seid Ärzte geworden.*

```
(R IHR SEID AERZTE GEWORDEN .)
((CMPLT ((IHR SEID AERZTE GEWORDEN %.)
        (DECL)
        1
        (START (IHR)
                (P2 P)
                (SEID)
                (V P2 S))
        2
        (MAIN+FVERB (IHR SEID)
                    (V S P)
                    (AERZTE)
                    (P3 P))
        3
        (FVERB+MAIN (IHR SEID AERZTE)
                    (V S P P3 P)
                    (GEWORDEN)
                    (S WP))
        4
        (MAINCL+NFVERB (IHR SEID AERZTE GEWORDEN)
                    (V P P)
                    (%.)
                    (V DECL))
        5)))
```

B.6 Various predicate constructions in subordinate clauses

B.6.1 *Weil Peter ein guter Arzt ist, ...*

```
(R WEIL PETER EIN GUTER ARZT IST)
((SUBCL+LASTVERB ((WEIL PETER EIN GUTER ARZT IST ,)
                (ADCL MS)
                1
                (START (WEIL)
                        (ADCL V)
                        (PETER)
                        (S3 MS))
                2
                (SUBCL+MAIN (WEIL PETER)
                            (ADCL V S3 MS)
                            (EIN)
                            (S3 MS -ER))
                3
                (SUBCL+MAIN (WEIL PETER EIN)
                            (ADCL V S3 MS S3 MS -ER)
                            (GUTER)
                            (-ER))
```

```
            4
            (DET+ADJ (WEIL PETER EIN GUTER)
                    (ADCL V S3 MS S3 MS -ER)
                    (ARZT)
                    (MS))
            5
            (DET+NOUN (WEIL PETER EIN GUTER ARZT)
                    (ADCL V S3 MS S3 MS)
                    (IST)
                    (V S3 S))
            6)))
```

B.6.2 *Weil Peter ein guter Arzt wird, ...*

```
(R WEIL PETER EIN GUTER ARZT WIRD)
((SUBCL+LASTVERB ((WEIL PETER EIN GUTER ARZT WIRD ,)
            (ADCL MS)
            1
            (START (WEIL)
                    (ADCL V)
                    (PETER)
                    (S3 MS))
            2
            (SUBCL+MAIN (WEIL PETER)
                    (ADCL V S3 MS)
                    (EIN)
                    (S3 MS -ER))
            3
            (SUBCL+MAIN (WEIL PETER EIN)
                    (ADCL V S3 MS S3 MS -ER)
                    (GUTER)
                    (-ER))
            4
            (DET+ADJ (WEIL PETER EIN GUTER)
                    (ADCL V S3 MS S3 MS -ER)
                    (ARZT)
                    (MS))
            5
            (DET+NOUN (WEIL PETER EIN GUTER ARZT)
                    (ADCL V S3 MS S3 MS)
                    (WIRD)
                    (V S3 WP))
            6)))
```

B.6.3 *Weil Peter ein guter Arzt geworden ist, ...*

```
(R WEIL PETER EIN GUTER ARZT GEWORDEN IST)
((SUBCL+LASTVERB ((WEIL PETER EIN GUTER ARZT GEWORDEN IST ,)
            (ADCL MS)
            1
            (START (WEIL)
                    (ADCL V)
                    (PETER)
                    (S3 MS))
            2
            (SUBCL+MAIN (WEIL PETER)
```

```
                              (ADCL V S3 MS)
                              (EIN)
                              (S3 MS -ER))
                 3
                 (SUBCL+MAIN (WEIL PETER EIN)
                              (ADCL V S3 MS S3 MS -ER)
                              (GUTER)
                              (-ER))
                 4
                 (DET+ADJ (WEIL PETER EIN GUTER)
                              (ADCL V S3 MS S3 MS -ER)
                              (ARZT)
                              (MS))
                 5
                 (DET+NOUN (WEIL PETER EIN GUTER ARZT)
                              (ADCL V S3 MS S3 MS)
                              (GEWORDEN)
                              (S WP))
                 6
                 (SUBCL+VERB (WEIL PETER EIN GUTER ARZT GEWORDEN)
                              (ADCL V MS S3 MS S)
                              (IST)
                              (V S3 S))
                 7)))
```

B.6.4 *Weil Peter ein guter Arzt werden wird, ...*

```
(R WEIL PETER EIN GUTER ARZT WERDEN WIRD)
((SUBCL+LASTVERB ((WEIL PETER EIN GUTER ARZT WERDEN WIRD ,)
                 (ADCL MS)
                 1
                 (START (WEIL)
                              (ADCL V)
                              (PETER)
                              (S3 MS))
                 2
                 (SUBCL+MAIN (WEIL PETER)
                              (ADCL V S3 MS)
                              (EIN)
                              (S3 MS -ER))
                 3
                 (SUBCL+MAIN (WEIL PETER EIN)
                              (ADCL V S3 MS S3 MS -ER)
                              (GUTER)
                              (-ER))
                 4
                 (DET+ADJ (WEIL PETER EIN GUTER)
                              (ADCL V S3 MS S3 MS -ER)
                              (ARZT)
                              (MS))
                 5
                 (DET+NOUN (WEIL PETER EIN GUTER ARZT)
                              (ADCL V S3 MS S3 MS)
                              (WERDEN)
                              (W WP INF))
                 6
```

```
                        (SUBCL+VERB (WEIL PETER EIN GUTER ARZT WERDEN)
                                    (ADCL V MS S3 MS W INF)
                                    (WIRD)
                                    (V S3 W))
                    7)))
```

B.6.5 *Weil Peter alt wird, ...*

```
(R WEIL PETER ALT WIRD)
((SUBCL+LASTVERB ((WEIL PETER ALT WIRD ,)
                  (ADCL MS)
                  1
                  (START (WEIL)
                         (ADCL V)
                         (PETER)
                         (S3 MS))
                  2
                  (SUBCL+MAIN (WEIL PETER)
                              (ADCL V S3 MS)
                              (ALT)
                              (ADJ))
                  3
                  (SUBCL+MAIN (WEIL PETER ALT)
                              (ADCL V S3 MS ADJ)
                              (WIRD)
                              (V S3 WP))
                  4)))
```

B.6.6 *Weil Peter klug ist, ...*

```
(R WEIL PETER KLUG IST)
((SUBCL+LASTVERB ((WEIL PETER KLUG IST ,)
                  (ADCL MS)
                  1
                  (START (WEIL)
                         (ADCL V)
                         (PETER)
                         (S3 MS))
                  2
                  (SUBCL+MAIN (WEIL PETER)
                              (ADCL V S3 MS)
                              (KLUG)
                              (ADJ))
                  3
                  (SUBCL+MAIN (WEIL PETER KLUG)
                              (ADCL V S3 MS ADJ)
                              (IST)
                              (V S3 S))
                  4)))
```

B.6.7 *Weil Peter alt werden wird, ...*

```
(R WEIL PETER ALT WERDEN WIRD)
((SUBCL+LASTVERB ((WEIL PETER ALT WERDEN WIRD ,)
                  (ADCL MS)
                  1
```

```
(START (WEIL)
       (ADCL V)
       (PETER)
       (S3 MS))
2
(SUBCL+MAIN (WEIL PETER)
            (ADCL V S3 MS)
            (ALT)
            (ADJ))
3
(SUBCL+MAIN (WEIL PETER ALT)
            (ADCL V S3 MS ADJ)
            (WERDEN)
            (W WP INF))
4
(SUBCL+VERB (WEIL PETER ALT WERDEN)
            (ADCL V S3 MS W INF)
            (WIRD)
            (V S3 W))
5)))
```

B.6.8 *Weil Peter klug geworden ist, ...*

```
(R WEIL PETER KLUG GEWORDEN IST)
((SUBCL+LASTVERB ((WEIL PETER KLUG GEWORDEN IST ,)
                 (ADCL MS)
                 1
                 (START (WEIL)
                        (ADCL V)
                        (PETER)
                        (S3 MS))
                 2
                 (SUBCL+MAIN (WEIL PETER)
                             (ADCL V S3 MS)
                             (KLUG)
                             (ADJ))
                 3
                 (SUBCL+MAIN (WEIL PETER KLUG)
                             (ADCL V S3 MS ADJ)
                             (GEWORDEN)
                             (S WP))
                 4
                 (SUBCL+VERB (WEIL PETER KLUG GEWORDEN)
                             (ADCL V S3 MS S)
                             (IST)
                             (V S3 S))
                 5)))
```

B.7 Passive constructions in declarative main clauses

B.7.1 *Peter ist von Maria ein Buch gegeben worden.*

```
(R PETER IST VON MARIA EIN BUCH GEGEBEN WORDEN .)
((CMPLT ((PETER IST VON MARIA EIN BUCH GEGEBEN WORDEN %.)
        (DECL)
        1
        (START (PETER)
               (D MS)
               (IST)
               (V S3 S))
        2
        (MAIN+FVERB (PETER IST)
                    (V S3 S D MS)
                    (VON)
                    (-AG (D)))
        3
        (FVERB+MAIN (PETER IST VON)
                    (V S3 S D MS -AG (D))
                    (MARIA)
                    (D FS))
        4
        (PREP+MAIN (PETER IST VON MARIA)
                   (V S3 S D MS -AG FS)
                   (EIN)
                   (S3 NS -ES))
        5
        (FVERB+MAIN (PETER IST VON MARIA EIN)
                    (V S D MS -AG FS NS -ES)
                    (BUCH)
                    (NS))
        6
        (DET+NOUN (PETER IST VON MARIA EIN BUCH)
                  (V S D MS -AG FS NS)
                  (GEGEBEN)
                  (WP D -AG))
        7
        (MAINCL+NFVERB (PETER IST VON MARIA EIN BUCH GEGEBEN)
                       (V S MS FS NS WP)
                       (WORDEN)
                       (S WP))
        8
        (MAINCL+NFVERB (PETER IST VON MARIA EIN BUCH GEGEBEN WORDEN)
                       (V MS FS NS)
                       (%.)
                       (V DECL))
        9)))
```

B.7.2 *Peter ist von Maria ein Buch gegeben.

```
(R PETER IST VON MARIA EIN BUCH GEGEBEN .)
[ERROR "Ungrammatical continuation at"
       ((MAINCL+NFVERB ((PETER IST VON MARIA EIN BUCH GEGEBEN)
                       (V S3 S A MS FS A NS WP D)
                       1
                       (START (PETER)
                              (A MS)
                              (IST)
                              (V S3 S))
```

```
                              2
                              (MAIN+FVERB (PETER IST)
                                          (V S3 S A MS)
                                          (VON)
                                          (-AG (D)))
                              3
                              (FVERB+MAIN (PETER IST VON)
                                          (V S3 S A MS -AG (D))
                                          (MARIA)
                                          (D FS))
                              4
                              (PREP+MAIN (PETER IST VON MARIA)
                                         (V S3 S A MS -AG FS)
                                         (EIN)
                                         (A NS -ES))
                              5
                              (FVERB+MAIN (PETER IST VON MARIA EIN)
                                          (V S3 S A MS -AG FS A NS -ES)
                                          (BUCH)
                                          (NS))
                              6
                              (DET+NOUN (PETER IST VON MARIA EIN BUCH)
                                        (V S3 S A MS -AG FS A NS)
                                        (GEGEBEN)
                                        (WP D -AG))
                              8))
            (*START ((%.)
                     (V DECL]
```

B.7.3 *Peter ist ein Buch gegeben worden.*

```
(R PETER IST EIN BUCH GEGEBEN WORDEN .)
((CMPLT ((PETER IST EIN BUCH GEGEBEN WORDEN %.)
         (DECL)
         1
         (START (PETER)
                (D MS)
                (IST)
                (V S3 S))
         2
         (MAIN+FVERB (PETER IST)
                     (V S3 S D MS)
                     (EIN)
                     (S3 NS -ES))
         3
         (FVERB+MAIN (PETER IST EIN)
                     (V S D MS NS -ES)
                     (BUCH)
                     (NS))
         4
         (DET+NOUN (PETER IST EIN BUCH)
                   (V S D MS NS)
                   (GEGEBEN)
                   (WP D -AG))
         5
         (MAINCL+NFVERB (PETER IST EIN BUCH GEGEBEN)
```

```
                        (V S MS NS WP -AG)
                        (WORDEN)
                        (S WP))
        6
        (MAINCL+NFVERB (PETER IST EIN BUCH GEGEBEN WORDEN)
                        (V MS NS -AG)
                        (%.)
                        (V DECL))
        8)))
```

B.7.4 *Peter wird von Maria ein Buch gegeben werden.*

```
(R PETER WIRD VON MARIA EIN BUCH GEGEBEN WERDEN .)
((CMPLT ((PETER WIRD VON MARIA EIN BUCH GEGEBEN WERDEN %.)
        (DECL)
        1
        (START (PETER)
                (D MS)
                (WIRD)
                (V S3 W))
        2
        (MAIN+FVERB (PETER WIRD)
                    (V S3 W D MS)
                    (VON)
                    (-AG (D)))
        3
        (FVERB+MAIN (PETER WIRD VON)
                    (V S3 W D MS -AG (D))
                    (MARIA)
                    (D FS))
        4
        (PREP+MAIN (PETER WIRD VON MARIA)
                   (V S3 W D MS -AG FS)
                   (EIN)
                   (S3 NS -ES))
        5
        (FVERB+MAIN (PETER WIRD VON MARIA EIN)
                    (V W D MS -AG FS NS -ES)
                    (BUCH)
                    (NS))
        6
        (DET+NOUN (PETER WIRD VON MARIA EIN BUCH)
                  (V W D MS -AG FS NS)
                  (GEGEBEN)
                  (WP D -AG))
        7
        (MAINCL+NFVERB (PETER WIRD VON MARIA EIN BUCH GEGEBEN)
                        (V W MS FS NS WP)
                        (WERDEN)
                        (W WP INF))
        8
        (MAINCL+NFVERB (PETER WIRD VON MARIA EIN BUCH GEGEBEN WERDEN)
                        (V MS FS NS INF)
                        (%.)
                        (V DECL))
        9)))
```

B.7.5 *Peter wird ein Buch gegeben werden.*

```
(R PETER WIRD EIN BUCH GEGEBEN WERDEN .)
((CMPLT ((PETER WIRD EIN BUCH GEGEBEN WERDEN %.)
        (DECL)
        1
        (START (PETER)
               (D MS)
               (WIRD)
               (V S3 W))
        2
        (MAIN+FVERB (PETER WIRD)
               (V S3 W D MS)
               (EIN)
               (S3 NS -ES))
        3
        (FVERB+MAIN (PETER WIRD EIN)
               (V W D MS NS -ES)
               (BUCH)
               (NS))
        4
        (DET+NOUN (PETER WIRD EIN BUCH)
               (V W D MS NS)
               (GEGEBEN)
               (WP D -AG))
        5
        (MAINCL+NFVERB (PETER WIRD EIN BUCH GEGEBEN)
               (V W MS NS WP -AG)
               (WERDEN)
               (W WP INF))
        6
        (MAINCL+NFVERB (PETER WIRD EIN BUCH GEGEBEN WERDEN)
               (V MS NS -AG INF)
               (%.)
               (V DECL))
        7)))
```

B.7.6 *Peter war von Maria ein Buch gegeben worden.*

```
(R PETER WAR VON MARIA EIN BUCH GEGEBEN WORDEN .)
((CMPLT ((PETER WAR VON MARIA EIN BUCH GEGEBEN WORDEN %.)
        (DECL)
        1
        (START (PETER)
               (D MS)
               (WAR)
               (V S3 S))
        2
        (MAIN+FVERB (PETER WAR)
                    (V S3 S D MS)
                    (VON)
                    (-AG (D)))
        3
        (FVERB+MAIN (PETER WAR VON)
                    (V S3 S D MS -AG (D))
                    (MARIA)
```

```
                    (D FS))
        4
(PREP+MAIN (PETER WAR VON MARIA)
           (V S3 S D MS -AG FS)
           (EIN)
           (S3 NS -ES))
        5
(FVERB+MAIN (PETER WAR VON MARIA EIN)
            (V S D MS -AG FS NS -ES)
            (BUCH)
            (NS))
        6
(DET+NOUN (PETER WAR VON MARIA EIN BUCH)
          (V S D MS -AG FS NS)
          (GEGEBEN)
          (WP D -AG))
        7
(MAINCL+NFVERB (PETER WAR VON MARIA EIN BUCH GEGEBEN)
               (V S MS FS NS WP)
               (WORDEN)
               (S WP))
        8
(MAINCL+NFVERB (PETER WAR VON MARIA EIN BUCH GEGEBEN WORDEN)
               (V MS FS NS)
               (%.)
               (V DECL))
        9)))
```

B.7.7 *Ein Buch ist Peter von Maria gegeben worden.*

```
(R EIN BUCH IST PETER VON MARIA GEGEBEN WORDEN .)
((CMPLT ((EIN BUCH IST PETER VON MARIA GEGEBEN WORDEN %.)
        (DECL)
        1
        (START (EIN)
               (S3 NS -ES)
               (BUCH)
               (NS))
        2
        (DET+NOUN (EIN BUCH)
                  (S3 NS)
                  (IST)
                  (V S3 S))
        3
        (MAIN+FVERB (EIN BUCH IST)
                    (V S NS)
                    (PETER)
                    (D MS))
        4
        (FVERB+MAIN (EIN BUCH IST PETER)
                    (V S NS D MS)
                    (VON)
                    (-AG (D)))
        5
        (NOUN+PREP (EIN BUCH IST PETER VON)
                   (V S NS D MS (D))
```

```
                        (MARIA)
                        (D FS))
                6
        (PREP+MAIN (EIN BUCH IST PETER VON MARIA)
                        (V S NS D MS FS)
                        (GEGEBEN)
                        (WP D -AG))
                7
        (MAINCL+NFVERB (EIN BUCH IST PETER VON MARIA GEGEBEN)
                        (V S NS MS FS WP -AG)
                        (WORDEN)
                        (S WP))
                8
        (MAINCL+NFVERB (EIN BUCH IST PETER VON MARIA GEGEBEN WORDEN)
                        (V NS MS FS -AG)
                        (%.)
                        (V DECL))
                9))
(CMPLT ((EIN BUCH IST PETER VON MARIA GEGEBEN WORDEN %.)
        (DECL)
        1
        (START (EIN)
                (S3 NS -ES)
                (BUCH)
                (NS))
        2
        (DET+NOUN (EIN BUCH)
                (S3 NS)
                (IST)
                (V S3 S))
        3
        (MAIN+FVERB (EIN BUCH IST)
                        (V S NS)
                        (PETER)
                        (D MS))
        4
        (FVERB+MAIN (EIN BUCH IST PETER)
                        (V S NS D MS)
                        (VON)
                        (-AG (D)))
        5
        (FVERB+MAIN (EIN BUCH IST PETER VON)
                        (V S NS D MS -AG (D))
                        (MARIA)
                        (D FS))
        6
        (PREP+MAIN (EIN BUCH IST PETER VON MARIA)
                        (V S NS D MS -AG FS)
                        (GEGEBEN)
                        (WP D -AG))
        7
        (MAINCL+NFVERB (EIN BUCH IST PETER VON MARIA GEGEBEN)
                        (V S NS MS FS WP)
                        (WORDEN)
                        (S WP))
```

```
     8
     (MAINCL+NFVERB (EIN BUCH IST PETER VON MARIA GEGEBEN WORDEN)
                    (V NS MS FS)
                    (%.)
                    (V DECL))
        9)))
```

B.7.8 *Von Maria ist ein Buch Peter gegeben worden.*

```
(R VON MARIA IST EIN BUCH PETER GEGEBEN WORDEN .)
((CMPLT ((VON MARIA IST EIN BUCH PETER GEGEBEN WORDEN %.)
        (DECL)
        1
        (START (VON)
               (-AG (D))
               (MARIA)
               (D FS))
        2
        (PREP+MAIN (VON MARIA)
                   (-AG FS)
                   (IST)
                   (V S3 S))
        3
        (MAIN+FVERB (VON MARIA IST)
                    (V S3 S -AG FS)
                    (EIN)
                    (S3 NS -ES))
        4
        (FVERB+MAIN (VON MARIA IST EIN)
                    (V S -AG FS NS -ES)
                    (BUCH)
                    (NS))
        5
        (DET+NOUN (VON MARIA IST EIN BUCH)
                  (V S -AG FS NS)
                  (PETER)
                  (D MS))
        6
        (FVERB+MAIN (VON MARIA IST EIN BUCH PETER)
                    (V S -AG FS NS D MS)
                    (GEGEBEN)
                    (WP D -AG))
        7
        (MAINCL+NFVERB (VON MARIA IST EIN BUCH PETER GEGEBEN)
                       (V S FS NS MS WP)
                       (WORDEN)
                       (S WP))
        8
        (MAINCL+NFVERB (VON MARIA IST EIN BUCH PETER GEGEBEN WORDEN)
                       (V FS NS MS)
                       (%.)
                       (V DECL))
           9)))
```

B.7.9 *Peter wurde ein Buch gegeben.*

```
(R PETER WURDE EIN BUCH GEGEBEN .)
((CMPLT ((PETER WURDE EIN BUCH GEGEBEN %.)
        (DECL)
        1
        (START (PETER)
               (D MS)
               (WURDE)
               (V S3 WP))
        2
        (MAIN+FVERB (PETER WURDE)
                    (V S3 WP D MS)
                    (EIN)
                    (S3 NS -ES))
        3
        (FVERB+MAIN (PETER WURDE EIN)
                    (V WP D MS NS -ES)
                    (BUCH)
                    (NS))
        4
        (DET+NOUN (PETER WURDE EIN BUCH)
                  (V WP D MS NS)
                  (GEGEBEN)
                  (WP D -AG))
        5
        (MAINCL+NFVERB (PETER WURDE EIN BUCH GEGEBEN)
                       (V MS NS -AG)
                       (%.)
                       (V DECL))
        6)))
```

B.7.10 *Peter wurde von Maria ein Buch gegeben.*

```
(R PETER WURDE VON MARIA EIN BUCH GEGEBEN .)
((CMPLT ((PETER WURDE VON MARIA EIN BUCH GEGEBEN %.)
        (DECL)
        1
        (START (PETER)
               (D MS)
               (WURDE)
               (V S3 WP))
        2
        (MAIN+FVERB (PETER WURDE)
                    (V S3 WP D MS)
                    (VON)
                    (-AG (D)))
        3
        (FVERB+MAIN (PETER WURDE VON)
                    (V S3 WP D MS -AG (D))
                    (MARIA)
                    (D FS))
        4
        (PREP+MAIN (PETER WURDE VON MARIA)
                   (V S3 WP D MS -AG FS)
                   (EIN)
                   (S3 NS -ES))
        5
```

```
            (FVERB+MAIN (PETER WURDE VON MARIA EIN)
                        (V WP D MS -AG FS NS -ES)
                        (BUCH)
                        (NS))
         6
            (DET+NOUN (PETER WURDE VON MARIA EIN BUCH)
                      (V WP D MS -AG FS NS)
                      (GEGEBEN)
                      (WP D -AG))
         7
            (MAINCL+NFVERB (PETER WURDE VON MARIA EIN BUCH GEGEBEN)
                           (V MS FS NS)
                           (%.)
                           (V DECL))
         8)))
```

B.7.11 *Das Buch ist geschrieben.*

```
(R DAS BUCH IST GESCHRIEBEN .)
((CMPLT ((DAS BUCH IST GESCHRIEBEN %.)
         (DECL)
         1
         (START (DAS)
                (S3 NS -E)
                (BUCH)
                (NS))
         2
         (DET+NOUN (DAS BUCH)
                   (S3 NS)
                   (IST)
                   (V S3 S))
         3
         (MAIN+FVERB (DAS BUCH IST)
                     (V S NS)
                     (GESCHRIEBEN)
                     (S -AG))
         4
         (MAINCL+NFVERB (DAS BUCH IST GESCHRIEBEN)
                        (V NS -AG)
                        (%.)
                        (V DECL))
         5)))
```

B.7.12 *Das Buch ist geschrieben worden.*

```
(R DAS BUCH IST GESCHRIEBEN WORDEN .)
((CMPLT ((DAS BUCH IST GESCHRIEBEN WORDEN %.)
         (DECL)
         1
         (START (DAS)
                (S3 NS -E)
                (BUCH)
                (NS))
         2
         (DET+NOUN (DAS BUCH)
                   (S3 NS)
```

```
                        (IST)
                        (V S3 S))
                3
                (MAIN+FVERB (DAS BUCH IST)
                        (V S NS)
                        (GESCHRIEBEN)
                        (WP -AG))
                4
                (MAINCL+NFVERB (DAS BUCH IST GESCHRIEBEN)
                        (V S NS WP -AG)
                        (WORDEN)
                        (S WP))
                5
                (MAINCL+NFVERB (DAS BUCH IST GESCHRIEBEN WORDEN)
                        (V NS -AG)
                        (%.)
                        (V DECL))
                6)))
```

B.7.13 *Das Buch wird bald geschrieben sein.*

```
(R DAS BUCH WIRD BALD GESCHRIEBEN SEIN .)
((CMPLT ((DAS BUCH WIRD BALD GESCHRIEBEN SEIN %.)
                (DECL)
                1
                (START (DAS)
                        (S3 NS -E)
                        (BUCH)
                        (NS))
                2
                (DET+NOUN (DAS BUCH)
                        (S3 NS)
                        (WIRD)
                        (V S3 W))
                3
                (MAIN+FVERB (DAS BUCH WIRD)
                        (V W NS)
                        (BALD)
                        (ADV-T))
                4
                (FVERB+MAIN (DAS BUCH WIRD BALD)
                        (V W NS ADV-T)
                        (GESCHRIEBEN)
                        (S -AG))
                5
                (MAINCL+NFVERB (DAS BUCH WIRD BALD GESCHRIEBEN)
                        (V W NS S -AG)
                        (SEIN)
                        (W S INF))
                6
                (MAINCL+NFVERB (DAS BUCH WIRD BALD GESCHRIEBEN SEIN)
                        (V NS -AG INF)
                        (%.)
                        (V DECL))
                7)))
```

B.7.14 *Das Buch wird geschrieben werden.*

```
(R DAS BUCH WIRD GESCHRIEBEN WERDEN .)
((CMPLT ((DAS BUCH WIRD GESCHRIEBEN WERDEN %.)
        (DECL)
        1
        (START (DAS)
               (S3 NS -E)
               (BUCH)
               (NS))
        2
        (DET+NOUN (DAS BUCH)
                  (S3 NS)
                  (WIRD)
                  (V S3 W))
        3
        (MAIN+FVERB (DAS BUCH WIRD)
                    (V W NS)
                    (GESCHRIEBEN)
                    (WP -AG))
        4
        (MAINCL+NFVERB (DAS BUCH WIRD GESCHRIEBEN)
                       (V W NS WP -AG)
                       (WERDEN)
                       (W WP INF))
        5
        (MAINCL+NFVERB (DAS BUCH WIRD GESCHRIEBEN WERDEN)
                       (V NS -AG INF)
                       (%.)
                       (V DECL))
        6)))
```

B.8   Q-Passives in declarative main clauses

B.8.1 *Das Mädchen ist zu überzeugen.*

```
(R DAS MAEDCHEN IST ZU UEBERZEUGEN .)
((CMPLT ((DAS MAEDCHEN IST ZU UEBERZEUGEN %.)
        (DECL)
        1
        (START (DAS)
               (S3 NS -E)
               (MAEDCHEN)
               (NS))
        2
        (DET+NOUN (DAS MAEDCHEN)
                  (S3 NS)
                  (IST)
                  (V S3 S))
        3
        (MAIN+FVERB (DAS MAEDCHEN IST)
                    (V S NS)
                    (ZU)
                    (Z))
```

```
            4
            (MAINCL+NFVERB (DAS MAEDCHEN IST ZU)
                           (V NS Q)
                           (UEBERZEUGEN)
                           (Q -AG))
            5
            (MAINCL+NFVERB (DAS MAEDCHEN IST ZU UEBERZEUGEN)
                           (V NS -AG)
                           (%.)
                           (V DECL))
        6)))
```

B.8.2 *Das Mädchen wird zu überzeugen sein.*

```
(R DAS MAEDCHEN WIRD ZU UEBERZEUGEN SEIN .)
((CMPLT ((DAS MAEDCHEN WIRD ZU UEBERZEUGEN SEIN %.)
        (DECL)
        1
        (START (DAS)
               (S3 NS -E)
               (MAEDCHEN)
               (NS))
        2
        (DET+NOUN (DAS MAEDCHEN)
                  (S3 NS)
                  (WIRD)
                  (V S3 W))
        3
        (MAIN+FVERB (DAS MAEDCHEN WIRD)
                    (V W NS)
                    (ZU)
                    (Z))
        4
        (MAINCL+NFVERB (DAS MAEDCHEN WIRD ZU)
                       (V NS Q W S)
                       (UEBERZEUGEN)
                       (Q -AG))
        5
        (MAINCL+NFVERB (DAS MAEDCHEN WIRD ZU UEBERZEUGEN)
                       (V NS W S -AG)
                       (SEIN)
                       (W S INF))
        6
        (MAINCL+NFVERB (DAS MAEDCHEN WIRD ZU UEBERZEUGEN SEIN)
                       (V NS -AG INF)
                       (%.)
                       (V DECL))
        7)))
```

B.8.3 *Die Mädchen sind zu überzeugen.*

```
(R DIE MAEDCHEN SIND ZU UEBERZEUGEN .)
((CMPLT ((DIE MAEDCHEN SIND ZU UEBERZEUGEN %.)
        (DECL)
        1
        (START (DIE)
```

```
                    (P3 P -EN)
                    (MAEDCHEN)
                    (P))
        2
        (DET+NOUN (DIE MAEDCHEN)
                    (P3 P)
                    (SIND)
                    (V P3 S))
        3
        (MAIN+FVERB (DIE MAEDCHEN SIND)
                    (V S P)
                    (ZU)
                    (Z))
        4
        (MAINCL+NFVERB (DIE MAEDCHEN SIND ZU)
                    (V P Q)
                    (UEBERZEUGEN)
                    (Q -AG))
        5
        (MAINCL+NFVERB (DIE MAEDCHEN SIND ZU UEBERZEUGEN)
                    (V P -AG)
                    (%.)
                    (V DECL))
        6)))
```

B.8.4 *Dem Mädchen ist zu helfen.*

```
(R DEM MAEDCHEN IST ZU HELFEN .)
((CMPLT ((DEM MAEDCHEN IST ZU HELFEN %.)
        (DECL)
        1
        (START (DEM)
                    (D NS -EN)
                    (MAEDCHEN)
                    (NS))
        2
        (DET+NOUN (DEM MAEDCHEN)
                    (D NS)
                    (IST)
                    (V S3 S))
        3
        (MAIN+FVERB (DEM MAEDCHEN IST)
                    (V S3 S D NS)
                    (ZU)
                    (Z))
        4
        (MAINCL+NFVERB (DEM MAEDCHEN IST ZU)
                    (V S3 D NS Q)
                    (HELFEN)
                    (Q S3 D -FA))
        5
        (MAINCL+NFVERB (DEM MAEDCHEN IST ZU HELFEN)
                    (V NS -FA)
                    (%.)
                    (V DECL))
        6)))
```

B.8.5 *Den Mädchen ist zu helfen.*

```
(R DEN MAEDCHEN IST ZU HELFEN .)
((CMPLT ((DEN MAEDCHEN IST ZU HELFEN %.)
        (DECL)
        1
        (START (DEN)
               (D PD -EN)
               (MAEDCHEN)
               (PD))
        2
        (DET+NOUN (DEN MAEDCHEN)
                  (D PD)
                  (IST)
                  (V S3 S))
        3
        (MAIN+FVERB (DEN MAEDCHEN IST)
                    (V S3 S D PD)
                    (ZU)
                    (Z))
        4
        (MAINCL+NFVERB (DEN MAEDCHEN IST ZU)
                       (V S3 D PD Q)
                       (HELFEN)
                       (Q S3 D -FA))
        5
        (MAINCL+NFVERB (DEN MAEDCHEN IST ZU HELFEN)
                       (V PD -FA)
                       (%.)
                       (V DECL))
        6)))
```

B.8.6 *Dem Mädchen wird bald geholfen sein.*

```
(R DEM MAEDCHEN WIRD BALD GEHOLFEN SEIN .)
((CMPLT ((DEM MAEDCHEN WIRD BALD GEHOLFEN SEIN %.)
        (DECL)
        1
        (START (DEM)
               (D NS -EN)
               (MAEDCHEN)
               (NS))
        2
        (DET+NOUN (DEM MAEDCHEN)
                  (D NS)
                  (WIRD)
                  (V S3 W))
        3
        (MAIN+FVERB (DEM MAEDCHEN WIRD)
                    (V S3 W D NS)
                    (BALD)
                    (ADV-T))
        4
        (FVERB+MAIN (DEM MAEDCHEN WIRD BALD)
                    (V S3 W D NS ADV-T)
```

```
                   (GEHOLFEN)
                   (S S3 D -AG))
         5
         (MAINCL+NFVERB (DEM MAEDCHEN WIRD BALD GEHOLFEN)
                   (V W NS S -AG)
                   (SEIN)
                   (W S INF))
         6
         (MAINCL+NFVERB (DEM MAEDCHEN WIRD BALD GEHOLFEN SEIN)
                   (V NS -AG INF)
                   (%.)
                   (V DECL))
         7)))
```

B.8.7 *Das Buch ist zu lesen.*

```
(R DAS BUCH IST ZU LESEN .)
((CMPLT ((DAS BUCH IST ZU LESEN %.)
         (DECL)
         1
         (START (DAS)
                (S3 NS -E)
                (BUCH)
                (NS))
         2
         (DET+NOUN (DAS BUCH)
                (S3 NS)
                (IST)
                (V S3 S))
         3
         (MAIN+FVERB (DAS BUCH IST)
                (V S NS)
                (ZU)
                (Z))
         4
         (MAINCL+NFVERB (DAS BUCH IST ZU)
                (V NS Q)
                (LESEN)
                (Q -AG))
         5
         (MAINCL+NFVERB (DAS BUCH IST ZU LESEN)
                (V NS -AG)
                (%.)
                (V DECL))
         6)))
```

B.8.8 *Das Buch ist von Maria zu lesen.*

```
(R DAS BUCH IST VON MARIA ZU LESEN .)
((CMPLT ((DAS BUCH IST VON MARIA ZU LESEN %.)
         (DECL)
         1
         (START (DAS)
                (S3 NS -E)
                (BUCH)
                (NS))
```

```
2
(DET+NOUN (DAS BUCH)
          (S3 NS)
          (IST)
          (V S3 S))
3
(MAIN+FVERB (DAS BUCH IST)
            (V S NS)
            (VON)
            (-AG (D)))
4
(FVERB+MAIN (DAS BUCH IST VON)
            (V S NS -AG (D))
            (MARIA)
            (D FS))
5
(PREP+MAIN (DAS BUCH IST VON MARIA)
           (V S NS -AG FS)
           (ZU)
           (Z))
6
(MAINCL+NFVERB (DAS BUCH IST VON MARIA ZU)
               (V NS -AG FS Q)
               (LESEN)
               (Q -AG))
7
(MAINCL+NFVERB (DAS BUCH IST VON MARIA ZU LESEN)
               (V NS FS)
               (%.)
               (V DECL))
8)))
```

B.8.9 *Das Buch ist dem Freund zu geben.*

```
(R DAS BUCH IST DEM FREUND ZU GEBEN .)
((CMPLT ((DAS BUCH IST DEM FREUND ZU GEBEN %.)
        (DECL)
        1
        (START (DAS)
               (S3 NS -E)
               (BUCH)
               (NS))
        2
        (DET+NOUN (DAS BUCH)
                  (S3 NS)
                  (IST)
                  (V S3 S))
        3
        (MAIN+FVERB (DAS BUCH IST)
                    (V S NS)
                    (DEM)
                    (D MS -EN))
        4
        (FVERB+MAIN (DAS BUCH IST DEM)
                    (V S NS D MS -EN)
                    (FREUND)
```

```
                   (MS))
       5
       (DET+NOUN (DAS BUCH IST DEM FREUND)
               (V S NS D MS)
               (ZU)
               (Z))
       6
       (MAINCL+NFVERB (DAS BUCH IST DEM FREUND ZU)
                      (V NS D MS W)
                      (GEBEN)
                      (W D))
       7
       (MAINCL+NFVERB (DAS BUCH IST DEM FREUND ZU GEBEN)
                      (V NS MS)
                      (%.)
                      (V DECL))
       8)))
```

B.8.10 *Das Buch wird dem Freund zu geben sein.*

```
(R DAS BUCH WIRD DEM FREUND ZU GEBEN SEIN %.)
((CMPLT ((DAS BUCH WIRD DEM FREUND ZU GEBEN SEIN %.)
       (DECL)
       1
       (START (DAS)
              (S3 NS -E)
              (BUCH)
              (NS))
       2
       (DET+NOUN (DAS BUCH)
               (S3 NS)
               (WIRD)
               (V S3 W))
       3
       (MAIN+FVERB (DAS BUCH WIRD)
               (V W NS)
               (DEM)
               (D MS -EN))
       4
       (FVERB+MAIN (DAS BUCH WIRD DEM)
               (V W NS D MS -EN)
               (FREUND)
               (MS))
       5
       (DET+NOUN (DAS BUCH WIRD DEM FREUND)
               (V W NS D MS)
               (ZU)
               (Z))
       6
       (MAINCL+NFVERB (DAS BUCH WIRD DEM FREUND ZU)

                      (V NS D MS Q W S)
                      (GEBEN)
                      (Q D -AG))
       7
       (MAINCL+NFVERB (DAS BUCH WIRD DEM FREUND ZU GEBEN)
```

```
                            (V NS MS W S -AG)
                            (SEIN)
                            (W S INF))
         8
      (MAINCL+NFVERB (DAS BUCH WIRD DEM FREUND ZU GEBEN SEIN)
                            (V NS MS -AG INF)
                            (%.)
                            (V DECL))
         9)))
```

B.8.11 *Dem Mädchen ist ein Buch zu geben.*

```
(R DEM MAEDCHEN IST EIN BUCH ZU GEBEN .)
((CMPLT ((DEM MAEDCHEN IST EIN BUCH ZU GEBEN %.)
         (DECL)
         1
      (START (DEM)
               (D NS -EN)
               (MAEDCHEN)
               (NS))
         2
      (DET+NOUN (DEM MAEDCHEN)
               (D NS)
               (IST)
               (V S3 S))
         3
      (MAIN+FVERB (DEM MAEDCHEN IST)
               (V S3 S D NS)
               (EIN)
               (S3 NS -ES))
         4
      (FVERB+MAIN (DEM MAEDCHEN IST EIN)
               (V S D NS NS -ES)
               (BUCH)
               (NS))
         5
      (DET+NOUN (DEM MAEDCHEN IST EIN BUCH)
               (V S D NS NS)
               (ZU)
               (Z))
         6
      (MAINCL+NFVERB (DEM MAEDCHEN IST EIN BUCH ZU)
               (V D NS NS Q)
               (GEBEN)
               (Q D -AG))
         7
      (MAINCL+NFVERB (DEM MAEDCHEN IST EIN BUCH ZU GEBEN)
               (V NS NS -AG)
               (%.)
               (V DECL))
         8)))
```

B.9   Passive in subordinate clauses

B.9.1 *Weil Peter von Maria ein Buch gegeben worden ist, lacht Susi.*

```
(R WEIL PETER VON MARIA EIN BUCH GEGEBEN WORDEN IST LACHT SUSI .)
((CMPLT ((WEIL PETER VON MARIA EIN BUCH GEGEBEN WORDEN IST , LACHT SUSI %.)
        (DECL)
        1
        (START (WEIL)
               (ADCL V)
               (PETER)
               (D MS))
        2
        (SUBCL+MAIN (WEIL PETER)
                    (ADCL V D MS)
                    (VON)
                    (-AG (D)))
        3
        (SUBCL+MAIN (WEIL PETER VON)
                    (ADCL V D MS -AG (D))
                    (MARIA)
                    (D FS))
        4
        (PREP+MAIN (WEIL PETER VON MARIA)
                   (ADCL V D MS -AG FS)
                   (EIN)
                   (S3 NS -ES))
        5
        (SUBCL+MAIN (WEIL PETER VON MARIA EIN)
                    (ADCL V D MS -AG FS S3 NS -ES)
                    (BUCH)
                    (NS))
        6
        (DET+NOUN (WEIL PETER VON MARIA EIN BUCH)
                  (ADCL V D MS -AG FS S3 NS)
                  (GEGEBEN)
                  (WP D -AG))
        7
        (SUBCL+VERB (WEIL PETER VON MARIA EIN BUCH GEGEBEN)
                    (ADCL V MS FS S3 NS INF WP)
                    (WORDEN)
                    (S WP))
        8
        (SUBCL+VERB (WEIL PETER VON MARIA EIN BUCH GEGEBEN WORDEN)
                    (ADCL V MS FS S3 NS S)
                    (IST)
                    (V S3 S))
        9
        (SUBCL+LASTVERB (WEIL PETER VON MARIA EIN BUCH GEGEBEN WORDEN IST ,)
                        (ADCL MS FS NS)
                        (LACHT)
                        (V S3))
        10
        (MAIN+FVERB (WEIL PETER VON MARIA EIN BUCH GEGEBEN WORDEN IST , LACHT)
                    (V S3 MS FS NS)
                    (SUSI)
                    (S3 FS))
        11
```

```
        (FVERB+MAIN (WEIL PETER VON MARIA EIN BUCH GEGEBEN
                                              WORDEN IST , LACHT SUSI)
                   (V MS FS NS FS)
                   (%.)
                   (V DECL))
        12)))
```

B.9.2 *Weil Peter ein Buch gegeben wird, lacht Susi.*

```
(R WEIL PETER EIN BUCH GEGEBEN WIRD LACHT SUSI .)
((CMPLT ((WEIL PETER EIN BUCH GEGEBEN WIRD , LACHT SUSI %.)
        (DECL)
        1
        (START (WEIL)
               (ADCL V)
               (PETER)
               (D MS))
        2
        (SUBCL+MAIN (WEIL PETER)
                    (ADCL V D MS)
                    (EIN)
                    (S3 NS -ES))
        3
        (SUBCL+MAIN (WEIL PETER EIN)
                    (ADCL V D MS S3 NS -ES)
                    (BUCH)
                    (NS))
        4
        (DET+NOUN (WEIL PETER EIN BUCH)
                  (ADCL V D MS S3 NS)
                  (GEGEBEN)
                  (WP D -AG))
        5
        (SUBCL+VERB (WEIL PETER EIN BUCH GEGEBEN)
                    (ADCL V MS S3 NS INF WP -AG)
                    (WIRD)
                    (V S3 WP))
        6
        (SUBCL+LASTVERB (WEIL PETER EIN BUCH GEGEBEN WIRD ,)
                        (ADCL MS NS)
                        (LACHT)
                        (V S3))
        7
        (MAIN+FVERB (WEIL PETER EIN BUCH GEGEBEN WIRD , LACHT)
                    (V S3 MS NS)
                    (SUSI)
                    (S3 FS))
        8
        (FVERB+MAIN (WEIL PETER EIN BUCH GEGEBEN WIRD , LACHT SUSI)
                    (V MS NS FS)
                    (%.)
                    (V DECL))
        9)))
```

B.9.3 *Der Mann, dem das Buch gegeben wurde, schläft.*

```
(R DER MANN DEM DAS BUCH GEGEBEN WURDE SCHLAEFT .)
((CMPLT ((DER MANN , DEM DAS BUCH GEGEBEN WURDE , SCHLAEFT %.)
        (DECL)
        1
        (START (DER)
               (S3 MS -E)
               (MANN)
               (MS))
        2
        (DET+NOUN (DER MANN)
                  (S3 MS)
                  (DEM)
                  (D MS -EN))
        3
        (NOUN+RELPRO (DER MANN , DEM)
                     (S3 V D)
                     (DAS)
                     (S3 NS -E))
        4
        (SUBCL+MAIN (DER MANN , DEM DAS)
                    (S3 V D S3 NS -E)
                    (BUCH)
                    (NS))
         5
        (DET+NOUN (DER MANN , DEM DAS BUCH)
                  (S3 V D S3 NS)
                  (GEGEBEN)
                  (WP D -AG))
        6
        (SUBCL+VERB (DER MANN , DEM DAS BUCH GEGEBEN)
                    (S3 V S3 NS INF WP -AG)
                    (WURDE)
                    (V S3 WP))
        7
        (SUBCL+LASTVERB (DER MANN , DEM DAS BUCH GEGEBEN WURDE ,)
                        (S3 NS)
                        (SCHLAEFT)
                        (V S3))
        8
        (MAIN+FVERB (DER MANN , DEM DAS BUCH GEGEBEN WURDE , SCHLAEFT)
                    (V NS)
                    (%.)
                    (V DECL))
        9)))
```

B.9.4 *Der Mann, dem von Maria das Buch gegeben worden ist, schläft.*

```
(R DER MANN DEM VON MARIA DAS BUCH GEGEBEN WORDEN IST SCHLAEFT .)
((CMPLT ((DER MANN , DEM VON MARIA DAS BUCH GEGEBEN WORDEN IST , SCHLAEFT %.)
        (DECL)
        1
        (START (DER)
               (S3 MS -E)
               (MANN)
               (MS))
        2
```

```
(DET+NOUN (DER MANN)
          (S3 MS)
          (DEM)
          (D MS -EN))
3
(NOUN+RELPRO (DER MANN , DEM)
             (S3 V D)
             (VON)
             (-AG (D)))
4
(SUBCL+MAIN (DER MANN , DEM VON)
            (S3 V D -AG (D))
            (MARIA)
            (D FS))
5
(PREP+MAIN (DER MANN , DEM VON MARIA)
           (S3 V D -AG FS)
           (DAS)
           (S3 NS -E))
6
(SUBCL+MAIN (DER MANN , DEM VON MARIA DAS)
            (S3 V D -AG FS S3 NS -E)
            (BUCH)
            (NS))
7
(DET+NOUN (DER MANN , DEM VON MARIA DAS BUCH)
          (S3 V D -AG FS S3 NS)
          (GEGEBEN)
          (WP D -AG))
8
(SUBCL+VERB (DER MANN , DEM VON MARIA DAS BUCH GEGEBEN)
            (S3 V FS S3 NS INF WP)
            (WORDEN)
            (S WP))
9
(SUBCL+VERB (DER MANN , DEM VON MARIA DAS BUCH GEGEBEN WORDEN)
            (S3 V FS S3 NS S)
            (IST)
            (V S3 S))
10
(SUBCL+LASTVERB (DER MANN , DEM VON MARIA DAS BUCH GEGEBEN WORDEN IST ,)
                (S3 FS NS)
                (SCHLAEFT)
                (V S3))
11
(MAIN+FVERB (DER MANN , DEM VON MARIA DAS BUCH GEGEBEN
                                             WORDEN IST , SCHLAEFT)
            (V FS NS)
            (%.)
            (V DECL))
12)))
```

B.9.5 *Das Buch, das von Maria dem Mann gegeben worden ist, liegt auf dem Tisch.*

(R DAS BUCH DAS VON MARIA DEM MANN GEGEBEN WORDEN IST LIEGT AUF DEM TISCH .)

```
((CMPLT ((DAS BUCH , DAS VON MARIA DEM MANN GEGEBEN WORDEN IST , LIEGT AUF
                                                        DEM TISCH %.)
        (DECL)
        1
        (START (DAS)
                (S3 NS -E)
                (BUCH)
                (NS))
        2
        (DET+NOUN (DAS BUCH)
                (S3 NS)
                (DAS)
                (S3 NS -E))
        3
        (NOUN+RELPRO (DAS BUCH , DAS)
                (S3 V S3)
                (VON)
                (-AG (D)))
        4
        (SUBCL+MAIN (DAS BUCH , DAS VON)
                (S3 V S3 -AG (D))
                (MARIA)
                (D FS))
        5
        (PREP+MAIN (DAS BUCH , DAS VON MARIA)
                (S3 V S3 -AG FS)
                (DEM)
                (D MS -EN))
        6
        (SUBCL+MAIN (DAS BUCH , DAS VON MARIA DEM)
                (S3 V S3 -AG FS D MS -EN)
                (MANN)
                (MS))
        7
        (DET+NOUN (DAS BUCH , DAS VON MARIA DEM MANN)
                (S3 V S3 -AG FS D MS)
                (GEGEBEN)
                (WP D -AG))
        8
        (SUBCL+VERB (DAS BUCH , DAS VON MARIA DEM MANN GEGEBEN)
                (S3 V S3 FS MS INF WP)
                (WORDEN)
                (S WP))
        9
        (SUBCL+VERB (DAS BUCH , DAS VON MARIA DEM MANN GEGEBEN WORDEN)
                (S3 V S3 FS MS S)
                (IST)
                (V S3 S))
        10
        (SUBCL+LASTVERB (DAS BUCH , DAS VON MARIA DEM MANN GEGEBEN WORDEN IST ,)
                (S3 FS MS)
                (LIEGT)
                (V S3 ADV-L))
        11
        (MAIN+FVERB (DAS BUCH , DAS VON MARIA DEM MANN GEGEBEN WORDEN IST , LIEGT)
```

```
                    (V ADV-L FS MS)
                    (AUF)
                    (ADV-L (D)))
          12
(FVERB+MAIN (DAS BUCH , DAS VON MARIA DEM MANN GEGEBEN WORDEN IST ,
                                                       LIEGT AUF)
                    (V FS MS (D))
                    (DEM)
                    (D MS -EN))
          13
(PREP+MAIN (DAS BUCH , DAS VON MARIA DEM MANN GEGEBEN WORDEN IST ,
                                                       LIEGT AUF DEM)
                    (V FS MS MS -EN)
                    (TISCH)
                    (MS))
          14
(DET+NOUN (DAS BUCH , DAS VON MARIA DEM MANN GEGEBEN WORDEN IST , LIEGT
                                                       AUF DEM TISCH)
                    (V FS MS MS)
                    (%.)
                    (V DECL))
          15)))
```

B.10   Q-passives in subordinate clauses

B.10.1 *Weil das Buch dem Kind zu geben ist ...*

```
(R WEIL DAS BUCH DEM KIND ZU GEBEN IST)
((SUBCL+LASTVERB ((WEIL DAS BUCH DEM KIND ZU GEBEN IST ,)
                    (ADCL NS)
                    1
                    (START (WEIL)
                            (ADCL V)
                            (DAS)
                            (S3 NS -E))
                    2
                    (SUBCL+MAIN (WEIL DAS)
                            (ADCL V S3 NS -E)
                            (BUCH)
                            (NS))
                    3
                    (DET+NOUN (WEIL DAS BUCH)
                            (ADCL V S3 NS)
                            (DEM)
                            (D NS -EN))
                    4
                    (SUBCL+MAIN (WEIL DAS BUCH DEM)
                            (ADCL V S3 NS D NS -EN)
                            (KIND)
                            (NS))
                    5
                    (DET+NOUN (WEIL DAS BUCH DEM KIND)
                            (ADCL V S3 NS D NS)
                            (ZU)
```

```
                        (Z))
            6
            (SUBCL+VERB (WEIL DAS BUCH DEM KIND ZU)
                        (ADCL V S3 NS D NS Z)
                        (GEBEN)
                        (Q D -AG))
            7
            (SUBCL+VERB (WEIL DAS BUCH DEM KIND ZU GEBEN)
                        (ADCL V S3 NS NS -AG S)
                        (IST)
                        (V S3 S))
            8)))
```

B.10.2 *Weil dem Kind zu helfen ist ...*

```
(R WEIL DEM KIND ZU HELFEN IST)
((SUBCL+LASTVERB ((WEIL DEM KIND ZU HELFEN IST ,)
                 (ADCL NS)
                 1
                 (START (WEIL)
                        (ADCL V)
                        (DEM)
                        (D NS -EN))
                 2
                 (SUBCL+MAIN (WEIL DEM)
                             (ADCL V D NS -EN)
                             (KIND)
                             (NS))
                 3
                 (DET+NOUN (WEIL DEM KIND)
                           (ADCL V D NS)
                           (ZU)
                           (Z))
                 4
                 (SUBCL+VERB (WEIL DEM KIND ZU)
                             (ADCL V D NS Z)
                             (HELFEN)
                             (Q S3 D -FA))
                 5
                 (SUBCL+VERB (WEIL DEM KIND ZU HELFEN)
                             (ADCL V NS S3 -FA S)
                             (IST)
                             (V S3 S))
                 6)))
```

B.10.3 *Weil dem Kind von Peter zu helfen ist ...*

```
(R WEIL DEM KIND VON PETER ZU HELFEN IST)
((SUBCL+LASTVERB ((WEIL DEM KIND VON PETER ZU HELFEN IST ,)
                 (ADCL NS MS)
                 1
                 (START (WEIL)
                        (ADCL V)
                        (DEM)
                        (D NS -EN))
                 2
```

```
            (SUBCL+MAIN (WEIL DEM)
                        (ADCL V D NS -EN)
                        (KIND)
                        (NS))
            3
            (DET+NOUN (WEIL DEM KIND)
                      (ADCL V D NS)
                      (VON)
                      (-AG (D)))
            4
            (SUBCL+MAIN (WEIL DEM KIND VON)
                        (ADCL V D NS -AG (D))
                        (PETER)
                        (D MS))
            5
            (PREP+MAIN (WEIL DEM KIND VON PETER)
                       (ADCL V D NS -AG MS)
                       (ZU)
                       (Z))
            6
            (SUBCL+VERB (WEIL DEM KIND VON PETER ZU)
                        (ADCL V D NS -AG MS Z)
                        (HELFEN)
                        (Q S3 D -FA))
            7
            (SUBCL+VERB (WEIL DEM KIND VON PETER ZU HELFEN)
                        (ADCL V NS -AG MS S3 -FA S)
                        (IST)
                        (V S3 S))
            8))
(SUBCL+LASTVERB ((WEIL DEM KIND VON PETER ZU HELFEN IST ,)
                 (ADCL NS MS)
                 1
                 (START (WEIL)
                        (ADCL V)
                        (DEM)
                        (D NS -EN))
                 2
                 (SUBCL+MAIN (WEIL DEM)
                             (ADCL V D NS -EN)
                             (KIND)
                             (NS))
                 3
                 (DET+NOUN (WEIL DEM KIND)
                           (ADCL V D NS)
                           (VON)
                           (-AG (D)))
                 4
                 (NOUN+PREP (WEIL DEM KIND VON)
                            (ADCL V D NS (D))
                            (PETER)
                            (D MS))
                 5
                 (PREP+MAIN (WEIL DEM KIND VON PETER)
                            (ADCL V D NS MS)
```

```
                        (ZU)
                        (Z))
            6
            (SUBCL+VERB (WEIL DEM KIND VON PETER ZU)
                        (ADCL V D NS MS Z)
                        (HELFEN)
                        (Q S3 D -FA))
            7
            (SUBCL+VERB (WEIL DEM KIND VON PETER ZU HELFEN)
                        (ADCL V NS MS S3 -FA S)
                        (IST)
                        (V S3 S))
         8)))
```

B.10.4 Weil dem Kind von Peter geholfen werden muss ...

```
(R WEIL DEM KIND VON PETER GEHOLFEN WERDEN MUSS)
((SUBCL+LASTVERB ((WEIL DEM KIND VON PETER GEHOLFEN WERDEN MUSS ,)
                  (ADCL NS MS)
                  1
                  (START (WEIL)
                         (ADCL V)
                         (DEM)
                         (D NS -EN))
                  2
                  (SUBCL+MAIN (WEIL DEM)
                              (ADCL V D NS -EN)
                              (KIND)
                              (NS))
                  3
                  (DET+NOUN (WEIL DEM KIND)
                            (ADCL V D NS)
                            (VON)
                            (-AG (D)))
                  4
                  (SUBCL+MAIN (WEIL DEM KIND VON)
                              (ADCL V D NS -AG (D))
                              (PETER)
                              (D MS))
                  5
                  (PREP+MAIN (WEIL DEM KIND VON PETER)
                             (ADCL V D NS -AG MS)
                             (GEHOLFEN)
                             (WP S3 D -AG))
                  6
                  (SUBCL+VERB (WEIL DEM KIND VON PETER GEHOLFEN)
                              (ADCL V NS MS WP S3)
                              (WERDEN)
                              (W WP INF))
                  7
                  (SUBCL+VERB (WEIL DEM KIND VON PETER GEHOLFEN WERDEN)
                              (ADCL V NS MS S3 W INF)
                              (MUSS)
                              (V S3 W))
               8))
    (SUBCL+LASTVERB ((WEIL DEM KIND VON PETER GEHOLFEN WERDEN MUSS ,)
```

```
(ADCL NS MS)
1
(START (WEIL)
        (ADCL V)
        (DEM)
        (D NS -EN))
2
(SUBCL+MAIN (WEIL DEM)
            (ADCL V D NS -EN)
            (KIND)
            (NS))
3
(DET+NOUN (WEIL DEM KIND)
          (ADCL V D NS)
          (VON)
          (-AG (D)))
4
(NOUN+PREP (WEIL DEM KIND VON)
           (ADCL V D NS (D))
           (PETER)
           (D MS))
5
(PREP+MAIN (WEIL DEM KIND VON PETER)
           (ADCL V D NS MS)
           (GEHOLFEN)
           (WP S3 D -AG))
6
(SUBCL+VERB (WEIL DEM KIND VON PETER GEHOLFEN)
            (ADCL V NS MS WP S3 -AG)
            (WERDEN)
            (W WP INF))
7
(SUBCL+VERB (WEIL DEM KIND VON PETER GEHOLFEN WERDEN)
            (ADCL V NS MS S3 -AG W INF)
            (MUSS)
            (V S3 W))
        8)))
```

B.10.5 *Das Kind, dem zu helfen ist, schläft auf dem Sofa.*

```
(R DAS KIND DEM ZU HELFEN IST SCHLAEFT AUF DEM SOFA .)
((CMPLT ((DAS KIND , DEM ZU HELFEN IST , SCHLAEFT AUF DEM SOFA %.)
        (DECL)
        1
        (START (DAS)
               (S3 NS -E)
               (KIND)
               (NS))
        2
        (DET+NOUN (DAS KIND)
                  (S3 NS)
                  (DEM)
                  (D NS -EN))
        3
        (NOUN+RELPRO (DAS KIND , DEM)
                     (S3 V D)
```

```
                    (ZU)
                    (Z))
        4
        (SUBCL+VERB (DAS KIND , DEM ZU)
                    (S3 V D Z)
                    (HELFEN)
                    (Q S3 D -FA))
        5
        (SUBCL+VERB (DAS KIND , DEM ZU HELFEN)
                    (S3 V S3 -FA S)
                    (IST)
                    (V S3 S))
        6
        (SUBCL+LASTVERB (DAS KIND , DEM ZU HELFEN IST ,)
                    (S3)
                    (SCHLAEFT)
                    (V S3))
        7
        (MAIN+FVERB (DAS KIND , DEM ZU HELFEN IST , SCHLAEFT)
                    (V)
                    (AUF)
                    (ADV-L (D)))
        8
        (FVERB+MAIN (DAS KIND , DEM ZU HELFEN IST , SCHLAEFT AUF)
                    (V (D))
                    (DEM)
                    (D NS -EN))
        9
        (PREP+MAIN (DAS KIND , DEM ZU HELFEN IST , SCHLAEFT AUF DEM)
                    (V NS -EN)
                    (SOFA)
                    (NS))
        10
        (DET+NOUN (DAS KIND , DEM ZU HELFEN IST , SCHLAEFT AUF DEM SOFA)
                    (V NS)
                    (%.)
                    (V DECL))
        11)))
```

B.10.6 *Das Kind, dem das Buch zu geben ist, schläft auf dem Sofa.*

```
(R DAS KIND DEM DAS BUCH ZU GEBEN IST SCHLAEFT AUF DEM SOFA .)
((CMPLT ((DAS KIND , DEM DAS BUCH ZU GEBEN IST , SCHLAEFT AUF DEM SOFA %.)
        (DECL)
        1
        (START (DAS)
                (S3 NS -E)
                (KIND)
                (NS))
        2
        (DET+NOUN (DAS KIND)
                (S3 NS)
                (DEM)
                (D NS -EN))
        3
        (NOUN+RELPRO (DAS KIND , DEM)
```

```
                        (S3 V D)
                        (DAS)
                        (S3 NS -E))
        4
        (SUBCL+MAIN (DAS KIND , DEM DAS)
                    (S3 V D S3 NS -E)
                    (BUCH)
                    (NS))
        5
        (DET+NOUN (DAS KIND , DEM DAS BUCH)
                  (S3 V D S3 NS)
                  (ZU)
                  (Z))
        6
        (SUBCL+VERB (DAS KIND , DEM DAS BUCH ZU)
                    (S3 V D S3 NS Z)
                    (GEBEN)
                    (Q D -AG))
        7
        (SUBCL+VERB (DAS KIND , DEM DAS BUCH ZU GEBEN)
                    (S3 V S3 NS -AG S)
                    (IST)
                    (V S3 S))
        8
        (SUBCL+LASTVERB (DAS KIND , DEM DAS BUCH ZU GEBEN IST ,)
                        (S3 NS)
                        (SCHLAEFT)
                        (V S3))
        9
        (MAIN+FVERB (DAS KIND , DEM DAS BUCH ZU GEBEN IST , SCHLAEFT)
                    (V NS)
                    (AUF)
                    (ADV-L (D)))
        10
        (FVERB+MAIN (DAS KIND , DEM DAS BUCH ZU GEBEN IST , SCHLAEFT AUF)
                    (V NS (D))
                    (DEM)
                    (D NS -EN))
        11
        (PREP+MAIN (DAS KIND , DEM DAS BUCH ZU GEBEN IST , SCHLAEFT AUF DEM)
                   (V NS NS -EN)
                   (SOFA)
                   (NS))
        12
        (DET+NOUN (DAS KIND , DEM DAS BUCH ZU GEBEN IST , SCHLAEFT AUF DEM SOFA)
                  (V NS NS)
                  (%.)
                  (V DECL))
        13)))
```

B.10.7 *Das Buch, das dem Kind zu geben sein wird,*

```
(R DAS BUCH DAS DEM KIND ZU GEBEN SEIN WIRD)
((SUBCL+LASTVERB ((DAS BUCH , DAS DEM KIND ZU GEBEN SEIN WIRD ,)
                  (S3 NS)
                  1
```

```
            (START (DAS)
                   (S3 NS -E)
                   (BUCH)
                   (NS))
            2
            (DET+NOUN (DAS BUCH)
                      (S3 NS)
                      (DAS)
                      (S3 NS -E))
            3
            (NOUN+RELPRO (DAS BUCH , DAS)
                         (S3 V S3)
                         (DEM)
                         (D NS -EN))
            4
            (SUBCL+MAIN (DAS BUCH , DAS DEM)
                        (S3 V S3 D NS -EN)
                        (KIND)
                        (NS))
            5
            (DET+NOUN (DAS BUCH , DAS DEM KIND)
                      (S3 V S3 D NS)
                      (ZU)
                      (Z))
            6
            (SUBCL+VERB (DAS BUCH , DAS DEM KIND ZU)
                        (S3 V S3 D NS Z)
                        (GEBEN)
                        (Q D -AG))
            7
            (SUBCL+VERB (DAS BUCH , DAS DEM KIND ZU GEBEN)
                        (S3 V S3 NS -AG S)
                        (SEIN)
                        (W S INF))
            8
            (SUBCL+VERB (DAS BUCH , DAS DEM KIND ZU GEBEN SEIN)
                        (S3 V S3 NS -AG W INF)
                        (WIRD)
                        (V S3 W))
            9))
(SUBCL+LASTVERB ((DAS BUCH , DAS DEM KIND ZU GEBEN SEIN WIRD ,)
                (A NS)
                1
                (START (DAS)
                       (A NS -E)
                       (BUCH)
                       (NS))
                2
                (DET+NOUN (DAS BUCH)
                          (A NS)
                          (DAS)
                          (S3 NS -E))
                3
                (NOUN+RELPRO (DAS BUCH , DAS)
                             (A V S3)
```

```
                              (DEM)
                              (D NS -EN))
            4
            (SUBCL+MAIN (DAS BUCH , DAS DEM)
                        (A V S3 D NS -EN)
                        (KIND)
                        (NS))
            5
            (DET+NOUN (DAS BUCH , DAS DEM KIND)
                      (A V S3 D NS)
                      (ZU)
                      (Z))
            6
            (SUBCL+VERB (DAS BUCH , DAS DEM KIND ZU)
                        (A V S3 D NS Z)
                        (GEBEN)
                        (Q D -AG))
            7
            (SUBCL+VERB (DAS BUCH , DAS DEM KIND ZU GEBEN)
                        (A V S3 NS -AG S)
                        (SEIN)
                        (W S INF))
            8
            (SUBCL+VERB (DAS BUCH , DAS DEM KIND ZU GEBEN SEIN)
                        (A V S3 NS -AG W INF)
                        (WIRD)
                        (V S3 W))
         9)))
```

B.11   Multiple modal infinitives in main clauses

B.11.1 *Der Mann hat das Buch schreiben wollen.*

```
(R DER MANN HAT DAS BUCH SCHREIBEN WOLLEN .)
((CMPLT ((DER MANN HAT DAS BUCH SCHREIBEN WOLLEN %.)
        (DECL)
        1
        (START (DER)
               (S3 MS -E)
               (MANN)
               (MS))
        2
        (DET+NOUN (DER MANN)
                  (S3 MS)
                  (HAT)
                  (V S3 H))
        3
        (MAIN+FVERB (DER MANN HAT)
                    (V H MS)
                    (DAS)
                    (A NS -E))
        4
        (FVERB+MAIN (DER MANN HAT DAS)
                    (V H MS A NS -E)
```

```
                        (BUCH)
                        (NS))
        5
        (DET+NOUN (DER MANN HAT DAS BUCH)
                  (V H MS A NS)
                  (SCHREIBEN)
                  (W A INF))
        6
        (MAINCL+NFVERB (DER MANN HAT DAS BUCH SCHREIBEN)
                       (V H MS NS W INF)
                       (WOLLEN)
                       (H W INF))
        7
        (MAINCL+NFVERB (DER MANN HAT DAS BUCH SCHREIBEN WOLLEN)
                       (V MS NS INF)
                       (%.)
                       (V DECL))
        8)))
```

B.11.2 *Der Mann wird das Buch schreiben wollen.*

```
(R DER MANN WIRD DAS BUCH SCHREIBEN WOLLEN .)
((CMPLT ((DER MANN WIRD DAS BUCH SCHREIBEN WOLLEN %.)
         (DECL)
         1
         (START (DER)
                (S3 MS -E)
                (MANN)
                (MS))
         2
         (DET+NOUN (DER MANN)
                   (S3 MS)
                   (WIRD)
                   (V S3 W))
         3
         (MAIN+FVERB (DER MANN WIRD)
                     (V W MS)
                     (DAS)
                     (A NS -E))
         4
         (FVERB+MAIN (DER MANN WIRD DAS)
                     (V W MS A NS -E)
                     (BUCH)
                     (NS))
         5
         (DET+NOUN (DER MANN WIRD DAS BUCH)
                   (V W MS A NS)
                   (SCHREIBEN)
                   (W A INF))
         6
         (MAINCL+NFVERB (DER MANN WIRD DAS BUCH SCHREIBEN)
                        (V MS NS INF)
                        (WOLLEN)
                        (H W INF))
         7
         (MAINCL+NFVERB (DER MANN WIRD DAS BUCH SCHREIBEN WOLLEN)
```

```
                        (V MS NS INF)
                        (%.)
                        (V DECL))
        8)))
```

B.11.3 *Der Mann hat das Buch schreiben können wollen.*

```
(R DER MANN HAT DAS BUCH SCHREIBEN KOENNEN WOLLEN .)
((CMPLT ((DER MANN HAT DAS BUCH SCHREIBEN KOENNEN WOLLEN %.)
        (DECL)
        1
        (START (DER)
                (S3 MS -E)
                (MANN)
                (MS))
        2
        (DET+NOUN (DER MANN)
                (S3 MS)
                (HAT)
                (V S3 H))
        3
        (MAIN+FVERB (DER MANN HAT)
                (V H MS)
                (DAS)
                (A NS -E))
        4
        (FVERB+MAIN (DER MANN HAT DAS)
                (V H MS A NS -E)
                (BUCH) ·
                (NS))
        5
        (DET+NOUN (DER MANN HAT DAS BUCH)
                (V H MS A NS)
                (SCHREIBEN)
                (W A INF))
        6
        (MAINCL+NFVERB (DER MANN HAT DAS BUCH SCHREIBEN)
                (V H MS NS W INF)
                (KOENNEN)
                (H W INF))
        7
        (MAINCL+NFVERB (DER MANN HAT DAS BUCH SCHREIBEN KOENNEN)
                (V MS NS INF)
                (WOLLEN)
                (H W INF))
        8
        (MAINCL+NFVERB (DER MANN HAT DAS BUCH SCHREIBEN KOENNEN WOLLEN)
                (V MS NS INF)
                (%.)
                (V DECL))
        9)))
```

B.11.4 *Der Mann hat dem Mädchen das Buch geben dürfen können wollen sollen mögen.*

```
(R DER MANN HAT DEM MAEDCHEN DAS BUCH GEBEN DUERFEN KOENNEN SOLLEN SOLLEN MOEGEN .)
```

```
((CMPLT ((DER MANN HAT DEM MAEDCHEN DAS BUCH GEBEN DUERFEN KOENNEN WOLLEN SOLLEN
                                                              MOEGEN %.)
        (DECL)
        1
        (START (DER)
               (S3 MS -E)
               (MANN)
               (MS))
        2
        (DET+NOUN (DER MANN)
                  (S3 MS)
                  (HAT)
                  (V S3 H))
        3
        (MAIN+FVERB (DER MANN HAT)
                    (V H MS)
                    (DEM)
                    (D NS -EN))
        4
        (FVERB+MAIN (DER MANN HAT DEM)
                    (V H MS D NS -EN)
                    (MAEDCHEN)
                    (NS))
        5
        (DET+NOUN (DER MANN HAT DEM MAEDCHEN)
                  (V H MS D NS)
                  (DAS)
                  (A NS -E))
        6
        (FVERB+MAIN (DER MANN HAT DEM MAEDCHEN DAS)
                    (V H MS D NS A NS -E)
                    (BUCH)
                    (NS))
        7
        (DET+NOUN (DER MANN HAT DEM MAEDCHEN DAS BUCH)
                  (V H MS D NS A NS)
                  (GEBEN)
                  (W D A INF))
        8
        (MAINCL+NFVERB (DER MANN HAT DEM MAEDCHEN DAS BUCH GEBEN)
                       (V H MS NS NS W INF)
                       (DUERFEN)
                       (H W INF))
        9
        (MAINCL+NFVERB (DER MANN HAT DEM MAEDCHEN DAS BUCH GEBEN DUERFEN)
                       (V MS NS NS INF)
                       (KOENNEN)
                       (H W INF))
        10
        (MAINCL+NFVERB (DER MANN HAT DEM MAEDCHEN DAS BUCH GEBEN DUERFEN KOENNEN)
                       (V MS NS NS INF)
                       (WOLLEN)
                       (H W INF))
        11
        (MAINCL+NFVERB (DER MANN HAT DEM MAEDCHEN DAS BUCH GEBEN
```

```
                                                DUERFEN KOENNEN WOLLEN)
            (V MS NS NS INF)
            (SOLLEN)
            (H W INF))
    12
    (MAINCL+NFVERB (DER MANN HAT DEM MAEDCHEN DAS BUCH GEBEN
                                        DUERFEN KOENNEN WOLLEN SOLLEN)
            (V MS NS NS INF)
            (MOEGEN)
            (H W INF))
    13
    (MAINCL+NFVERB (DER MANN HAT DEM MAEDCHEN DAS BUCH GEBEN
                                DUERFEN KOENNEN WOLLEN SOLLEN MOEGEN)
            (V MS NS NS INF)
            (%.)
            (V DECL))
    14)))
```

B.12   Multiple modal infinitives in subordinate clauses

B.12.1 *Weil der Mann den Teller sehen können wollte, ...*

```
(R WEIL DER MANN DEN TELLER SEHEN KOENNEN WOLLTE)
((SUBCL+LASTVERB ((WEIL DER MANN DEN TELLER SEHEN KOENNEN WOLLTE ,)
            (ADCL MS)
            1
            (START (WEIL)
                    (ADCL V)
                    (DER)
                    (S3 MS -E))
            2
            (SUBCL+MAIN (WEIL DER)
                    (ADCL V S3 MS -E)
                    (MANN)
                    (MS))
            3
            (DET+NOUN (WEIL DER MANN)
                    (ADCL V S3 MS)
                    (DEN)
                    (A MS -EN))
            4
            (SUBCL+MAIN (WEIL DER MANN DEN)
                    (ADCL V S3 MS A MS -EN)
                    (TELLER)
                    (MS))
            5
            (DET+NOUN (WEIL DER MANN DEN TELLER)
                    (ADCL V S3 MS A MS)
                    (SEHEN)
                    (W A INF))
            6
            (SUBCL+VERB (WEIL DER MANN DEN TELLER SEHEN)
```

```
                              (ADCL V S3 MS MS W INF)
                              (KOENNEN)
                              (H W INF))
                7
                (SUBCL+VERB (WEIL DER MANN DEN TELLER SEHEN KOENNEN)
                              (ADCL V S3 MS MS W INF)
                              (WOLLTE)
                              (V S3 W))
                8)))
```

B.12.2 *Weil der Mann den Teller hat sehen können, lacht Susi.*

```
(R WEIL DER MANN DEN TELLER HAT SEHEN KOENNEN LACHT SUSI .)
((CMPLT ((WEIL DER MANN DEN TELLER HAT SEHEN KOENNEN , LACHT SUSI %.)
        (DECL)
        1
        (START (WEIL)
               (ADCL V)
               (DER)
               (S3 MS -E))
        2
        (SUBCL+MAIN (WEIL DER)
                     (ADCL V S3 MS -E)
                     (MANN)
                     (MS))
        3
        (DET+NOUN (WEIL DER MANN)
                   (ADCL V S3 MS)
                   (DEN)
                   (A MS -EN))
        4
        (SUBCL+MAIN (WEIL DER MANN DEN)
                     (ADCL V S3 MS A MS -EN)
                     (TELLER)
                     (MS))
        5
        (DET+NOUN (WEIL DER MANN DEN TELLER)
                   (ADCL V S3 MS A MS)
                   (HAT)
                   (V S3 H))
        6
        (SUBCL+VERB (WEIL DER MANN DEN TELLER HAT)
                     (ADCL INF H MS A MS)
                     (SEHEN)
                     (W A INF))
        7
        (SUBCL+VERB (WEIL DER MANN DEN TELLER HAT SEHEN)
                     (ADCL INF H MS MS W INF)
                     (KOENNEN)
                     (H W INF))
        8
        (SUBCL+LASTVERB (WEIL DER MANN DEN TELLER HAT SEHEN KOENNEN ,)
                         (ADCL)
                         (LACHT)
                         (V S3))
        9
```

```
         (MAIN+FVERB (WEIL DER MANN DEN TELLER HAT SEHEN KOENNEN , LACHT)
                    (V S3)
                    (SUSI)
                    (S3 FS))
      10
         (FVERB+MAIN (WEIL DER MANN DEN TELLER HAT SEHEN KOENNEN , LACHT SUSI)
                    (V FS)
                    (%.)
                    (V DECL))
      11)))
```

B.12.3 *Weil der Mann den Teller sehen können hat, lacht Susi.*

```
(R WEIL DER MANN DEN TELLER SEHEN KOENNEN HAT LACHT SUSI)
[ERROR "Ungrammatical continuation at"
      ((SUBCL+VERB ((WEIL DER MANN , DEN TELLER SEHEN KOENNEN ,
                         HAT)
                   (ADCL INF H P)
                   1
                   (START (WEIL)
                         (ADCL V)
                         (DER)
                         (S3 MS -E))
                   2
                   (SUBCL+MAIN (WEIL DER)
                         (ADCL V S3 MS -E)
                         (MANN)
                         (MS))
                   3
                   (DET+NOUN (WEIL DER MANN)
                         (ADCL V S3 MS)
                         (DEN)
                         (A MS -EN))
                   4
                   (NOUN+RELPRO (WEIL DER MANN , DEN)
                         (ADCL V S3 V A)
                         (TELLER)
                         (P3 P))
                   5
                   (SUBCL+MAIN (WEIL DER MANN , DEN TELLER)
                         (ADCL V S3 V A P3 P)
                         (SEHEN)
                         (W A INF))
                   6
                   (SUBCL+VERB (WEIL DER MANN , DEN TELLER SEHEN)
                         (ADCL V S3 V P3 P W INF)
                         (KOENNEN)
                         (V P3 W))
                   7
                   (SUBCL+LASTVERB (WEIL DER MANN , DEN TELLER SEHEN KOENNEN ,
                         (ADCL V S3 P)
                         (HAT)
                         (V S3 H))
                   8))
      (START ((LACHT)
             (V S3]
```

B.12.4 *Weil der Mann den Teller sehen können wird, lacht Susi.*

```
(R WEIL DER MANN DEN TELLER SEHEN KOENNEN WIRD LACHT SUSI .)
((CMPLT ((WEIL DER MANN DEN TELLER SEHEN KOENNEN WIRD , LACHT SUSI %.)
        (DECL)
        1
        (START (WEIL)
               (ADCL V)
               (DER)
               (S3 MS -E))
        2
        (SUBCL+MAIN (WEIL DER)
                    (ADCL V S3 MS -E)
                    (MANN)
                    (MS))
        3
        (DET+NOUN (WEIL DER MANN)
                  (ADCL V S3 MS)
                  (DEN)
                  (A MS -EN))
        4
        (SUBCL+MAIN (WEIL DER MANN DEN)
                    (ADCL V S3 MS A MS -EN)
                    (TELLER)
                    (MS))
        5
        (DET+NOUN (WEIL DER MANN DEN TELLER)
                  (ADCL V S3 MS A MS)
                  (SEHEN)
                  (W A INF))
        6
        (SUBCL+VERB (WEIL DER MANN DEN TELLER SEHEN)
                    (ADCL V S3 MS MS W INF)
                    (KOENNEN)
                    (H W INF))
        7
        (SUBCL+VERB (WEIL DER MANN DEN TELLER SEHEN KOENNEN)
                    (ADCL V S3 MS MS W INF)
                    (WIRD)
                    (V S3 W))
        8
        (SUBCL+LASTVERB (WEIL DER MANN DEN TELLER SEHEN KOENNEN WIRD ,)
                        (ADCL MS)
                        (LACHT)
                        (V S3))
        9
        (MAIN+FVERB (WEIL DER MANN DEN TELLER SEHEN KOENNEN WIRD , LACHT)
                    (V S3 MS)
                    (SUSI)
                    (S3 FS))
        10
        (FVERB+MAIN (WEIL DER MANN DEN TELLER SEHEN KOENNEN WIRD , LACHT SUSI)
                    (V MS FS)
                    (%.)
                    (V DECL))
        11)))
```

B.12.5 *Der Mann, der das Buch lesen gewollt hat, ...*

```
(R DER MANN DER DAS BUCH LESEN GEWOLLT HAT)
((SUBCL+LASTVERB ((DER MANN , DER DAS BUCH LESEN GEWOLLT HAT ,)
                (S3 NS)
                1
                (START (DER)
                       (S3 MS -E)
                       (MANN)
                       (MS))
                2
                (DET+NOUN (DER MANN)
                          (S3 MS)
                          (DER)
                          (S3 MS -E))
                3
                (NOUN+RELPRO (DER MANN , DER)
                             (S3 V S3)
                             (DAS)
                             (A NS -E))
                4
                (SUBCL+MAIN (DER MANN , DER DAS)
                            (S3 V S3 A NS -E)
                            (BUCH)
                            (NS))
                5
                (DET+NOUN (DER MANN , DER DAS BUCH)
                          (S3 V S3 A NS)
                          (LESEN)
                          (W A INF))
                6
                (SUBCL+VERB (DER MANN , DER DAS BUCH LESEN)
                            (S3 V S3 NS W INF)
                            (GEWOLLT)
                            (W H))
                7
                (SUBCL+VERB (DER MANN , DER DAS BUCH LESEN GEWOLLT)
                            (S3 V S3 NS H)
                            (HAT)
                            (V S3 H))
                8)))
```

B.12.6 **Der Mann, der das Buch lesen wollen hat, ...*

```
(R DER MANN DER DAS BUCH LESEN WOLLEN HAT)
[ERROR "Ungrammatical continuation at"
     ((SUBCL+VERB ((DER MANN , DER DAS BUCH LESEN WOLLEN)
                  (S3 V S3 NS W INF)
                  1
                  (START (DER)
                         (S3 MS -E)
                         (MANN)
                         (MS))
                  2
                  (DET+NOUN (DER MANN)
                            (S3 MS)
```

```
                        (DER)
                        (S3 MS -E))
                3
                (NOUN+RELPRO (DER MANN , DER)
                        (S3 V S3)
                        (DAS)
                        (A NS -E))
                4
                (SUBCL+MAIN (DER MANN , DER DAS)
                        (S3 V S3 A NS -E)
                        (BUCH)
                        (NS))
                5
                (DET+NOUN (DER MANN , DER DAS BUCH)
                        (S3 V S3 A NS)
                        (LESEN)
                        (W A INF))
                6
                (SUBCL+VERB (DER MANN , DER DAS BUCH LESEN)
                        (S3 V S3 NS W INF)
                        (WOLLEN)
                        (H W INF))
            7))
    (START ((HAT)
            (V S3 A]
```

B.12.7 *Der Mann, der das Buch hat lesen wollen, ...*

```
(R DER MANN DER DAS BUCH HAT LESEN KOENNEN)
((SUBCL+LASTVERB ((DER MANN , DER DAS BUCH HAT LESEN WOLLEN ,)
                (S3)
                1
                (START (DER)
                        (S3 MS -E)
                        (MANN)
                        (MS))
                2
                (DET+NOUN (DER MANN)
                        (S3 MS)
                        (DER)
                        (S3 MS -E))
                3
                (NOUN+RELPRO (DER MANN , DER)
                        (S3 V S3)
                        (DAS)
                        (A NS -E))
                4
                (SUBCL+MAIN (DER MANN , DER DAS)
                        (S3 V S3 A NS -E)
                        (BUCH)
                        (NS))
                5
                (DET+NOUN (DER MANN , DER DAS BUCH)
                        (S3 V S3 A NS)
                        (HAT)
                        (V S3 H))
```

```
                    6
                    (SUBCL+VERB (DER MANN , DER DAS BUCH HAT)
                                (S3 INF H A NS)
                                (LESEN)
                                (W A INF))
                    7
                    (SUBCL+VERB (DER MANN , DER DAS BUCH HAT LESEN)
                                (S3 INF H NS W INF)
                                (WOLLEN)
                                (H W INF))
                8))
(SUBCL+VERB ((DER MANN , DER DAS BUCH HAT LESEN WOLLEN)
            (S3 INF H NS W INF)
            1
            (START (DER)
                   (S3 MS -E)
                   (MANN)
                   (MS))
            2
            (DET+NOUN (DER MANN)
                      (S3 MS)
                      (DER)
                      (S3 MS -E))
            3
            (NOUN+RELPRO (DER MANN , DER)
                         (S3 V S3)
                         (DAS)
                         (A NS -E))
            4
            (SUBCL+MAIN (DER MANN , DER DAS)
                        (S3 V S3 A NS -E)
                        (BUCH)
                        (NS))
            5
            (DET+NOUN (DER MANN , DER DAS BUCH)
                      (S3 V S3 A NS)
                      (HAT)
                      (V S3 H))
            6
            (SUBCL+VERB (DER MANN , DER DAS BUCH HAT)
                        (S3 INF H A NS)
                        (LESEN)
                        (W A INF))
            7
            (SUBCL+VERB (DER MANN , DER DAS BUCH HAT LESEN)
                        (S3 INF H NS W INF)
                        (WOLLEN)
                        (H W INF))
            8)))
```

B.12.8 Der Mann, der das Buch lesen können gewollt hat,

```
(R DER MANN DER DAS BUCH LESEN KOENNEN GEWOLLT HAT)
((SUBCL+LASTVERB ((DER MANN , DER DAS BUCH LESEN KOENNEN GEWOLLT HAT ,)
                 (S3 NS)
                 1
```

```
              (START (DER)
                     (S3 MS -E)
                     (MANN)
                     (MS))
          2
          (DET+NOUN (DER MANN)
                    (S3 MS)
                    (DER)
                    (S3 MS -E))
          3
          (NOUN+RELPRO (DER MANN , DER)
                       (S3 V S3)
                       (DAS)
                       (A NS -E))
          4
          (SUBCL+MAIN (DER MANN , DER DAS)
                      (S3 V S3 A NS -E)
                      (BUCH)
                      (NS))
          5
          (DET+NOUN (DER MANN , DER DAS BUCH)
                    (S3 V S3 A NS)
                    (LESEN)
                    (W A INF))
          6
          (SUBCL+VERB (DER MANN , DER DAS BUCH LESEN)
                      (S3 V S3 NS W INF)
                      (KOENNEN)
                      (H W INF))
          7
          (SUBCL+VERB (DER MANN , DER DAS BUCH LESEN KOENNEN)
                      (S3 V S3 NS W INF)
                      (GEWOLLT)
                      (W H))
          8
          (SUBCL+VERB (DER MANN , DER DAS BUCH LESEN KOENNEN GEWOLLT)
                      (S3 V S3 NS H)
                      (HAT)
                      (V S3 H))
          9)))
```

B.12.9 *Der Mann, der das Buch Maria hat geben können wollen, ...*

```
(R DER MANN DER DAS BUCH MARIA HAT GEBEN KOENNEN WOLLEN)
((SUBCL+LASTVERB ((DER MANN , DER DAS BUCH MARIA HAT GEBEN KOENNEN WOLLEN ,)
                 (S3)
                 1
                 (START (DER)
                        (S3 MS -E)
                        (MANN)
                        (MS))
                 2
                 (DET+NOUN (DER MANN)
                           (S3 MS)
                           (DER)
                           (S3 MS -E))
```

```
              3
              (NOUN+RELPRO (DER MANN , DER)
                           (S3 V S3)
                           (DAS)
                           (A NS -E))
              4
              (SUBCL+MAIN (DER MANN , DER DAS)
                          (S3 V S3 A NS -E)
                          (BUCH)
                          (NS))
              5
              (DET+NOUN (DER MANN , DER DAS BUCH)
                        (S3 V S3 A NS)
                        (MARIA)
                        (D FS))
              6
              (SUBCL+MAIN (DER MANN , DER DAS BUCH MARIA)
                          (S3 V S3 A NS D FS)
                          (HAT)
                          (V S3 H))
              7
              (SUBCL+VERB (DER MANN , DER DAS BUCH MARIA HAT)
                          (S3 INF H A NS D FS)
                          (GEBEN)
                          (W D A INF))
              8
              (SUBCL+VERB (DER MANN , DER DAS BUCH MARIA HAT GEBEN)
                          (S3 INF H NS FS W INF)
                          (KOENNEN)
                          (H W INF))
              9
              (SUBCL+VERB (DER MANN , DER DAS BUCH MARIA HAT GEBEN KOENNEN)
                          (S3 INF H NS FS W INF)
                          (WOLLEN)
                          (H W INF))
              10))
(SUBCL+VERB ((DER MANN , DER DAS BUCH MARIA HAT GEBEN KOENNEN WOLLEN)
             (S3 INF H NS FS W INF)
              1
              (START (DER)
                     (S3 MS -E)
                     (MANN)
                     (MS))
              2
              (DET+NOUN (DER MANN)
                        (S3 MS)
                        (DER)
                        (S3 MS -E))
              3
              (NOUN+RELPRO (DER MANN , DER)
                           (S3 V S3)
                           (DAS)
                           (A NS -E))
              4
              (SUBCL+MAIN (DER MANN , DER DAS)
```

```
                        (S3 V S3 A NS -E)
                        (BUCH)
                        (NS))
            5
        (DET+NOUN (DER MANN , DER DAS BUCH)
                        (S3 V S3 A NS)
                        (MARIA)
                        (D FS))
            6
        (SUBCL+MAIN (DER MANN , DER DAS BUCH MARIA)
                        (S3 V S3 A NS D FS)
                        (HAT)
                        (V S3 H))
            7
        (SUBCL+VERB (DER MANN , DER DAS BUCH MARIA HAT)
                        (S3 INF H A NS D FS)
                        (GEBEN)
                        (W D A INF))
            8
        (SUBCL+VERB (DER MANN , DER DAS BUCH MARIA HAT GEBEN)
                        (S3 INF H NS FS W INF)
                        (KOENNEN)
                        (H W INF))
            9
        (SUBCL+VERB (DER MANN , DER DAS BUCH MARIA HAT GEBEN KOENNEN)
                        (S3 INF H NS FS W INF)
                        (WOLLEN)
                        (H W INF))
        10)))
```

B.13   Obligatory versus optional adverbs

B.13.1 *Peter wohnte früher in Hamburg.*

```
(R PETER WOHNTE FRUEHER IN HAMBURG .)
((CMPLT ((PETER WOHNTE FRUEHER IN HAMBURG %.)
        (DECL)
        1
        (START (PETER)
                (S3 MS)
                (WOHNTE)
                (V S3 ADV-L))
        2
        (MAIN+FVERB (PETER WOHNTE)
                (V ADV-L MS)
                (FRUEHER)
                (ADV-T))
        3
        (FVERB+MAIN (PETER WOHNTE FRUEHER)
                (V ADV-L MS)
                (IN)
                (ADV-L (D)))
        4
        (FVERB+MAIN (PETER WOHNTE FRUEHER IN)
```

```
                        (V MS (D))
                        (HAMBURG)
                        (D NS))
            5
            (PREP+MAIN (PETER WOHNTE FRUEHER IN HAMBURG)
                        (V MS NS)
                        (%.)
                        (V DECL))
            6)))
```

B.13.2 *In Hamburg wohnte früher Peter.*

```
(R IN HAMBURG WOHNTE FRUEHER PETER .)
((CMPLT ((IN HAMBURG WOHNTE FRUEHER PETER %.)
        (DECL)
        1
        (START (IN)
                (ADV-L (D))
                (HAMBURG)
                (D NS))
          2
        (PREP+MAIN (IN HAMBURG)
                    (ADV-L NS)
                    (WOHNTE)
                    (V S3 ADV-L))
            3
        (MAIN+FVERB (IN HAMBURG WOHNTE)
                    (V S3 NS)
                    (FRUEHER)
                    (ADV-T))
            4
        (FVERB+MAIN (IN HAMBURG WOHNTE FRUEHER)
                    (V S3 NS)
                    (PETER)
                    (S3 MS))
            5
        (FVERB+MAIN (IN HAMBURG WOHNTE FRUEHER PETER)
                    (V NS MS)
                    (%.)
                    (V DECL))
            6)))
```

B.13.3 *Früher wohnte Peter in Hamburg.*

```
(R FRUEHER WOHNTE PETER IN HAMBURG .)
((CMPLT ((FRUEHER WOHNTE PETER IN HAMBURG %.)
        (DECL)
        1
        (START (FRUEHER)
                (ADV-T)
                (WOHNTE)
                (V S3 ADV-L))
          2
        (MAIN+FVERB (FRUEHER WOHNTE)
                    (V S3 ADV-L)
                    (PETER)
```

```
                       (S3 MS))
         3
         (FVERB+MAIN (FRUEHER WOHNTE PETER)
                     (V ADV-L MS)
                     (IN)
                     (ADV-L (D)))
         4
         (FVERB+MAIN (FRUEHER WOHNTE PETER IN)
                     (V MS (D))
                     (HAMBURG)
                     (D NS))
         5
         (PREP+MAIN (FRUEHER WOHNTE PETER IN HAMBURG)
                    (V MS NS)
                    (%.)
                    (V DECL))
       6)))
```

B.13.4 *Peter wohnte.*

```
(R PETER WOHNTE .)
[ERROR "Ungrammatical continuation at"
      ((MAIN+FVERB ((PETER WOHNTE)
                    (V ADV-L MS)
                    1
                    (START (PETER)
                           (S3 MS)
                           (WOHNTE)
                           (V S3 ADV-L))
                   2))
       (*START ((%.)
                (V DECL]
```

B.13.5 *In Hamburg wohnte Peter früher.*

```
(R IN HAMBURG WOHNTE PETER FRUEHER .)
((CMPLT ((IN HAMBURG WOHNTE PETER FRUEHER %.)
         (DECL)
         1
         (START (IN)
                (ADV-L (D))
                (HAMBURG)
                (D NS))
         2
         (PREP+MAIN (IN HAMBURG)
                    (ADV-L NS)
                    (WOHNTE)
                    (V S3 ADV-L))
         3
         (MAIN+FVERB (IN HAMBURG WOHNTE)
                     (V S3 NS)
                     (PETER)
                     (S3 MS))
         4
         (FVERB+MAIN (IN HAMBURG WOHNTE PETER)
                     (V NS MS)
```

```
                    (FRUEHER)
                    (ADV-T))
          5
          (FVERB+MAIN (IN HAMBURG WOHNTE PETER FRUEHER)
                      (V NS MS)
                      (%.)
                      (V DECL))
          6)))
```

B.13.6 *Peter hat früher in Hamburg gewohnt.*

```
(R PETER HAT FRUEHER IN HAMBURG GEWOHNT .)
((CMPLT ((PETER HAT FRUEHER IN HAMBURG GEWOHNT %.)
        (DECL)
        1
        (START (PETER)
               (S3 MS)
               (HAT)
               (V S3 H))
          2
          (MAIN+FVERB (PETER HAT)
                      (V H MS)
                      (FRUEHER)
                      (ADV-T))
          3
          (FVERB+MAIN (PETER HAT FRUEHER)
                      (V H MS ADV-T)
                      (IN)
                      (ADV-L (D)))
          4
          (FVERB+MAIN (PETER HAT FRUEHER IN)
                      (V H MS ADV-T ADV-L (D))
                      (HAMBURG)
                      (D NS))
          5
          (PREP+MAIN (PETER HAT FRUEHER IN HAMBURG)
                     (V H MS ADV-T ADV-L NS)
                     (GEWOHNT)
                     (H ADV-L))
          6
          (MAINCL+NFVERB (PETER HAT FRUEHER IN HAMBURG GEWOHNT)
                         (V MS NS)
                         (%.)
                         (V DECL))
          7)))
```

B.13.7 *Früher hat Peter in Hamburg gewohnt.*

```
(R FRUEHER HAT PETER IN HAMBURG GEWOHNT .)
((CMPLT ((FRUEHER HAT PETER IN HAMBURG GEWOHNT %.)
        (DECL)
        1
        (START (FRUEHER)
               (ADV-T)
               (HAT)
               (V S3 H))
```

```
        2
        (MAIN+FVERB (FRUEHER HAT)
                    (V S3 H ADV-T)
                    (PETER)
                    (S3 MS))
        3
        (FVERB+MAIN (FRUEHER HAT PETER)
                    (V H ADV-T MS)
                    (IN)
                    (ADV-L (D)))
        4
        (FVERB+MAIN (FRUEHER HAT PETER IN)
                    (V H ADV-T MS ADV-L (D))
                    (HAMBURG)
                    (D NS))
        5
        (PREP+MAIN (FRUEHER HAT PETER IN HAMBURG)
                   (V H ADV-T MS ADV-L NS)
                   (GEWOHNT)
                   (H ADV-L))
        6
        (MAINCL+NFVERB (FRUEHER HAT PETER IN HAMBURG GEWOHNT)
                       (V MS NS)
                       (%.)
                       (V DECL))
        7)))
```

B.13.8 *In Hamburg hat Peter früher gewohnt.*

```
(R IN HAMBURG HAT PETER FRUEHER GEWOHNT .)
((CMPLT ((IN HAMBURG HAT PETER FRUEHER GEWOHNT %.)
         (DECL)
         1
         (START (IN)
                (ADV-L (D))
                (HAMBURG)
                (D NS))
         2
         (PREP+MAIN (IN HAMBURG)
                    (ADV-L NS)
                    (HAT)
                    (V S3 H))
         3
         (MAIN+FVERB (IN HAMBURG HAT)
                     (V S3 H ADV-L NS)
                     (PETER)
                     (S3 MS))
         4
         (FVERB+MAIN (IN HAMBURG HAT PETER)
                     (V H ADV-L NS MS)
                     (FRUEHER)
                     (ADV-T))
         5
         (FVERB+MAIN (IN HAMBURG HAT PETER FRUEHER)
                     (V H ADV-L NS MS ADV-T)
                     (GEWOHNT)
```

```
                    (H ADV-L))
        6
   (MAINCL+NFVERB (IN HAMBURG HAT PETER FRUEHER GEWOHNT)
                    (V NS MS)
                    (%.)
                    (V DECL))
        7)))
```

B.13.9 *Früher hat Peter gewohnt.*

```
(R FRUEHER HAT PETER GEWOHNT .)
[ERROR "Ungrammatical continuation at"
     ((MAINCL+NFVERB ((FRUEHER HAT PETER GEWOHNT)
                     (V S3 A MS ADV-L)
                     1
                     (START (FRUEHER)
                            (ADV-T)
                            (HAT)
                            (V S3 H))
                     2
                     (MAIN+FVERB (FRUEHER HAT)
                                 (V S3 H ADV-T)
                                 (PETER)
                                 (A MS))
                     3
                     (FVERB+MAIN (FRUEHER HAT PETER)
                                 (V S3 H ADV-T A MS)
                                 (GEWOHNT)
                                 (H ADV-L))
                     4))
        (START ((%.)
                (V DECL]
```

B.14   The preposition *hinter* in various constructions

B.14.1 *Hinter dem Berg wohnt Maria.*

```
(R HINTER DEM BERG WOHNT MARIA .)
((CMPLT ((HINTER DEM BERG WOHNT MARIA %.)
         (DECL)
         1
         (START (HINTER)
                (ADV-L (D))
                (DEM)
                (D MS -EN))
         2
         (PREP+MAIN (HINTER DEM)
                    (ADV-L MS -EN)
                    (BERG)
                    (MS))
         3
         (DET+NOUN (HINTER DEM BERG)
```

```
                    (ADV-L MS)
                    (WOHNT)
                    (V S3 ADV-L))
        4
        (MAIN+FVERB (HINTER DEM BERG WOHNT)
                    (V S3 MS)
                    (MARIA)
                    (S3 FS))
        5
        (FVERB+MAIN (HINTER DEM BERG WOHNT MARIA)
                    (V MS FS)
                    (%.)
                    (V DECL))
        6)))
```

B.14.2 *Das Haus hinter dem Berg gehört Maria.*

```
(R DAS HAUS HINTER DEM BERG GEHOERT MARIA .)
((CMPLT ((DAS HAUS HINTER DEM BERG GEHOERT MARIA %.)
        (DECL)
        1
        (START (DAS)
               (S3 NS -E)
               (HAUS)
               (NS))
        2
        (DET+NOUN (DAS HAUS)
                  (S3 NS)
                  (HINTER)
                  (ADV-L (D)))
        3
        (NOUN+PREP (DAS HAUS HINTER)
                   (S3 NS (D))
                   (DEM)
                   (D MS -EN))
        4
        (PREP+MAIN (DAS HAUS HINTER DEM)
                   (S3 NS MS -EN)
                   (BERG)
                   (MS))
        5
        (DET+NOUN (DAS HAUS HINTER DEM BERG)
                  (S3 NS MS)
                  (GEHOERT)
                  (V S3 D))
        6
        (MAIN+FVERB (DAS HAUS HINTER DEM BERG GEHOERT)
                    (V D NS MS)
                    (MARIA)
                    (D FS))
        7
        (FVERB+MAIN (DAS HAUS HINTER DEM BERG GEHOERT MARIA)
                    (V NS MS FS)
                    (%.)
                    (V DECL))
        8)))
```

B.14.3 *Das Haus, hinter dem die Katze schläft, gehört Maria.*

```
(R DAS HAUS HINTER DEM DIE KATZE SCHLAEFT GEHOERT MARIA .)
((CMPLT ((DAS HAUS , HINTER DEM DIE KATZE SCHLAEFT , GEHOERT MARIA %.)
        (DECL)
        1
        (START (DAS)
               (S3 NS -E)
               (HAUS)
               (NS))
        2
        (DET+NOUN (DAS HAUS)
                  (S3 NS)
                  (HINTER)
                  (ADV-L (D)))
        3
        (NOUN+SUBPREP (DAS HAUS , HINTER)
                      (S3 NS V (D))
                      (DEM)
                      (D NS -EN))
        4
        (SUBPREP+PRO (DAS HAUS , HINTER DEM)
                     (S3 NS V)
                     (DIE)
                     (S3 FS -E))
        5
        (SUBCL+MAIN (DAS HAUS , HINTER DEM DIE)
                    (S3 NS V S3 FS -E)
                    (KATZE)
                    (FS))
        6
        (DET+NOUN (DAS HAUS , HINTER DEM DIE KATZE)
                  (S3 NS V S3 FS)
                  (SCHLAEFT)
                  (V S3))
        7
        (SUBCL+LASTVERB (DAS HAUS , HINTER DEM DIE KATZE SCHLAEFT ,)
                        (S3 NS FS)
                        (GEHOERT)
                        (V S3 D))
        8
        (MAIN+FVERB (DAS HAUS , HINTER DEM DIE KATZE SCHLAEFT , GEHOERT)
                    (V D NS FS)
                    (MARIA)
                    (D FS))
        9
        (FVERB+MAIN (DAS HAUS , HINTER DEM DIE KATZE SCHLAEFT , GEHOERT MARIA)
                    (V NS FS FS)
                    (%.)
                    (V DECL))
        10)))
```

B.14.4 *Das Haus, das hinter dem Berg liegt, gehört Maria.*

```
(R DAS HAUS DAS HINTER DEM BERG LIEGT GEHOERT MARIA .)
((CMPLT ((DAS HAUS , DAS HINTER DEM BERG LIEGT , GEHOERT MARIA %.)
```

```
(DECL)
1
(START (DAS)
       (S3 NS -E)
       (HAUS)
       (NS))
2
(DET+NOUN (DAS HAUS)
          (S3 NS)
          (DAS)
          (S3 NS -E))
3
(NOUN+RELPRO (DAS HAUS , DAS)
             (S3 V S3)
             (HINTER)
             (ADV-L (D)))
4
(SUBCL+MAIN (DAS HAUS , DAS HINTER)
            (S3 V S3 ADV-L (D))
            (DEM)
            (D MS -EN))
5
(PREP+MAIN (DAS HAUS , DAS HINTER DEM)
           (S3 V S3 ADV-L MS -EN)
           (BERG)
           (MS))
6
(DET+NOUN (DAS HAUS , DAS HINTER DEM BERG)
          (S3 V S3 ADV-L MS)
          (LIEGT)
          (V S3 ADV-L))
7
(SUBCL+LASTVERB (DAS HAUS , DAS HINTER DEM BERG LIEGT ,)
                (S3 MS)
                (GEHOERT)
                (V S3 D))
8
(MAIN+FVERB (DAS HAUS , DAS HINTER DEM BERG LIEGT , GEHOERT)
            (V D MS)
            (MARIA)
            (D FS))
9
(FVERB+MAIN (DAS HAUS , DAS HINTER DEM BERG LIEGT , GEHOERT MARIA)
            (V MS FS)
            (%.)
            (V DECL))
10)))
```

B.14.5 *Die Katze ist hinter dem Haus.*

```
(R DIE KATZE IST HINTER DEM HAUS .)
((CMPLT ((DIE KATZE IST HINTER DEM HAUS %.)
        (DECL)
        1
        (START (DIE)
               (S3 FS -E)
```

```
            (KATZE)
            (FS))
    2
(DET+NOUN (DIE KATZE)
            (S3 FS)
            (IST)
            (V S3 S))
    3
(MAIN+FVERB (DIE KATZE IST)
            (V S FS)
            (HINTER)
            (ADV-L (D)))
    4
(AUX-PRED (DIE KATZE IST HINTER)
            (V FS (D))
            (DEM)
            (D NS -EN))
    5
(PREP+MAIN (DIE KATZE IST HINTER DEM)
            (V FS NS -EN)
            (HAUS)
            (NS))
    6
(DET+NOUN (DIE KATZE IST HINTER DEM HAUS)
            (V FS NS)
            (%.)
            (V DECL))
    7)))
```

B.15 Adsentential clauses and adverbs in various positions

B.15.1 *Nachdem der Mann gestern geschlafen hatte, las er ein Buch.*

```
(R NACHDEM DER MANN GESTERN GESCHLAFEN HATTE  LAS ER EIN BUCH .)
((CMPLT ((NACHDEM DER MANN GESTERN GESCHLAFEN HATTE , LAS ER EIN BUCH %.)
            (DECL)
            1
(START (NACHDEM)
            (ADCL V)
            (DER)
            (S3 MS -E))
            2
(SUBCL+MAIN (NACHDEM DER)
            (ADCL V S3 MS -E)
            (MANN)
            (MS))
            3
(DET+NOUN (NACHDEM DER MANN)
            (ADCL V S3 MS)
            (GESTERN)
            (ADV-T))
            4
```

```
(SUBCL+MAIN (NACHDEM DER MANN GESTERN)
            (ADCL V S3 MS ADV-T)
            (GESCHLAFEN)
            (H))
5
(SUBCL+VERB (NACHDEM DER MANN GESTERN GESCHLAFEN)
            (ADCL V S3 MS ADV-T INF H)
            (HATTE)
            (V S3 H))
6
(SUBCL+LASTVERB (NACHDEM DER MANN GESTERN GESCHLAFEN HATTE ,)
                (ADCL MS)
                (LAS)
                (V S3 A))
7
(MAIN+FVERB (NACHDEM DER MANN GESTERN GESCHLAFEN HATTE , LAS)
            (V S3 A MS)
            (ER)
            (S3))
8
(FVERB+MAIN (NACHDEM DER MANN GESTERN GESCHLAFEN HATTE , LAS ER)
            (V A MS)
            (EIN)
            (A NS -ES))
9
(FVERB+MAIN (NACHDEM DER MANN GESTERN GESCHLAFEN HATTE , LAS ER EIN)
            (V MS NS -ES)
            (BUCH)
            (NS))
10
(DET+NOUN (NACHDEM DER MANN GESTERN GESCHLAFEN HATTE , LAS ER EIN BUCH)
          (V MS NS)
          (%.)
          (V DECL))
11)))
```

B.15.2 *Der Mann las gestern ein Buch, nachdem er geschlafen hatte.*

```
(R DER MANN LAS GESTERN EIN BUCH NACHDEM ER GESCHLAFEN HATTE .)
((CMPLT ((DER MANN LAS GESTERN EIN BUCH , NACHDEM ER GESCHLAFEN HATTE %.)
         (DECL)
         1
         (START (DER)
                (S3 MS -E)
                (MANN)
                (MS))
         2
         (DET+NOUN (DER MANN)
                   (S3 MS)
                   (LAS)
                   (V S3 A))
         3
         (MAIN+FVERB (DER MANN LAS)
                     (V A MS)
                     (GESTERN)
                     (ADV-T))
```

```
4
(FVERB+MAIN (DER MANN LAS GESTERN)
            (V A MS)
            (EIN)
            (A NS -ES))
5
(FVERB+MAIN (DER MANN LAS GESTERN EIN)
            (V MS NS -ES)
            (BUCH)
            (NS))
6
(DET+NOUN (DER MANN LAS GESTERN EIN BUCH)
          (V MS NS)
          (NACHDEM)
          (ADCL V))
7
(FVERB+MAIN (DER MANN LAS GESTERN EIN BUCH , NACHDEM)
            (V MS NS V)
            (ER)
            (S3))
8
(SUBCL+MAIN (DER MANN LAS GESTERN EIN BUCH , NACHDEM ER)
            (V MS NS V S3)
            (GESCHLAFEN)
            (H))
9
(SUBCL+VERB (DER MANN LAS GESTERN EIN BUCH , NACHDEM ER GESCHLAFEN)
            (V MS NS V S3 INF H)
            (HATTE)
            (V S3 H))
10
(SUBCL+LASTVERB (DER MANN LAS GESTERN EIN BUCH , NACHDEM ER GESCHLAFEN
                                                            HATTE ,)

                (V MS NS)
                (%.)
                (V DECL))
11)))
```

B.15.3 *Ein Buch las der Mann gestern, nachdem er geschlafen hatte.*

```
(R EIN BUCH LAS DER MANN GESTERN NACHDEM ER GESCHLAFEN HATTE .)
((CMPLT ((EIN BUCH LAS DER MANN GESTERN , NACHDEM ER GESCHLAFEN HATTE %.)
         (DECL)
         1
         (START (EIN)
                (A NS -ES)
                (BUCH)
                (NS))
         2
         (DET+NOUN (EIN BUCH)
                   (A NS)
                   (LAS)
                   (V S3 A))
         3
         (MAIN+FVERB (EIN BUCH LAS)
```

```
                          (V S3 NS)
                          (DER)
                          (S3 MS -E))
          4
          (FVERB+MAIN (EIN BUCH LAS DER)
                      (V NS MS -E)
                      (MANN)
                      (MS))
          5
          (DET+NOUN (EIN BUCH LAS DER MANN)
                    (V NS MS)
                    (GESTERN)
                    (ADV-T))
          6
          (FVERB+MAIN (EIN BUCH LAS DER MANN GESTERN)
                      (V NS MS)
                      (NACHDEM)
                      (ADCL V))
          7
          (FVERB+MAIN (EIN BUCH LAS DER MANN GESTERN , NACHDEM)
                      (V NS MS V)
                      (ER)
                      (S3))
          8
          (SUBCL+MAIN (EIN BUCH LAS DER MANN GESTERN , NACHDEM ER)
                      (V NS MS V S3)
                      (GESCHLAFEN)
                      (H))
          9
          (SUBCL+VERB (EIN BUCH LAS DER MANN GESTERN , NACHDEM ER GESCHLAFEN)
                      (V NS MS V S3 INF H)
                      (HATTE)
                      (V S3 H))
          10
          (SUBCL+LASTVERB (EIN BUCH LAS DER MANN GESTERN , NACHDEM ER GESCHLAFEN
                                                                       HATTE ,)
                          (V NS MS)
                          (%.)
                          (V DECL))
          11)))
```

B.15.4 *Gestern nachdem er geschlafen hatte, las der Mann ein Buch.*

```
(R GESTERN NACHDEM ER GESCHLAFEN HATTE LAS DER MANN EIN BUCH .)
((CMPLT ((GESTERN NACHDEM ER GESCHLAFEN HATTE , LAS DER MANN EIN BUCH %.)
         (DECL)
         1
         (START (GESTERN)
                (ADV-T)
                (NACHDEM)
                (ADCL V))
         2
         (ADV+ADV (GESTERN NACHDEM)
                  (ADV-T ADCL V)
                  (ER)
                  (S3))
```

```
   3
(SUBCL+MAIN (GESTERN NACHDEM ER)
            (ADV-T ADCL V S3)
            (GESCHLAFEN)
            (H))
   4
(SUBCL+VERB (GESTERN NACHDEM ER GESCHLAFEN)
            (ADV-T ADCL V S3 INF H)
            (HATTE)
            (V S3 H))
   5
(SUBCL+LASTVERB (GESTERN NACHDEM ER GESCHLAFEN HATTE ,)
                (ADV-T ADCL)
                (LAS)
                (V S3 A))
   6
(MAIN+FVERB (GESTERN NACHDEM ER GESCHLAFEN HATTE , LAS)
            (V S3 A)
            (DER)
            (S3 MS -E))
   7
(FVERB+MAIN (GESTERN NACHDEM ER GESCHLAFEN HATTE , LAS DER)
            (V A MS -E)
            (MANN)
            (MS))
   8
(DET+NOUN (GESTERN NACHDEM ER GESCHLAFEN HATTE , LAS DER MANN)
          (V A MS)
          (EIN)
          (A MS -ES))
   9
(FVERB+MAIN (GESTERN NACHDEM ER GESCHLAFEN HATTE , LAS DER MANN EIN)
            (V MS NS -ES)
            (BUCH)
            (NS))
   10
(DET+NOUN (GESTERN NACHDEM ER GESCHLAFEN HATTE , LAS DER MANN EIN BUCH)
          (V MS NS)
          (%.)
          (V DECL))
   11)))
```

B.16   Relative clause agreement

B.16.1 *Der Mann gab der Frau das Buch, die das Kind gesehen hatte.*

```
(R DER MANN GAB DER FRAU DAS BUCH DIE DAS KIND GESEHEN HATTE .)
((CMPLT ((DER MANN GAB DER FRAU DAS BUCH , DIE DAS KIND GESEHEN HATTE %.)
         (DECL)
         1
         (START (DER)
                (S3 MS -E)
                (MANN)
                (MS))
```

```
2
(DET+NOUN (DER MANN)
          (S3 MS)
          (GAB)
          (V S3 D A))
3
(MAIN+FVERB (DER MANN GAB)
            (V D A MS)
            (DER)
            (D FS -EN))
4
(FVERB+MAIN (DER MANN GAB DER)
            (V A MS FS -EN)
            (FRAU)
            (FS))
5
(DET+NOUN (DER MANN GAB DER FRAU)
          (V A MS FS)
          (DAS)
          (A NS -E))
6
(FVERB+MAIN (DER MANN GAB DER FRAU DAS)
            (V MS FS NS -E)
            (BUCH)
            (NS))
7
(DET+NOUN (DER MANN GAB DER FRAU DAS BUCH)
          (V MS FS NS)
          (DIE)
          (S3 FS -E))
8
(NOUN+RELPRO (DER MANN GAB DER FRAU DAS BUCH , DIE)
             (V MS NS V S3)
             (DAS)
             (A NS -E))
9
(SUBCL+MAIN (DER MANN GAB DER FRAU DAS BUCH , DIE DAS)
            (V MS NS V S3 A NS -E)
            (KIND)
            (NS))
10
(DET+NOUN (DER MANN GAB DER FRAU DAS BUCH , DIE DAS KIND)
          (V MS NS V S3 A NS)
          (GESEHEN)
          (H A))
11
(SUBCL+VERB (DER MANN GAB DER FRAU DAS BUCH , DIE DAS KIND GESEHEN)
            (V MS NS V S3 NS INF H)
            (HATTE)
            (V S3 H))
12
(SUBCL+LASTVERB (DER MANN GAB DER FRAU DAS BUCH , DIE DAS KIND
                                                GESEHEN HATTE ,)
                (V MS NS NS)
                (%.)
```

```
                             (V DECL))
          13))
(CMPLT ((DER MANN GAB DER FRAU DAS BUCH , DIE DAS KIND GESEHEN HATTE %.)
          (DECL)
          1
          (START (DER)
                 (S3 MS -E)
                 (MANN)
                 (MS))
          2
          (DET+NOUN (DER MANN)
                    (S3 MS)
                    (GAB)
                    (V S3 D A))
          3
          (MAIN+FVERB (DER MANN GAB)
                      (V D A MS)
                      (DER)
                      (D FS -EN))
          4
          (FVERB+MAIN (DER MANN GAB DER)
                      (V A MS FS -EN)
                      (FRAU)
                      (FS))
          5
          (DET+NOUN (DER MANN GAB DER FRAU)
                    (V A MS FS)
                    (DAS)
                    (A NS -E))
          6
          (FVERB+MAIN (DER MANN GAB DER FRAU DAS)
                      (V MS FS NS -E)
                      (BUCH)
                      (NS))
          7
          (DET+NOUN (DER MANN GAB DER FRAU DAS BUCH)
                    (V MS FS NS)
                    (DIE)
                    (A FS -E))
          8
          (NOUN+RELPRO (DER MANN GAB DER FRAU DAS BUCH , DIE)
                       (V MS NS V A)
                       (DAS)
                       (S3 NS -E))
          9
          (SUBCL+MAIN (DER MANN GAB DER FRAU DAS BUCH , DIE DAS)
                      (V MS NS V A S3 NS -E)
                      (KIND)
                      (NS))
          10
          (DET+NOUN (DER MANN GAB DER FRAU DAS BUCH , DIE DAS KIND)
                    (V MS NS V A S3 NS)
                    (GESEHEN)
                    (H A))
          11
```

```
        (SUBCL+VERB (DER MANN GAB DER FRAU DAS BUCH , DIE DAS KIND GESEHEN)
                (V MS NS V S3 NS INF H)
                (HATTE)
                (V S3 H))
        12
        (SUBCL+LASTVERB (DER MANN GAB DER FRAU DAS BUCH , DIE DAS KIND
                                                        GESEHEN HATTE ,)
                        (V MS NS NS)
                        (%.)
                        (V DECL))
        13)))
```

B.16.2 *Der Mann gab der Frau das Buch, das das Kind gesehen hatte.*

```
(R DER MANN GAB DER FRAU DAS BUCH DAS DAS KIND GESEHEN HATTE .)
((CMPLT ((DER MANN GAB DER FRAU DAS BUCH , DAS DAS KIND GESEHEN HATTE %.)
        (DECL)
        1
        (START (DER)
                (S3 MS -E)
                (MANN)
                (MS))
        2
        (DET+NOUN (DER MANN)
                (S3 MS)
                (GAB)
                (V S3 D A))
        3
        (MAIN+FVERB (DER MANN GAB)
                (V D A MS)
                (DER)
                (D FS -EN))
        4
        (FVERB+MAIN (DER MANN GAB DER)
                (V A MS FS -EN)
                (FRAU)
                (FS))
        5
        (DET+NOUN (DER MANN GAB DER FRAU)
                (V A MS FS)
                (DAS)
                (A NS -E))
        6
        (FVERB+MAIN (DER MANN GAB DER FRAU DAS)
                (V MS FS NS -E)
                (BUCH)
                (NS))
        7
        (DET+NOUN (DER MANN GAB DER FRAU DAS BUCH)
                (V MS FS NS)
                (DAS)
                (S3 NS -E))
        8
        (NOUN+RELPRO (DER MANN GAB DER FRAU DAS BUCH , DAS)
                (V MS FS V S3)
                (DAS)
```

```
                        (A NS -E))
         9
      (SUBCL+MAIN (DER MANN GAB DER FRAU DAS BUCH , DAS DAS)
                  (V MS FS V S3 A NS -E)
                  (KIND)
                  (NS))
         10
      (DET+NOUN (DER MANN GAB DER FRAU DAS BUCH , DAS DAS KIND)
                (V MS FS V S3 A NS)
                (GESEHEN)
                (H A))
         11
      (SUBCL+VERB (DER MANN GAB DER FRAU DAS BUCH , DAS DAS KIND GESEHEN)
                  (V MS FS V S3 NS INF H)
                  (HATTE)
                  (V S3 H))
         12
      (SUBCL+LASTVERB (DER MANN GAB DER FRAU DAS BUCH , DAS DAS KIND
                                                  GESEHEN HATTE ,)
                      (V MS FS NS)
                      (%.)
                      (V DECL))
         13))
(CMPLT ((DER MANN GAB DER FRAU DAS BUCH , DAS DAS KIND GESEHEN HATTE %.)
       (DECL)
         1
      (START (DER)
             (S3 MS -E)
             (MANN)
             (MS))
         2
      (DET+NOUN (DER MANN)
                (S3 MS)
                (GAB)
                (V S3 D A))
         3
      (MAIN+FVERB (DER MANN GAB)
                  (V D A MS)
                  (DER)
                  (D FS -EN))
         4
      (FVERB+MAIN (DER MANN GAB DER)
                  (V A MS FS -EN)
                  (FRAU)
                  (FS))
         5
      (DET+NOUN (DER MANN GAB DER FRAU)
                (V A MS FS)
                (DAS)
                (A NS -E))
         6
      (FVERB+MAIN (DER MANN GAB DER FRAU DAS)
                  (V MS FS NS -E)
                  (BUCH)
                  (NS))
```

```
7
(DET+NOUN (DER MANN GAB DER FRAU DAS BUCH)
          (V MS FS NS)
          (DAS)
          (A NS -E))
8
(NOUN+RELPRO (DER MANN GAB DER FRAU DAS BUCH , DAS)
             (V MS FS V A)
             (DAS)
             (S3 NS -E))
9
(SUBCL+MAIN (DER MANN GAB DER FRAU DAS BUCH , DAS DAS)
            (V MS FS V A S3 NS -E)
            (KIND)
            (NS))
10
(DET+NOUN (DER MANN GAB DER FRAU DAS BUCH , DAS DAS KIND)
          (V MS FS V A S3 NS)
          (GESEHEN)
          (H A))
11
(SUBCL+VERB (DER MANN GAB DER FRAU DAS BUCH , DAS DAS KIND GESEHEN)
            (V MS FS V S3 NS INF H)
            (HATTE)
            (V S3 H))
12
(SUBCL+LASTVERB (DER MANN GAB DER FRAU DAS BUCH , DAS DAS KIND
                                              GESEHEN HATTE ,)
                (V MS FS NS)
                (%.)
                (V DECL))
13)))
```

B.16.3 *Der Mann hat der Frau das Buch gegegen, die das Kind gesehen hatte.*

```
(R DER MANN HAT DER FRAU DAS BUCH GEGEBEN DIE DAS KIND GESEHEN HATTE .)
((CMPLT ((DER MANN HAT DER FRAU DAS BUCH GEGEBEN , DIE DAS KIND GESEHEN HATTE %.)
         (DECL)
         1
         (START (DER)
                (S3 MS -E)
                (MANN)
                (MS))
         2
         (DET+NOUN (DER MANN)
                   (S3 MS)
                   (HAT)
                   (V S3 H))
         3
         (MAIN+FVERB (DER MANN HAT)
                     (V H MS)
                     (DER)
                     (D FS -EN))
         4
         (FVERB+MAIN (DER MANN HAT DER)
                     (V H MS D FS -EN)
```

```
                              (FRAU)
                              (FS))
              5
          (DET+NOUN (DER MANN HAT DER FRAU)
                    (V H MS D FS)
                    (DAS)
                    (A NS -E))
              6
          (FVERB+MAIN (DER MANN HAT DER FRAU DAS)
                      (V H MS D FS A NS -E)
                      (BUCH)
                      (NS))
              7
          (DET+NOUN (DER MANN HAT DER FRAU DAS BUCH)
                    (V H MS D FS A NS)
                    (GEGEBEN)
                    (H D A))
              8
          (MAINCL+NFVERB (DER MANN HAT DER FRAU DAS BUCH GEGEBEN)
                         (V MS FS NS)
                         (DIE)
                         (S3 FS -E))
              9
          (NOUN+RELPRO (DER MANN HAT DER FRAU DAS BUCH GEGEBEN , DIE)
                       (V MS NS V S3)
                       (DAS)
                       (A NS -E))
              10
          (SUBCL+MAIN (DER MANN HAT DER FRAU DAS BUCH GEGEBEN , DIE DAS)
                      (V MS NS V S3 A NS -E)
                      (KIND)
                      (NS))
              11
          (DET+NOUN (DER MANN HAT DER FRAU DAS BUCH GEGEBEN , DIE DAS KIND)
                    (V MS NS V S3 A NS)
                    (GESEHEN)
                    (H A))
              12
          (SUBCL+VERB (DER MANN HAT DER FRAU DAS BUCH GEGEBEN , DIE DAS KIND
                                                                    GESEHEN)
                      (V MS NS V S3 NS INF H)
                      (HATTE)
                      (V S3 H))
              13
          (SUBCL+LASTVERB (DER MANN HAT DER FRAU DAS BUCH GEGEBEN , DIE DAS
                                                      KIND GESEHEN HATTE ,)
                          (V MS NS NS)
                          (%.)
                          (V DECL))
           14))
    (CMPLT ((DER MANN HAT DER FRAU DAS BUCH GEGEBEN , DIE DAS KIND GESEHEN HATTE %.)
           (DECL)
           1
           (START (DER)
                  (S3 MS -E)
```

```
          (MANN)
          (MS))
2
(DET+NOUN (DER MANN)
          (S3 MS)
          (HAT)
          (V S3 H))
3
(MAIN+FVERB (DER MANN HAT)
            (V H MS)
            (DER)
            (D FS -EN))
4
(FVERB+MAIN (DER MANN HAT DER)
            (V H MS D FS -EN)
            (FRAU)
            (FS))
5
(DET+NOUN (DER MANN HAT DER FRAU)
          (V H MS D FS)
          (DAS)
          (A NS -E))
6
(FVERB+MAIN (DER MANN HAT DER FRAU DAS)
            (V H MS D FS A NS -E)
            (BUCH)
            (NS))
7
(DET+NOUN (DER MANN HAT DER FRAU DAS BUCH)
          (V H MS D FS A NS)
          (GEGEBEN)
          (H D A))
8
(MAINCL+NFVERB (DER MANN HAT DER FRAU DAS BUCH GEGEBEN)
               (V MS FS NS)
               (DIE)
               (A FS -E))
9
(NOUN+RELPRO (DER MANN HAT DER FRAU DAS BUCH GEGEBEN , DIE)
             (V MS NS V A)
             (DAS)
             (S3 NS -E))
10
(SUBCL+MAIN (DER MANN HAT DER FRAU DAS BUCH GEGEBEN , DIE DAS)
            (V MS NS V A S3 NS -E)
            (KIND)
            (NS))
11
(DET+NOUN (DER MANN HAT DER FRAU DAS BUCH GEGEBEN , DIE DAS KIND)
          (V MS NS V A S3 NS)
          (GESEHEN)
          (H A))
12
(SUBCL+VERB (DER MANN HAT DER FRAU DAS BUCH GEGEBEN ,
                                        DIE DAS KIND GESEHEN)
```

```
                    (V MS NS V S3 NS INF H)
                    (HATTE)
                    (V S3 H))
        13
        (SUBCL+LASTVERB (DER MANN HAT DER FRAU DAS BUCH GEGEBEN , DIE
                                            DAS KIND GESEHEN HATTE ,)
                        (V MS NS NS)
                        (%.)
                        (V DECL))
        14)))
```

B.16.4 *Der Mann hat der Frau das Buch gegeben, das das Kind gesehen hatte.*

```
(R DER MANN HAT DER FRAU DAS BUCH GEGEBEN DAS DAS KIND GESEHEN HATTE .)
((CMPLT ((DER MANN HAT DER FRAU DAS BUCH GEGEBEN , DAS DAS KIND GESEHEN HATTE %.)
        (DECL)
        1
        (START (DER)
               (S3 MS -E)
               (MANN)
               (MS))
        2
        (DET+NOUN (DER MANN)
                  (S3 MS)
                  (HAT)
                  (V S3 H))
        3
        (MAIN+FVERB (DER MANN HAT)
                    (V H MS)
                    (DER)
                    (D FS -EN))
        4
        (FVERB+MAIN (DER MANN HAT DER)
                    (V H MS D FS -EN)
                    (FRAU)
                    (FS))
        5
        (DET+NOUN (DER MANN HAT DER FRAU)
                  (V H MS D FS)
                  (DAS)
                  (A NS -E))
        6
        (FVERB+MAIN (DER MANN HAT DER FRAU DAS)
                    (V H MS D FS A NS -E)
                    (BUCH)
                    (NS))
        7
        (DET+NOUN (DER MANN HAT DER FRAU DAS BUCH)
                  (V H MS D FS A NS)
                  (GEGEBEN)
                  (H D A))
        8
        (MAINCL+NFVERB (DER MANN HAT DER FRAU DAS BUCH GEGEBEN)
                       (V MS FS NS)
                       (DAS)
                       (S3 NS -E))
```

```
        9
        (NOUN+RELPRO (DER MANN HAT DER FRAU DAS BUCH GEGEBEN , DAS)
                    (V MS FS V S3)
                    (DAS)
                    (A NS -E))
        10
        (SUBCL+MAIN (DER MANN HAT DER FRAU DAS BUCH GEGEBEN , DAS DAS)
                    (V MS FS V S3 A NS -E)
                    (KIND)
                    (NS))
        11
        (DET+NOUN (DER MANN HAT DER FRAU DAS BUCH GEGEBEN , DAS DAS KIND)
                  (V MS FS V S3 A NS)
                  (GESEHEN)
                  (H A))
        12
        (SUBCL+VERB (DER MANN HAT DER FRAU DAS BUCH GEGEBEN ,
                                            DAS DAS KIND GESEHEN)
                    (V MS FS V S3 NS INF H)
                    (HATTE)
                    (V S3 H))
        13
        (SUBCL+LASTVERB (DER MANN HAT DER FRAU DAS BUCH GEGEBEN ,
                                        DAS DAS KIND GESEHEN HATTE ,)
                        (V MS FS NS)
                        (%.)
                        (V DECL))
        14))
(CMPLT ((DER MANN HAT DER FRAU DAS BUCH GEGEBEN , DAS DAS KIND GESEHEN HATTE %.)
        (DECL)
        1
        (START (DER)
               (S3 MS -E)
               (MANN)
               (MS))
        2
        (DET+NOUN (DER MANN)
                  (S3 MS)
                  (HAT)
                  (V S3 H))
        3
        (MAIN+FVERB (DER MANN HAT)
                    (V H MS)
                    (DER)
                    (D FS -EN))
        4
        (FVERB+MAIN (DER MANN HAT DER)
                    (V H MS D FS -EN)
                    (FRAU)
                    (FS))
        5
        (DET+NOUN (DER MANN HAT DER FRAU)
                  (V H MS D FS)
                  (DAS)
                  (A NS -E))
```

```
       6
       (FVERB+MAIN (DER MANN HAT DER FRAU DAS)
                   (V H MS D FS A NS -E)
                   (BUCH)
                   (NS))
       7
       (DET+NOUN (DER MANN HAT DER FRAU DAS BUCP)
                 (V H MS D FS A NS)
                 (GEGEBEN)
                 (H D A))
       8
       (MAINCL+NFVERB (DER MANN HAT DER FRAU DAS BUCH GEGEBEN)
                      (V MS FS NS)
                      (DAS)
                      (A NS -E))
       9
       (NOUN+RELPRO (DER MANN HAT DER FRAU DAS BUCH GEGEBEN , DAS)
                    (V MS FS V A)
                    (DAS)
                    (S3 NS -E))
       10
       (SUBCL+MAIN (DER MANN HAT DER FRAU DAS BUCH GEGEBEN , DAS DAS)
                   (V MS FS V A S3 NS -E)
                   (KIND)
                   (NS))
       11
       (DET+NOUN (DER MANN HAT DER FRAU DAS BUCH GEGEBEN , DAS DAS KIND)
                 (V MS FS V A S3 NS)
                 (GESEHEN)
                 (H A))
       12
       (SUBCL+VERB (DER MANN HAT DER FRAU DAS BUCH GEGEBEN ,
                                          DAS DAS KIND GESEHEN)
                   (V MS FS V S3 NS INF H)
                   (HATTE)
                   (V S3 H))
       13
       (SUBCL+LASTVERB (DER MANN HAT DER FRAU DAS BUCH GEGEBEN ,
                                      DAS DAS KIND GESEHEN HATTE ,)
                       (V MS FS NS)
                       (%.)
                       (V DECL))
       14)))
```

B.16.5 *Der Mann, der gestern das Buch kaufte, schläft auf dem Sofa.*

```
(R DER MANN DER GESTERN DAS BUCH KAUFTE SCHLAEFT AUF DEM SOFA .)
((CMPLT ((DER MANN , DER GESTERN DAS BUCH KAUFTE , SCHLAEFT AUF DEM SOFA %.)
        (DECL)
        1
        (START (DER)
               (S3 MS -E)
               (MANN)
               (MS))
        2
        (DET+NOUN (DER MANN)
```

```
                    (S3 MS)
                    (DER)
                    (S3 MS -E))
         3
(NOUN+RELPRO (DER MANN , DER)
                    (S3 V S3)
                    (GESTERN)
                    (ADV-T))
         4
(SUBCL+MAIN (DER MANN , DER GESTERN)
                    (S3 V S3 ADV-T)
                    (DAS)
                    (A NS -E))
         5
(SUBCL+MAIN (DER MANN , DER GESTERN DAS)
                    (S3 V S3 ADV-T A NS -E)
                    (BUCH)
                    (NS))
         6
(DET+NOUN (DER MANN , DER GESTERN DAS BUCH)
                    (S3 V S3 ADV-T A NS)
                    (KAUFTE)
                    (V S3 A))
         7
(SUBCL+LASTVERB (DER MANN , DER GESTERN DAS BUCH KAUFTE ,)
                    (S3 NS)
                    (SCHLAEFT)
                    (V S3))
         8
(MAIN+FVERB (DER MANN , DER GESTERN DAS BUCH KAUFTE , SCHLAEFT)
                    (V NS)
                    (AUF)
                    (ADV-L (D)))
         9
(FVERB+MAIN (DER MANN , DER GESTERN DAS BUCH KAUFTE , SCHLAEFT AUF)
                    (V NS (D))
                    (DEM)
                    (D NS -EN))
         10
(PREP+MAIN (DER MANN , DER GESTERN DAS BUCH KAUFTE , SCHLAEFT AUF DEM)
                    (V NS NS -EN)
                    (SOFA)
                    (NS))
         11
(DET+NOUN (DER MANN , DER GESTERN DAS BUCH KAUFTE , SCHLAEFT AUF DEM SOFA
                    (V NS NS)
                    (%.)
                    (V DECL))
         12)))
```

B.16.6 *Das Buch, in dem der Mann gestern las, liegt auf dem Sofa.*

```
(R DAS BUCH IN DEM DER MANN GESTERN LAS LIEGT AUF DEM SOFA .)
((CMPLT ((DAS BUCH , IN DEM DER MANN GESTERN LAS , LIEGT AUF DEM SOFA %.)
                    (DECL)
         1
```

```
(START (DAS)
       (S3 NS -E)
       (BUCH)
       (NS))
2
(DET+NOUN (DAS BUCH)
          (S3 NS)
          (IN)
          (ADV-L (D)))
3
(NOUN+SUBPREP (DAS BUCH , IN)
              (S3 NS V ADV-L (D))
              (DEM)
              (D NS -EN))
4
(SUBPREP+PRO (DAS BUCH , IN DEM)
             (S3 NS V ADV-L)
             (DER)
             (S3 MS -E))
5
(SUBCL+MAIN (DAS BUCH , IN DEM DER)
            (S3 NS V ADV-L S3 MS -E)
            (MANN)
            (MS))
6
(DET+NOUN (DAS BUCH , IN DEM DER MANN)
          (S3 NS V ADV-L S3 MS)
          (GESTERN)
          (ADV-T))
7
(SUBCL+MAIN (DAS BUCH , IN DEM DER MANN GESTERN)
            (S3 NS V ADV-L S3 MS ADV-T)
            (LAS)
            (V S3 ADV-L))
8
(SUBCL+LASTVERB (DAS BUCH , IN DEM DER MANN GESTERN LAS ,)
                (S3 NS MS)
                (LIEGT)
                (V S3 ADV-L))
9
(MAIN+FVERB (DAS BUCH , IN DEM DER MANN GESTERN LAS , LIEGT)
            (V ADV-L NS MS)
            (AUF)
            (ADV-L (D)))
10
(FVERB+MAIN (DAS BUCH , IN DEM DER MANN GESTERN LAS , LIEGT AUF)
            (V NS MS (D))
            (DEM)
            (D NS -EN))
11
(PREP+MAIN (DAS BUCH , IN DEM DER MANN GESTERN LAS , LIEGT AUF DEM)
           (V NS MS NS -EN)
           (SOFA)
           (NS))
12
```

```
        (DET+NOUN (DAS BUCH , IN DEM DER MANN GESTERN LAS , LIEGT AUF DEM SOFA)
                (V NS MS NS)
                (%.)
                (V DECL))
        13)))
```

B.16.7 *Der Mann, dem der Freund gestern das Buch gab, schläft auf dem Sofa.*

```
(R DER MANN DEM DER FREUND GESTERN DAS BUCH GAB SCHLAEFT AUF DEM SOFA %.)
((CMPLT ((DER MANN , DEM DER FREUND GESTERN DAS BUCH GAB , SCHLAEFT AUF DEM
                                                          SOFA %.)
        (DECL)
        1
        (START (DER)
                (S3 MS -E)
                (MANN)
                (MS))
        2
        (DET+NOUN (DER MANN)
                (S3 MS)
                (DEM)
                (D MS -EN))
        3
        (NOUN+RELPRO (DER MANN , DEM)
                (S3 V D)
                (DER)
                (S3 MS -E))
        4
        (SUBCL+MAIN (DER MANN , DEM DER)
                (S3 V D S3 MS -E)
                (FREUND)
                (MS))
        5
        (DET+NOUN (DER MANN , DEM DER FREUND)
                (S3 V D S3 MS)
                (GESTERN)
                (ADV-T))
        6
        (SUBCL+MAIN (DER MANN , DEM DER FREUND GESTERN)
                (S3 V D S3 MS ADV-T)
                (DAS)
                (A NS -E))
        7
        (SUBCL+MAIN (DER MANN , DEM DER FREUND GESTERN DAS)
                (S3 V D S3 MS ADV-T A NS -E)
                (BUCH)
                (NS))
        8
        (DET+NOUN (DER MANN , DEM DER FREUND GESTERN DAS BUCH)
                (S3 V D S3 MS ADV-T A NS)
                (GAB)
                (V S3 D A))
        9
        (SUBCL+LASTVERB (DER MANN , DEM DER FREUND GESTERN DAS BUCH GAB ,)
                (S3 MS NS)
```

```
                        (SCHLAEFT)
                        (V S3))
      10
(MAIN+FVERB (DER MANN , DEM DER FREUND GESTERN DAS BUCH GAB , SCHLAEFT)
            (V MS NS)
            (AUF)
            (ADV-L (D)))
      11
(FVERB+MAIN (DER MANN , DEM DER FREUND GESTERN DAS BUCH
                                                 GAB , SCHLAEFT AUF)
            (V MS NS (D))
            (DEM)
            (D NS -EN))
      12
(PREP+MAIN (DER MANN , DEM DER FREUND GESTERN DAS BUCH
                                                GAB , SCHLAEFT AUF DEM)
           (V MS NS NS -EN)
           (SOFA)
           (NS))
      13
(DET+NOUN (DER MANN , DEM DER FREUND GESTERN DAS BUCH
                                             GAB , SCHLAEFT AUF DEM SOFA)
          (V MS NS NS)
          (%.)
          (V DECL))
      14)))
```

B.16.8 *Der Mann, dessen Buch Maria liest, schläft auf dem Sofa.*

```
(R DER MANN DESSEN BUCH MARIA LIEST SCHLAEFT AUF DEM SOFA .)
((CMPLT ((DER MANN , DESSEN BUCH MARIA LIEST , SCHLAEFT AUF DEM SOFA %.)
         (DECL)
         1
         (START (DER)
                (S3 MS -E)
                (MANN)
                (MS))
         2
         (DET+NOUN (DER MANN)
                   (S3 MS)
                   (DESSEN)
                   (A MS NS -ES))
         3
         (NOUN+RELPRO (DER MANN , DESSEN)
                      (S3 V A NS -ES)
                      (BUCH)
                      (NS))
         4
         (DET+NOUN (DER MANN , DESSEN BUCH)
                   (S3 V A NS)
                   (MARIA)
                   (S3 FS))
         5
         (SUBCL+MAIN (DER MANN , DESSEN BUCH MARIA)
                     (S3 V A NS S3 FS)
                     (LIEST)
```

```
                    (V S3 A))
      6
(SUBCL+LASTVERB (DER MANN , DESSEN BUCH MARIA LIEST ,)
                (S3 NS FS)
                (SCHLAEFT)
                (V S3))
      7
(MAIN+FVERB (DER MANN , DESSEN BUCH MARIA LIEST , SCHLAEFT)
            (V NS FS)
            (AUF)
            (ADV-L (D)))
      8
(FVERB+MAIN (DER MANN , DESSEN BUCH MARIA LIEST , SCHLAEFT AUF)
            (V NS FS (D))
            (DEM)
            (D NS -EN))
      9
(PREP+MAIN (DER MANN , DESSEN BUCH MARIA LIEST , SCHLAEFT AUF DEM)
           (V NS FS NS -EN)
           (SOFA)
           (NS))
      10
(DET+NOUN (DER MANN , DESSEN BUCH MARIA LIEST , SCHLAEFT AUF DEM SOFA)
          (V NS FS NS)
          (%.)
          (V DECL))
      11)))
```

B.17   Sentential complements

B.17.1 *Das Kind, das der Frau die Katze gab, hat geglaubt, dass sie gerne in dem schönen alten Haus wohnen würde.*

```
(R DAS KIND DAS DER FRAU DIE KATZE GAB HAT GEGLAUBT DASS SIE GERNE IN DEM
                              SCHOENEN ALTEN HAUS WOHNEN WUERDE .)
((CMPLT ((DAS KIND , DAS DER FRAU DIE KATZE GAB , HAT GEGLAUBT , DASS SIE
                GERNE IN DEM SCHOENEN ALTEN HAUS WOHNEN WUERDE %.)
        (DECL)
        1
        (START (DAS)
               (S3 NS -E)
               (KIND)
               (NS))
        2
        (DET+NOUN (DAS KIND)
                  (S3 NS)
                  (DAS)
                  (S3 NS -E))
        3
        (NOUN+RELPRO (DAS KIND , DAS)
                     (S3 V S3)
                     (DER)
                     (D FS -EN))
        4
```

```
(SUBCL+MAIN (DAS KIND , DAS DER)
            (S3 V S3 D FS -EN)
            (FRAU)
            (FS))
5
(DET+NOUN (DAS KIND , DAS DER FRAU)
          (S3 V S3 D FS)
          (DIE)
          (A FS -E))
6
(SUBCL+MAIN (DAS KIND , DAS DER FRAU DIE)
            (S3 V S3 D FS A FS -E)
            (KATZE)
            (FS))
7
(DET+NOUN (DAS KIND , DAS DER FRAU DIE KATZE)
          (S3 V S3 D FS A FS)
          (GAB)
          (V S3 D A))
8
(SUBCL+LASTVERB (DAS KIND , DAS DER FRAU DIE KATZE GAB ,)
                (S3 FS)
                (HAT)
                (V S3 H))
9
(MAIN+FVERB (DAS KIND , DAS DER FRAU DIE KATZE GAB , HAT)
            (V H FS)
            (GEGLAUBT)
            (H SC))
10
(MAINCL+NFVERB (DAS KIND , DAS DER FRAU DIE KATZE GAB , HAT GEGLAUBT)
               (V FS SC)
               (DASS)
               (SC V))
11
(FVERB+MAIN (DAS KIND , DAS DER FRAU DIE KATZE GAB,
                                          HAT GEGLAUBT , DASS)
            (V FS V)
            (SIE)
            (S3 FS))
12
(SUBCL+MAIN (DAS KIND , DAS DER FRAU DIE KATZE GAB ,
                                     HAT GEGLAUBT , DASS SIE)
            (V FS V S3 FS)
            (GERNE)
            (ADV-M))
13
(SUBCL+MAIN (DAS KIND , DAS DER FRAU DIE KATZE GAB ,
                                     HAT GEGLAUBT , DASS SIE GERNE)
            (V FS V S3 FS ADV-M)
            (IN)
            (ADV-L (D)))
14
(SUBCL+MAIN (DAS KIND , DAS DER FRAU DIE KATZE GAB ,
                                     HAT GEGLAUBT , DASS SIE GERNE IN)
```

```
                      (V FS V S3 FS ADV-M ADV-L (D))
                      (DEM)
                      (D NS -EN))
              15
              (PREP+MAIN (DAS KIND , DAS DER FRAU DIE KATZE GAB ,
                                    HAT GEGLAUBT , DASS SIE GERNE IN DEM)
                      (V FS V S3 FS ADV-M ADV-L NS -EN)
                      (SCHOENEN)
                      (-EN))
              16
              (DET+ADJ (DAS KIND , DAS DER FRAU DIE KATZE GAB , HAT GEGLAUBT , DASS
                                            SIE GERNE IN DEM SCHOENEN)
                      (V FS V S3 FS ADV-M ADV-L NS -EN)
                      (ALTEN)
                      (-EN))
              17
              (DET+ADJ (DAS KIND , DAS DER FRAU DIE KATZE GAB , HAT GEGLAUBT , DASS
                                            SIE GERNE IN DEM SCHOENEN ALTEN)
                      (V FS V S3 FS ADV-M ADV-L NS -EN)
                      (HAUS)
                      (NS))
              18
              (DET+NOUN (DAS KIND , DAS DER FRAU DIE KATZE GAB , HAT GEGLAUBT , DASS
                                            SIE GERNE IN DEM SCHOENEN ALTEN HAUS)
                      (V FS V S3 FS ADV-M ADV-L NS)
                      (WOHNEN)
                      (W ADV-L INF))
              18
              (SUBCL+VERB (DAS KIND , DAS DER FRAU DIE KATZE GAB , HAT GEGLAUBT ,
                               DASS SIE GERNE IN DEM SCHOENEN ALTEN HAUS WOHNEN)
                      (V FS V S3 FS ADV-M NS W INF)
                      (WUERDE)
                      (V S3 W))
              19
              (SUBCL+LASTVERB (DAS KIND , DAS DER FRAU DIE KATZE GAB , HAT GEGLAUBT ,
                               DASS SIE GERNE IN DEM SCHOENEN ALTEN HAUS WOHNEN WUERDE ,)
                          (V FS FS NS)
                          (%.)
                          (V DECL))
              20))
  (CMPLT ((DAS KIND , DAS DER FRAU DIE KATZE GAB , HAT GEGLAUBT , DASS SIE GERNE
                                  IN DEM SCHOENEN ALTEN HAUS WOHNEN WUERDE %.)
          (DECL)
          1
          (START (DAS)
                  (S3 NS -E)
                  (KIND)
                  (NS))
          2
          (DET+NOUN (DAS KIND)
                  (S3 NS)
                  (DAS)
                  (A NS -E))
          3
          (NOUN+RELPRO (DAS KIND , DAS)
```

```
                          (S3 V A)
                          (DER)
                          (D FS -EN))
       4
(SUBCL+MAIN (DAS KIND , DAS DER)
            (S3 V A D FS -EN)
            (FRAU)
            (FS))
       5
(DET+NOUN (DAS KIND , DAS DER FRAU)
          (S3 V A D FS)
          (DIE)
          (S3 FS -E))
       6
(SUBCL+MAIN (DAS KIND , DAS DER FRAU DIE)
            (S3 V A D FS S3 FS -E)
            (KATZE)
            (FS))
       7
(DET+NOUN (DAS KIND , DAS DER FRAU DIE KATZE)
          (S3 V A D FS S3 FS)
          (GAB)
          (V S3 D A))
       8
(SUBCL+LASTVERB (DAS KIND , DAS DER FRAU DIE KATZE GAB ,)
                (S3 FS)
                (HAT)
                (V S3 H))
       9
(MAIN+FVERB (DAS KIND , DAS DER FRAU DIE KATZE GAB , HAT)
            (V H FS)
            (GEGLAUBT)
            (H SC))
       10
(MAINCL+NFVERB (DAS KIND , DAS DER FRAU DIE KATZE GAB , HAT GEGLAUBT)
               (V FS SC)
               (DASS)
               (SC V))
       11
(FVERB+MAIN (DAS KIND , DAS DER FRAU DIE KATZE GAB ,
                                          HAT GEGLAUBT , DASS)
            (V FS V)
            (SIE)
            (S3 FS))
       12
(SUBCL+MAIN (DAS KIND , DAS DER FRAU DIE KATZE GAB ,
                                      HAT GEGLAUBT , DASS SIE)
            (V FS V S3 FS)
            (GERNE)
            (ADV-M))
       13
(SUBCL+MAIN (DAS KIND , DAS DER FRAU DIE KATZE GAB ,
                                  HAT GEGLAUBT , DASS SIE GERNE)
            (V FS V S3 FS ADV-M)
            (IN)
```

```
                   (ADV-L (D)))
       14
       (SUBCL+MAIN (DAS KIND , DAS DER FRAU DIE KATZE GAB ,
                                        HAT GEGLAUBT , DASS SIE GERNE IN)
                   (V FS V S3 FS ADV-M ADV-L (D))
                   (DEM)
                   (D NS -EN))
       15
       (PREP+MAIN (DAS KIND , DAS DER FRAU DIE KATZE GAB ,
                                        HAT GEGLAUBT , DASS SIE GERNE IN DEM)
                  (V FS V S3 FS ADV-M ADV-L NS -EN)
                  (SCHOENEN)
                  (-EN))
       16
       (DET+ADJ (DAS KIND , DAS DER FRAU DIE KATZE GAB ,
                                 HAT GEGLAUBT , DASS SIE GERNE IN DEM SCHOENEN)
                (V FS V S3 FS ADV-M ADV-L NS -EN)
                (ALTEN)
                (-EN))
       17
       (DET+ADJ (DAS KIND , DAS DER FRAU DIE KATZE GAB ,
                            HAT GEGLAUBT , DASS SIE GERNE IN DEM SCHOENEN ALTEN)
                (V FS V S3 FS ADV-M ADV-L NS -EN)
                (HAUS)
                (NS))
       18
       (DET+NOUN (DAS KIND , DAS DER FRAU DIE KATZE GAB ,
                      HAT GEGLAUBT , DASS SIE GERNE IN DEM SCHOENEN ALTEN HAUS)
                 (V FS V S3 FS ADV-M ADV-L NS)
                 (WOHNEN)
                 (W ADV-L INF))
       19
       (SUBCL+VERB (DAS KIND , DAS DER FRAU DIE KATZE GAB, HAT GEGLAUBT ,
                            DASS SIE GERNE IN DEM SCHOENEN ALTEN HAUS WOHNEN)
                   (V FS V S3 FS ADV-M NS W INF)
                   (WUERDE)
                   (V S3 W))
       20
       (SUBCL+LASTVERB (DAS KIND , DAS DER FRAU DIE KATZE GAB , HAT GEGLAUBT ,
                       DASS SIE GERNE IN DEM SCHOENEN ALTEN HAUS WOHNEN WUERDE ,)
                       (V FS FS NS)
                       (%.)
                       (V DECL))
       21)))
```

B.17.2 *Peter glaubt, dass Maria den Brief lesen wird.*

```
(R PETER GLAUBT DASS MARIA DEN BRIEF LESEN WIRD .)
((CMPLT ((PETER GLAUBT , DASS MARIA DEN BRIEF LESEN WIRD %.)
        (DECL)
        1
        (START (PETER)
               (S3 MS)
               (GLAUBT)
               (V S3 SC))
        2
```

```
(MAIN+FVERB (PETER GLAUBT)
            (V SC MS)
            (DASS)
            (SC V))
     3
(FVERB+MAIN (PETER GLAUBT , DASS)
            (V MS V)
            (MARIA)
            (S3 FS))
     4
(SUBCL+MAIN (PETER GLAUBT , DASS MARIA)
            (V MS V S3 FS)
            (DEN)
            (A MS -E))
     5
(SUBCL+MAIN (PETER GLAUBT , DASS MARIA DEN)
            (V MS V S3 FS A NS -E)
            (BRIEF)
            (MS))
     6
(DET+NOUN (PETER GLAUBT , DASS MARIA DEN BRIEF)
            (V MS V S3 FS A MS)
            (LESEN)
            (W A INF))
     7
(SUBCL+VERB (PETER GLAUBT , DASS MARIA DEN BRIEF LESEN)
            (V MS V S3 FS MS W INF)
            (WIRD)
            (V S3 W))
     8
(SUBCL+LASTVERB (PETER GLAUBT , DASS MARIA DEN BRIEF LESEN WIRD ,)
                (V MS FS MS)
                (%.)
                (V DECL))
     9)))
```

B.17.3 *Peter weiss, dass Maria den Brief gelesen hat.*

```
(R PETER WEISS DASS MARIA DEN BRIEF GELESEN HAT .)
((CMPLT ((PETER WEISS , DASS MARIA DEN BRIEF GELESEN HAT %.)
        (DECL)
        1
        (START (PETER)
               (S3 MS)
               (WEISS)
               (V S3 SC I))
          2
        (MAIN+FVERB (PETER WEISS)
                    (V SC I MS)
                    (DASS)
                    (SC V))
            3
        (FVERB+MAIN (PETER WEISS , DASS)
                    (V MS V)
                    (MARIA)
```

```
                       (S3 FS))
          4
          (SUBCL+MAIN  (PETER WEISS , DASS MARIA)
                       (V MS V S3 FS)
                       (DEN)
                       (A MS -E))
          5
          (SUBCL+MAIN  (PETER WEISS , DASS MARIA DEN)
                       (V MS V S3 FS A MS -E)
                       (BRIEF)
                       (NS))
          6
          (DET+NOUN    (PETER WEISS , DASS MARIA BRIEF)
                       (V MS V S3 FS A MS)
                       (GELESEN)
                       (H A))
          7
          (SUBCL+VERB  (PETER WEISS , DASS MARIA DEN BRIEF GELESEN)
                       (V MS V S3 FS MS INF H)
                       (HAT)
                       (V S3 H))
          8
          (SUBCL+LASTVERB (PETER WEISS , DASS MARIA DEN BRIEF GELESEN HAT ,)
                          (V MS FS MS)
                          (%.)
                          (V DECL))
          9))
```

B.17.4 **Peter glaubt, warum Maria den Brief lesen wird.*

```
(R PETER GLAUBT WARUM MARIA DEN BRIEF LESEN WIRD .)
[ERROR "Ungrammatical continuation at"
        ((FVERB+MAIN ((PETER GLAUBT WARUM MARIA)
                     (V MS FS)
                     1
                     (START (PETER)
                            (A MS)
                            (GLAUBT)
                            (V S3 A))
                     2
                     (MAIN+FVERB (PETER GLAUBT)
                             (V S3 MS)
                             (WARUM)
                             (ADV-C I))
                     3
                     (FVERB+MAIN (PETER GLAUBT WARUM)
                             (V S3 MS I)
                             (MARIA)
                             (S3 FS))
                     4))
        (START ((DEN)
                (A MS -E]
```

B.17.5 *Peter weiss warum Maria den Brief lesen wird.*

```
(R PETER WEISS WARUM MARIA DEN BRIEF LESEN WIRD .)
((CMPLT ((PETER WEISS WARUM MARIA DAS BUCH LESEN WIRD %.)
        (DECL)
        1
        (START (PETER)
               (S3 MS)
               (WEISS)
               (V S3 SC I))
        2
        (MAIN+FVERB (PETER WEISS)
                    (V SC I MS)
                    (WARUM)
                    (ADV-C I))
        3
        (FVERB+MAIN (PETER WEISS WARUM)
                    (V V ADV-C)
                    (MARIA)
                    (S3 FS))
        4
        (SUBCL+MAIN (PETER WEISS WARUM MARIA)
                    (V V ADV-C S3 FS)
                    (DEN)
                    (A MS -E))
        5
        (SUBCL+MAIN (PETER WEISS WARUM MARIA DEN)
                    (V V ADV-C S3 FS A MS -E)
                    (BRIEF)
                    (MS))
        6
        (DET+NOUN (PETER WEISS WARUM MARIA DEN BRIEF)
                  (V V ADV-C S3 FS A MS)
                  (LESEN)
                  (W A INF))
        7
        (SUBCL+VERB (PETER WEISS WARUM MARIA DEN BRIEF LESEN)
                    (V V ADV-C S3 FS MS W INF)
                    (WIRD)
                    (V S3 W))
        8
        (SUBCL+LASTVERB (PETER WEISS WARUM MARIA DEN BRIEF LESEN WIRD ,)
                        (V FS MS)
                        (%.)
                        (V DECL))
        9))
```

B.18   Infinitives with *zu* in main clauses

B.18.1 *Maria ist leicht zu überzeugen.*

```
(R MARIA IST LEICHT ZU UEBERZEUGEN .)
((CMPLT ((MARIA IST LEICHT ZU UEBERZEUGEN %.)
        (DECL)
        1
        (START (MARIA)
```

```
                    (S3 FS)
                    (IST)
                    (V S3 S))
            2
            (MAIN+FVERB (MARIA IST)
                        (V S FS)
                        (LEICHT)
                        (ADJ S))
            0
            (AUX-PRED (MARIA IST LEICHT)
                      (V FS S)
                      (ZU)
                      (Z))
            4
            (MAINCL+NFVERB (MARIA IST LEICHT ZU)
                           (V FS Q)
                           (UEBERZEUGEN)
                           (Q -AG))
            5
            (MAINCL+NFVERB (MARIA IST LEICHT ZU UEBERZEUGEN)
                           (V FS -AG)
                           (%.)
                           (V DECL))
            6)))
```

B.18.2 *Es ist leicht Maria zu überzeugen.*

```
(R ES IST LEICHT MARIA ZU UEBERZEUGEN .)
((CMPLT ((ES IST LEICHT MARIA ZU UEBERZEUGEN %.)
         (DECL)
         1
         (START (ES)
                (S3)
                (IST)
                (V S3 S))
         2
         (MAIN+FVERB (ES IST)
                     (V S)
                     (LEICHT)
                     (ADJ S))
         3
         (AUX-PRED (ES IST LEICHT)
                   (V S)
                   (MARIA)
                   (A FS))
         4
         (FVERB+MAIN (ES IST LEICHT MARIA)
                     (V S A FS)
                     (ZU)
                     (Z))
         5
         (MAINCL+NFVERB (ES IST LEICHT MARIA ZU)
                        (V A FS W)
                        (UEBERZEUGEN)
                        (W A INF))
         6
```

```
    (MAINCL+NFVERB (ES IST LEICHT MARIA ZU UEBERZEUGEN)
                   (V FS INF)
                   (%.)
                   (V DECL))
    7)))
```

B.18.3 *Maria ist bereit zu singen.*

```
(R MARIA IST BEREIT ZU SINGEN .)
((CMPLT ((MARIA IST BEREIT ZU SINGEN %.)
        (DECL)
        1
        (START (MARIA)
               (S3 FS)
               (IST)
               (V S3 S))
        2
        (MAIN+FVERB (MARIA IST)
                    (V S FS)
                    (BEREIT)
                    (ADJ S))
        3
        (AUX-PRED (MARIA IST BEREIT)
                  (V FS S)
                  (ZU)
                  (Z))
        4
        (MAINCL+NFVERB (MARIA IST BEREIT ZU)
                       (V FS Q)
                       (SINGEN)
                       (Q -FA))
        5
        (MAINCL+NFVERB (MARIA IST BEREIT ZU SINGEN)
                       (V FS -FA)
                       (%.)
                       (V DECL))
        6)))
```

B.18.4 *Maria versucht zu singen.*

```
(R MARIA VERSUCHT ZU SINGEN .)
((CMPLT ((MARIA VERSUCHT ZU SINGEN %.)
        (DECL)
        1
        (START (MARIA)
               (S3 FS)
               (VERSUCHT)
               (V S3 Z))
        2
        (MAIN+FVERB (MARIA VERSUCHT)
                    (V Z FS)
                    (ZU)
                    (Z))
        3
        (MAINCL+NFVERB (MARIA VERSUCHT ZU)
                       (V FS W)
```

```
                         (SINGEN)
                         (W INF))
         4
         (MAINCL+NFVERB (MARIA VERSUCHT ZU SINGEN)
                         (V FS INF)
                         (%.)
                         (V DECL))
         5)))
```

B.18.5 *Maria hat versucht das Buch zu lesen.*

```
(R MARIA HAT VERSUCHT DAS BUCH ZU LESEN .)
((CMPLT ((MARIA HAT VERSUCHT DAS BUCH ZU LESEN %.)
         (DECL)
         1
         (START (MARIA)
                (A FS)
                (HAT)
                (V S3 H))
         2
         (MAIN+FVERB (MARIA HAT)
                     (V S3 H A FS)
                     (VERSUCHT)
                     (H Z))
         3
         (MAINCL+NFVERB (MARIA HAT VERSUCHT)
                        (V S3 A FS Z)
                        (DAS)
                        (S3 NS -E))
         4
         (FVERB+MAIN (MARIA HAT VERSUCHT DAS)
                     (V A FS Z NS -E)
                     (BUCH)
                     (NS))
         5
         (DET+NOUN (MARIA HAT VERSUCHT DAS BUCH)
                   (V A FS Z NS)
                   (ZU)
                   (Z))
         6
         (MAINCL+NFVERB (MARIA HAT VERSUCHT DAS BUCH ZU)
                        (V A FS NS W)
                        (LESEN)
                        (W A INF))
         7
         (MAINCL+NFVERB (MARIA HAT VERSUCHT DAS BUCH ZU LESEN)
                        (V FS NS INF)
                        (%.)
                        (V DECL))
         8)))
```

B.18.6 *Maria versuchte dem Freund einen Brief zu geben.*

```
(R MARIA VERSUCHTE DEM FREUND EINEN BRIEF ZU GEBEN .)
((CMPLT ((MARIA VERSUCHTE DEM FREUND EINEN BRIEF ZU GEBEN %.)
         (DECL)
```

```
        1
        (START (MARIA)
                (S3 FS)
                (VERSUCHTE)
                (V S3 Z))
        2
        (MAIN+FVERB (MARIA VERSUCHTE)
                    (V Z FS)
                    (DEM)
                    (D MS -EN))
        3
        (SUBCL+MAIN (MARIA VERSUCHTE DEM)
                    (V Z FS D MS -EN)
                    (FREUND)
                    (MS))
        4
        (DET+NOUN (MARIA VERSUCHTE DEM FREUND)
                  (V Z FS D MS)
                  (EINEN)
                  (A MS -EN))
        5
        (SUBCL+MAIN (MARIA VERSUCHTE DEM FREUND EINEN)
                    (V Z FS D MS A MS -EN)
                    (BRIEF)
                    (MS))
        6
        (DET+NOUN (MARIA VERSUCHTE DEM FREUND EINEN BRIEF)
                  (V Z FS D MS A MS)
                  (ZU)
                  (Z))
        7
        (MAINCL+NFVERB (MARIA VERSUCHTE DEM FREUND EINEN BRIEF ZU)
                       (V FS D MS A MS W)
                       (GEBEN)
                       (W D A INF))
        8
        (MAINCL+NFVERB (MARIA VERSUCHTE DEM FREUND EINEN BRIEF ZU GEBEN)
                       (V FS MS MS INF)
                       (%.)
                       (V DECL))
        9)))
```

B.18.7 *Dem Freund ist zu helfen.*

```
(R DEM FREUND IST ZU HELFEN .)
((CMPLT ((DEM FREUND IST ZU HELFEN %.)
        (DECL)
        1
        (START (DEM)
               (D MS -EN)
               (FREUND)
               (MS))
        2
        (DET+NOUN (DEM FREUND)
                  (D MS)
                  (IST)
```

```
                    (V S3 S))
        3
        (MAIN+FVERB (DEM FREUND IST)
                    (V S3 S D MS)
                    (ZU)
                    (Z))
        4
        (MAINCL+NFVERB (DEM FREUND IST ZU)
                       (V S3 D MS W)
                       (HELFEN)
                       (W S3 D -FA))
        5
        (MAINCL+NFVERB (DEM FREUND IST ZU HELFEN)
                       (V MS -FA)
                       (%.)
                       (V DECL))
        6)))
```

B.18.8 *Es ist dem Freund zu helfen.*

```
(R ES IST DEM FREUND ZU HELFEN .)
((CMPLT ((ES IST DEM FREUND ZU HELFEN %.)
        (DECL)
        1
        (START (ES)
               (S3)
               (IST)
               (V S3 S))
        2
        (MAIN+FVERB (ES IST)
                    (V S)
                    (DEM)
                    (D MS -EN))
        3
        (FVERB+MAIN (ES IST DEM)
                    (V S D MS -EN)
                    (FREUND)
                    (MS))
        4
        (DET+NOUN (ES IST DEM FREUND)
                  (V S D MS)
                  (ZU)
                  (Z))
        5
        (MAINCL+NFVERB (ES IST DEM FREUND ZU)
                       (V D MS W)
                       (HELFEN)
                       (W D INF))
        6
        (MAINCL+NFVERB (ES IST DEM FREUND ZU HELFEN)
                       (V MS INF)
                       (%.)
                       (V DECL))
        7)))
```

B.18.9 *Dem Freund wird zu helfen sein.*

```
(R DEM FREUND WIRD ZU HELFEN SEIN .)
((CMPLT ((DEM FREUND WIRD ZU HELFEN SEIN %.)
        (DECL)
        1
        (START (DEM)
               (D MS -EN)
               (FREUND)
               (MS))
        2
        (DET+NOUN (DEM FREUND)
                  (D MS)
                  (WIRD)
                  (V S3 W))
        3
        (MAIN+FVERB (DEM FREUND WIRD)
                    (V S3 W D MS)
                    (ZU)
                    (Z))
        4
        (MAINCL+NFVERB (DEM FREUND WIRD ZU)
                       (V S3 D MS Q W S)
                       (HELFEN)
                       (Q S3 D -FA))
        5
        (MAINCL+NFVERB (DEM FREUND WIRD ZU HELFEN)
                       (V MS W S -FA)
                       (SEIN)
                       (W S INF))
        6
        (MAINCL+NFVERB (DEM FREUND WIRD ZU HELFEN SEIN)
                       (V MS -FA INF)
                       (%.)
                       (V DECL))
        7)))
```

B.18.10 *Es wird dem Freund zu helfen sein.*

```
(R ES WIRD DEM FREUND ZU HELFEN SEIN .)
((CMPLT ((ES WIRD DEM FREUND ZU HELFEN SEIN %.)
        (DECL)
        1
        (START (ES)
               (S3)
               (WIRD)
               (V S3 W))
        2
        (MAIN+FVERB (ES WIRD)
                    (V W)
                    (DEM)
                    (D MS -EN))
        3
        (FVERB+MAIN (ES WIRD DEM)
                    (V W D MS -EN)
                    (FREUND)
                    (MS))
        4
```

```
(DET+NOUN (ES WIRD DEM FREUND)
          (V W D MS)
          (ZU)
          (Z))
     5
(MAINCL+NFVERB (ES WIRD DEM FREUND ZU)
               (V D MS Q W S)
               (HELFEN)
               (Q D -FA))
     6
(MAINCL+NFVERB (ES WIRD DEM FREUND ZU HELFEN)
               (V MS W S -FA)
               (SEIN)
               (W S INF))
     7
(MAINCL+NFVERB (ES WIRD DEM FREUND ZU HELFEN SEIN)
               (V MS -FA INF)
               (%.)
               (V DECL))
     8)))
```

B.18.11 *Dem Freund ist leicht zu helfen.*

```
(R DEM FREUND IST LEICHT ZU HELFEN .)
((CMPLT ((DEM FREUND IST LEICHT ZU HELFEN %.)
        (DECL)
        1
        (START (DEM)
               (D MS -EN)
               (FREUND)
               (MS))
        2
        (DET+NOUN (DEM FREUND)
                  (D MS)
                  (IST)
                  (V S3 S))
        3
        (MAIN+FVERB (DEM FREUND IST)
                    (V S3 S D MS)
                    (LEICHT)
                    (ADJ S))
        4
        (AUX-PRED (DEM FREUND IST LEICHT)
                  (V S3 D MS S)
                  (ZU)
                  (Z))
        5
        (MAINCL+NFVERB (DEM FREUND IST LEICHT ZU)
                       (V S3 D MS W)
                       (HELFEN)
                       (W S3 D -FA))
        6
        (MAINCL+NFVERB (DEM FREUND IST LEICHT ZU HELFEN)
                       (V MS -FA)
                       (%.)
                       (V DECL))
```

```
        7)))
```

B.18.12 *Es ist leicht dem Freund zu helfen.*

```
(R ES IST LEICHT DEM FREUND ZU HELFEN .)
((CMPLT ((ES IST LEICHT DEM FREUND ZU HELFEN %.)
        (DECL)
        1
        (START (ES)
               (S3)
               (IST)
               (V S3 S))
        2
        (MAIN+FVERB (ES IST)
                    (V S)
                    (LEICHT)
                    (ADJ S))
        3
        (AUX-PRED (ES IST LEICHT)
                  (V S)
                  (DEM)
                  (D MS -EN))
        4
        (FVERB+MAIN (ES IST LEICHT DEM)
                    (V S D MS -EN)
                    (FREUND)
                    (MS))
        5
        (DET+NOUN (ES IST LEICHT DEM FREUND)
                  (V S D MS)
                  (ZU)
                  (Z))
        6
        (MAINCL+NFVERB (ES IST LEICHT DEM FREUND ZU)
                       (V D MS W)
                       (HELFEN)
                       (W D INF))
        7
        (MAINCL+NFVERB (ES IST LEICHT DEM FREUND ZU HELFEN)
                       (V MS INF)
                       (%.)
                       (V DECL))
        8)))
```

B.18.13 *Leicht ist es dem Freund zu helfen.*

```
(R LEICHT IST ES DEM FREUND ZU HELFEN .)
((CMPLT ((LEICHT IST ES DEM FREUND ZU HELFEN %.)
        (DECL)
        1
        (START (LEICHT)
               (ADJ S)
               (IST)
               (V S3 S))
        2
        (AUX-PRED (LEICHT IST)
```

```
                    (V S3 S)
                    (ES)
                    (S3))
        3
        (FVERB+MAIN (LEICHT IST ES)
                    (V S)
                    (DEM)
                    (D MS -EN))
        4
        (FVERB+MAIN (LEICHT IST ES DEM)
                    (V S D MS -EN)
                    (FREUND)
                    (MS))
        5
        (DET+NOUN (LEICHT IST ES DEM FREUND)
                    (V S D MS)
                    (ZU)
                    (Z))
        6
        (MAINCL+NFVERB (LEICHT IST ES DEM FREUND ZU)
                    (V D MS W)
                    (HELFEN)
                    (W D INF))
        7
        (MAINCL+NFVERB (LEICHT IST ES DEM FREUND ZU HELFEN)
                    (V MS INF)
                    (%.)
                    (V DECL))
        8)))
```

B.18.14 *Es ist dem Freund leicht zu helfen.

```
(R ES IST DEM FREUND LEICHT ZU HELFEN .)
[ERROR "Ungrammatical continuation at"
        ((DET+NOUN ((ES IST DEM FREUND)
                    (V S3 S A D MS)
                    1
                    (START (ES)
                            (A)
                            (IST)
                            (V S3 S))
                    2
                    (MAIN+FVERB (ES IST)
                            (V S3 S A)
                            (DEM)
                            (D MS -EN))
                    3
                    (FVERB+MAIN (ES IST DEM)
                            (V S3 S A D MS -EN)
                            (FREUND)
                            (MS))
                    4))
        (START ((LEICHT)
                (ADJ S]
```

B.18.15 Es ist dem Freund schnell zu helfen.

```
(R ES IST DEM FREUND SCHNELL ZU HELFEN %.)
((CMPLT ((ES IST DEM FREUND SCHNELL ZU HELFEN %.)
        (DECL)
        1
        (START (ES)
               (S3)
               (IST)
               (V S3 S))
        2
        (MAIN+FVERB (ES IST)
                    (V S)
                    (DEM)
                    (D MS -EN))
        3
        (FVERB+MAIN (ES IST DEM)
                    (V S D MS -EN)
                    (FREUND)
                    (MS))
        4
        (DET+NOUN (ES IST DEM FREUND)
                  (V S D MS)
                  (SCHNELL)
                  (ADV-M))
        5
        (FVERB+MAIN (ES IST DEM FREUND SCHNELL)
                    (V S D MS ADV-M)
                    (ZU)
                    (Z))
        6
        (MAINCL+NFVERB (ES IST DEM FREUND SCHNELL ZU)
                       (V D MS ADV-M W)
                       (HELFEN)
                       (W D INF))
        7
        (MAINCL+NFVERB (ES IST DEM FREUND SCHNELL ZU HELFEN)
                       (V MS INF)
                       (%.)
                       (V DECL))
        8)))
```

B.18.16 *Dem Freund ist schnell zu helfen.*

```
(R DEM FREUND IST SCHNELL ZU HELFEN .)
((CMPLT ((DEM FREUND IST SCHNELL ZU HELFEN %.)
        (DECL)
        1
        (START (DEM)
               (D MS -EN)
               (FREUND)
               (MS))
        2
        (DET+NOUN (DEM FREUND)
                  (D MS)
                  (IST)
                  (V S3 S))
        3
```

```
            (MAIN+FVERB (DEM FREUND IST)
                        (V S3 S D MS)
                        (SCHNELL)
                        (ADV-M))
            4
            (FVERB+MAIN (DEM FREUND IST SCHNELL)
                        (V S3 S D MS ADV-M)
                        (ZU)
                        (Z))
            5
            (MAINCL+NFVERB (DEM FREUND IST SCHNELL ZU)
                           (V S3 D MS ADV-M W)
                           (HELFEN)
                           (W S3 D -FA))
            6
            (MAINCL+NFVERB (DEM FREUND IST SCHNELL ZU HELFEN)
                           (V MS -FA)
                           (%.)
                           (V DECL))
            7)))
```

B.18.17 *Peter hat dem Freund zu helfen.*

```
(R PETER HAT DEM FREUND ZU HELFEN .)
((CMPLT ((PETER HAT DEM FREUND ZU HELFEN %.)
         (DECL)
         1
         (START (PETER)
                (S3 MS)
                (HAT)
                (V S3 H))
         2
         (MAIN+FVERB (PETER HAT)
                     (V H MS)
                     (DEM)
                     (D MS -EN))
         3
         (FVERB+MAIN (PETER HAT DEM)
                     (V H MS D MS -EN)
                     (FREUND)
                     (MS))
         4
         (DET+NOUN (PETER HAT DEM FREUND)
                   (V H MS D MS)
                   (ZU)
                   (Z))
         5
         (MAINCL+NFVERB (PETER HAT DEM FREUND ZU)
                        (V MS D MS W)
                        (HELFEN)
                        (W D INF))
         6
         (MAINCL+NFVERB (PETER HAT DEM FREUND ZU HELFEN)
                        (V MS MS INF)
                        (%.)
                        (V DECL))
```

```
      7)))
```

B.18.18 *Peter hat das Buch zu lesen.*

```
(R PETER HAT DEN BRIEF ZU LESEN .)
((CMPLT ((PETER HAT DEN BRIEF ZU LESEN %.)
        (DECL)
        1
        (START (PETER)
               (S3 MS)
               (HAT)
               (V S3 H))
        2
        (MAIN+FVERB (PETER HAT)
                    (V H MS)
                    (DEN)
                    (A MS -E))
        3
        (FVERB+MAIN (PETER HAT DEN)
                    (V H MS A MS -E)
                    (BRIEF)
                    (MS))
        4
        (DET+NOUN (PETER HAT DEN BRIEF)
                  (V H MS A MS)
                  (ZU)
                  (Z))
        5
        (MAINCL+NFVERB (PETER HAT DEN BRIEF ZU)
                       (V MS A MS W)
                       (LESEN)
                       (W A INF))
        6
        (MAINCL+NFVERB (PETER HAT DEN BRIEF ZU LESEN)
                       (V MS MS INF)
                       (%.)
                       (V DECL))
      7))
```

B.18.19 *Der Mann wird den Brief zu lesen haben.*

```
(R DER MANN WIRD DEN BRIEF ZU LESEN HABEN .)
((CMPLT ((DER MANN WIRD DEN BRIEF ZU LESEN HABEN %.)
        (DECL)
        1
        (START (DER)
               (S3 MS -E)
               (MANN)
               (MS))
        2
        (DET+NOUN (DER MANN)
                  (S3 MS)
                  (WIRD)
                  (V S3 W))
        3
        (MAIN+FVERB (DER MANN WIRD)
```

```
                    (V W MS)
                    (DEN)
                    (A MS -EN))
       4
       (FVERB+MAIN (DER MANN WIRD DEN)
                    (V W MS A MS -EN)
                    (BRIEF)
                    (MS))
       5
       (DET+NOUN (DER MANN WIRD DEN BRIEF)
                    (V W MS A MS)
                    (ZU)
                    (Z))
       6
       (MAINCL+NFVERB (DER MANN WIRD DEN BRIEF ZU)
                    (V MS A MS Q W S)
                    (LESEN)
                    (W A INF))
       7
       (MAINCL+NFVERB (DER MANN WIRD DEN BRIEF ZU LESEN)
                    (V MS MS Q S INF)
                    (HABEN)
                    (Q S))
       8
       (MAINCL+NFVERB (DER MANN WIRD DEN BRIEF ZU LESEN HABEN)
                    (V MS MS INF)
                    (%.)
                    (V DECL))
       9)))
```

B.19   Infinitives with *zu* in subordinate clauses

B.19.1 *Weil Maria leicht zu überzeugen ist, ...*

```
(R WEIL MARIA LEICHT ZU UEBERZEUGEN IST)
((SUBCL+LASTVERB ((WEIL MARIA LEICHT ZU UEBERZEUGEN IST ,)
                    (ADCL FS)
                    1
                    (START (WEIL)
                            (ADCL V)
                            (MARIA)
                            (S3 FS))
                    2
                    (SUBCL+MAIN (WEIL MARIA)
                            (ADCL V S3 FS)
                            (LEICHT)
                            (ADJ))
                    3
                    (SUBCL+VERB (WEIL MARIA LEICHT)
                            (ADCL V S3 FS ADJ)
                            (ZU)
                            (Z))
                    4
                    (SUBCL+VERB (WEIL MARIA LEICHT ZU)
```

```
                              (ADCL V S3 FS ADJ Z)
                              (UEBERZEUGEN)
                              (Q -AG))
             5
           (SUBCL+VERB (WEIL MARIA LEICHT ZU UEBERZEUGEN)
                              (ADCL V S3 FS ADJ -AG S)
                              (IST)
                              (V S3 S))
             6)))
```

B.19.2 *Der Freund, dem leicht zu helfen ist, ...*

```
(R DER FREUND DEM LEICHT ZU HELFEN IST)
((SUBCL+LASTVERB ((DER FREUND , DEM LEICHT ZU HELFEN IST ,)
                (S3)
                1
                (START (DER)
                       (S3 MS -E)
                       (FREUND)
                       (MS))
                2
                (DET+NOUN (DER FREUND)
                       (S3 MS)
                       (DEM)
                       (D MS -EN))
                3
                (NOUN+RELPRO (DER FREUND , DEM)
                       (S3 V D)
                       (LEICHT)
                       (ADJ))
                4
                (SUBCL+VERB (DER FREUND , DEM LEICHT)
                       (S3 V D ADJ)
                       (ZU)
                       (Z))
                5
                (SUBCL+VERB (DER FREUND , DEM LEICHT ZU)
                       (S3 V D ADJ Z)
                       (HELFEN)
                       (Q S3 D -FA))
                6
                (SUBCL+VERB (DER FREUND , DEM LEICHT ZU HELFEN)
                       (S3 V ADJ S3 -FA S)
                       (IST)
                       (V S3 S))
                7)))
```

B.19.3 *Weil dem Freund zu helfen ist, ...*

```
(R WEIL DEM FREUND ZU HELFEN IST)
((SUBCL+LASTVERB ((WEIL DEM FREUND ZU HELFEN IST ,)
                (ADCL MS)
                1
                (START (WEIL)
                       (ADCL V)
                       (DEM)
```

```
                      (D MS -EN))
          2
          (SUBCL+MAIN (WEIL DEM)
                      (ADCL V D MS -EN)
                      (FREUND)
                      (MS))
          3
          (DET+NOUN (WEIL DEM FREUND)
                    (ADCL V D MS)
                    (ZU)
                    (Z))
          4
          (SUBCL+VERB (WEIL DEM FREUND ZU)
                      (ADCL V D MS Z)
                      (HELFEN)
                      (Q S3 D -FA))
          5
          (SUBCL+VERB (WEIL DEM FREUND ZU HELFEN)
                      (ADCL V MS S3 -FA S)
                      (IST)
                      (V S3 S))
          6)))
```

B.19.4 *Weil dem Freund zu helfen sein wird, ...*

```
(R WEIL DEM FREUND ZU HELFEN SEIN WIRD)
((SUBCL+LASTVERB ((WEIL DEM FREUND ZU HELFEN SEIN WIRD ,)
                 (ADCL MS)
                 1
                 (START (WEIL)
                        (ADCL V)
                        (DEM)
                        (D MS -EN))
                 2
                 (SUBCL+MAIN (WEIL DEM)
                             (ADCL V D MS -EN)
                             (FREUND)
                             (MS))
                 3
                 (DET+NOUN (WEIL DEM FREUND)
                           (ADCL V D MS)
                           (ZU)
                           (Z))
                 4
                 (SUBCL+VERB (WEIL DEM FREUND ZU)
                             (ADCL V D MS Z)
                             (HELFEN)
                             (Q S3 D -FA))
                 5
                 (SUBCL+VERB (WEIL DEM FREUND ZU HELFEN)
                             (ADCL V MS S3 -FA S)
                             (SEIN)
                             (W S INF))
                 6
                 (SUBCL+VERB (WEIL DEM FREUND ZU HELFEN SEIN)
                             (ADCL V MS S3 -FA W INF)
```

```
                    (WIRD)
                    (V S3 W))
         7)))
```

B.19.5 *Weil dem Mädchen leicht zu helfen ist, ...*

```
(R WEIL DEM MAEDCHEN LEICHT ZU HELFEN IST)
((SUBCL+LASTVERB ((WEIL DEM MAEDCHEN LEICHT ZU HELFEN IST ,)
                 (ADCL NS)
                 1
                 (START (WEIL)
                        (ADCL V)
                        (DEM)
                        (D NS -EN))
                 2
                 (SUBCL+MAIN (WEIL DEM)
                             (ADCL V D NS -EN)
                             (MAEDCHEN)
                             (NS))
                 3
                 (DET+NOUN (WEIL DEM MAEDCHEN)
                           (ADCL V D NS)
                           (LEICHT)
                           (ADJ))
                 4
                 (SUBCL+VERB (WEIL DEM MAEDCHEN LEICHT)
                             (ADCL V D NS ADJ)
                             (ZU)
                             (Z))
                 5
                 (SUBCL+VERB (WEIL DEM MAEDCHEN LEICHT ZU)
                             (ADCL V D NS ADJ Z)
                             (HELFEN)
                             (Q S3 D -FA))
                 6
                 (SUBCL+VERB (WEIL DEM MAEDCHEN LEICHT ZU HELFEN)
                             (ADCL V NS ADJ S3 -FA S)
                             (IST)
                             (V S3 S))
          7)))
```

B.19.6 *Das Buch, das zu lesen ist, ...*

```
(R DAS BUCH DAS ZU LESEN IST)
((SUBCL+LASTVERB ((DAS BUCH , DAS ZU LESEN IST ,)
                 (S3)
                 1
                 (START (DAS)
                        (S3 NS -E)
                        (BUCH)
                        (NS))
                 2
                 (DET+NOUN (DAS BUCH)
                           (S3 NS)
                           (DAS)
                           (S3 NS -E))
```

```
                    3
                    (NOUN+RELPRO (DAS BUCH , DAS)
                                 (S3 V S3)
                                 (ZU)
                                 (Z))
                    4
                    (SUBCL+VERB (DAS BUCH , DAS ZU)
                                (S3 V S3 Z)
                                (LESEN)
                                (Q -AG))
                    5
                    (SUBCL+VERB (DAS BUCH , DAS ZU LESEN)
                                (S3 V S3 -AG S)
                                (IST)
                                (V S3 S))
                    6))
  (SUBCL+LASTVERB ((DAS BUCH , DAS ZU LESEN IST ,)
                    (A)
                    1
                    (START (DAS)
                           (A NS -E)
                           (BUCH)
                           (NS))
                    2
                    (DET+NOUN (DAS BUCH)
                              (A NS)
                              (DAS)
                              (S3 NS -E))
                    3
                    (NOUN+RELPRO (DAS BUCH , DAS)
                                 (A V S3)
                                 (ZU)
                                 (Z))
                    4
                    (SUBCL+VERB (DAS BUCH , DAS ZU)
                                (A V S3 Z)
                                (LESEN)
                                (Q -AG))
                    5
                    (SUBCL+VERB (DAS BUCH , DAS ZU LESEN)
                                (A V S3 -AG S)
                                (IST)
                                (V S3 S))
                    6)))
```

B.19.7 *Das Buch, das zu lesen sein wird, ...*

```
(R DAS BUCH DAS ZU LESEN SEIN WIRD)
((SUBCL+LASTVERB ((DAS BUCH , DAS ZU LESEN SEIN WIRD ,)
                  (S3)
                  1
                  (START (DAS)
                         (S3 NS -E)
                         (BUCH)
                         (NS))
                  2
```

```
                (DET+NOUN (DAS BUCH)
                        (S3 NS)
                        (DAS)
                        (S3 NS -E))
                3
                (NOUN+RELPRO (DAS BUCH , DAS)
                        (S3 V S3)
                        (ZU)
                        (Z))
                4
                (SUBCL+VERB (DAS BUCH , DAS ZU)
                        (S3 V S3 Z)
                        (LESEN)
                        (Q -AG))
                5
                (SUBCL+VERB (DAS BUCH , DAS ZU LESEN)
                        (S3 V S3 -AG S)
                        (SEIN)
                        (W S INF))
                6
                (SUBCL+VERB (DAS BUCH , DAS ZU LESEN SEIN)
                        (S3 V S3 -AG W INF)
                        (WIRD)
                        (V S3 W))
                7))
(SUBCL+LASTVERB ((DAS BUCH , DAS ZU LESEN SEIN WIRD ,)
                (A)
                1
                (START (DAS)
                        (A NS -E)
                        (BUCH)
                        (NS))
                2
                (DET+NOUN (DAS BUCH)
                        (A NS)
                        (DAS)
                        (S3 NS -E))
                3
                (NOUN+RELPRO (DAS BUCH , DAS)
                        (A V S3)
                        (ZU)
                        (Z))
                4
                (SUBCL+VERB (DAS BUCH , DAS ZU)
                        (A V S3 Z)
                        (LESEN)
                        (Q -AG))
                5
                (SUBCL+VERB (DAS BUCH , DAS ZU LESEN)
                        (A V S3 -AG S)
                        (SEIN)
                        (W S INF))
                6
                (SUBCL+VERB (DAS BUCH , DAS ZU LESEN SEIN)
                        (A V S3 -AG W INF)
```

```
                              (WIRD)
                              (V S3 W))
                7)))
```

B.19.8 *Das Buch, das dem Mädchen zu geben sein wird, ...*

```
(R DAS BUCH DAS DEM MAEDCHEN ZU GEBEN SEIN WIRD)
((SUBCL+LASTVERB ((DAS BUCH , DAS DEM MAEDCHEN ZU GEBEN SEIN
                   WIRD ,)
                  (S3 NS)
                  1
                  (START (DAS)
                         (S3 NS -E)
                         (BUCH)
                         (NS))
                  2
                  (DET+NOUN (DAS BUCH)
                            (S3 NS)
                            (DAS)
                            (S3 NS -E))
                  3
                  (NOUN+RELPRO (DAS BUCH , DAS)
                               (S3 V S3)
                               (DEM)
                               (D NS -EN))
                  4
                  (SUBCL+MAIN (DAS BUCH , DAS DEM)
                              (S3 V S3 D NS -EN)
                              (MAEDCHEN)
                              (NS))
                  5
                  (DET+NOUN (DAS BUCH , DAS DEM MAEDCHEN)
                            (S3 V S3 D NS)
                            (ZU)
                            (Z))
                  6
                  (SUBCL+VERB (DAS BUCH , DAS DEM MAEDCHEN ZU)
                              (S3 V S3 D NS Z)
                              (GEBEN)
                              (Q D -AG))
                  7
                  (SUBCL+VERB (DAS BUCH , DAS DEM MAEDCHEN ZU GEBEN)
                              (S3 V S3 NS -AG S)
                              (SEIN)
                              (W S INF))
                  8
                  (SUBCL+VERB (DAS BUCH , DAS DEM MAEDCHEN ZU GEBEN
                                   SEIN)
                              (S3 V S3 NS -AG W INF)
                              (WIRD)
                              (V S3 W))
                  9))
 (SUBCL+LASTVERB ((DAS BUCH , DAS DEM MAEDCHEN ZU GEBEN SEIN
                   WIRD ,)
                  (A NS)
                  1
```

```
            (START (DAS)
                   (A NS -E)
                   (BUCH)
                   (NS))
        2
        (DET+NOUN (DAS BUCH)
                   (A NS)
                   (DAS)
                   (S3 NS -E))
        3
        (NOUN+RELPRO (DAS BUCH , DAS)
                     (A V S3)
                     (DEM)
                     (D NS -EN))
        4
        (SUBCL+MAIN (DAS BUCH , DAS DEM)
                    (A V S3 D NS -EN)
                    (MAEDCHEN)
                    (NS))
        5
        (DET+NOUN (DAS BUCH , DAS DEM MAEDCHEN)
                   (A V S3 D NS)
                   (ZU)
                   (Z))
        6
        (SUBCL+VERB (DAS BUCH , DAS DEM MAEDCHEN ZU)
                    (A V S3 D NS Z)
                    (GEBEN)
                    (Q D -AG))
        7
        (SUBCL+VERB (DAS BUCH , DAS DEM MAEDCHEN ZU GEBEN)
                    (A V S3 NS -AG S)
                    (SEIN)
                    (W S INF))
        8
        (SUBCL+VERB (DAS BUCH , DAS DEM MAEDCHEN ZU GEBEN
                         SEIN)
                    (A V S3 NS -AG W INF)
                    (WIRD)
                    (V S3 W))
        9)))
```

B.19.9 *Der Brief, den Peter zu lesen hat, ...*

```
(R DER BRIEF DEN PETER ZU LESEN HAT)
((SUBCL+LASTVERB ((DER BRIEF , DEN PETER ZU LESEN HAT ,)
                 (S3 MS)
        1
        (START (DER)
               (S3 MS -E)
               (BRIEF)
               (MS))
            2
            (DET+NOUN (DER BRIEF)
                      (S3 MS)
                      (DEN)
```

```
                           (A MS -EN))
              3
              (NOUN+RELPRO (DER BRIEF , DEN)
                           (S3 V A)
                           (PETER)
                           (S3 MS))
              4
              (SUBCL+MAIN (DER BRIEF , DEN PETER)
                           (S3 V A S3 MS)
                           (ZU)
                           (Z))
              5
              (SUBCL+VERB (DER BRIEF , DEN PETER ZU)
                           (S3 V A S3 MS Z)
                           (LESEN)
                           (W A INF))
              6
              (SUBCL+VERB (DER BRIEF , DEN PETER ZU LESEN)
                           (S3 V S3 MS INF H)
                           (HAT)
                           (V S3 H))
              7)))
```

B.20   Separable verbal prefixes

B.20.1 *Gestern sah der Mann das Wort im Lexikon nach.*

```
(R GESTERN SAH DER MANN DAS WORT IM LEXIKON NACH .)
((CMPLT ((GESTERN SAH DER MANN DAS WORT IM LEXIKON NACH %.)
        (DECL)
        1
        (START (GESTERN)
               (ADV-T)
               (SAH)
               (V S3 A DE1))
        2
        (MAIN+FVERB (GESTERN SAH)
                    (V S3 A DE1)
                    (DER)
                    (S3 MS -E))
        3
        (FVERB+MAIN (GESTERN SAH DER)
                    (V A DE1 MS -E)
                    (MANN)
                    (MS))
        4
        (DET+NOUN (GESTERN SAH DER MANN)
                  (V A DE1 MS)
                  (DAS)
                  (A NS -E))
        5
        (FVERB+MAIN (GESTERN SAH DER MANN DAS)
                    (V DE1 MS NS -E)
                    (WORT)
```

```
                          (NS))
          6
          (DET+NOUN (GESTERN SAH DER MANN DAS WORT)
                    (V DE1 MS NS)
                    (IM)
                    (ADV-L NS -EN))
          7
          (FVERB+MAIN (GESTERN SAH DER MANN DAS WORT IM)
                      (V DE1 MS NS NS -EN)
                      (LEXIKON)
                      (NS))
          8
          (DET+NOUN (GESTERN SAH DER MANN DAS WORT IM LEXIKON)
                    (V DE1 MS NS NS)
                    (NACH)
                    (DE1))
          9
          (MAINCL+NFVERB (GESTERN SAH DER MANN DAS WORT IM LEXIKON NACH)
                         (V MS NS NS)
                         (%.)
                         (V DECL))
          10))
 (CMPLT ((GESTERN SAH DER MANN DAS WORT IM LEXIKON NACH %.)
          (DECL)
          1
          (START (GESTERN)
                 (ADV-T)
                 (SAH)
                 (V S3 A DE1))
          2
          (MAIN+FVERB (GESTERN SAH)
                      (V S3 A DE1)
                      (DER)
                      (S3 MS -E))
          3
          (FVERB+MAIN (GESTERN SAH DER)
                      (V A DE1 MS -E)
                      (MANN)
                      (MS))
          4
          (DET+NOUN (GESTERN SAH DER MANN)
                    (V A DE1 MS)
                    (DAS)
                    (A NS -E))
          5
          (FVERB+MAIN (GESTERN SAH DER MANN DAS)
                      (V DE1 MS NS -E)
                      (WORT)
                      (NS))
          6
          (DET+NOUN (GESTERN SAH DER MANN DAS WORT)
                    (V DE1 MS NS)
                    (IM)
                    (ADV-L NS -EN))
          7
```

```
(NOUN+PREP (GESTERN SAH DER MANN DAS WORT IM)
           (V DE1 MS NS NS -EN)
           (LEXIKON)
           (NS))
8
(DET+NOUN (GESTERN SAH DER MANN DAS WORT IM LEXIKON)
          (V DE1 MS NS NS)
          (NACH)
          (DE1))
9
(MAINCL+NFVERB (GESTERN SAH DER MANN DAS WORT IM LEXIKON NACH)
               (V MS NS NS)
               (%.)
               (V DECL))
10)))
```

B.20.2 *Gestern hat der Mann das Wort im Lexikon nachgesehen.*

```
(R GESTERN HAT DER MANN DAS WORT IM LEXIKON NACHGESEHEN %.)
((CMPLT ((GESTERN HAT DER MANN DAS WORT IM LEXIKON NACHGESEHEN %.)
        (DECL)
        1
        (START (GESTERN)
               (ADV-T)
               (HAT)
               (V S3 H))
        2
        (MAIN+FVERB (GESTERN HAT)
                    (V S3 H)
                    (DER)
                    (S3 MS -E))
        3
        (FVERB+MAIN (GESTERN HAT DER)
                    (V H MS -E)
                    (MANN)
                    (MS))
        4
        (DET+NOUN (GESTERN HAT DER MANN)
                  (V H MS)
                  (DAS)
                  (A NS -E))
        5
        (FVERB+MAIN (GESTERN HAT DER MANN DAS)
                    (V H MS A NS -E)
                    (WORT)
                    (NS))
        6
        (DET+NOUN (GESTERN HAT DER MANN DAS WORT)
                  (V H MS A NS)
                  (IM)
                  (ADV-L NS -EN))
        7
        (FVERB+MAIN (GESTERN HAT DER MANN DAS WORT IM)
                    (V H MS A NS ADV-L NS -EN)
                    (LEXIKON)
                    (NS))
```

```
        8
        (DET+NOUN (GESTERN HAT DER MANN DAS WORT IM LEXIKON)
                  (V H MS A NS ADV-L NS)
                  (NACHGESEHEN)
                  (H A))
        9
        (MAINCL+NFVERB (GESTERN HAT DER MANN DAS WORT IM LEXIKON NACHGESEHEN)
                       (V MS NS NS)
                       (%.)
                       (V DECL))
        10))
(CMPLT ((GESTERN HAT DER MANN DAS WORT IM LEXIKON NACHGESEHEN %.)
        (DECL)
        1
        (START (GESTERN)
               (ADV-T)
               (HAT)
               (V S3 H))
        2
        (MAIN+FVERB (GESTERN HAT)
                    (V S3 H)
                    (DER)
                    (S3 MS -E))
        3
        (FVERB+MAIN (GESTERN HAT DER)
                    (V H MS -E)
                    (MANN)
                    (MS))
        4
        (DET+NOUN (GESTERN HAT DER MANN)
                  (V H MS)
                  (DAS)
                  (A NS -E))
        5
        (FVERB+MAIN (GESTERN HAT DER MANN DAS)
                    (V H MS A NS -E)
                    (WORT)
                    (NS))
        6
        (DET+NOUN (GESTERN HAT DER MANN DAS WORT)
                  (V H MS A NS)
                  (IM)
                  (ADV-L NS -EN))
        7
        (NOUN+PREP (GESTERN HAT DER MANN DAS WORT IM)
                   (V H MS A NS NS -EN)
                   (LEXIKON)
                   (NS))
        8
        (DET+NOUN (GESTERN HAT DER MANN DAS WORT IM LEXIKON)
                  (V H MS A NS NS)
                  (NACHGESEHEN)
                  (H A))
        9
        (MAINCL+NFVERB (GESTERN HAT DER MANN DAS WORT IM LEXIKON NACHGESEHEN)
```

```
                    (V MS NS NS)
                    (%.)
                    (V DECL))
        10)))
```

B.20.3 *Der Mann sah das Wort nach dem Essen nach.*

```
(R DER MANN SAH DAS WORT NACH DEM ESSEN NACH .)
((CMPLT ((DER MANN SAH DAS WORT NACH DEM ESSEN NACH %.)
        (DECL)
        1
        (START (DER)
               (S3 MS -E)
               (MANN)
               (MS))
        2
        (DET+NOUN (DER MANN)
               (S3 MS)
               (SAH)
               (V S3 A DE1))
        3
        (MAIN+FVERB (DER MANN SAH)
               (V A DE1 MS)
               (DAS)
               (A NS -E))
        4
        (FVERB+MAIN (DER MANN SAH DAS)
               (V DE1 MS NS -E)
               (WORT)
               (NS))
        5
        (DET+NOUN (DER MANN SAH DAS WORT)
               (V DE1 MS NS)
               (NACH)
               (ADV-T (D)))
        6
        (FVERB+MAIN (DER MANN SAH DAS WORT NACH)
               (V DE1 MS NS (D))
               (DEM)
               (D NS -EN))
        7
        (PREP+MAIN (DER MANN SAH DAS WORT NACH DEM)
               (V DE1 MS NS NS -EN)
               (ESSEN)
               (NS))
        8
        (DET+NOUN (DER MANN SAH DAS WORT NACH DEM ESSEN)
               (V DE1 MS NS NS)
               (NACH)
               (DE1))
        9
        (MAINCL+NFVERB (DER MANN SAH DAS WORT NACH DEM ESSEN NACH)
               (V MS NS NS)
               (%.)
               (V DECL))
        10))
```

```
(CMPLT ((DER MANN SAH DAS WORT NACH DEM ESSEN NACH %.)
        (DECL)
        1
        (START (DER)
               (S3 MS -E)
               (MANN)
               (MS))
        2
        (DET+NOUN (DER MANN)
                  (S3 MS)
                  (SAH)
                  (V S3 A DE1))
        3
        (MAIN+FVERB (DER MANN SAH)
                    (V A DE1 MS)
                    (DAS)
                    (A NS -E))
        4
        (FVERB+MAIN (DER MANN SAH DAS)
                    (V DE1 MS NS -E)
                    (WORT)
                    (NS))
        5
        (DET+NOUN (DER MANN SAH DAS WORT)
                  (V DE1 MS NS)
                  (NACH)
                  (ADV-T (D)))
        6
        (NOUN+PREP (DER MANN SAH DAS WORT NACH)
                   (V DE1 MS NS (D))
                   (DEM)
                   (D NS -EN))
        7
        (PREP+MAIN (DER MANN SAH DAS WORT NACH DEM)
                   (V DE1 MS NS NS -EN)
                   (ESSEN)
                   (NS))
        8
        (DET+NOUN (DER MANN SAH DAS WORT NACH DEM ESSEN)
                  (V DE1 MS NS NS)
                  (NACH)
                  (DE1))
        9
        (MAINCL+NFVERB (DER MANN SAH DAS WORT NACH DEM ESSEN NACH)
                       (V MS NS NS)
                       (%.)
                       (V DECL))
        10)))
```

B.21   Yes/no-interrogatives

B.21.1 *Hat der junge Mann dem Kind gestern eine Puppe gegeben?*

(R HAT DER JUNGE MANN DEM KIND GESTERN EINE PUPPE GEGEBEN ?)

```
((CMPLT ((HAT DER JUNGE MANN DEM KIND GESTERN EINE PUPPE GEGEBEN ?)
        (INTERROG)
        1
        (START (HAT)
                (V S3 H)
                (DER)
                (S3 MS -E))
        2
        (?FV+MAIN (HAT DER)
                (V I H MS -E)
                (JUNGE)
                (-E))
        3
        (DET+ADJ (HAT DER JUNGE)
                (V I H MS -E)
                (MANN)
                (MS))
        4
        (DET+NOUN (HAT DER JUNGE MANN)
                (V I H MS)
                (DEM)
                (D NS -EN))
        5
        (FVERB+MAIN (HAT DER JUNGE MANN DEM)
                (V I H MS D NS -EN)
                (KIND)
                (NS))
        6
        (DET+NOUN (HAT DER JUNGE MANN DEM KIND)
                (V I H MS D NS)
                (GESTERN)
                (ADV-T))
        7
        (FVERB+MAIN (HAT DER JUNGE MANN DEM KIND GESTERN)
                (V I H MS D NS ADV-T)
                (EINE)
                (A FS -E))
        8
        (FVERB+MAIN (HAT DER JUNGE MANN DEM KIND GESTERN EINE)
                (V I H MS D NS ADV-T A FS -E)
                (PUPPE)
                (FS))
        9
        (DET+NOUN (HAT DER JUNGE MANN DEM KIND GESTERN EINE PUPPE)
                (V I H MS D NS ADV-T A FS)
                (GEGEBEN)
                (H D A))
        10
        (MAINCL+NFVERB (HAT DER JUNGE MANN DEM KIND GESTERN EINE PUPPE GEGEBEN)
                        (V I MS NS FS)
                        (?)
                        (I INTERROG))
        11)))
```

B.21.2 *Gab der junge Mann dem Kind gestern eine Puppe?*

```
(R GAB DER JUNGE MANN DEM KIND GESTERN EINE PUPPE ?)
((CMPLT ((GAB DER JUNGE MANN DEM KIND GESTERN EINE PUPPE ?)
        (INTERROG)
        1
        (START (GAB)
                (V S3 D A)
                (DER)
                (S3 MS -E))
        2
        (?FV+MAIN (GAB DER)
                (V I D A MS -E)
                (JUNGE)
                (-E))
        3
        (DET+ADJ (GAB DER JUNGE)
                (V I D A MS -E)
                (MANN)
                (MS))
        4
        (DET+NOUN (GAB DER JUNGE MANN)
                (V I D A MS)
                (DEM)
                (D NS -EN))
        5
        (FVERB+MAIN (GAB DER JUNGE MANN DEM)
                (V A MS NS -EN)
                (KIND)
                (NS))
        6
        (DET+NOUN (GAB DER JUNGE MANN DEM KIND)
                (V A MS NS)
                (GESTERN)
                (ADV-T))
        7
        (FVERB+MAIN (GAB DER JUNGE MANN DEM KIND GESTERN)
                (V A MS NS)
                (EINE)
                (A FS -E))
        8
        (FVERB+MAIN (GAB DER JUNGE MANN DEM KIND GESTERN EINE)
                (V MS NS FS -E)
                (PUPPE)
                (FS))
        9
        (DET+NOUN (GAB DER JUNGE MANN DEM KIND GESTERN EINE PUPPE)
                (V MS NS FS)
                (?)
                (I INTERROG))
        10)))
```

B.21.3 *Gab eine Puppe dem Kind gestern die junge Frau?*

```
(R GAB EINE PUPPE DEM KIND GESTERN DIE JUNGE FRAU ?)
((CMPLT ((GAB EINE PUPPE DEM KIND GESTERN DIE JUNGE FRAU ?)
        (INTERROG)
        1
```

```
        (START (GAB)
               (V S3 D A)
               (EINE)
               (S3 FS -E))
        2
        (?FV+MAIN (GAB EINE)
                  (V I D A FS -E)
                  (PUPPE)
                  (FS))
        3
        (DET+NOUN (GAB EINE PUPPE)
                  (V I D A FS)
                  (DEM)
                  (D NS -EN))
        4
        (FVERB+MAIN (GAB EINE PUPPE DEM)
                    (V A FS NS -EN)
                    (KIND)
                    (NS))
        5
        (DET+NOUN (GAB EINE PUPPE DEM KIND)
                  (V A FS NS)
                  (GESTERN)
                  (ADV-T))
        6
        (FVERB+MAIN (GAB EINE PUPPE DEM KIND GESTERN)
                    (V A FS NS)
                    (DIE)
                    (A FS -E))
        7
        (FVERB+MAIN (GAB EINE PUPPE DEM KIND GESTERN DIE)
                    (V FS NS FS -E)
                    (JUNGE)
                    (-E))
        8
        (DET+ADJ (GAB EINE PUPPE DEM KIND GESTERN DIE JUNGE)
                 (V FS NS FS -E)
                 (FRAU)
                 (FS))
        9
        (DET+NOUN (GAB EINE PUPPE DEM KIND GESTERN DIE JUNGE FRAU)
                  (V FS NS FS)
                  (?)
                  (I INTERROG))
        10))
(CMPLT ((GAB EINE PUPPE DEM KIND GESTERN DIE JUNGE FRAU ?)
        (INTERROG)
        1
        (START (GAB)
               (V S3 D A)
               (EINE)
               (A FS -E))
        2
        (?FV+MAIN (GAB EINE)
                  (V I S3 D FS -E)
```

```
                      (PUPPE)
                      (FS))
        3
        (DET+NOUN (GAB EINE PUPPE)
                  (V I S3 D FS)
                  (DEM)
                  (D NS -EN))
        4
        (FVERB+MAIN (GAB EINE PUPPE DEM)
                    (V S3 FS NS -EN)
                    (KIND)
                    (NS))
        5
        (DET+NOUN (GAB EINE PUPPE DEM KIND)
                  (V S3 FS NS)
                  (GESTERN)
                  (ADV-T))
        6
        (FVERB+MAIN (GAB EINE PUPPE DEM KIND GESTERN)
                    (V S3 FS NS)
                    (DIE)
                    (S3 FS -E))
        7
        (FVERB+MAIN (GAB EINE PUPPE DEM KIND GESTERN DIE)
                    (V FS NS FS -E)
                    (JUNGE)
                    (-E))
        8
        (DET+ADJ (GAB EINE PUPPE DEM KIND GESTERN DIE JUNGE)
                 (V FS NS FS -E)
                 (FRAU)
                 (FS))
        9
        (DET+NOUN (GAB EINE PUPPE DEM KIND GESTERN DIE JUNGE FRAU)
                  (V FS NS FS)
                  (?)
                  (I INTERROG))
        10)))
```

B.21.4 *Der junge Mann hat dem Kind gestern eine Puppe gegeben?*

```
(R DER JUNGE MANN HAT DEM KIND GESTERN EINE PUPPE GEGEBEN ?)
((CMPLT ((DER JUNGE MANN HAT DEM KIND GESTERN EINE PUPPE GEGEBEN ?)
         (INTERROG)
         1
         (START (DER)
                (S3 MS -E)
                (JUNGE)
                (-E))
         2
         (DET+ADJ (DER JUNGE)
                  (S3 MS -E)
                  (MANN)
                  (MS))
         3
         (DET+NOUN (DER JUNGE MANN)
```

```
                  (S3 MS)
                  (HAT)
                  (V S3 H))
        4
        (MAIN+FVERB (DER JUNGE MANN HAT)
                    (V H MS)
                    (DEM)
                    (D NS -EN))
        5
        (FVERB+MAIN (DER JUNGE MANN HAT DEM)
                    (V H MS D NS -EN)
                    (KIND)
                    (NS))
        6
        (DET+NOUN (DER JUNGE MANN HAT DEM KIND)
                  (V H MS D NS)
                  (GESTERN)
                  (ADV-T))
        7
        (FVERB+MAIN (DER JUNGE MANN HAT DEM KIND GESTERN)
                    (V H MS D NS ADV-T)
                    (EINE)
                    (A FS -E))
        8
        (FVERB+MAIN (DER JUNGE MANN HAT DEM KIND GESTERN EINE)
                    (V H MS D NS ADV-T A FS -E)
                    (PUPPE)
                    (FS))
        9
        (DET+NOUN (DER JUNGE MANN HAT DEM KIND GESTERN EINE PUPPE)
                  (V H MS D NS ADV-T A FS)
                  (GEGEBEN)
                  (H D A))
        10
        (MAINCL+NFVERB (DER JUNGE MANN HAT DEM KIND GESTERN EINE PUPPE GEGEBEN)
                       (V MS NS FS)
                       (?)
                       (I INTERROG))
        11)))
```

B.22   Wh-interrogatives

B.22.1 *Wer gab dem Kind gestern eine Puppe?*

```
(R WER GAB DEM KIND GESTERN EINE PUPPE ?)
((CMPLT ((WER GAB DEM KIND GESTERN EINE PUPPE ?)
         (INTERROG)
         1
         (START (WER)
                (S3 I)
                (GAB)
                (V S3 D A))
         2
         (MAIN+FVERB (WER GAB)
```

```
                    (V D A I)
                    (DEM)
                    (D NS -EN))
        3
    (FVERB+MAIN (WER GAB DEM)
                    (V A NS -EN)
                    (KIND)
                    (NS))
        4
    (DET+NOUN (WER GAB DEM KIND)
                    (V A NS)
                    (GESTERN)
                    (ADV-T))
        5
    (FVERB+MAIN (WER GAB DEM KIND GESTERN)
                    (V A NS)
                    (EINE)
                    (A FS -E))
        6
    (FVERB+MAIN (WER GAB DEM KIND GESTERN EINE)
                    (V NS FS -E)
                    (PUPPE)
                    (FS))
        7
    (DET+NOUN (WER GAB DEM KIND GESTERN EINE PUPPE)
                    (V NS FS)
                    (?)
                    (I INTERROG))
        8)))
```

B.22.2 *Wer gab gestern wem eine Puppe?*

```
(R WER GAB GESTERN WEM EINE PUPPE ?)
((CMPLT ((WER GAB GESTERN WEM EINE PUPPE ?)
        (INTERROG)
        1
    (START (WER)
            (S3 I)
            (GAB)
            (V S3 D A))
        2
    (MAIN+FVERB (WER GAB)
                    (V D A I)
                    (GESTERN)
                    (ADV-T))
        3
    (FVERB+MAIN (WER GAB GESTERN)
                    (V D A)
                    (WEM)
                    (D I))
        4
    (FVERB+MAIN (WER GAB GESTERN WEM)
                    (V A I)
                    (EINE)
                    (A FS -E))
        5
```

```
(FVERB+MAIN (WER GAB GESTERN WEM EINE)
            (V FS -E)
            (PUPPE)
            (FS))
   6
(DET+NOUN (WER GAB GESTERN WEM EINE PUPPE)
            (V FS)
            (?)
            (I INTERROG))
   7)))
```

B.22.3 *Der Junge Mann gab wem gestern eine Puppe?*

```
(R DER JUNGE MANN GAB GESTERN WEM EINE PUPPE ?)
((CMPLT ((DER JUNGE MANN GAB GESTERN WEM EINE PUPPE ?)
         (INTERROG)
   1
(START (DER)
       (S3 MS -E)
       (JUNGE)
       (-E))
   2
(DET+ADJ (DER JUNGE)
         (S3 MS -E)
         (MANN)
         (MS))
   3
(DET+NOUN (DER JUNGE MANN)
          (S3 MS)
          (GAB)
          (V S3 D A))
   4
(MAIN+FVERB (DER JUNGE MANN GAB)
            (V D A MS)
            (GESTERN)
            (ADV-T))
   5
(FVERB+MAIN (DER JUNGE MANN GAB GESTERN)
            (V D A MS)
            (WEM)
            (D I))
   6
(FVERB+MAIN (DER JUNGE MANN GAB GESTERN WEM)
            (V A MS I)
            (EINE)
            (A FS -E))
   7
(FVERB+MAIN (DER JUNGE MANN GAB GESTERN WEM EINE)
            (V MS FS -E)
            (PUPPE)
            (FS))
   8
(DET+NOUN (DER JUNGE MANN GAB GESTERN WEM EINE PUPPE)
          (V MS FS)
          (?)
          (I INTERROG))
```

```
        9)))
```

B.22.4 *Was gab der junge Mann gestern dem Kind?*

```
(R WAS GAB DER JUNGE MANN GESTERN DEM KIND ?)
((CMPLT ((WAS GAB DER JUNGE MANN GESTERN DEM KIND ?)
        (INTERROG)
        1
        (START (WAS)
               (A I)
               (GAB)
               (V S3 D A))
        2
        (MAIN+FVERB (WAS GAB)
                    (V S3 D I)
                    (DER)
                    (S3 MS -E))
        3
        (FVERB+MAIN (WAS GAB DER)
                    (V D MS -E)
                    (JUNGE)
                    (-E))
        4
        (DET+ADJ (WAS GAB DER JUNGE)
                 (V D MS -E)
                 (MANN)
                 (MS))
        5
        (DET+NOUN (WAS GAB DER JUNGE MANN)
                  (V D MS)
                  (GESTERN)
                  (ADV-T))
        6
        (FVERB+MAIN (WAS GAB DER JUNGE MANN GESTERN)
                    (V D MS)
                    (DEM)
                    (D NS -EN))
        7
        (FVERB+MAIN (WAS GAB DER JUNGE MANN GESTERN DEM)
                    (V MS NS -EN)
                    (KIND)
                    (NS))
        8
        (DET+NOUN (WAS GAB DER JUNGE MANN GESTERN DEM KIND)
                  (V MS NS)
                  (?)
                  (I INTERROG))
        9)))
```

B.22.5 *Wo wohnt Peter?*

```
(R WO WOHNT PETER ?)
((CMPLT ((WO WOHNT PETER ?)
        (INTERROG)
        1
        (START (WO)
```

```
              (ADV-L I)
              (WOHNT)
              (V S3 ADV-L))
      2
      (MAIN+FVERB (WO WOHNT)
                  (V S3 I)
                  (PETER)
                  (S3 MS))
      3
      (FVERB+MAIN (WO WOHNT PETER)
                  (V MS)
                  (?)
                  (I INTERROG))
      4)))
```

B.22.6 *Warum hat der Mann dem Kind die Puppe gegeben?*

```
(R WARUM HAT DER MANN DEM KIND DIE PUPPE GEGEBEN ?)
((CMPLT ((WARUM HAT DER MANN DEM KIND DIE PUPPE GEGEBEN ?)
         (INTERROG)
      1
      (START (WARUM)
             (ADV-C I)
             (HAT)
             (V S3 H))
      2
      (MAIN+FVERB (WARUM HAT)
                  (V S3 H I)
                  (DER)
                  (S3 MS -E))
      3
      (FVERB+MAIN (WARUM HAT DER)
                  (V H MS -E)
                  (MANN)
                  (MS))
      4
      (DET+NOUN (WARUM HAT DER MANN)
                (V H MS)
                (DEM)
                (D NS -EN))
      5
      (FVERB+MAIN (WARUM HAT DER MANN DEM)
                  (V H MS D NS -EN)
                  (KIND)
                  (NS))
      6
      (DET+NOUN (WARUM HAT DER MANN DEM KIND)
                (V H MS D NS)
                (DIE)
                (A FS -E))
      7
      (FVERB+MAIN (WARUM HAT DER MANN DEM KIND DIE)
                  (V H MS D NS A FS -E)
                  (PUPPE)
                  (FS))
      8
```

```
(DET+NOUN (WARUM HAT DER MANN DEM KIND DIE PUPPE)
          (V H MS D NS A FS)
          (GEGEBEN)
          (H D A))
9
(MAINCL+NFVERB (WARUM HAT DER MANN DEM KIND DIE PUPPE GEGEBEN)
               (V MS NS FS)
               (?)
               (I INTERROG))
10)))
```

B.22.7 *Warum hat der Mann dem Kind die Puppe gegeben, das gestern in die Schule kam?*

```
(R WARUM HAT DER MANN DEM KIND DIE PUPPE GEGEBEN DAS GESTERN IN DIE SCHULE KAM ?)
((CMPLT ((WARUM HAT DER MANN DEM KIND DIE PUPPE GEGEBEN , DAS GESTERN IN DIE
                                                         SCHULE KAM ?)
        (INTERROG)
        1
        (START (WARUM)
               (ADV-C I)
               (HAT)
               (V S3 H))
        2
        (MAIN+FVERB (WARUM HAT)
                    (V S3 H I)
                    (DER)
                    (S3 MS -E))
        3
        (FVERB+MAIN (WARUM HAT DER)
                    (V H MS -E)
                    (MANN)
                    (MS))
        4
        (DET+NOUN (WARUM HAT DER MANN)
                  (V H MS)
                  (DEM)
                  (D NS -EN))
        5
        (FVERB+MAIN (WARUM HAT DER MANN DEM)
                    (V H MS D NS -EN)
                    (KIND)
                    (NS))
        6
        (DET+NOUN (WARUM HAT DER MANN DEM KIND)
                  (V H MS D NS)
                  (DIE)
                  (A FS -E))
        7
        (FVERB+MAIN (WARUM HAT DER MANN DEM KIND DIE)
                    (V H MS D NS A FS -E)
                    (PUPPE)
                    (FS))
        8
        (DET+NOUN (WARUM HAT DER MANN DEM KIND DIE PUPPE)
                  (V H MS D NS A FS)
```

```
                    (GEGEBEN)
                    (H D A))
          9
          (MAINCL+NFVERB (WARUM HAT DER MANN DEM KIND DIE PUPPE GEGEBEN)
                         (V MS NS FS)
                         (DAS)
                         (S3 NS -E))
          10
          (NOUN+RELPRO (WARUM HAT DER MANN DEM KIND DIE PUPPE GEGEBEN , DAS)
                       (V MS FS V S3)
                       (GESTERN)
                       (ADV-T))
          11
          (SUBCL+MAIN (WARUM HAT DER MANN DEM KIND DIE PUPPE GEGEBEN , DAS GESTERN)
                      (V MS FS V S3 ADV-T)
                      (IN)
                      (ADV-D (A)))
          12
          (SUBCL+MAIN (WARUM HAT DER MANN DEM KIND DIE PUPPE GEGEBEN , DAS
                                                           GESTERN IN)
                      (V MS FS V S3 ADV-T ADV-D (A))
                      (DIE)
                      (A FS -E))
          13
          (PREP+MAIN (WARUM HAT DER MANN DEM KIND DIE PUPPE GEGEBEN , DAS GESTERN
                                                                  IN DIE)
                     (V MS FS V S3 ADV-T ADV-D FS -E)
                     (SCHULE)
                     (FS))
          14
          (DET+NOUN (WARUM HAT DER MANN DEM KIND DIE PUPPE GEGEBEN , DAS GESTERN
                                                               IN DIE SCHULE)
                    (V MS FS V S3 ADV-T ADV-D FS)
                    (KAM)
                    (V S3))
          15
          (SUBCL+LASTVERB (WARUM HAT DER MANN DEM KIND DIE PUPPE GEGEBEN , DAS
                                                       GESTERN IN DIE SCHULE KAM ,)
                          (V MS FS FS)
                          (?)
                          (I INTERROG))
          16)))
```

B.22.8 *Warum hat der Mann dem Kind die Puppe gegeben, die es gestern in der Schule gesehen hatte?*

```
(R WARUM HAT DER MANN DEM KIND DIE PUPPE GEGEBEN DIE ES GESTERN IN DER SCHULE
                                                     GESEHEN HATTE ?)
((CMPLT ((WARUM HAT DER MANN DEM KIND DIE PUPPE GEGEBEN , DIE ES GESTERN IN DER
                                                     SCHULE GESEHEN HATTE ?)
         (INTERROG)
         1
         (START (WARUM)
                (ADV-C I)
                (HAT)
                (V S3 H))
```

```
2
(MAIN+FVERB (WARUM HAT)
            (V S3 H I)
            (DER)
            (S3 MS -E))
3
(FVERB+MAIN (WARUM HAT DER)
            (V H MS -E)
            (MANN)
            (MS))
4
(DET+NOUN (WARUM HAT DER MANN)
          (V H MS)
          (DEM)
          (D NS -EN))
5
(FVERB+MAIN (WARUM HAT DER MANN DEM)
            (V H MS D NS -EN)
            (KIND)
            (NS))
6
(DET+NOUN (WARUM HAT DER MANN DEM KIND)
          (V H MS D NS)
          (DIE)
          (A FS -E))
7
(FVERB+MAIN (WARUM HAT DER MANN DEM KIND DIE)
            (V H MS D NS A FS -E)
            (PUPPE)
            (FS))
8
(DET+NOUN (WARUM HAT DER MANN DEM KIND DIE PUPPE)
          (V H MS D NS A FS)
          (GEGEBEN)
          (H D A))
9
(MAINCL+NFVERB (WARUM HAT DER MANN DEM KIND DIE PUPPE GEGEBEN)
               (V MS NS FS)
               (DIE)
               (S3 FS -E))
10
(NOUN+RELPRO (WARUM HAT DER MANN DEM KIND DIE PUPPE GEGEBEN , DIE)
             (V MS NS V S3)
             (ES)
             (A))
11
(SUBCL+MAIN (WARUM HAT DER MANN DEM KIND DIE PUPPE GEGEBEN , DIE ES)
            (V MS NS V S3 A)
            (GESTERN)
            (ADV-T))
12
(SUBCL+MAIN (WARUM HAT DER MANN DEM KIND DIE PUPPE GEGEBEN , DIE ES
                                                             GESTERN)
            (V MS NS V S3 A ADV-T)
            (IN)
```

```
                        (ADV-L (D)))
        13
        (SUBCL+MAIN (WARUM HAT DER MANN DEM KIND DIE PUPPE GEGEBEN , DIE ES
                                                            GESTERN IN)
                        (V MS NS V S3 A ADV-T ADV-L (D))
                        (DER)
                        (D FS -EN))
        14
        (PREP+MAIN (WARUM HAT DER MANN DEM KIND DIE PUPPE GEGEBEN , DIE ES
                                                            GESTERN IN DER)
                        (V MS NS V S3 A ADV-T ADV-L FS -EN)
                        (SCHULE)
                        (FS))
        15
        (DET+NOUN (WARUM HAT DER MANN DEM KIND DIE PUPPE GEGEBEN , DIE ES
                                                        GESTERN IN DER SCHULE)
                        (V MS NS V S3 A ADV-T ADV-L FS)
                        (GESEHEN)
                        (H A))
        16
        (SUBCL+VERB (WARUM HAT DER MANN DEM KIND DIE PUPPE GEGEBEN , DIE ES
                                                    GESTERN IN DER SCHULE GESEHEN)
                        (V MS NS V S3 ADV-T ADV-L FS INF H)
                        (HATTE)
                        (V S3 H))
        17
        (SUBCL+LASTVERB (WARUM HAT DER MANN DEM KIND DIE PUPPE GEGEBEN , DIE
                                        ES GESTERN IN DER SCHULE GESEHEN HATTE ,)
                        (V MS NS FS)
                        (?)
                        (I INTERROG))
        18))


(CMPLT ((WARUM HAT DER MANN DEM KIND DIE PUPPE GEGEBEN , DIE ES GESTERN IN
                                                DER SCHULE GESEHEN HATTE ?)
        (INTERROG)
        1
        (START (WARUM)
                (ADV-C I)
                (HAT)
                (V S3 H))
        2
        (MAIN+FVERB (WARUM HAT)
                (V S3 H I)
                (DER)
                (S3 MS -E))
        3

        (FVERB+MAIN (WARUM HAT DER)
                (V H MS -E)
                (MANN)
                (MS))
        4
        (DET+NOUN (WARUM HAT DER MANN)
                (V H MS)
```

```
            (DEM)
            (D NS -EN))
5
(FVERB+MAIN (WARUM HAT DER MANN DEM)
            (V H MS D NS -EN)
            (KIND)
            (NS))
6
(DET+NOUN (WARUM HAT DER MANN DEM KIND)
            (V H MS D NS)
            (DIE)
            (A FS -E))
7
(FVERB+MAIN (WARUM HAT DER MANN DEM KIND DIE)
            (V H MS D NS A FS -E)
            (PUPPE)
            (FS))
8
(DET+NOUN (WARUM HAT DER MANN DEM KIND DIE PUPPE)
            (V H MS D NS A FS)
            (GEGEBEN)
            (H D A))
9
(MAINCL+NFVERB (WARUM HAT DER MANN DEM KIND DIE PUPPE GEGEBEN)
            (V MS NS FS)
            (DIE)
            (A FS -E))
10
(NOUN+RELPRO (WARUM HAT DER MANN DEM KIND DIE PUPPE GEGEBEN , DIE)
            (V MS NS V A)
            (ES)
            (S3))
11
(SUBCL+MAIN (WARUM HAT DER MANN DEM KIND DIE PUPPE GEGEBEN , DIE ES)
            (V MS NS V A S3)
            (GESTERN)
            (ADV-T))
12
(SUBCL+MAIN (WARUM HAT DER MANN DEM KIND DIE PUPPE GEGEBEN , DIE ES
                                                          GESTERN)
            (V MS NS V A S3 ADV-T)
            (IN)
            (ADV-L (D)))
13
(SUBCL+MAIN (WARUM HAT DER MANN DEM KIND DIE PUPPE GEGEBEN , DIE ES
                                                          GESTERN IN)
            (V MS NS V A S3 ADV-T ADV-L (D))
            (DER)
            (D FS -EN))
14
(PREP+MAIN (WARUM HAT DER MANN DEM KIND DIE PUPPE GEGEBEN , DIE ES
                                                          GESTERN IN DER)
            (V MS NS V A S3 ADV-T ADV-L FS -EN)
            (SCHULE)
            (FS))
```

```
15
(DET+NOUN (WARUM HAT DER MANN DEM KIND DIE PUPPE GEGEBEN , DIE ES
                                              GESTERN IN DER SCHULE)
          (V MS NS V A S3 ADV-T ADV-L FS)
          (GESEHEN)
          (H A))
16
(SUBCL+VERB (WARUM HAT DER MANN DEM KIND DIE PUPPE GEGEBEN , DIE ES
                                          GESTERN IN DER SCHULE GESEHEN)
            (V MS NS V S3 ADV-T ADV-L FS INF H)
            (HATTE)
            (V S3 H))
17
(SUBCL+LASTVERB (WARUM HAT DER MANN DEM KIND DIE PUPPE GEGEBEN , DIE
                              ES GESTERN IN DER SCHULE GESEHEN HATTE ,)
                (V MS NS FS)
                (?)
                (I INTERROG))
18)))
```

C. A selection of ECAT test examples

Like DCAT, ECAT's development was based on expanding sets of test examples. The present appendix presents computer-generated derivations of 114 selected test sentences of English. For an overview see appendix D, which contains a list of the sample derivations in this book.

The greatest initial difficulty in writing ECAT was the design of a suitable category system. Once the categories described in 5.1 and 5.2 were established, it took three weeks to expand the parser to its present scope. ECAT is extremely fast: none of the following derivations takes more than a fraction of a second.

The following sample derivations illustrate the descriptive scope of the parser, as well as serving as a reference for building further constructions into the transition network of the grammar. A program which samples all combinations performed by a particular rule, e.g. all combinations performed by /ADD-VERB, is an excellent tool for exploiting the information contained in a large set of left-associative sample derivations. Study of such a set will lead to a simpler and more principled formulation of the rule in question.

C.1 List of category segments used in ECAT and ELEX

In ECAT/ELEX the name of a category segment indicating a valency position is usually different from that of the segment indicating a compatible argument. For example, the accusative valency position A in the category (V A SH) of *John read* may be filled by a noun phrase of category SH, S-H, PH, P-H, :S3, etc. In other words, in ECAT the category segments used to indicate the 'slot' differ from those indicating the 'filler'; compatibility between a given valency position and an argument is specified in the linguistic rules of the parser. In some instances, the valency position has the same name as the argument, e.g. *John has* of category (V HV) combines with *given* of category (HV D A) into *John has given* of category (V D A). But such cases of categorial correspondence with identity are the exception in ECAT/ELEX.

1. **A** (accusative, indicates valency position for a noun phrase, e.g. (saw ((V N A))).)

2. **AG** (agent, indicates valency position for an optional by-phrase, e.g. *John was given a book* of category (V AG SH), and represents result category of preposition (by ((AG NP))).)

3. **B** ('be', indicates valency position for a present participle, e.g. (am ((V S1 B))), and represents result category of present participle verb forms, e.g. (giving ((B D A))).)

4. **C** (consonant, represents singular determiners combining with nouns and adjectives beginning with a consonant, e.g. (a ((C))).)

5. **-C** (no-consonant, represents singular determiners combining with nouns and adjectives beginning with a vowel, e.g. (an ((-C))).)

6. **CH** (consonant human, represents singular nouns beginning with a consonant and denoting a person, e.g. (man ((CH))).)

7. **C-H** (consonant non-human, represents singular nouns beginning with a consonant and denoting a thing, e.g. (car ((C-H))).)

8. **-CH** (no-consonant human, represents singular nouns beginning with a vowel and denoting a person, e.g. (uncle ((-CH))).)

9. **-C-H** (no-consonant non-human, represents singular nouns beginning with a vowel and denoting a thing, e.g. (auto ((-C-H))).)

10. **D** (dative, indicates valency position for a noun phrase, e.g. (gave ((V N D A))).)

11. **DECL** (declarative, result category of a complete declarative sentence, e.g. (%. ((DECL V))).)

12. **DO** ('do', third segment of verb forms in the *do* paradigm, e.g. (does ((V S3 DO))).)

13. **HV** ('have', indicates valency position for a past participle, e.g. (have ((V N HV))), and represents result category of past participles, e.g. (given ((HV D A)).)

14. **INTERROG** (interrogative, result category of a complete interrogative sentence, e.g. (? ((INTERROG V))).)

15. **M** (modal, third segment of modal verbs, e.g. (could ((V N M))).)

16. **N** (nominative, indicates valency position for noun phrases of all persons and numbers, e.g (gave ((V N D A))).)

17. **NM** (nominative, indicates valency position for noun phrases of all numbers and persons except the first and third person singular, e.g. (are ((V NM B))).)

18. **NOM** (nominative, indicates valency position for noun phrases of all persons and numbers except the third person singular, e.g. (give ((V NOM D A))).)

19. **NP** (noun phrase, indicates noun phrase valency position which does not assign a case, e.g. (to ((TO NP))).)

20. **P1** (plural first person, represents noun phrases of first person plural marked for nominative, e.g. (we ((P1))).

21. **P3** (plural third person, represents noun phrases of third person plural marked for nominative, e.g. (they ((P3))).

22. **:P3** (oblique plural third person, represents noun phrases of third person plural which cannot fill a nominative valency position, e.g (them (:P3))).)

23. **PH** (plural human, represents plural nouns denoting persons, e.g. (men ((PH))) or (uncles ((PH))), and plural noun phrases denoting persons, e.g. *all men.*)

24. **:PH** (oblique plural human, represents plural noun phrases denoting persons which cannot fill a nominative valency position, e.g. (us ((:PH)))

25. **P-H** (plural non-human, represents plural nouns denoting things, e.g. (cars ((P-H))) or (autos ((P-H))), and plural noun phrases denoting things, e.g. *all cars.*)

26. **PNM** (post nominal modifier, represents result category of prepositional phrases used as post nominal modifiers, e.g. (by ((PNM NP))) as in *the book by Mary.*

27. **S** (singular, represents singular determiners which have no agreement restrictions on the first letter of the next word, e.g. (every ((S))), *an old*, or *a beautiful old.*)

28. **S1** (singular first person, indicates a valency position for first person singular nominative, e.g. (am ((V S1 B))), and represents first person singular noun phrases marked for nominative case, e.g. (I ((S1))).

29. **S3** (singular third person, indicates a valency position for third person singular nominative, e.g. (gives ((V S3 D A))), and represents third person singular noun phrases marked for nominative case, e.g. (he ((S3))) and (she ((S3))).)

30. **SC** (subordinate clause, indicates a valency position for a subordinate clause, e.g. *Mary said that* of category (V SC), and represents category subordinating conjunctions, e.g. (that ((SC)))

31. **SH** (singular human, represents singular noun phrases denoting a person, e.g. (John ((SH))) or *the man.*)

32. **:SH** (oblique singular human, represents singular noun phrases denoting a person which cannot fill nominative valency positions, e.g. (me ((:SH))), (him ((:SH))), and (her ((:SH))).

33. **S-H** (singular non-human, represents singular noun phrases denoting a thing, e.g. *the car.*)

34. **TO** ('to', indicates a valency position for a to-phrase, e.g. (gave ((V N A TO))), and represents result category of preposition (to ((TO NP))).)

35. **U** (universal, represents determiners which have no agreement restrictions on the first letter of the next word or on whether it is singular or plural, e.g. (the ((U))).)

36. **V** (verb, indicates a valency position for a declarative sentence, e.g. (DECL V), and represents the result category of finite verbs, e.g. (was ((V S3 B))), and sentence starts containing a finite verb, e.g. *John was* of category (V B).)

37. **VI** (verb interrogative, indicates a valency position for an interrogative sentence, e.g (INTERROG VI), and represents result category of sentence starts marked for interrogative mood, e.g. *Was John* of category (VI B), or *Who was* of category (VI B).)

38. **WH** (w-phrase human, represents interrogative noun phrases used as relative and interrogative pronouns, e.g. (who ((WH))).)

39. **:WH** (oblique w-phrase human, represents interrogative noun phrases used as relative and interrogative pronouns (whom ((:WH))).)

40. **W-H** (w-phrase non-human, represents interrogative noun phrases used as relative pronouns, e.g. (which ((W-H))) and (what ((W-H))).)

41. **WP** (w-phrase plural, represents plural interrogative noun phrases, e.g. *which books* or *which men* of category (WP).)

42. **WS** (w-phrase singular, represents singular interrogative noun phrases, e.g. *which book* or *which man* of category (WS).)

43. **WU** (w-phrase universal, represents interrogative determiners without agreement restrictions on the first letter of the next word or on whether it is singular or plural, e.g. (which ((WU))).)

44. **#** (subclause delimiter, introduced by rules such as /ADD-NOM and /START-RELCL, e.g. *Who did Mary say that John* of category (VI SC SH # WH SH).)

C.2   Active voice constructions using the verb *give*

C.2.1 *John gave Mary a beautiful book.*

```
(R John gave Mary a beautiful book .)
((*CMPLT ((John gave Mary a beautiful book %.)
         (DECL)
         1
         (*START (John)
                 (SH)
                 (gave)
                 (V N D A))
         2
         (*NOM+FVERB (John gave)
                     (V D A)
                     (Mary)
                     (SH))
         3
         (*FVERB+MAIN (John gave Mary)
                      (V A SH)
                      (a)
                      (C))
         4
         (*FVERB+MAIN (John gave Mary a)
                      (V C SH)
                      (beautiful)
                      (CA))
         5
         (*DET+ADJ (John gave Mary a beautiful)
                   (V S SH)
                   (book)
                   (C-H))
         6
         (*DET+NOUN (John gave Mary a beautiful book)
                    (V SH S-H)
                    (%.)
                    (DECL V))
         7)))
```

C.2.2 *John might give Mary an old book.*

```
(R John might give Mary an old book .)
((*CMPLT ((John might give Mary an old book %.)
         (DECL)
         1
         (*START (John)
                 (SH)
                 (might)
                 (V N M))
         2
         (*NOM+FVERB (John might)
                     (V M)
                     (give)
                     (V NOM D A))
```

```
        3
        (*ADD-VERB (John might give)
                  (V D A)
                  (Mary)
                  (SH))
        4
        (*FVERB+MAIN (John might give Mary)
                     (V A SH)
                     (an)
                     (-C))
        5
        (*FVERB+MAIN (John might give Mary an)
                     (V -C SH)
                     (old)
                     (-CA))
        6
        (*DET+ADJ (John might give Mary an old)
                  (V S SH)
                  (book)
                  (C-H))
        7
        (*DET+NOUN (John might give Mary an old book)
                   (V SH S-H)
                   (%.)
                   (DECL V))
        8)))
```

C.2.3 *The man could have given Mary a book.*

```
(R the man could have given Mary a book .)
((*CMPLT ((the man could have given Mary a book %.)
         (DECL)
         1
         (*START (the)
                 (U)
                 (man)
                 (CH))
         2
         (*DET+NOUN (the man)
                    (SH)
                    (could)
                    (V N M))
         3
         (*NOM+FVERB (the man could)
                     (V M)
                     (have)
                     (V NOM HV))
         4
         (*ADD-VERB (the man could have)
                    (V HV)
                    (given)
                    (HV D A))
         5
         (*ADD-VERB (the man could have given)
                    (V D A)
                    (Mary)
```

```
                    (SH))
            6
            (*FVERB+MAIN (the man could have given Mary)
                        (V A SH)
                        (a)
                        (C))
            7
            (*FVERB+MAIN (the man could have given Mary a)
                        (V C SH)
                        (book)
                        (C-H))
            8
            (*DET+NOUN (the man could have given Mary a book)
                        (V SH S-H)
                        (%.)
                        (DECL V))
            9)))
```

C.2.4 *John gave a beautiful old book to the young girl.*

```
(R John gave a beautiful old book to the young girl .)
((*CMPLT ((John gave a beautiful old book to the young girl %.)
            (DECL)
            1
            (*START (John)
                    (SH)
                    (gave)
                    (V N A TO))
            2
            (*NOM+FVERB (John gave)
                        (V A TO)
                        (a)
                        (C))
            3
            (*FVERB+MAIN (John gave a)
                        (V C TO)
                        (beautiful)
                        (CA))
            4
            (*DET+ADJ (John gave a beautiful)
                        (V S TO)
                        (old)
                        (-CA))
            5
            (*DET+ADJ (John gave a beautiful old)
                        (V S TO)
                        (book)
                        (C-H))
            6
            (*DET+NOUN (John gave a beautiful old book)
                        (V TO S-H)
                        (to)
                        (TO NP))
            7
            (*FVERB+MAIN (John gave a beautiful old book to)
                        (V NP S-H)
```

```
                      (the)
                      (U))
          8
          (*PREP+NP (John gave a beautiful old book to the)
                    (V U S-H)
                    (young)
                    (CA))
          9
          (*DET+ADJ (John gave a beautiful old book to the young)
                    (V U S-H)
                    (girl)
                    (CH))
          10
          (*DET+NOUN (John gave a beautiful old book to the young girl)
                     (V S-H SH)
                     (%.)
                     (DECL V))
          11)))
```

C.2.5 *John could have given a book to Mary.*

```
(R John could have given a book to Mary .)
((*CMPLT ((John could have given a book to Mary %.)
          (DECL)
          1
          (*START (John)
                  (SH)
                  (could)
                  (V N M))
          2
          (*NOM+FVERB (John could)
                      (V M)
                      (have)
                      (V NOM HV))
          3
          (*ADD-VERB (John could have)
                     (V HV)
                     (given)
                     (HV A TO))
          4
          (*ADD-VERB (John could have given)
                     (V A TO)
                     (a)
                     (C))
          5
          (*FVERB+MAIN (John could have given a)
                       (V C TO)
                       (book)
                       (C-H))
          6
          (*DET+NOUN (John could have given a book)
                     (V TO S-H)
                     (to)
                     (TO NP))
          7
          (*FVERB+MAIN (John could have given a book to)
```

```
                         (V NP S-H)
                         (Mary)
                         (SH))
        8
        (*PREP+NP (John could have given a book to Mary)
                         (V S-H SH)
                         (%.)
                         (DECL V))
        9)))
```

C.2.6 *The man could be giving a beautiful book to the woman.*

```
(R the man could be giving a beautiful book to the woman .)
((*CMPLT ((the man could be giving a beautiful book to the woman %.)
         (DECL)
         1
         (*START (the)
                 (U)
                 (man)
                 (CH))
         2
         (*DET+NOUN (the man)
                 (SH)
                 (could)
                 (V N M))
         3
         (*NOM+FVERB (the man could)
                  (V M)
                  (be)
                  (M B))
         4
         (*ADD-VERB (the man could be)
                 (V B)
                 (giving)
                 (B A TO))
         5
         (*ADD-VERB (the man could be giving)
                 (V A TO)
                 (a)
                 (C))
         6
         (*FVERB+MAIN (the man could be giving a)
                  (V C TO)
                  (beautiful)
                  (CA))
         7
         (*DET+ADJ (the man could be giving a beautiful)
                 (V S TO)
                 (book)
                 (C-H))
         8
         (*DET+NOUN (the man could be giving a beautiful book)
                 (V TO S-H)
                 (to)
                 (TO NP))
         9
```

```
(*FVERB+MAIN (the man could be giving a beautiful book to)
            (V NP S-H)
            (the)
            (U))
10
(*PREP+NP (the man could be giving a beautiful book to the)
          (V U S-H)
          (woman)
          (CH))
11
(*DET+NOUN (the man could be giving a beautiful book to the woman)
           (V S-H SH)
           (%.)
           (DECL V))
12)))
```

C.3 Passive voice constructions using the verb give

C.3.1 The man was given a book by Mary.

```
(R the man was given a book by Mary .)
((*CMPLT ((the man was given a book by Mary %.)
         (DECL)
         1
         (*START (the)
                 (U)
                 (man)
                 (CH))
         2
         (*DET+NOUN (the man)
                    (SH)
                    (was)
                    (V S3 B))
         3
         (*NOM+FVERB (the man was)
                     (V B)
                     (given)
                     (HV D A))
         4
         (*ADD-VERB (the man was given)
                    (V A AG)
                    (a)
                    (C))
         5
         (*FVERB+MAIN (the man was given a)
                      (V C AG)
                      (book)
                      (C-H))
         6
         (*DET+NOUN (the man was given a book)
                    (V AG S-H)
                    (by)
```

```
                        (AG NP))
            7
            (*FVERB+MAIN (the man was given a book by)
                        (V NP S-H)
                        (Mary)
                        (SH))
            8
            (*PREP+NP (the man was given a book by Mary)
                        (V C H SH)
                        (%.)
                        (DECL V))
            9))
(*CMPLT ((the man was given a book by Mary %.)
            (DECL)
            1
            (*START (the)
                        (U)
                        (man)
                        (CH))
            2
            (*DET+NOUN (the man)
                        (SH)
                        (was)
                        (V S3 B))
            3
            (*NOM+FVERB (the man was)
                        (V B)
                        (given)
                        (HV D A))
            4
            (*ADD-VERB (the man was given)
                        (V A AG)
                        (a)
                        (C))
            5
            (*FVERB+MAIN (the man was given a)
                        (V C AG)
                        (book)
                        (C-H))
            6
            (*DET+NOUN (the man was given a book)
                        (V AG S-H)
                        (by)
                        (PNM NP))
            7
            (*NOUN+PNM (the man was given a book by)
                        (V NP AG)
                        (Mary)
                        (SH))
            8
            (*PREP+NP (the man was given a book by Mary)
                        (V AG SH)
                        (%.)
                        (DECL V))
            9)))
```

C.3.2 *The man might have been given a book.*

```
(R the man might have been given a book .)
((*CMPLT ((the man might have been given a book %.)
         (DECL)
         1
         (*START (the)
                 (U)
                 (man)
                 (CH))
         2
         (*DET+NOUN (the man)
                    (SH)
                    (might)
                    (V N M))
         3
         (*NOM+FVERB (the man might)
                     (V M)
                     (have)
                     (V NOM HV))
         4
         (*ADD-VERB (the man might have)
                    (V HV)
                    (been)
                    (HV B))
         5
         (*ADD-VERB (the man might have been)
                    (V B)
                    (given)
                    (HV D A))
         6
         (*ADD-VERB (the man might have been given)
                    (V A AG)
                    (a)
                    (C))
         7
         (*FVERB+MAIN (the man might have been given a)
                      (V C AG)
                      (book)
                      (C-H))
         8
         (*DET+NOUN (the man might have been given a book)
                    (V AG S-H)
                    (%.)
                    (DECL V))
         9)))
```

C.3.3 *A book might have been given to John by Mary.*

```
(R a book might have been given to John by Mary .)
((*CMPLT ((a book might have been given to John by Mary %.)
         (DECL)
         1
         (*START (a)
                 (C)
                 (book)
```

```
                (C-H))
        2
        (*DET+NOUN (a book)
                   (S-H)
                   (might)
                   (V N M))
        3
        (*NOM+FVERB (a book might)
                    (V M)
                    (have)
                    (V NOM HV))
        4
        (*ADD-VERB (a book might have)
                   (V HV)
                   (been)
                   (HV B))
        5
        (*ADD-VERB (a book might have been)
                   (V B)
                   (given)
                   (HV A TO))
        6
        (*ADD-VERB (a book might have been given)
                   (V TO AG)
                   (to)
                   (TO NP))
        7
        (*FVERB+MAIN (a book might have been given to)
                     (V NP AG)
                     (John)
                     (SH))
        8
        (*PREP+NP (a book might have been given to John)
                  (V AG SH)
                  (by)
                  (AG NP))
        9
        (*FVERB+MAIN (a book might have been given to John by)
                     (V NP SH)
                     (Mary)
                     (SH))
        10
        (*PREP+NP (a book might have been given to John by Mary)
                  (V SH SH)
                  (%.)
                  (DECL V))
        11)))
```

C.3.4 *A book might have been given to John.*

```
(R a book might have been given to John .)
((*CMPLT ((a book might have been given to John %.)
         (DECL)
         1
         (*START (a)
                 (C)
```

```
                (book)
                (C-H))
        2
        (*DET+NOUN  (a book)
                   (S-H)
                   (might)
                   (V N M))
        3
        (*NOM+FVERB (a book might)
                    (V M)
                    (have)
                    (V NOM HV))
        4
        (*ADD-VERB  (a book might have)
                    (V HV)
                    (been)
                    (HV B))
        5
        (*ADD-VERB  (a book might have been)
                    (V B)
                    (given)
                    (HV A TO))
        6
        (*ADD-VERB  (a book might have been given)
                    (V TO AG)
                    (to)
                    (TO NP))
        7
        (*FVERB+MAIN (a book might have been given to)
                     (V NP AG)
                     (John)
                     (SH))
        8
        (*PREP+NP   (a book might have been given to John)
                    (V AG SH)
                    (%.)
                    (DECL V))
        9)))
```

C.3.5 *A book was given John by Mary.*

```
(R a book was given John by Mary .)
((*CMPLT ((a book was given John by Mary %.)
         (DECL)
         1
         (*START (a)
                 (C)
                 (book)
                 (C-H))
         2
         (*DET+NOUN (a book)
                    (S-H)
                    (was)
                    (V S3 B))
         3
         (*NOM+FVERB (a book was)
```

```
                      (V B)
                      (given)
                      (HV D A))
         4
         (*ADD-VERB (a book was given)
                      (V A AG)
                      (John)
                      (SH))
         5
         (*FVERB+MAIN (a book was given John)
                      (V AG SH)
                      (by)
                      (AG NP))
         6
         (*FVERB+MAIN (a book was given John by)
                      (V NP SH)
                      (Mary)
                      (SH))
         7
         (*PREP+NP (a book was given John by Mary)
                      (V SH SH)
                      (%.)
                      (DECL V))
         8)))
```

C.3.6 *A book was given John.*

```
(R a book was given John .)
((*CMPLT ((a book was given John %.)
         (DECL)
         1
         (*START (a)
                   (C)
                   (book)
                   (C-H))
         2
         (*DET+NOUN (a book)
                   (S-H)
                   (was)
                   (V S3 B))
         3
         (*NOM+FVERB (a book was)
                      (V B)
                      (given)
                      (HV D A))
         4
         (*ADD-VERB (a book was given)
                      (V A AG)
                      (John)
                      (SH))
         5
         (*FVERB+MAIN (a book was given John)
                      (V AG SH)
                      (%.)
                      (DECL V))
         6)))
```

C.4   Genitive constructions

C.4.1 *John's book is beautiful.*

```
(R John's book is beautiful .)
((*CMPLT ((John's book is beautiful %.)
         (DECL)
         1
         (*START (John's)
                 (U)
                 (book)
                 (C-H))
         2
         (*DET+NOUN (John's book)
                    (S-H)
                    (is)
                    (V S3 B))
         3
         (*NOM+FVERB (John's book is)
                     (V B)
                     (beautiful)
                     (CA))
         4
         (*ADD-VERB (John's book is beautiful)
                    (V)
                    (%.)
                    (DECL V))
         5)))
```

C.4.2 **John's book are beautiful .*

```
(R John's book are beautiful .)
[ERROR "Ungrammatical continuation at:" ((*DET+NOUN ((John's book)
                                                     (S-H)
                                                     1
                                                     (*START (John's)
                                                             (U)
                                                             (book)
                                                             (C-H))
                                                     2))

            (*START ((are)
                     (V NM B]
```

C.4.3 *John's books are beautiful.*

```
(R John's books are beautiful %.)
((*CMPLT ((John's books are beautiful %.)
         (DECL)
         1
         (*START (John's)
                 (U)
                 (books)
                 (P-H))
         2
         (*DET+NOUN (John's books)
                    (P-H)
```

```
                    (are)
                    (V IM B))
        3
        (*NOM+FVERB (John's books are)
                    (V B)
                    (beautiful)
                    (CA))
        4
        (*ADD-VERB (John's books are beautiful)
                    (V)
                    (%.)
                    (DECL V))
        5)))
```

C.4.4 *John's books is beautiful.

```
(R John's books is beautiful %.)
[ERROR "Ungrammatical continuation at:" ((*DET+NOUN ((John's books)
                                                     (P-H)
                                                     1
                                                     (*START (John's)
                                                             (U)
                                                             (books)
                                                             (P-H))
                                          2))
        (*START ((is)
                 (V S3 B]
```

C.4.5 The old man's book is beautiful.

```
(R the old man's book is beautiful .)
((*CMPLT ((the old man's book is beautiful %.)
         (DECL)
         1
         (*START (the)
                 (U)
                 (old)
                 (-CA))
         2
         (*DET+ADJ (the old)
                 (U)
                 (man's)
                 (CA))
         3
         (*DET+ADJ (the old man's)
                 (U)
                 (book)
                 (C-H))
         4
         (*DET+NOUN (the old man's book)
                 (S-H)
                 (is)
                 (V S3 B))
         5
         (*NOM+FVERB (the old man's book is)
                 (V B)
```

```
                    (beautiful)
                    (CA))
        6
   (*ADD-VERB (the old man's book is beautiful)
              (V)
              (%.)
              (DECL V))
        7)))
```

C.5 Auxiliaries taking noun phrases as the second argument

C.5.1 *John has many beautiful books.*

```
(R John has many beautiful books .)
((*CMPLT ((John has many beautiful books %.)
         (DECL)
         1
         (*START (John)
                 (SH)
                 (has)
                 (V S3 HV))
         2
         (*NOM+FVERB (John has)
                     (V HV)
                     (many)
                     (P))
         3
         (*FVERB+MAIN (John has many)
                      (V P)
                      (beautiful)
                      (CA))
         4
         (*DET+ADJ (John has many beautiful)
                   (V P)
                   (books)
                   (P-H))
         5
         (*DET+NOUN (John has many beautiful books)
                    (V P-H)
                    (%.)
                    (DECL V))
         6)))
```

C.5.2 *John has a beautiful book.*

```
(R John has a beautiful book .)
((*CMPLT ((John has a beautiful book %.)
         (DECL)
         1
         (*START (John)
                 (SH)
```

```
                    (has)
                    (V S3 HV))
        2
        (*NOM+FVERB (John has)
                    (V HV)
                    (a)
                    (C))
        3
        (*FVERB+MAIN (John has a)
                    (V C)
                    (beautiful)
                    (CA))
        4
        (*DET+ADJ (John has a beautiful)
                    (V S)
                    (book)
                    (C-H))
        5
        (*DET+NOUN (John has a beautiful book)
                    (V S-H)
                    (%.)
                    (DECL V))
        6)))
```

C.5.3 *John has beautiful book.*

```
(R John has beautiful book %.)
[ERROR "Ungrammatical continuation at:" ((*FVERB+MAIN ((John has beautiful)
                                        (V P)
                                        1
                                        (*START (John)
                                                (SH)
                                                (has)
                                                (V S3 HV))
                                        2
                                        (*NOM+FVERB
                                         (John has)
                                         (V HV)
                                         (beautiful)
                                         (CA))
                                        3))

        (*START ((book)
                (C-H]
```

C.5.4 *You are a beautiful young woman.*

```
(R you are a beautiful young woman .)
((*CMPLT ((you are a beautiful young woman %.)
        (DECL)
        1
        (*START (you)
                (PH)
                (are)
                (V NM B))
        2
        (*NOM+FVERB (you are)
```

```
                        (V B)
                        (a)
                        (C))
           3
           (*FVERB+MAIN (you are a)
                        (V C)
                        (beautiful)
                        (CA))
           4
           (*DET+ADJ (you are a beautiful)
                        (V S)
                        (young)
                        (CA))
           5
           (*DET+ADJ (you are a beautiful young)
                        (V S)
                        (woman)
                        (CH))
           6
           (*DET+NOUN (you are a beautiful young woman)
                        (V SH)
                        (%.)
                        (DECL V))
           7)))
```

C.6   Auxiliaries taking an adjective as the second argument

C.6.1 *You are beautiful.*

```
(R you are beautiful .)
((*CMPLT ((you are beautiful %.)
          (DECL)
          1
          (*START (you)
                  (PH)
                  (are)
                  (V NM B))
          2
          (*NOM+FVERB (you are)
                      (V B)
                      (beautiful)
                      (CA))
          3
          (*ADD-VERB (you are beautiful)
                     (V)
                     (%.)
                     (DECL V))
          4)))
```

C.7 Nominative agreement and the auxiliary *be*

C.7.1 *You are women.*

```
(R you are women .)
((*CMPLT ((you are women %.)
         (DECL)
         1
         (*START (you)
                 (PH)
                 (are)
                 (V NM B))
         2
         (*NOM+FVERB (you are)
                     (V B)
                     (women)
                     (PH))
         3
         (*FVERB+MAIN (you are women)
                      (V PH)
                      (%.)
                      (DECL V))
         4)))
```

C.7.2 *He is a good doctor.*

```
(R he is a good doctor .)
((*CMPLT ((he is a good doctor %.)
         (DECL)
         1
         (*START (he)
                 (S3)
                 (is)
                 (V S3 B))
         2
         (*NOM+FVERB (he is)
                     (V B)
                     (a)
                     (C))
         3
         (*FVERB+MAIN (he is a)
                      (V C)
                      (good)
                      (CA))
         4
         (*DET+ADJ (he is a good)
                   (V S)
                   (doctor)
                   (CH))
         5
         (*DET+NOUN (he is a good doctor)
                    (V SH)
                    (%.)
                    (DECL V))
         6)))
```

C.7.3 *We are good doctors.*

```
(R we are good doctors .)
((*CMPLT ((we are good doctors %.)
         (DECL)
         1
         (*START (we)
                 (P1)
                 (are)
                 (V IM B))
         2
         (*NOM+FVERB (we are)
                     (V B)
                     (good)
                     (CA))
         3
         (*FVERB+MAIN (we are good)
                      (V P)
                      (doctors)
                      (PH))
         4
         (*DET+NOUN (we are good doctors)
                    (V PH)
                    (%.)
                    (DECL V))
         5)))
```

C.7.4 **You is good doctors.*

```
(R you is good doctors .)
[ERROR "Ungrammatical continuation at:" ((*START ((you)
                                                   (PH)))
        (*START ((is)
                 (V S3 B]
```

C.7.5 *You are beautiful women.*

```
(R you are beautiful women .)
((*CMPLT ((you are beautiful women %.)
         (DECL)
         1
         (*START (you)
                 (PH)
                 (are)
                 (V IM B))
         2
         (*NOM+FVERB (you are)
                     (V B)
                     (beautiful)
                     (CA))
         3
         (*FVERB+MAIN (you are beautiful)
                      (V P)
                      (women)
                      (PH))
         4
```

```
          (*DET+NOUN (you are beautiful women)
                    (V PH)
                    (%.)
                    (DECL V))
          5)))
```

C.7.6 *I am a collector of old beautiful books.*

```
(R I am a collector of old beautiful books .)
((*CMPLT ((I am a collector of old beautiful books %.)
          (DECL)
          1
          (*START (I)
                  (S1)
                  (am)
                  (V S1 B))
          2
          (*NOM+FVERB (I am)
                      (V B)
                      (a)
                      (C))
          3
          (*FVERB+MAIN (I am a)
                       (V C)
                       (collector)
                       (C-H))
          4
          (*DET+NOUN (I am a collector)
                     (V S-H)
                     (of)
                     (PNM NP))
          5
          (*NOUN+PNM (I am a collector of)
                     (V NP)
                     (old)
                     (-CA))
          6
          (*PREP+NP (I am a collector of old)
                    (V -CA)
                    (beautiful)
                    (CA))
          7
          (*DET+ADJ (I am a collector of old beautiful)
                    (V P)
                    (books)
                    (P-H))
          8
          (*DET+NOUN (I am a collector of old beautiful books)
                     (V P-H)
                     (%.)
                     (DECL V))
          9)))
```

C.8 Yes/no-interrogatives and related declaratives

C.8.1 *Mary said that?*

```
(R Mary said that ?)
((*CMPLT ((Mary said that ?)
         (INTERROG)
         1
         (*START (Mary)
                 (SH)
                 (said)
                 (V N A))
         2
         (*NOM+FVERB (Mary said)
                     (V A)
                     (that)
                     (SC))
         3
         (*FVERB+MAIN (Mary said that)
                      (V)
                      (?)
                      (INTERROG V))
         4)))
```

C.8.2 *Mary said that.*

```
(R Mary said that .)
((*CMPLT ((Mary said that %.)
         (DECL)
         1
         (*START (Mary)
                 (SH)
                 (said)
                 (V N A))
         2
         (*NOM+FVERB (Mary said)
                     (V A)
                     (that)
                     (SC))
         3
         (*FVERB+MAIN (Mary said that)
                      (V)
                      (%.)
                      (DECL V))
         4)))
```

C.8.3 *Does John love Mary?*

```
(R does John love Mary ?)
((*CMPLT ((does John love Mary ?)
         (INTERROG)
         1
         (*START (does)
                 (V S3 DO)
```

```
                    (John)
                    (SH))
            2
            (*FVERB+NOM (does John)
                        (VI DO SH)
                        (love)
                        (V NOM A))
            3
            (*ADD-VERB (does John love)
                        (VI A SH)
                        (Mary)
                        (SH))
            4
            (*FVERB+MAIN (does John love Mary)
                        (VI SH SH)
                        (?)
                        (INTERROG V))
            5)))
```

C.8.4 *Does John love Mary.

```
(R does John love Mary .)
[ERROR "Ungrammatical continuation at:" ((*FVERB+MAIN ((does John love Mary)
                                                       (VI SH SH)
                                                       1
                                                       (*START (does)
                                                               (V S3 DO)
                                                               (John)
                                                               (SH))
                                                       2
                                                       (*FVERB+NOM
                                                         (does John)
                                                         (VI DO SH)
                                                         (love)
                                                         (V NOM A))
                                                       3
                                                       (*ADD-VERB
                                                         (does John love)
                                                         (VI A SH)
                                                         (Mary)
                                                         (SH))
                                                       4))
        (*START ((%.)
                 (DECL V]
```

C.8.5 *John loves Mary?*

```
(R John loves Mary ?)
((*CMPLT ((John loves Mary ?)
         (INTERROG)
         1
         (*START (John)
                 (SH)
                 (loves)
                 (V S3 A))
```

```
            2
            (*NOM+FVERB (John loves)
                        (V A)
                        (Mary)
                        (SH))
            3
            (*FVERB+MAIN (John loves Mary)
                         (V SH)
                         (?)
                         (INTERROG V))
            4)))
```

C.8.6 *John loves Mary.*

```
(R John loves Mary .)
((*CMPLT ((John loves Mary %.)
         (DECL)
         1
         (*START (John)
                 (SH)
                 (loves)
                 (V S3 A))
         2
         (*NOM+FVERB (John loves)
                     (V A)
                     (Mary)
                     (SH))
         3
         (*FVERB+MAIN (John loves Mary)
                      (V SH)
                      (%.)
                      (DECL V))
         4)))
```

C.8.7 *Did Mary give John the book?*

```
(R did Mary give John the book ?)
((*CMPLT ((did Mary give John the book ?)
         (INTERROG)
         1
         (*START (did)
                 (V N DO)
                 (Mary)
                 (SH))
         2
         (*FVERB+NOM (did Mary)
                     (VI DO SH)
                     (give)
                     (V NOM D A))
         3
         (*ADD-VERB (did Mary give)
                    (VI D A SH)
                    (John)
                    (SH))
         4
         (*FVERB+MAIN (did Mary give John)
```

C.8 Yes/no-interrogatives and related declaratives 451

```
                    (VI A SH SH)
                    (the)
                    (U))
        5
        (*FVERB+MAIN (did Mary give John the)
                    (VI U SH SH)
                    (book)
                    (C-H))
        6
        (*DET+NOUN (did Mary give John the book)
                    (VI SH SH S-H)
                    (?)
                    (INTERROG V))
        7)))
```

C.8.8 Did Mary give the book to John?

```
(R did Mary give the book to John ?)
((*CMPLT ((did Mary give the book to John ?)
        (INTERROG)
        1
        (*START (did)
                (V N DO)
                (Mary)
                (SH))
        2
        (*FVERB+NOM (did Mary)
                    (VI DO SH)
                    (give)
                    (V NOM A TO))
        3
        (*ADD-VERB (did Mary give)
                    (VI A TO SH)
                    (the)
                    (U))
        4
        (*FVERB+MAIN (did Mary give the)
                    (VI U TO SH)
                    (book)
                    (C-H))
        5
        (*DET+NOUN (did Mary give the book)
                    (VI TO SH S-H)
                    (to)
                    (TO NP))
        6
        (*FVERB+MAIN (did Mary give the book to)
                    (VI NP SH S-H)
                    (John)
                    (SH))
        7
        (*PREP+NP (did Mary give the book to John)
                    (VI SH S-H SH)
                    (?)
                    (INTERROG V))
        8)))
```

C.8.9 *Has Mary given John the book?*

```
(R has Mary given John the book ?)
((*CMPLT ((has Mary given John the book ?)
         (INTERROG)
         1
         (*START (has)
                 (V S3 HV)
                 (Mary)
                 (SH))
         2
         (*FVERB+NOM (has Mary)
                     (VI HV SH)
                     (given)
                     (HV D A))
         3
         (*ADD-VERB (has Mary given)
                    (VI D A SH)
                    (John)
                    (SH))
         4
         (*FVERB+MAIN (has Mary given John)
                      (VI A SH SH)
                      (the)
                      (U))
         5
         (*FVERB+MAIN (has Mary given John the)
                      (VI U SH SH)
                      (book)
                      (C-H))
         6
         (*DET+NOUN (has Mary given John the book)
                    (VI SH SH S-H)
                    (?)
                    (INTERROG V))
         7)))
```

C.8.10 *Has Mary given the book to John?*

```
(R has Mary given the book to John ?)
((*CMPLT ((has Mary given the book to John ?)
         (INTERROG)
         1
         (*START (has)
                 (V S3 HV)
                 (Mary)
                 (SH))
         2
         (*FVERB+NOM (has Mary)
                     (VI HV SH)
                     (given)
                     (HV A TO))
         3
         (*ADD-VERB (has Mary given)
                    (VI A TO SH)
                    (the)
```

```
                    (U))
          4
          (*FVERB+MAIN (has Mary given the)
                      (VI U TO SH)
                      (book)
                      (C-H))
          5
          (*DET+NOUN (has Mary given the book)
                     (VI TO SH S-H)
                     (to)
                     (TO NP))
          6
          (*FVERB+MAIN (has Mary given the book to)
                      (VI NP SH S-H)
                      (John)
                      (SH))
          7
          (*PREP+NP (has Mary given the book to John)
                    (VI SH S-H SH)
                    (?)
                    (INTERROG V))
          8)))
```

C.8.11 *Did Mary read the book?*

```
(R did Mary read the book ?)
((*CMPLT ((did Mary read the book ?)
         (INTERROG)
         1
         (*START (did)
                 (V N DO)
                 (Mary)
                 (SH))
         2
         (*FVERB+NOM (did Mary)
                     (VI DO SH)
                     (read)
                     (V NOM A))
         3
         (*ADD-VERB (did Mary read)
                    (VI A SH)
                    (the)
                    (U))
         4
         (*FVERB+MAIN (did Mary read the)
                     (VI U SH)
                     (book)
                     (C-H))
         5
         (*DET+NOUN (did Mary read the book)
                    (VI SH S-H)
                    (?)
                    (INTERROG V))
         6)))
```

C.8.12 *Has Mary read the book?*

```
(R has Mary read the book ?)
((*CMPLT ((has Mary read the book ?)
         (INTERROG)
         1
         (*START (has)
                 (V S3 HV)
                 (Mary)
                 (SH))
         2
         (*FVERB+NOM (has Mary)
                 (VI HV SH)
                 (read)
                 (HV A))
         3
         (*ADD-VERB (has Mary read)
                 (VI A SH)
                 (the)
                 (U))
         4
         (*FVERB+MAIN (has Mary read the)
                 (VI U SH)
                 (book)
                 (C-H))
         5
         (*DET+NOUN (has Mary read the book)
                 (VI SH S-H)
                 (?)
                 (INTERROG V))
         6)))
```

C.8.13 *Could Mary have read the book?*

```
(R could Mary have read the book ?)
((*CMPLT ((could Mary have read the book ?)
         (INTERROG)
         1
         (*START (could)
                 (V N M)
                 (Mary)
                 (SH))
         2
         (*FVERB+NOM (could Mary)
                 (VI M SH)
                 (have)
                 (V NOM HV))
         3
         (*ADD-VERB (could Mary have)
                 (VI HV SH)
                 (read)
                 (HV A))
         4
         (*ADD-VERB (could Mary have read)
                 (VI A SH)
                 (the)
                 (U))
         5
```

```
            (*FVERB+MAIN (could Mary have read the)
                         (VI U SH)
                         (book)
                         (C-H))
         6
         (*DET+NOUN (could Mary have read the book)
                    (VI SH S-H)
                    (?)
                    (INTERROG V))
         7)))
```

C.8.14 *Was Mary reading a book?*

```
(R was Mary reading a book ?)
((*CMPLT ((was Mary reading a book ?)
         (INTERROG)
         1
         (*START (was)
                 (V S1 B)
                 (Mary)
                 (SH))
         2
         (*FVERB+NOM (was Mary)
                     (VI B SH)
                     (reading)
                     (B A))
         3
         (*ADD-VERB (was Mary reading)
                    (VI A SH)
                    (a)
                    (C))
         4
         (*FVERB+MAIN (was Mary reading a)
                      (VI C SH)
                      (book)
                      (C-H))
         5
         (*DET+NOUN (was Mary reading a book)
                    (VI SH S-H)
                    (?)
                    (INTERROG V))
         6)))
```

C.9 Wh–interrogatives

C.9.1 *Who does Mary love?*

```
(R who does Mary love ?)
((*CMPLT ((who does Mary love ?)
         (INTERROG)
         1
         (*START (who)
                 (WH)
                 (does)
```

```
                          (V S3 DO))
              2
              (*TOP-MAIN (who does)
                          (VI S3 DO WH)
                          (Mary)
                          (SH))
              3
              (*FVERB+NOM (who does Mary)
                          (VI DO WH SH)
                          (love)
                          (V NOM A))
              4
              (*ADD-VERB (who does Mary love)
                          (VI SH)
                          (?)
                          (INTERROG V))
              5)))
```

C.9.2 *Who doesn't love Mary?*

```
(R who doesn't love Mary ?)
((*CMPLT ((who doesn't love Mary ?)
          (INTERROG)
          1
          (*START (who)
                  (WH)
                  (doesn't)
                  (V S3 DO))
          2
          (*NOM+FVERB (who doesn't)
                      (VI DO)
                      (love)
                      (V NOM A))
          3
          (*ADD-VERB (who doesn't love)
                      (VI A)
                      (Mary)
                      (SH))
          4
          (*FVERB+MAIN (who doesn't love Mary)
                       (VI SH)
                       (?)
                       (INTERROG V))
          5)))
```

C.9.3 *Who loves Mary?*

```
(R who loves Mary ?)
((*CMPLT ((who loves Mary ?)
          (INTERROG)
          1
          (*START (who)
                  (WH)
                  (loves)
                  (V S3 A))
```

```
        2
        (*NOM+FVERB (who loves)
                    (VI A)
                    (Mary)
                    (SH))
        3
        (*FVERB+MAIN (who loves Mary)
                     (VI SH)
                     (?)
                     (INTERROG V))
        4)))
```

C.9.4 *Whom doesn't Mary love?*

```
(R whom doesn't Mary love ?)
((*CMPLT ((whom doesn't Mary love ?)
         (INTERROG)
         1
         (*START (whom)
                 (:WH)
                 (doesn't)
                 (V S3 DO))
         2
         (*TOP-MAIN (whom doesn't)
                    (VI S3 DO :WH)
                    (Mary)
                    (SH))
         3
         (*FVERB+NOM (whom doesn't Mary)
                     (VI DO :WH SH)
                     (love)
                     (V NOM A))
         4
         (*ADD-VERB (whom doesn't Mary love)
                    (VI SH)
                    (?)
                    (INTERROG V))
         5)))
```

C.9.5 **Whom loves Mary?*

```
(R whom loves Mary ?)
[ERROR "Ungrammatical continuation at:" ((*START ((whom)
                                                  (:WH)))
       (*START ((loves)
                (P-H]
```

C.9.6 *Mary said what?*

```
(R Mary said what ?)
((*CMPLT ((Mary said what ?)
         (INTERROG)
         1
         (*START (Mary)
                 (SH)
```

```
                        (said)
                        (V ■ A))
            2
            (*NOM+FVERB (Mary said)
                        (V A)
                        (what)
                        (W-H))
            3
            (*FVERB+MAIN (Mary said what)
                        (VI)
                        (?)
                        (INTERROG V))
            4)))
```

C.9.7 *Mary said what.

```
(R Mary said what .)
[ERROR "Ungrammatical continuation at:" ((*FVERB+MAIN ((Mary said what)
                                              (VI)
                                              1
                                              (*START (Mary)
                                                      (SH)
                                                      (said)
                                                      (V ■ A))
                                              2
                                              (*NOM+FVERB
                                                (Mary said)
                                                (V A)
                                                (what)
                                                (W-H))
                                              3))
```

```
            (*START ((%.)
                     (DECL V]
```

C.9.8 Who gave what to whom?

```
(R who gave what to whom ?)
((*CMPLT ((who gave what to whom ?)
         (INTERROG)
         1
         (*START (who)
                 (WH)
                 (gave)
                 (V ■ A TO))
         2
         (*NOM+FVERB (who gave)
                     (VI A TO)
                     (what)
                     (W-H))
         3
         (*FVERB+MAIN (who gave what)
                     (VI TO)
                     (to)
                     (TO NP))
         4
         (*FVERB+MAIN (who gave what to)
```

```
                        (VI NP)
                        (whom)
                        (:WH))
             5
             (*PREP+NP (who gave what to whom)
                        (VI)
                        (?)
                        (INTERROG V))
             6)))
```

C.9.9 *Who did Mary give a book?*

```
(R who did Mary give a book ?)
((*CMPLT ((who did Mary give a book ?)
          (INTERROG)
          1
          (*START (who)
                  (WH)
                  (did)
                  (V N DO))
          2
          (*TOP-MAIN (who did)
                     (VI N DO WH)
                     (Mary)
                     (SH))
          3
          (*FVERB+NOM (who did Mary)
                      (VI DO WH SH)
                      (give)
                      (V NOM D A))
          4
          (*ADD-VERB (who did Mary give)
                     (VI A SH)
                     (a)
                     (C))
          5
          (*FVERB+MAIN (who did Mary give a)
                       (VI C SH)
                       (book)
                       (C-H))
          6
          (*DET+NOUN (who did Mary give a book)
                     (VI SH S-H)
                     (?)
                     (INTERROG V))
          7)))
```

C.9.10 *Whom did Mary give a book?*

```
(R whom did Mary give a book ?)
((*CMPLT ((whom did Mary give a book ?)
          (INTERROG)
          1
          (*START (whom)
                  (:WH)
                  (did)
```

```
                         (V I DO))
            2
            (*TOP-MAIN (whom did)
                       (VI I DO :WH)
                       (Mary)
                       (SH))
            3
            (*FVERB+NOM (whom did Mary)
                        (VI DO :WH SH)
                        (give)
                        (V NOM D A))
            4
            (*ADD-VERB (whom did Mary give)
                       (VI A SH)
                       (a)
                       (C))
            5
            (*FVERB+MAIN (whom did Mary give a)
                         (VI C SH)
                         (book)
                         (C-H))
            6
            (*DET+NOUN (whom did Mary give a book)
                       (VI SH S-H)
                       (?)
                       (INTERROG V))
            7)))
```

C.9.11 *Who did Mary give a book to?*

```
(R who did Mary give a book to ?)
((*CMPLT ((who did Mary give a book to ?)
          (INTERROG)
          1
          (*START (who)
                  (WH)
                  (did)
                  (V I DO))
          2
          (*TOP-MAIN (who did)
                     (VI I DO WH)
                     (Mary)
                     (SH))
          3
          (*FVERB+NOM (who did Mary)
                      (VI DO WH SH)
                      (give)
                      (V NOM A TO))
          4
          (*WH+VERB (who did Mary give)
                    (VI A TO WH SH)
                    (a)
                    (C))
          5
          (*FVERB+MAIN (who did Mary give a)
                       (VI C TO WH SH)
```

```
                         (book)
                         (C-H))
            6
            (*DET+NOUN (who did Mary give a book)
                       (VI TO WH SH S-H)
                       (to)
                       (TO NP))
            7
            (*FVERB+MAIN (who did Mary give a book to)
                         (VI S-H)
                         (?)
                         (INTERROG V))
            8)))
```

C.9.12 Who did Mary give to John?

```
(R who did Mary give to John ?)
((*CMPLT ((who did Mary give to John ?)
          (INTERROG)
          1
          (*START (who)
                  (WH)
                  (did)
                  (V N DO))
          2
          (*TOP-MAIN (who did)
                     (VI N DO WH)
                     (Mary)
                     (SH))
          3
          (*FVERB+NOM (who did Mary)
                      (VI DO WH SH)
                      (give)
                      (V NOM A TO))
          4
          (*ADD-VERB (who did Mary give)
                     (VI TO SH)
                     (to)
                     (TO NP))
          5
          (*FVERB+MAIN (who did Mary give to)
                       (VI NP SH)
                       (John)
                       (SH))
          6
          (*PREP+NP (who did Mary give to John)
                    (VI SH SH)
                    (?)
                    (INTERROG V))
          7)))
```

C.9.13 What did Mary say?

```
(R what did Mary say ?)
((*CMPLT ((what did Mary say ?)
          (INTERROG)
```

```
       1
       (*START (what)
               (W-H)
               (did)
               (V I DO))
       2
       (*TOP-MAIN (what did)
                  (VI I DO W-H)
                  (Mary)
                  (SH))
       3
       (*FVERB+NOM (what did Mary)
                   (VI DO W-H SH)
                   (say)
                   (V NOM A))
       4
       (*ADD-VERB (what did Mary say)
                  (VI SH)
                  (?)
                  (INTERROG V))
       5)))
```

C.9.14 *Who could Mary have seen?*

```
(R who could Mary have seen ?)
((*CMPLT ((who could Mary have seen ?)
          (INTERROG)
          1
          (*START (who)
                  (WH)
                  (could)
                  (V I M))
          2
          (*TOP-MAIN (who could)
                     (VI I M WH)
                     (Mary)
                     (SH))
          3
          (*FVERB+NOM (who could Mary)
                      (VI M WH SH)
                      (have)
                      (V NOM HV))
          4
          (*NOM+FVERB (who could Mary have)
                      (VI HV WH SH)
                      (seen)
                      (HV A))
          5
          (*ADD-VERB (who could Mary have seen)
                     (VI SH)
                     (?)
                     (INTERROG V))
          6)))
```

C.9.15 *Who could have seen Mary?*

```
(R who could have seen Mary ?)
((*CMPLT ((who could have seen Mary ?)
         (INTERROG)
         1
         (*START (who)
                 (WH)
                 (could)
                 (V N M))
         2
         (*NOM+FVERB (who could)
                     (VI M)
                     (have)
                     (V NOM HV))
         3
         (*ADD-VERB (who could have)
                    (VI HV)
                    (seen)
                    (HV A))
         4
         (*ADD-VERB (who could have seen)
                    (VI A)
                    (Mary)
                    (SH))
         5
         (*FVERB+MAIN (who could have seen Mary)
                      (VI SH)
                      (?)
                      (INTERROG V))
         6)))
```

C.9.16 *Who could Mary have given the book?*

```
(R who could Mary have given the book ?)
((*CMPLT ((who could Mary have given the book ?)
         (INTERROG)
         1
         (*START (who)
                 (WH)
                 (could)
                 (V N M))
         2
         (*TOP-MAIN (who could)
                    (VI N M WH)
                    (Mary)
                    (SH))
         3
         (*FVERB+NOM (who could Mary)
                     (VI M WH SH)
                     (have)
                     (V NOM HV))
         4
         (*NOM+FVERB (who could Mary have)
                     (VI HV WH SH)
                     (given)
                     (HV D A))
         5
```

```
(*ADD-VERB (who could Mary have given)
          (VI A SH)
          (the)
          (U))
6
(*FVERB+MAIN (who could Mary have given the)
             (VI U SH)
             (book)
             (C-H))
7
(*DET+NOUN (who could Mary have given the book)
           (VI SH S-H)
           (?)
           (INTERROG V))
8)))
```

C.9.17 *Who could Mary have given the book to?*

```
(R who could Mary have given the book to ?)
((*CMPLT ((who could Mary have given the book to ?)
          (INTERROG)
          1
          (*START (who)
                  (WH)
                  (could)
                  (V N M))
          2
          (*TOP-MAIN (who could)
                     (VI N M WH)
                     (Mary)
                     (SH))
          3
          (*FVERB+NOM (who could Mary)
                      (VI M WH SH)
                      (have)
                      (V NOM HV))
          4
          (*NOM+FVERB (who could Mary have)
                      (VI HV WH SH)
                      (given)
                      (HV A TO))
          5
          (*ADD-VERB (who could Mary have given)
                     (VI A TO WH SH)
                     (the)
                     (U))
          6
          (*FVERB+MAIN (who could Mary have given the)
                       (VI U TO WH SH)
                       (book)
                       (C-H))
          7
          (*DET+NOUN (who could Mary have given the book)
                     (VI TO WH SH S-H)
                     (to)
                     (TO NP))
```

```
8
(*FVERB+MAIN (who could Mary have given the book to)
            (VI S-H)
            (?)
            (INTERROG V))
9)))
```

C.10   The interrogative determiner *which*

C.10.1 *Which book did John read?*

```
(R which book did John read ?)
((*CMPLT ((which book did John read ?)
         (INTERROG)
         1
         (*START (which)
                 (WU)
                 (book)
                 (C-H))
         2
         (*DET+NOUN (which book)
                    (WS)
                    (did)
                    (V N DO))
         3
         (*TOP-MAIN (which book did)
                    (VI N DO WS)
                    (John)
                    (SH))
         4
         (*FVERB+NOM (which book did John)
                     (VI DO WS SH)
                     (read)
                     (V NOM A))
         5
         (*ADD-VERB (which book did John read)
                    (VI SH)
                    (?)
                    (INTERROG V))
         6)))
```

C.10.2 **Which book did John read.*

```
(R which book did John read .)
[ERROR "Ungrammatical continuation at:"
     ((*ADD-VERB ((which book did John read)
                  (VI SH)
                  1
                  (*START (which)
                          (WU)
                          (book)
                          (C-H))
                  2
                  (*DET+NOUN (which book)
```

```
                              (WS)
                              (did)
                              (V I DO))
                3
                (*TOP-MAIN (which book did)
                           (VI I DO WS)
                           (John)
                           (SH))
                4
                (*FVERB+NOM (which book did John)
                            (VI DO WS SH)
                            (read)
                            (V NOM A))
                    5))
        (*START ((%.)
                 (DECL V]
```

C.10.3 *John read which book?*

```
87_(R John read which book ?)
((*CMPLT ((John read which book ?)
         (INTERROG)
         1
         (*START (John)
                 (SH)
                 (read)
                 (V I A))
         2
         (*NOM+FVERB (John read)
                     (V A)
                     (which)
                     (WU))
         3
         (*FVERB+MAIN (John read which)
                      (VI U)
                      (book)
                      (C-H))
         4
         (*DET+NOUN (John read which book)
                    (VI S-H)
                    (?)
                    (INTERROG V))
             5)))
```

C.10.4 **John read which book.*

```
(R John read which book .)
[ERROR "Ungrammatical continuation at:" ((*DET+NOUN ((John read which book)
                                                     (VI S-H)
                                                     1
                                                     (*START (John)
                                                             (SH)
                                                             (read)
                                                             (V I A))
                                                     2
                                                     (*NOM+FVERB
```

```
                                             (John read)
                                             (V A)
                                             (which)
                                             (WU))
                                          3
                                          (*FVERB+MAIN
                                             (John read which)
                                             (VI U)
                                             (book)
                                             (C-H))
                                          4))
          (*START ((%.)
                   (DECL V]
```

C.11   *That*-clauses

C.11.1 *Mary says that John loves Susi.*

```
(R Mary says that John loves Susi .)
((*CMPLT ((Mary says that John loves Susi %.)
          (DECL)
          1
          (*START (Mary)
                  (SH)
                  (says)
                  (V S3 A))
          2
          (*NOM+FVERB (Mary says)
                      (V A)
                      (that)
                      (SC))
          3
          (*START-SUBCL (Mary says that)
                        (V SC)
                        (John)
                        (SH))
          4
          (*ADD-NOM (Mary says that John)
                    (V SC SH *)
                    (loves)
                    (V S3 A))
          5
          (*NOM+FVERB (Mary says that John loves)
                      (V A)
                      (Susi)
                      (SH))
          6
          (*FVERB+MAIN (Mary says that John loves Susi)
                       (V SH)
                       (%.)
                       (DECL V))
          7)))
```

C.11.2 *Mary believes that John said that Susi was reading a book.*

```
(R Mary believes that John said that Susi was reading a book .)
((*CMPLT ((Mary believes that John said that Susi was reading a book %.)
         (DECL)
         1
         (*START (Mary)
                 (SH)
                 (believes)
                 (V S3 A))
         2
         (*NOM+FVERB (Mary believes)
                 (V A)
                 (that)
                 (SC))
         3
         (*START-SUBCL (Mary believes that)
                 (V SC)
                 (John)
                 (SH))
         4
         (*ADD-NOM (Mary believes that John)
                 (V SC SH *)
                 (said)
                 (V N A))
         5
         (*NOM+FVERB (Mary believes that John said)
                 (V A)
                 (that)
                 (SC))
         6
         (*START-SUBCL (Mary believes that John said that)
                 (V SC)
                 (Susi)
                 (SH))
         7
         (*ADD-NOM (Mary believes that John said that Susi)
                 (V SC SH *)
                 (was)
                 (V S3 B))
         8
         (*NOM+FVERB (Mary believes that John said that Susi was)
                 (V B)
                 (reading)
                 (B A))
         9
         (*ADD-VERB (Mary believes that John said that Susi was reading)
                 (V A)
                 (a)
                 (C))
         10
         (*FVERB+MAIN (Mary believes that John said that Susi was reading a)
                 (V C)
                 (book)
                 (C-H))
         11
         (*DET+NOUN (Mary believes that John said that Susi was reading a
```

```
                             book)
                  (V S-H)
                  (%.)
                  (DECL V))
       12)))
```

C.11.3 *Mary believes John said Susi was reading a book.*

```
(R Mary believes John said Susi was reading a book %.)
((*CMPLT ((Mary believes John said Susi was reading a book %.)
         (DECL)
         1
         (*START (Mary)
                 (SH)
                 (believes)
                 (V S3 A))
         2
         (*NOM+FVERB (Mary believes)
                     (V A)
                     (John)
                     (SH))
         3
         (*START-SUBCL (Mary believes John)
                       (V SC SH *)
                       (said)
                       (V N A))
         4
         (*NOM+FVERB (Mary believes John said)
                     (V A)
                     (Susi)
                     (SH))
         5
         (*START-SUBCL (Mary believes John said Susi)
                       (V SC SH *)
                       (was)
                       (V S3 B))
         6
         (*NOM+FVERB (Mary believes John said Susi was)
                     (V B)
                     (reading)
                     (B A))
         7
         (*ADD-VERB (Mary believes John said Susi was reading)
                    (V A)
                    (a)
                    (C))
         8
         (*FVERB+MAIN (Mary believes John said Susi was reading a)
                      (V C)
                      (book)
                      (C-H))
         9
         (*DET+NOUN (Mary believes John said Susi was reading a book)
                    (V S-H)
                    (%.)
                    (DECL V))
```

```
     10)))
```

C.12   Wh-interrogatives with *that*-clauses

C.12.1 *Who does Mary say that John loves?*

```
(R who does Mary say that John loves ?)
((*CMPLT ((who does Mary say that John loves ?)
         (INTERROG)
         1
         (*START (who)
                 (WH)
                 (does)
                 (V S3 DO))
         2
         (*TOP-MAIN (who does)
                 (VI S3 DO WH)
                 (Mary)
                 (SH))
         3
         (*FVERB+NOM (who does Mary)
                 (VI DO WH SH)
                 (say)
                 (V NOM A))
         4
         (*WH+VERB (who does Mary say)
                 (VI A WH SH)
                 (that)
                 (SC))
         5
         (*START-SUBCL (who does Mary say that)
                 (VI SC WH SH)
                 (John)
                 (SH))
         6
         (*ADD-NOM (who does Mary say that John)
                 (VI SC SH # WH SH)
                 (loves)
                 (V S3 A))
         7
         (*NOM+FVERB (who does Mary say that John loves)
                 (VI SH)
                 (?)
                 (INTERROG V))
         8)))
```

C.12.2 **Who says Mary that John loves?*

```
(R who says Mary that John loves ?)
[ERROR "Ungrammatical continuation at:" ((*FVERB+MAIN ((who says Mary)
                                                       (VI SH)
                                                       1
                                                       (*START (who)
                                                               (WH)
```

```
                                                        (says)
                                                        (V S3 A))
                                                2
                                               (*NOM+FVERB
                                                (who says)
                                                (VI A)
                                                (Mary)
                                                (SH))
                                              3))
            (*START ((that)
                     (SC]
```

C.12.3 *Who says that Mary loves John?*

```
(R who says that Mary loves John ?)
((*CMPLT ((who says that Mary loves John ?)
         (INTERROG)
         1
         (*START (who)
                 (WH)
                 (says)
                 (V S3 A))
         2
         (*NOM+FVERB (who says)
                     (VI A)
                     (that)
                     (SC))
         3
         (*START-SUBCL (who says that)
                       (VI SC)
                       (Mary)
                       (SH))
         4
         (*ADD-NOM (who says that Mary)
                   (VI SC SH #)
                   (loves)
                   (V S3 A))
         5
         (*NOM+FVERB (who says that Mary loves)
                     (VI A)
                     (John)
                     (SH))
         6
         (*FVERB+MAIN (who says that Mary loves John)
                      (VI SH)
                      (?)
                      (INTERROG V))
         7)))
```

C.12.4 *Who says Mary loves John?*

```
(R who says Mary loves John ?)
((*CMPLT ((who says Mary loves John ?)
         (INTERROG)
         1
         (*START (who)
```

```
                    (WH)
                    (says)
                    (V S3 A))
         2
         (*NOM+FVERB (who says)
                    (VI A)
                    (Mary)
                    (SH))
         3
         (*START-SUBCL (who says Mary)
                    (VI SC SH #)
                    (loves)
                    (V S3 A))
         4
         (*NOM+FVERB (who says Mary loves)
                    (VI A)
                    (John)
                    (SH))
         5
         (*FVERB+MAIN (who says Mary loves John)
                    (VI SH)
                    (?)
                    (INTERROG V))
         6)))
```

C.12.5 *Who did Mary say that John doesn't like?*

```
(R who did Mary say that John doesn't like ?)
((*CMPLT ((who did Mary say that John doesn't like ?)
         (INTERROG)
         1
         (*START (who)
                    (WH)
                    (did)
                    (V N DO))
         2
         (*TOP-MAIN (who did)
                    (VI N DO WH)
                    (Mary)
                    (SH))
         3
         (*FVERB+NOM (who did Mary)
                    (VI DO WH SH)
                    (say)
                    (V NOM A))
         4
         (*WH+VERB (who did Mary say)
                    (VI A WH SH)
                    (that)
                    (SC))
         5
         (*START-SUBCL (who did Mary say that)
                    (VI SC WH SH)
                    (John)
                    (SH))
         6
```

```
        (*ADD-NOM (who did Mary say that John)
                (VI SC SH # WH SH)
                (doesn't)
                (V S3 DO))
        7
        (*NOM+FVERB (who did Mary say that John doesn't)
                (VI DO WH SH)
                (like)
                (V NOM A))
        8
        (*ADD-VERB (who did Mary say that John doesn't like)
                (VI SH)
                (?)
                (INTERROG V))
        9)))
```

C.12.6 *Who says Mary that Bill believes that John loves?

```
(R who says Mary  that Bill believes that John loves ?)
[ERROR "Ungrammatical continuation at:" ((*FVERB+MAIN ((who says Mary)
                                                (VI SH)
                                                1
                                                (*START (who)
                                                        (WH)
                                                        (says)
                                                        (V S3 A))
                                                2
                                                (*NOM+FVERB
                                                 (who says)
                                                 (VI A)
                                                 (Mary)
                                                 (SH))
                                                3))
        (*START ((that)
                (SC]
```

C.12.7 Who does Mary say that Bill believes that John loves?

```
(R who does Mary say that Bill believes that John loves ?)
((*CMPLT ((who does Mary say that Bill believes that John loves ?)
        (INTERROG)
        1
        (*START (who)
                (WH)
                (does)
                (V S3 DO))
        2
        (*TOP-MAIN (who does)
                (VI S3 DO WH)
                (Mary)
                (SH))
        3
        (*FVERB+NOM (who does Mary)
                (VI DO WH SH)
                (say)
                (V NOM A))
```

```
4
(*WH+VERB (who does Mary say)
         (VI A WH SH)
         (that)
         (SC))
5
(*START-SUBCL (who does Mary say that)
              (VI SC WH SH)
              (Bill)
              (SH))
6
(*ADD-NOM (who does Mary say that Bill)
          (VI SC SH # WH SH)
          (believes)
          (V S3 A))
7
(*WH+VERB (who does Mary say that Bill believes)
          (VI A # WH SH)
          (that)
          (SC))
8
(*START-SUBCL (who does Mary say that Bill believes that)
              (VI SC # WH SH)
              (John)
              (SH))
9
(*ADD-NOM (who does Mary say that Bill believes that John)
          (VI SC SH # # WH SH)
          (loves)
          (V S3 A))
10
(*NOM+FVERB (who does Mary say that Bill believes that John loves)
            (VI SH)
            (?)
            (INTERROG V))
11)))
```

C.13   Passives in subordinate clauses

C.13.1 *Mary says that John was given a book by Susi.*

```
(R Mary says that John was given a book by Susi %.)
((*CMPLT ((Mary says that John was given a book by Susi %.)
         (DECL)
         1
         (*START (Mary)
                 (SH)
                 (says)
                 (V S3 A))
         2
         (*NOM+FVERB (Mary says)
                     (V A)
                     (that)
                     (SC))
```

```
            3
            (*START-SUBCL (Mary says that)
                       (V SC)
                       (John)
                       (SH))
            4
            (*ADD NOM (Mary says that John)
                       (V SC SH #)
                       (was)
                       (V S3 B))
            5
            (*NOM+FVERB (Mary says that John was)
                       (V B)
                       (given)
                       (HV D A))
            6
            (*ADD-VERB (Mary says that John was given)
                       (V A AG)
                       (a)
                       (C))
            7
            (*FVERB+MAIN (Mary says that John was given a)
                       (V C AG)
                       (book)
                       (C-H))
            8
            (*DET+NOUN (Mary says that John was given a book)
                       (V AG S-H)
                       (by)
                       (AG NP))
            9
            (*FVERB+MAIN (Mary says that John was given a book by)
                       (V NP S-H)
                       (Susi)
                       (SH))
            10
            (*PREP+NP (Mary says that John was given a book by Susi)
                       (V S-H SH)
                       (%.)
                       (DECL V))
            11))
(*CMPLT ((Mary says that John was given a book by Susi %.)
         (DECL)
         1
         (*START (Mary)
                (SH)
                (says)
                (V S3 A))
         2
         (*NOM+FVERB (Mary says)
                (V A)
                (that)
                (SC))
         3
         (*START-SUBCL (Mary says that)
```

```
                      (V SC)
                      (John)
                      (SH))
         4
         (*ADD-NOM (Mary says that John)
                   (V SC SH #)
                   (was)
                   (V S3 B))
         5
         (*NOM+FVERB (Mary says that John was)
                   (V B)
                   (given)
                   (HV D A))
         6
         (*ADD-VERB (Mary says that John was given)
                   (V A AG)
                   (a)
                   (C))
         7
         (*FVERB+MAIN (Mary says that John was given a)
                   (V C AG)
                   (book)
                   (C-H))
         8
         (*DET+NOUN (Mary says that John was given a book)
                   (V AG S-H)
                   (by)
                   (PNM NP))
         9
         (*NOUN+PNM (Mary says that John was given a book by)
                   (V NP AG)
                   (Susi)
                   (SH))
         10
         (*PREP+NP (Mary says that John was given a book by Susi)
                   (V AG SH)
                   (%.)
                   (DECL V))
         11)))
```

C.13.2 *The man who was given a book by Mary is intelligent.*

```
(R the man who was given a book by Mary is intelligent %.)
((*CMPLT ((the man who was given a book by Mary is intelligent %.)
         (DECL)
         1
         (*START (the)
                 (U)
                 (man)
                 (CH))
         2
         (*DET+NOUN (the man)
                   (SH)
                   (who)
                   (WH))
         3
```

```
          (*START-RELCL (the man who)
                    (SH WS #)
                    (was)
                    (V S3 B))
          4
          (*NOM+FVERB (the man who was)
                    (SH B)
                    (given)
                    (HV D A))
          5
          (*ADD-VERB (the man who was given)
                    (SH A AG)
                    (a)
                    (C))
          6
          (*FVERB+MAIN (the man who was given a)
                    (SH C AG)
                    (book)
                    (C-H))
          7
          (*DET+NOUN (the man who was given a book)
                    (SH AG S-H)
                    (by)
                    (AG NP))
          8
          (*FVERB+MAIN (the man who was given a book by)
                    (SH NP S-H)
                    (Mary)
                    (SH))
          9
          (*PREP+NP (the man who was given a book by Mary)
                    (SH S-H SH)
                    (is)
                    (V S3 B))
          10
          (*NOM+FVERB (the man who was given a book by Mary is)
                    (V B)
                    (intelligent)
                    (-CA))
          11
          (*ADD-VERB (the man who was given a book by Mary is
                         intelligent)
                    (V)
                    (%.)
                    (DECL V))
          12))
(*CMPLT ((the man who was given a book by Mary is intelligent %.)
          (DECL)
          1
          (*START (the)
                  (U)
                  (man)
                  (CH))
          2
          (*DET+NOUN (the man)
```

```
                    (SH)
                    (who)
                    (WH))
       3
       (*START-RELCL (the man who)
                    (SH WS *)
                    (was)
                    (V S3 B))
       4
       (*NOM+FVERB (the man who was)
                    (SH B)
                    (given)
                    (HV D A))
       5
       (*ADD-VERB (the man who was given)
                    (SH A AG)
                    (a)
                    (C))
       6
       (*FVERB+MAIN (the man who was given a)
                    (SH C AG)
                    (book)
                    (C-H))
       7
       (*DET+NOUN (the man who was given a book)
                    (SH AG S-H)
                    (by)
                    (PNM NP))
       8
       (*NOUN+PNM (the man who was given a book by)
                    (SH NP AG)
                    (Mary)
                    (SH))
       9
       (*PREP+NP (the man who was given a book by Mary)
                    (SH AG SH)
                    (is)
                    (V S3 B))
       10
       (*NOM+FVERB (the man who was given a book by Mary is)
                    (V B)
                    (intelligent)
                    (-CA))
       11
       (*ADD-VERB (the man who was given a book by Mary is
                        intelligent)
                    (V)
                    (%.)
                    (DECL V))
        12)))
```

C.14 Relative clauses modifying sentence final noun phrases

C.14.1 *I know the man who loves Mary.*

```
(R I know the man who loves Mary .)
((*CMPLT ((I know the man who loves Mary %.)
         (DECL)
         1
         (*START (I)
                 (S1)
                 (know)
                 (V I A))
         2
         (*NOM+FVERB (I know)
                     (V A)
                     (the)
                     (U))
         3
         (*FVERB+MAIN (I know the)
                      (V U)
                      (man)
                      (CH))
         4
         (*DET+NOUN (I know the man)
                    (V SH)
                    (who)
                    (WH))
         5
         (*START-RELCL (I know the man who)
                       (V WS *)
                       (loves)
                       (V S3 A))
         6
         (*NOM+FVERB (I know the man who loves)
                     (V A)
                     (Mary)
                     (SH))
         7
         (*FVERB+MAIN (I know the man who loves Mary)
                      (V SH)
                      (%.)
                      (DECL V))
         8)))
```

C.14.2 *I know the man who has read the book.*

```
(R I know the man who has read the book .)
((*CMPLT ((I know the man who has read the book %.)
         (DECL)
         1
         (*START (I)
                 (S1)
                 (know)
                 (V I A))
```

```
      2
      (*NOM+FVERB (I know)
                 (V A)
                 (the)
                 (U))
      3
      (*FVERB+MAIN (I know the)
                 (V U)
                 (man)
                 (CH))
      4
      (*DET+NOUN (I know the man)
                 (V SH)
                 (who)
                 (WH))
      5
      (*START-RELCL (I know the man who)
                 (V WS #)
                 (has)
                 (V S3 HV))
      6
      (*NOM+FVERB (I know the man who has)
                 (V HV)
                 (read)
                 (HV A))
      7
      (*ADD-VERB (I know the man who has read)
                 (V A)
                 (the)
                 (U))
      8
      (*FVERB+MAIN (I know the man who has read the)
                 (V U)
                 (book)
                 (C-H))
      9
      (*DET+NOUN (I know the man who has read the book)
                 (V S-H)
                 (%.)
                 (DECL V))
      10)))
```

C.14.3 *I know the man who will be reading the book.*

```
(R I know the man who will be reading the book %.)
((*CMPLT ((I know the man who will be reading the book %.)
         (DECL)
      1
      (*START (I)
              (S1)
              (know)
              (V N A))
      2
      (*NOM+FVERB (I know)
                 (V A)
                 (the)
```

```
                  (U))
        3
        (*FVERB+MAIN (I know the)
                     (V U)
                     (man)
                     (CH))
        4
        (*DET+NOUN (I know the man)
                    (V SH)
                    (who)
                    (WH))
        5
        (*START-RELCL (I know the man who)
                       (V WS #)
                       (will)
                       (V N M))
        6
        (*NOM+FVERB (I know the man who will)
                     (V M)
                     (be)
                     (M B))
        7
        (*ADD-VERB (I know the man who will be)
                    (V B)
                    (reading)
                    (B A))
        8
        (*ADD-VERB (I know the man who will be reading)
                    (V A)
                    (the)
                    (U))
        9
        (*FVERB+MAIN (I know the man who will be reading the)
                     (V U)
                     (book)
                     (C-H))
        10
        (*DET+NOUN (I know the man who will be reading the book)
                    (V S-H)
                    (%.)
                    (DECL V))
        11)))
```

C.14.4 *I have the book which Mary didn't read.*

```
(R I have the book which Mary didn't read .)
((*CMPLT ((I have the book which Mary didn't read %.)
         (DECL)
         1
         (*START (I)
                 (S1)
                 (have)
                 (V NOM HV))
         2
         (*NOM+FVERB (I have)
                     (V HV)
```

```
                        (the)
                        (U))
        3
        (*FVERB+MAIN (I have the)
                        (V U)
                        (book)
                        (C-H))
        4
        (*DET+NOUN (I have the book)
                        (V S-H)
                        (which)
                        (W-H))
        5
        (*START-RELCL (I have the book which)
                          (V WS *)
                          (Mary)
                          (SH))
        6
        (*ADD-NOM (I have the book which Mary)
                        (V WS SH *)
                        (didn't)
                        (V N DO))
        7
        (*NOM+FVERB (I have the book which Mary didn't)
                          (V DO WS)
                          (read)
                          (V NOM A))
        8
        (*ADD-VERB (I have the book which Mary didn't read)
                          (V)
                          (%.)
                          (DECL V))
        9)))
```

C.14.5 *I have the book which Mary didn't give to John.*

```
(R I have the book which Mary didn't give to John .)
((*CMPLT ((I have the book which Mary didn't give to John %.)
          (DECL)
          1
          (*START (I)
                    (S1)
                    (have)
                    (V NOM HV))
          2
          (*NOM+FVERB (I have)
                          (V HV)
                          (the)
                          (U))
          3
          (*FVERB+MAIN (I have the)
                          (V U)
                          (book)
                          (C-H))
          4
          (*DET+NOUN (I have the book)
```

```
                   (V S-H)
                   (which)
                   (W-H))
        5
     (*START-RELCL (I have the book which)
                   (V WS #)
                   (Mary)
                   (SH))
        6
     (*ADD-NOM (I have the book which Mary)
                   (V WS SH #)
                   (didn't)
                   (V N DO))
        7
     (*NOM+FVERB (I have the book which Mary didn't)
                   (V DO WS)
                   (give)
                   (V NOM A TO))
        8
     (*ADD-VERB (I have the book which Mary didn't give)
                   (V TO)
                   (to)
                   (TO NP))
        9
     (*FVERB+MAIN (I have the book which Mary didn't give to)
                   (V NP)
                   (John)
                   (SH))
        10
     (*PREP+NP (I have the book which Mary didn't give to John)
                   (V SH)
                   (%.)
                   (DECL V))
        11)))
```

C.14.6 *I have the book that Mary didn't give to John.*

```
(R I have the book that Mary didn't give to John %.)
((*CMPLT ((I have the book that Mary didn't give to John %.)
          (DECL)
          1
     (*START (I)
             (S1)
             (have)
             (V NOM HV))
          2
     (*NOM+FVERB (I have)
             (V HV)
             (the)
             (U))
          3
     (*FVERB+MAIN (I have the)
             (V U)
             (book)
             (C-H))
          4
```

```
(*DET+NOUN (I have the book)
          (V S-H)
          (that)
          (SC))
5
(*START-RELCL (I have the book that)
             (V WS *)
             (Mary)
             (SH))
6
(*ADD-NOM (I have the book that Mary)
          (V WS SH *)
          (didn't)
          (V N DO))
7
(*NOM+FVERB (I have the book that Mary didn't)
            (V DO WS)
            (give)
            (V NOM A TO))
8
(*ADD-VERB (I have the book that Mary didn't give)
           (V TO)
           (to)
           (TO NP))
9
(*FVERB+MAIN (I have the book that Mary didn't give to)
             (V NP)
             (John)
             (SH))
10
(*PREP+NP (I have the book that Mary didn't give to John)
          (V SH)
          (%.)
          (DECL V))
11)))
```

C.14.7 *I have the book which Mary didn't give John.*

```
(R I have the book which Mary didn't give John %.)
((*CMPLT ((I have the book which Mary didn't give John %.)
         (DECL)
         1
         (*START (I)
                 (S1)
                 (have)
                 (V NOM HV))
         2
         (*NOM+FVERB (I have)
                     (V HV)
                     (the)
                     (U))
         3
         (*FVERB+MAIN (I have the)
                      (V U)
                      (book)
                      (C-H))
```

```
4
(*DET+NOUN (I have the book)
          (V S-H)
          (which)
          (W-H))
5
(*START-RELCL (I have the book which)
              (V WS *)
              (Mary)
              (SH))
6
(*ADD-NOM (I have the book which Mary)
          (V WS SH *)
          (didn't)
          (V N DO))
7
(*NOM+FVERB (I have the book which Mary didn't)
            (V DO WS)
            (give)
            (V NOM D A))
8
(*ADD-VERB (I have the book which Mary didn't give)
           (V A)
           (John)
           (SH))
9
(*FVERB+MAIN (I have the book which Mary didn't give John)
             (V SH)
             (%.)
             (DECL V))
10)))
```

C.14.8 *I have the book that Mary didn't give John.*

```
(R I have the book that Mary didn't give John %.)
((*CMPLT ((I have the book that Mary didn't give John %.)
         (DECL)
1
(*START (I)
        (S1)
        (have)
        (V NOM HV))
2
(*NOM+FVERB (I have)
            (V HV)
            (the)
            (U))
3
(*FVERB+MAIN (I have the)
             (V U)
             (book)
             (C-H))
4
(*DET+NOUN (I have the book)
           (V S-H)
           (that)
```

```
                    (SC))
         5
         (*START-RELCL (I have the book that)
                       (V WS #)
                       (Mary)
                       (SH))
         6
         (*ADD-NOM (I have the book that Mary)
                   (V WS SH #)
                   (didn't)
                   (V I DO))
         7
         (*NOM+FVERB (I have the book that Mary didn't)
                     (V DO WS)
                     (give)
                     (V NOM D A))
         8
         (*ADD-VERB (I have the book that Mary didn't give)
                    (V A)
                    (John)
                    (SH))
         9
         (*FVERB+MAIN (I have the book that Mary didn't give John)
                      (V SH)
                      (%.)
                      (DECL V))
      10)))
```

C.15   Relative clauses modifying mid-sentence noun phrases

C.15.1 *John gave the girl who read the book a cookie.*

```
(R John gave the girl who read the book a cookie .)
((*CMPLT ((John gave the girl who read the book a cookie %.)
         (DECL)
         1
         (*START (John)
                 (SH)
                 (gave)
                 (V I D A))
         2
         (*NOM+FVERB (John gave)
                     (V D A)
                     (the)
                     (U))
         3
         (*FVERB+MAIN (John gave the)
                      (V U A)
                      (girl)
                      (CH))
         4
         (*DET+NOUN (John gave the girl)
```

```
                    (V A SH)
                    (who)
                    (WH))
         5
         (*START-RELCL (John gave the girl who)
                       (V WS # A)
                       (read)
                       (V I A))
         6
         (*NOM+FVERB (John gave the girl who read)
                     (V A A)
                     (the)
                     (U))
         7
         (*FVERB+MAIN (John gave the girl who read the)
                      (V U A)
                      (book)
                      (C-H))
         8
         (*DET+NOUN (John gave the girl who read the book)
                    (V A S-H)
                    (a)
                    (C))
         9
         (*FVERB+MAIN (John gave the girl who read the book a)
                      (V C S-H)
                      (cookie)
                      (C-H))
         10
         (*DET+NOUN (John gave the girl who read the book a cookie)
                    (V S-H S-H)
                    (%.)
                    (DECL V))
         11)))
```

C.15.2 *John didn't give the girl who didn't read the book a cookie.*

```
(R John didn't give the girl who didn't read the book a cookie %.)
((*CMPLT ((John didn't give the girl who didn't read the book a cookie %.)
         (DECL)
         1
         (*START (John)
                 (SH)
                 (didn't)
                 (V I DO))
         2
         (*NOM+FVERB (John didn't)
                     (V DO)
                     (give)
                     (V NOM D A))
         3
         (*ADD-VERB (John didn't give)
                    (V D A)
                    (the)
                    (U))
         4
```

```
(*FVERB+MAIN (John didn't give the)
             (V U A)
             (girl)
             (CH))
5
(*DET+NOUN (John didn't give the girl)
             (V A SH)
             (who)
             (WH))
6
(*START-RELCL (John didn't give the girl who)
             (V WS # A)
             (didn't)
             (V N DO))
7
(*NOM+FVERB (John didn't give the girl who didn't)
             (V DO A)
             (read)
             (V NOM A))
8
(*ADD-VERB (John didn't give the girl who didn't read)
             (V A A)
             (the)
             (U))
9
(*FVERB+MAIN (John didn't give the girl who didn't read the)
             (V U A)
             (book)
             (C-H))
10
(*DET+NOUN (John didn't give the girl who didn't read the book)
             (V A S-H)
             (a)
             (C))
11
(*FVERB+MAIN (John didn't give the girl who didn't read the book a)
             (V C S-H)
             (cookie)
             (C-H))
12
(*DET+NOUN (John didn't give the girl who didn't read the book a
                   cookie)
             (V S-H S-H)
             (%.)
             (DECL V))
13)))
```

C.15.3 *John gave the girl who gave the man a book a cookie.*

```
(R John gave the girl who gave the man a book a cookie .)
((*CMPLT ((John gave the girl who gave the man a book a cookie %.)
        (DECL)
        1
        (*START (John)
                (SH)
                (gave)
```

```
                (V I D A))
        2
        (*NOM+FVERB (John gave)
                    (V D A)
                    (the)
                    (U))
        3
        (*FVERB+MAIN (John gave the)
                     (V U A)
                     (girl)
                     (CH))
        4
        (*DET+NOUN (John gave the girl)
                   (V A SH)
                   (who)
                   (WH))
        5
        (*START-RELCL (John gave the girl who)
                      (V WS # A)
                      (gave)
                      (V I D A))
        6
        (*NOM+FVERB (John gave the girl who gave)
                    (V D A A)
                    (the)
                    (U))
        7
        (*FVERB+MAIN (John gave the girl who gave the)
                     (V U A A)
                     (man)
                     (CH))
        8
        (*DET+NOUN (John gave the girl who gave the man)
                   (V A A SH)
                   (a)
                   (C))
        9
        (*FVERB+MAIN (John gave the girl who gave the man a)
                     (V C A SH)
                     (book)
                     (C-H))
        10
        (*DET+NOUN (John gave the girl who gave the man a book)
                   (V A SH S-H)
                   (a)
                   (C))
        11
        (*FVERB+MAIN (John gave the girl who gave the man a book a)
                     (V C SH S-H)
                     (cookie)
                     (C-H))
        12
        (*DET+NOUN (John gave the girl who gave the man a book a cookie)
                   (V SH S-H S-H)
                   (%.)
```

```
                    (DECL V))
           13)))
```

C.15.4 *John didn't give the girl who didn't give the man a book a cookie.*

```
(R John didn't give the girl who didn't give the man a book a cookie %.)
((*CMPLT ((John didn't give the girl who didn't give the man a book a cookie
              %.)
         (DECL)
         1
         (*START (John)
                 (SH)
                 (didn't)
                 (V N DO))
         2
         (*NOM+FVERB (John didn't)
                     (V DO)
                     (give)
                     (V NOM D A))
         3
         (*ADD-VERB (John didn't give)
                    (V D A)
                    (the)
                    (U))
         4
         (*FVERB+MAIN (John didn't give the)
                      (V U A)
                      (girl)
                      (CH))
         5
         (*DET+NOUN (John didn't give the girl)
                    (V A SH)
                    (who)
                    (WH))
         6
         (*START-RELCL (John didn't give the girl who)
                       (V WS * A)
                       (didn't)
                       (V N DO))
         7
         (*NOM+FVERB (John didn't give the girl who didn't)
                     (V DO A)
                     (give)
                     (V NOM D A))
         8
         (*ADD-VERB (John didn't give the girl who didn't give)
                    (V D A A)
                    (the)
                    (U))
         9
         (*FVERB+MAIN (John didn't give the girl who didn't give the)
                      (V U A A)
                      (man)
                      (CH))
         10
         (*DET+NOUN (John didn't give the girl who didn't give the man)
```

```
                    (V A A SH)
                    (a)
                    (C))
        11
        (*FVERB+MAIN (John didn't give the girl who didn't give the man a)
                    (V C A SH)
                    (book)
                    (C-H))
        12
        (*DET+NOUN (John didn't give the girl who didn't give the man a
                        book)
                    (V A SH S-H)
                    (a)
                    (C))
        13
        (*FVERB+MAIN (John didn't give the girl who didn't give the man a
                        book a)
                    (V C SH S-H)
                    (cookie)
                    (C-H))
        14
        (*DET+NOUN (John didn't give the girl who didn't give the man a
                        book a cookie)
                    (V SH S-H S-H)
                    (%.)
                    (DECL V))
        15)))
```

C.15.5 *John gave the girl who Mary gave a cookie a book.*

```
(R John gave the girl who Mary gave a cookie a book %.)
((*CMPLT ((John gave the girl who Mary gave a cookie a book %.)
        (DECL)
        1
        (*START (John)
                (SH)
                (gave)
                (V N D A))
        2
        (*NOM+FVERB (John gave)
                    (V D A)
                    (the)
                    (U))
        3
        (*FVERB+MAIN (John gave the)
                    (V U A)
                    (girl)
                    (CH))
        4
        (*DET+NOUN (John gave the girl)
                    (V A SH)
                    (who)
                    (WH))
        5
        (*START-RELCL (John gave the girl who)
                    (V WS # A)
```

```
                       (Mary)
                       (SH))
      6
   (*ADD-NOM (John gave the girl who Mary)
             (V WS SH # # A)
             (gave)
             (V N D A))
      7
   (*NOM+FVERB (John gave the girl who Mary gave)
               (V A # A)
               (a)
               (C))
      8
   (*FVERB+MAIN (John gave the girl who Mary gave a)
                (V C A)
                (cookie)
                (C-H))
      9
   (*DET+NOUN (John gave the girl who Mary gave a cookie)
              (V A S-H)
              (a)
              (C))
      10
   (*FVERB+MAIN (John gave the girl who Mary gave a cookie a)
                (V C S-H)
                (book)
                (C-H))
      11
   (*DET+NOUN (John gave the girl who Mary gave a cookie a
                    book)
              (V S-H S-H)
              (%.)
              (DECL V))
      12)))
```

C.16   Relative clauses modifying sentence initial noun phrases

C.16.1   *The man who gave Mary a book loves Susi.*

```
(R the man who gave Mary a book loves Susi .)
((*CMPLT ((the man who gave Mary a book loves Susi %.)
         (DECL)
         1
      (*START (the)
              (U)
              (man)
              (CH))
         2
      (*DET+NOUN (the man)
                 (SH)
                 (who)
                 (WH))
```

```
3
(*START-RELCL (the man who)
              (SH WS *)
              (gave)
              (V N D A))
4
(*NOM+FVERB (the man who gave)
              (SH D A)
              (Mary)
              (SH))
5
(*FVERB+MAIN (the man who gave Mary)
              (SH A SH)
              (a)
              (C))
6
(*FVERB+MAIN (the man who gave Mary a)
              (SH C SH)
              (book)
              (C-H))
7
(*DET+NOUN (the man who gave Mary a book)
              (SH SH S-H)
              (loves)
              (V S3 A))
8
(*NOM+FVERB (the man who gave Mary a book loves)
              (V A)
              (Susi)
              (SH))
9
(*FVERB+MAIN (the man who gave Mary a book loves Susi)
              (V SH)
              (%.)
              (DECL V))
10)))
```

C.16.2 *The man who didn't read the book loves Mary.*

```
(R the man who didn't read the book loves Mary .)
((*CMPLT ((the man who didn't read the book loves Mary %.)
         (DECL)
1
(*START (the)
         (U)
         (man)
         (CH))
2
(*DET+NOUN (the man)
              (SH)
              (who)
              (WH))
3
(*START-RELCL (the man who)
              (SH WS *)
              (didn't)
```

```
                  (V I DO))
    4
(*NOM+FVERB (the man who didn't)
            (SH DO)
            (read)
            (V NOM A))
    5
(*ADD-VERB (the man who didn't read)
            (SH A)
            (the)
            (U))
    6
(*FVERB+MAIN (the man who didn't read the)
             (SH U)
             (book)
             (C-H))
    7
(*DET+NOUN (the man who didn't read the book)
           (SH S-H)
           (loves)
           (V S3 A))
    8
(*NOM+FVERB (the man who didn't read the book loves)
            (V A)
            (Mary)
            (SH))
    9
(*FVERB+MAIN (the man who didn't read the book loves Mary)
             (V SH)
             (%.)
             (DECL V))
    10)))
```

C.16.3 *The man who could have been reading the book loves Mary.*

```
(R the man who could have been reading the book loves Mary .)
((*CMPLT ((the man who could have been reading the book loves Mary %.)
         (DECL)
    1
(*START (the)
        (U)
        (man)
        (CH))
    2
(*DET+NOUN (the man)
           (SH)
           (who)
           (WH))
    3
(*START-RELCL (the man who)
              (SH WS *)
              (could)
              (V I M))
    4
(*NOM+FVERB (the man who could)
            (SH M)
```

```
                    (have)
                    (V NOM HV))
        5
    (*ADD-VERB (the man who could have)
               (SH HV)
               (been)
               (HV B))
        6
    (*ADD-VERB (the man who could have been)
               (SH B)
               (reading)
               (B A))
        7
    (*ADD-VERB (the man who could have been reading)
               (SH A)
               (the)
               (U))
        8
    (*FVERB+MAIN (the man who could have been reading the)
               (SH U)
               (book)
               (C-H))
        9
    (*DET+NOUN (the man who could have been reading the book)
               (SH S-H)
               (loves)
               (V S3 A))
        10
    (*NOM+FVERB (the man who could have been reading the book loves)
               (V A)
               (Mary)
               (SH))
        11
    (*FVERB+MAIN (the man who could have been reading the book loves
                        Mary)
               (V SH)
               (%.)
               (DECL V))
        12)))
```

C.17   The relative pronoun *who* as subject and object

C.17.1   *The man who loves Mary is reading a book.*

```
(R the man who loves Mary is reading a book .)
((*CMPLT ((the man who loves Mary is reading a book %.)
          (DECL)
          1
          (*START (the)
                  (U)
                  (man)
                  (CH))
```

```
2
(*DET+NOUN (the man)
          (SH)
          (who)
          (WH))
3
(*START-RELCL (the man who)
              (SH WS *)
              (loves)
              (V S3 A))
4
(*NOM+FVERB (the man who loves)
            (SH A)
            (Mary)
            (SH))
5
(*FVERB+MAIN (the man who loves Mary)
             (SH SH)
             (is)
             (V S3 B))
6
(*NOM+FVERB (the man who loves Mary is)
            (V B)
            (reading)
            (B A))
7
(*ADD-VERB (the man who loves Mary is reading)
           (V A)
           (a)
           (C))
8
(*FVERB+MAIN (the man who loves Mary is reading a)
             (V C)
             (book)
             (C-H))
9
(*DET+NOUN (the man who loves Mary is reading a book)
           (V S-H)
           (%.)
           (DECL V))
10)))
```

C.17.2 *The man who Mary loves is reading a book.*

```
(R the man who Mary loves is reading a book .)
((*CMPLT ((the man who Mary loves is reading a book %.)
         (DECL)
         1
         (*START (the)
                 (U)
                 (man)
                 (CH))
         2
         (*DET+NOUN (the man)
                    (SH)
                    (who)
```

```
                            (WH))
                3
                (*START-RELCL (the man who)
                            (SH WS #)
                            (Mary)
                            (SH))
                4
                (*ADD-NOM (the man who Mary)
                            (SH WS SH #)
                            (loves)
                            (V S3 A))
                5
                (*NOM+FVERB (the man who Mary loves)
                            (SH)
                            (is)
                            (V S3 B))
                6
                (*NOM+FVERB (the man who Mary loves is)
                            (V B)
                            (reading)
                            (B A))
                7
                (*ADD-VERB (the man who Mary loves is reading)
                            (V A)
                            (a)
                            (C))
                8
                (*FVERB+MAIN (the man who Mary loves is reading a)
                            (V C)
                            (book)
                            (C-H))
                9
                (*DET+NOUN (the man who Mary loves is reading a book)
                            (V S-H)
                            (%.)
                            (DECL V))
                10)))
```

C.17.3 *The man who doesn't love Mary is reading a book.*

```
(R the man who doesn't love Mary is reading a book .)
((*CMPLT ((the man who doesn't love Mary is reading a book %.)
            (DECL)
            1
            (*START (the)
                    (U)
                    (man)
                    (CH))
            2
            (*DET+NOUN (the man)
                    (SH)
                    (who)
                    (WH))
            3
            (*START-RELCL (the man who)
                    (SH WS #)
```

```
                        (doesn't)
                        (V S3 DO))
        4
  (*NOM+FVERB (the man who doesn't)
              (SH DO)
              (love)
              (V NOM A))
        5
  (*ADD-VERB (the man who doesn't love)
              (SH A)
              (Mary)
              (SH))
        6
  (*FVERB+MAIN (the man who doesn't love Mary)
               (SH SH)
               (is)
               (V S3 B))
        7
  (*NOM+FVERB (the man who doesn't love Mary is)
              (V B)
              (reading)
              (B A))
        8
  (*ADD-VERB (the man who doesn't love Mary is reading)
              (V A)
              (a)
              (C))
        9
  (*FVERB+MAIN (the man who doesn't love Mary is reading a)
               (V C)
               (book)
               (C-H))
        10
  (*DET+NOUN (the man who doesn't love Mary is reading a book)
             (V S-H)
             (%.)
             (DECL V))
        11)))
```

C.17.4 *The man who Mary doesn't love is reading a book.*

```
(R the man who Mary doesn't love is reading a book .)
((*CMPLT ((the man who Mary doesn't love is reading a book %.)
         (DECL)
         1
  (*START (the)
          (U)
          (man)
          (CH))
         2
  (*DET+NOUN (the man)
             (SH)
             (who)
             (WH))
         3
  (*START-RELCL (the man who)
```

```
                        (SH WS *)
                        (Mary)
                        (SH))
        4
        (*ADD-NOM (the man who Mary)
                  (SH WS SH *)
                  (doesn't)
                  (V S3 DO))
        5
        (*NOM+FVERB (the man who Mary doesn't)
                    (SH DO WS)
                    (love)
                    (V NOM A))
        6
        (*ADD-VERB (the man who Mary doesn't love)
                   (SH)
                   (is)
                   (V S3 B))
        7
        (*NOM+FVERB (the man who Mary doesn't love is)
                    (V B)
                    (reading)
                    (B A))
        8
        (*ADD-VERB (the man who Mary doesn't love is reading)
                   (V A)
                   (a)
                   (C))
        9
        (*FVERB+MAIN (the man who Mary doesn't love is reading a)
                     (V C)
                     (book)
                     (C-H))
        10
        (*DET+NOUN (the man who Mary doesn't love is reading a book)
                   (V S-H)
                   (%.)
                   (DECL V))
        11)))
```

C.17.5 *The man who didn't give Mary a book loves Susi.*

```
(R the man who didn't give Mary a book loves Susi .)
((*CMPLT ((the man who didn't give Mary a book loves Susi %.)
         (DECL)
        1
        (*START (the)
                (U)
                (man)
                (CH))
        2
        (*DET+NOUN (the man)
                   (SH)
                   (who)
                   (WH))
        3
```

```
        (*START-RELCL (the man who)
                (SH WS #)
                (didn't)
                (V N DO))
     4
     (*NOM+FVERB (the man who didn't)
                (SH DO)
                (give)
                (V NOM D A))
     5
     (*ADD-VERB (the man who didn't give)
                (SH D A)
                (Mary)
                (SH))
     6
     (*FVERB+MAIN (the man who didn't give Mary)
                (SH A SH)
                (a)
                (C))
     7
     (*FVERB+MAIN (the man who didn't give Mary a)
                (SH C SH)
                (book)
                (C-H))
     8
     (*DET+NOUN (the man who didn't give Mary a book)
                (SH SH S-H)
                (loves)
                (V S3 A))
     9
     (*NOM+FVERB (the man who didn't give Mary a book loves)
                (V A)
                (Susi)
                (SH))
     10
     (*FVERB+MAIN (the man who didn't give Mary a book loves Susi)
                (V SH)
                (%.)
                (DECL V))
        11)))
```

C.17.6 *The man who Mary didn't give a book to loves Susi.*

```
(R the man who Mary didn't give a book to loves Susi %.)
((*CMPLT ((the man who Mary didn't give a book to loves Susi %.)
        (DECL)
        1
        (*START (the)
                (U)
                (man)
                (CH))
        2
        (*DET+NOUN (the man)
                (SH)
                (who)
                (WH))
```

```
3
(*START-RELCL (the man who)
              (SH WS #)
              (Mary)
              (SH))
4
(*ADD-NOM (the man who Mary)
              (SH WS SH #)
              (didn't)
              (V N DO))
5
(*NOM+FVERB (the man who Mary didn't)
              (SH DO WS)
              (give)
              (V NOM A TO))
6
(*WH+VERB (the man who Mary didn't give)
              (SH A TO WS)
              (a)
              (C))
7
(*FVERB+MAIN (the man who Mary didn't give a)
              (SH C TO WS)
              (book)
              (C-H))
8
(*DET+NOUN (the man who Mary didn't give a book)
              (SH TO WS S-H)
              (to)
              (TO NP))
9
(*FVERB+MAIN (the man who Mary didn't give a book to)
              (SH)
              (loves)
              (V S3 A))
10
(*NOM+FVERB (the man who Mary didn't give a book to loves)
              (V A)
              (Susi)
              (SH))
11
(*FVERB+MAIN (the man who Mary didn't give a book to loves Susi)
              (V SH)
              (%.)
              (DECL V))
12)))
```

C.18   Mixing relative clauses and *that*-clauses

C.18.1 *The man who saw that John loves Mary is reading a book.*

```
(R the man who saw that John loves Mary is reading a book .)
((*CMPLT ((the man who saw that John loves Mary is reading a book %.)
         (DECL)
```

```
1
(*START (the)
        (U)
        (man)
        (CH))
2
(*DET+NOUN (the man)
           (SH)
           (who)
           (WH))
3
(*START-RELCL (the man who)
              (SH WS #)
              (saw)
              (V N A))
4
(*NOM+FVERB (the man who saw)
            (SH A)
            (that)
            (SC))
5
(*START-SUBCL (the man who saw that)
              (SH SC)
              (John)
              (SH))
6
(*ADD-NOM (the man who saw that John)
          (SH SC SH #)
          (loves)
          (V S3 A))
7
(*NOM+FVERB (the man who saw that John loves)
            (SH A)
            (Mary)
            (SH))
8
(*FVERB+MAIN (the man who saw that John loves Mary)
             (SH SH)
             (is)
             (V S3 B))
9
(*NOM+FVERB (the man who saw that John loves Mary is)
            (V B)
            (reading)
            (B A))
10
(*ADD-VERB (the man who saw that John loves Mary is reading)
           (V A)
           (a)
           (C))
11
(*FVERB+MAIN (the man who saw that John loves Mary is reading a)
             (V C)
             (book)
             (C-H))
```

```
12
(*DET+NOUN (the man who saw that John loves Mary is reading a book)
           (V S-H)
           (%.)
           (DECL V))
13)))
```

C.18.2 *The man who said that Mary loves him sleeps.*

```
(R the man who said that Mary loves him sleeps .)
((*CMPLT ((the man who said that Mary loves him sleeps %.)
         (DECL)
         1
         (*START (the)
                 (U)
                 (man)
                 (CH))
         2
         (*DET+NOUN (the man)
                    (SH)
                    (who)
                    (WH))
         3
         (*START-RELCL (the man who)
                       (SH WS #)
                       (said)
                       (V N A))
         4
         (*NOM+FVERB (the man who said)
                     (SH A)
                     (that)
                     (SC))
         5
         (*START-SUBCL (the man who said that)
                       (SH SC)
                       (Mary)
                       (SH))
         6
         (*ADD-NOM (the man who said that Mary)
                   (SH SC SH #)
                   (loves)
                   (V S3 A))
         7
         (*NOM+FVERB (the man who said that Mary loves)
                     (SH A)
                     (him)
                     (:S3))
         8
         (*FVERB+MAIN (the man who said that Mary loves him)
                      (SH)
                      (sleeps)
                      (V S3))
         9
         (*NOM+FVERB (the man who said that Mary loves him sleeps)
                     (V)
                     (%.)
```

```
                          (DECL V))
              10)))
```

C.18.3 *I know the man who John said Mary believes that Susi loves.*

```
(R I know the man who John said Mary believes that Susi loves %.)
((*CMPLT ((I know the man who John said Mary believes that Susi
              loves %.)
          (DECL)
          1
          (*START (I)
                  (S1)
                  (know)
                  (V N A))
          2
          (*NOM+FVERB (I know)
                      (V A)
                      (the)
                      (U))
          3
          (*FVERB+MAIN (I know the)
                       (V U)
                       (man)
                       (CH))
          4
          (*DET+NOUN (I know the man)
                     (V SH)
                     (who)
                     (WH))
          5
          (*START-RELCL (I know the man who)
                        (V WS #)
                        (John)
                        (SH))
          6
          (*ADD-NOM (I know the man who John)
                    (V WS SH #)
                    (said)
                    (V N A))
          7
          (*WH+VERB (I know the man who John said)
                    (V A WS SH #)
                    (Mary)
                    (SH))
          8
          (*START-SUBCL (I know the man who John said Mary)
                        (V SC SH # WS SH #)
                        (believes)
                        (V S3 A))
          9
          (*WH+VERB (I know the man who John said Mary believes)
                    (V A # WS SH #)
                    (that)
                    (SC))
          10
          (*START-SUBCL (I know the man who John said Mary believes
```

```
                        that)
                    (V SC # WS SH #)
                    (Susi)
                    (SH))
        11
        (*ADD-NOM (I know the man who John said Mary believes that
                    Susi)
                (V SC SH # # WS SH #)
                (loves)
                (V S3 A))
        12
        (*NOM+FVERB (I know the man who John said Mary believes
                    that Susi loves)
                (V SH)
                (%.)
                (DECL V))
        13)))
```

C.18.4 *I know the man who John said that Mary believes that Susi loves.*

```
(R I know the man who John said that Mary believes that Susi loves %.)
((*CMPLT ((I know the man who John said that Mary believes that Susi
        loves %.)
        (DECL)
        1
        (*START (I)
                (S1)
                (know)
                (V N A))
        2
        (*NOM+FVERB (I know)
                    (V A)
                    (the)
                    (U))
        3
        (*FVERB+MAIN (I know the)
                    (V U)
                    (man)
                    (CH))
        4
        (*DET+NOUN (I know the man)
                    (V SH)
                    (who)
                    (WH))
        5
        (*START-RELCL (I know the man who)
                    (V WS #)
                    (John)
                    (SH))
        6
        (*ADD-NOM (I know the man who John)
                (V WS SH #)
                (said)
                (V N A))
        7
        (*WH+VERB (I know the man who John said)
```

```
                      (V A WS SH #)
                      (that)
                      (SC))
          8
     (*START-SUBCL (I know the man who John said that)
                      (V SC WS SH #)
                      (Mary)
                      (SH))
          9
     (*ADD-NOM (I know the man who John said that Mary)
                      (V SC SH # WS SH #)
                      (believes)
                      (V S3 A))
          10
     (*WH+VERB (I know the man who John said that Mary believes)
                      (V A # WS SH #)
                      (that)
                      (SC))
          11
     (*START-SUBCL (I know the man who John said that Mary
                            believes that)
                      (V SC # WS SH #)
                      (Susi)
                      (SH))
          12
     (*ADD-NOM (I know the man who John said that Mary believes
                            that Susi)
                      (V SC SH # # WS SH #)
                      (loves)
                      (V S3 A))
          13
     (*NOM+FVERB (I know the man who John said that Mary
                            believes that Susi loves)
                      (V SH)
                      (%.)
                      (DECL V))
          14)))
```

C.19   Wh-interrogatives with relative clauses

C.19.1 *Who loves the man who gave Mary a book?*

```
(R who loves the man who gave Mary a book ?)
((*CMPLT ((who loves the man who gave Mary a book ?)
          (INTERROG)
          1
     (*START (who)
             (WH)
             (loves)
             (V S3 A))
          2
     (*NOM+FVERB (who loves)
                 (VI A)
                 (the)
```

```
                     (U))
          3
          (*FVERB+MAIN (who loves the)
                      (VI U)
                      (man)
                      (CH))
          4
          (*DET+NOUN (who loves the man)
                      (VI SH)
                      (who)
                      (WH))
          5
          (*START-RELCL (who loves the man who)
                      (VI WS #)
                      (gave)
                      (V N D A))
          6
          (*NOM+FVERB (who loves the man who gave)
                      (VI D A)
                      (Mary)
                      (SH))
          7
          (*FVERB+MAIN (who loves the man who gave Mary)
                      (VI A SH)
                      (a)
                      (C))
          8
          (*FVERB+MAIN (who loves the man who gave Mary a)
                      (VI C SH)
                      (book)
                      (C-H))
          9
          (*DET+NOUN (who loves the man who gave Mary a book)
                      (VI SH S-H)
                      (?)
                      (INTERROG V))
          10)))
```

C.19.2 *Who loves the man whom Mary gave a book to?*

```
(R who loves the man whom Mary gave a book to ?)
((*CMPLT ((who loves the man whom Mary gave a book to ?)
          (INTERROG)
          1
          (*START (who)
                  (WH)
                  (loves)
                  (V S3 A))
          2
          (*NOM+FVERB (who loves)
                      (VI A)
                      (the)
                      (U))
          3
          (*FVERB+MAIN (who loves the)
                      (VI U)
```

```
                        (man)
                        (CH))
        4
        (*DET+NOUN (who loves the man)
                        (VI SH)
                        (whom)
                        (:WH))
        5
        (*START-RELCL (who loves the man whom)
                        (VI WS #)
                        (Mary)
                        (SH))
        6
        (*ADD-NOM (who loves the man whom Mary)
                        (VI WS SH #)
                        (gave)
                        (V N A TO))
        7
        (*WH+VERB (who loves the man whom Mary gave)
                        (VI A TO WS SH #)
                        (a)
                        (C))
        8
        (*FVERB+MAIN (who loves the man whom Mary gave a)
                        (VI C TO WS SH)
                        (book)
                        (C-H))
        9
        (*DET+NOUN (who loves the man whom Mary gave a book)
                        (VI TO WS SH S-H)
                        (to)
                        (TO NP))
        10
        (*FVERB+MAIN (who loves the man whom Mary gave a book to)
                        (VI S-H)
                        (?)
                        (INTERROG V))
        11)))
```

C.20   Declaratives and interrogatives with "Wh-movement"

C.20.1 *Mary said that John doesn't believe that Susi read the book.*

```
(R Mary said that John doesn't believe that Susi read the book %.)
((*CMPLT ((Mary said that John doesn't believe that Susi read the book %.)
                (DECL)
        1
        (*START (Mary)
                (SH)
                (said)
                (V N A))
        2
```

```
(*NOM+FVERB (Mary said)
            (V A)
            (that)
            (SC))
3
(*START-SUBCL (Mary said that)
              (V SC)
              (John)
              (SH))
4
(*ADD-NOM (Mary said that John)
          (V SC SH *)
          (doesn't)
          (V S3 DO))
5
(*NOM+FVERB (Mary said that John doesn't)
            (V DO)
            (believe)
            (V NOM A))
6
(*ADD-VERB (Mary said that John doesn't believe)
           (V A)
           (that)
           (SC))
7
(*START-SUBCL (Mary said that John doesn't believe that)
              (V SC)
              (Susi)
              (SH))
8
(*ADD-NOM (Mary said that John doesn't believe that Susi)
          (V SC SH *)
          (read)
          (V N A))
9
(*NOM+FVERB (Mary said that John doesn't believe that Susi read)
            (V A)
            (the)
            (U))
10
(*FVERB+MAIN (Mary said that John doesn't believe that Susi read
                 the)
             (V U)
             (book)
             (C-H))
11
(*DET+NOUN (Mary said that John doesn't believe that Susi read the
               book)
           (V S-H)
           (%.)
           (DECL V))
12)))
```

C.20.2 *Which book did Mary say that John doesn't believe that Susi read?*

(R which book did Mary say that John doesn't believe that Susi read ?)

```
((*CMPLT ((which book did Mary say that John doesn't believe that Susi read ?)
         (INTERROG)
         1
         (*START (which)
                 (WU)
                 (book)
                 (C-H))
         2
         (*DET+NOUN (which book)
                    (WS)
                    (did)
                    (V N DO))
         3
         (*TOP-MAIN (which book did)
                    (VI N DO WS)
                    (Mary)
                    (SH))
         4
         (*FVERB+NOM (which book did Mary)
                     (VI DO WS SH)
                     (say)
                     (V NOM A))
         5
         (*WH+VERB (which book did Mary say)
                   (VI A WS SH)
                   (that)
                   (SC))
         6
         (*START-SUBCL (which book did Mary say that)
                       (VI SC WS SH)
                       (John)
                       (SH))
         7
         (*ADD-NOM (which book did Mary say that John)
                   (VI SC SH # WS SH)
                   (doesn't)
                   (V S3 DO))
         8
         (*NOM+FVERB (which book did Mary say that John doesn't)
                     (VI DO WS SH)
                     (believe)
                     (V NOM A))
         9
         (*WH+VERB (which book did Mary say that John doesn't believe)
                   (VI A WS SH)
                   (that)
                   (SC))
         10
         (*START-SUBCL (which book did Mary say that John doesn't believe
                              that)
                       (VI SC WS SH)
                       (Susi)
                       (SH))
         11
         (*ADD-NOM (which book did Mary say that John doesn't believe that
```

```
                          Susi)
                 (VI SC SH # WS SH)
                 (read)
                 (V N A))
        12
        (*NOM+FVERB (which book did Mary say that John doesn't believe that
                          Susi read)
                 (VI SH)
                 (?)
                 (INTERROG V))
        13)))
```

C.20.3 *John believes that Mary gave Bill a book.*

```
(R John believes that Mary gave Bill a book .)
((*CMPLT ((John believes that Mary gave Bill a book %.)
         (DECL)
         1
         (*START (John)
                 (SH)
                 (believes)
                 (V S3 A))
         2
         (*NOM+FVERB (John believes)
                 (V A)
                 (that)
                 (SC))
         3
         (*START-SUBCL (John believes that)
                 (V SC)
                 (Mary)
                 (SH))
         4
         (*ADD-NOM (John believes that Mary)
                 (V SC SH #)
                 (gave)
                 (V N D A))
         5
         (*NOM+FVERB (John believes that Mary gave)
                 (V D A)
                 (Bill)
                 (SH))
         6
         (*FVERB+MAIN (John believes that Mary gave Bill)
                 (V A SH)
                 (a)
                 (C))
         7
         (*FVERB+MAIN (John believes that Mary gave Bill a)
                 (V C SH)
                 (book)
                 (C-H))
         8
         (*DET+NOUN (John believes that Mary gave Bill a book)
                 (V SH S-H)
                 (%.)
```

```
                    (DECL V))
        9)))
```

C.20.4 *Who does John believe Mary gave a book?*

```
(R who does John believe Mary gave a book ?)
((*CMPLT ((who does John believe Mary gave a book ?)
         (INTERROG)
         1
         (*START (who)
                 (WH)
                 (does)
                 (V S3 DO))
         2
         (*TOP-MAIN (who does)
                    (VI S3 DO WH)
                    (John)
                    (SH))
         3
         (*FVERB+NOM (who does John)
                     (VI DO WH SH)
                     (believe)
                     (V NOM A))
         4
         (*WH+VERB (who does John believe)
                   (VI A WH SH)
                   (Mary)
                   (SH))
         5
         (*START-SUBCL (who does John believe Mary)
                       (VI SC SH # WH SH)
                       (gave)
                       (V N D A))
         6
         (*NOM+FVERB (who does John believe Mary gave)
                     (VI A SH)
                     (a)
                     (C))
         7
         (*FVERB+MAIN (who does John believe Mary gave a)
                      (VI C SH)
                      (book)
                      (C-H))
         8
         (*DET+NOUN (who does John believe Mary gave a book)
                    (VI SH S-H)
                    (?)
                    (INTERROG V))
         9)))
```

C.20.5 *John believes that Mary gave a book to Bill.*

```
(R John believes that Mary gave a book to Bill .)
((*CMPLT ((John believes that Mary gave a book to Bill %.)
         (DECL)
         1
```

```
(*START (John)
        (SH)
        (believes)
        (V S3 A))
2
(*NOM+FVERB (John believes)
            (V A)
            (that)
            (SC))
3
(*START-SUBCL (John believes that)
              (V SC)
              (Mary)
              (SH))
4
(*ADD-NOM (John believes that Mary)
          (V SC SH *)
          (gave)
          (V N A TO))
5
(*NOM+FVERB (John believes that Mary gave)
            (V A TO)
            (a)
            (C))
6
(*FVERB+MAIN (John believes that Mary gave a)
             (V C TO)
             (book)
             (C-H))
7
(*DET+NOUN (John believes that Mary gave a book)
           (V TO S-H)
           (to)
           (TO NP))
8
(*FVERB+MAIN (John believes that Mary gave a book to)
             (V NP S-H)
             (Bill)
             (SH))
9
(*PREP+NP (John believes that Mary gave a book to Bill)
          (V S-H SH)
          (%.)
          (DECL V))
10)))
```

C.20.6 *Who does John believe that Mary gave the book to ?*

```
(R who does John believe that Mary gave the book to ?)
((*CMPLT ((who does John believe that Mary gave the book to ?)
         (INTERROG)
1
(*START (who)
        (WH)
        (does)
        (V S3 DO))
```

```
    2
(*TOP-MAIN (who does)
          (VI S3 DO WH)
          (John)
          (SH))
    3
(*FVERB+NOM (who does John)
          (VI DO WH SH)
          (believe)
          (V NOM A))
    4
(*WH+VERB (who does John believe)
          (VI A WH SH)
          (that)
          (SC))
    5
(*START-SUBCL (who does John believe that)
          (VI SC WH SH)
          (Mary)
          (SH))
    6
(*ADD-NOM (who does John believe that Mary)
          (VI SC SH # WH SH)
          (gave)
          (V N A TO))
    7
(*WH+VERB (who does John believe that Mary gave)
          (VI A TO # WH SH)
          (the)
          (U))
    8
(*FVERB+MAIN (who does John believe that Mary gave the)
             (VI U TO WH SH)
             (book)
             (C-H))
    9
(*DET+NOUN (who does John believe that Mary gave the book)
          (VI TO WH SH S-H)
          (to)
          (TO NP))
    10
(*FVERB+MAIN (who does John believe that Mary gave the book to)
             (VI S-H)
             (?)
             (INTERROG V))
 11)))
```

C.21   Subordinate clauses with and without com plementizers

C.21.1 *The man whom John said that Mary loves sleeps.*

(R the man whom John said that Mary loves sleeps .)

```
((*CMPLT ((the man whom John said that Mary loves sleeps %.)
         (DECL)
         1
         (*START (the)
                 (U)
                 (man)
                 (CH))
         2
         (*DET+NOUN (the man)
                 (SH)
                 (whom)
                 (:WH))
         3
         (*START-RELCL (the man whom)
                 (SH WS #)
                 (John)
                 (SH))
         4
         (*ADD-NOM (the man whom John)
                 (SH WS SH #)
                 (said)
                 (V N A))
         5
         (*WH+VERB (the man whom John said)
                 (SH A WS SH #)
                 (that)
                 (SC))
         6
         (*START-SUBCL (the man whom John said that)
                 (SH SC WS SH #)
                 (Mary)
                 (SH))
         7
         (*ADD-NOM (the man whom John said that Mary)
                 (SH SC SH # WS SH #)
                 (loves)
                 (V S3 A))
         8
         (*NOM+FVERB (the man whom John said that Mary loves)
                 (SH SH)
                 (sleeps)
                 (V S3))
         9
         (*NOM+FVERB (the man whom John said that Mary loves sleeps)
                 (V)
                 (%.)
                 (DECL V))
         10)))
```

C.21.2 The man John said that Mary loves sleeps.

```
(R the man John said that Mary loves sleeps .)
((*CMPLT ((the man John said that Mary loves sleeps %.)
         (DECL)
         1
         (*START (the)
```

```
                      (U)
                      (man)
                      (CH))
           2
           (*DET+NOUN (the man)
                      (SH)
                      (John)
                      (SH))
           3
           (*START-RELCL (the man John)
                      (SH WS SH #)
                      (said)
                      (V N A))
           4
           (*WH+VERB (the man John said)
                      (SH A WS SH #)
                      (that)
                      (SC))
           5
           (*START-SUBCL (the man John said that)
                      (SH SC WS SH #)
                      (Mary)
                      (SH))
           6
           (*ADD-NOM (the man John said that Mary)
                      (SH SC SH # WS SH #)
                      (loves)
                      (V S3 A))
           7
           (*NOM+FVERB (the man John said that Mary loves)
                      (SH SH)
                      (sleeps)
                      (V S3))
           8
           (*NOM+FVERB (the man John said that Mary loves sleeps)
                      (V)
                      (%.)
                      (DECL V))
           9)))
```

C.21.3 *The man John said Mary loves sleeps.*

```
(R the man John said Mary loves sleeps %.)
((*CMPLT ((the man John said Mary loves sleeps %.)
           (DECL)
           1
           (*START (the)
                      (U)
                      (man)
                      (CH))
           2
           (*DET+NOUN (the man)
                      (SH)
                      (John)
                      (SH))
           3
```

```
          (*START-RELCL (the man John)
                        (SH WS SH #)
                        (said)
                        (V N A))
      4
          (*WH+VERB (the man John said)
                    (SH A WS SH #)
                    (Mary)
                    (SH))
      5
          (*START-SUBCL (the man John said Mary)
                        (SH SC SH # WS SH #)
                        (loves)
                        (V S3 A))
      6
          (*NOM+FVERB (the man John said Mary loves)
                      (SH SH)
                      (sleeps)
                      (V S3))
      7
          (*NOM+FVERB (the man John said Mary loves sleeps)
                      (V)
                      (%.)
                      (DECL V))
      8)))
```

C.21.4 *The man whom John said that Mary believes that Susi loves sleeps.*

```
(R the man whom John said that Mary believes that Susi loves sleeps .)
((*CMPLT ((the man whom John said that Mary believes that Susi loves sleeps %.
          )
         (DECL)
      1
         (*START (the)
                 (U)
                 (man)
                 (CH))
      2
         (*DET+NOUN (the man)
                    (SH)
                    (whom)
                    (:WH))
      3
         (*START-RELCL (the man whom)
                       (SH WS #)
                       (John)
                       (SH))
      4
         (*ADD-NOM (the man whom John)
                   (SH WS SH #)
                   (said)
                   (V N A))
      5
         (*WH+VERB (the man whom John said)
                   (SH A WS SH #)
                   (that)
```

```
                      (SC))
          6
          (*START-SUBCL (the man whom John said that)
                        (SH SC WS SH #)
                        (Mary)
                        (SH))
          7
          (*ADD-NOM (the man whom John said that Mary)
                    (SH SC SH # WS SH #)
                    (believes)
                    (V S3 A))
          8
          (*WH+VERB (the man whom John said that Mary believes)
                    (SH A # WS SH #)
                    (that)
                    (SC))
          9
          (*START-SUBCL (the man whom John said that Mary believes that)
                        (SH SC # WS SH #)
                        (Susi)
                        (SH))
          10
          (*ADD-NOM (the man whom John said that Mary believes that Susi)
                    (SH SC SH # # WS SH #)
                    (loves)
                    (V S3 A))
          11
          (*NOM+FVERB (the man whom John said that Mary believes that Susi
                          loves)
                      (SH SH)
                      (sleeps)
                      (V S3))
          12
          (*NOM+FVERB (the man whom John said that Mary believes that Susi
                          loves sleeps)
                      (V)
                      (%.)
                      (DECL V))
          13)))
```

C.21.5 *The man John said Mary believes Susi loves sleeps.*

```
(R the man John said Mary believes Susi loves sleeps %.)
((*CMPLT ((the man John said Mary believes Susi loves sleeps %.)
         (DECL)
         1
         (*START (the)
                 (U)
                 (man)
                 (CH))
         2
         (*DET+NOUN (the man)
                    (SH)
                    (John)
                    (SH))
         3
```

```
(*START-RELCL (the man John)
              (SH WS SH #)
              (said)
              (V N A))
4
(*WH+VERB (the man John said)
          (SH A WS SH #)
          (Mary)
          (SH))
5
(*START-SUBCL (the man John said Mary)
              (SH SC SH # WS SH #)
              (believes)
              (V S3 A))
6
(*WH+VERB (the man John said Mary believes)
          (SH A # WS SH #)
          (Susi)
          (SH))
7
(*START-SUBCL (the man John said Mary believes Susi)
              (SH SC SH # # WS SH #)
              (loves)
              (V S3 A))
8
(*NOM+FVERB (the man John said Mary believes Susi loves)
            (SH SH)
            (sleeps)
            (V S3))
9
(*NOM+FVERB (the man John said Mary believes Susi loves sleeps)
            (V)
            (%.)
            (DECL V))
10)))
```

D. List of computer-generated sample derivations

For easier reference, the sample sentences of chapter 3 and 4 and the test examples of appendices B and C are listed below. About half a dozen examples from chapter 4 are repeated in appendix B for systematic reasons. Due to the recursive nature of the grammars, DCAT and ECAT each parse an indefinite number of sentences. The derivations presented in this book were chosen to illustrate specific grammatical issues arising within the left-associative approach. Before each sentence, the location of the corresponding derivation is indicated in parentheses.

D.1 The DCAT derivations

Chapter 3

1. (3.3.4) *Der schöne alte Tisch* / the beautiful old table

2. (3.3.8) *der Tisch* / the table

3. (3.4.1) *Ich schlafe.* / I sleep. - I am asleep.

4. (3.4.2) *Du schläfst.* / You sleep. - You are asleep.

5. (3.4.4) *Der Mann gab dem Mädchen ein Buch.* / The man gave the girl a book.

6. (3.5.2) *Der gab einem das.* / He gave someone that.

7. (3.5.4) *Peter kaufte die kleinen.* / Peter bought the small (ones).

8. (3.5.5) *Peter kaufte die kleinen grünen.* / Peter bought the small green (ones).

9. (3.5.6) *Peter kaufte die kleinen grünen Tomaten.* / Peter bought the small green tomatoes.

10. (3.5.7) *Peter kaufte die, die so bitter schmecken.* / Peter bought the (ones) that taste so bitter.

11. (3.5.8) *Peter kaufte die kleinen, die so bitter schmecken.* / Peter bought the small (ones) that taste so bitter.

12. (3.5.9) *Peter kaufte die kleinen grünen, die so bitter schmecken.* / Peter bought the small green (ones) that taste so bitter.

13. (3.5.10) *Peter kaufte die kleinen grünen Tomaten, die so bitter schmecken.* / Peter bought the small green tomatoes that taste so bitter.

14. (3.5.13) *Peter schwieg.* / Peter was silent.

15. (3.5.14) *Peter, der Maria das Buch gegeben hatte, schwieg.* / Peter, who had given the book to Mary, was silent.

16. (3.5.16) *Maria liest gerne Bücher.* / Mary likes to read books.

17. (3.5.17) *Maria liest gerne Bücher, die traurig enden.* / Mary likes to read books that have sad endings.

18. (3.4.19) *Maria liest gerne gute.* / Mary likes to read good (ones).

19. (3.5.20) *Maria liest gerne gute lange.* / Mary likes to read good long (ones).

20. (3.5.21) *Maria liest gern gute lange, die traurig enden.* / Mary likes to read good long (ones) that have sad endings.

21. (3.5.22) *Maria liest gern gute lange Bücher, die traurig enden.* / Mary likes to read good long books that have sad endings.

Chapter 4

22. (4.1.1) *Das Mädchen gab dem Kind den Teller.* / The girl gave the child the plate.

23. (4.1.2) **Das Mädchen dem Kind gab den Teller.* / The girl gave the child the plate.

24. (4.1.5) **Das Mädchen gab dem Kind den Teller ein Buch.*

25. (4.1.6) *Dem Kind gab das Mädchen den Teller.* / The girl gave the child the plate.

26. (4.1.7) *Das Mädchen hat dem Kind den Teller gegeben.* / The girl has given the child the plate.

27. (4.1.9) *Dem Kind hat das Mädchen den Teller gegeben.* / The girl has given the child the plate.

28. (4.1.10) *Der schöne alte Tisch, den Peter kaufte,* / The beautiful old table that Peter bought

29. (4.1.14) *Früher wohnte Peter in Hamburg.* / Peter lived in Hamburg earlier.

30. (4.1.15) *Weil Peter früher gern in Hamburg wohnte,* / Because Peter had earlier liked living in Hamburg,

31. (4.2.1) *Dem Mann wurde von dem Mädchen ein Buch gegeben.* / The man was given a book by the girl.

32. (4.2.2) *Das Mädchen hat dem Mann ein Buch gegeben.* / The girl has given the man a book.

33. (4.2.3) *Peter ist ein guter Arzt geworden.* / Peter has become a good doctor.

34. (4.2.4) *Der Mann, dem von dem Mädchen ein Buch gegeben wurde,* / The man who was given a book by the girl

35. (4.2.5) *Peter ist von Maria gesehen worden.* / Peter has been seen by Mary.

36. (4.2.6) *Peter wird von Maria gesehen werden.* / Peter will be seen by Mary.

37. (4.2.7) *Der Mann, der von Maria gesehen worden ist,* / The man who has been seen by Mary

38. (4.2.8) *Peter hätte ein guter Arzt werden können.* / Peter could have become a good doctor.

39. (4.2.9) *Weil Peter ein guter Arzt hätte werden können,* / Because Peter could have become a good doctor

40. (4.2.10) *Weil Peter ein guter Arzt werden können wollte,* / Because Peter wanted to be able to become a good doctor

41. (4.3.1) *Der Mann, den die Frau, die das Kind, das schläft, liebt, sieht,* / The man whom the woman who the child who sleeps loves sees

42. (4.3.2) *Der Mann, den die Frau sieht, die das Kind liebt, das schläft,* / The man whom the woman sees who the child who sleeps loves

43. (4.4.1) *Dem Kind, das geschlafen hatte, gab Maria einen Teller.* / Mary gave a plate to the child who had slept.

44. (4.4.2) *Hatte Maria einen Teller?* / Did Mary have a plate?

45. (4.4.13) *Peter gab Maria Susi.* / Peter gave Mary to Susi. Peter gave Susi to Mary. Mary gave Peter to Susi. Mary gave Susi to Peter. Susi gave Peter to Mary. Susi gave Mary to Peter.

46. (4.4.14) *Der Mann brachte dem Mädchen ein Buch aus München.* / From Munich the man brought the girl a book. The man brought the girl a book made in Munich.

47. (4.4.17) *Das Haus, aus dem Maria kam, gehört Peter.* / The house out of which Mary came is owned by Peter.

48. (4.5.2) *Gegessen hat Maria den Apfel.* / Mary has eaten the appel.

49. (4.5.3) *Den Apfel hat Maria gegessen.* / Mary has eaten the appel.

50. (4.5.9) *Das Haus an dem See gehört Maria.* / The house on the lake belongs to Mary.

51. (4.5.10) *Das Haus am See gehört Maria.*

52. (4.5.13) *Das Buch ist von Maria zu lesen.* / The book is to be read by Mary.

53. (4.5.14) *Das Buch ist schwierig zu lesen.* / The book is difficult to read.

54. (4.5.15) *Maria ist ein junges Mädchen.* / Mary is a young girl.

55. (4.5.16) *Maria ist ein junges Mädchen.* / Mary is a young girl.

56. (4.5.17) *Maria ist in der Schule.* / Mary is in the school.

Appendix B

B.2 Declaratives with finite main verbs

57. (B.2.1) *Das Mädchen gab dem Kind den Teller.*

58. (B.2.2) *Das Mädchen gab den Teller dem Kind.*

59. (B.2.3) *Dem Kind gab das Mädchen den Teller.*

60. (B.2.4) *Dem Kind gab den Teller das Mädchen.*

61. (B.2.5) *Den Teller gab das Mädchen dem Kind.*

62. (B.2.6) *Den Teller gab dem Kind das Mädchen.*

B.3 Declaratives with auxiliary and non-finite main verb

63. (B.3.1) *Das Mädchen hat dem Kind den Teller gegeben.*

64. (B.3.2) *Das Mädchen hat den Teller dem Kind gegeben.*

65. (B.3.3) *Dem Kind hat das Mädchen den Teller gegeben.*

66. (B.3.4) *Dem Kind hat den Teller das Mädchen gegeben.*

67. (B.3.5) *Den Teller hat das Mädchen dem Kind gegeben.*

68. (B.3.6) *Den Teller hat dem Kind das Mädchen gegeben.*

B.4 Declaratives with topicalized non-finite verb

69. (B.4.1) *Gegeben hat das Mädchen dem Kind den Teller.*

70. (B.4.2) *Gegeben hat das Mädchen den Teller dem Kind.*

71. (B.4.3) *Gegeben hat den Teller das Mädchen dem Kind.*

72. (B.4.4) *Gegeben hat den Teller dem Kind das Mädchen.*

73. (B.4.5) *Gegeben hat dem Kind das Mädchen den Teller.*

74. (B.4.6) *Gegeben hat dem Kind den Teller das Mädchen.*

75. (B.4.7) **Gegeben dem Kind hat den Teller das Mädchen.*

B.5 Various predicate constructions in declarative main clauses

76. (B.5.1) *Der Film wird gut sein.*

77. (B.5.2) *Die Suppe wird gut werden.*

78. (B.5.3) *Das kleine Mädchen ist nachhause gekommen.*

79. (B.5.4) *Es ist jetzt an der Zeit.*

80. (B.5.5) *Peter ist ein guter Freund.*

81. (B.5.6) *Peter hat einen guten Freund.*

82. (B.5.7) *Der Brief ist leicht geschrieben.*

83. (B.5.8) *Peter hat Freunde.*

84. (B.5.9) *Peter hat viele Freunde.*

85. (B.5.10) *Peter hat viele gute Freunde, die ihm oft helfen.*

86. (B.5.11) *Ihr wurdet Ärzte.*

87. (B.5.12) *Ihr wolltet Ärzte werden.*

88. (B.5.13) *Ihr seid Ärzte geworden.*

B.6 Various predicate constructions in subordinate clauses

89. (B.6.1) *Weil Peter ein guter Arzt ist,*

90. (B.6.2) *Weil Peter ein guter Arzt wird,*

91. (B.6.3) *Weil Peter ein guter Arzt geworden ist,*

92. (B.6.4) *Weil Peter ein guter Arzt werden wird,*

93. (B.6.5) *Weil Peter alt wird,*

94. (B.6.6) *Weil Peter klug ist,*

95. (B.6.7) *Weil Peter alt werden wird,*

96. (B.6.8) *Weil Peter klug geworden ist,*

B.7 Passive constructions in declarative main clauses

97. (B.7.1) *Peter ist von Maria ein Buch gegeben worden.*

98. (B.7.2) **Peter ist von Maria ein Buch gegeben.*

99. (B.7.3) *Peter ist ein Buch gegeben worden.*

100. (B.7.4) *Peter wird von Maria ein Buch gegeben werden.*

101. (B.7.5) *Peter wird ein Buch gegeben werden.*

102. (B.7.6) *Peter war von Maria ein Buch gegeben worden.*

103. (B.7.7) *Ein Buch ist Peter von Maria gegeben worden.*

104. (B.7.8) *Von Maria ist ein Buch Peter gegeben worden.*

105. (B.7.9) *Peter wurde ein Buch gegeben.*

106. (B.7.10) *Peter wurde von Maria ein Buch gegeben.*

107. (B.7.11) *Das Buch ist geschrieben.*

108. (B.7.12) *Das Buch ist geschrieben worden.*

109. (B.7.13) *Das Buch wird bald geschrieben sein.*

110. (B.7.14) *Das Buch wird geschrieben werden.*

B.8 Q-Passives in declarative main clauses

111. (B.8.1) *Das Mädchen ist zu überzeugen.*

112. (B.8.2) *Das Mädchen wird zu überzeugen sein.*

113. (B.8.3) *Die Mädchen sind zu überzeugen.*

114. (B.8.4) *Dem Mädchen ist zu helfen.*

115. (B.8.5) *Den Mädchen ist zu helfen.*

116. (B.8.6) *Dem Mädchen wird bald geholfen sein.*

117. (B.8.7) *Das Buch ist zu lesen.*

118. (B.8.8) *Das Buch ist von Maria zu lesen.*

119. (B.8.9) *Das Buch ist dem Freund zu geben.*

120. (B.8.10) *Das Buch wird dem Freund zu geben sein.*

121. (B.8.11) *Dem Mädchen ist ein Buch zu geben.*

B.9 Passives in subordinate clauses

122. (B.9.1) *Weil Peter von Maria ein Buch gegeben worden ist, lacht Susi.*

123. (B.9.2) *Weil Peter ein Buch gegeben wird, lacht Susi.*

124. (B.9.3) *Der Mann, dem das Buch gegeben wurde, schläft.*

125. (B.9.4) *Der Mann, dem von Maria das Buch gegeben worden ist, schläft.*

126. (B.9.5) *Das Buch, das von Maria dem Mann gegeben worden ist, liegt auf dem Tisch.*

B.10 Q-passives in subordinate clauses

127. (B.10.1) *Weil das Buch dem Kind zu geben ist,*

128. (B.10.2) *Weil dem Kind zu helfen ist,*

129. (B.10.3) *Weil dem Kind von Peter zu helfen ist,*

130. (B.10.4) *Weil dem Kind von Peter geholfen werden muss,*

131. (B.10.5) *Das Kind, dem zu helfen ist, schläft auf dem Sofa.*

132. (B.10.6) *Das Kind, dem das Buch zu geben ist, schläft auf dem Sofa.*

133. (B.10.7) *Das Buch, das dem Kind zu geben sein wird,*

B.11 Multiple modal infinitives in main clauses

134. (B.11.1) *Der Mann wird das Buch schreiben wollen.*

135. (B.11.2) *Der Mann hat das Buch schreiben wollen.*

136. (B.11.3) *Der Mann hat das Buch schreiben können wollen.*

137. (B.11.4) *Der Mann hat dem Mädchen das Buch geben dürfen können wollen sollen mögen.*

B.12 Multiple modal infinitives in subordinate clauses

138. (B.12.1) *Weil der Mann den Teller sehen können wollte,*

139. (B.12.2) *Weil der Mann den Teller hat sehen können, lacht Susi.*

140. (B.12.3) **Weil der Mann den Teller sehen können hat, lacht Susi*

141. (B.12.4) *Weil der Mann den Teller sehen können wird, lacht Susi.*

142. (B.12.5) *Der Mann, der das Buch lesen gewollt hat,*

143. (B.12.6) **Der Mann, der das Buch lesen wollen hat,*

144. (B.12.7) *Der Mann, der das Buch hat lesen wollen,*

145. (B.12.8) *Der Mann, der das Buch lesen können gewollt hat,*

146. (B.12.9) *Der Mann, der das Buch Maria hat geben können wollen,*

B.13 Obligatory versus optional adverbs

147. (B.13.1) *Peter wohnte früher in Hamburg.*

148. (B.13.2) *In Hamburg wohnte Peter früher.*

149. (B.13.3) *Früher wohnte Peter in Hamburg.*

150. (B.13.4) **Peter wohnte.*

151. (B.13.5) *In Hamburg wohnte Peter früher.*

152. (B.13.6) *Peter hat früher in Hamburg gewohnt.*

153. (B.13.7) *Früher hat Peter in Hamburg gewohnt.*

154. (B.13.8) *In Hamburg hat Peter früher gewohnt.*

155. (B.13.9) **Früher hat Peter gewohnt.*

156. (B.13.10) **Früher hat Peter gewohnt.*

B.14 The preposition *hinter* in various constructions

157. (B.14.1) *Hinter dem Berg wohnt Maria.*

158. (B.14.2) *Das Haus hinter dem Berg gehört Maria.*

159. (B.14.3) *Das Haus, hinter dem die Katze schläft, gehört Maria.*

160. (B.14.4) *Das Haus, das hinter dem Berg liegt, gehört Maria.*

161. (B.14.5) *Die Katze ist hinter dem Haus.*

B.15 Adsentential clauses and adverbs in various positions

162. (B.15.1) *Nachdem der Mann gestern geschlafen hatte, las er ein Buch.*

163. (B.15.2) *Der Mann las gestern ein Buch, nachdem er geschlafen hatte.*

164. (B.15.3) *Ein Buch las der Mann gestern, nachdem er geschlafen hatte.*

165. (B.15.4) *Gestern nachdem er geschlafen hatte, las der Mann ein Buch.*

B.16 Relative clause agreement

166. (B.16.1) *Der Mann gab der Frau das Buch, die das Kind gesehen hatte.*

167. (B.16.2) *Der Mann gab der Frau das Buch, das das Kind gesehen hatte.*

168. (B.16.3) *Der Mann hat der Frau das Buch gegeben, die das Kind gesehen hatte.*

169. (B.16.4) *Der Mann hat der Frau das Buch gegeben, das das Kind gesehen hatte.*

170. (B.16.5) *Der Mann, der gestern das Buch kaufte, schläft auf dem Sofa.*

171. (B.16.6) *Das Buch in dem der Mann gestern las, liegt auf dem Sofa.*

172. (B.16.7) *Der Mann, dem der Freund gestern das Buch gab, schläft auf dem Sofa.*

173. (B.16.8) *Der Mann, dessen Buch Maria liest, schläft auf dem Sofa.*

B.17 Sentential complements

174. (B.17.1) *Das Kind, das der Frau die Katze gab, hat geglaubt, dass sie gerne in dem schoenen alten Haus wohnen würde.*

175. (B.17.2) *Peter glaubt, dass Maria den Brief lesen wird.*

176. (B.17.3) *Peter weiss, dass Maria den Brief gelesen hat.*

177. (B.17.4) **Peter glaubt, warum Maria den Brief gelesen hat.*

178. (B.17.5) *Peter weiss, warum Maria den Brief lesen wird.*

B.18 Infinitives with *zu* in main clauses

179. (B.18.1) *Maria ist leicht zu überzeugen.*

180. (B.18.2) *Es ist leicht Maria zu überzeugen.*

181. (B.18.3) *Maria ist bereit zu singen.*

182. (B.18.4) *Maria versucht zu singen.*

183. (B.18.5) *Maria hat versucht das Buch zu lesen.*

184. (B.18.6) *Maria versuchte dem Freund einen Brief zu geben.*

185. (B.18.7) *Dem Freund ist zu helfen.*

186. (B.18.8) *Es ist dem Freund zu helfen.*

187. (B.18.9) *Dem Freund wird leicht zu helfen sein.*

188. (B.18.10) *Es wird dem Freund zu helfen sein.*

189. (B.18.11) *Dem Freund ist leicht zu helfen.*

190. (B.18.12) *Es ist leicht dem Freund zu helfen.*

191. (B.18.13) *Leicht ist es dem Freund zu helfen.*

192. (B.18.14) **Es ist dem Freund leicht zu helfen.*

193. (B.18.15) *Es ist dem Freund schnell zu helfen.*

194. (B.18.16) *Dem Freund ist schnell zu helfen.*

195. (B.18.17) *Peter hat dem Freund zu helfen.*

196. (B.18.18) *Peter hat das Buch zu lesen.*

197. (B.18.19) *Der Mann wird den Brief zu lesen haben.*

B.19 Infinitives with *zu* in subordinate clauses

198. (B.19.1) *Weil Maria leicht zu überzeugen ist.*

199. (B.19.2) *Der Freund, dem leicht zu helfen ist,*

200. (B.19.3) *Weil dem Freund zu helfen ist,*

201. (B.19.4) *Weil dem Freund zu helfen sein wird,*

202. (B.19.5) *Weil dem Mädchen leicht zu helfen ist,*

203. (B.19.6) *Das Buch, das zu lesen ist,*

204. (B.19.7) *Das Buch, das zu lesen sein wird,*

205. (B.19.8) *Das Buch, das dem Mädchen zu geben sein wird*

206. (B.19.9) *Der Brief, den Peter zu lesen hat,*

B.20 Separable verbal prefixes

207. (B.20.1) *Gestern sah der Mann das Wort im Lexikon nach.*

208. (B.20.2) *Gestern hat der Mann das Wort im Lexikon nachgesehen.*

209. (B.20.3) *Der Mann sah das Wort nach dem Essen nach.*

B.21 Yes/no-interrogatives

210. (B.21.1) *Hat der junge Mann dem Kind gestern eine Puppe gegeben?*

211. (B.21.2) *Gab der junge Mann dem Kind gestern eine Puppe?*

212. (B.21.3) *Gab eine Puppe dem Kind gestern die junge Frau?*

213. (B.21.4) *Der junge Mann hat dem Kind gestern eine Puppe gegeben?*

B.22 Wh-interrogatives

214. (B.22.1) *Wer gab dem Kind gestern eine Puppe?*

215. (B.22.2) *Wer gab gestern wem eine Puppe?*

216. (B.22.3) *Der junge Mann gab gestern wem eine Puppe?*

217. (B.22.4) *Was gab der junge Mann gestern dem Kind?*

218. (B.22.5) *Wo wohnt Peter?*

219. (B.22.6) *Warum hat der Mann dem Kind die Puppe gegeben?*

220. (B.22.7) *Warum hat der Mann dem Kind die Puppe gegeben, das gestern in die Schule kam?*

221. (B.22.8) *Warum hat der Mann dem Kind die Puppe gegeben, die es gestern in der Schule gesehen hatte?*

D.2   The ECAT derivations

Appendix C

C.2 Active voice constructions using the verb *give*

222. (C.2.1) *John gave Mary a beautiful book.*

223. (C.2.2) *John might give Mary an old book.*

224. (C.2.3) *The man could have given Mary a book.*

225. (C.2.4) *John gave a beautiful old book to the young girl.*

226. (C.2.5) *John could have given a book to Mary.*

227. (C.2.6) *The man could be giving a beautiful book to the woman.*

C.3 Passive voice constructions using the verb *give*

228. (C.3.1) *The man was given a book by Mary.*

229. (C.3.2) *The man might have been given a book.*

230. (C.3.3) *A book might have been given to John by Mary.*

231. (C.3.4) *A book might have been given to John.*

232. (C.3.5) *A book was given John by Mary.*

233. (C.3.6) *A book was given John.*

C.4 Genitive constructions

234. (C.4.1) *John's book is beautiful.*

235. (C.4.2) **John's book are beautiful .*

236. (C.4.3) *John's books are beautiful.*

237. (C.4.4) **John's books is beautiful.*

238. (C.4.5) *The old man's book is beautiful.*

C.5 Auxiliaries taking quantified noun phrases as the second argument

239. (C.5.1)*John has many beautiful books.*

240. (C.5.2)*John has a beautiful book.*

241. (C.5.3)**John has beautiful book.*

242. (C.5.4)*You are a beautiful young woman.*

C.6 Auxiliary taking an adjective as the second argument

243. (C.6.1) *You are beautiful.*

C.7 Nominative argreement in the case of the auxiliary *be*

244. (C.7.1) *You are women.*

245. (C.7.2) *He is a good doctor.*

246. (C.7.3) *We are good doctors.*

247. (C.7.4) **You is good doctors.*

248. (C.7.5) *You are beautiful women.*

249. (C.7.6) *I am a collector of old beautiful books.*

C.8 Yes/no-interrogatives and related declaratives

250. (C.8.1) *Mary said that.*

251. (C.8.2) *Mary said that?*

252. (C.8.3) *Does John love Mary?*

253. (C.8.4) **Does John love Mary.*

254. (C.8.5) *John loves Mary?*

255. (C.8.6) *John loves Mary.*

256. (C.8.7) *Did Mary give John the book?*

257. (C.8.8) *Did Mary give the book to John?*

258. (C.8.9) *Has Mary given John the book?*

259. (C.8.10) *Has Mary given the book to John?*

260. (C.8.11) *Did Mary read the book?*

261. (C.8.12) *Has Mary read the book?*

262. (C.8.13) *Could Mary have read the book?*

263. (C.8.14) *Was Mary reading a book?*

C.9 Wh-interrogatives

264. (C.9.1) *Who does Mary love?*

265. (C.9.2) *Who doesn't love Mary?*

266. (C.9.3) *Who loves Mary?*

267. (C.9.4) *Whom doesn't Mary love?*

268. (C.9.5) **Whom loves Mary?*

269. (C.9.6) *Mary said what?*

270. (C.9.7) **Mary said what.*

271. (C.9.8) *Who gave what to whom?*

272. (C.9.9) *Who did Mary give a book?*

273. (C.9.10) *Whom did Mary give a book?*

274. (C.9.11) *Who did Mary give a book to?*

275. (C.9.12) *Who did Mary give to John?*

276. (C.9.13) *What did Mary say?*

277. (C.9.14) *Who could Mary have seen?*

278. (C.9.15) *Who could have seen Mary?*

279. (C.9.16) *Who could Mary have given the book?*

280. (C.9.17) *Who could Mary have given the book to?*

C.10 The interrogative determiner *which*

281. (C.10.1) *Which book did John read?*

282. (C.10.2) **Which book did John read.*

283. (C.10.3) *John read which book?*

284. (C.10.4) **John read which book.*

C.11 *That*-clauses

285. (C.11.1) *Mary says that John loves Susi.*

286. (C.11.2) *Mary believes that John said that Susi was reading a book.*

287. (C.11.3) *Mary believes John said Susi was reading a book.*

C.12 Wh-interogatives with *that*-clauses

288. (C.12.1) *Who does Mary say that John loves?*

289. (C.12.2) **Who says Mary that John loves?*

290. (C.12.3) *Who says that Mary loves John?*

291. (C.12.4) *Who says Mary loves John?*

292. (C.12.5) *Who did Mary say that John doesn't like?*

293. (C.12.6) **Who says Mary that Bill believes that John loves?*

294. (C.12.7) *Who does Mary say that Bill believes that John loves?*

C.13 Passive in subordinate clauses

295. (C.13.1) *Mary says that John was given a book by Susi.*

296. (C.13.2) *the man who was given a book by Mary is intelligent.*

C.14 Relative clauses modifying sentence final noun phrases

297. (C.14.1) *I know the man who loves Mary.*

298. (C.14.2) *I know the man who has read the book.*

299. (C.14.3) *I know the man who will be reading the book.*

300. (C.14.4) *I have the book which Mary didn't read.*

301. (C.14.5) *I have the book which Mary didn't give to John.*

302. (C.14.6) *I have the book that Mary didn't give to John.*

303. (C.14.7) *I have the book which Mary didn't give John.*

304. (C.14.8) *I have the book that Mary didn't give John.*

C.15 Relative clauses modifying mid-sentence noun phrases

305. (C.15.1) *John gave the girl who read the book a cookie.*

306. (C.15.2) *John didn't give the girl who didn't read the book a cookie.*

307. (C.15.3) *John gave the girl who gave the man a book a cookie.*

308. (C.15.4) *John didn't give the girl who didn't give the man a book a cookie.*

309. (C.15.5) *John gave the girl who Mary gave a cookie a book.*

C.16 Relative clauses modifying sentence initial noun phrases

310. (C.16.1) *The man who gave Mary a book loves Susi.*

311. (C.16.2) *The man who didn't read the book loves Mary.*

312. (C.16.3) *The man who could have been reading the book loves Mary.*

C.17 The relative pronoun *who* as subject and as object

313. (C.17.1) *The man who loves Mary is reading a book.*

314. (C.17.2) *The man who Mary loves is reading a book.*

315. (C.17.3) *The man who doesn't love Mary is reading a book.*

316. (C.17.4) *The man who Mary doesn't love is reading a book.*

317. (C.17.5) *The man who didn't give Mary a book loves Susi.*

318. (C.17.6) *The man who Mary didn't give a book to loves Susi.*

C.18 Mixing relative clauses and *that*-clauses

319. (C.18.1) *The man who saw that John loves Mary is reading a book.*

320. (C.18.2) *The man who said that Mary loves him sleeps.*

321. (C.18.3) *I know the man who John said Mary believes that Susi loves.*

322. (C.18.4) *I know that the man who John said that Mary believes that Susi loves.*

C.19 Wh-Interrogatives with relative clauses

323. (C.19.1) *Who loves the man who gave Mary a book?*

324. (C.19.2) *Who loves the man whom Mary gave a book to?*

C.20 Declaratives and interrogatives with "Wh-movement"

325. (C.20.1) *Mary said that John doesn't believe that Susi read the book.*

326. (C.20.2) *Which book did Mary say that John doesn't believe that Susi read?*

327. (C.20.3) *John believes that Mary gave Bill a book.*

328. (C.20.4) *Who does John believe Mary gave a book ?*

329. (C.20.5) *John believes that Mary gave a book to Bill.*

330. (C.20.6) *Who does John believe that Mary gave the book to?*

C.21 Subordinate clauses with and without complementizers

331. (C.21.1) *The man whom John said that Mary loves sleeps.*

332. (C.21.2) *The man John said that Mary loves sleeps.*

333. (C.21.3) *The man John said Mary loves sleeps.*

334. (C.21.4) *The man whom John said that Mary believes that Susi loves sleeps.*

335. (C.21.5) *The man John said Mary believes Susi loves sleeps.*

References

Abelson, H. and G. Sussman 1985. *The Structure and Interpretation of Computer Programs*, MIT Press, Cambridge.

Adjukiewicz, K. 1929. *"Logicze Podstawy Naucania"*, The Foundations of Teaching.

Aho, A.V., and J.D. Ullman 1972. *The Theory of Parsing, Translation, and Compiling. Vol.I: Parsing*, Prentice Hall, Englewood Cliffs, New Jersey.

Akmajian , A., S. Steele, and T. Wasow 1979. "The Category AUX in Universal Grammar", Linguistic Inquiry 10.1.

Bar-Hillel, Y. 1953. *"A Quasi-arithmetical Notation for Syntactic Description"*, Language 29.

Bresnan, J. (Ed.) 1982. *The Mental Representation of Grammatical Relations*, MIT-Press, Cambridge, Massachusetts

Charniak,E., C.Riesbeck, and D.McDermott 1980. *Artificial Intelligence Programming*, Lawrence Erlbaum, Hillsdale, New Jersey.

Chomsky, N. 1957. *Syntactic Structures*, Mouton, The Hague.

Chomsky, N. 1981. *Lectures on Government and Binding*, Foris Publications, Dordrecht, Holland.

Clocksin, W.F. and C.S. Mellish 1984. *Programming in Prolog*, Springer-Verlag, Berlin.

Curme, G. 1947. *English Grammar*, Barnes and Noble, New York.

Erman, L.D., F. Hayes-Roth, V.R. Lesser, and D.R. Reddy 1980. "The Hearsay-II Speech-Understanding System: Integrating Knowledge to Resolve Uncertainty", Computing Surveys, Vol.12, No.2.

Gazdar, G., E. Klein, G. Pullum, and I. Sag 1985. *Generalized Phrase Structure Grammar*, Harvard University Press: Cambridge, Massachusetts, and Blackwell: Oxford.

Hausser, R. 1984. *Surface Compositional Grammar*, Wilhelm Fink Verlag, Munich.

Jackendoff, R. 1977. *X-Syntax: A Study of Phrase Structure*, Linguistic Inquiry Monograph 2, MIT.

Jespersen, O. 1938. *Growth and Structure of the English Language*, Basil Blackwell, Oxford.

King, M., ed. 1983. *Parsing Natural Language*, Academic Press, London.

Lesniewski, S. 1929. *"Grundzüge eines neuen Systems der Grundlage der Mathematik"*, Fundamenta Mathematicae, Warsaw.

Post, E. 1936. *"Finite Combinatory Processes — Formulation I"*, Journal of Symbolic Logic, I.

McCarthy, J. 1960. *"Recursive Functions of Symbolic Expressions and Their Computation by Machine"*, Communications of the ACM, Vol.7.

Matthews, P.H. 1981. *Syntax*, Cambridge University Press, Cambridge, England.

Montague, R. 1974. *Formal Philosophy*, Yale University Press, New Haven, CT.

Rich, E. 1983. *Artificial Intelligence*, McGraw-Hill Book Company, New York.

Teitelman et al. 1983. *Interlisp Reference Manual*, Xerox Corporation, Palo Alto, California.

Vennemann, T. 1980. "Remarks on grammatical relations", Linguistics in the Morning Calm, ed. by the Linguistic Society of Korea, Seoul: Hanshin, Korea.

Weyhrauch,R. 1980. "Prolegomena to a Formal Theory of Mechanical Reasoning", Artificial Intelligence.

Winograd, T. 1983. *Language as a Cognitive Process: Syntax*, Addison-Wesley Publishing Company, Reading, Massachusetts

Winston, P. 1977. *Artificial Intelligence*, (2nd ed. 1984), Addison-Wesley Publishing Company, Reading, Massachusetts.

Printed in the United States
by Baker & Taylor Publisher Services